VIETNAM

WELCOME TO VIETNAM

With everything from superb cuisine to stunning landscapes, this corner of Southeast Asia dazzles the senses. Peaceful paddy fields give way to frenetic urban centers like Ho Chi Minh City and Hanoi, where the youthful population rushes to embrace the future. Boutiques fill the French colonial buildings in enchanting Hoi An; in the north, a world away, are Sapa's ethnic markets. Around Vietnam, lush jungles and jagged karst peaks beckon adventurers. Absorb it all but take time to relax, perhaps on the long, alluring coastline with its world-class beaches.

TOP REASONS TO GO

★ **History:** From Hue's Imperial City to the Cu Chi tunnels, Vietnam's past enthralls.

★ **Cuisine:** Fresh herbs, fiery chilies, fragrant noodle dishes—*pho* is just the beginning.

★ **Postcard Views**: Misty mountains, vibrant green rice paddies, and sapphire seascapes.

★ **Cool Cities:** The buzzing streets of Ho Chi Minh City and Hanoi reward exploration.

★ **Islands:** Isolated Con Dao, blissful Phu Quoc, and rugged Cat Ba are tropical escapes.

★ **Boating:** Cruises in Halong Bay, boat rides through the Mekong Delta—Vietnam is best by boat.

12
TOP EXPERIENCES
Vietnam offers terrific experiences that should be on every traveler's list. Here are Fodor's top picks for a memorable trip.

1 Halong Bay

Thousands of limestone karsts jut skyward from emerald waters in this UNESCO World Heritage–listed seascape. The best way to see it is to hop by boat between islands, including scenic Cat Ba, home to a national park. *(Ch. 6)*

2 The Imperial City, Hue

The jewel of Hue's Citadel, this sprawling complex of majestic palaces and evocative temples brings the magnificence of Vietnam's royal dynasties to life. *(Ch. 5)*

3 Markets

From Hanoi's bustling Old Quarter to floating outposts in the Mekong Delta, markets reveal colorful slices of local life. Plunge right in, and haggle like you mean it. *(Ch. 2–8)*

4 Ho Chi Minh City

Rapidly modernizing, HCMC is a jolt of urban energy unlike anywhere else in the country. The frenetic pace (that traffic!) is tempered by peaceful pagodas, parks, and cafés. *(Ch. 2)*

5 Street Food

Devour a delicious bowl of *pho* on a bustling corner, or follow the fragrant smoke emanating from a sidewalk brazier, where marinated pork sizzles. *(Chs 2–8).*

6 Vietnam War Legacy

Museums pay tribute, but for a different perspective on the war, look underground—the vast Cu Chi tunnel network is a monument to Vietnamese tenacity. *(Ch. 2)*

7 Phong Nha Ke Bang National Park

Untamed jungle, vast imagination-defying limestone caves, and underground rivers make this spectacular region irresistible to adventurers. *(Ch. 5)*

8 Hoi An

French colonial architecture, historic traders' houses, and atmospheric temples are among the charms of Hoi An that are easily discovered on a riverside stroll. *(Ch. 5)*

9 Beaches and Islands

Two thousand miles of tropical coastline ensure that the white sands of a postcard are never far away. Islands like Phu Quoc *(pictured)* combine idyllic beaches and diving. *(Ch. 3)*

10 Hill Stations

Built by the French as health retreats, hill stations such as Dalat *(pictured)* make a cool contrast to the steamy lowlands—think misty peaks and rugged scenery. *(Ch. 4)*

11 Sapa

Home to ethnic minorities, this northern mountain town is also the jumping-off point for some compelling sights, including Fansipan, Vietnam's tallest summit. *(Ch. 8)*

12 The Mekong Delta

This patchwork of waterways and floating markets, mangrove swamps, and brilliant green rice paddies is best explored by boat, but bike tours provide a fun alternative. *(Ch. 3)*

CONTENTS

1 **EXPERIENCE VIETNAM** 13
What's Where 14
Need To Know 16
Vietnam Today 18
If You Like 20
Flavors of Vietnam 22
People of Vietnam 24
History You Can See 26
Vietnam Made Easy 31
Great Itineraries 32

2 **HO CHI MINH CITY** 37
Orientation and Planning 39
Exploring 47
Where to Eat 58
Where to Stay 70
Nightlife and Performing Arts 75
Sports and the Outdoors 79
Shopping 81
Side Trips from Ho Chi Minh City . . 88

3 **THE MEKONG DELTA** 107
Orientation and Planning 109
Northern Mekong Delta 115
Phu Quoc Island 125
South-Central Mekong Delta 134

4 **THE SOUTH-CENTRAL COAST
& HIGHLANDS** 147
Orientation and Planning 149
The Southern Coast 153
Nha Trang 162
The Central Highlands 172
North of Nha Trang 190

5 **THE CENTRAL COAST** 195
Orientation and Planning 197
Hoi An 203
Danang and Nearby 225

Hue 241
Phong Nha Ke Bang
National Park 258

6 **HALONG BAY AND NORTH-
CENTRAL VIETNAM** 265
Orientation and Planning 267
Ninh Binh and Nearby 271
Haiphong 279
Halong Bay and Nearby 285

7 **HANOI** 301
Orientation and Planning 302
Exploring 311
Where to Eat 326
Where to Stay 338
Nightlife and Performing Arts . . . 342
Sports and the Outdoors 347
Shopping 349
Side Trips from Hanoi 354

8 **THE NORTHWEST** 361
Orientation and Planning 364
Sapa and Nearby 371
Dien Bien Phu and Nearby 381

9 **SIDE TRIP TO
ANGKOR WAT** 389
Orientation and Planning 390
Exploring 394
Where to Eat 403
Where to Stay 406
Nightlife and Performing Arts . . . 409
Shopping 411
Books and Movies 414
Vietnam Vocabulary 416

TRAVEL SMART VIETNAM . . . 423
Index 447
About Our Writers 455

CONTENTS

MAPS

Ho Chi Minh City 48

Beyond the City Center 55

Where to Eat and Stay in
Ho Chi Minh City 60–61

Side Trips from
Ho Chi Minh City 89

The Mekong Delta. 110

Phu Quoc Island. 126

South Central Coast and
Highlands. 151

Nha Trang. 163

Dalat. 176

The Central Coast. 198

Hoi An. 206–207

Danang 228

Hue. 242–243

Halong Bay and
North Central Vietnam. 268

Ninh Binh and Nearby 272

Haiphong 280

Halong Bay and Nearby 286

Hanoi 306–307

The Old Quarter. 313

The French Quarter. 316

Around the Ho Chi Minh
Mausoleum and West Lake 320

Where to Eat and Stay
in Hanoi. 328–329

Side Trips from Hanoi 355

The Northwest. 365

Cambodia. 391

Angkor Wat. 399

Where to Stay and Eat in
Siem Reap 404

ABOUT THIS GUIDE

Fodor's Recommendations

Everything in this guide is worth doing—we don't cover what isn't—but exceptional sights, hotels, and restaurants are recognized with additional accolades. Fodor's Choice★ indicates our top recommendations. Care to nominate a new place? Visit Fodors.com/contact-us.

Trip Costs

We list prices wherever possible to help you budget well. Hotel and restaurant price categories from $ to $$$$ are noted alongside each recommendation. For hotels, we include the lowest cost of a standard double room in high season. For restaurants, we cite the average price of a main course at dinner or, if dinner isn't served, at lunch. For attractions, we always list adult admission fees; discounts are usually available for children, students, and senior citizens.

Hotels

Our local writers vet every hotel to recommend the best overnights in each price category, from budget to expensive. Unless otherwise specified, you can expect private bath, phone, and TV in your room. For expanded hotel reviews, visit Fodors.com.

Top Picks		Hotels &
★ Fodor's Choice		Restaurants
		🏨 Hotel
Listings		🛏 Number of
✉ Address		rooms
📭 Branch address		🍽 Meal plans
☎ Telephone		✕ Restaurant
🖶 Fax		🪑 Reservations
⊕ Website		👔 Dress code
📧 E-mail		☐ No credit cards
💳 Admission fee		$ Price
⊘ Open/closed		
times		**Other**
Ⓜ Subway		⇨ See also
✛ Directions or		☞ Take note
Map coordinates		🏌 Golf facilities

Restaurants

Unless we state otherwise, restaurants are open for lunch and dinner daily. We mention dress code only when there's a specific requirement and reservations only when they're essential or not accepted. To make restaurant reservations, visit Fodors.com.

Credit Cards

The hotels and restaurants in this guide typically accept credit cards. If not, we'll say so.

EUGENE FODOR

Hungarian-born Eugene Fodor (1905–91) began his travel career as an interpreter on a French cruise ship. The experience inspired him to write *On the Continent* (1936), the first guidebook to receive annual updates and discuss a country's way of life as well as its sights. Fodor later joined the U.S. Army and worked for the OSS in World War II. After the war, he kept up his intelligence work while expanding his guidebook series. During the Cold War, many guides were written by fellow agents who understood the value of insider information. Today's guides continue Fodor's legacy by providing travelers with timely coverage, insider tips, and cultural context.

EXPERIENCE VIETNAM

WHAT'S WHERE

Numbers refer to chapters.

2 Ho Chi Minh City. Still called Saigon by many, Ho Chi Minh City is a rapidly expanding metropolis, one full of contrasts. The downtown core is quite walkable and most major sites—from the French-built Notre Dame Cathedral to the War Remnants Museum and the Reunification Palace—can be visited on foot.

3 The Mekong Delta. Running through the upper delta is the Mekong River, dotted with small fertile islands where fruit grows in abundance. The rest is a patchwork of waterways, mangrove swamps, and brilliant green rice paddies that run into the emerald South China Sea.

4 The South Central Coast and Highlands. Two of Vietnam's most popular resort towns are here—ocean-side Nha Trang and the cool mountain retreat of Dalat. Farther north are the isolated towns of Pleiku and Kon Tum—good jumping-off points for treks into the forests and visits to hill-tribe villages.

5 The Central Coast. The towns of Hue and Hoi An provide a fascinating glimpse of Vietnam's history. UNESCO site Hoi An is an ancient trading and fishing town where many buildings remain as they were 200 years ago.

Hue's Imperial City and palatial royal tombs are impressive reminders of the country's regal past.

6 Halong Bay and North Central Vietnam. Staying overnight on a boat on Halong Bay and kayaking among the islands of the Cat Ba archipelago, are just two of the popular outdoor activities in the picturesque North Central region.

7 Hanoi. The capital of Vietnam is also its cultural hub. Despite the chaotic motorbike traffic, this city of majestic lakes, wide tree-lined boulevards, and hauntingly familiar French colonial architecture remains quite charming, despite serious overcrowding.

8 The Northwest. Many ethnic minorities live in the beautiful highlands of the north, where views of the rice terraces and surrounding fields are truly stunning. The area around the mountain town of Sapa is a magnet for avid trekkers and amateur hikers alike.

9 Angkor Wat. Siem Reap's spectacular Angkor temple complex makes neighboring Cambodia an essential side trip.

CHINA

Ha Giang
Cao Bang
Lao Cai
Sapa
8
Tuyen Quang
Lang Son
Luan Chau
Thai Nguyen
Son La
Phu Lang Thuong
Dien
Bien Phu
HANOI
Hai Duong
Hon Gai
7
Haiphong
Thai Binh
Luang
Prabang
6
Ninh Binh
Thanh Hoa
1
VIETNAM
HAINAN
ISLAND

LAOS
Vinh
Ha Tinh
Gulf of Tonkin

VIENTIANE

Udon Thani
Dong Hoi

Dong Ha
THAILAND
9 1
Hue
Danang
5
Hoi An
Ubon Ratchathani
14
Nakhon Ratchasima
Quang Ngai
1
Kon Tum

Pleiku
Qui Nhon
9
Siem Reap
14
Tuy Hoa

CAMBODIA
Buon Me Thuot
4
Nha Trang
14
Dalat
PHNOM
PENH
1
VIETNAM
Tay Ninh
14
Thu Dao Mot
Bien Hoa
Phan Thiet
3
Mui Ne
Long Xuyen
My Tho
Ho Chi Minh City
PHU QUOC
ISLAND
Can Tho
Vinh Long
2
Soc Trang
Tra Vinh
Bac Lieu
1
MOUTHS OF THE MEKONG

South China Sea

Gulf of Thailand

NEED TO KNOW

Hanoi

Gulf of Tonkin

VIETNAM

Gulf of Thailand

AT A GLANCE

Capital: Hanoi

Population: 93,421,835

Currency: dong

Money: ATMs common in cities; cash more common than credit.

Language: Vietnamese

Country Code: 84

Emergencies: 113 (Police), 114 (Fire), 115 (Ambulance)

Driving: On the right

Electricity: 220v/50 cycles

Time: 12 hours ahead of New York

Documents: Up to 30 days visa on arrival

Mobile Phones: GSM (900 and 1800 bands)

Major Mobile Companies: Viettel Mobile, MobiFone, Vinaphone

WEBSITES

Vietnam National Administration of Tourism: ⊕ www.vietnamtourism.com

Vietnam Travel: ⊕ www.vietnamtravel.org

The InsideVietnam Blog: ⊕ www.insidevietnamblog.com

GETTING AROUND

✈ **Air Travel:** Major international airports in Hanoi, Danang, and Ho Chi Minh City.

🚌 **Bus Travel:** Public buses are affordable but crowded, uncomfortable, and make multiple stops.

🚗 **Car Travel:** Driving in Vietnam is notoriously hectic and visitors are strongly discouraged from attempting to drive in the country.

🚆 **Train Travel:** Trains are a comfortable way to get around Vietnam, and are safer and a bit more luxurious than local buses.

PLAN YOUR BUDGET

	HOTEL ROOM	MEAL	ATTRACTIONS
Low Budget	200,000 VND	40,000 VND	Hanoi Fine Arts Museum admission, 20,000 VND
Mid Budget	850,000 VND	80,000 VND	Vietnam Museum of Ethnology admission, 40,000 VND
High Budget	5,000,000 VND	250,000 VND	The Hue Citadel admission, 105,000 VND

WAYS TO SAVE

Stay somewhere with free breakfast. Many budget hotels offer free breakfast to guests.

Eat street food. Food stalls are cheap and plentiful and are a great place to try regional specialties.

Travel by *cyclo.* These three-wheeled bicycle taxis, are among the cheapest way to get around Vietnamese towns.

Stick to free attractions. If you're really tight for cash, attractions such as markets cost nothing.

PLAN YOUR TIME

Hassle Factor	High. Vietnam is far away no matter how you approach it, and you'll need to make at least one layover, usually somewhere in Asia.
3 days	With only three days in Vietnam, your best bet is to stick to Hanoi with a side trip to Halong Bay.
1 week	If you only have one week in the country, you might be better off limiting your trip to either Hanoi and surrounding sites of the north or Ho Chi Minh City and the southern beaches.
2 weeks	With two weeks in Vietnam, you'll have time to visit the top sites of Hanoi and Ho Chi Minh City as well as Nha Trang, Hoi An, Hue, and Halong Bay.

WHEN TO GO

High Season: Vietnam has two high seasons: November–March in the south and July and August in the north. Christmas and Western New Year are popular with travelers and rates will be higher, while the most expensive time to travel is during Tet, in January of February.

Low Season: Because of Vietnam's different climate zones, high season in the south (November–March) is low season in the north, and vice versa. The Mekong Delta region is always hot and humid, but off-season travelers to the north will find temperatures pleasant.

Value Season: April–June and September–November offer the best value in Vietnam. You won't have to fight for accommodations or elbow room at major sites and you'll still be able to enjoy peak season weather in some parts of the country. The south is still very hot and it will rain, though not all day.

BIG EVENTS

January–February: The lunar New Year, or Tet is marked with family visits and special foods.

Apri–May: Grandiose firework displays light the skies over the Han River during the Danang International Fireworks Competition.

September: Tet Trung Thu marks the autumn harvest with moon gazing and special moon cakes.

December: The Khmer people celebrate the Ghe Ngo Festival with offerings to the moon and boat races.

READ THIS

■ **Catfish and Mandala,** Andrew X. Pham. A Vietnamese-American man travels by bicycle to Vietnam.

■ **The Lotus Eaters,** Tatjana Soli. An American war photojournalist gets into a love triangle.

■ **The Quiet American,** Graham Greene. A journalist and a CIA agent experience the Indochina War.

WATCH THIS

■ **Indochine.** A French plantation owner raises a Vietnamese girl as if she were her own daughter.

■ **The Scent of Green Papaya.** A Vietnamese servant ends up in a love affair with one of her employers.

■ **Full Metal Jacket.** U.S. Marines experience the Vietnam War.

EAT THIS

■ **Bánh mì**: filled baguette sandwiches

■ **Pho**: hearty noodle soup

■ **Chè dâu do** sweet Azuki beans in coconut milk

■ **Bánh xèo**: stuffed pancakes seasoned with turmeric

■ **Nôm**: a salad often served with shreds of meat

■ **Bún riêu**: a soup of meat and vermicelli noodles

VIETNAM TODAY

Vietnam is a place of lush, natural beauty, from the low-lying deltas of the south and the mountainous central highlands to the bold architectural rice terraces of the north. Over a thousand miles long and only 31 miles wide at its narrowest, with a total area slightly larger than New Mexico, Vietnam is home to an estimated 90 million people, with the majority born after 1975. Visitors discover vibrant culture, one that includes an elegantly crumbling European heritage, and a deliciously exotic street food scene. This is certainly the time to visit: Vietnam is a country obsessed with the future, rushing headlong toward a dream of first-world prosperity with an irrepressible energy. Despite centuries of war and poverty, the Vietnamese people have an obvious enjoyment of life. It's the locals who are the real secret; their warm smiles, curiosity, and humor are what make a visit here so unforgettable.

Government

Since 1975, the Socialist Republic of Vietnam has been a one-party state, with the only legal political party being the Communist Party of Vietnam. Members of the Communist Party and independents are eligible to run for office and at the last election, in 2011, the largest number of independents ever—four—were elected to the 500-seat National Assembly in Hanoi.

In Vietnam, the Prime Minister is the head of government, responsible to the national assembly, while the President is the head of state. Both are part of a 16-member Politburo, the nation's highest decision-making body, with the power to implement policy approved by the Communist Party's National Congress and parliament. The machinations of power are murky, and little reported in Vietnam, where the government or Communist Party directly or indirectly owns most of the media. The government faces many challenges, including the widening gap between rich and poor, territorial disputes with its large and populous neighbor, China, and the pollution and environmental degradation that accompany modernization.

Economy

Vietnam's economy has mostly bounced back from the global financial crisis, which ended the country's run of 7% annual growth. Economic growth is hampered, however, by an entrenched culture of corruption in business, as well as the inefficiencies and mismanagement of state-run firms, which account for 40% of the GDP. The resurgence is most visible in the major cities, where soaring glass-and-chrome skyscrapers; new roads, bridges, and tunnels continue to be built; alongside a plethora of new up-market restaurants and five-star hotels. The other side of Vietnam's economic story is told outside of the cities, where 70% of the population is still engaged in agriculture, often small-scale enterprises that provide only a subsistence living.

The vast economic divide is only increasing. The rise of urban overcrowding has led to rapidly growing shanty towns, particularly in Hanoi and Ho Chi Minh City, though residents' access to basic services is better than in many Asian cities. Meanwhile, private jets and high-end vehicles are now must-have accessories among the country's elite, and Rolls Royce and Prada are the latest luxury brands to establish a presence in Hanoi.

Such displays of wealth are in stark contrast to the situation post-1975, when the nation was plunged into poverty after the imposition of a Soviet-style closed market

economy. Realizing things weren't working, the government introduced *doi moi* (renovation) economic reforms in 1986, which included opening up a socialist market economy at home, allowing free trade, and renewing diplomatic relations to encourage foreign investment.

The Legacy of War

Despite the ongoing visible affects of the American use of Agent Orange, including third-generation birth defects and environmental devastation, the Vietnamese have moved on from the atrocities of the period of war that stretched from 1955 to 1975. (A Vietnamese victims' rights group failed to have their case heard in the U.S. Supreme Court in 2009, though efforts for compensation continue.) It comes as a surprise to some travelers that little resentment toward Americans remains among the general Vietnamese population, who are more interested in the future than the past. It is also the case that the government has encouraged this attitude. And with 42% of the population aged under 25, the end of the Vietnam war in 1975 is practically ancient history. Vietnam's young people are more concerned with becoming rich (and sometimes famous), in order to buy the latest iPhones, cars, and fancy new apartments.

Some visitors to Vietnam are offended by the various Vietnamese museums and memorials dedicated to the last war. It's important to remember that these government-owned facilities are designed to reinforce the government's own position domestically. The use of propaganda is still very much in evidence, for example in the War Remnants Museum in Ho Chi Minh City, where graphic images are displayed alongside explanatory text that presents the North Vietnamese side.

Family

Vietnamese life still revolves around the family, even in the rapidly developing big cities. Modern Vietnamese society, like 1950s America, asks young people to study hard, complete a university degree, and then, as soon as possible, start a family. Children are often overindulged, and older people are shown a respect little seen in Western society today.

A two-child policy exists in Vietnam. Enforcement is not as harsh as in China, but employees of state-owned enterprises who have a third or subsequent child are fined for their fertility, usually in the form of losing monthly bonuses and being denied promotions. Children are considered a blessing, sons more so than daughters because sons can carry on the family name through their children. (Vietnamese wives don't assume their husband's family name.) The eldest son is responsible for caring for his parents later in life, although often all the children contribute financially to the care of their parents. Most people still follow the tradition of expecting a new bride to move into her husband's family home after marriage, even nowadays with an estimated 73% of women of working age in paid employment.

If you're traveling with kids, expect them to be fussed over and touched (cheek pinches are common). If you're of grandparenting age, expect to be shown solicitous and attentive respect, and to be applauded for being healthy and wealthy enough to travel. However, if you are a childless or single woman of a certain age, you may have to explain your "bad luck."

IF YOU LIKE

Beaches

Vietnam's beach culture is not nearly as overdeveloped as neighboring Thailand's. The country's long stretch of pristine coast—more than 2,000 miles—is still a working shoreline, with fishing families who row daily into the surf in tiny, oval-shape boats woven from reed and rattan. Some cities along the coast, such as Nha Trang, Danang, and Phan Thiet have actively developed tourism but haven't fallen victim to being overrun by visitors.

An Bang and Cam Am. In Danang, hit the waves at My Khe (known as China Beach to U.S. servicemen during the Vietnam war) or Non Nuoc Beach. Both are very pleasant and popular with locals and expats. The undertows here can be strong, so be cautious when swimming far out.

Danang. For those who prefer their beach with some city rather than seclusion, Danang offers a good compromise. It's less than 30 minutes' drive from UNESCO site Hoi An Ancient Town, which itself has two beaches.

Nha Trang. A 6-km (3.7-mile) stretch of white sand hugs the edge of the city, separating it from the crystal clear waters that beckon beachgoers from around the country. All manner of water sports can easily be organized, including excellent diving, as well as PADI-certification courses and day trips to Nha Trang's outlying islands.

Phu Quoc. What was once an untouched paradise is quickly becoming more developed, but there are still stretches of beach with the immaculate white sand and cerulean waters of a postcard. Go far enough from the big hotels and you may well have a sandy swath of beach all to yourself.

Outdoor Adventure

Northern Vietnam is a favorite of trekkers. The verdant rice terraces, snow-capped mountains, and rolling green hills will, sometimes literally, take your breath away. Cycling in the lush Mekong Delta, or boating in Halong Bay offers adventure of a gentler kind, while Phong Na Khe National Park is a bucket-list destination for adventurers.

Halong Bay. For an outdoor experience that won't leave you panting, hop in a kayak and paddle around UNESCO site Halong Bay, exploring caves and ogling the limestone karst formations that appear to be floating. Heavily touristed yes, but one look and you'll know why.

The Mekong Delta. Cycling the Mekong Delta is the best way to get up close with the cities and towns along the water—and to exercise while doing it. Tours both day and overnight can be booked from Hanoi and Ho Chi Minh and are generally all-inclusive, with a solid mountain bike and helmet provided. Though the terrain is flat, these rides are best suited for those with at least a moderate degree of fitness.

Phong Na Khe Be National Park. Home to the world's largest cave, this national park in Central Vietnam offers some of the best outdoor activities in the country among untamed jungle. Try your hand at ziplining, kayaking the rapids, or boating into a river cave.

Sapa. This was once a French hill station and today is one of the most popular bases for hikers, with a wide variety of restaurants. Unfortunately, the flocks of tourists mean loads of hawkers, but that hasn't spoiled the views. Mist hangs ethereally above the rice terraces.

Shopping

As in much of Southeast Asia, you'll find plenty of custom-made clothing in silks and linens, ceramics, elegant black-and-red lacquer ware, and intricate wood-carvings of Buddhas and animals. In well-touristed places, fair trade and social enterprise shops are growing in popularity and are a wonderful way to support the local economy. **Hanoi.** The contemporary art scene here is booming, although paintings can get pricey. Hit the pavement in Hanoi's Old Quarter and you'll pass shops selling stationery, shoes, bolts of silk and silk clothing, accessories, and lacquer ware.

Hoi An. Hundreds of tailor shops line the streets here and made-to-measure clothing can be turned around in just 48 hours—sometimes less for simple pieces. The best way to get exactly what you want is to bring something to be copied. Shoes and bags can also be custom made.

Ho Chi Minh City. The boutique scene here is small but growing, with chic shops selling clothing, accessories, home goods, and high-quality lacquer ware from local designers. Alternatively, immerse yourself in the colorful chaos of Bin Tanh market. The crowds can be overwhelming, as can the abundance of goods, but it's certainly an authentic Vietnamese market experience.

Sapa. The market here, in northern Vietnam, is the place to go to buy the hill tribes' beautifully embroidered fabrics, indigo-dyed clothing, as well as other handicrafts and food staples. If you're in town long enough, you can even have your own clothes embroidered with colorful traditional designs.

Shrines and Places of Worship

While Vietnam's government says it's an atheist state, shared beliefs and practices, such as paying respects to ancestors, are still prevalent. Both Buddhist and Catholic homes and businesses have altars to ancestors.

Cao Dai Holy See. Though this colorful temple is 90 km (56 miles) from Ho Chi Minh City, it can be easily combined with a day trip to the Cu Chi Tunnels. The temple is devoted to Caodaism, a contemporary Vietnamese religion based on an amalgamation of Eastern and Western thought.

Marble Mountains. Twenty minutes' drive south of Danang are the Marble Mountains. The climb to the summit of Thuy Son, one of the five mountains, is literally breathtaking; it's 150 steps (there's an elevator, too), but you'll be rewarded with shrines hidden inside caves and grottoes and sweeping views of Danang.

Perfume Pagoda. Every spring, thousands make the pilgrimage to Perfume (Huong) Pagoda, a day trip from Hanoi complete with cable car and boat rides. This complex of Buddhist temples and shrines is carved into the limestone of the Huong Tich Mountains.

Tran Quac Pagoda. On an island just off Hanoi's West Lake is the city's oldest Buddhist pagoda, dating back to the 6th century. Its peaceful shoreline location makes it a popular spot for watching the sun set. In the pagoda's leafy garden is a Bodhi tree, believed to have grown from a cutting from the original Bodhi tree under which the Buddha found enlightenment.

FLAVORS OF VIETNAM

Thousands of Years in the Making

For centuries, Vietnamese cooks have been adapting the techniques, ingredients, and recipes of conquering overlords, trading partners, and neighboring nations, to create a cuisine that is arguably the best in the world, and certainly one of the healthiest. The flavors of Vietnam are fresh and light, featuring herbs such as basil, Vietnamese mint, lemongrass, and coriander/cilantro. The versatile fish sauce known as *nuoc mam* makes an appearance at most meals, as does seafood, and rice noodles, fresh vegetables, rice, and lime juice.

Vietnam's three main areas, the North, Central, and South, each have their own regional variations, reflecting their different climates, cultures, and traditions. In the north, which has a distinct winter, ginger and dill are commonly used, as are some Chinese spices. The food of the Central region is the spiciest in Vietnam and includes everyday home cooking, as well as the elaborate Imperial cuisine developed during the Nguyen Dynasty. In the lush, tropical south, there's a stronger focus on salads and herbs, which are added to soups or used as wraps.

Vietnamese dishes balance textures and flavors by blending spicy, sour, bitter, salty, and sweet. Each dish should appeal to all five senses, too, and great attention is paid to the colors, spices, textures, and presentation of even the most humble dishes. The Vietnamese also follow the Chinese belief that each meal should contain a ying-yang balance of "hot" and "cooling" foods.

Noodles

Vietnam has a plethora of noodle dishes, from stir-fries to soups containing noodles made from rice, tapioca, and wheat, and sometimes a combination.

Bun rieu and hoan thanh mi. In the north, the noodle specialty is *bun rieu,* featuring thin rice noodles and a tomato-y broth made with pounded rice paddy crab. The Chinese influence in this region is also apparent, for example, in the popular noodle dish *hoan thanh mi.* Said aloud, it's clear that hoan thanh is the local adaption of wonton, while mi is Vietnamese for wheat noodle.

Mi Quang and cao lau. Central Vietnam's Quang Nam province, which contains the cities of Hoi An and Danang, is home to some of Vietnam's most delicious noodle soups, in the form of *mi Quang,* a savory half-soup, half-salad noodle dish with pork, prawn, quail eggs, and rice cracker shards. Equally popular is *cao lau,* which uses local noodles with an almost mythical backstory, along with pork and fresh herbs. According to the local belief, cao lau noodles are only authentic if they are made from water from a certain Hoi An well and the ash of a particular type of tree found on nearby Cham Island.

Pho. Perhaps the most famous Vietnamese food, and the unofficial national dish, *pho* (pronounced "fuh"), is a tangle of silky rice noodles and beef (which can be raw and sliced thin) or chicken in a fragrant broth with hints of roasted onion, ginger, star anise, cinnamon, and cloves, garnished with coriander, onion, green onion, and bean sprouts; this is a must-try dish. True foodies will enjoy the subtle changes in the way pho is prepared and served as they travel through Vietnam. In the South, an array of accoutrements, including a basket of fresh herbs, is served alongside a bowl of pho but in the north, Hanoians believe the broth should be so good, nothing needs to be added, so minimal accompaniments are provided. Once

you get down into the Mekong Delta, the pork and prawn noodle soup known as *hu tieu* is more common than pho.

Rice

The fact that the Vietnamese word for rice, *com,* is the same as the word for food indicates how important this rice staple is to the Vietnamese diet.

Com tam dishes. Throughout Vietnam, rice restaurants offer cheap home-cooked meals to working people. Called *com binh dan* in the central regions and *com tam* in the South, these places are where adventurous visitors can try a range of dishes using the time-honored travelers' point-and-order method. The signature com tam dish is barbecued pork marinated in fish sauce, garlic, and palm sugar, and a slice of Vietnamese quiche—an egg pie containing noodles, wood ear mushrooms, and ground pork. Other dishes often on display in the glass-fronted com stalls include *ca kho to* (caramelized fish in claypot) and *thit kho tau* (pork and duck eggs stewed in coconut juice).

Rice cakes and snacks. Sticky rice is a sweet anytime-of-day snack, although in Ho Chi Minh City it's most common to see food vendors pushing carts of colorful sticky rice—purple, black, and green—after dark. Rice is also used to make a range of delicious steamed crepes and savory cakes, such as *banh cuon*—rice crepes loosely stuffed with pork and mushroom, and topped with fried shallots and fish sauce—and *banh beo,* bite-size rice cakes topped with dried shrimp powder and green onion oil.

Rice wine There are many forms of rice wine, including the Central Vietnamese *ruoi can,* a sticky rice wine prepared in six-liter vats and consumed communally through giant straws, and snake wine, where whole snakes are infused in rice wine or grain alcohol, seen most often in tourist shops.

Banh mi, wraps, and rolls

Banh mi. One of the most obvious culinary legacies of the almost 100 years of French rule, *banh mi* is the Vietnamese version of a baguette. There are a few different varieties of banh mi, with the most popular being banh mi *thit,* a crisp-on-the-outside and fluffy-on-the-inside baguette with pâté, slices of Vietnamese sausage, strips of cucumber, pickled carrot and radish, fresh herbs, and slices of chili. Banh mi *op la* is a great on-the-go breakfast, filled with a fried egg, soy sauce, and strips of cucumber. There's also a roast pork and barbecue sauce version, banh mi *heo quay.* The best banh mi vendors will lightly toast the baguette before slicing it open, filling it with fresh ingredients, wrapping it in a square of paper secured with an elastic band, and presenting the warm parcel to the customer.

Cuon Diep. Vietnamese cuisine also features a range of other wrapped and rolled delights, some of which are prerolled, such as *cuon diep* (mustard leaf wraps), while others are a wrap-your-own affair, customable with a vast array of herbs, meats, and salad items.

Spring rolls and summer rolls. The most famous of Vietnam's various wraps and rolls are its fried spring rolls. Known as *nem* in the north and *cha gio* in the South, fried spring rolls are stuffed with pork, prawn, and crab. *Goi cuon,* known as summer rolls or fresh spring rolls, consist of rice paper wrapped around vermicelli, pork, shrimp, and fresh chives.

PEOPLE OF VIETNAM

Visit any of the hill tribes and the variety of different ethnicities and cultures that make up Vietnam becomes readily apparent. The country has 54 ethnic groups recognized by the government, from the majority Khin—who make up more than 85% of the population—to the tiny Brau group, who are believed to number fewer than 400.

The Khin tend to live in urban areas and, socioeconomically, are at the top. The ethnic minority groups, however—especially the smallest—face a number of problems. These include lack of access to adequate education, health care, and public services. Without education, these groups—in particular those living in remote, mountainous regions with agrarian economies—are unable to acquire knowledge and increase production. Though there are government programs aimed at improving the lives of Vietnam's rural minorities, they are not very effective, and many live below the poverty line. For some ethnic minority groups, such as those in the hill tribes around Sapa, tourism has provided a major boon to the economy.

If you can't make it to the hill-tribe villages, the next best thing is a visit to Vietnam Museum of Ethnology in Hanoi. The fantastic exhibits showcase nearly 300 photographs and some 700 objects, including costumes, musical instruments, weapons, and hunting implements. On the museum's grounds are reconstructed homes from a dozen ethnic groups that visitors are welcome to explore. What follows is an overview of some of the groups you may see on your travels.

Kinh (Population: 74,000,000) The Kinh originated from what is now southern China and northern Vietnam, and the Kinh living over the border in China are known as the Gin. Today the highest concentrations of Kinh are in Ho Chi Minh City and Hanoi. You're unlikely to be able to recognize any Kinh by their outfits; as most live in urban centers, they dress just as in the West. Vietnam's majority ethnic group speaks standard Vietnamese.

Tay (Population: 1,700,000) The country's second largest ethnic group makes up just 2% of the population. The Tay tend to live in Quang Ninh province, home to Halong Bay, and in Sapa, in Lao Cai province. Traditionally, the Tay society was an agrarian one, with most Tay living in fertile areas and growing rice and corn. Today, many Tay have intermarried and live in ethnically mixed villages or in towns. The group speaks Tay, a Tai language that includes standard Thai and Laotian. Traditional clothing is made from homegrown cotton, dyed with indigo and usually without embroidery or embellishments. Women wear both skirts and trousers.

Muong (Population: 1,300,000) It's believed that the Muong are the most closely related to the ethnic Vietnamese (Kinh). They reside in northern Vietnam's mountainous regions, in Hoa Binh and Thanh Hoa provinces. Far from the Chinese border and high in the mountains, the Muong were not influenced by the Chinese as other ethnic minority groups were. The economy is agrarian and the Muong attend markets and trade goods. The group speaks Muong, closely related to Vietnamese. Women generally wear a plain white fabric headscarf, short blouses, usually with small side slits, ankle-length skirts with an embroidered floral border, and silver key chains hanging from the waist.

Khmer Krom (Population: 1,200,000) These are the indigenous Khmer (present day Cambodians) who live along the southern Mekong Delta, past Cambodia. The group takes its name from the Khmer word "krom," which means "below," implying south of Cambodia. The area where the Khmer Krom live is not technically a disputed territory—it's considered Vietnam—but there are associations of exiled Khmer Krom who want self-determination for the Khmer Krom in Vietnam. The clothing worn in public by most Khmer Krom is unlikely to give them away; women are usually in a simple blouse and *sampot* (a long rectangular cloth worn as a skirt) and men wear shirts tucked into sarongs. Some Khmer Krom may also dress in Western clothing. Many practice Theravada Buddhism. They speak Vietnamese and Khmer, which differ from neighboring languages in that they aren't tonal.

Hmong (Population: 1,100,000) Within Vietnam, the Hmong have several subgroups, including the Red, White, Flower, Striped, Green, and Black Hmong. The Hmong economy was traditionally agrarian, but an influx of tourists into places like Sapa has helped jumpstart a tourism sector. The Hmong wear and produce beautiful textiles with intricate embroidery. In their colorful embroidered skirts and jackets, the Flower Hmong women are the most recognizable. Other Hmong generally wear black skirts or trousers, a black jacket with colorful trim, and sometimes a peaked black turban. Depending on the group, the outfit is accessorized with an embroidered belt or waistband. At Sapa Market, dozens of Hmong women gather to sell jewelry, handicrafts, and textiles. In doing so, they've changed the traditional Hmong family structure; no longer is the man the head of every household. The Hmong/Mong speak Hmong.

Gia Rai (Population: 500,000) This group, also known as the Jarai, lives primarily in Vietnam's Central Highlands (a few thousand live in Cambodia). The Gia Rai culture is matrilineal. Theirs is an agricultural society, and the Gia Rai grow crops and raise pigs, chicken, buffaloes, oxen, and horses. Cloth and basket weaving are popular, and back baskets are often used to transport loads. The Gia Rai were originally animists (those who believe nonhuman entities have spirits), but visits by American missionaries have resulted in several thousand converts to Christianity. The Gia Rai speak Gia Rai, a Malayo-Polynesian language, as well as Vietnamese. Gia Rai men wear white or striped loin clothes (*toai*) and sometimes a short black jacket. Women dress in long indigo sarongs with designs on the hem and a long-sleeve black top with colorful sleeves.

Cham (Population: 170,000) When the Ancient Kingdom of Champa was annexed by Vietnam, many Cham fled to present-day Hainan (China), Trengganu (Malaysia), and south to Cambodia. Today, the Cham in Vietnam live in the central part of the country, including in Ho Chi Minh City. Many are Hindu (compared to the Muslim Cham in Cambodia). In Vietnam, the group speaks Cham and Vietnamese. Most Cham living in urban centers dress in mostly Western clothing. Those who live in more rural areas wear a sarong, with men wearing a shirt on top and women wearing a form-fitting blouse. Both sexes use turbans or head wraps.

HISTORY YOU CAN SEE

Ancient Vietnam and Chinese Domination

Inhabited since the Paleolithic era, which began more than 2.6 million years ago, the origins of the earliest settlers in Vietnam are mostly lost in the mists of time. The first of the Hung Kings, Hung Vuong, came to power in 2879 BC, in the northern Red River Delta, naming his kingdom Van Lang. According to legend, Hung Vuong was the eldest son of an immortal mountain fairy called Au Co. It's unsurprising that in a country famous for its cuisine, food plays a role in the story of its founding—the first Hung King is credited with teaching his subjects how to grow rice. The reign of all 18 Hung Kings is known as the Hong Bang period, which lasted for about 2,500 years until 258 BC. Around this time, the Vietnam of today was divided into three states: Van Lang in the north, the Champa Kingdom in the center, and the Indian-influenced Cambodian Kingdom of Funan in the south. Over the course of several centuries, these states waged ongoing battles for land and power. The first of four periods of Chinese domination of northern Vietnam began in 111 BC with the Han–Nanyue War and continued for 10 centuries, introducing the Chinese language, Confucianism, and advanced agricultural techniques to the area. During Chinese domination, Vietnam was known as Annam, then Tinh Hai. Chinese rule ended in AD 938 when provincial governor Ngo Quyen took control of the military and fended off the Chinese in the Battle of Bach Dang River, north of modern-day Haiphong. The mandarin system (a highly regulated system of elite groups of bureaucratic scholars that governed the civil service) remained in place for about 1,000 years after Vietnam became a sovereign nation.

What To See

The Chinese influence on Vietnam is pervasive; it can be seen in every **temple** and **pagoda,** which are very Chinese in style with Chinese characters used throughout, and in every home, where the practice of ancestor worship continues to be observed. The Chinese influence is also evident in **art,** especially the techniques used to produce ceramics, as well as the visual references to the Chinese-introduced themes of Confucianism, Mahayana Buddhism, and Taoism. Few actual relics remain, as sovereign Vietnam—past and present—does not like to be reminded of its domination by its

ca. 1300 BC	The Dong Son are the earliest recorded civilization in what is now Vietnam.
AD 100	The Champa Kingdom emerges near present-day Danang.
939–1400	The early Chinese dynastic period sees the rise and fall of many ruling families.
1413–28	The Chinese Ming Empire reconquers Vietnam and occupies the country, forcing further taxes, servitude, and Chinese culture on the Vietnamese.
1428	The Chinese officially recognize Vietnam's independence following the Lam Son uprising.
1627	Alexandre de Rhodes, a French Jesuit missionary, adapts spoken Vietnamese to the Roman alphabet. The country splits into the Trinh and the Nguyen dynasty.
1802	Emperor Gia Long unites Vietnam. French missionary activity begins to spread as the Nguyen emperors develop a mutually tolerant relationship with the French.

populous northern neighbor. Instead, every city and town names its **streets** after the national heroes who helped *repel* the Chinese, Hai Ba Trung (the two sisters Trung), and Thi Sach (one of the Trung sister's husbands). You'll see these names frequently as you travel around Vietnam.

The Lost Kingdom of Champa

Little is known of the Cham, a powerful maritime empire that ruled the central and southern lowlands of Vietnam for more than 900 years, leaving behind exquisite temple complexes and fanciful Hindu sculptures. Like the Funan Kingdom, the Kingdom of Champa was based on strong trade links with India. The Cham culture adopted Indianized art forms and architectural styles as well as written Sanskrit. From AD 2nd to 13th century, Amaravati, now known as Quang Nam province in central Vietnam, was the capital of the Champa Kingdom, with the city of Lam Ap Pho the kingdom's center for sea trade. Lam Ap Pho, later called Faifo, and now Hoi An, was a key stop on the Spice Route between the Persian Gulf and China.

What To See

About 50 km (31 miles) from the former Cham port of Hoi An is the most famous of all the Cham temple complexes in Vietnam, **My Son,** which predates Angkor Wat in Cambodia. It was heavily damaged by carpet bombing during the Vietnam War. **The Po Nagar Cham Towers** in Nha Trang, the **Poshanu Towers** in Phan Thiet, and the **Thap Doi Cham Towers in Quy Nhon** are also relics of the mysterious kingdom. Locals still pay their respects at the old shrines, and the sites themselves are shown the same respect as temples and pagodas (when visiting, adults should have their knees and shoulders covered). The **Danang Museum of Cham Sculpture** houses the world's largest collection of Cham artifacts and sculptures, including many representations of the Hindu *linga* and *yoni* (male and female sex organs).

Dynastic Vietnam

Ngo Quyen's military defeat of the Chinese in AD 938 marked the start of the short-lived Ngo Dynasty. The Ngo Dynasty was followed by the Dinh Dynasty, during which time the country was renamed Dai Co Viet, literally Great Viet Land. Plotting and politicking was rife during these years, as was the ever-present threat of foreign invasion, leading to the rise and fall of many ruling families, now known as the Early Le, Ly, Tran, Ho, Le, and Nguyen dynasties. The emperors

1887	The French create the Indochinese Union in order to end Vietnamese expansion into Cambodia and Laos, ending the unified Vietnamese state created by Gia Long.	1930	Ho Chi Minh and his colleagues form the Indochinese Communist Party in Hong Kong.
1890	Ho Chi Minh, Communist revolutionary leader, is born as Nguyen Sinh Cung. In 1911 he leaves Vietnam. Over the next 30 years he works in France and spends time in Moscow, becoming involved with the Communist movement.	1940	The French Vichy government peacefully capitulates to Japanese occupation of Vietnam. The Japanese leave the French administration in place as the most efficient way of controlling the region during World War II.

of these dynasties ruled with absolute power, in charge of the judicial system and the armed forces. During this time, the rulers were expanding south, battling the Kingdom of Champa in what is now central Vietnam and the Angkor Empire of modern-day Cambodia, as well as fending off incursions from the north, including several Mongol attacks ordered by Kublai Khanh. In 1802 Emperor Gia Long united the country for the first time, named the new nation Viet Nam (Southern Viet), and designated Hue the capital. This heralded the beginning of the 143-year Nguyen Dynasty, which ended in 1847 when Emperor Tu Duc ceded administration of the country to the French. This association with the French means Vietnam's current leaders don't favorably regard the Nguyen Dynasty, even though the founder of the dynasty, Emperor Gia Long (1762–1820), is credited with being the first to unify Vietnam's north and south.

What To See

The Imperial capital was moved to Thang Long (Ascending Dragon), now known as **Hanoi,** in the 11th century during the Ly Dynasty. Hanoi's **Temple of Literature,** built by Ly Thanh Tong, the third emperor of the Ly Dynasty, remains in excellent condition, and is one of the city's most popular sights. **Ngoc Son Temple** in the middle of Hanoi's Hoan Kiem Lake is dedicated to Tran Hung Dao, the Supreme Commander of Vietnam during the Tran Dynasty, who helped repel the Mongol hordes in the 13th century. The former capital of **Hue** is now home to the country's highest concentration of Imperial architecture, including the UNESCO-listed **Citadel** and the **royal tombs** of the Nguyen Dynasty emperors Minh Mang, Gia Long, and Tu Duc.

French Indochina

The French had a presence in Vietnam from the early 17th century, when Jesuit missionaries arrived, quickly graduating from saving souls to involving themselves in diplomacy and politics. The ruling Nguyen Dynasty attempted to expel the Catholics, and in response, France launched a military attack on Danang in 1847. Saigon was seized two years later and by 1883 Emperor Tu Duc had signed a treaty making north and central Vietnam a French protectorate. The French colonial era was to last until 1954. During this time the French divided Vietnam into three administrative areas—Tonkin, Annam, and Cochin-China—and set about ambitiously building roads, bridges,

1945	At Japan's defeat, the Viet Minh takes over large portions of the country. Famine kills 2 million.
1946	Ongoing tensions between the French and the Viet Minh lead to the outbreak of the French-Indochina War.
1954–55	French defeat leads to the division of Vietnam at the 17th parallel. The United States begins to provide direct aid and to train the South Vietnamese army.
1959–66	American military support to the south increases. The Gulf of Tonkin

	incident (1964) prompts the first American bombing of North Vietnam. The first U.S. combat troops arrive (1965) and ground war begins.
1967–70	The Vietnam War enters its bloodiest phase. American forces number 540,000, and there are heavy casualties on both sides. U.S. troop casualties eventually total more than 58,000. Total Vietnamese death toll is an estimated 2.1 million from 1954 to 1975.

1

public buildings, and the Hanoi to Saigon railway, which is still used today. In 1941, the man born Nguyen Sinh Cung but better known by his assumed name of Ho Chi Minh, returned to Vietnam after decades abroad to lead the anti-French independence movement, the Viet Minh. The resistance that followed World War II, with Communist China supporting the Viet Minh, is known as the First Indochina War, which lasted until 1954. The Vietnamese defeated the French at Dien Bien Phu, marking the end of the French-Indochina War. Agreement was reached among France, Britain, the United States, and the Soviet Union as part of the Geneva Accords to cease hostilities in Indochina and to divide Vietnam temporarily at the 17th parallel. Hundreds of thousands of refugees, mostly Vietnamese Catholics worried that religious tolerance will not be practiced in the Viet Minh–controlled north, fled to the south with U.S. Navy assistance.

What To See

Colonial architecture can be found throughout Vietnam, some dilapidated and decrepit, some beautifully maintained. In Hanoi's **French Quarter,** crumbling colonial facades line the streets between landmark colonial buildings, such as the **Metropole** and the **Opera House.** Spanning the Red River is the cantilever **Long Bien Bridge,** designed by Gustave Eiffel of Eiffel Tower fame. In Ho Chi Minh City, the former **Hotel de Ville,** the **Central Post Office**—another masterpiece by the prolific Eiffel—and the Opera House are the most prominent public buildings from the colonial era. The existence of highland towns such as **Dalat,** with its large French villas, and **Sapa** are also credited to the former French rulers, who set up hill stations there to escape the oppressive heat of the lowlands.

War with the Americans

During the Cold War, the long-running military and political standoff between the United States and the USSR, much of the foreign policy of the United States was directed by the Domino Theory. This was the belief that allowing one country to fall to Communism would cause a stain of red to flow across the world's geopolitical maps, and Asia would be lost to Russian domination. Despite the forces on the ground in Vietnam since 1950, in the interest of "containment," American involvement in the North-South war through 1964 mainly involved financially

1969–70	Paris peace talks continue. Ho Chi Minh dies of natural causes in Hanoi. Troop withdrawal begins.
1975	The fall of Saigon. The United States retreats as Communist forces capture Saigon on April 30.
1978–79	Hanoi signs a friendship pact with the Soviet Union. Vietnam invades Cambodia in 1978 and remains in armed conflict until 1989, effectively ending the "killing fields" there.
1986	Vietnam commits to doi moi, the reform of socialist economic policies into a more market-oriented system.
1994	The United States ends its economic embargo on Vietnam. Economic rebuilding continues, through IMF and World Bank loans, and foreign investments.
2000–01	Bill Clinton is the first U.S. president to visit since the end of the war. The country celebrates the 25th anniversary of the Fall of Saigon. Vietnamese stock exchange opens.
2008	The global economic crash halts a decade of rapid economic growth.
2013	Vietnam's 90th million citizen is born.

assisting the French and then the South Vietnamese government in their conflict with Communist North Vietnam. By December 1965, however, there were more than 184,000 U.S. troops in Vietnam, and by 1967 there were almost half a million. Extensive carpet-bombing did little to impede the growth and advance of the Communist Viet Cong army, and both sides continued to suffer heavy casualties over the next four years. In the West, the public began questioning U.S. involvement in the war—and the government's claim it was winning—in the wake of the 1968 Tet Offensive, when the Viet Cong launched coordinated surprise attacks against U.S. troops in more than 1,000 cities and towns throughout Vietnam. Public support for the war in the United States declined further when news broke of the brutal My Lai Massacre, a mass killing of unarmed Vietnamese civilians by American troops the same year (1968). After much negotiation, the Paris Peace Accords were signed, and on January 27, 1973, a ceasefire was called and the United States withdrew, leaving a skeleton ground crew to advise the South Vietnamese Army. On April 30, 1975, Vietnam was "liberated" when North Vietnamese tanks crashed through the Independence Palace in Saigon, marking the end of the war.

What To See

The tanks that remain guarding the front of the **Reunification Palace** in Ho Chi Minh City are perhaps the starkest reminder of the victory of the north over the south. Evidence of the brutalities of the last war abound at the various museums throughout the country, including Ho Chi Minh City's grueling **War Remnants Museum** and Hanoi's **Military History Museum** and **Ho Chi Minh Museum.** You can also explore the **Cu Chi Tunnels,** the extensive network of underground tunnels used by the Viet Cong just outside of Ho Chi Minh City, as well as the horrific prisons used by the South Vietnamese government, including the infamous **Tiger Cages,** on Con Dao Islands.

Reunification and Afterward

A decade of brutal Communist rule followed the "liberation" of Southern Vietnam in 1975, with harsh reprisals for those linked to the Southern government and military. The reprisals, the reeducation camps, and the grinding poverty of this period led to a mass exodus from Southern Vietnam, with an estimated 2 million people leaving the country. In 1994 the United States. lifted the trade embargo on Vietnam and a year later the two countries normalized relations. Vietnam's ascension to the World Trade Organization in 2006 further opened the doors to foreign investment and contributed to the resurgence of Vietnam's economy. Vietnam's move toward a market economy and the resumption of commercial flights between the two countries in 2004, also seemed to be the catalyst for many Overseas Vietnamese, known as Viet Kieu, to return to Vietnam.

What To See

The gleaming skyscrapers in Hanoi, Danang, and Ho Chi Minh City, including the 68-story **Bitexco Financial Tower,** signify Vietnam's heady postwar rush toward capitalism. One of the most noticeable signs of international investment can be seen in the **food and retail landscape,** with foreign brands such as Coca-Cola, KFC, McDonald's, Louis Vuitton, and branches of Korea's giant Lotte conglomerate increasingly visible.

VIETNAM MADE EASY

What vaccines do I need?

All travelers should have routine vaccines up-to-date (these include MMR, diphtheria-tetanus-pertussis). Hepatitis A and typhoid can be contracted through contaminated food and water; you should not let this stop you from eating street food, but stick to bottled water. In the United States, the hepatitis A vaccine is nearly 100% effective; it's given in two doses six months apart. If you don't have time to get both doses, the Immunization Action Coalition says it's still well worth it to get just the first dose. The typhoid vaccine is 50%–80% effective and can be taken orally. The risk of malaria is extremely low.

Will I be safe?

Violent crime against tourists is extremely rare. Women traveling alone in Vietnam are unlikely to face any harassment. Most common is petty crime—pickpocketing, bag-snatching, and scamming. ATMs are everywhere in the big cities, so you needn't carry around large amounts of cash. In crowded areas, or when riding in cyclos or on motorcycles, don't wear your camera or sunglasses around your neck, and keep a firm grip on your bag. When you arrive at the airport, go to the taxi stand; don't get in the car with anyone who comes up to you. Beyond scams, the major safety hazard is Vietnam's chaotic traffic. Many intersections have no traffic lights; even if they do, the flow of traffic won't stop even though the light has changed. The safest way to cross the street is to latch on to locals; follow them closely and you'll get across safely. If there's no one you can cross with, be brave. Scary as it may be, step into the street and start moving forward without hesitation; the scooters will go around you.

Are there cultural sensitivities of which I should be aware?

Just as in other Asian countries, the concept of "face" is very important. You can give face, lose face, and help others save face. As face can be a tricky concept for foreigners, the safest way to give it is to compliment someone's family or their business acumen. Even if you are upset with a vendor, be careful not to publicly shame them, which will cause a loss of face. When meeting people, you can shake as we do in the West, but locals may do so with both hands, and bow slightly as a sign of respect—especially if you're meeting someone elderly. Use common sense: do not bring up the Vietnam War (which Vietnamese people call the American War) unless you are with your guide at one of the war museums. At religious sites, cover your shoulders and knees. Otherwise, modesty is not an issue in Vietnam, and women will run into no problems wearing shorts and tank tops.

Do people speak English?

Given that English proficiency in Vietnam is low and few foreigners visiting Vietnam speak Vietnamese, it's surprisingly easy to get around. In Ho Chi Minh City and Hanoi, where the urban population tends to be educated, English-speakers are most prevalent. Nearly all teenagers and university-aged people speak some English, and they're often happy to help. When in doubt, write it out: some locals can read English much better than they can speak it. Anywhere that's on the tourist circuit, from Sapa south to Phu Quoc, has vendors used to speaking basic English. In places that see crowds of visitors, such as the big cities and Hoi An, even some taxi drivers understand very simple English directions (left, right, stop).

GREAT ITINERARIES

ESSENTIAL VIETNAM, 10 DAYS

Visitors to Vietnam mostly follow the main transport route, Highway 1, known as the spine of Vietnam. The distances involved in traversing this long, skinny country means most visitors fly, rather than travel by road, to take in the major cities—the bustling hub of Ho Chi Minh City, the beachfront resort town of Nha Trang, the ancient trading port of Hoi An, the former Imperial capital of Hue, and the cultural and political capital of Hanoi. A visit to Vietnam isn't complete, however, without a visit to the mesmerizing Mekong Delta, and the captivating Halong Bay. This Essential Vietnam itinerary covers all these must-see attractions, but we've provided optional add-ons for those who have more time to explore further afield.

Days 1–2: Ho Chi Minh City

Arrive in Ho Chi Minh City (Saigon) and hit an ATM before heading to your hotel by taxi. Spend the first day visiting top sites including the **Reunification Palace,** the **Central Post Office,** and the **Notre Dame Cathedral** in bustling District 1, as well as the controversial **War Remnants Museum.** Take a **nighttime food tour** (essential to book these ahead of time to avoid disappointment) for an overview of the country's delicious and varied cuisine. On the second day, rise early to join an organized day tour to the **Cu Chi Tunnels,** accessible by car or boat on the Saigon River. Stretching from all the way to Cambodia, this network of underground tunnels was used by the Viet Cong during the war. Further your Vietnamese food education with the set menu at **Cyclo Resto.**

Day 3: Mekong Delta
(Excursions from HCMC take 7–9 hours)

Take an organized tour to the **Mekong Delta.** For richer insights into life on the delta, with its networks of waterways and narrow motorbike-only paths, fruit orchards, rice paddies, busy markets, and friendly locals, take a river cruise with **Les Rives** or a reputable bicycle tour, such as those offered by **Mekong Bike Tours.**

Day 4: Nha Trang
(1 hour by plane from Ho Chi Minh City, 7½ hours by train)

Take a one-hour flight from Ho Chi Minh City to **Nha Trang.** Consider this your most relaxing destination in your Vietnam travels, and take full advantage of every moment. Check into one of the luxury resorts that line Nha Trang's coastline. Between spa treatments and beach walks, take a boat trip to the nearby island of **Hon Mun** for an afternoon dive or snorkel. For a taste of culture, squeeze in a visit to the **Po Nagar Cham Towers** before an evening meal at one of Nha Trang's celebrated restaurants.

Days 5 and 6: Hoi An
(1 hour and 15 minutes by plane to Danang, then a 45-minute taxi ride to Hoi An)

Home to French and Chinese architecture, tailor shops, art galleries, and the 16th-century **Japanese Covered Bridge,** Hoi An is an easy place to fall in love with. Catch a flight from Nha Trang to Danang (and then a taxi to Hoi An), and upon arrival, spend some time getting lost in the **Old Quarter.** Sip on traditional Vietnamese coffee, get fitted for a custom-tailored suit, and shop to your heart's content. Visit the famed Chinese-built **Assembly Halls,** and if you have time, take a bicycle tour of the surrounding countryside.

Dedicate the morning of Day 6 to sampling Vietnamese cuisine. Participate in a **cooking course** or join a culinary tour through the Central Market, the best place to try local dishes like *cao lau* (rice noodles) and *banh bao vac* (steamed dumplings). Spend the rest of the day at the **My Son Sanctuary,** the former religious capital of the Champa kingdom. Dating back to the 4th century, this archaeological site is an hour's drive from Hoi An. For less history and more relaxation, swap My Son for an afternoon at **An Bang Beach,** a favorite with locals, known for its warm waters, soft sand, and excellent seafood restaurants.

Day 7: Hue
(About 2½ hours by train or 3 hours by bus from Danang)

Traveling by train to Hue will give you some spectacular views of the South China Sea on one side and the Hai Van Pass on the other. After checking into your hotel, get your history fix with a full day exploring the top three sites: **The Citadel,** the **Thien Mu Pagoda,** and one of the impressive **mausoleums** that pay tribute to past emperors. Be sure to reach the pagoda by way of dragon boat along the **Perfume River.** Dine in the tourist district near Chu Van An Street, or venture to a converted colonial villa to dine at **Les Jardins De La Carambole.**

Day 8: Hanoi
(1 hour and 10 minutes by plane or 14½ hours by train from Hue)

Catch a morning flight from Hue one hour north to Hanoi. Plan to spend a full day in the city and account for the 45-minute drive from the airport to downtown Hanoi. Wander the bustling streets of **Old Quarter,** stopping along the way to shop or enjoy a cold one on **Bia Hoi corner,** the beer mecca of Hanoi. Visit the **Temple of Literature** and the nearby **Fine Arts Museum,** or stroll around the picturesque **Hoan Kiem Lake;** its northern shore is home to Jade Island where Ngoc Son Temple stands. Be sure to sample *pho* at dinner, especially because this popular rice noodle dish originated in northern Vietnam. Finish the day with a live performance at the **Hanoi Opera House** or the **Thang Long Water Puppet Theater.** Try to get an early night before your 8 am shuttle to Halong Bay. Most hotels will store luggage for guests who take day or overnight trips to the coast.

Day 9: Halong Bay
(Excursions from Hanoi take 11–12 hours)

Travel by shuttle four hours to **Halong Bay.** Select a tour company offering trips to floating villages, historic caves, pristine beaches, and **Cat Ba Island.** Organize the tour company ahead of time, as this is a long day. As Halong Bay's largest island, Cat Ba is home to lakes, waterfalls, caves, and a national park where the endangered Langur monkey lives.

Day 10: Hanoi

End your trip with a day of history and culture. Begin with a visit to **Ho Chi Minh's Mausoleum and Residence.** This memorial in Ba Dinh Square gets extremely crowded, so be sure to arrive early. Spend some time strolling through this area, which includes the pretty **One Pillar Pagoda.** Head back to the Old Quarter for dinner and a musical performance of Ca Tru. This ceremonial singing can best be enjoyed at the **Thang Long Ca Tru Theater.** Grab a nightcap at one of the rooftop lounge bars in this charming district.

PHU QUOC ISLAND EXTENSION, 2–3 DAYS

(1 hour by plane from Ho Chi Minh City)

A tropical island paradise with long, lovely beaches, warm turquoise water, and swathes of jungle, **Phu Quoc** is the perfect backdrop for winding down, no matter what form of relaxation you prefer. It makes for a great side trip from Ho Chi Minh City.

Follow days 1–2 of Essential Vietnam itinerary.

Day 3

Fly from Ho Chi Minh City to Phu Quoc, just 12 km (7½ miles) from the southeast coast of Cambodia. If your idea of relaxation is the full five-star resort experience, spend today holed up in your resort enjoying the amenities. If you're the type that can't stand still, organize some transport (motorbike, taxi, or car-with-driver) and set out to explore Phu Quoc's **beaches.**

Watch the sun sink into the South China Sea with a cocktail at **On The Rocks,** Mango Bay Resort's in-house restaurant at **Ong Lang Beach,** then enjoy some delicious Asian fusion cuisine as the waves caress the rocks under the deck.

Day 4

Explore the undersea delights of Phu Quoc with a half-day diving or snorkeling tour with **Rainbow Divers.** Spend the afternoon recovering on a deck chair at **Rory's Beach Bar** and a long late-afternoon walk along the beach to your dinner destination, **The Spice House** at Cassia Cottage.

Day 5

Allocate several hours to swimming, sunbathing, or spa-ing, then some laid-back exploring of some of Phu Quoc's sights. You could head south of **Duong Dong Town,** stopping at **Ngoc Hien Pearl** and the **Coconut Tree Prison** en route to the northern stretches of **Sao Beach.** After a bit of swimming, loop around to **Suoi Tranh** for a lovely rain forest walk to the waterfall. Get back to Duong Dong Town in time to watch the sun set from the pier near the **Dinh Cau Night Market,** then dive into the market for a local-style barbecue seafood dinner. Have a postprandial drink and maybe some exquisite tapas at **Itaca Resto Lounge.**

Day 6

Fly back to Ho Chi Minh City, and take the ferry to Hai Tien to begin your Mekong Delta explorations.

CON DAO ISLANDS EXTENSION, 2–3 DAYS

(1 hour by plane from Ho Chi Minh City)

These islands offer some of the most unspoiled tropical landscapes in Vietnam, a short flight from Ho Chi Minh City.

Follow days 1–2 of Essential Vietnam itinerary.

Day 3

Fly to these undiscovered and mostly undeveloped islands with beautiful beaches, clear waters, and a large **national park** teeming with exotic plants and animals, including the endangered green and hawksbill turtles. For a luxurious retreat, stay at the high-end eco-lodge, **Six Senses Con Dao,** and indulge in some pampering at the in-house spa and some serious relaxing in your private plunge-pool. After a long walk along the beach, enjoy a seafood dinner at the resort's **By The Beach** restaurant. Night owls can visit **Hang Duong Cemetery** for the atmospheric midnight ceremony honoring the martyred teenager Vo Thi Sau.

Day 4

Organize some transport for a morning of island exploration, taking in **Van Son Tu Pagoda, Hang Duong Cemetery,** and the **Con Dao Museum,** where you can arrange to visit the nearby **Phu Hai Prison** the next day. If you're on Con Dao between May and October you'll be able to take a **turtle-nesting tour,** which usually starts with a mid-afternoon pickup and includes an overnight stay on an outer island.

Day 5

You'll be delivered back to the mainland mid-morning after your nocturnal turtle nesting observations. Perk yourself up with a coffee at the **Con Son Café,** then begin some gentle ambling, stopping off at the **Old French Governor's House** on the way to **Phu Hai Prison.** Dine at the delightful **Thu Ba,** which specializes in fresh-caught seafood.

MEKONG DELTA EXTENSION, 4 DAYS

The lush Mekong Delta, with its fascinating river life, fruit orchards, and friendly locals, requires some time to explore, especially if you're keen to gain insights into local life.

Follow days 1–2 of Essential Vietnam itinerary.

Day 3

(Can Tho is 3 hours by bus from Ho Chi Minh City)

Travel to the capital of the Mekong Delta, **Can Tho.** Break the journey in the charming town of **Sa Dec,** the childhood home of French author Marguerite Duras, and take some time to explore the streets fronting the river, the **Huynh Thuy Le Ancient House,** and the narrow pathways lined by flower farms. At the end of your long journey, stretch your legs in Can Tho with a walk along the river front, then watch the sun set from **L'Escale,** the rooftop restaurant at the **Nam Bo Boutique Hotel.**

Days 4–5

Spend Days 4 and 5 experiencing local Mekong Delta life with a **homestay** at Nguyen Shack Homestay or Green Village Homestay or an **overnight river cruise** with Bassac Cruises.

Day 6

Travel to fascinating **Chau Doc,** where the Cham people worship at the **Murbarak Mosque,** the local Buddhists pray at shrines on **Sam Mountain,** and river folk operate floating fish farms under their houses. Allocate several hours to exploring Sam Mountain, and finish your tour with a cocktail at **Nui Sam Lodge,** with its stunning views of the rice paddies and flood plains of the Mekong Delta. From

Chau Doc, you can travel back to Ho Chi Minh City. Sapa Extension, 4 Days

(8 hours by train from Hanoi)

The former French hill station of **Sapa**, in the misty Tonkinese Alps near the Chinese border, is famous for its stunning scenery, the colorful traditional dress of the local ethnic minority people, and its proximity to **Mount Fansipan**, Vietnam's highest peak. Traveling through this region, on foot or by road, will take you past picturesque rice terraces, tiny ethnic villages, and cold, clear mountain streams.

Follow days 1–10 of the Essential Vietnam itinerary.

Day 11

Take the overnight train from Hanoi to **Lao Cai,** where minibuses await to run visitors further up the mountain to Sapa, which overlooks misty rice terraces. If you want to avoid an early-morning arrival, consider taking the bus, which uses the new Noi Bai–Lao Cai highway. Spend your first day exploring the township, which is full of wandering vendors in traditional dress selling all manner of handicrafts.

Days 12–14

Rise early to start your **multiday trek** of the beautiful countryside that surrounds Sapa, past terraced rice fields and through a range of ethnic minority villages. Try to end your trek on a Saturday so you can spend Sunday doing a day trip to the **Bac Ha Market,** 110 km (68.4 miles) from Sapa, home of the very colorful Flower H'mong ethnic minority people. When your trek is over, return to Hanoi.

ANGKOR WAT EXTENSION

(Siem Reap is 1 hour by plane from Ho Chi Minh City)

The Kingdom of Cambodia, which evolved from the powerful Khmer Empire that ruled Laos, Thailand, and Southern Vietnam, is home to the magnificent 12th-century temple complex known as **Angkor Wat**. A side trip here makes for an unforgettable experience.

Follow days 1–2 of Essential Vietnam itinerary.

Day 3: Siem Reap

Don't plan to see any temples on the day you arrive. Instead, take some time to wander around the **Old Market**, visit the **Angkor National Museum,** and organize your tickets to the Angkor Temple Complex (you'll need passport photos). Dine at **Mie Cafe** for a taste of up-market Khmer and Khmer-fusion dining.

Days 4–5: Angkor Wat

Rise early (and we mean very early) to catch the sunrise at **Angkor Wat,** the complex's main temple. Afterwards, ask your tuk-tuk driver or local guide to whisk you away from the crowds to a deserted temple to enjoy the picnic breakfast your hotel has provided. If you time it right, you can do one of the classic circuits without encountering the crowds until mid- or late morning. Talk to your guide or tuk-tuk driver about when the group tours arrive at each site and see if you can beat them there. Head back to town for lunch and a well-deserved afternoon nap.

On Day 5, explore some of the temples you may have missed the previous day. These excursions can be hot, dusty, and quite tiring, so aim to arrive early and finish up before lunch. Spend your afternoon shopping or wandering around **Siem Reap.**

HO CHI
MINH CITY

Updated by
Barbara Adam

Romantically referred to by the French as the Pearl of the Orient, Ho Chi Minh City today is a super-charged city of sensory overload. Motorbikes zoom day and night along the wide boulevards, through the narrow back alleys and past vendors pushing handcarts hawking goods of all descriptions. Still called Saigon by most residents, this is Vietnam's largest city and the engine driving the country's current economic resurgence, but despite its frenetic pace, it's a friendlier place than Hanoi and locals will tell you the food—simple, tasty, and incorporating many fresh herbs— is infinitely better than in the capital.

This is a city full of surprises. The madness of the city's traffic—witness the oddball things that are transported on the back of motorcycles—is countered by tranquil pagodas, peaceful parks, quirky coffee shops, and whole neighborhoods hidden down tiny alleyways, although some of these quiet spots can be difficult to track down. Life in Ho Chi Minh City is lived in public: on the back of motorcycles, on the sidewalks, and in the parks. Even when its residents are at home, they're still on display. With many living rooms opening onto the street, grandmothers napping, babies being rocked, and food being prepared, are all in full view of passersby.

Icons of the past endure in the midst of the city's headlong rush into capitalism. The Hotel Continental, immortalized in Graham Greene's *The Quiet American,* continues to stand on the corner of old Indochina's most famous thoroughfare, the rue Catinat, known to American G.I.s during the Vietnam War as Tu Do (Freedom) Street and renamed Dong Khoi (Uprising) Street by the Communists. The city still has its ornate opera house and its old French city hall, the Hôtel de Ville. The broad colonial boulevards leading to the Saigon River and the gracious stucco villas are other remnants of the French colonial presence. Grisly reminders of the more recent past can be seen at the city's war-related museums. Residents, however, prefer to look forward rather than back and are often perplexed by tourists' fascination with a war that ended 40 years ago.

The Chinese influence on the country is still very much in evidence in the Cholon district, the city's Chinatown, but the modern office towers and international hotels that mark the skyline symbolize Vietnam's fixation on the future.

2

TOP REASONS TO GO

The buzz: On every street corner there are people eating, drinking, and laughing, kids playing, old men napping, and someone selling something. The noise, the smells, the traffic, the honking . . . it's all part of the mesmerizing chaos that makes this city unforgettable to everyone who visits.

The food: Saigonese are the ultimate foodies, dedicating a large part of each day to discussing what and where to eat. This is evident in the proliferation of local eating places, where style is unimportant, the options are almost endless, and everything is delicious.

The architecture: Vietnam's former French rulers left behind wide well-planned streets and handsome colonial architecture. Old Saigon is, unfortunately, disappearing at quite a rate, but highlights—some crumbling, some well-maintained—sit proudly among the modern skyscrapers.

The history: Chinese and French influence on the city is still in evidence—in the pagodas, the colonial architecture, and the food.

The coffee: Modern Ho Chi Minh City has a strong café culture. Everywhere you turn you'll see people at streetside cafés, watching the world go by over their glass of *ca phe*.

ORIENTATION AND PLANNING

GETTING ORIENTED

Ho Chi Minh City sprawls across a large region, stretching all the way north to Cu Chi near the border of Tay Ninh Province, and south to the upper reaches of the Mekong Delta. The part of the city formerly known as Saigon covered only two of the 14 current districts of Ho Chi Minh City: Districts 1 and 3, which are home to the highest concentration of tourist sites, hotels, restaurants, and bars. Most areas of interest to visitors are here, although the city's Chinatown, known as Cholon, in District 5 and part of District 6 is also worth exploring. Outlying districts, including Districts 2 and 7, contain newer expat-centric areas, which warrant a visit for dining and entertainment rather than sightseeing.

Downtown Ho Chi Minh City is walkable nowadays, with mostly even sidewalks clear of parked motorbikes and street vendors. Outside of the main business area, however, the streets and sidewalks are chaotic, making a leisurely stroll a difficult proposition.

Around Dong Khoi Street. At the heart of Old Saigon in District 1, this historic thoroughfare links the area around Notre Dame Cathedral to the Saigon River, with many of the city's main attractions along the way. Always bustling, its upscale shopping and restaurants and a mix of French-colonial and modern high-rise buildings give it something of a European vibe, which extends to nearby streets such as tree-lined Le Duan and lovely Nguyen Hue street. Behind all of this is an intricate maze of busy hems (alleys).

Around Pham Ngu Lao. This is the famous "backpacker area," long a magnet for budget travelers, which centers on the intersection of Pham

Ngu Lao and De Tham streets. It's full of markets, hostel accommodations, lively bars, and an international mix of travelers seeking the "real" Ho Chi Minh City.

District 3. Stretching west from Nguyen Thi Minh Kai Street, District 3 is also at the heart of downtown, but streets are narrower (beware rush hour) and it has a more residential, less touristy feel.

Beyond the Center. To the southwest of the central hub, Cholon has been home to the city's large Chinese community since the 1680s, while the new suburbs of Thao Dien in District 2 and Phu My Hung in District 7, which have become expat enclaves of hip bars and great restaurants.

PLANNING

WHEN TO GO

The best time to visit the city is during the cooler dry season, roughly between November and April. Don't discount a visit during rainy season, which runs from about May through October, as most days dawn clear and blue and the afternoon rain showers can be waited out in a café or a museum. During the Christmas season, downtown is lit up with the most astounding Christmas lights and odd decorations, including nativity-themed "caves." The center of town becomes a traffic gridlock at night as people drive in to look at the lights. If you're traveling through Vietnam during Tet, the lunar or Chinese New Year (the date changes each year according to the phases of the moon), you are better off being in Ho Chi Minh City rather than a rural area, where everything will be shut.

GETTING HERE AND AROUND

Traffic can often be quite hectic and very noisy, and taxis tend to be the best bet for getting around. Avoid taxi scams and unreliable meters by choosing Vinasun or Mai Linh taxis—one will cruise by within a few minutes, no matter where you are in the city.

Addresses in Ho Chi Minh City often contain words such as district (quan), ward (phuong), or road/street (duong). Odd- and even-numbered addresses are usually on opposite sides of the street. The ward name or number can be important because on many long streets, the numbering reverts to 1 at the ward boundary. Places located down a *hem* (alley) will have a sometimes-confusing address containing a multitude of numbers, such as "26/78 Something Street." To find this address, go down the *hem* at 26 Something Street and find building number 78.

AIR TRAVEL

Ho Chi Minh City's Tan Son Nhat Airport, about 7 km (4 miles) north of the city center, is Vietnam's largest, with a domestic and an international terminal. Direct international flights are available from major cities in Europe, Australia, and other parts of Asia, including Cambodia's Siem Reap and Phnom Penh. It takes about 10 minutes to walk between terminals along a covered walkway, so it's a relatively easy airport in which to transit.

Ho Chi Minh City is also served by domestic flights from just about any airport in the country, including the major tourist destinations of Hanoi, Hue, Danang (for Hoi An), Dalat, Nha Trang, Phu Quoc, and Con Dao.

Airport Information Tan Son Nhat Airport ✉ *Hoang Van Thu, Tan Binh District* ☎ *028/3848–5383* ⊕ *vietnamairport.vn*

TRANSFERS Hotels that offer airport transfers usually charge a premium for this service, and you'll probably pay two or three times what it would cost in a taxi. To take a taxi, ignore the touts who congregate outside the arrivals hall, turn left and look for someone with a clipboard and a Mai Linh or Vinasun taxi company uniform. Tell them your destination and they'll organize a taxi for you, although it might take some time and local travelers are likely to jump to the front of the line. It takes 20 to 45 minutes to get downtown, depending on the traffic, and the fare should be between 130,000d and 170,000d. There's a 15,000d taxi exit toll that will be added to the fare shown on the meter. Saigon Air Taxi has a monopoly at Tan Son Nhat airport and at some government-owned hotels in the city. If you purchase a prepaid Saigon Air voucher at the airport (not recommended), do not pay the driver any additional sum. Only take a Saigon Air taxi if you can't find a Vinasun or Mai Linh taxi.

Taxi Contacts Mai Linh ☎ *028/3838–3838* ⊕ *www.mailinh.vn.* **Saigon Air Taxi** ☎ *028/3811–7234* ⊕ *www.saigonair.com.vn.* **Vinasun** ☎ *028/3827–2727* ⊕ *www.vinasuntaxi.com*

BIKE TRAVEL

Ho Chi Minh City was built for bicycles, though the sheer volume of motor traffic these days can make cycling a challenge. But once you work out how the traffic flows, cycling can be an enjoyable way to get around, especially if you want to explore some of the quieter reaches of the city. Consider a half- or full-day bicycle tour to get started. Bicycles can be rented from several shops, all outside the central business area, for about 300,000d a day, with the per-day rate dropping for weekly rentals. You can also rent panniers and racks. Saigon Cycles is in District 7, about 20 minutes by taxi from downtown, and this newer district has some cycling trails that are an easy introduction to pedaling in the city. Similarly, The Bike Shop, in District 2, is in a quiet location well suited to cycling, but try to avoid school drop-off and pick-up times.

Bike Contacts The Bike Shop ✉ *250 Nguyen Van Huong, Thao Dien, District 2* ☎ *028/3744–6405* ⊙ *Tues.–Sun. 10–6:30.* **Saigon Cycles** ✉ *Shop 51/1 Sky Garden 2, Tan Phuong, Phu My Hung, District 7* ☎ *028/5410–3114* ⊕ *xedapcaocap.com.*

BOAT TRAVEL

Vina Express run hydrofoils every two hours between Ho Chi Minh City and Vung Tau.

Contact Vina Express ✉ *2 Nguyen Hue St., District 1* ☎ *028/3827–7555* ⊕ *www.vinaexpress.com.vn*

BUS TRAVEL

There are several reputable bus companies that offer regular departures from Ho Chi Minh City on comfortable, air-conditioned coaches to major towns and cities in the Mekong Delta and points north. It pays to do a bit of research on the latest road conditions leading to a chosen destination before deciding whether to take the bus, the train, or a flight.

Ho Chi Minh City has a number of bus stations. More than 200 big and small bus companies operate out of Mien Dong Station, 7 km (4 miles) east of District 1, from destinations including Vung Tau, Phan Thiet, Dalat, Nha Trang, and places in the central highlands. Buses from the Mekong Delta arrive at and depart from Mien Tay Station. An Suong Station, a 45-minute taxi ride from downtown, serves Tay Ninh. Ho Chi Minh City bus stations have no central office. Instead each bus company that uses the bus station has a ticket office, most with a waiting area. Disembarking passengers are accosted by an array of taxi and *xe om* drivers, but bus companies may offer a free minibus shuttle to bigger, more convenient bus stations. The shuttles can be very cramped, and information is very difficult to elicit if you don't speak Vietnamese, so if you plan to take the easier option of a taxi to downtown, consider pushing through the throng to find a trusted brand, such as Mai Linh or Vinasun. Some bus stations, including Mien Tay, have their own taxi company, which means you have to get past the "approved" drivers to find Mai Linh or Vinasun taxis, which will be waiting outside. Using public buses to get around the city can be time consuming and confusing. Your best bet is Ben Thanh station; buses depart here for all corners of the city, including Cholon. Inside the covered waiting area, there's often a uniformed bus company official who speaks enough English to assist wide-eyed travelers.

Bus Contacts An Suong Station (*Ben Xe An Suong*). ✉ *Hwy. 22, Ba Dien, Hoc Mon District* ☎ *028/3883–2517* **Ben Thanh Station** (*Tram dieu hanh Sai Gon*). ✉ *Ben Thanh Roundabout, District 1.* **Cholon Station** ✉ *86 Trang Tu, District 5* ☎ *028/3854–8313.* **Mien Dong Station** (*Ben Xe Mien Dong*). ✉ *292 Dinh Bo Linh, Binh Thanh District* ☎ *028/3899–1607.* **Mien Tay Station** (*Ben Xe Mien Tay*). ✉ *395 Kinh Duong Vuong, Binh Tan District.* **September 23 Park Station** ✉ *Pham Ngu Lao St., District 1.* **Tay Ninh Station** ✉ *Le Dai Hanh St., Tan Binh Station, Tan Binh District*

CAR TRAVEL

Most car rental places offer car-and-driver rental, which can give you great freedom to explore the city and surrounding areas without having to deal with the chaotic traffic. Hiring a car and driver for a full day starts at about 1,180,000d for a four-seater and 1,288,000d for a seven-seater, although the fee is based on where you want to go. The drivers will speak basic English only—enough to decide a route and organize meeting points, but not enough to provide any commentary or act as a tour guide. For getting around within the city, taxis are often more useful; with a rented car, your driver will have to find somewhere to park in a city designed for bicycles, not automobiles. Most of the bigger hotels in Ho Chi Minh City can arrange short- or long-term car-and-driver rentals, Sinh Tourist can also assist, or you can contact Bali

Limousines, ETravelVietnam (a branch of government-owned Saigon Tourist), or Avis, the latter with locations downtown and at the airport.

Car Contacts **Avis** ☎ 028/5445–8537 ⊕ *washington.avis.com.* .**Bali Limousines** ☎ 028/3974–9749 ⊕ *www.balilimo.vn.* **ETravelVietnam** ☎ 090/928–4554 ⊕ *www.etravelvietnam.com.* **Sinh Tourist** ✉ *123 Ly Tu Trong St., District 1* ☎ *093/633–6468* ⊕ *sinhcafetravel.com.*

CYCLO TRAVEL

This form of travel is quite comfortable, and the slow and gentle rhythm of the pedaling makes for a strangely peaceful experience on the busy roads. Cyclo Resto offers reputable two-hour cyclo tours of the city, day or night, for a flat fee of 300,000d per person (*see Tours*). Unless part of an organized tour, cyclos (*xich lo*) should be avoided at all costs. The freelance cyclo drivers who lurk at Ben Thanh Market and in the backpacker area in District 1 are notorious for ripping off trusting tourists.

MOTORBIKE TRAVEL

Saigon Scooter Centre is a professional and reliable motorbike rental option set up by a British enthusiast, which has a fleet of well-maintained scooters and motorbikes ranging from classic Vespas to KTM touring bikes, available daily, weekly or for longer. Bikes can be rented here and dropped off at most towns and cities in Vietnam, and a luggage service can be arranged. The motorbikes at Chi's Cafe are similarly reliable and the rental fees are very reasonable, from 120,000d a day. There are also outlets that advertise sales and repurchase for those who want to buy a motorbike in Ho Chi Minh City and sell it back to the company at their branch in Hanoi. The reliability of motorbike rental and sales places varies widely; most expect up-front payment, and some ask for a deposit or to hold your passport as security against the rented motorbike.

Motorbike Contacts **Chi's Café.** ✉ *40/31 Bui Vien, District 1* ☎ *0903/643–446* ⊕ *www.chiscafe.com.* **Saigon Scooter Centre** ✉ *Cong Hoa Garden Industrial Zone, 20 Cong Hoa, Tan Binh District* ☎ *028/6681–2362* ⊕ *www.saigonscootercentre.com* ☉ *Closed Mon.*

TAXIS AND MOTORBIKE TAXI TRAVEL

One of the quickest—and scariest—ways around the city is riding on the back of a motorbike taxi, known as a Honda om or a xe om (*xe* means transportation, *om* means hug, and Honda is the most popular brand of motorbike in Vietnam). These days the xe om drivers who hang out in Ho Chi Minh City's tourist centers expect to be paid the same as a taxi fare for a journey that's far less comfortable and far more dangerous than in a taxi. Motorbike taxi drivers who are based outside of the tourist centers often don't speak much English. A quick five-minute trip should cost no more than 20,000d.

For regular taxis, the recommended companies are Mai Linh and Vinasun. Mai Linh taxis are either all green or white and green, and Vinasun taxis are white with a red stripe. The drivers of both companies wear a uniform with a tie and should have an ID card on the dash. Meters start automatically—if you are trying to catch a taxi that has a passenger disembarking, you'll be asked to shut the door and then open it again to reset the meter. Fares are relatively cheap, but vary depending on whether you're in a four-seater or a seven-seater. Flagfall starts from 65 cents, plus 70–81 cents per kilometer; fares drop slightly at the 26-km (16-mile) mark. Waiting time is charged at 9 cents per four minutes. ■ TIP➔ **Check the name and the livery of the cab carefully as there are many fake taxis roaming the streets, often with one or two letters different from the company they're copying.**

Taxi Contacts **Mai Linh** ☎ *028/3838–3838* ⊕ *www.mailinh.vn.* .**Vinasun** ☎ *028/3827–2727* ⊕ *www.vinasuntaxi.com.*

TRAIN TRAVEL

Trains connecting Ho Chi Minh City with coastal towns to the north arrive and depart from the Saigon Railway Station (Ga Sai Gon) in District 3, about 1 km (½ mile) from the downtown area of District 1. Two main train services depart from here. The Reunification Express travels along Vietnam's "spine" stopping at centers including Nha Trang, Danang, Hue, and finally—about 33 hours after leaving Ho Chi Minh City—Hanoi. A second train service runs from Ho Chi Minh City to Phan Thiet, 20 km (12 miles) from the resort town of Mui Ne. Hotels and travel agents can organize tickets for a small fee, which usually amounts to less than a taxi fare to the Saigon Railway ticketing office.

Train Contacts **Saigon Railway Station** (*Ga Sai Gon*). ✉ *1 Nguyen Thong, District 3* ☎ *028/3931–8952* ⊕ *www.gasaigon.com.vn.* **Saigon Railway ticketing office** ✉ *275C Pham Ngu Lao, District 1* ☎ *028/3836–7640, 028/3837– 7660* ☻ *Closed Sun.*

MONEY

International and local ATMs are scattered throughout the city. The local banks have a per-transaction limit of about 2 million dong (about $94) so to minimize international withdrawal fees, look for international bank ATMs, such as HSBC, Citibank, and ANZ. If exploring rural areas outside of Ho Chi Minh City's sprawl, it's a good idea to take plenty of low denomination bills, as small shops and stalls frequently have difficulty changing large bills.

TOURS

Ho Chi Minh City has a two-tier tour industry, with older operations offering adventurous budget (and sometimes uncomfortable) options to the backpacker market, and a fledgling service catering to more upscale travelers. Reliability tends to come at a price. A number of companies offer city tours, on foot or by motorbike, and many reputable travel agencies can recommend an English-speaking guide to give you a personalized tour. Reliable new operators also offer food tours and bicycle tours. Day and multiday excursions outside of Ho Chi Minh City are easy to arrange, and an organized tour is the easiest option.

TOUR OPERATORS

Back of the Bike Tours. Hop on the pillion of a motorbike for one of this company's three tours showcasing the city and the best of its street food. The company was set up by an American chef to share his love of Vietnamese street food with international visitors, and though he has now gone home, he left the business in the capable hands of his friend and fellow chef, Fred. Custom tours are also available, by bike, van, or car. ☎ *028/6298–5659* ⊕ *backofthebiketours.com* ✉ *From: 1,008,000d.*

Buffalo Tours. A well-regarded travel and tour company, set up by a Hanoian doctor in 1994, Buffalo Tours offers day tours in and around Ho Chi Minh City as well as side trips to surrounding areas and longer itineraries throughout Indochina and Thailand. ✉ *157 Pasteur St., ground fl., District 3* ☎ *028/3827–9170* ⊕ *www.buffalotours.com* ✉ *Half-day tours start from 768,000d.*

Cyclo Resto. If you're interested in a cyclo tour, the only way to avoid the super-scammy cyclo drivers that cruise downtown looking for victims is to go with an organized tour, such as the two-hour fixed price tours offered by this company. ✉ *6/28 Cach Mang Thang Tam St., District 1* ☎ *028/6680–4235* ⊕ *www.cycloresto.com.vn* ✉ *From: 300,000d.*

Fodor's Choice **Exo Travel.** This professional Asian-based tour company caters to dis-
★ cerning and adventurous travelers with a range of day and half-day tours, side trips from Ho Chi Minh City, and country and region-wide itineraries. Formerly known as Exotissimo, the company has tour desks in the lobby of the New World Hotel and the Sofitel and there's also small office at 41 Thao Dien Street in District 2. ✉ *261–263 Phan Xich Long St., Phu Nhuan* ☎ *028/3995–9898* ⊕ *www.exotravel.com* ✉ *From: 660,000d for a half-day city tour.*

FAMILY **Les Rives.** Luxury speedboat tours of the Mekong Delta, the Cu Chi Tunnels, and Can Gio mangrove reserve are led by entertaining professional tour guides who forgo the places popular with budget tour operators in favor of taking small groups to interesting local areas. Going by boat makes these places, which are not always easy to access, seem much closer to Ho Chi Minh City. Tours include hotel pickup, as well as food and drinks. Options include the Cu Chi Tunnels by bicycle and boat, a Cu Chi tour that includes a cooking course, and a Vespa tour. ☎ *0128/592–0018* ⊕ *lesrivesexperience.com* ✉ *From: 1,700,000d.*

Saigon and Cholon Heritage Tours. Historian and author Tim Doling leads two four-hour tours that trace Ho Chi Minh City's development from a Khmer fishing village to the current booming metropolis and Cholon's growth from a tiny Minh Hương settlement to the current sprawling Chinatown. These fascinating tours involve walking interspersed with minibus or car transportation. A minimum of three people are required for a tour to depart. ☎ *0128/579–4800* ⊕ *www.historicvietnam.com* ✉ *From: 1,000,000d.*

Saigon Cooking Class. Saigon Cooking Class by Hoa Tuc offers four-hour tours (on foot or by motorbike) that promise to unlock some of the city's street food secrets. The tours visit a market and small eateries in some of the lesser-known parts of Ho Chi Minh City. As the name suggests, cooking classes are also available. ✉ *74/7 Hai Ba Trung St., District 1* ☎ *028/3825–8485* ⊕ *saigoncookingclass.com* ✉ *From: 1,068,000d.*

Saigon Street Eats. The Vietnamese-Australian couple who run these laid-back foodie tours really make you feel as if you're hanging out with friends who are keen to show you the best and tastiest parts of their city. Saigon Street Eats also caters to those who aren't keen on motorbikes, with a morning walking tour and a "scaredy-cat option" of taking taxis instead of motorbikes on their evening tours. Delicious, informative, and fun, the tours offer many insights into local life and Ho Chi Minh City's street food scene, which can be somewhat intimidating. Tours include pickups from most downtown hotels. ☎ *0908/449–408* ⊕ *www. saigonstreeteats.com* ✉ *From: 1,100,000d.*

Saigon Tourist. One of Vietnam's oldest travel companies, Saigon Tourist is a government-owned conglomerate comprising eight travel service companies, 54 hotels, 13 resorts, and 28 restaurants. The main Saigon Tourist brand offers packaged tours throughout Vietnam and Indochina, day tours, car (with driver) rental, visa services, and flight and accommodations bookings. ✉ *49 Le Thanh Ton St., District 1* ☎ *028/3827–9279* 🖷 *28/3822–4987* ⊕ *www.saigontourist.net* ✉ *From: 1,046,000d for a half-day tour* ✉ *Budget office in Café Apricot: 187A Pham Ngu Lao St., District 1* ☎ *028/835–4539* ⊕ *www.saigon-tourist. com.*

Saigon Unseen. Set up by two Australians, both named Adam, who share a passion for Ho Chi Minh City and urban photography, Saigon Unseen offers three informative and photo-centric half-day tours of their adopted home. Tours include hotel pickups from most downtown hotels. Bookings are taken by email only. ✉ *saigonunseen@gmail.com* ⊕ *www.saigonunseen.com* ✉ *From: 534,000d.*

The Sinh Tourist. One of the more reputable budget tour agencies in the backpacker area, the Sinh Tourist (formerly known as Sinh Café) offers a range of tours in and around Ho Chi Minh City ranging from day trips to Cu Chi and Vung Tau and longer itineraries to Cambodia or Hanoi. A full-day city tour includes visits to pagodas, Cholon, the Reunification Palace, and the War Remnants Museum. Walk-in prices are much cheaper than those advertised on the website, but be aware that you get what you pay for. ✉ *246–248 De Tham St., District 1* ☎ *028/3838–9597* ⊕ *www.thesinhtourist.vn* ✉ *From: 160,000d.*

Fodor's Choice ★ **Sophie's Art Tour.** These fascinating four-hour art tours conducted by British art historian Sophie Hughes examine Vietnam's recent history through the eyes of its artists. The tour includes visits to private collections and galleries as well as the Ho Chi Minh City Fine Arts Museum, where Sophie points out the highlights, including the war artists, who needed less equipment than photographers to record the realities of the battlefield. The tour is just as much a stimulating narrative journey as it is a visual one. Family tours are also available on request. ☎ *0121/8303–742* ⊕ *sophiesarttour.com* ✉ *From: 1,100,000d.*

Stu's Explorer Club. One of the newest tour companies in town, Stu's Explorer Club, set up by British birder Stu Palmer, offers two-day jungle trips from Ho Chi Minh City. The two-day Rumbles in the Jungle, which can be done by self-driving a motorbike or taking a private car, includes a jungle trek, overnight camping, and a morning hike to a lake for a swim. Camping equipment, permits, hearty meals, and guide are all included. ☎ *0933/752–402* ✉ *2,500,000d by private vehicle, 2,000,000d if self-driving (own motorbike required).*

Vietnam Bike Tours. This is a reliable company that offers multiday bicycle tours from Ho Chi Minh City, as well as half- and full-day trips around the city and to the Cu Chi Tunnels, Can Gio mangrove forest, the port city of Vung Tau, and the Mekong Delta. The outfitter also organizes the popular free Sunday Bike Ride, which departs every Sunday at 6:30 am from the Ben Thanh Market in District 1. ⊠ *163–165 Tran Hung Dao St., Level 6, District 1* ☎ *028/6653–0372* ⊕ *www.vietnambiketours. com* ✉ *From: 3,374,000d per person.*

XO Tours. The initials stand for *xe om* (motorbike taxi) but these are motorbike taxi tours with a difference—all the tour guides are female, dressed in the traditional *ao dai,* and offering in-depth local knowledge with a unique perspective. Choose from a shopping tour, a foodie tour, or a highlight-of-the-sights tour, all of which are fun, friendly, and informative. Hotel pickups are included in the price. ☎ *0933/083–727* ⊕ *xotours.vn* ✉ *From: 855,000d.*

VISITOR INFORMATION

There is no official tourist information center in Ho Chi Minh City. Any signs you see claiming to offer tourist information is actually a travel agency that will try to sell you a tour. Hotel tour desk are usually the best source of information, but be aware that some concierges and travel desks will only recommend activities that will pay them a commission.

EXPLORING

Ho Chi Minh City is a fascinating destination, but a chronic lack of infrastructure, not to mention oppressive heat and seasonal rains, can make navigation difficult. A fearless visitor might embrace the chaos by jumping on the back of a xe om (motorbike taxi) with a hit-list of cultural attractions and must-eat street food dishes, but most visitors prefer to traverse the city by taxi. Whatever your mode of transportation, spread your sightseeing over two or three days and let yourself unwind—despite the pulsating street life, this is also a city of soul-soothing spas, hidden cafés, and rooftop bars.

AROUND DONG KHOI STREET

District 1 is the center of old Saigon and Dong Khoi Street, toward the eastern edge, is the neighborhood's historic main thoroughfare. It's a pleasant tree-lined street running down to the Saigon River from Notre Dame Cathedral and the Central Post Office. These buildings, among many other fine examples here, date from the French colonial era, when the street was known as rue Catinat. Another name change occurred in the 1960s and '70s, when, known as Tu Do Street, it was Saigon's red-light district. Since then, the seedy element has been replaced by plenty of chic shopping, eating, and drinking, but it tends to be more costly here than elsewhere in the city. Around Dong Khoi Street, broad Nguyen Hue and Le Loi boulevards converge at the Hotel de Ville (now the People's Committee building), the historic Opera House, and the

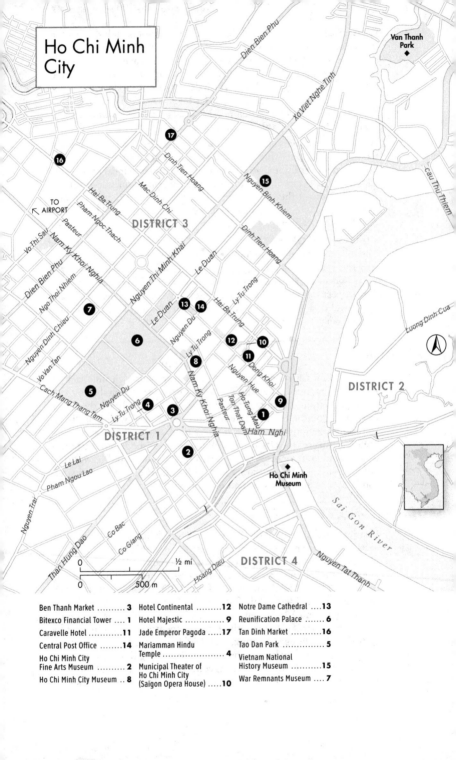

Ho Chi Minh City

TO AIRPORT ←

DISTRICT 3

DISTRICT 1

DISTRICT 2

DISTRICT 4

Van Thanh Park

Ho Chi Minh Museum

Sai Gon River

½ mi
500 m

Ben Thanh Market **3**

Bitexco Financial Tower **1**

Caravelle Hotel **11**

Central Post Office **14**

Ho Chi Minh City
Fine Arts Museum **2**

Ho Chi Minh City Museum .. **8**

Hotel Continental **12**

Hotel Majestic **9**

Jade Emperor Pagoda **17**

Mariamman Hindu
Temple **4**

Municipal Theater of
Ho Chi Minh City
(Saigon Opera House) **10**

Notre Dame Cathedral **13**

Reunification Palace **6**

Tan Dinh Market **16**

Tao Dan Park **5**

Vietnam National
History Museum **15**

War Remnants Museum **7**

Hotel Continental, and the former presidential palace (now called the Reunification Palace) is on the northern boundary of the area.

TOP ATTRACTIONS

Fodor'sChoice
★

Central Post Office (*Buu Dien Trung Tam*). Be sure to go inside to check out the huge map of old Indochina in this classic French colonial building, designed by French architect Gustave Eiffel (of Eiffel Tower fame) and completed in 1891. In addition to the usual mail services, there are phones, fax machines, and a small gift shop. ⊠ *2 Cong xa Paris, District 1* ☉ *Daily 7:30–7:30.*

Fodor'sChoice
★

Reunification Palace (*Dinh Doc Lap*). This is one of the more potent symbols of the Vietnam War. On April 30, 1975, a North Vietnamese Army tank smashed through the main gate of what was then known as the Independence Palace, ending one of the bloodiest conflicts in living memory. The current boxy building replaced the elegant French colonial–style Norodom Palace, which was bombed by fighter jets in 1962 in an unsuccessful attempt to assassinate South Vietnam's President Ngo Dinh Diem. The jet, along with the tanks that ended the war, is on display on the grounds. Free guides are available inside the palace, which remains as it was on that fateful day in 1975, albeit slightly more worn. The time-capsule nature of the palace offers a fascinating insight into the high life of 1960s Saigon, when bigwigs would enjoy tea and movie screenings in plush rooms upstairs, while the war effort was directed from the spartan concrete warren in the basement. The gardens cover 18 hectares (44 acres) of lush lawn and shady trees, and a large fountain in front of the palace redirects the bad luck that could flow into the palace from the broad boulevard of Le Duan Street, according to the principles of feng shui. ⊠ *135 Nam Ky Khoi Nghia St., District 1* ☏ *028/3829–4117* ⊕ *www.dinhdoclap.gov.vn* ☏ *30,000d* ☉ *Daily 7:30–11:30, 1–4:30.*

WORTH NOTING

Bitexco Financial Tower. A symbol of contemporary Ho Chi Minh City, the 68-floor Bitexco Financial Tower is the city's tallest building, and you can enjoy high-altitude views from the Saigon Skydeck on the 49th floor. This deck features interactive screens that provide information about a selection of streets and sites below. Another way to enjoy the view—although it comes at quite a price—is to grab a bite at the Eon51 Café on the 50th floor, enjoy French cuisine at Eon51 Fine Dining, or have a sunset drink at Eon51 Heli Bar. ⊠ *2 Hai Trieu, District 1* ☏ *028/3915–6868 Skydeck information* ⊕ *www.saigonskydeck.com* ☏ *192,000d.*

Caravelle Hotel. Most of the foreign correspondents stayed at this hotel during the Vietnam War, and during the 1968 Tet Offensive, journalists filmed the battle from the rooftop. A major renovation in 1998 added a modern 24-story building to the original 10-story hotel that officially opened on Christmas Eve in 1959. ⇨ *See also Where to Stay.* ⊠ *19 Lam Son Sq., District 1* ☏ *028/3823–4999* ⊕ *www.caravellehotel.com.*

Ho Chi Minh City Museum (*Bao Tang Thanh Pho Ho Chi Minh*). Completed in 1890, the building has been the residence for the French governor of Cochin China, the Japanese governor during Vietnam's brief

Ho Chi Minh City History

Bordered by the Thi Nghe Channel to the north, the Ben Nghe Channel to the south, and the Saigon River to the east, the city has served as a natural fortress and has been fought over by countless people during the past 2,000 years. The ancient empire of Funan used the area as a trading post, and the Khmer kingdom of Angkor transformed Prey Nokor, as Ho Chi Minh City was called, into a flourishing center of trade protected by a standing army. By the 14th century, while under Khmer rule, the city attracted Arab, Cham, Chinese, Malaysian, and Indian merchants. It was then known as the gateway to the Kingdom of Champa, the sister empire to Angkor.

In 1674 the lords of the Nguyen clan in Hue established a customs post at Prey Nokor to cash in on the region's growing commercial traffic. Saigon, as the Vietnamese called it, became an increasingly important administrative post. The building in 1772 of a 6-km (4-mile) trench on the western edge of old Saigon, in what is now District 5, marked the shift in control in the south from Khmer rule to Nguyen rule from Hue. Further Vietnamese consolidation came in 1778 with the development of Cholon, Saigon's Chinese city, as a second commercial hub in the area that is now District 5.

In 1789 the Nguyen lords moved their power base from Hue to Saigon, following attacks by rebels from the village of Tay Son. Unhappy with the way the Nguyen lords had been running the country, the rebels massacred most of the Nguyen clan and took control of the government—briefly. In 1802, Prince Nguyen Anh, the last surviving heir to the Nguyen dynasty, defeated the Tay Son ruler—with French backing—regaining power and uniting Vietnam. He moved the capital back to Hue and declared himself Emperor Gia Long.

In quelling the Tay Son rebels, Gia Long's request for French assistance, which was readily provided, came at a price. In exchange for their help, Gia Long promised the French territorial concessions in Vietnam. Although the French Revolution and the Napoleonic Wars temporarily delayed any French claims, Gia Long's decision eventually cost Vietnam dearly. In 1859, the French, tired of waiting for the Vietnamese emperor to give them what they felt they deserved, seized Saigon and made it the capital of their new colony, Cochin China. This marked the beginning of an epoch of colonial-style feudalism and indentured servitude for many Vietnamese in the highlands. The catastrophe that was to overtake Saigon and the rest of Vietnam during the latter half of the 20th century was a direct result of French colonial interference.

Japanese occupation, and the envoy of Bao Dai, the last empeor of Vietnam, and also served as the Supreme Court. Since 1975, it's been a museum (formerly known as the Museum of the Revolution) with a strong focus on the Vietnamese struggle against the French and Americans. Displays focus on famous marches, military battles, and anti-French and anti-American activists. Exhibits include photos of historical events, uprisings, student demonstrations, and the self-immolation of the monk Thich Quang Duc as a protest against the war. The building itself is as interesting as many of the exhibits inside: a neoclassic design, it has huge columns outside and 19th-century ballrooms with lofty ceilings inside. Beneath the building are concrete bunkers and tunnels connecting to the Reunification Palace. It was here that President Ngo Dinh Diem (1901–63) and his notorious brother Ngo Dinh Nhu hid before being caught and eventually executed in 1963. Outside on the grounds are Soviet tanks, an American helicopter, and antiaircraft guns. ⊠ *65 Ly Tu Trong St., District 1* ☎ *028/3829–9741* ⊕ *www.hcmc-museum. edu.vn* ⊡ *15,000d* ☼ *Daily 8–5.*

Hotel Continental. In French colonial days, the Hotel Continental's open-air terrace—then known as Café de la Hien—was the town's most sought-after lunch spot; during the Vietnam War, journalists and diplomats met there to discuss the latest events. Now, the terrace has been enclosed and renamed La Dolce Vita Café. The hotel features in Graham Greene's *The Quiet American* and the author himself was a long-time resident in room 214 and a regular at La Bourgeois Restaurant. ⇨ *See also Where to Stay.* ⊠ *132–134 Dong Khoi St., District 1* ☎ *028/3829–9201* ⊕ *continentalsaigon.com.*

Hotel Majestic. Built in the late 19th century, the Majestic was one of the first French colonial hotels, and it still has the elegant style to show for it. Head to the rooftop bar for an excellent view of the Saigon River. ⇨ *See also Where to Stay.* ⊠ *1 Dong Khoi St., District 1* ☎ *028/829–5514* ⊕ *www.majesticsaigon.com.vn.*

Municipal Theater of Ho Chi Minh City (Saigon Opera House) (*Nha Hat Thanh Pho*). This colonial-style theater was built by the French in 1899 as Saigon's opera house. Later it housed the National Assembly of South Vietnam, the congress of the South Vietnamese government. After 1975, when South Vietnam ceased to be, it became a theater again (⇨ *see also Nightlife and Performing Arts*). ⊠ *7 Lam Son Sq., District 1* ☎ *028/3823–7419.*

Notre Dame Cathedral (*Nha Tho Duc Ba*). Officially known as the Basilica of Our Lady of Immaculate Conception, this neo-Romanesque cathedral, built by the French in 1880, was once a prominent presence on the city skyline. Spanish, Portuguese, and French missionaries introduced Catholicism to Vietnam as early as the 16th century and today there are approximately 6 million Catholics in Vietnam, the fifth-largest Christian population in Asia. The Mass celebrated at 9:30 am on Sunday is quite a sight, as hundreds of faithful converge on the church and stand in the surrounding square. The service includes short sections in English and French. ⊠ *1 Cong Xa Paris, at top of Dong Khoi St., District 1.*

AROUND PHAM NGU LAO

Pham Ngu Lao used to be the shorthand reference to the backpacker area, which is between September 23 Park along Pham Ngu Lao Street and Bui Vien Street. The area is still thriving and still popular with budget travelers of all ages, but many come here simply to experience the lively cultural mix of international travelers and locals going about their business. There are the requisite backpacker bars and eateries here, but also a growing number of upscale restaurants.

Ben Thanh Market. This bustling, historic market is worth a visit for the people-watching opportunities alone, but there is also plenty of shopping and eating to partake in. The market, which traces its history back to the 17th century, is a good place to score deals on textiles, clothing, and artisanal crafts—if you're willing to haggle for a price. Food vendors at Ben Thanh offer authentic local snacks, should all that shopping and haggling work up your appetite. ⊠ *Le Lai St. and Le Loi Ave., District 1.*

Ho Chi Minh City Fine Arts Museum (*Bao Tang My Thuat Thanh Pho Ho Chi Minh*). Spread over three floors in a reportedly haunted French colonial villa known as Chu Hoa's (Uncle Fire's) mansion, the city's Fine Arts Museum offers a comprehensive run through the main stages of Vietnamese art. Strolling around is a pleasant experience, but sadly there is scant information to enlighten visitors. To really understand the significance of what's on display, curious sightseers should consider a guided tour (⇨ *see also Tours*). ⊠ *97A Pho Duc Chinh, District 1* ☎ *028/3829–4441* ☜ *10,000d* ☉ *Tues.–Sun. 9–4:45.*

Mariamman Hindu Temple (*Chua Ba Mariamman*). Vivid statues and colorful floral offerings at this Hindu temple create a microcosm of India in the streets of Saigon. Before the temple was returned to the Hindu community in the early 1990s, the government used it as a factory for making joss sticks (incense) and for processing dried fish. Today it serves a small congregation of Tamil Hindus, but some Vietnamese and Chinese locals also revere it as a holy space. ⊠ *45 Truong Dinh St., District 1* ☉ *Daily 7–7.*

FAMILY
Fodor'sChoice
★
Tao Dan Park. This huge park, a block behind the Reunification Palace, has a little something for everyone: walking paths for strolling or jogging; tall trees for shade; open areas where exercise classes are held in the mornings and evenings; a miniature Cham tower; a replica Hung King Temple; and an extensive children's playground. There's also a coffee stand, known as the bird café, at the the Cach Mang Thang Tam entrance, and every morning bird fanciers bring their feathered friends here for singing practice. Do pull up a plastic chair and enjoy the ruckus and the theater of finicky owners trying to position their birds in order to generate the loudest birdsong. The birds are usually taken home by 9 am—by motorbike, which is a spectacle in itself. ⊠ *Entrances on Nguyen Thi Minh Khai, Trung Dinh, and Cach Mang Thang Tam Sts., District 1.*

DISTRICT 3

The densely populated District 3 sprawls from the border of District 1 toward the airport. Its plethora of eateries draws Saigonese foodies from throughout the city to converge on the street food joints, drinking restaurants, and more upscale dining establishments from dusk until the early hours of the morning.

Jade Emperor Pagoda (*Chua Ngoc Hoang, Phuoc Hai Tu, Chua Phuoc Hai*). The Cantonese community built this structure—the finest Chinese pagoda in Ho Chi Minh City—in 1909. A mixture of Taoist, Buddhist, and ethnic myths provides the sources for the small pagoda's multitude of statues and carvings, incorporating just about everything from the *King of Hell* to a *Buddha of the Future*. Slowly strolling around the interior to view them may be preferable to attempting to decipher the significance of each of the numerous, distinct deities. Take a moment to note the main altar, the side panel's depiction of hell, and, in the side room, the miniature female figures representing the range of human qualities. There are usually a few vendors at the entrance selling turtles. Buddhists believe that releasing these turtles into the pagoda's turtle pond will generate merit. ⊠ *73 Mai Thi Luu St., District 3* ☎ *Free* ☽ *Daily 7–6.*

Tan Dinh Market (*Cho Tan Dinh*). This authentic local wet market, full of stalls selling fresh flowers, fruit, vegetables, meat, and seafood, also has a strip of eating places fronting Nguyen Huu Cau Street. The narrow inside aisles are lined with stalls selling a range of haberdashery, clothing, and shoes, none of which would really appeal to Westerners unless they're seeking a quirky souvenir. ⊠ *Corner of Hai Ba Trung and Nguyen Huu Cau Sts., District 1.*

War Remnants Museum (*Bao Tang Chung Tich Chien Tranh*). This is a grueling museum focused on the horrors of the Vietnam War, known as the American War in Vietnam, with indoor exhibitions featuring graphic photographs of dismembered bodies and dead children and babies. Outside the machines of war (fighter planes, tanks, howitzers, bombs) are displayed and there's a re-creation of the infamous tiger cages of Con Dao prison island. Don't feel obliged to visit, the Vietnam-American War is old news for the majority of Vietnam's population, who were born after the conflict ended. If you do go, take Kleenex and a stoic demeanor. Expect to see the war from a different perspective, one that's unabashedly critical of the United States and its activities in Vietnam decades ago. ⊠ *28 Vo Van Tan St., District 3* ☎ *028/3930–5587* ⊕ *www.baotangchungtichchientranh.vn* ☎ *15,000d* ☽ *Daily 7:30–noon, 1:30–5.*

Vietnam National History Museum (*Bao Tang Lich Su Quoc Gia*). A little way to the northeast of the War Remnants Museum, via Thi Minh Khai Street, is a lush, riverside environment where the Vietnam National Museum of History is sited on the grounds of Saigon Zoo and Botanical Gardens. Much of Vietnam's history, and consequently its identity today, has been influenced by outsiders. In ancient times the Khmer and Chinese empires occupied large portions of modern-day Vietnam, and in more recent times the country has been partially or completely occupied by French, Japanese, and American forces. The museum is an excellent place to get Vietnamese perspective on these events as well as some unexpected surprises, most notably the oldest mummy ever found in the country. The English introductions in the museum's exhibits are extremely helpful. ⊠ *Saigon Zoo and Botanical Gardens, 2 Nguyen Binh Khiem St., District 1* ☎ *028/3829–8146* ⊕ *baotanglichsu. vn* ☎ *15,000d* ☽ *Tues.–Sun. 8–11:30, 1:30–5.*

BEYOND THE CITY CENTER

Several interesting sights lie outside of the center, some of them in far-flung areas of the city, such as the Buddhist-themed Suoi Tien amusement park and the Ao Dai Museum in District 9, the Dam Sen pair of parks in District 11, and the many quirky cafés of Phu Nhuan District. There are modern residential suburbs in District 2 and District 7, where expats and wealthy Vietnamese live in large villas with swimming pools and gardens. Though they don't have any notable sights, these areas can be worth visiting for the shopping and dining options.

Southwest of central Ho Chi Minh City is Cholon, a Chinese sister-city-within-the-city, which takes up most of District 5 and a small part of District 6. This was and still is the heart of Chinese culture in the city. There's no discernible entry point into its rabbit warren of small streets with wall-to-wall houses, shops, and eateries. Hai Thuong Lan Ong road is worth a peek for the aromatic apothecaries, and Luong Nhu Hoc—home to stores selling all kinds of ritualistic costumes, ornaments, and opera masks—is a great spot to pick up souvenirs.

The French supported the Chinese in Vietnam because of their success in commerce and their apolitical outlook—the Chinese seldom supported Vietnamese Nationalist struggles. The Communists, on the other hand, saw Cholon as a bastion of capitalism, and the area suffered greatly after 1975. Later, in 1979, during the war between Vietnam and China, Cholon was again targeted, since it was considered a potential center of fifth columnists (pro-Chinese agitators). Many of the first boat people to flee Vietnam were Chinese-Vietnamese from Cholon. Now, after having made money in Australia, Canada, and the United States, many have returned to Saigon and are among the city's wealthiest residents.

The pagodas concentrated around Nguyen Trai and Tran Hung Dao streets can be navigated on foot. Bright blue, yellow, red, orange, and gold cover the pagodas in a dazzling display that would put mating peacocks to shame. Getting lost in Cholon's back streets can be interesting, but also hot, tiring, and noisy. For a good overview of the suburb, consider a motorbike tour that can whizz you through the crowded narrow alleys.

TOP ATTRACTIONS

Fodor's Choice ★ **Ao Dai Museum.** Honoring Vietnam's national dress, this private museum is set on stunningly picturesque grounds that are a very long way from downtown. Once you pay the admission fee, a guide will take you to the two beautiful wooden exhibition houses, which showcase *ao dais* from the 17th century to the modern day. Smaller kids will like feeding the fish and playing *ao dai* quoits (and generally letting off steam on the verdant lawns if they're all city-ed out). Expect basic English only, this place is— amazingly—still off the tourist radar. ⊠ *206/19/30 Long Thuan St., District 9* ☎ *090/801–8086* ⊕ *baotangaodaivietnam.com* 🖃 *100,000d* ⊗ *Tues.–Sun. 8:30–5:30.*

Cholon Mosque. Built in 1932 by Tamil Muslims, the Cholon Mosque now serves the city's Indonesian and Malaysian Muslim community. Notice how much simpler the mosque is than the pagodas in the area,

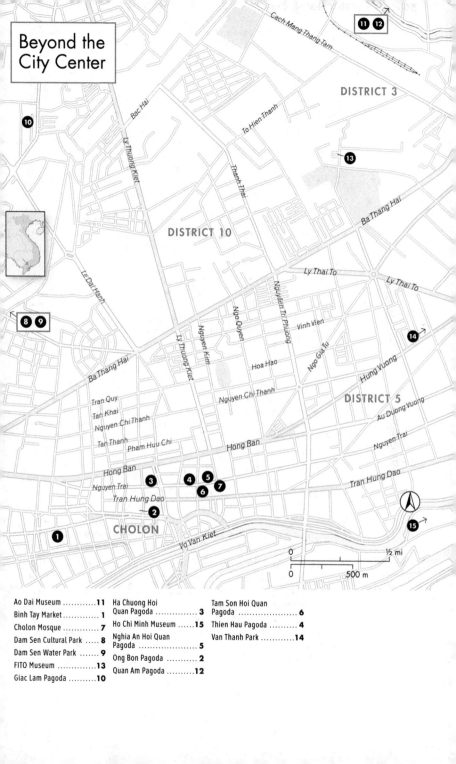

Beyond the City Center

Ao Dai Museum **11**
Binh Tay Market **1**
Cholon Mosque **7**
Dam Sen Cultural Park **8**
Dam Sen Water Park **9**
FITO Museum **13**
Giac Lam Pagoda **10**

Ha Chuong Hoi
Quan Pagoda **3**
Ho Chi Minh Museum **15**
Nghia An Hoi Quan
Pagoda **5**
Ong Bon Pagoda **2**
Quan Am Pagoda **12**

Tam Son Hoi Quan
Pagoda **6**
Thien Hau Pagoda **4**
Van Thanh Park **14**

which are characterized by exuberant ornamentation and bright colors. ⊠ *641 Nguyen Trai St., District 5.*

FAMILY   **Dam Sen Water Park.** For a rollicking day out for kids of all ages, this park has a variety of slides and pools (one with a wave machine), a zipline, and a lazy river ride. Compared to water parks in more developed countries, Dam Sen is a little rough around the edges but that doesn't it stop it from being an exhilarating day out. Children have to be taller than 1.4 meters (4 feet 6 inches) to go on the larger slides but there's a range of medium slides for smaller kids and a toddler play area. English signage and language skills are limited but the staff do try hard.

■TIP→ **On weekdays there are usually no lines for the rides.** Lockers are available (15,000d) and you're given a small waterproof tube to hold your money, valuables, and the locker key. There are also several food kiosks within the park. It can take up to an hour to get here from District 1 when traffic is heavy, or about 40 minutes in light traffic. ⊠ *3 Hoa Bien, District 11* ☎ *028/3858–8418* ⊕ *www.damsenwaterpark. com.vn* ⊠ *130,000d before 4 pm, 110,000d after 4 pm* ☉ *Mon.–Sat. 9–6, Sun. and public holidays 8:30–6.*

Fodor's Choice   **FITO Museum** (*Museum of Traditional Vietnamese Medicine*). The out-
★   side of this museum showcasing the history of traditional Vietnamese medicine might be plain, but inside it's a fabulous carved wooden wonderland, with the interior of an authentic antique house on the third floor and a re-created Cham-style gazebo on the rooftop. Displays, enhanced by audio-visuals and drawing on nearly 3,000 items in the collection, range from Stone-Age pots to 3rd-century coins (for coin-rubbing therapy), ancient texts, bronze kettles, and a range of cutting, chopping, and storing utensils. The concluding part of the introductory film (subtitled in English) and the shop at the exit are a reminder that this is a private museum, set up by Fito Pharma. It's well worth a visit for the insight into traditional Vietnamese daily life through the ages. ⊠ *41 Hoang Du Khuong St., District 10* ☎ *028/3864–2430* ⊕ *www. fitomuseum.com.vn* ⊠ *50,000d* ☉ *Daily 8:30–5.*

Giac Lam Pagoda. One of the oldest pagodas in Ho Chi Minh City, Giac Lam Pagoda was built in 1744 in the jungle outside of the city of Gia Dinh. Outside the walls of the pagoda now lies the urban sprawl of Ho Chi Minh City. Inside, however, are peaceful gardens containing a bodhi tree imported from Sri Lanka in 1953, a seven-story stupa, and the pagoda itself. Prayers are held every evening at 6 pm. ⊠ *118D Lac Long Quan St., Tan Binh District* ☎ *028/3865–3933* ☉ *Daily 8–8.*

Quan Am Pagoda. Busy scenes in lacquer, ceramic, gold, and wood illustrate traditional Chinese stories at this pagoda, built in 1816 by a congregation of Fujian refugees from China. Many legendary and divine beings, some dressed in elaborately embroidered robes, are portrayed, as some simple rural scenes representing the birthplaces of the original members of the congregation. Be prepared for a stifling cloud of incense when you enter—this is still one of Cholon's most active pagodas. ⊠ *12 Lao Tu St. (parallel to Hung Vuong and Nguyen Trai Sts.), District 5.*

Thien Hau Pagoda (*Chua Ba*). Sailors used to come to be blessed at this pagoda dedicated to Thien Hau, the goddess of the sea and protector of fisherfolk and mariners. On the main dais are three statues of the goddess, each flanked by two guardians. Note also the figure of Long Mau, guardian of mothers and babies. The turtles living on the grounds are considered sacred animals and are a symbol of longevity. The Cantonese congregation built this pagoda at the beginning of the 19th century. ⊠ *710 Nguyen Trai St., District 5.*

FAMILY
Fodor's Choice
★

Van Thanh Park. A large government-owned tourist park, Van Thanh is a lovely escape from Ho Chi Minh City's urban chaos, with its artificial lake, restaurants, swimming pool, and small children's playground. The food isn't brilliant but dining in a little hut over the lake is fun, and the grounds and buildings are picturesque "ancient Vietnam" style. Entry to the pool, which gets very crowded on weekends, is 20,000d. ⊠ *48/10 Dien Bien Phu, Binh Thanh District* ☎ *028/3512–3026* ⊕ *binhquoiresort.com.vn.*

WORTH NOTING

Binh Tay Market. This wholesale market, in a colonial-era Chinese-style building about a half-hour drive from downtown, is not so much a shopping destination (unless you want to buy spices or textiles) as a spectacle to behold, particularly if you get here before 8 am to savor the frenetic atmosphere at its peak. With more than 2,000 stalls, Binh Tay can get pretty chaotic. In the central courtyard a small shrine honors the market's founder, Quach Dam (1863–1927), a disabled Chinese immigrant who started out collecting scrap before making his fortune. The food court inside serves a wide variety of Vietnamese street food and Chinese-influenced dishes—great for a replenishing brunch after an early arrival. ⊠ *57A Thap Muoi, District 6.*

FAMILY
Dam Sen Cultural Park. Next door to Dam Sen Water Park (⇨ *see below*), this attraction has an amusement park as well as its cultural aspects, which makes it a good choice for a family outing. You can enjoy traditional Vietnamese handicrafts, games, and folk song performances and then view a range of cultural reproductions, which include an ancient Roman square and a Japanese teahouse and peach blossom garden. If the kids get restless, head for the roller coaster, bumper cars, Ferris wheel, and other rides. Tamer activities include swan boats to pedal, an extensive aquarium, animal enclosures, a bowling alley, and a movie theater. There are food and drink outlets throughout the park. ■ TIP→ **Trying to visit both the cultural and the water park in the one day is not recommended.** ⊠ *3 Hoa Binh St., District 11* ☎ *028/3963–2483* ⊕ *www.damsenpark.com.vn* 🎫 *180,000d* ⏱ *Weekdays 8–6, weekends 8–9 (to 10 on public holidays).*

Ha Chuong Hoi Quan Pagoda. Like many other pagodas built by Fujian congregations, this one is dedicated to Thien Hau, goddess of the sea and protector of fisherfolk and sailors. It has four stone pillars encircled by painted dragons, brought from China when the pagoda was constructed in the 19th century. Also note the scenes in ceramic relief on the roof and the murals next to the main altar. ⊠ *802 Nguyen Trai St., District 5.*

Ho Chi Minh Museum (*Nha Rong*). This example of early French colonial architecture in Vietnam, nicknamed the Dragon House (Nha Rong), could be considered more interesting than most of the displays within. Sitting by quayside on Ben Nghe Channel, at far end of Ham Nghi, it was constructed in 1863 as the original French customs house; any individuals coming to colonial Saigon would have had to pass through the building once they docked at the port. Ho Chi Minh passed through here in 1911 on the way to his 30-year sojourn around Europe and America. Inside are some of his personal belongings, including his journals, fragments of his clothing, and his rubber sandals. Uncle Ho, as he's now affectionately known, was an ascetic type of guy, known for wearing sandals made only from tires; these are now scattered in museums around the country. ⊠ *Saigon Port, 1 Nguyen Tat Thanh St., District 4* ☎ *028/3940–2060* ⊕ *www.baotanghochiminh.vn* ✉ *10,000d* ⊙ *Tues.–Sun. 7:30–11:30, 1:30–5.*

Nghia An Hoi Quan Pagoda. This pagoda, built by the Chaozhou Chinese congregation in 1872, is worth seeing for its elaborate woodwork. There are intricately carved wooden boats and a large figure of the deified Chinese general Quan Cong's sacred red horse, as well as representations of Quan Cong himself with two guardians. A festival dedicated to Quan Cong takes place here every year on the 13th day of the first lunar month. ⊠ *678 Nguyen Trai St., District 5.*

Ong Bon Pagoda (*Chua Ong Bon or Nhi Phu Hoi Quan*). Many deities are represented at this pagoda, but the main attraction is Ong Bon himself, the guardian of happiness and virtue. Ong Bong is also responsible for wealth, so people bring fake paper money to burn in the pagoda's furnace in his honor, hoping the year ahead will bring financial rewards to their families. The centerpiece of the pagoda is an elaborately carved wood-and-gold altar and a finely crafted statue of Ong Bon. Look for the intricately painted murals of lions, tigers, and dragons. ⊠ *264 Hai Thuong Lan Ong Blvd., at Phung Hung St., District 5.*

Tam Son Hoi Quan Pagoda (*Chua Ba Chua*). The Chinese Fujian congregation built this lavishly decorated pagoda dedicated to Me Sanh, the goddess of fertility, in the 19th century. Women—and some men—pray to the goddess to bring them children. Many other deities are represented here as well: Thien Hau, the goddess of the sea and protector of fisherfolk and sailors; Ong Bon, the guardian of happiness and virtue; and Quan Cong, the deified general, depicted with a long beard and his sacred red horse. ⊠ *118 Trieu Quang Phuc St., District 5* ☎ *028/3856–6655.*

WHERE TO EAT

Dining options in Ho Chi Minh City run the gamut from fine dining in secluded air-conditioned splendor to sidewalk eateries where the food is cooked in makeshift open-air kitchens. The dynamism and energy of the city is reflected in a dining scene bursting with international options and a host of fusion choices in between.

The city's middle classes love nothing more than descending on the latest dining craze, so do note locals' recommendations and follow the crowds to the latest hotspot. Despite the Saigonese's love for the flashy "new next big thing," there's also a somewhat reluctant loyalty to the French cuisine of their former colonial rulers. Ho Chi Minh City is home to many French restaurants, from casual Parisian-style bistros to the full starched linen and paired wine experience. Most of Ho Chi Minh City's international restaurants are in and around Districts 1 and 3, although there are several excellent options in the expat areas of Districts 2 and 7.

Meals are serious business in Ho Chi Minh City, and between noon and 1 pm most office workers and public servants take a lunch break. Dinner is generally served any time after about 6 pm and eating (and drinking) can continue until 1 am or later.

Use the coordinates (✣ B2) at the end of each listing to locate a site on the corresponding map.

WHAT IT COSTS

	$	$$	$$$	$$$$
Restaurants	Under 70,000d	70,000d–270,000d	271,000d–400,000d	over 401,000d

Prices in the reviews are the average cost of a main course at dinner or, if dinner isn't served, at lunch.

AROUND DONG KHOI STREET

$$ MEDITERRANEAN FAMILY

🍴 **Au Parc.** Midway between the Reunification Palace and Notre Dame cathedral, overlooking the tall trees of April 30 Park, this is a great place to linger in exotic surroundings, whether for a meal or just a coffee. The flavors are Mediterranean and Middle Eastern, the staff is attentive, and the location is prime. The appeal of Au Parc, in a restored colonial-era shop front, is further enhanced by the children's playroom upstairs, which is supervised by a nanny on weekends from 11 am to 4 pm. [$] *Average main: 180000d* ✉ *23 Han Thuyen St., District 1* ☎ *028/3829–2772* 🌐 *auparcsaigon.com* ✣ *F3.*

$$$ JAPANESE

🍴 **Blanchy Street.** Japanese fusion cuisine here is inspired by chefs' experience at Michelin-starred Nobu in London. Martin Brito and Yogo Oba have created a menu that's as stylish and contemporary as the restaurant's interior. The sushi selection is sublime, as is the selection of hot and cold Japanese-style dishes, and most can be paired with something from the restaurant's extensive wine list, including a sake selection. [$] *Average main: 350000d* ✉ *74/3 Hai Ba Trung, District 1* ☎ *028/3823–8793* 🌐 *blanchystreet.weebly.com* ✍ *Reservations essential* ✣ *G4.*

$$ VIETNAMESE Fodor's Choice ★

🍴 **Hatvala.** A haven for tea lovers seeking the best Vietnamese brews, Hatvala also serves premium local coffee and casual Vietnamese fusion dining in a narrow two-story building decorated with natural fibers. Hatvala offers tastings showcasing poetically named teas such as Mountain Mist

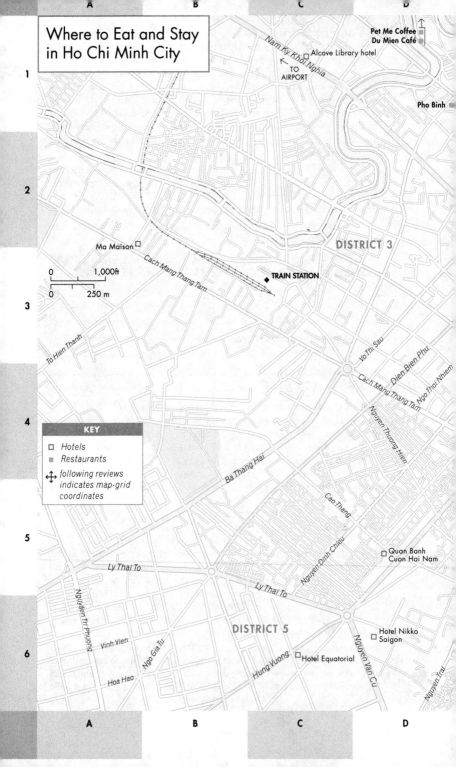

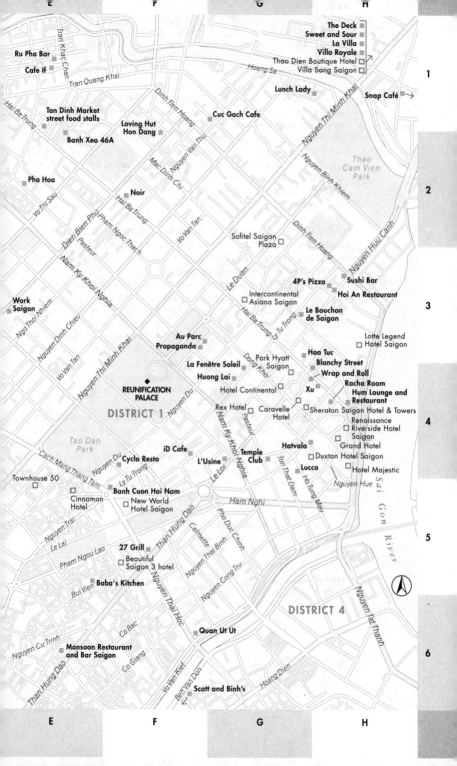

White Tea, Fish Hook Green Tea, and Autumn Jade Jasmine Tea, which are available for purchase. All the teas are grown in Vietnam's misty and mountainous north, mostly by hill tribes who process the leaves using traditional methods. $ *Average main: 170000d* ✉ *44 Nguyen Hue St., District 1* ☎ *028/3824–1534* ⊕ *hatvala.com* ⚓ *G4.*

$$$
VIETNAMESE
Fodor's Choice
★

✕ **Hoa Tuc.** The name translates as opium poppy, and this chic little eatery is in a corner of the former *La Manufacture d'Opium*, the French-controlled opium refinery and warehouse. It offers contemporary Vietnamese cuisine with knockout flavors and a wine list that works with local flavors. The art deco interior is elegant, with wrought iron chairs, cast iron lamps, quirky purple accents, and a leafy outdoor terrace. Standout dishes include mustard leaf rolls, pink pomelo, squid, and crab salad, and soft shell crabs in green rice batter with passionfruit sauce. This is a great place to try one of the local specialties—soursop smoothie—if you are nervous of the streetside drinks stands. ■ TIP→ **Hoa Tuc shares its passion for Vietnamese food with its Saigon Cooking Class (daily except Monday), conducted above the restaurant.** $ *Average main: 370000d* ✉ *74/7 Hai Ba Trung St., District 1* ☎ *028/3825–1676* ⊕ *www.hoatuc.com/wordpress* ⚓ *H3.*

$$
VEGETARIAN
Fodor's Choice
★

✕ **Hum Lounge and Restaurant.** Classy surroundings, attentive staff, and amazing cocktails are good reasons to come here, but it's the mouthwatering pan-Asian food that's the highlight, regularly winning over meat lovers who have reluctantly accompanied their vegetarian partners and friends. The menu is full of appealing health-conscious descriptions, and the food is as visually appealing as it is delicious. Unlike traditional vegetarian places in Vietnam, Hum uses garlic and onion and serves alcohol. ■ TIP→ **The cucumber and ginger martini is highly recommended.** $ *Average main: 170000d* ✉ *2 Thi Sach St., District 1* ☎ *028/3823–8920* ⊕ *www.hum-vegetarian.vn* ⚓ *H4.*

$$
VIETNAMESE

✕ **Huong Lai.** In a prime location on Ly Tu Trong Street, Huong Lai serves up traditional Southern Vietnamese home cooking with a very high feel-good factor—all the staffers are orphans and disadvantaged young people, given a helping hand by the philanthropic Japanese owner, who calls his enterprise a training restaurant. The interior is delightfully rustic, the service is friendly, the English language skills excellent, the food is authentic, and over the course of more than a decade, Huong Lai has launched around 60 young people into careers in the five-star hospitality sector. $ *Average main: 160000d* ✉ *38 Ly Tu Trong St., District 1* ☎ *028/3822–6814* ⊕ *www.huonglai2001saigon.com* ⚓ *G4.*

$$$
INTERNATIONAL

✕ **La Fenêtre Soleil.** A Ho Chi Minh City institution that's outlasted many flash-in-the-pan dining and entertainment ventures over the years, La Fenêtre Soleil is laid-back and bohemian during the day, elegant and intimate at night, and jazz-funkily groovy after 9 pm (⇨ *see also Nightlife*). The menu features a mix of Western, Vietnamese fusion, and Indonesian cuisine, which, strangely, works; the interior is eclectically arty, with exposed brick walls, chandeliers, a baby grand piano, comfortable couches, and a gauzy drapes. It's possible to arrive early for coffee and an online work session and stay throughout the day until late evening. $ *Average main: 275000d* ✉ *44 Ly Tu Trong St., 1st fl., District 1* ☎ *028/3824–5994* ⊕ *www.lafenetresoleil.com* ⚓ *G4.*

$$$ | FRENCH | Fodor's Choice ★

🍴 **Le Bouchon de Saigon.** This French bistro ticks all the right boxes, with red gingham tablecloths, friendly staff, a free glass of sparkling wine on arrival, and a menu that includes what could be a contender for the world's best French onion soup and a great take on *moules frites* (mussels and fries). Reservations are recommended as this place is usually buzzing. [$] *Average main: 350000d* ✉ *40 Thai Van Lung St., District 1* ☎ *028/3829–9263* 🌐 *www.lebouchondesaigon.com* ✥ *G3.*

$$$ | ITALIAN

🍴 **Lucca.** Downstairs is an atmospheric wine bar, upstairs is a classy Italian restaurant that wouldn't seem out of place in New York. Here, you'll find a menu of authentic pizzas, pastas, and mains such as *Saltimbocca alla Romana* (veal and prosciutto, cooked in white wine and butter) as well as a delicious selection of desserts. A finer dining experience than is the norm for Ho Chi Minh City, Lucca is equally suitable for a business lunch or a romantic evening. [$] *Average main: 390000d* ✉ *88 Ho Tung Mau St., District 1* ☎ *028/3915–3692* 🌐 *www.luccasaigon.com* ✥ *G4.*

$$ | CAFÉ | Fodor's Choice ★

🍴 **L'Usine.** Industrial chic meets arthouse in a colonial villa at this café with a retail space—or fashion boutique and art gallery with a café area, depending on your point of view (⇨ *see also Shopping*). The food is contemporary café fusion fare, with a range of salads, sandwiches—including a very tasty Vietnamese caramelized pork and herb number—and cold cut platters. If you're hankering after cupcakes, you will be very happy indeed. There's a second, equally dynamic outlet comprising a lifestyle store and panini bar, at 70B Le Loi St in District 1. [$] *Average main: 140000d* ✉ *151/1 Dong Khoi, 1st fl., District 1* ✥ *Turn into alley at 151 Dong Khoi and pass art shops. At parking area, turn right and walk toward stairwell where a sign points up to L'Usine on 1st floor* ☎ *028/6674–9565* 🌐 *lusinespace.tumblr.com* ✥ *F4.*

$$ | VIETNAMESE | Fodor's Choice ★

🍴 **Propaganda.** Serving what is described as "redesigned" Vietnamese cuisine with a focus on fresh ingredients, the sleek and artsy Propaganda does nontraditional takes on traditional dishes, especially fresh spring (summer) rolls. You can avoid menu confusion by choosing the 450,000d discovery menu of four courses, three glasses of wine, and organic green tea. Midway between the Reunification Palace and the Notre Dame Cathedral, Propaganda is the perfect spot to recharge during a long hot day of sightseeing, while admiring some (you guessed it) wartime propaganda art. [$] *Average main: 150000d* ✉ *21 Han Thuyen St., District 1* ☎ *028/3822–9048* 🌐 *www.propaganda.vn* ✥ *F4.*

$$$ | ASIAN FUSION | Fodor's Choice ★

🍴 **Racha Room.** The hippest new eatery in town, the Racha Room serves up Thai fusion food as well as artisan cocktails (prepared by a bartender imported from Melbourne, Australia) in a small but groovy space, with exposed brick walls, graffiti art, and funky music. Since opening its doors in September 2014, the place has proved a hit with locals, expats, and travelers alike for its bold flavors and overall grooviness, so reservations are recommended. [$] *Average main: 300000d* ✉ *12–14 Mac Thi Buoi St., District 1* ☎ *0908/791–412* ✍ *Reservations essential* ✥ *H4.*

$$$ | VIETNAMESE | Fodor's Choice ★

🍴 **Temple Club.** One of Ho Chi Minh City's most memorable places to grab a meal or coffee, the charming, atmospheric Temple Club occupies a heritage building that was formerly the guest quarters for the Hindu temple across the street. The main dining room and the lounge at the rear are both ideal for special occasions or a romantic meal in an unforgettable space. The menu features classic Vietnamese fare—try the fresh shrimp and pork salad rolls or the grilled fish in banana leaf—but the star of the show is the place itself, from the lantern-lit corridor through which you enter the restaurant to the Asian art and colonial-style furnishings. $ *Average main: 300000d* ✉ *29–31 Ton That Thiep St., District 1* ☎ *028/3829–9244* ⊕ *templeclub.com.vn* ✢ *G4.*

$$
VIETNAMESE

✕ **Wrap and Roll.** The flagship of this fabulously named chain (with the tag line "it's only wrap and roll but I like it") does a surprisingly good take on traditional Vietnamese street food dishes, many of which require wrapping or rolling. If actual street food freaks you out, with its proximity to traffic, noise, and dirt, this is a quiet, clean, lime green, and air-conditioned alternative. Service can be slow, but they serve beer here. $ *Average main: 95000d* ✉ *62 Hai Ba Trung St., District 1* ☎ *028/3822–2166* ⊕ *wrap-roll.com* ▤ *No credit cards* ✢ *H4.*

$$$$
VIETNAMESE
Fodor's Choice
★

✕ **Xu.** A posh restaurant-lounge serving traditional Vietnamese food, fine wines, and highly creative cocktails might seem a bit incongruous, but Xu offers all this and more. The food is exquisite, if pricey (three-course tasting menus start at 918,265d), but you can expect the highest standards of quality in terms of food preparation, service, and surroundings. The bar downstairs gets lively in the evening thanks to a generous happy hour from 5:30 to 8:30 pm Monday to Saturday, with half-price cocktails. A classic martini or an edible concoction blasted with liquid nitrogen—the choice is yours. Smart-casual wear is expected in the evening. $ *Average main: 1200000d* ✉ *71–75 Hai Ba Trung St., District 1* ☎ *028/3824–8468* ⊕ *www.xusaigon.com* ⚐ *Reservations essential* ✢ *H4.*

AROUND PHAM NGU LAO

$$$$
INTERNATIONAL

✕ **27 Grill.** With service that's usually as sleek as the interior design, 27 Grill, associated with the glitzy Chill Bar on the 26th floor, has the best steaks and one of the best views in town, as well as an extensive wine list. If you can drag your eyes away from the view of Ho Chi Minh City at night, you can watch the two Danish chefs at work at the charcoal grill in the marble and stainless steel open kitchen. This is one of the few places in town to have a dress code (no flip-flops, shorts, or tank tops). It also bans pregnant women and children under 18 after 9 pm. $ *Average main: 1000000d* ✉ *AB Tower, 76A Le Lai St., 27th fl., District 1* ☎ *028/3827–2372* ⊕ *www.chillsaigon.com* ◔ *No lunch* ✢ *F5.*

$$
INDIAN

✕ **Baba's Kitchen.** Slap-bang in the heart of the backpacker district, this is a gem of an Indian restaurant, serving a great selection of curries, tandoori, tikka, vegetarian dishes, breads, and Southern Indian specialties. It's an unassuming, clean, and friendly little place, but if you don't feel like venturing out, they deliver throughout Ho Chi Minh City. $ *Average main: 100000d* ✉ *164 Bui Vien St., District 1* ☎ *028/3838–6661* ⊕ *www.babaskitchen.in* ✢ *E5.*

$
VIETNAMESE
Fodor's Choice
★

✕ **Banh Cuon Hai Nam.** Always packed with locals, this narrow eatery serves up Ho Chi Minh City's best *banh cuon* (steamed rice-flour crepes stuffed with minced/ground pork and woodear mushrooms) and an excellent version of the Central Vietnamese *banh beo* (steamed rice-flour pancakes topped with prawn). Just order the first three items on the menu and you'll be in foodie heaven in no time. ■ TIP➔ **This**

HO CHI MINH CITY'S CAFÉ CULTURE

Cafés aren't just for coffee in Ho Chi Minh City, they're an important part of the fabric of society. In this crowded city, jammed full of multigenerational homes, cafés offer an element of peace and privacy. They're cheap places for young people to hang out and for friends of all ages to meet and shoot the breeze. To attract the crowds among so much competition, all kinds of novelty and hidden coffee shops have sprung up. **L'Usine** in Dong Khoi led the charge, with its industrial chic café and retail space hidden down an alley and up a flight of dingy stairs. Now "hidden" cafés are de rigueur, just about every old apartment block has one. The trend includes novelty cafés, such as **Pet Me Coffee,** and "design" cafés like **Du Mien** in Phu Nhuan District and **Villa Royale** in District 2. With Ho Chi Minh City one of the hot new destination for digital nomads and location independent types, there are also a host of cafés catering to this techie crowd, including **Work Saigon,** an all-in-one co-working space and coffee shop.

place is off the tourist trail so be patient with the staffers, who are not very experienced in dealing with non-Vietnamese speakers. [$] *Average main: 60000d* ✉ *11A Cao Thang St., District 3* ☎ *028/3839–3394* ✍ *Reservations not accepted* ✣ *F5.*

$$ VIETNAMESE Fodor's Choice ★ 🍴 **Cyclo Resto.** Delicious authentic Southern Vietnamese home cooking is the focus of this simple restaurant, which has a set menu of five dishes: spring rolls, shrimp and wintermelon soup, stir-fried vegetables, snakehead fish in claypot, lemongrass chicken, rice, and fruit. Near the end of an alley near one of the city's busiest roundabouts, the interior is plain and functional, with bamboo chairs and white walls covered in reviews written by happy customers. Cyclo Resto, run by the engaging and enterprising Mr. An, also offers three- to four-hour cooking classes and two-hour cyclo tours of the city (⇨ *see Tours*). [$] *Average main: 130000d* ✉ *6/28 Cach mang Thang Tam St., District 1* ☎ *028/6680–4235* 🌐 *www.cycloresto.com.vn* ▭ *No credit cards* ✣ *F4.*

$ VIETNAMESE 🍴 **ID Café.** One of the front-runners in the new wave of modern Vietnamese cafés that cater to the young switched-on set, ID Café is popular with digital nomads, bloggers, locals, expats, and tourists alike. They come for its groovy interior design, high speed internet, coffee, and very tasty food, including several vegetarian options. There's another branch at 63 Tu Xuong Street in District 3. [$] *Average main: 65000d* ✉ *34D Thu Khoa Huan St., District 1* ☎ *028/3822–2901* 🌐 *www.idcafe.net* ✣ *F4.*

$$ ASIAN FAMILY Fodor's Choice ★ 🍴 **Monsoon Restaurant and Bar Saigon.** Take a culinary tour of Vietnam, Myanmar, Laos, Thailand, and Cambodia within the confines of this stylish-yet-relaxed restaurant that offers authentic traditional dishes from all five Southeast Asian countries. The interior is part industrial chic, part Asian resort, and often used as a backdrop for art exhibitions. The menu is as beautiful as the surroundings, the staff is attentive, the food is delicious, and there's a kid's play area in the upstairs section. Call ahead to reserve the best seat in the house, a four-poster bed with sheer curtains (but be warned, it only seats four, sitting cross-legged

around a small table). $ *Average main: 120000d* ✉ *1 Cao Ba Nha St., District 1* ☎ *028/6290–8899* ✣ *E6.*

$$ AMERICAN Fodor's Choice ★ 🍴 **Quan Ut Ut.** This American barbecue joint is wildly popular among locals, who love the tasty ribs, the craft beer, the cheeky menu, and the laid-back vibe. It was set up by an American, Australian, and French trio, who charm the local dining scene with shared plates, communal park-bench style tables, stripped back surroundings, and low prices. The most popular menu items are the ribs and the big, spicy Italian sausage, each coming with three free sides. You can choose whether to eat with a knife and fork or chopsticks. A second outlet, created out of shipping containers, is due to open in March 2015 at 60 Truong Sa Street, in Binh Thanh District. $ *Average main: 150000d* ✉ *168 Vo Van Kiet St., District 1* ☎ *028/3914–4500* 🌐 *www.quanutut.com* ✍ *Reservations not accepted* ⏲ *No lunch* ✣ *F6.*

DISTRICT 3

$$ VIETNAMESE 🍴 **Banh Xeo 46A.** A no-frills, family-run institution, Banh Xeo 46A is the go-to place for one of southern Vietnam's most cherished culinary creations: *banh xeo* (literally, "sizzling cake")—a crispy pancake made with rice flour, coconut milk, and a smidgen of turmeric, and filled with bean sprouts, onion, shrimp, and pork. Place a slice in a giant mustard leaf, add a clump of herbs and greens, roll it all up, and dunk it in a fish sauce-based dip laced with chilies. The menu has been expanded to include other Vietnamese dishes but the *banh xeo* is still the star. There's a room with air-conditioning, but sitting outside is more fun, especially in the evening. $ *Average main: 120000d* ✉ *46A Dinh Cong Trang St., off Hai Ba Trung St., District 3* ☎ *028/3824–1110* ✍ *Reservations not accepted* 💳 *No credit cards* ✣ *E2.*

$$ VIETNAMESE 🍴 **Café If.** In a beautifully renovated French Colonial villa that evokes the romance of a bygone age, Café If serves up MSG-free Vietnamese fare with a slight French influence. The leafy courtyard is a great spot for a predinner cocktail before taking a seat in the main dining room, formerly the villa's grand salon. The prix-fixe lunch, geared toward busy office workers, can be great value. The extensive dinner menu can be quite daunting, but don't be afraid to ask for some assistance. $ *Average main: 200000d* ✉ *38 Dang Dung St., District 1* ☎ *028/3846–9853* 🌐 *cafeif.com* ✣ *E1.*

$$$ INTERNATIONAL Fodor's Choice ★ 🍴 **Noir.** A new concept for Ho Chi Minh City—dining in pitch blackness, served by vision impaired waiters—and one that's been a huge hit since Noir opened its doors in mid-2014. The theory is that because sight is our dominant sense, if you take it away other senses are heightened, resulting in a more intense experience of the food's aromas and taste. Diners divest themselves of light-emitting devices such as mobile phones and order two- or three-course Eastern, Western, or vegetarian set menus in a well-lit entry area before entering the blacked-out dining room. Noir's founders and kitchen team have extensive fine dining experience, which is evident once the first morsel is navigated through the darkness to awaiting taste buds. After the meal, diners learn the specifics of the dishes they've enjoyed. $ *Average main: 385000d* ✉ *178 Hai Ba*

Trung St., District 1 ☎ 028/6263–2525 🌐 www.noirdininginthedark.com ⊙ No lunch ✣ F2.

$ VIETNAMESE ✕ **Pho Binh.** Even today, long after the war, you couldn't guess this little pho shop's secret: in an upstairs room here, a resistance cell planned the Ho Chi Minh City attacks of the 1968 Tet Offensive. After a delicious bowl of beef or chicken pho arrives, foreign visitors are usually presented with a photo album and guest book. It's usually possible to visit the humble room (for 10,000d per person), which remains much the same—except it now has the grand title, Command Post Office of Subdivision 6 in the General Offensive and Uprising of the Tet Offensive in 1968. The name of the shop, by the way, means "peace soup." *$ Average main: 60000d ✉ 7 Ly Chinh Thang St., District 3 ☎ 028/3848–3775 ▭ No credit cards ✣ D1.*

$ VIETNAMESE ✕ **Pho Hoa.** This place is usually packed with locals slurping up huge bowls of noodle soup, served alongside fried doughnuts and the usual Southern-style selection of condiments and herbs. It's basic, the ground floor area is open to the street, and there's also an air-conditioned room upstairs. Some say the quality of the pho has dropped off since Pho Hoa registered on the tourist radar, but it still seems to satisfy the hordes of locals who descend daily and the soup is still a thousand times tastier than the stuff served up by chain restaurants. *$ Average main: 60000d ✉ 260C Pasteur St., District 3 ☎ 028/3829–7943 ▭ No credit cards ✣ E2.*

$$ VIETNAMESE ✕ **Ru Pho Bar.** Tucked into an alley on the very edge of District 1, this little eatery serves simple Vietnamese dishes, including very tasty pho noodle soup, in a homey atmosphere. Popular with locals at lunchtime for its set meals, Ru Pho Bar is a quiet, cheap-and-cheerful nighttime dining option with a friendly young staff. *$ Average main: 95000d ✉ 27E Tran Nhat Duat St., District 1 ☎ 093/858–8303 🌐 ruphobar.weebly.com ✣ E1.*

$ VIETNAMESE ✕ **Tan Dinh Market street food stands** (*Cho Tan Dinh*). Sample some of Ho Chi Minh City's best street food from the vendors at the front of Tan Dinh Market (Cho Tan Dinh). The *bun rieu* (noodle soup with rice paddy crab and tofu) and *nuoung suon* (barbecued pork) are especially recommended, as is *che*, the Vietnamese dessert-in-a-glass that's a popular afternoon snack. The vendors here have limited English but they are familiar with the fine art of point-and-order. *$ Average main: 60000d ✉ Corner of Hai Ba Trung and Nguyen Huu Cau Sts., District 3 ▭ No credit cards ✣ E2.*

$$ CAFÉ Fodor's Choice ★ ✕ **Work Saigon.** A café and co-working space, popular with the location-independent and webpreneur types based in the city, Work Saigon's cafeteria's is as hip as its clientele, serving great coffee in repurposed jam jars and doing a great take on modern café food. The Wi-Fi is fast and the working area is practical, with standing desks and one and two-person working desks. There's also a small pool and garden area where the Work Saigon team shows movies during the nonrainy season. *$ Average main: 140000d ✉ 267/2 Dien Bien Phu, District 3 ☎ 0121/600–8334 🌐 www.worksaigon.com ✣ E3.*

BEYOND THE CENTER

$$ PIZZA Fodor's Choice ★ ✕ **4P's Pizza.** The centerpiece of this stylish, immensely popular Japanese-owned restaurant is not a sushi bar but a brick oven, and the thin-crust pizzas it produces are truly worthy of Naples. You can opt for classic creations such as prosciutto margherita or something a little more experimental, like flower pizza (with edible blooms such as pumpkin, leek, and daylily) or teriyaki chicken with seaweed. Italian-style appetizers and pasta dishes are also available, as is a cheese platter featuring handmade cheeses from the 4P's cheese factory near Dalat. Customers who can't get a seat will stand by the bar just for a slice of the mouthwatering pizza. Reservations should be made days in advance—yes, it's *that* popular. [$] *Average main: 250000d* ✉ *8/15 Le Thanh Ton St., District 1* ☎ *0120/789–4444* 🌐 *www.pizza4ps.com* ✍ *Reservations essential* ✣ *H3.*

$$$$ CONTEMPORARY Fodor's Choice ★ ✕ **The Deck.** A stylish lounge and restaurant on the banks of the slow-flowing Saigon River, The Deck is a place to spoil yourself with sublime seafood-focused pan-Asian cuisine, fine wines, and professional service. The beauty of the entry courtyard, with its tall trees, black marble pond, and potted lotus plants, is almost forgotten once you enter the restaurant, where the river views take center stage. The weekend champagne brunches are sophisticated yet casual and the executive set lunches are perfectly suited to the business community. The Deck has one of the best happy hours in town, with 50% off cocktails from 4 pm to 7 pm; it also has a luxury boat providing shuttle service from District 1, sunset cruises, and guided tours of the Cu Chi Tunnels. [$] *Average main: 410000d* ✉ *38 Nguyen U Di St., Thao Dien, District 2* ☎ *028/3744–6632* 🌐 *thedecksaigon.com* ✣ *H1.*

$ VIETNAMESE ✕ **Du Mien Café.** A classic example of the Ho Chi Minh City "architecture café," this is a great spot to while away several hours drinking coffee, meeting friends, working online, or just enjoying the greenery, the waterfall, and the interior design. The menu features standard Vietnamese dishes at reasonable prices; it doesn't aspire to being outstanding, but the average quality suits the locals who come to grab a quick lunch or coffee during the day. At night the place is packed with groups of young people and couples on dates. [$] *Average main: 60000d* ✉ *48/9A Ho Bieu Chanh St., Phu Nhuan* ☎ *028/3844–3054* ✣ *D1.*

$$$$ VIETNAMESE ✕ **Hoi An Restaurant.** Designed to look like a beautiful "ancient house" from Hoi An with a high teak ceiling, dark wooden furniture, and silk lanterns, this restaurant serves attractively presented Central Vietnamese cuisine from Hoi An and the former Imperial capital, Hue. It mainly serves the tourist market and although the prices are on the high side, the food rarely disappoints. You'll have the option of a set menu or à la carte. [$] *Average main: 745000d* ✉ *11 Le Thanh Ton St., District 1* ☎ *028/3823–7694* 🌐 *www.orientalsaigon.com.vn* ✣ *G3.*

$$$$ FRENCH Fodor's Choice ★ ✕ **La Villa.** An experience rather than a meal, La Villa serves elegant but not pretentious fine French dining on a quiet street in District 2's Thao Dien area. Whether you sit in the garden by the pool, surrounded by fairy lights and greenery, or inside in the airy salon, the attentive service and the cuisine will make it a night to remember. For an extra-special meal, try the Menu Villa Gourmet and for something extra-extra special ask for Chef Thierry's wine pairings from the extensive wine list. Don't

miss the homemade Camembert Calvados (apple brandy camembert) from the cheese cart. $ *Average main: 1290000d* ⊠ *14 Ngo Quang Huy St., Thao Dien, District 2* ☎ *028/3898–2082* ⊕ *www.lavilla-restaurant. com.vn* ⌲ *Reservations essential* ⊘ *Closed Sun.* ✛ *H1*

$$ ✕ **Loving Hut Hoa Dang.** This is a bright and clean vegan restaurant cater-
VEGETARIAN   ing to local Buddhists, who are full-time or part-time vegetarians—some just forsake meat twice a month, on the full and half moon. An extensive range of fresh and delicious Vietnamese vegan dishes features on the menu, many using mock-meat made from tofu, lentils, or beans (meaning there's actually no beef in a dish labeled, for instance, beef with pepper sauce). Not only is the menu in English, it also includes pictures . . . and the prepared dishes really do look as appealing and colorful as they do in the menu. $ *Average main: 160000d* ⊠ *38 Huynh Khuong Ninh St., District 2* ☎ *028/3820–9702* ⊟ *No credit cards* ✛ *F2.*

$ ✕ **Lunch Lady.** A quirk of fate made the ever-smiling Nguyen Thi Thanh
VIETNAMESE   an international television superstar, yet fame has not wrought many changes to her humble food stand under a tree in an alley near the Saigon River. The Lunch Lady, who famously served celebrity chef Anthony Bourdain on his *No Reservations* TV show in 2009, has a rolling menu of a different dish every day. She speaks very little English but manages to serve visitors from around the world with very little fuss. It's a not-too-confronting way to try street food local-style, at tiny plastic tables and chairs on the sidewalk. ■ TIP➔ **It's not compulsory to eat the fresh spring rolls/summer rolls that are served once you sit down, but if you try one, you will be charged for the whole plate.** $ *Average main: 40000d* ⊠ *1A 1B C/C Nguyen Dinh Chiet, District 1* ☎ *0933/887–922* ⌲ *Reservations not accepted* ⊟ *No credit cards* ⊘ *No dinner* ✛ *H1.*

$ ✕ **Pet Me Coffee.** Drinks, ice cream, and yogurt (not food) are served
CAFÉ   here, but that's not the main attraction, this is a bird-petting café where you can end up with a miniature owl, a parakeet, or a cockatoo at your table. The more delicate birds, including African parrots and a toucan, at the front of the café aren't for petting, but the smaller birds are. The staff will usually present you with a bird after you've ordered. $ *Average main: 45000d* ⊠ *179 Tran Huy Lieu St., Phu Nhuan* ☎ *0917/096–677* ⊕ *petmeshop.com* ⊟ *No credit cards* ✛ *D1.*

$$ ✕ **Scott and Binh's.** Promising a taste of "home," burly American Scott
AMERICAN   and his wife Duc deliver with super-friendly service and American comfort food, including burgers, sandwiches, pasta, and mains such as Chili Roast Pork Tenderloin and Jamaican Jerk Swordfish. Expect personal attention, especially if you order cocktails, and honest American home-style cooking using as many local ingredients as possible. The food and the welcoming atmosphere (and possibly the purple velvet couches) at this tiny eatery adjacent to a hotel have given Scott and Binh's a local following of expats, locals, and travelers. It opens for brunch on weekends. $ *Average main: 175000d* ⊠ *15–17 Cao Trieu Phat St., Phu My Hung, District 7* ☎ *0948/901–465* ⊕ *bizuhotel.com/scottbinhs* ⊘ *Closed Mon. No lunch* ✛ *F6.*

$$ ✕ **Snap Café.** Serving a mish-mash of international, Tex-Mex, and Viet-
CAFÉ   namese fare, Snap is a family-oriented café-restaurant with a resort
FAMILY   style that seems to demand an ocean view; instead, the large thatched

hut overlooks a children's playground. Popular with the local expat community, Snap caters to nonfamilies with its quieter library section tucked away on one side (with a free two-for-one book exchange) beside a beautiful manicured tropical garden. The restaurant tries hard to please all comers, with burger nights, quiz nights, movie nights, live music, a pool table, and an extensive menu. The staff is friendly, especially to kids, but service is at times slow. [$] *Average main: 180000d* ✉ *32 Tran Ngoc Dien St., Thao Dien, District 2* ☎ *028/3519–4282* 🌐 *snap.com.vn* ✣ *H1.*

$$ JAPANESE 🍴 **Sushi Bar.** One of the first Japanese restaurants in Ho Chi Minh City's "Little Tokyo," the flagship restaurant of what is now a chain of sushi outlets remains one of the best Japanese joints in town. Tuck into fresh sushi, sashimi, hand rolls, and bento sets in the lively downstairs dining room or in a private room upstairs. [$] *Average main: 200000d* ✉ *2 Le Thanh Ton St., District 1* ☎ *028/3823–8042* 🌐 *sushibar-vn.com* ✣ *H3.*

$ CAFÉ FAMILY 🍴 **Sweet and Sour.** A pretty pink café specializing in cupcakes and macaroons, Sweet and Sour supplies many cafés in town, including L'Usine in Dong Khoi Street. Sweet and Sour is super-cute, with a little doll's house to keep kids happy and a champagne menu to keep the parents happy. Also serves great coffee. [$] *Average main: 50000d* ✉ *9 Ngo Quang Huy, Thao Dien, District 2* ☎ *028/3519–1568* 🌐 *sweetandsour.vn* ✣ *H1.*

$$ CAFÉ Fodor's Choice ★ 🍴 **Villa Royale.** World-class tea, cakes, pastries, and Australian café-style comfort food is served among antiques, objets d'art, and other treasures collected by globetrotting chef and hotelier David Campbell. It's a very exotic feeling, to be sitting on a vintage couch surrounded by beautiful things, using the free Wi-Fi and sipping top-quality TWG teas. High tea, brunch, or lunch can be served inside the antiques shop, on the terrace, or in the elaborate gazebo outside. The menu offers various baked goods, sandwiches, pies, and dishes such as lasagna and quiche. It's a great place to try Australian favorites such as lamingtons (chocolate cake with coconut), coconut ice, sausage rolls, and fritters. [$] *Average main: 170000d* ✉ *8 Dang Huu Pho St., Thao Dien, District 2* ☎ *028/3744–4897* 🌐 *www.villaroyaletreasures.com* ⏲ *Closed Mon. and public holidays. No dinner* ✣ *H1.*

WHERE TO STAY

Most visitors stay in Districts 1 and 3—the center of old Saigon—where the highest proportion of the museums, galleries, restaurants, bars, and nightclubs are found. The gracious old colonial hotels are here, too, as are many newer international hotels. Free Wi-Fi is ubiquitous, but service can be hit-or-miss. When in doubt, just remember that location trumps facilities. Look for bargains during Ho Chi Minh City's low season, from May to October, when some hotels discount their room rates to entice visitors during the rainy season.

WHAT IT COSTS			
$	$$	$$$	$$$$
Hotels	Under 750,000d	750,000d–1 million d	1.1 million d–2.5 million d	over 2.6 million d

Prices in the reviews are the lowest cost of a standard double room in high season.

AROUND DONG KHOI STREET

$$$$ **Caravelle Hotel.** Extensive renovations have freshened up this iconic
HOTEL hotel, which opened to the public on Christmas Eve 1959 and has entertained VIPs from around the globe throughout its storied history. **Pros:** imbued with Vietnam War mystique; convenient location; legendary bar. **Cons:** not the best value in its price range. $ *Rooms from: 4680000d ⊠ 19–23 Lam Son Sq., District 1 ☎ 028/3823–4999 ⊕ www. caravellehotel.com ⤳ 335 rooms, 31 suites* ¶⊙¶ *No meals* ✦ G4.

$$$$ **Duxton Hotel Saigon.** A comfortable hotel in a prime central loca-
HOTEL tion, the Duxton has an impressive marble lobby, attentive and helpful staff, and spacious rooms. **Pros:** great city views from the seventh floor and up; accommodating staff. **Cons:** the swimming pool area is rather small; some parts of the hotel are showing their age. $ *Rooms from: 43000000d ⊠ 63 Nguyen Hue St., District 1 ☎ 028/3822–2999 ⊕ www.saigon.duxtonhotels.com ⤳ 181 rooms, 6 suites, 4 apartments* ¶⊙¶ *Breakfast* ✦ G4.

$$$$ **Grand Hotel.** Although more modest than the Majestic or the Conti-
HOTEL nental hotels, this pleasant old colonial establishment evokes a bygone era of Francophone Saigon in the heart of the old Rue Catinat, where it's been since 1930. **Pros:** as locations go, this is as central as you get; river views from some rooms on upper floors. **Cons:** service can be indifferent at times. $ *Rooms from: 2700000d ⊠ 8 Dong Khoi St., District 1 ☎ 028/3915–5555 ⊕ www.grandhotel.vn ⤳ 215 rooms, 15 suites* ¶⊙¶ *No meals* ✦ G4.

$$$ **Hotel Continental.** History buffs head for this French colonial style
HOTEL hotel, where Graham Greene's classic *The Quiet American* was set and
Fodor's Choice the author himself stayed (in room 214); it was also the meeting place
★ of journalists and diplomats during the Vietnam War. **Pros:** central location; it's one of the city's historic sights. **Cons:** rooms facing the street are noisy—ask for one overlooking the inner courtyard. $ *Rooms from: 2240000d ⊠ 132–134 Dong Khoi, District 1 ☎ 028/3829–9201 ⊕ www.continentalvietnam.com ⤳ 55 rooms, 32 suites* ¶⊙¶ *No meals* ✦ G4.

$$$$ **Hotel Majestic.** On the waterfront overlooking the Saigon River, this is
HOTEL one of Vietnam's truly great colonial hotels, steeped with nostalgia and old-world charm that has been accumulating since 1925. **Pros:** great central location. **Cons:** government owned, which sometimes affects service standards. $ *Rooms from: 3200000d ⊠ 1 Dong Khoi St., District 1 ☎ 028/3829–5517 ⊕ www.majesticsaigon.com.vn ⤳ 93 rooms, 29 suites* ¶⊙¶ *No meals* ✦ H4.

$$$$ **Intercontinental Asiana Saigon.** One of the newest luxury hotels in
HOTEL town, this place wows with a flashy lobby and world-class amenities,

but the rooms are warm and inviting, with understated elegance in neutral tones. **Pros:** central location; attentive service; higher floors have great views. **Cons:** adjoins a labyrinthine shopping and dining complex, which can be noisy. $ *Rooms from: 4500000d* ⊠ *Hai Ba Trung and Le Duan Sts., District 1* ☎ *028/3520–9999* ⊕ *www.ihg.com* ⚲ *286 rooms, 19 suites* ⎰⎱ *Breakfast* ♧ *G3.*

$$$$
HOTEL

⬚ **Lotte Legend Hotel Saigon.** Pleasant and luxurious, this riverfront business-centric hotel, part of the giant Korean-owned Lotte chain, has fancy marble bathrooms and spacious rooms with floor-to-ceiling windows for great views. **Pros:** great location; professional and courteous staff; extensive breakfast buffet. **Cons:** the smell from the smoking floors can leak onto the nonsmoking floors; rooms on lower floors get street noise. $ *Rooms from: 3780000d* ⊠ *2A–4A Ton Duc Thang St., District 1* ☎ *028/3823–3333* ⊕ *www.lottehotel.com* ⚲ *283 rooms* ⎰⎱ *Breakfast* ♧ *H3.*

$$$$
HOTEL
Fodor'sChoice
★

⬚ **Park Hyatt Saigon.** Arguably one of the top international luxury hotels in Ho Chi Minh City, the Park Hyatt Saigon has a hard-to-beat location close to the major downtown attractions. **Pros:** world-class rooms and facilities; ideal location in District 1; beautiful swimming pool. **Cons:** standard rooms are on the small side; restaurants are a bit overpriced. $ *Rooms from: 6235000d* ⊠ *2 Lam Son Sq., District 1* ☎ *028/3824–1234* ⊕ *www.saigon.park.hyatt.com* ⚲ *223 rooms, 21 suites* ⎰⎱ *Breakfast* ♧ *G4.*

$$$$
HOTEL

⬚ **Renaissance Riverside Hotel Saigon.** Part of the Marriott group, the Renaissance Riverside offers comfortable elegance in a central location and its relaxing pool area, on the 21st floor, has panoramic views of the city. **Pros:** great riverside location; in walking distance of many downtown sights; accommodating staff. **Cons:** the lobby café and rooftop bar are very expensive; city-view rooms look out on an office block across the way. $ *Rooms from: 3280000d* ⊠ *8–15 Ton Duc Thang St., District 1* ☎ *028/3822–0033* ⊕ *www.marriott.com* ⚲ *332 rooms, 17 suites* ⎰⎱ *No meals* ♧ *H4.*

$$$$
HOTEL
Fodor'sChoice
★

⬚ **Rex Hotel.** If it's history you're after, the Rex has it in spades: it played a major role in the Vietnam War, hosting the American Information Service's daily "five o'clock follies" press briefings, and the 1976 unification of North and South Vietnam was announced in the same room. **Pros:** a great sense of history; friendly and helpful staff; central location. **Cons:** food and beverage prices can be extortionate. $ *Rooms from: 4063000d* ⊠ *141 Nguyen Hue St., District 1* ☎ *028/3829–2185* ⊕ *www.rexhotelvietnam.com* ⚲ *129 rooms, 98 suites* ⎰⎱ *No meals* ♧ *G4.*

$$$$
HOTEL

⬚ **Sheraton Saigon Hotel and Towers.** An older, but scrupulously maintained hotel in one of Ho Chi Minh City's premier streets, the Sheraton Saigon has all the amenities and standards of service you'd expect from the Starwood Hotels chain. **Pros:** central location; exemplary service; top-notch facilities. **Cons:** some rooms don't have great views; the hotel is in need of a spruce-up. $ *Rooms from: 4500000d* ⊠ *88 Dong Khoi St., District 1* ☎ *028/3827–2828/9* ⊕ *www.starwoodhotels.com* ⚲ *401 rooms, 84 suites* ⎰⎱ *No meals* ♧ *G4.*

AROUND PHAM NGU LAO

$ HOTEL
Beautiful Saigon 3 Hotel. If luxury and amenities aren't critical but a good deal is, this is one of the best options in District 1—a solid budget choice in the backpacker district, not far from many restaurants and bars. **Pros:** central location; good value; Wi-Fi in all rooms. **Cons:** being in the backpacker area can be tiresome; basic amenities. [$] *Rooms from: 747000d* ✉ *40/27 Bui Vien St., District 1* ☎ *028/3920–4874* 🌐 *www.beautifulsaigon3hotel.com* 🛏 *18 rooms* 🍴 *Breakfast* ✥ *F5.*

$$$ HOTEL Fodor's Choice ★
Cinnamon Hotel. This boutique hotel is so friendly—it offers a free foot massage as well as a welcome drink—that many guests never want to leave. **Pros:** wonderful service; within walking distance to downtown and the backpacker area. **Cons:** no elevator; rooms facing the street can be a bit noisy. [$] *Rooms from: 1500000d* ✉ *74 Le Thi Rieng St., District 1* ☎ *028/3926–0130* 🌐 *www.cinnamonhotel.net* 🛏 *10 rooms* 🍴 *Breakfast* ✥ *E5.*

$$$$ HOTEL
Hotel Nikko Saigon. Minimalist Japanese elegance and attentive service are the hallmarks of this hotel, right on the border of District 1 and District 5. **Pros:** spacious rooms; fifth-floor outdoor swimming pool is a great spot to unwind after a hot day of sightseeing; spa and fitness center. **Cons:** even though the hotel is in District 1, it's 20 minutes from downtown by taxi, longer during peak hours. [$] *Rooms from: 3500000d* ✉ *235 Nguyen Van Cu St., District 1* ☎ *028/3925–7777* 🌐 *www.hotelnikkosaigon.com.vn* 🛏 *285 room, 49 suites* 🍴 *No meals* ✥ *D6.*

$$$ HOTEL
New World Hotel Saigon. This was the first modern high-rise hotel in Ho Chi Minh City, and though it's looking a little tired these days, the central location, business amenities, gym, tennis court, and pool make it a good choice for business travelers. **Pros:** great location, opposite September 23 park and a short walk to the Ben Thanh Market; friendly staff. **Cons:** some rooms get street and bar noise. [$] *Rooms from: 2130000d* ✉ *76 Le Lai St., District 1* ☎ *028/3822–8888* 🌐 *saigon.newworldhotels.com* 🛏 *507 rooms, 26 suites* 🍴 *Breakfast* ✥ *F5.*

$ HOTEL
Townhouse 50. Clean and stylish, this minihotel/hostel has a great laid-back feel and friendly helpful staff and is a great option if you're on a budget or traveling solo. **Pros:** huge amounts of style and comfort for the price; very welcoming atmosphere. **Cons:** slightly out of the way, but for this price, who's complaining? [$] *Rooms from: 682000d* ✉ *50E Bui Thi Xuan St., District 1* ☎ *0903/740–924* 🛏 *11 rooms, 2 dormitories* 🍴 *Breakfast* ✥ *E5.*

DISTRICT 3

$$$ B&B/INN
Ma Maison. A small family-run boutique hotel outside the city center, Ma Maison is an affordable alternative to the city's international properties and a comfortable retreat from downtown that's ideal for solo travelers or couples. **Pros:** urban retreat feel; excellent service. **Cons:** surrounding area has little to offer; house rules, such as removing shoes, rub some guests the wrong way. [$] *Rooms from: 1900000d* ✉ *656/52 Cach Mang Thang Tam St., District 3* ☎ *028/3846–0263* 🌐 *www.mamaison.vn* 🛏 *12 rooms* 🍴 *Breakfast* ✥ *A2.*

BEYOND THE CITY CENTER

$$$
HOTEL
⌨ **Alcove Library Hotel.** This is a great option if you're looking for a bit of glamour slap-bang in the middle of local life, and a stylish alternative to the big downtown hotels. **Pros:** a quiet retreat from the chaos of downtown; free Wi-Fi, mineral water and beverages. **Cons:** some walls show scuff marks; 20 minutes by taxi from downtown and the tourist attractions. $ *Rooms from: 1350000d* ✉ *133A Nguyen Dinh Chinh St., Phu Nhuan* ☎ *028/6256–9966* ⊕ *www.alcovehotel.com.vn* ↩ *23 rooms, 3 suites* ❘◎❘ *Breakfast* ✛ *C1.*

$$$
HOTEL
⌨ **Hotel Equatorial.** Part of a Malaysian-owned chain of five-star hotels, the Equatorial has provided the only upscale accommodations in District 5 for years, with spacious rooms, an excellent seafood restaurant, and impeccable service. **Pros:** the only luxury option in District 5; live entertainment in the lounge Thursday to Saturday. **Cons:** 15 to 20 minutes from downtown (but the hotel offers a regular free shuttle service). $ *Rooms from: 2325000d* ✉ *242 Tran Binh Trong, District 5* ☎ *028/3839–7777* ⊕ *www.hotel-equatorial-hcmc.com* ↩ *327 rooms, 6 suites* ❘◎❘ *No meals* ✛ *C6.*

$$$$
HOTEL
⌨ **Sofitel Saigon Plaza.** With its renovation complete, this super-stylish hotel has elegant French and Vietnamese influences throughout, from the imposing lobby to the tasteful rooms to the sultry Boudoir Lounge on the ground floor. **Pros:** has a boutique hotel feel, despite its size; regular shuttle bus to the Ben Thanh Market; excellent fitness center. **Cons:** slightly out of the way on Le Duan Boulevard; closer to the zoo than the Reunification Palace. $ *Rooms from: 3833000d* ✉ *17 Le Duan Blvd., District 1* ☎ *028/3824–1555* ⊕ *www.sofitel.com* ↩ *275 rooms, 11 suites* ❘◎❘ *No meals* ✛ *G2.*

$$$$
HOTEL
Fodor's Choice
★
⌨ **Thao Dien Boutique Hotel.** Part of the scenic riverfront Thao Dien Village complex, this welcoming boutique hotel on landscaped grounds is a celebration of textures, with a giant knitted installation in the lobby and rooms combining corduroy cushions, muslin drapes, and polished cement floors. **Pros:** visually appealing urban hideaway with friendly staff. **Cons:** there's no boat shuttle service, making downtown a long taxi ride away, especially during rush hours. $ *Rooms from: 3600000d* ✉ *189–197 Nguyen Van Huong St., District 2* ☎ *028/3744–2222* ⊕ *www.thaodienvillage.com* ↩ *18 rooms, 2 suites* ❘◎❘ *Breakfast* ✛ *H1.*

$$$$
HOTEL
Fodor's Choice
★
⌨ **Villa Song Saigon.** Channeling the elegance of the French colonial era with soaring ceilings and wooden floorboards, the three-story Villa Song is an ode to art and interior design and became a favorite with discerning travelers as soon as it opened at the end of 2013. **Pros:** all-day breakfast, free minibar, and the lush landscaped saltwater pool make relaxing all too easy; regular shuttle boats to District 1. **Cons:** no elevator; the location outside of the main part of Thao Dien means there are few dining options within walking distance. $ *Rooms from: 5000000d* ✉ *197/2 Nguyen Van Huong St., Thao Dien, District 2* ☎ *028/3744–6090* ⊕ *www.villasong.com* ↩ *18 rooms, 5 suites* ❘◎❘ *Breakfast* ✛ *H1.*

NIGHTLIFE AND PERFORMING ARTS

As a thriving business hub, Ho Chi Minh City works hard and plays hard. You'll find plenty of lively bars and nightclubs all across District 1. The performing arts are largely represented by the Saigon Opera House and the French-government funded Idecaf venue, which both hold regular concerts. English-language films either have Vietnamese subtitles or are dubbed (very loudly) into Vietnamese. If you want to see one, make sure you get a ticket to a subtitled screening so that you can hear the original soundtrack. For movie screening times in English, visit ⊕ *dimovie.vn.*

NIGHTLIFE

AROUND DONG KHOI STREET

BARS AND PUBS

Apocalypse Now. Apocalypse Now, one of the oldest clubs in Saigon, is loud, fun, and always packed with a cross section of expatriates and foreign tourists. It's the after-hours place to go in the city. Amiable pimps and local prostitutes shoot pool while hordes of foreigners drink tequila and vodka and dance until dawn. But keep in mind these words of warning: always take a taxi, not a cyclo, back to your hotel (cabs line up outside); cyclo drivers have been known to steal from inebriated foreigners. Also, you should leave any jewelry, including watches, at your hotel; there are pickpockets at this nightspot. ⊠ *2C Thi Sach St., District 1* ☎ *08/825–6124.*

Blanchy's Tash. Since opening in 2012, Blanchy's Tash has become one of the city's most popular late-night haunts, attracting a mix of expats, tourists, and locals. If downstairs gets too crowded for your tastes, head for the rooftop terrace on the third floor. The three-hour-long happy hour on weeknights is a great value for a flash bar in a major city. For those curious about the peculiar name, it honors the moustache of Paul Blanchy, a colonial entrepreneur who made his fortune cultivating pepper and went on to become the first mayor of Saigon (1895–1901). ⊠ *95 Hai Ba Trung, District 1* ☎ *090/902–8293* ⊕ *www.blanchystash. com* ⊗ *5 pm–3 am028.*

Broma. A small, trendy bar, Broma stocks an impressive array of bottled beers from all corners of the globe, and the bar staff mix an excellent cocktail. If you're looking for a little local flavor, try the eye-opening *Rum bo Hue* (made with fresh basil, coriander, mint, chili pepper, rum, lemon, and roasted cinnamon). Make sure to sit in the open-air lounge on the top floor, where you will be right in between two of the city's flashiest skyscrapers (Saigon Times Square and Bitexco Financial Tower). The only drawback is the music, as customers often hijack the sound system. ⊠ *41 Nguyen Hue St., District 1* ☎ *028/382–36838* ⊗ *4 pm–2 am.*

Game On. Ho Chi Minh City's newest sports bar, Game On is sleek and satisfying, with cold beer, traditional pub grub, salads, and Asian options. Live broadcasts of sports from around the world include all football codes, golf, Formula 1 motor racing, boxing, and cricket on three projection screens and 10 large-screen TVs. It does a rather good breakfast, too. ✉ *115 Ho Tung Mau St., District 1* ☎ *028/6251–9898* ⊕ *www.gameonsaigon.com* ⊙ *Daily 8 am to late.*

Nguyen Trung Truc Street. If you're looking to enjoy a fun, laid-back night out, Nguyen Trung Truc Street is home to a string of cheap and cheerful bar-and-grill joints that attract scores of locals throughout the evening. Even though there is indoor seating, everyone is on the street. Ongoing entertainment is provided by fire-breathers and clusters of guitar-strumming, crooning customers. Xua va Nay (*33 Nguyen Trung Truc*) is the most popular restaurant, but farther up the street Saigon Xua va Nay (no relation) is just as good, and Saigon Night repeats the winning formula. To get started, order a round of Saigon beer and a plate of pork ribs (*suon nuong*). The street party continues until midnight. ✉ *District 1.*

O'Brien's Factory. An Irish pub with pool tables, exposed brick walls, friendly staff, and pretty fine food, O'Brien's Factory is a great place to relax, meet new friends, and enjoy live music on Tuesday and Saturday nights. ✉ *74/A3 Hai Ba Trung St., District 1* ☎ *028/3829–3198* ⊙ *Mon.–Sat. 11 am–midnight; Sun. 5 pm–midnight.*

CAFÉS
Bootleg DJ Café. Casual minimalist café by day, DJ lounge by night, Bootleg serves up excellent coffee, cocktails, panini, and, as you would expect from a joint set up by a DJ, great music, including electro-jazz, lounge, tech house, techno, and electronica. Food prices increase by 20% after 10 pm. ✉ *9 Le Thanh Ton St., District 1* ☎ *090/7760–9202* ⊕ *www.bootlegsaigon.com.*

Café RuNam. A newcomer to Ho Chi Minh City's to-be-seen scene, RuNam justifies its prices with stylish interiors and Vietnamese coffee prepared in a golden *fin* (filter)—slightly pretentious, perhaps, but still a fun place to hang out with the city's movers and shakers while enjoying great local coffee. During the day it's good for people-watching, too. Operated by a company that owns several café chains, its odd mix of Vietnamese and Western dishes can be hit or miss. ✉ *96 Mac Thi Buoi, District 1* ☎ *028/3825–8883* ⊕ *caferunam.com.*

DANCE CLUBS
Lush. Lush's longevity in the ever-changing nightclub scene of Ho Chi Minh City is a tribute to its eternal grooviness and cool beats, a combination that attracts a clientele of young Vietnamese, tourists, and expats. The indoor and outdoor sections can get crowded on Tuesday (Ladies Night), Friday, and Saturday. ✉ *2 Ly Tu Trong St., District 1* ☎ *028/3824–2496* ⊕ *www.lush.vn* ⊙ *Daily 8 pm–2 am.*

MUSIC CLUBS
Carmen. Flamenco music meets Hobbit house in this charming dimly lit bar; a great spot for an entertaining night out, although it can get smoky. The live music, performed by Vietnamese and Filipino artists, begins at 9 pm. ✉ *8 Ly Tu Trong St., District 1* ☎ *028/3829–7699* ⊙ *Daily 7 pm–midnight.*

La Fenêtre Soleil. This is the only Indonesian restaurant (⇨ *see also Where to Eat*) in this city that turns into a nightclub after 9 pm. Enjoy live music seven days a week at lunchtime as well as at nighttime in the artsy bohemian-style lounge/bar/café on the first floor. La Fenêtre de Soleil hosts regular Sunday night jam sessions and salsa nights on Wednesday. ⊠ *44 Ly Tu Trong St., Level 1, District 1* ☎ *028/3824–5994* ⊕ *lafenetresoleil.com* ⊗ *Daily 10 am–midnight.*

WINE BAR

Le Rendez-vous de Saigon. A newcomer to Ho Chi Minh's nightlife scene, Le Rendez-vous Saigon is a wine bistro with a large selection of new- and old-world wines, which can be enjoyed, along with delicious French bar food, in the welcoming wine bar downstairs or the luxurious lounge upstairs. There's live music Wednesday to Saturday. ⊠ *9A Ngo Van Nam St., District 1* ☎ *028/6291–0396* ⊕ *www.lerendezvousdesaigon. com.*

AROUND PHAM NGU LAO

BARS AND PUBS

OMG. A leafy rooftop bar that looks out over the hypnotic traffic chaos of the Ben Thanh Market roundabout, OMG (Original, Musical, Gastronomic) is a hip to-be-seen venue that does great cocktails and Asian fusion cuisine. ⊠ *Tan Hai Long Hotel, 15–19 Nguyen An Ninh St., rooftop, District 1* ☎ *0937/200–222* .

DANCE CLUBS

Gossip. The always-packed Gossip, a trendy Singaporean-run nightspot, is a favorite late-night haunt of models, celebrities, and high rollers. The crowd is decidedly young and Vietnamese, and the music loud and pulsating with a slant toward techno and house. The service is unusually attentive (in a good way). ⊠ *79 Tran Hung Dao St., District 1* ☎ *028/6682–3318* ⊕ *www.gossipclub.vn* ⊗ *Daily 6:30 pm–2 am.*

WINE BARS

Chill (Skybar). Far above the bustling crowds, Chill is an impressive open bar on the 26th floor of one of the city's modern office blocks. With unimpeded views of downtown Ho Chi Minh City and beyond, this is a dramatic vantage point to watch the sun go down and the metropolis's lights go on. It's a slick, pricey venue that attracts plenty of glamorous, well-heeled guests, but it's worth a splurge. (Entry to 27 Grill is through Chill.) ■ TIP➔ **Gentlemen, make sure you slip on some casual wear lest you have to borrow the dreaded "trousers and shoes for lend."** ⊠ *AB Tower, 76a Le Lai St., rooftop* ☎ *028/382–72372* ⊕ *www. chillsaigon.com* ⊗ *5:30 pm–2 am.*

PERFORMING ARTS

AROUND DONG KHOI STREET

FILM

BHD Bitexco (*Icon 68 cinema*). Seven screens show local and international movies. ⊠ *Bitexco Icon 68, 2 Hai Trieu St., Levels 3 and 4, District 1* ☎ *028/6267–0670* ⊕ *bhdstar.vn.*

MUSIC AND THEATER

Idecaf. Vietnam's institute of cultural exchange with France regularly hosts performances by local and visiting musicians and theater groups. Look for the *hoat dong van hoa* (cultural events) tab on the Vietnamese site for details of upcoming shows. ⊠ *31 Thai Van Lung St., District 1* ☎ *028/3829–5451* ⊕ *www.idecaf.gov.vn (French and Vietnamese only).*

Fodor's Choice
★ **Municipal Theater of Ho Chi Minh City (Saigon Opera House)** (*Nha Hat Thanh Pho*). The French colonial Opera House is one of the icons of downtown Ho Chi Minh City. It was built in 1897 and modeled on the Petit Palais in Paris, which was completed the same year. It was originally as lavish inside as it was out, with a revolving stage and a three-tiered, 800-seat gallery. Some of the more ornate fixtures were removed in the 1940s and from 1956 it was the home of the National Assembly of South Vietnam. It became a theater again in 1975 and is now the permanent headquarters of the Ho Chi Minh City Ballet and Symphony Orchestra. Check the website for details of upcoming ballet, musical, and cultural performances. ⊠ *7 Lam Son Sq., District 1* ☎ *028/3823–7419* ⊕ *www.hbso.org.vn.*

AROUND PHAM NGU LAO

FILM

Galaxy Cinema Nguyen Du. Three screens showing local and international new release films. ⊠ *116 Nguyen Du St., District 1* ☎ *028/3823–5235* ⊕ *www.galaxycine.vn.*

Galaxy Cinema Nguyen Trai. Three screens show local and international new release movies. ⊠ *Citi Plaza Supermarket, 230 Nguyen Trai St., District 1* ☎ *028/3920–6688* ⊕ *www.galaxycine.vn.*

MUSIC

Conservatory of Music (*Nhac Vien Thanh Pho Ho Chi Minh*). This is the only regular venue in town for classical music performances. The theater's main season is from September through June; it's generally closed in summer except when there are special concerts by visiting orchestras. Check the "notice" section of the website for performance times. ⊠ *112 Nguyen Du St., District 1* ☎ *028/3822–5841* ⊕ *www.hcmcons.vn.*

THEATER

Golden Dragon Water Puppet Theater. Three times a day, talented water puppeteers perform this folk art from the Red River Delta in Vietnam's north. The show is narrated in Vietnamese by a troupe of singers, accompanied by traditional musicians but there is no English translation or any explanation that the 50-minute show does not tell just one story, but scenes from daily life and skits based on Vietnamese folk tales. Expect to get a little wet if you sit in the front row—it's OK to scream if you get splashed, it's all part of the fun. ■ TIP→ **Explore the nearby Tao Dan Park before or after a show.** ⊠ *55B Nguyen Thi Minh Khai St., District 1* ☎ *028/3930–2196* ⊕ *www.goldendragonwaterpuppet.com.*

BEYOND THE CITY CENTER
FILM
CGV Megastar Crescent Mall. One of the newest movie theater chains in Ho Chi Minh City shows local and international movies, dubbed and subtitled. ⊠ *Crescent Mall, Nguyen Van Linh, 5th fl., District 7* ☎ *028/5412–2222* ⊕ *www.cgv.vn.*

CGV Megastar Parkson Paragon ⊠ *Parkson Paragon, 3 Nguyen Luong Bang, 5th fl., District 7* ☎ *028/5416–0088* ⊕ *www.cgv.vn.*

THEATER
Thu Do Theater. This is the place to catch a performance of *Cai Luong,* the traditional Southern Vietnamese folk opera featuring elaborate costumes and makeup, with the singing accompanied by *dan tranh,* the Vietnamese zither. The website is in Vietnamese and the theater reception staff have limited English so it's best you get some local help organizing tickets. Performances usually run from 8 to 10:30 pm. ⊠ *125A Chau Van Liem St., District 5* ☎ *028/3855–5226* ⊕ *www.cailuong.org. vn (Vietnamese only).*

SPORTS AND THE OUTDOORS

Sporting amenities are somewhat limited within the city, but do include some unexpected facilities, and there are several golf courses in and around the city.

BOWLING
Saigon Superbowl. This is a popular bowling alley with 24 lanes, an electronic games arcade, and food court, all within walking distance from the airport. It's ideal for whiling away a few hours if you've got a long stopover and can't face the taxi ride into District 1. ⊠ *A43 Truong Son St., Tan Binh District* ☎ *028/3848–8888* ⊕ *sbvn.com.vn* ☉ *Daily 9 am–midnight.*

DIVING
Rainbow Divers. Vietnam's only PADI dive centers are operated by Rainbow Divers, whose Ho Chi Minh City HQ is considered the gateway to dive travel throughout Vietnam. You can start your PADI training here in the city (in the Thao Dien, An Phu area) and combine it with trips to regional areas. Other outlets are in Nha Trang, Hoi An, Phu Quoc, Con Dao, and Whale Island. ⊠ *Buddha Bar, 7 Thao Dien St., District 2* ☎ *0913/408–146* ⊕ *www.divevietnam.com.*

GOLF
Dong Nai Golf Resort. It takes about an hour to reach this scenic course, about 50 km (30 miles) outside of Ho Chi Minh City. Designed by Ward W. Northrup, it's considered one of the most challenging courses in Southeast Asia, with hills and natural ponds. The location, at the bottom of a valley, ensures stable playing conditions year-round, with little wind. ⊠ *Off National Hwy. 1A, Trang Bom District, Dong Nai* ☎ *061/386–6288* ⊕ *dongnaigolf.com.vn* ⊠ *From 1,000,000d on weekdays* ⚲ *27 holes, 10381 yards, par 72.*

Saigon South Golf Club. This compact nine-hole par three golf course and driving range is the closest golf course to downtown Ho Chi Minh City. The greens are well-maintained and while not the most exciting course around, it's very accessible from downtown. ⊠ *Nguyen Van Linh, District 7* ☎ *028/5411–2001* ⊕ *www.saigonsouth.com* ✉ *From 433,000d on weekdays, including caddy* 🏌 *9 holes, 1160 yards, par 3* ⊗ *Daily 6 am–9:30 pm.*

Song Be Golf Resort. This 27-hole USGA standard championship course, 20 km (12 miles) outside the city, was built on former fruit and coconut orchards and is considered one of the most challenging layouts in Vietnam, with 10 lakes. The nine-hole Desert Course is Song Be's most feared, with its long, narrow fairways and complex bunkers that require some strategizing. The nine-hole Lotus Course and the nine-hole Palm Course are prettier than the Desert Course, with several lakes and large undulating greens. ⊠ *77 Binh Duong Blvd., Lai Thieu, Thuan An* ☎ *0274/3756–660* ⊕ *songbegolf.com* ✉ *1,659,000d weekdays, 2,499,000d weekends* 🏌 *27 holes, 6374 yards, par 72.*

Twin Doves Golf Club. Visitors need to reserve a week or two in advance to play at this private club, but will be rewarded with a 27-hole international standard championship course featuring woodland, lakes, rolling hills, and tree-lined fairways. Of Twin Doves' three courses—Luna, Mare, and Sole—Mare is considered the most challenging. ⊠ *368 Tran Ngoc Len, Hoa Phu, Thu Dau Mot, Binh Duong Province* ☎ *0274/386–0211* ⊕ *twindovesgolf.vn* ✉ *Visitor fees from 1,175,000d weekdays* 🏌 *27 holes, 7282 yards, par 72.*

Vietnam Golf and Country Club. This course, 20 km (12 miles) from downtown Ho Chi Minh City, was the country's first 36-hole golf course, set on a woodland estate. The 7,106-yard West Course, which features tree-lined fairways, has twice hosted the Vietnam Open Asian PGA Tour. The 6,946-yard East Course, designed by Lee Trevino, is more challenging, with many bunkers and water hazards and fast greens. ■ TIP→ Fees are lowest on Monday but the promotional rate does attract the crowds. ⊠ *Club House, Long Thanh My, District 9* ☎ *028/6280–0101* ⊕ *vietnamgolfcc.com* ✉ *Mon. 660,000d for 9 holes, 1,150,000d for 18 holes; Wed. 810,000d for 9 holes, 1,450,000d for 18 holes; Tues., Thurs., and Fri. 1,371,000d for 9 holes, 2,284,000d for 18 holes; weekends and holidays 1,805,000d for 9 holes, 3,009,000d for 18 holes* 🏌 *West Course: 18 holes, 7106 yards, par 36; East Course: 18 holes, 6946 yards, par 36.*

ROCK CLIMBING

X-Rock Climbing. Here you can tackle a bouldering wall 3 meters (10 feet) high and 8 meters (26 feet) long, with several different routes for climbers of all abilities. ⊠ *Phan Dinh Phung Sport Center, 75 Nguyen Dinh Chieu St., District 3* ☎ *028/6278–5794* ⊕ *www.xrockclimbing.com* ✉ *200,000d for day pass* ⊗ *Daily 8 am–9 pm.*

BUYING ANTIQUES IN HO CHI MINH CITY

Unless you have permission from the Ministry of Culture, it's against the law for you to take antiques out of Vietnam, and anyone found carrying antiques at the airport must hand them over to the authorities. This policy is unevenly enforced, however, and there's a vast gray area of what is and isn't an antique; often it's up to the whims of individual customs officers to decide. If you buy a fake article that looks like an antique, be sure to get a receipt in Vietnamese with the shop owner's signature guaranteeing the object is not genuine. Without it, you'll run into big trouble at customs. If you do decide to spend big bucks on the real thing (genuine antiques don't come cheaply in Vietnam), be sure you know what you're buying. It's very difficult to distinguish between genuine and fake items, when both sell at comparable prices. In particular, beware of restored antique timepieces, which often have a 1950s Rolex face, for example, covering the much cheaper hardware of a 1970s Seiko.

SHOPPING

There's a growing trend in Ho Chi Minh City's shopping scene of in-the-know locals and expats opening up enticing boutiques selling fair trade items, housewares, and very stylish locally made items, ranging from fashion to coffee cups.

Considered a traditional fine art of Vietnam, lacquerware is beautiful, long-lasting and—best of all for those with luggage weight restrictions—light. Most tourist shops and markets hawk the same kind of budget lacquerware. Higher quality items come at a price and are usually found in specialty shops. Some of the newer high-rise shopping complexes in downtown Ho Chi Minh City are home to high-end international brands, such as Versace, Jimmy Choo, and Prada. On the other end of the scale, markets offer a cheap and cheerful experience. They are generally open from sunrise until sunset, although some vendors just outside the markets stay open later.

By law, all transactions should be completed using dong, even if prices are quoted in U.S. dollars.

AROUND DONG KHOI STREET

Continuing a tradition dating to the time when it was French Saigon's main shopping thoroughfare, Dong Khoi Street between Le Loi (also a shopping street) and the river, is lined with shops selling jewelry, clothing, art, lacquerware, wood carvings, and other souvenirs mostly to tourists—which doesn't mean there aren't good finds.

ANTIQUES AND ANTIQUE REPLICAS

Nguyen Freres. Antique replicas here include prints of old colonial Saigon and *Dong Ho* folk woodcut paintings. There's also a treasure trove of clothing, fabrics, and craft items. ⊠ *2 Dong Khoi St., District 1* ☎ *028/3823–9459.*

ART

Mai's Gallery. This private gallery houses some of the works of Vietnamese and international artists collected by art lover Tuyet Mai, who has the dual aim of showcasing local artists and exposing locals to international works. Mai's Gallery, part of the 3A Station shopping and art area in an alley near the Saigon River, regularly hosts exhibitions and experimental arts events. ⊠ *3A-B Ton Duc Thang, District 1* ☎ *028/2241–0990* ⊕ *www.maisgallery.vn* ☉ *Daily 8 am–9 pm.*

CLOTHING

Mai Lam. Self-taught designer Mai Lam's sumptuous store in the Continental Hotel is worth visiting even if you have no intention of buying, but beware, the designs are bewitching, from hand-embroidered and embellished U.S. army jackets to soft and floaty embroidered blouses and jeans adorned with embroidered peacocks and phoenixes. ⊠ *Continental Hotel, 132–134 Dong Khoi St., District 1* ☎ *028/3827–2733* ⊕ *www.mailam.com.vn.*

Ninh Khuong. The flagship store of a small local chain selling cute-as-a-button linen and cotton baby and kids clothing and embroidered homewares. The fish-shape baby sleeping bags are likely to make you squeal. ⊠ *42 Le Loi St., District 1* ☎ *028/3824–7456* ⊕ *www.ninhkhuong.vn.*

Tuyet Lan Orchids Silk. This cute little shop has a selection of ready-made clothing in Western sizes and a fast and efficient tailoring service. The clothing is mostly women's but there is a small range of men's items, including ties, as well as a range of handbags, scarves, and jewelry. ■ TIP➔ **Allow at least two days for tailoring, even though the shop assistants may tell you they can do a one-day turnaround—some extra fitting and final adjustments may make all the difference to your purchase.** There's a second outlet at 71B Dong Khoi Street. ⊠ *84 Le Loi St., District 1* ☎ *028/3829–9754.*

CRAFTS

Mekong Creations. Set up by an NGO to assist women in remote villages in Vietnam and Cambodia, Mekong Creations stocks beautifully handcrafted items made from papier mache, silk, bamboo (including seven models of bamboo bicycles) and water hyacinth, as well as handmade quilts. ⊠ *68 Le Loi St., 1st fl., District 1* ☎ *028/2210–3110* ⊕ *www.mekong-creations.org.*

GIFTS AND SOUVENIRS

Fodor's Choice ★ **L'Usine.** This chic, capacious boutique stocks stylish international brands of casual clothing for men and women, like summer dresses by Trois Filles and denims and T-shirts from Universal Works, but there's so much more than apparel to browse here. The variety of trendy imported electronic goods, stationery, and accessories includes Lomography cameras, Moleskine notebooks, and Sunday Somewhere sunglasses. International travelers might be more interested in the array of stylish, made-in-Vietnam products. Keep an eye out for placemats by Very Ngon Homewares and lamps by District 8. The eponymous café upstairs (⇨ *see Where to Eat*) is an excellent spot for brunch and coffee. ⊠ *151/1 Dong Khoi St., District 1* ☎ *028/3521–0702* ⊕ *www.lusinespace.com.*

Saigon Kitsch. Just as the name implies, Saigon Kitsch offers a treasure trove of entertaining knickknacks—mugs, badges, stickers, coasters, laptop bags, shot glasses, ashtrays—all emblazoned with Socialist period slogans or quirky Vietnam-themed motifs. It's the perfect place to grab a sack full of souvenirs for friends and family back home. It's also worth wandering upstairs to Dogma, another store where you can buy reproductions of vintage revolutionary period propaganda art and T-shirts. ⊠ *43 Ton That Thiep St., District 1* ☎ *028/3821–8019.*

HOUSEWARES

Authentique Home. Nearly hidden down a little alley, Authentique Home sells a range of ceramics, tablewear, embroidered purses and handbags, and cushions, as well as beautifully crafted wooden furniture. There's a second outlet at 113 Le Thanh Ton Street. ⊠ *71/1 Mac Thi Buoi St., District 1* ☎ *028/3823–8811* ⊕ *authentiquehome.com.*

JEWELRY

Fodor's Choice ★ **Gallery Vivekkevin.** The founder of Gallery Vivekkevin presents his own luxurious contemporary jewelry, as well as collections from artists from around Asia, in ways that elevate the jewelers from craftspeople to artists. Even if you'd rather not splurge for jewelry while on holidays, this stark white gallery and retail outlet is worth popping in for a quick peek. The intricate creations on display are mind-blowing. ⊠ *35 Dong Khoi St., District 1* ☎ *028/6291–8162* ⊕ *www.galleryvivekkevin.com* ⊗ *Daily 9:30–8.*

LACQUERWARE

Nga Art and Craft. Finely crafted Vietnamese lacquerware in traditional and modern designs, as well as a range of wooden products, are all made at Nga's factory in District 9. ⊠ *81 Mac Thi Buoi St., District 1* ☎ *028/3823–8356* ⊕ *www.huongngafinearts.vn.*

MALLS AND SHOPPING CENTERS

3A Station. A collection of designer clothing boutiques and handicraft and jewelry shops, 3A (Alternative Art Area) Station is located alongside a café, an art gallery, and an outdoor exhibition space. The retail and art spaces surround a pedestrian-only courtyard plastered with graffiti—a popular backdrop for Ho Chi Minh's amateur and professional photographers. ⊠ *3A Ton Duc Thang St., District 1.*

Lucky Plaza. The recently renovated Lucky Plaza spans an entire city block, with entrances in Nguyen Hue and Dong Khoi streets, and is stuffed full of stalls selling clothing, shoes, handbags, lacquerware, watches, DVDs, jewelry, sunglasses, and souvenirs. ⊠ *38 Nguyen Hue St., District 1* ☎ *028/3827–1155.*

Parkson Plaza. The first and most central of the Parkson chain of shopping centers, Parkson Plaza has a wide range of fashion, cosmetics, homewares, appliances, and kitchenware, as well as a small supermarket on the top floor. ⊠ *35 Bis–45 Le Thanh Ton St., District 1* ☎ *028/ 3827–7636* ⊕ *www.parkson.com.vn.*

Taka Plaza. Downtown's "hidden" shopping mall, Taka Plaza has a small entrance on Nam Ky Khoi Nghia Street and a second, deliciously local, entrance down an alley off Le Loi Street. Inside is a hodgepodge of small stalls selling clothing, handbags, branded items, souvenirs, and accessories. Bargaining is expected here. ⊠ *102 Nam Ky Khoi Nghia St., District 1.*

Union Square. This upscale, faux-colonial shopping mall has high-end shops such as Ralph Lauren, Mont Blanc, and Piaget, as well as more mid-range options. The food court has cafés and fast-food outlets such as KFC and Thai Express. ⊠ *171 Dong Khoi St., District 1* ☎ *028/3825–8855* ⊕ *www.unionsquare.vn.*

FAMILY **Vincom Center.** Five levels of retail therapy in a shiny new glass and chrome skyscraper include an eclectic mix of high end fashion brands, such as Jimmy Choo and Versace, and well known mid-range options, such as Gap and a branch of the British Debenhams department store. There are multiple dining options, a CGV movie theater on the sixth floor, and a Kids Zone on one of the basement floors, with a play area for young children and a large arcade for older kids. ⊠ *72 Le Thanh Ton St., District 1* ☎ *028/3936–9999* ⊕ *www.vincomshoppingmall.com.*

MARKETS

Saigon Square I. A huge conglomeration of tiny stalls hawking all kinds of clothing, footwear, accessories, and electronics, Saigon Square is a great place to restock on threadbare beachwear: shorts, T-shirts, swim suits, flip-flops, children's clothing, sunglasses, hats, and whatever else you may have worn out while on vacation. Some haggling is required, even when an item has a price tag attached. Generally, the more you buy, the bigger the discount. Note that all transactions are cash-only. ⊠ *77 Nam Ky Khoi Nghia St., District 1.*

SHOES AND LEATHER GOODS

Anupa. Beautifully soft handmade leather handbags and accessories here are all one-of-a-kind, often featuring unusual intricate details, such as fish leather and tourmaline. ⊠ *9 Dong Du St., District 1* ☎ *028/3822–2394* ⊕ *anupa.net* ⊙ *Daily 9 am to 8 pm.*

Ipa Nima. The beautifully embellished handbags here, which are sold at high-end boutiques around the world, are considered by some to be the ultimate style souvenir from Vietnam. There's a smaller Ipa Nima shop at 71 Pasteur Street. ⊠ *77–79 Dong Khoi St., District 1* ☎ *028/3822–3277* ⊕ *ipa-nima.com.*

Tran Quoc Lan. This little cobbler shop can custom-make shoes in as little as a week, either copying an existing shoe or replicating one of the samples on display. Expect to pay 1,490,000d and up—not bad for a hand-stitched pair made with quality leather, likely to be a long-lasting reminder of your trip to Vietnam. ⊠ *97 Le Thanh Ton St., District 1* ☎ *028/3829–5453.*

SPA

Jasmine Total Body Wellness Spa. This boutique spa offers a range of face and body treatments, waxing, manicures and pedicures for men and women. There's also a small hair salon on the ground floor. ⊠ *45 Ton That Thiep St., District 1* ☎ *028/3827–2737* ⊕ *www.jasminespa.vn.*

TEXTILES AND SEWING

Catherine Denoual Maison. French fashion editor-turned-designer Catherine Denoual creates soft and luxurious hand-embroidered bed and table linens in elegant neutral colors, many with a dragonfly motif. The linen and other homewares in her flagship store have been described as contemporary heirlooms for their elegance and attention to detail. ✉ *15C Thi Sach St., District 1* ☎ *028/3823–9394* ⊕ *catherinedenoual. com.*

XQ. The hand-embroidered silk "paintings" created here have to be seen to be believed. They come in a range of styles, from traditional Vietnamese scenes to photograph-quality portraits. The artists work on the top floor, and the lower floors showcase their work, together with a small range of men's and women's clothes and accessories (scarves, ties, and fans). There's another outlet at 106 Le Loi Street, and also in Dalat, Nha Trang, Danang, Hoi An, and Hanoi. ✉ *37 Dong Khoi St., District 1* ☎ *008/3823–9581* ⊕ *tranhtheuxq.com.*

AROUND PHAM NGU LAO

ANTIQUES AND ANTIQUE REPLICAS

Antique Street. The vendors in this short street crammed with shops might claim their wares are genuine, but the truth is they're mostly replicas—interesting and beautiful, but definitely not worth the first price quoted. It's a great street for browsing, especially if you're into old photographs, but it will test your negotiating skills. ✉ *Le Cong Kieu St., District 1, Ho Chi Minh City.*

ART

Fodor's Choice ★ **Galerie Quynh.** Vietnam's best-known contemporary art gallery showcases various art forms, from drawing and painting to video and installation art, in a large factory-turned-exhibition space a stone's throw from Ho Chi Minh's backpacker district. Set up in 2003 by Quynh Pham, who fled Vietnam for the United States at the end of the Vietnam War, Galerie Quynh focuses on encouraging young artists and developing an arts infrastructure within Vietnam. The gallery has a second art space downtown on Dong Khoi Street. ✉ *65 De Tham St., District 1, Ho Chi Minh City* ☎ *028/3836–8019* ⊕ *galeriequynh.com* ⊙ *Tues.–Sat. 10–6.*

GIFTS AND SOUVENIRS

Ginko Concept Store. A tiny little T-shirt shop that opened in 2007 has grown into a concept store promoting natural, organic, and sustainable souvenirs. As well as its own Ginko T-shirts, the spiffy-looking store also stocks clothing, housewares, toys, and collectibles from local designers and artisans, such as Mekong Belle stationery and gifts and Archie Eco Shoes. Many of the brands in the stores are produced by charities and NGOs. Ginko also has outlets at 10 Le Loi and 54–56 Bui Vien streets. ✉ *254 De Tham St., District 1, Ho Chi Minh City* ☎ *028/6270–5928* ⊕ *www.ginkgo-vietnam.com.*

MARKETS

Ben Thanh Market (*Cho Ben Thanh*). Built in 1914 and renovated in 1985, the sprawling Ben Thanh Market has 3,000 booths. The outlets at the front are tourist-orientated, selling clothing, shoes, bags, and lacquerware; in the middle there's food and at the back fresh produce. The vendors can be incredibly pushy and pickpockets often roam the narrow aisles. There are better places to pick up souvenirs and much better places to eat. Once a must-see in Ho Chi Minh City, now it's a place best avoided, although it's a handy landmark, lying as it does between the central business district and the backpacker's area. ⊠ *At intersection of Tran Hung Dao, Le Loi, and Ham Nghi Sts., District 1, Ho Chi Minh City.*

Yersin Market (*Cho Dan Sinh*). Once the go-to place for army surplus items and Vietnam War memorabilia, this market now has an eclectic range of hardware and camping supplies alongside the military-esque products. So if you're in the market for a Zippo cigarette lighter, a hand truck, an army-green hatchet, or a life jacket, this is the place for you. ⊠ *104 Yersin St., District 1, Ho Chi Minh City.*

SPA

Cat Moc Spa. A calm and peaceful day spa a short distance from Ho Chi Minh City's backpacker district, Cat Moc Spa specializes in half-day pampering packages, with a menu of facials, massages, body treatments, hand and foot care, and a Japanese-style shampoo and blow dry service. ⊠ *61 Tran Dinh Xu, District 1, Ho Chi Minh City* ☎ *028/6295–8926* ⊕ *www.catmocspa.com.*

DISTRICT 3

ART

Craig Thomas Gallery. Regularly hosting exhibitions of painting, sculpture, and mixed media by emerging and mid-career Vietnamese artists, this gallery also has a satellite exhibition space in the Thao Dien neighborhood of District 2. ⊠ *27i Tran Nhat Duat St., District 1, Ho Chi Minh City* ☎ *0903–888–431* ⊕ *cthomasgallery.com* ☉ *Tues.–Sun. afternoon, or by appointment.*

CLOTHING

Massimo Ferrari. High-end bespoke menswear at this boutique features handmade shoes, suits, and shirts, as well as bags and sunglasses. If you can't make it to the District 3 store, you can arrange a consultation in your hotel room. ⊠ *42–A1 Tran Quoc Thao St., District 3, Ho Chi Minh City* ☎ *028/3930–6212* ⊕ *massimoferrariboutique.com.*

MARKET

Ban Co (Chessboard) Market. A great example of a local wet market selling fresh fruit, vegetables, meat, seafood, and homewares. The aisles are narrow and crowded and full of locals doing their daily (sometimes second- or third-daily) market runs. Food, coffee, and other drinks are available if you need a recharge. It's all done by 4 pm. ⊠ *664 Nguyen Dinh Chieu St., District 3, Ho Chi Minh City.*

SPA

La Maison de l'Apothiquaire. Down a romantic leafy lane, this is an elegant day spa in a beautifully renovated colonial villa. The spa has a full range of face and body treatments, manicures and pedicures, as well as a yoga studio. L'Apothiquaire also has a smaller salon downtown, at 100 Mac Thi Buoi Street in District 1. ⊠ *64A Trung Dinh St., District 3, Ho Chi Minh City* ☎ *028/3932–5181* ⊕ *www.lapothiquaire.com.*

BEYOND THE CITY CENTER

ANTIQUES AND ANTIQUE REPLICAS

Villa Royale. This tea house and antiques shop offers an eclectic mix of small, large, and very large collectibles, objets d'art, art, silverware, and vintage furnishings from Europe, North Africa, and Asia, collected by globetrotting Australian chef and hotelier David Campbell. David exercises his chef muscles in the tea house (⇨ *see Where to Eat*). ⊠ *8 Dang Huu Pho St., Thao Dien, District 2, Ho Chi Minh City* ☎ *028/3744–4897* ⊕ *www.villaroyaletreasures.com* ☾ *Closed Mon. and public holidays.*

ART

San Art. Independent, artist-initiated, and nonprofit, this contemporary art space hosts regular exhibitions, including some that only partially satisfy the government censor. It also hosts workshops, lectures, and artist presentations. Check the website for upcoming events, some of which take place off-site. ⊠ *3 Me Linh St., Binh Thanh District, Ho Chi Minh City* ☎ *028/3840–0898* ⊕ *www.san-art.org.*

VinSpace. Regular art exhibitions are hosted in this boutique art studio in District 2's Thao Dien area, and it also runs workshops for adults and children. It's particularly popular with expats for its regular Wine and Canvas painting evenings and Coffee and Canvas morning sessions. Some events are held at VinSpace Garage at 95 Pasteur Street in District 1. ⊠ *6 Le Van Mien St., District 2, Ho Chi Minh City* ☎ *028/3519–4581* ⊕ *vin-space.com.*

MALLS AND SHOPPING CENTERS

Crescent Mall. Ho Chi Minh City's newest shopping complex, Crescent Mall in the Phu My Hung expat area, has just about everything you could want in one shopping experience: a supermarket, an eight-screen movie theater, fashion boutiques, specialty shops, restaurants and cafés, furniture and homewares, electronics, and a children's entertainment area. ⊠ *Ton Dat Tien St., Phu My Hung, District 7, Ho Chi Minh City* ☎ *028/5413–3333* ⊕ *www.the-crescent.com.*

Parkson Paragon. This shopping mall has many international fashion and accessory outlets, such as Levis, Coach, and Bobbi Brown, as well as local brands Vera, Nino Maxx, and N&M. Like all the big malls in Ho Chi Minh City, there's also a dizzying array of dining and entertainment options, including a movie theater. ⊠ *Nguyen Luong Bang St., District 7, Ho Chi Minh City* ☎ *028/5410–8108* ⊕ *www.parkson.com.vn.*

Saigon Square II. With the same name, this has virtually identical stock as the older more central Saigon Square I in Nam Ky Khoi Nghia Street.

Expect to find clothing, sunglasses, iPhone covers, bags, winter jackets, and women's shoes. Prices aren't fixed so you'll have to flex your haggling muscles. ⊠ *7–9 Ton Duc Thang, District 1, Ho Chi Minh City.*

MARKETS

Binh Tay Market (*Cho Binh Tay*). This Cholon market carries wholesale items that can be purchased in small amounts by anyone: kitchenware, baskets, plastic goods (barrettes, magnets, toys, shopping bags, wigs, you name it), hats (traditional conical, straw, baseball caps), shoes, and food. With more than 2,000 stalls, Binh Tay can get get pretty chaotic. Head to the central courtyard where a statue of market founder Quach Dam (1863–1927) presides over a slightly more peaceful area. ⊠ *Hau Giang Blvd., District 6, Ho Chi Minh City* ⊕ *www.chobinhtay.gov.vn.*

Flower Market. Ho Chi Minh City's flower market is a vibrant and colorful affair. Busiest early in the morning when the bulk of the wholesale trade is conducted, the market continues to trade until mid-afternoon. ⊠ *Ho Thi Ky St., District 10, Ho Chi Minh City.*

SIDE TRIPS FROM HO CHI MINH CITY

Some of the destinations around Ho Chi Minh City can be visited as day trips; others may take a few days. Some excursions are more rugged, adventurous trips through forests and islands; others will take you to sandy beaches and seaside resorts.

CU CHI

Fodor'sChoice ★   *70 km (44 miles) northwest of Ho Chi Minh City.*

Cu Chi, now an outlying district of Ho Chi Minh City, was the Vietcong base of operations during the last war. The base was underground, in a vast system of tunnels that thwarted allied detection for most of the war. The tunnels are now regarded as a symbol of the resilience and enterprising nature of the Vietnamese people.

GETTING HERE AND AROUND

The easiest and best way to visit is on an organized tour, although it's possible to get to the tunnel complexes independently. It takes about 90 minutes to drive to Cu Chi in either a hired car with driver or a taxi. Negotiate a day rate with an operator at Mai Linh or Vinasun taxi companies rather than using the meter. Expect to pay around 1,500,500d.

TOURS

Organized tours can be arranged through reputable travel agents or hotel tour desks. The super-budget option involves strolling into any travel shop in the backpacker district—they'll be able to get you on a bus tour the following day for 110,000d or thereabouts, not including the entrance fee and lunch. Most bus tours offer the option of combining the Cu Chi Tunnels with a visit to the Cao Dai Holy See in Tay Ninh. Taking a boat tour to the Cu Chi Tunnels is faster and cooler, although more expensive, than going by road. Several companies offer boat tours, but Les Rives is probably the best.

AMBODIA

Suong

Phumi Krek

Bo Tuc

Ap Loc Thanh

Phuoc Binh   14

Dang Boa

An Loc

Dia Die Bunard

Xa Loc Ninh

Don Luan

14

Cat Tien
National Park

Bao Loc

Da Hoa

Tay Ninh

Tri Tram

Phu Giao

Xa Phuong Lam

Xa Hieu Tin

Krong
Svay Rieng

Xom Ben Co

14

Ap Bau Bang

Xom Trum Thap

Tan Uyen

Xa Gia Kiem

Ben Co

Trang Bang

Cu Chi

Ho Chi Minh City

Binh Trung

Ap Tham Thien

Ham Tan

1

51

Ap Ca Hoan

Thu Thua

50

Long Le

Ho Coc

Can Gio

Phuoc Le

Ho Tram

Ap Bac

Khiem
Ich

Can Duoc

Long Hai

Ben Tranh

Xom Vam Lang

Vung Tau

Cho Mo

30

Long Xuyen

Sa Dec

Go Cong

Thot Not

Vinh Long

Sung Hieu

50

Xom Cua Tieu

My Tho

91

Can Tho

Ap An Diem

Thoi Thuan

Ap An Thuan

53

Tra Vinh

Thanh Phu

ach Goi

61

Tie Can

Thanh
Phong

Vi Thanh

1

Mac Bat

Ap Tram

Long My

Ba Dong

Vinh Quoi

Soc Trang

Ap Ca Coi

Thanh Tri

Ap Dau Giong

Vinh Loi   Giong Me

Gia Rai

Xom Vam
Cai Cung

MEKONG RIVER

DELTA

MOUTHS OF THE MEKONG

South China Sea

Con Dao
Islands

0   40 mi

0   40 km

Side Trips from
Ho Chi Minh City

Les Rives. This reputable river-based tour company, which operates small group tours, offers an insightful half-day tour to the Cu Chi Tunnels that starts with a 7 am hotel pickup, and includes a pleasant journey on their luxury speedboat, a guided tour of the Cu Chi site, and lunch. Les Rives also offers several full-day tour options that take in Cu Chi and include cycling, a countryside tour, or a Vesper tour of Ho Chi Minh City, and a cooking class. ☎ *028/3827–5000* ⊕ *lesrivesexperience.com* ✉ *From 1,799,000d.*

Sinh Tourist. Catering to backpackers, this company has a daily tour to the Cu Chi Tunnels, departing at 1 pm. It's really nothing more than an air-conditioned bus that shuttles you to the tunnel site. ✉ *246–248 De Tham, Ho Chi Minh City* ☎ *028/3838–9593* ⊕ *www.thesinhtourist. vn* ✉ *From 85,000d.*

Urban Adventures. Daily five- to six-hour day tours to the Cu Chi Tunnels complex are accompanied by local English-speaking guides. The tours, which include bus transportation, usually visit a family to learn about local life and culture. ☎ *0909/904–100* ⊕ *www.urbanadventures. com* ✉ *From 875,500d.*

Vietnam Bike Tours. For a more vigorous Cu Chi Tunnels experience, try this bike and cruise itinerary, starting with a leisurely cruise to Cu Chi, a visit to the complex, then some cycling through back roads, past rubber plantations and rice paper making operations, and transfers back to Ho Chi Minh City by private minivan. The tour price includes an English-speaking local guide, breakfast, lunch, bicycles and safety gear, support vehicle, and boat and minivan transfers. ☎ *028/6653–0372* ⊕ *www.vietnambiketours.com* ✉ *From 3,374,000d per person, based on 2 people on tour; the price falls if more people join the group.*

EXPLORING

Cu Chi Tunnels (*Dia Dao Cu Chi*). A 250 km (155 mile) underground network of field hospitals, command posts, living quarters, eating quarters, and traps, the Cu Chi Tunnels illustrate the Vietcong's ingenuity in the face of overwhelming odds.

Work on the tunnels began in 1948 to combat the French and continued into the '70s, the extensive underground network made it possible for the Vietcong in the '60s not only to withstand blanket bombings and to communicate with other distant Vietcong enclaves but to command a sizable rural area that was in dangerous proximity (a mere 35 km [22 miles]) to Saigon. After the South Vietnam President Ngo Dinh Diem regime's ill-fated "strategic hamlet program" of 1963, disenchanted peasants who refused to move fled to Cu Chi to avoid the aerial bombardments. In fact, the stunning Tet Offensive of 1968 was masterminded and launched from the Cu Chi Tunnels nerve center, with weapons crafted by an enthusiastic assembly line of Vietcong-controlled Cu Chi villagers. Despite extensive ground operations and sophisticated chemical warfare—and even after declaring the area a free-fire zone—American troops were incapable of controlling the area. In the late 1960s B-52 bombing reduced the area to a wasteland, but the Vietnamese Communists and the National Liberation Front managed to hang on.

There are two Cu Chi Tunnel tourist areas, which both have tunnels that have been expanded to accommodate "big size" tourists. These larger tunnels are still claustrophobically small, however, and much too snug for anyone who is genuinely big-size. Most guided tours go to **Ben Dinh,** where the firing range (M16 bullets are 40,000d each, AK47 bullets are 45,000d each) is right next to the souvenir shop. This "fun" feature does make an awful racket.

Ben Duoc is a much prettier site and is usually less crowded than Ben Dinh, with the added advantage of having its firing range farther away from the tunnel area. What makes Ben Duoc the more pleasant site is the on-site temple and restaurant: Ben Duoc Temple of Martyr Memorial is surrounded by lush green gardens; while the Dia Dao Restaurant is a nice location for lunch.

The ticket price includes an official guide, who will show you the tunnels, the air vents, living quarters and explain the recreated booby traps, the mechanized mannequins making bombs and traps and the real-life people making sandals from tires.

Both sites are owned by the government and visiting both is not recommended, as the displays are the same. ✉ *Phu My Hung Ward, Cu Chi District, Ho Chi Minh City* ☎ *028/3794–8830 administration, 028/3794–8820 Ben Duoc site, 028/3794–6442 Ben Dinh site* ⊕ *www. diadaocuchi.com.vn* ✒ *90,000d for each site* ⊙ *Daily 7–5.*

Ben Dinh. Most guided tours go to Ben Dinh, so it can get very crowded, which only adds to the claustrophobic feel of the tunnels. The firing range (M16 bullets are 32,000d each, AK47 bullets are 42,600d each) is right next to the souvenir shop, and this "fun" feature does make an awful racket. ✉ *Cu Chi District, Ho Chi Minh City.*

Ben Duoc. A much prettier site, with a temple and on-site restaurant, Ben Duoc and usually less crowded than Ben Dinh, and has the added advantage of having its firing range farther away from the tunnel area. The Temple of Martyr Memorial here is surrounded by lush green gardens, and the Dia Dao Restaurant is a nice location for lunch. ✉ *Cu Chi District, Ho Chi Minh City.*

Cu Chi Wildlife Rescue Station. A cooperative program between local NGO, Wildlife At Risk, and the Ho Chi Minh City Forest Protection Department, the wildlife rescue station helps rehabilitate animals confiscated from illegal wildlife traders. Expect to see rescued bears, gibbons, langurs, loris, wild cats, pangolins, turtles, monitors, and many species of birds at the 0.4-hectare (1-acre) sanctuary. The sanctuary is about 1½ hours drive by car from Ho Chi Minh City, longer by public bus. ✉ *50 Duong 15 St., Cho Cu Ha Hamlet* ☎ *028/3794–7045, 098–428–1190, for reservations* ⊕ *www.wildlifeatrisk.org* ✒ *200,000d* ⊙ *Daily 7:30–11:30 and 1–4:30 (by reservation only)* ☞ *For reservation, call center manager Mr Lam on number given here, then go to Wildlife At Risk's Ho Chi Minh City office, at 202/10 Nguyen Xi St., Binh Thanh, to pay entry fee; take receipt to show at rescue station.*

TAY NINH

95 km (59 miles) northwest of Ho Chi Minh City.

Generally a visit to Tay Ninh is part of a day trip to the Cu Chi Tunnels arranged through one of the travel agencies in Saigon. A guide will accompany you, explain the history of the Cao Dai sect, and take you through the temple, usually to watch the midday service.

GETTING HERE AND AROUND

Tay Ninh's Cao Dai Holy See is usually an included stop on a Cu Chi bus tour (⇨ *see Cu Chi Tunnels for details*). Buses to Tay Ninh depart Ho Chi Minh City's An Suong bus depot regularly; the fare is about 65,000d each way. Getting to Tay Ninh by taxi or renting a car with driver will take about 2½ hours and a day trip will cost around 200,000d.

Bus contacts Dong Phuoc ☎ *028/3883–0477 in Ho Chi Minh City, 066/377–7777 in Tay Ninh.* **Kim Ngan** ☎ *028/3718–6857, 066/377–2255 in Tay Ninh.*

EXPLORING

Cao Dai Holy See (*Toa Thanh Tay Ninh*). The town of Tay Ninh is home to Cao Daism, an indigenous hybrid religion founded in 1926 by a mystic named Ngo Minh Chieu, and its impressive and brightly colored temple, the Cao Dai Holy See. The noon ceremony (others are held at 6 am, 6 pm, and midnight) at the temple is a fascinating and colorful religious vignette. A finely tuned hierarchical procession of men and women of all ages parades through the temple's great hall, where painted columns twined with carved dragons support sky-blue arched vaulting. Panels of stained glass with a cosmic-eye motif punctuate the walls. You are permitted to watch and take snapshots from the mezzanine. Ignore any feeling of complicity in what appears to be a collective voyeuristic sacrilege; the ceremony goes on as though you were not there. ⊠ *Hoa Thanh District* ⊕ *caodai.com.vn.*

CAN GIO

60 km (37 miles) southeast of Ho Chi Minh City.

A maze of channels, inlets, and tiny hamlets hidden among swamp and forest, Can Gio has only appeared on the tourist radar within the last few years and so the amenities and services, set up to service the domestic tourist market, are quite basic. To make the most of a visit, going with a reputable tour company or a private tour guide is highly recommended. Tours usually include stops at the Rung Sac Guerilla Base, the Vam Sat eco zone, and sometimes the very brown Can Gio Beach. Without a guide, or at least someone who speaks Vietnamese, in your group, Can Gio can be a confusing and disappointing place to visit.

GETTING HERE AND AROUND

Can Gio is best visited with a tour guide or on an organized tour and there are many options for touring Can Gio's mangrove areas to view the wildlife. Driving here from Ho Chi Minh City takes about two hours and includes a ferry crossing. Hiring a taxi for a day trip will cost about1,500,500d , plus the fee for the ferry crossing—10,000 each way.

Cao Daism

Cao Daism incorporates elements of the major world religions—Buddhism, Confucianism, Taoism, Christianity, and Islam—as well as Vietnamese spiritualism. The religion fuses a Mahayana Buddhist code of ethics with Taoist and Confucian components. Sprinkled into the mix are elements of Roman Catholicism, the cult of ancestors, Vietnamese superstition, and over-the-top interior decoration that encompasses a fantastic blend of Asian and European architectural styles. Cao Daism has grown from its original 26,000 members to a present-day membership of 3 million. Meditation and communicating with spiritual worlds via earthly mediums or seances are among its primary practices. Despite its no-holds-barred decorative tendencies, Cao Daism emphasizes abstinence from luxury and sensuality as well as vegetarianism as a means of escaping the reincarnation cycle. Although the priesthood is strictly nonprofessional, clergy must remain celibate.

Key beliefs

Perhaps most important, the Cao Daists believe the divine revelation has undergone three iterations: God's word presented itself first through Lao-tzu and other Buddhist, Confucianist, and Taoist players; then through a second set of channelers such as Jesus, Muhammad, Moses, Confucius, and Buddha. Whether because of the fallibility of these human agents or because of the changing set of human needs, the Cao Daists believe the divine transmission was botched. They see themselves as the third and final expression— the "third alliance between God and man." Because anyone can take part in this alliance, even Westerners like Joan of Arc, Victor Hugo, and William Shakespeare have been added to the Cao Dai roster.

Cao Daism and politics

During World War II, the Cao Daists were armed and financed by the Japanese, whom the sect saw as also fighting the government. After the war, the Cao Daists gained the backing of the French in return for their support against the Vietminh. After the French left in the late '50s, the South Vietnamese government made a point to destroy the Cao Daists as a military force, which caused many members of the sect to turn to the Communists, and the area became an anti–South Vietnamese stronghold. But when the Communists came to power in 1975, they repossessed the sect's land, and Cao Daism lost most of its remaining power. Today the religion is tolerated but is no longer involved in politics.

TOUR CONTACTS

Les Rives. Take a luxury speed boat to Can Gio to explore the area with a knowledgeable English-speaking guide, who will introduce you to the local wildlife, including bats, monkeys, and crocodiles. The full-day small-group tour includes breakfast and lunch. ☎ 0128/592–0018 ⊕ lesrivesexperience.com 2,263,000d.

Saigon Riders. Leap onto the back of a motorbike cruiser and hit the highway (and a local wooden ferry) to explore Can Gio with local English-speaking guides/drivers. This full-day tour takes country roads to the biosphere reserve for some wildlife watching and lunch, with an option to travel father to Monkey Island. ☎ *0913–767–113* ⊕ *www.saigonriders.vn* ✉ *2,320,000d per person (minimum 2 people).*

EXPLORING

Can Gio UNESCO Biosphere Reserve. This mangrove forest, officially part of Ho Chi Minh City, covers an area the size of Singapore. The old forest was destroyed by aerial bombing and defoliants—primarily Agent Orange—during the Vietnam War because it had been a regular hiding place for the Vietcong, who would fire mortars at the supply ships on the Saigon River. Residents of the area were forced to leave, and it wasn't until 1978 that surviving Can Gio families returned, replanted the forest, and gradually resettled. Surprisingly, the area's wild animals also returned, and today there are monkeys, wild boar, deer, and leopards, long-tailed macaques, crocodiles, birds and giant fruitbats, although not all are easy to spot.

In 2000, the area was declared a UNESCO Biosphere Reserve and the local economy is now supported by various eco-tourism ventures. Under the Can Gio Biosphere Reserve model, families live inside the reserve conducting small-scale aquaculture ventures to help preserve what's known as the "lungs of Ho Chi Minh City."

The government-owned Saigon Tourist has a "eco forest park" on Monkey Island that includes a bizarre animal circus with monkeys and crocodiles. ✉ *Rung Sac, Can Gio.*

VUNG TAU

130 km (80 miles) southeast of Ho Chi Minh City.

Known as Cap St-Jacques during colonial times, Vung Tau was a popular beach resort for the French and later, during the Vietnam War, it became a major United States and Australian army base. The area was later taken over by the Soviet Union as a concession for helping Hanoi win the war. The Soviets used the Vung Tau port as a navy base and drilled for oil off the coast. Following the collapse of the Soviet Union, many Russians left, although Vung Tau is still home to many, who are mostly still involved in the area's oil industry.

Vung Tau is an easy getaway from Ho Chi Minh City, although not as popular as the resort town of Mui Ne farther along the coast. Tourism amenities are aimed at domestic tourists, who have a different set of expectations from international visitors. Vung Tau's quirkiness, rather than its beaches, makes it an interesting place to visit.

The city, which has made its fortune from the oil industry, is a good base for exploring the beaches along the coast: Long Hai, Ho Coc, and Ho Tram.

GETTING HERE AND AROUND

Buses leave at regular intervals during the day from Ho Chi Minh City to Vung Tau. The journey takes 2 to 2½ hours and costs from about 100,000d. Minibuses run by Mai Linh Express and Rang Dong depart from Mien Dong bus station at 292 Dinh Bo Linh Street in Binh Thanh District. Hoa Mai buses depart for Vung Tau from 44 Nguyen Thai

Binh Street in District 1. In Vung Tau, Hoa Mai offers a pickup service that must be reserved in advance.

It's possible to get to Vung Tau by taxi from Ho Chi Minh City. Agree a rate with the taxi company operator rather than use the meter. A one-way trip should cost around 1,000,000d. Hiring a taxi for the day to take you to Vung Tau and back to Ho Chi Minh City should cost around 2,040,000d. Three reliable taxi companies ply the streets of Vung Tau. They can be hired on a daily basis.

Bus Contacts Hoa Mai ⊠ *Ho Chi Minh City* ☎ *028/3821–8928, 064/3531–982 Vung Tau number, to organize pickup* ⊕ *hoamaivungtau.com.vn.* **Mai Linh Express** ⊠ *Ho Chi Minh City* ☎ *028/3511–7888* ⊕ *www.mailinh.vn.* **Rang Dong** ⊠ *Ho Chi Minh City* ☎ *028/3894–5808* **Vung Tau Bus Station** ⊠ *192 Nam Ky Khoi Nhgia St.* ☎ *064/385–9727.*

Ferry Contacts Vina Express ⊠ *Vung Tau* ☎ *028/3827–7555* ⊕ *www. vinaexpress.com.vn.*

Taxi Contacts Mai Linh ☎ *064/356–5656* ⊕ *www.mailinh.vn* **Petro Taxi** ☎ *064/381–8181* **Vinasun** ☎ *064/372–7009* ⊕ *www.vinasuntaxi.com*

EXPLORING
TOP ATTRACTIONS
Christ the King Statue (*Tuong Dai Chua Kito Vua*). Rio has Christ the Redeemer overlooking the city, Vung Tau has Christ the King, a 32-meter (105-feet) -high statue on a 4-meter (13-feet) -high platform atop Mount Nho, looking out over the South China Sea with his arms outstretched. Even though tackling the 847 steps up Mount Nho is a challenge in the hot and steamy conditions, expect to be overtaken by tiny Vietnamese grandmothers in thick acrylic suits. Take plenty of water. There's a little shop at the top selling drinks and snacks, and an art gallery inside Jesus's legs, but the opening hours seem to change to suit the caretakers' own schedules. ⊠ *2 Ha Long St.*

Niet Ban Tinh Xa Pagoda (*Phat Nam Pagoda, Chua Phat Nam*). Completed in 1974, this pagoda at the base of Nho Mountain, is considered one of Vung Tau's most beautiful. The serene garden in front of the pagoda represents Buddha achieving the state of Nirvana. The most famous part of the complex, however, is the 12-meter (39-feet) -long Reclining Buddha statue. ⊠ *Ha Long* 🎫 *Free* ☉ *Daily 7–4.*

Thich Ca Phat Dai Pagoda. This Theravada Buddhism temple, built between 1961 and 1963, is on the northwestern face of Lon Mountain. The highlights are a 10-meter (33-feet) -high gleaming white Buddha statue and the climb up the steps to its base, through beautiful gardens and jungle. Alongside the steps is a series of statues depicting Buddha's life. Pilgrims from all over Vietnam visit the pagoda, which has a Zen Buddhist monastery on site. ⊠ *608 Tran Phu St.* 🎫 *Free* ☉ *Daily 7–4.*

White Palace (*Bach Dinh*). Built in 1898, the White Palace has variously served as the French governor's residence, a retreat of Bao Dai, the last emperor of Vietnam, and the president of South Vietnam's summer house. The villa is now a slightly worn museum with a ground-floor exhibition of late 17th- and early 18th-century Chinese artifacts recovered from a shipwreck near the Con Dao Islands. On the upper floors there's the now-shopworn living quarters of the last resident. Despite its tired air, the White Palace is worth visiting for the views of the South China Sea and the lush tropical grounds. ⊠ *12 Tran Phu St.* ☏ *0254/810–124, 0254/852–605* 🖙 *15,000d* ⊗ *Daily 7–5.*

WORTH NOTING

Front Beach Park (*Cong Vien Bai Truoc*). One of Vung Tau's more quirky sights, Front Beach Park, sometimes called Statue Park, has a children's playground, fitness stations, walking trails, and an extensive collection of statues, including some that are quite racy for conservative Vietnam. ⊠ *Quang Trung.*

FAMILY **Ho May Eco-Tourism Park** (*Cloud Lake Resort*). Disregard the name—Ho May is a theme park, not an eco-tourism destination, but it offers a host of fun activities, starting with a 500-meter (1,640-foot) -long cable-car ride to the entrance atop Lon Mountain. The 20 hectare (50 acre) park features two artificial lakes connected by a man-made waterfall, and other attractions range from swan-shape paddle boats and carriage rides, to thrill rides, ziplining, horseback-riding, paintball, and go-kart racing. There are also enclosures containing deer, ostrich, boar, porcupines, and peacocks, and an animal circus. ⊠ *Cable Car Station 1, 1A Tran Phu* ☏ *064/385–6078* ⊕ *www.captreovungtau.vn* 🖙 *300,000d, including cable car* ⊗ *Daily 7 am–11 pm.*

Hon Ba Island. Only accessible at low tide across treacherous slippery rocks, Hon Ba Island is home to the Mieu Ba (lady) temple, dedicated to the patron goddess of sailors and fishermen. If you visit, watch the tide carefully to make sure you don't get stranded. There's no food or fresh water on the island. ⊠ *Off southern tip of Back Beach.*

Vung Tau Lighthouse (*Ngon hai dang Vung Tau*). Built by the French during colonial times to guide ships into the Saigon port, the still-operational 18-meter (59-feet) -high lighthouse sits at the top of Small Mountain, at the end of a steep and winding road, still protected by four old French cannon. The lighthouse balcony offers a spectacular 360-degree view of Vung Tau and the South China Sea. If you take a taxi to the lighthouse, ask the driver to wait for you because there are not going to be any passing taxis to hail and it's a very long walk back down the mountain. ⊠ *Hai Dang* 🖙 *20,000d* ⊗ *Daily 7–5.*

BEACHES

Back Beach (*Bai Sau*). Vung Tau's most popular beach has golden sands that stretch for miles, but it's not the prettiest or the cleanest beach around. Quiet on weekdays, it's crowded on weekends, with locals who will be playing volleyball, football, and jogging. Back Beach is fine for swimming, but be aware that all the locals swim fully clothed so parading around in a swimsuit is going to attract some stares. There are showers at the Imperial Hotel's Beach Club, which has a 200,000d entry fee. **Amenities:** food and drink; showers. **Best for:** sunset; swimming; walking. ⊠ *Thuy Van.*

WHERE TO EAT

$ ✕ **Banh Khot Goc Vu Sua.** *Banh khot* (tiny rice flour pancakes topped with
VIETNAMESE shrimp that you wrap in baby mustard leaves) is Vung Tau's signature dish and locals rate Banh Khot Goc Vu Sua as the best in class. This is

simple, inexpensive, and 100% delicious local street food—maybe not for the faint-hearted or weak-stomached, but adventurous foodies will enjoy the whole *banh khot* experience, sitting on tiny chairs in a big tin shed that fills with smoke every time a new batch is cooked. [$] *Average main: 30000d* ✉ *14 Nguyen Truong To St.* ☎ *064/352–3465* ✍ *Reservations not accepted* 🕒 *No dinner.*

$$ VIETNAMESE Fodor's Choice ★ 🍴 **Ganh Hao.** This sprawling seafront eatery is regarded as the best seafood place in town for a very good reason: the food here is delicious, and the spring (or summer) rolls are highly recommended. Like many Vietnamese places, the interior design takes a back seat to the food and the view. It's pricier than the more local joints farther along Tran Phu Street, but you get what you pay for, which in this case, aside from the great food, is English-speaking staff, an English menu, and servers used to dealing with international tourists. [$] *Average main: 250000d* ✉ *3 Tran Phu St.* ☎ *064/355–0909.*

$$ SEAFOOD 🍴 **Hai San Thanh Phat.** If eating fresh-caught seafood in a tin shed on the waterfront alongside rowdy locals is your thing, this is definitely the place for you. Communication can be a struggle here, but it's a worthwhile one if you end up with a few cold beers and several plates of seafood. The prawns barbecued with chili and salt (*tom nuong muoi ot*) is highly recommended. **TIP→ Make sure you go to the restaurant on the water side of the street; ignore the guys across the road who will try to get your attention.** [$] *Average main: 150000d* ✉ *334 Tran Phu St.* ☎ *064/355–0595* 💳 *No credit cards.*

$$ EASTERN EUROPEAN 🍴 **Kozac.** The interior is a bit worn-around-the-edges but this Ukrainian restaurant—Vietnam does have a knack for the unexpected—serves some tasty Eastern European, Western and Asian dishes, along with Russian, Vietnamese, and imported beers, in a friendly atmosphere. If you need a break from Vietnamese food, this will hit the spot. [$] *Average main: 175000d* ✉ *7 Nguyen Tri Phuong* ☎ *064/356–3776* 🌐 *kozakmamay.com.*

WHERE TO STAY

$$$$ RESORT Fodor's Choice ★ 🏨 **Binh An Village.** With all the charm of a stylish and intimate lodging and the upscale amenities of an oceanfront resort, Binh An Village provides the best of both worlds. **Pros:** a relaxing and stylish getaway with great views of the South China Sea. **Cons:** slightly too far from town to walk anywhere. [$] *Rooms from: 2566000d* ✉ *1 Tran Phu St.* ☎ *064/351–0016* 🌐 *www.binhanvillage.com* 🛏 *3 rooms, 2 suites, 5 villas* 🍽 *Breakfast.*

$$$$ HOTEL 🏨 **Imperial Hotel.** With its slightly over-the-top French chateau interiors and large, sumptuous rooms, the Imperial is certainly the fanciest hotel in Vung Tau (you can even hire a butler!). **Pros:** prime location across from the beach, accessed via a pedestrian overpass; sea views; friendly staff. **Cons:** could be considered kitschy; service doesn't always live up to the style. [$] *Rooms from: 3638000d* ✉ *159–163 Thuy Van St.* ☎ *064/362–8888* 🌐 *www.imperialhotel.vn* 🛏 *132 rooms, 12 suites* 🍽 *Breakfast.*

$$$ RESORT FAMILY 🏨 **Lan Rung Resort and Spa.** The elaborate Italianate touches that abound here will either impress you or tickle your funny-bone (a game of spot-the-plaster-cherubs anyone?). **Pros:** restaurant and pool; great sea

views; overall very child-friendly. **Cons:** service can be patchy; restaurant is a bit overpriced. [$] *Rooms from: 1300000d* ✉ *3–6 Ha Long St.* ☎ *064/352–6010* 🌐 *www.lanrung.com.vn* 🛏 *68 rooms, 12 suites* 🍴 *No meals.*

NIGHTLIFE

Vung Tau, unfortunately, has a seedy side at night, with lots of girly bars full of drunk and obnoxious oil rig workers, but there are a couple of places that are more acceptable.

Fodor's Choice ★ **Haven Beach Lounge.** Snag one of the comfy waterfront couches here and you'll be in a prime location for sunset drinks. If you're peckish, this small intimate bar has a short menu of Western comfort food (everything is 100,000d), including bangers and mash, chicken and mushroom pie, beef casserole, and a few vegetarian options. If you pine for a hookah by the water, this place has what it takes to make you happy. ✉ *166 Tran Phu St.* 🌐 *www.havenvungtau.com* 🕒 *Daily 11 am–late.*

Matilda's Pub. A smart-casual bar run by an Australian couple, Matilda's Pub is one of Vung Tau's most popular watering holes for travelers and expats. The pub offers a range of Western and Vietnamese dishes at very reasonable prices, and does a great breakfast, too. ✉ *6 Nguyen Du St.* ☎ *0933/216–425* 🌐 *matildaspub.com.vn.*

SPORTS AND THE OUTDOORS

GOLF

Paradise Resort Golf Club. This 27-hole golf course has a patchy track record when it comes to course maintenance but the caddies are regarded as some of the best in Vietnam. With a challenging links-style design, players must contend with sea breezes while enjoying great ocean views. ✉ *1 Thuy Van* ☎ *064/385–9697* 🌐 *www.golfparadise.com.vn* 🎫 *From: 1,100,000d* ⛳ *27 holes, 6840 yards, par 72.*

LONG HAI

15 km (9 miles) east of Vung Tau, 170 km (105 miles) southeast of Ho Chi Minh City.

There's not much to Long Hai aside from a beautiful beach and an interesting temple with views of the beach. It's close enough to Vung Tau to make a nice day trip, but it's probably not worth the long drive from Ho Chi Minh City for the beach alone.

GETTING HERE AND AROUND

It takes about 30 minutes by car to Long Hai from Vung Tau, and a 3½-hour excursion by taxi will cost about 648,000d. It's also possible to hire a car with driver in Ho Chi Minh City for a day trip, a journey of about 2½ hours each way.

EXPLORING

Fodor's Choice ★ **Dinh Co Temple.** Le Thi Hong Thuy, a 16-year-old girl, washed up on Long Hai Beach nearly 200 years ago and the locals buried her on Co Son Hill. According to legend, her ghost began visiting seafarers and warning them of impending bad weather, and she is now regarded as a goddess who protects the local fishing fleet. This temple is dedicated to her, and every year, on the 10th, 11th, and 12th days of the second lunar month, the it hosts the Nghinh Co Festival, which includes a colorful parade and boat races, and attracts thousands of people from surrounding regions. The views of Long Hai Beach and beyond from the temple terraces are magnificent. ⊠ *Off Rd. 6, Long Hai* 🖃 *Free* ☉ *Daily 7–4.*

Long Hai Beach. This beach is about a 2½-hour drive from Ho Chi Minh City and 15 km (9 miles) along the coast from Vung Tau, but it feels like it's worlds away. Opposite the Dinh Co Temple, a series of shacks offer deck chairs for rent, as well as food and drinks. The beach is not patrolled but the water is calm with no surf and the golden sand stretches for miles. **Amenities:** food and drink. **Best for:** sunsets; swimming; walking. ⊠ *Rd. 6, Long Hai.*

HO TRAM

45 km (28 miles) east of Vung Tau, 113 km (70 miles) southeast of Ho Chi Minh City.

There's not much to Ho Tram apart from a very long—and very beautiful—stretch of golden sand beach. Two upscale resorts front the beach but it's possible to find your own secluded little patch.

GETTING HERE AND AROUND

The two resorts at Ho Tram both offer shuttle buses between Ho Chi Minh City and their properties, each about a 2½-hour drive, starting at 500,000d. It's also possible to get a bus from Ho Chi Minh City or Vung Tau to Xuyen Moc bus depot. From there, it's about a 350,000d taxi fare to either of the resorts. Hiring a seven-seat taxi in Vung Tau for a day-long (5½ hours) excursion to Ho Tram should cost around 1,400,000. Taxis between the two resorts cost about 400,000d, including the round trip and two hours' waiting time while you are there.

WHERE TO STAY

$$$$
RESORT
FAMILY
The Grand Ho Tram Strip. Billing itself as Asia's only beachfront integrated resort, this is a massive new hotel, casino, and golf complex set along an exquisite white-sand beach. **Pros:** gambling, golfing and one of Vietnam's biggest spas are a few steps away; amenities are sparkling new. **Cons:** there's not much in the surrounding area; to eat outside the complex your only option is to take a taxi to the other resort. Ⓢ *Rooms from: 6300000d* ⊠ *Phuoc Thuan, Xuyen Moc, Ho Tram* ☎ *064/378–8888* ⊕ *www.thegrandhotramstrip.com* 🛏 *481 rooms, 60 suites* ⦿❘ *Breakfast.*

$$$$
RESORT
Fodor's Choice
★
Ho Tram Beach Resort and Spa. Capturing the romantic notion of a traditional Vietnamese village, Ho Tram Beach Resort's wood-and-tile bungalows and villas, along with two beautifully landscaped pools, a children's playground, a charming spa and Gecko Restaurant, are scattered throughout a casuarina forest that opens onto a beautiful stretch of beach. **Pros:** the surroundings are such that you can't help but relax; daily shuttle to Ho Chi Minh City. **Cons:** quite remote; if you want to eat elsewhere, the closest place is the Grand Ho Tram Strip resort. Ⓢ *Rooms from: 3080000d* ⊠ *Phuoc Thuan, Xuyen Moc, Ho Tram* ☎ *064/3781–525* ⊕ *www.hotramresort.com* 🛏 *63 rooms, 5 suites* ⦿❘ *Breakfast.*

SPORTS AND THE OUTDOORS
GOLF
The Bluffs Ho Tram Strip. This is a Greg Norman–designed links-style course has stunning views of the South China Sea from the dunes behind Ho Tram Beach. It's well worth the 120-km (75-mile) drive, which takes about 2½ hours, southeast of Ho Chi Minh City. The course flows over and around sand dunes and players must contend with strong sea breezes throughout the year. The golf course is associated with The Grand Ho Tram Strip integrated resort. ✉ *Phuoc Thuan, Xuyen Moc, Vung Tau* ☎ *0254/378–8888* ⊕ *thebluffshotram.com* ✉ *From 1,900,000d for 18 holes on weekdays* ⚑ *18 holes, 6855 yards, par 71.*

CON DAO ISLANDS

Fodor's Choice ★ *100 km (62 miles) off the southern tip of Vietnam, about 50 minutes by plane from Ho Chi Minh City.*

One of Vietnam's star attractions, this stunning archipelago of 16 islands has picturesque beaches, jungles teeming with wildlife, and a fabulous marine environment. In 1983, most of the archipelago was designated a national park to protect the flora, fauna, and marine life and, aside from a few national park personnel, most of the islands are uninhabited. They are an important nesting ground for Green and Hawksbill turtles, and every year from May to October it's possible to watch the turtles lay their eggs on the beaches of Bay Canh, Hon Cau, and Hon Tre islands.

Marco Polo called it Kondor when he stopped by in 1292, and it was known by the French as Poulo Condore, with Poulo believed to be a corruption of the Malay word for island, pulau. Emperor Gia Long ceded the islands to France in 1787 in exchange for military assistance, but the treaty didn't hold and 74 years later, when the islands officially came under French control, a penal settlement was established to house those accused of anti-French activities. Many of the founding fathers of modern Vietnam spent time in the jails of Con Dao.

The South Vietnamese took over the prison in 1954, incarcerating their own political prisoners, and the Americans, with the South Vietnamese, built a prison camp here during the Vietnam War. For the 113 years the main island of this beautiful archipelago was used as a prison island, the place was known as "hell on earth," and all told, an estimated 20,000 people died miserable deaths on Con Dao—Nationalist and Communist prisoners as well as revolutionary insurgents and criminals from all over the French Empire. Some traces of the horror remain, but only one of Con Dao's cemeteries still exists; it alone has 2,000 graves, of victims of the struggles from the 1940s to the 1970s.

Con Son, also called Con Dao, is the main island of the archipelago and feels like a country town, with little traffic and a very laid-back air. The population currently stands at about 30,000.

The Con Dao Islands today, with their fascinating history and beautiful natural environment, are still relatively unspoiled—and unknown. It's still possible to explore Con Son on foot and not see another non-Vietnamese person (unless you pop into one of the dive shops) or drive along deserted roads to deserted beaches. However, this will change soon. A secret this good doesn't keep. Unfortunately.

GETTING HERE AND AROUND

The airport is on the northern end of the main island of Con Son (also called Con Dao) and most hotels provide a free pickup service. Taxis and shared minibuses are also available outside the terminal. Vietnam Airline Service Company (VASCO) operates several flights a day to Con Dao from Ho Chi Minh City, which take about 50 minutes and cost around 1,700,000d one-way.

Traffic on Con Dao is fairly placid, making the prospect of driving a motorbike less daunting than in other places in Vietnam. Motorbike rentals can be arranged through the hotels.

Air Travel Contacts Con Dao Airport (*Co Ong Airport, Sang Bay Co Ong*). ⊠ *Co Ong, Con Son, Con Dao* ☎ *0254/383–1973* ⊕ *en.vietnamairport.vn/ page/107/airports/con-dao-airport.* **Vietnam Airline Service Company (VASCO)** ⊠ *Con Dao Airport, Con Son, Con Dao* ☎ *0254/3831–995* ⊕ *www. vasco.com.vn.*

EXPLORING

TOP ATTRACTIONS

Con Dao Museum (*Bao Tang Con Dao*). This vast museum, which opened in late 2013, has interesting and impressive exhibits that explore the themes (with signs in English and Vietnamese) of Con Dao's natural environment and people, the island's history as a prison island, and Con Dao today. The displays provide some insights into the island's history and its role in Vietnam's long struggle for independence. ⊠ *Nguyen Hue, Con Son, Con Dao* ☎ *0254/383–1009* 🎫 *Free* ☉ *Daily 7:30– 11:30, 1:30–4:30.*

Fodor'sChoice
★
Hang Duong Cemetery. The graves of more than 2,000 former prisoners (now considered war martyrs), who died during the 113 years Con Dao was used as a prison, are contained in this cemetery. The vast site, which covers nearly 2 square kilometers, contains victory monuments as well as marked, unmarked, and communal graves. Every night between 11 pm and midnight, Vietnamese pilgrims, bringing flowers, fruit, roast chickens, and paper offerings, visit the grave of national heroine Vo Thi Sau, who was executed in 1952 at age 19. The air around the grave becomes thick with the smoke of incense as the pilgrims pray and ask Vo Thi Sau for special favors, such as money and improved social standing. It's a very atmospheric ritual and no one seems to mind visitors attending and taking (discreet) photographs. Cemetery attendants are on-site to ensure proper conduct. ⊠ *Nguyen Anh Ninh, Con Son, Con Dao.*

Phu Hai Prison. Con Dao's oldest prison, Phu Hai was built by the French in 1862. It is now a grisly monument to the appalling conditions in the prisons, with mannequins in some of the chambers providing a potent visual representation of the lives of the prisoners. The church inside the prison complex was never used. Guided tours of this and the other prisons on Con Dao can be arranged at the Con Dao Museum next door with one day's notice. ⊠ *Le Van Viet, Con Son, Con Dao* 🎫 *20,000d* ☉ *Daily 8–11:30, 1:30–5.*

Van Son Tu Pagoda (*Nui Mot*). The name translates as Cloudy Hill Palace, and it's a picturesque place to visit, not so much for the temple—even though it is quite beautiful—but for the panoramic view it offers of Con Dao Town, An Hai Lake, and Con Son Bay below. The temple was built in 1964 for the prison officers and government officials stationed on Con Dao and is now considered a memorial to the martyrs who died during Vietnam's fight for independence. ✉ *Nguyen Doc Thuan, Con Son, Con Dao* 🎫 *Free* 🕐 *Daily 7:30–11:30, 1:30–5.*

WORTH NOTING

Bay Canh Island. This small islet east of Con Son, Con Dao's main island, is covered by rain forest and mangroves and its Cat Lon beach is a turtle nesting ground from April to September each year. Visitors can hike up to a small lighthouse in the island's northeast, built 226 meters (740 feet) above sea level by the French in 1884 and still operational today. Tours to the island can be organized through the National Park headquarters. ✉ *Con Dao* ⊕ *www.condaopark.com.vn.*

Hon Cau Island. Other than Con Son, Hon Cau (Big Island) is the only island in the archipelago with a water source. It was also used as a prison island by the French—one of the more notable inmates was the late Vietnamese Prime Minister, Pham Van Dong, who was incarcerated here from 1930 to 1931. Hon Cau is home to a turtle nesting beach and the tours offered by the national park headquarters includes a visit to the prison site, as well as snorkeling along the coral reefs just offshore. ✉ *Con Dao* ☎ *0254/383–0669* ⊕ *www.condaopark.com.vn.*

Old French Governor's House (*Dinh Chua Dao*). The former home of the Con Dao Museum, this house now contains somewhat confusing exhibits (signage in Vietnamese and French) outlining the history of Con Son's prisons. Admission is free and the entryway is presided over by a giant bust of Ho Chi Minh. Take time to stroll around the grounds, which have some exotic animals in pens at the rear. ✉ *Ton Duc Thang St., Con Son, Con Dao.*

Tiger Cages. A delegation of United States congressmen discovered the cramped tiger cages during an official visit to Con Dao in 1970, departing from their planned tour to follow a map drawn by a former prisoner. Photographs of the inhumane conditions were published in *Life* magazine in July 1970 and the international uproar that followed led to 180 men and 300 women being transferred from the cages to other prisons (or, in some cases, to psychiatric institutions). Mannequins rather than people now display the terrible conditions of the cages, which were hidden between a cluster of three prisons: Phu Tuong; Phu Son; and Phu Tho. Entry is through Phu Tuong Prison, built by the French in 1940. Guided tours of Phu Tuong and the other prisons on Con Dao can be arranged at the Con Dao Museum with one day's notice. ✉ *Nguyen Van Cu St., Con Son, Con Dao* 🎫 *20,000d* 🕐 *Daily 8–11:30, 1:30–5.*

Tre Lon Island. An important turtle nesting ground is here, and the jungle that covers the island is home to a variety of different species including some rare birds. Tours to the island, which can be booked at the National Park headquarters, usually include snorkeling. Underwater highlights include giant clams as well as fish and coral. ✉ *Con Dao* ☎ *0254/383–0669* 🌐 *www.condaopark.com.vn.*

BEACHES

An Hai Beach. The beauty of An Hai Beach has been marred somewhat by the stalled construction of a pier across from the Con Son Café. Turn your back on the mess and walk south, along the casurina-lined sand to get that deserted tropical island mood. **Amenities:** food and drink. **Best for:** solitude; sunrise; sunset; walking. ✉ *Nguyen Duc Thuan St., Con Dao.*

Dam Trau Beach. A few short years ago this was a pristine deserted wonderland of clear water and soft white sand. Now there's a collection of ramshackle huts on the beach hawking food, drinks, and deck chairs, but privacy can still be found by swimming around the rocks on the southern end of the beach. The beach is 200 meters down a rutted dirt track, which can be very slippery after rain. Look for the sign near the airport on Co Ong Street. It's a nice spot to watch the sunset, although traversing the track back to the main road in the dark can be treacherous if you're on a motorbike or bicycle. **Amenities:** food and drink. **Best for:** sunsets; swimming; solitude. ✉ *Co Ong St., Con Dao.*

Dat Doc Beach. Most of this beautiful crescent of white sand and calm blue waters is the private domain of the luxurious Six Senses Con Dao resort. There is a steep and narrow track leading down to the beach, just north of the resort entrance, for those who'd like to (discreetly) explore the beach. **Amenities:** none. **Best for:** solitude; sunrise; swimming; walking. ✉ *Bai Dat Doc, Con Dao.*

Lo Voi Beach. Locals seem to prefer walking along Nguyen Van Cuu Street's sidewalk at dawn and dusk rather than on this long white-sand beach, which is usually dotted with the round basket-boats the fishermen use to get to shore. Despite being right in town, Lo Voi Beach is usually deserted during the day. Fishing boats moored just offshore make this beautiful beach even more picturesque. **Amenities:** none. **Best for:** solitude; sunrise; sunset; swimming; walking. ✉ *Nguyen Van Cuu St., Con Dao.*

WHERE TO EAT

$$ CAFÉ Fodor's Choice ★

🍴 **Bar200.** More of a café than a bar, this tiny place makes fantastic sandwiches, salads, and pizzas as well as a great Western breakfast and Italian coffee. Tucked in behind the market, Bar200 is also the clubhouse for Senses Diving and the friendly staff can assist with general tourist information and motorbike rentals. The interior is simple, yet welcoming, with wooden blinds, rattan tables and chairs, and photos and propaganda art on the walls. The tiny veranda is a great spot from which to watch Con Son daily life. [$] *Average main: 120000d* ✉ *Pham Dong St., Con Son, Con Dao* ☎ *0254/363–0024* 🌐 *www.divecondao.com.*

$$$$ ASIAN FUSION

🍴 **By The Beach.** Nonguests are welcome at the luxury Six Senses Con Dao's main restaurant, which is the perfect venue for a romantic meal of freshly caught local seafood and fine wine overlooking Dat Doc Beach. It's just as stunning by moonlight as it is during the day. The menu is Asian fusion with a hint of French influence. [$] *Average main: 450000d*

⊠ *Dat Doc Beach, Con Dao* ☎ *0254/383–1222* ⊕ *www.sixsenses.com* ⚲ *Reservations essential.*

$$ ✗ **Café Infiniti.** Half a block north from the market, this small fan-cooled
CAFÉ café has a basic but eclectic style featuring driftwood, rope, and hessian, and its menu is designed for travelers, with pizza, burgers, and a small selection of Vietnamese dishes. The breakfast menu offers an extensive range of international breakfasts, including the full English. There are regular barbecue nights and Vietnamese street food nights. Staffers are friendly, with reasonably good English, and are happy for guests to stay until the wee hours. $ *Average main: 165000d* ⊠ *Tran Huy Lieu St., Con Son, Con Dao* ☎ *0254/383–0083.*

$ **Con Son Café.** This is a cute and simple drinks-only café consisting of
CAFÉ a few tables and umbrellas set under the trees in front of the former French Maison des Passagers (Customs House). The simple setup gives customers a great view of An Hai Beach, making it an ideal spot for sunset drinks. It's open from 7 am to 11 pm, and plans to introduce a menu of simple food are in the pipeline. ⊠ *Ton Duc Thang St., Con Son, Con Dao* ☎ *0908/099–919* ⊗ *Closed when it rains.*

$$ ✗ **Thu Ba.** A visit to Con Son isn't complete without a meal at Thu Ba.
VIETNAMESE Chef Thu Ba works her magic in the kitchen while her daughter Thuy
Fodor's Choice works the guests in the homey front section, recommending dishes from
★ the extensive menu full of Vietnamese seafood, pork, and beef dishes (the slipper lobster is highly recommended). Western and Vietnamese options are available for breakfast and Thu Ba can also prepare picnics for hikers and campers. $ *Average main: 150000d* ⊠ *Vo Thi Sau St., 7th Area, Con Son, Con Dao* ☎ *0254/383–0255.*

$$ ✗ **Tri Ky.** A spartan open-air local joint that's been the go-to place for
SEAFOOD domestic tourists to Con Dao for years, Tri Ky is worth a visit if you love fresh well-cooked seafood and don't mind ordering using basic English and sign language and exercising patience with the servers. The menu has pictures and some (sometimes strange) English but their grasp of English is too limited to assist with recommendations. The specialty is *oc ban tay* (hand snail), try it stir-fried with garlic—it tastes a lot better than it sounds! $ *Average main: 175000d* ⊠ *5 Nguyen Duc Thuan St., Con Son, Con Dao* ☎ *0254/383–0294.*

WHERE TO STAY

$$$ ⌂ **ATC Con Dao Resort.** The great location, with an equally great pool
RESORT and spacious guest rooms in renovated French colonial villas, is some compensation for the rather tired interior and limited breakfast. **Pros:** walking distance to all many of the sights on Con Dao and right across the road from the beach. **Cons:** the language barrier means some minor problems can snowball into major headaches. $ *Rooms from: 1130000d* ⊠ *8 Ton Duc Thang St., Con Son, Con Dao* ☎ *0254/383–0456* ⊕ *www.atcvietnam.com* ➴ *58 rooms, 2 villas* ▭ *No credit cards* ❑ *Breakfast.*

$ ⌂ **Con Dao Sea Cabanas** (*Con Dao Camping*). Two rows of cute little
HOTEL A-frame huts in a lovely garden right on the beachfront, this place has the basics covered with king-size beds and mod-cons such as Wi-Fi, cable television, fridges, air-conditioning, and a little café in a bamboo hut. **Pros:** great location and amazing views of Lo Voi Beach.

Cons: heavy rain on the tin roof can very loud; a stalled pier construction site next door could resume operations, although no one is sure what's happening with the project. $ *Rooms from: 745000d* ✉ *2 Nguyen Duc Thuan St., Con Son, Con Dao* ☎ *0254/383–1555* ⊕ *www. condaoseacabanas.com* ⤳ *22 rooms* ⦿ *No meals.*

$
B&B/INN

⊟ **Hotel Quynh Anh.** The rooms at this shiny new family-run guesthouse are spacious, clean, and bright, with above-average Vietnamese-style bathrooms, and it's just a few blocks from the Con Dao Market. **Pros:** one of the cheaper options on Con Dao; within walking distance to eating places. **Cons:** the staff, while lovely, speak very little English; not on the beach. $ *Rooms from: 550000d* ✉ *15 Le Duan St., Con Son, Con Dao* ☎ *0254/383–1999* ⤳ *16 rooms* ⊟ *No credit cards* ⦿ *No meals.*

$$$
HOTEL

⊟ **Saigon Con Dao.** The pick of the big beachfront hotels, Saigon Con Dao has a great location—next to the former French governor's mansion, in front of Phu Hai Son prison, and within walking distance of most of the town's other attractions. **Pros:** beautiful pool area; close to many attractions and restaurants. **Cons:** amenities and service standards can seem somewhat lacking to overseas guests. $ *Rooms from: 1690000d* ✉ *18–24 Ton Duc Thang, Con Son, Con Dao* ☎ *0254/383– 0336* ⊕ *www.saigoncondao.com* ⤳ *107 rooms, 8 suites* ⦿ *Breakfast.*

$$$
RESORT
FAMILY
Fodor's Choice
★

⊟ **Six Senses Con Dao.** A luxurious yet laid-back eco-lodge on a stunning crescent of beach, Six Senses Con Dao's private villas are a heavenly retreat from everyday life with excellent amenities like private infinity pools. **Pros:** incredibly relaxing; superb dining; first-rate spa; family-friendly. **Cons:** 5 km (3 miles) from town, where you might want to seek out alternatives to the resort's high restaurant prices. $ *Rooms from: 14500000d* ✉ *Dat Doc Beach, Con Son, Con Dao* ☎ *0254/383–1222* ⊕ *www.sixsenses.com* ⤳ *50 villas* ⦿ *No meals.*

SPORTS AND THE OUTDOORS

DIVING AND SNORKELING

Dive! Dive! Dive!. Larry and his friendly team run snorkeling and diving trips from the island's only custom-built dive boat (which has a freshwater shower), as well as certification courses and "try" dives. Daily two-dive trips set out from the shop at 8:45 am and include drinks, snacks, and a light lunch. Custom itineraries are also available, including multiday trips, diving-and-camping trips, and night dives. Larry, who has lived in Vietnam for 25 years, is a mine of information, and there's someone on staff who speaks at least one of the following languages: English, French, German, and Spanish. ✉ *Nguyen Hue St., Con Son, Con Dao* ☎ *0254/383–0701* ⊕ *www.dive-condao.com* ⊟ *Snorkeling from 918,000d, 1-dive drips from 1,920,000d.*

Rainbow Divers. This is a seasonal operation on Con Dao, leading daily dive and snorkel trips during the nonrainy season from April to September. From 2015, Rainbow Divers will be based at The Rainbow, a new bar and dive center next to Phi Yen Hotel. ✉ *The Rainbow, Ton Duc Thang St., Con Son, Con Dao* ☎ *0905/577–671* ⊕ *www.divevietnam. com* ⊟ *Snorkeling-only trips from 958,000d; 2-dive scuba trips from 3,100,000d.*

Senses Diving. Set up by two Brits and a South African in February 2013, Senses Diving operates snorkeling and diving trips around the archipelago on the *Poulo Condore*, a 17-meter (56-foot) converted Vietnamese fishing boat. The three owners are all certified PADI Master Scuba Diver Trainers and the outfit runs two-dive/snorkeling trips every day, departing at 9 am. There are also "try" dives for first-timers, night dives, and dive courses, including open water, advanced open water, and rescue certification. It's all run from the little Bar200, which doubles as the clubhouse and office. ⊠ *Bar200, Pham Van Dong St., Con Son, Con Dao* ☎ *0254/363–0024* ⊕ *divecondao.com* ✉ *3,360,000d for a 2-dive trip, including all equipment, taxes, marine park fees, and lunch. Snorkeling starts at 1,000,000d.*

HIKING

There are a number of (paved and unpaved) hiking trails on Con Dao. Maps and other information are available from the National Park office, the Dive Dive Dive shop, and Senses Diving. National Park rangers lead guided treks on Con Son as well as the smaller islands, including multiday treks. Easy options on Con Son that don't need a guide include a hike up to So Ray plantation, now home to some quite aggressive long-tailed macaques, and then down to the rocky Ong Dong Beach and back. The hike takes about five hours.

Con Dao National Park Office ⊠ *29 Vo Thi Sau St., Con Son, Con Dao* ☎ *0254/383–0669* ⊕ *www.condaopark.com.vn.*

WILDLIFE-WATCHING

FAMILY **National Park Turtle Nesting Tours.** Green and hawksbill turtles come to 13 of Con Dao's beaches between May and October each year to lay their eggs. The National Park offers overnight turtle nesting tours to Bay Canh Island for a minimum of two people. The baby turtles hatch from mid-August to December and you can also organize turtle hatching tours through the National Park office. ⊠ *Con Dao National Park headquarters, 29 Vo Thi Sau St., Con Son, Con Dao* ☎ *0254/383–0150* ⊕ *www.condaopark.com.vn* ✉ *From 2,840,000d.*

THE MEKONG
DELTA

Updated by
Barbara Adam

The Mekong Delta (Cuu Long) is a destination like no other. Innumerable rivers, canals, tributaries, and rivulets overflow with fish, and the rich alluvial soil helps produce an abundance of rice, fruit, and vegetables. Lush tropical orchards, floating markets, quaint towns, delicious food, emerald-green rice paddies, and lazy brown rivers and canals add to the photogenic wonder of the place. It's a land touched by ancient and modern cultures, from the Funanese to the Khmer, Cham, and Vietnamese.

Slicing through the heart of the delta is the Mekong River, also known as Song Cuu Long, or River of the Nine Dragons. Descending from the Tibetan plateau, the river runs through China, separates Myanmar (Burma) from Laos, skirts Thailand, passes through Cambodia, and flows through Vietnam into the South China Sea. The river carries fertile soil deposits at a rate of 2,500 to 50,000 cubic meters per second, which created the delta and continues its expansion. As it enters Vietnam, the river divides into two arteries: the Tien Giang (Upper River), which splinters at My Tho and Vinh Long into several seaward tributaries, and the Hau Giang (Lower River or Bassac River), which passes through Chau Doc, Long Xuyen, and Can Tho en route to the sea. The river's many islands are famous for their beautiful fruit gardens and orchards, and the year-round hot and humid climate is ideal for tropical fruits, such as pomelo, coconut, jackfruit, pineapple, and papaya.

Dotting the endless fields of rice paddies, farmers in conical hats evoke the classic image of Vietnam. These days enough rice is produced to feed the country *and* to export abroad. Vietnam is now the world's third largest exporter of rice—a remarkable feat considering that as recently as the early 1990s the country was importing this food staple.

The northern delta, with its fruit farms and rice fields, is the most accessible from Ho Chi Minh City, with day trips possible to My Tho and Vinh Long. The south-central delta encompasses the Ca Mau Peninsula, which juts into the sea from Soc Trang. Can Tho is the major center, a pleasant town with just enough tourist infrastructure for a comfortable stay. In the Mekong's southern section, steamy mangrove swamps and thick palm forests thrive on the flat, flooded delta, creating a haven for water birds, including some rare species.

To make the most of a visit to the Mekong Delta, a homestay is recommended, for the access they give to local communities and river life. A number of quite comfortable options are available. Most of the delta is pancake-flat, making it ideal for exploration by bicycle, and the services of a good guide will get you into a network of lanes that don't appear on maps—intricate tracks that are the heart of Mekong Delta life.

TOP REASONS TO GO

Rice paddies: There's something uniquely soothing about the Mekong Delta's rice paddies. Whether they're photogenically brilliantly green or postharvest brown, there's usually a buffalo standing around, accompanied by a white water bird. Sam Mountain, just outside Chau Doc, is the perfect vantage point.

River life: Get out on the water to see Mekong Delta life in action. Everything revolves around the water, which provides the region's main form of transportation.

Floating markets: Boats chock-full of locally grown produce congregate at certain points in the river to trade, advertising their wares by hoisting them up on a flagpole-like stick.

Homestays: There are several upscale homestay options well off the tourist trail that make a great base for cycling, walking, or boating through Delta communities.

Cham culture: The ancient kingdom of Champa ruled this region from the 7th to the 18th century, and pockets of Cham descendants remain, along with a smattering of beautiful temples.

ORIENTATION AND PLANNING

GETTING ORIENTED

The Mekong Delta stretches from the Plain of Reeds in the northern reaches to the wet mangrove forests of Ca Mau at the southernmost tip. Some parts of this sprawling region can be somewhat difficult to travel around because of the poor state of the roads. More than any other destination in Vietnam, tours are a recommended way to travel around the delta for short trips as logistics can prove awkward. Most tour operators offer hotel pickup and transportation from Ho Chi Minh City, though bear in mind river cruises will not begin until you reach the top of the delta. Sadly, there is an overabundance of cheap, generic tours operating in the Mekong Delta. The best advice is to choose a quality, reputable—and more expensive—tour company that will lead you down the roads and rivers less traveled. In many cases, you can continue your travels on to Phu Quoc Island (or even Cambodia) after exploring the delta.

Northern Mekong Delta. The most accessible area from Ho Chi Minh City can be interesting if you only have a few days, taking in My Tho, Vinh Long, and Chau Doc, a jumping-off point to Cambodia. Farther along the coast, Ha Tien is the gateway to Phu Quoc Island.

Phu Quoc Island. This rapidly developing island has powder-white sand beaches and a growing number of luxury resorts, many set right on the beach with views of the beautiful warm turquoise waters. The island has so far managed to retain its idyllic charm, and is a great spot for some laid-back exploring of remote beaches and jungle.

Southcentral Mekong Delta. Can Tho, at the heart of the Mekong Delta, is an ideal base for exploring the deeper parts of the delta. Southeast

The Mekong Delta

of Can Tho is Soc Trang and Tra Vinh, both with large Khmer populations, and farther south still is the pleasant city of Ca Mau.

PLANNING

WHEN TO GO

The best time to tour the Mekong Delta is during the dry season, from October to May. During the rainy season, from May to September, a large portion of the region is under water and inaccessible. A number of interesting festivals are held in the Mekong Delta, but without a guide or a local to explain what's going on, these can be rather confusing spectacles. Attending one of these festivals should be organized well in advance, as accommodations book up early. The Khmer communities in Soc Trang and Tra Vinh hold the three-day Ooc Om Boc (or Ok Om Bok) festival each year on the 13th to 15th days of the 10th lunar month. The highlight of the festival, a combination of moon worship and prayers for a good harvest, is the racing of slender wooden snake-shaped Ngo boats. The Khmer communities in Soc Trang and Tra Vinh also celebrate the Khmer New Year, Chol Chnam Thmay, usually in mid-April (the date is determined by an ancient Khmer calendar, not the lunar calendar that guides most other celebrations in the region.) The celebrations feature a lot of good-natured water splashing as well as family feasts and pagoda visits.

GETTING HERE AND AROUND

AIR TRAVEL

There are three airports in the Mekong Delta—in Can Tho, Ca Mau, and on Phu Quoc Island. A taxi from any of the three to your hotel will be around 108,000d. Regular flights from Hanoi and Danang arrive at the Can Tho International Airport, 9 km (5½ miles) from the city center. VietJet and Vietnam Airlines fly to this airport, which only really becomes international when chartered flights arrive, usually during Tet. Round-trip fares start at $41 from Danang and $70 from Hanoi. Ca Mau Airport is about 3 km (2 miles) from the center of Ca Mau. Vietnam Aviation Service Company (VASCO) operates one flight a day each way between Ho Chi Minh City and Ca Mau. Round-trip airfare starts at around $188.

Phu Quoc International Airport, 10 km (6 miles) from the main town of Duong Dong, opened in 2012 and is now Vietnam's fifth busiest airport. Direct flights arrive regularly from Hanoi, Ho Chi Minh City, Can Tho, Singapore, and Siem Reap in Cambodia. VASCO operates daily flights between Phu Quoc, Ho Chi Minh City, and Can Tho, and flies between Hanoi and Phu Quoc four times a week. Vietnam Airlines operates daily flights to and from Hanoi, two flights a week to and from Singapore, and three flights a week to and from Siem Reap. Jetstar Pacific operates daily flights to and from Ho Chi Minh City. Airfares can be quite reasonable, especially if you snag a promotional deal. Most resorts have an airport transfer service, and taxis and xe om drivers meet scheduled flights.

Airline Contacts Jetstar Pacific ☎ *1900–1550 hotline within Vietnam, 28/3547–3550 for callers outside Vietnam* ⊕ *www.jetstar.com.* **VietJet**

☎ 0477/399–1166 Phu Quoc office, 028/3551–6220 Ho Chi Minh City ⊕ www. vietjetair.com .**Vietnam Aviation Service Company (VASCO)** ⊠ B114 Bach Dang St., Tan Binh District, Ca Mau ☎ 028/3842–2790 ⊕ www.vasco.com.vn./

Airport Contacts Ca Mau Airport ⊠ 1A Ca Mau, Ca Mau ☎ 0290/383–6436 .**Can Tho International Airport** ⊠ 179B Le Hong Phong, Can Tho ☎ 0292/384–4301 ⊕ www.canthoairport.com. **Phu Quoc International Airport** ⊠ Duong To, Phu Quoc ☎ 0277/3384–8077 ⊕ www.phuquocinternationalairport.com.

BOAT TRAVEL

Despite improved infrastructure, traveling around the Mekong Delta may still require river crossings and boats can provide one of the most interesting and relaxed means of exploring. There are many tour operators, offering everything from short half-day to multiday cruises (⇨ *see also Tours*). Keep in mind that you get what you pay for, so it's worth a little extra cost to guarantee reliability and safety. In the case of ferries, if you're on a bus or in a private car, there's no need to do anything but enjoy the view. If you're traveling by motorbike, just follow the herd to the drive-up ticket window and wait for the next departure. Two ferry companies operate between Phu Quoc and the mainland. Superdong is the faster service, with three services a day between Phu Quoc and Ha Tien (about 1½ hours, 350,000d) and another three between Phu Quoc and Rach Gia (about 2 hours, 20 minutes; 195,000d). Thanh Thoi is the slower service, mainly for cars and heavy equipment. Thanh Thoi operates three services a day between Phu Quoc and Ha Tien, each taking 2 hours and 15 minutes; one adult ticket costs 185,000d and a ticket for a motorbike costs 80,000d.

Ferry Contacts Superdong ⊠ 10 30 Thang 4, Duong Dong, Phu Quoc ☎ 0297/398–0111 ⊕ www.superdong.com.vn. **Thanh Thoi** ☎ 0297/395–7239 ⊕ thanhthoi.vn.

BUS TRAVEL

From Ho Chi Minh City, you can board buses for all major towns in the Mekong Delta at Mien Tay Bus Terminal (⊠ *395 Kinh Duong Vuong, An Lac Ward, Binh Tan District*). More than 750 buses depart daily for Mekong Delta provinces, serving about 13,000 customers. Bus transportation is extremely cheap and usually quite comfortable. A one-way ticket to Can Tho, for example, will cost around 129,000d, while a one-way ticket to Ca Mau will cost around 200,000d. Be aware that there's usually no toilet on these buses, but most journeys include regular stops at tourist centers with food, drinks, and washrooms. Phuong Trang, sometimes known as Futa Buslines, has the most extensive network of routes through the Mekong Delta, with smaller companies, such as Hoang Vinh and Thanh Buoi, specializing in certain routes.

Bus Contacts Hoang Vinh ☎ 028/2241–6665 *Ho Chi Minh City, 0299/ 362–7627 Soc Trang.* **Hung Cuong** ☎ 028/3857–2624. **Kumho Samco** ⊠ *Ca Mau* ☎ 028/3511–4432 ⊕ *www.kumhosamco.com.vn.* **Phuong Trang** ⊠ *Ca Mau* ☎ 028/3830–9309 ⊕ *www.futabuslines.com.vn.* **Thanh Buoi** ☎ 028/3833–3999.

TAXI TRAVEL

Mai Linh is the most reputable taxi company throughout Vietnam, although you may find local taxis are cheaper in the Mekong Delta. If in doubt, ask your hotel to call you a cab.

Contacts Ca Mau Taxi ✉ *Ca Mau* ☎ *0290/383-7837* **Ha Tien Taxi** ☎ *0297/385-2569* **Mai Linh Taxi** ☎ *0290/378-7878 Ca Mau,* ☎ *0296/392-2266 Chau Doc,* ☎ *0292/382-8282 Can Tho,* ☎ *0297/395-6956 Ha Tien,* ☎ *0297/399-7799 Phu Quoc,* ☎ *0299/386-8868 Soc Trang,* ☎ *0273/387-8787 My Tho* ⊕ *www.mailinh.vn.*

RESTAURANTS

You can expect wonderful seafood and quality vegetarian dishes throughout the Mekong Delta. The more popular tourist spots, such as Can Tho and Chau Doc, offer a variety of dining options, from relatively fine dining to backpacker spots offering a mix of Vietnamese and Western dishes. In other towns, options are confined to street stalls and local places, where finding an English menu can be a lottery. Local food is cheap, usually delicious, and always an adventure if you don't speak Vietnamese.

One renowned Mekong Delta specialty to seek out is Ca Tai Tuong, a grilled "elephant ear fish." Rice is a staple, and the region is famous for its noodle soups, including *hu tieu* (pork, prawn, and usually some offal) and *bun nuoc leo* (a murky pork noodle soup with thin fresh rice noodles). *Banh mi* (baguettes) are another cheap, easy, and tasty option.

Fruit exists in abundance, so much so that carrying fruit with you doesn't make sense. Buy it, eat it, and before you're hungry again you'll pass another fruit seller—or one will pass you; commerce is very mobile in Vietnam.

WHAT IT COSTS			
$	$$	$$$	$$$$
Restaurants	Under 60,000d	60,000d–150,000d	151,000d–250,000d	over 250,000d
Hotels	Under 600,000d	600,000d–900,000d	901,000d–1,500,000d	over 1,500,000d

Prices in the reviews are the average cost of a main course at dinner or, if dinner is not served, at lunch. Prices in the reviews are the lowest cost of a standard double room in high season.

HOTELS

While some parts of the Mekong Delta receive few foreign visitors—and this is evident when it comes to dining and accommodation options—there's a growing number of boutique and luxury hotels and resorts in the Delta Many hotels in the parts of the Mekong delta less traveled by Westerners are state owned, which means service standards are lackluster, or targeted at local business travelers, who don't seem to require very pleasant environs.

For expanded reviews, facilities, and current deals, visit Fodors.com.

TOURS

Acqua Mekong. The decadent 62-meter (205-foot) *Aqua Mekong* cruises the Mekong between Ho Chi Minh City and Cambodia, with three-, four-, and seven-day itineraries. The floating five-star hotel, complete with luxurious suites, a plunge pool, spa, and one of Asia's best chefs onboard—the award-winning David Thompson—stops at fascinating off-the-beaten-path places, where shore excursions give you authentic insights into local life. ☎ *866/603–3687 in U.S. and Canada* ⊕ *www. aquaexpeditions.com* ✉ *3-night cruises start at 70,662,000d.*

Fodor's Choice ★ **Bassac Cruises.** Can Tho–based Bassac Cruises has a fleet of three elegant wooden cruisers with comfortable air-conditioned cabins, each with a cozy private bathroom, and public areas that are so well laid-out that it's possible to socialize with other guests or find some privacy in one of the covered or open lounge and dining areas. All three vessels—*Bassac I* is a converted rice barge, while the *Bassac II* and *Bassac III* were purpose-built for touring the Mekong Delta—were designed with passenger comfort and safety in mind, with quiet engines and air-conditioning systems, and safety features throughout. ✉ *144 Hai Ba Trung St., Can Tho* ☎ *0292/382–9540* ⊕ *transmekong.com* ✉ *From: 5,670,000d.*

Exo Travel. The staff at this experienced and professional tour company can help with customized itineraries and join-in tours through the Mekong Delta. They can also provide personal tour guides for those who want to delve deep into the Mekong Delta where little English is spoken. ✉ *261–263 Phan Xich Long, Phu Nhuan, Ho Chi Minh City* ☎ *028/3995–9898* ⊕ *www.exotravel.com* ✉ *From: $80 for a basic 1-day excursion.*

Fodor's Choice ★ **Innoviet.** A Mekong Delta–focused boutique travel agency offering small group tours that take people off the beaten path, Innoviet has itineraries ranging from day trips from Ho Chi Minh City to five-day tours of the delta. Long distance travel is by private car, while in the Mekong guests experience various forms of transportation, ranging from *xeo loi* bicycle trailers to bicycles and sampans. Private tours can also be arranged. ✉ *161 Bui Vien, District 1, Ho Chi Minh City* ☎ *028/2216–5303* ⊕ *innoviet.com* ✉ *From: $68 for a day excursion.*

L'Amant. Inspired by the 1930s "golden age" of travel, *L'Amant* is a 39-meter cruiser with 12 stylish air-conditioned cabins that offers one-to six-night cruises of the Mekong Delta, most departing from My Tho or nearby Cai Be. The cruises allow you to explore the waterways and villages of the Mekong Delta in relaxed and comfortable elegance. The on-board dining, which makes the most of fresh local Mekong Delta produce, is particularly delicious. Staff can help arrange transfers to the starting point and from the finishing point of the tours. ✉ *Long Giang Cruiser Company, 82–3, St. 7, An Phu, Ho Chi Minh City* ☎ *028/6281–0222* ⊕ *www.lamant-cruises.com* ✉ *From: 9,700,000d for a 2-day, 1-night cruise.*

Mekong Bike Tours. One- to seven-day all-inclusive bicycle tours of the Mekong Delta will take you along back roads and laneways that don't appear on any maps (not even Google Maps!). With friendly, experienced English-speaking cycle guides, Mekong Bike Tours specialize in unique routes that show local life. All tours include vehicular backup, accommodations, drinks, snacks, and meals; most itineraries start in Ho Chi Minh City, with some trips meandering through the delta to Phu Quoc Island or Cambodia. ✉ *459/1 Tran Hung Dao, District 1, Ho Chi Minh City* ☎ *028/3601–7671* ⊕ *www.mekongbiketours.com* 💲 *From: $150.*

Vietnam Birding. Set up by British bird enthusiast Richard Craik, Vietnam Birding offers customized and join-in bird-watching tours throughout Indochina, including to the Mekong Delta. Vietnam Birding is also experienced in general tourism and so can help arrange an itinerary that includes relaxation, cultural sites, cruises, and other vacation activities. Make contact well in advance of your trip—their services are in very high demand. ✉ *BTT Bldg., 32–34 Ngo Duc Ke, Room 902, District 1, Ho Chi Minh City* ☎ *028/3827–3766* ⊕ *www.vietnambirding.com* 💲 *Overnight trips from $400.*

NORTHERN MEKONG DELTA

It's possible to dip into the northern reaches of the Mekong Delta from Ho Chi Minh City, either as a one-day taster or a longer exploration that includes one or more overnight stays. This region contains all the iconic Mekong Delta attractions: green rice paddies, tropical orchards, bustling markets, and a host of riverine commerce.

Closest to Ho Chi Minh City is My Tho, and, along with its near neighbor Ben Tre, this city is popular with day-trippers. Like most large centers, these towns are not as interesting as the local life that surrounds them—on the river islands, on the river itself, and in the narrow motorbike- and bicycle-only network of local lanes. The city of Vinh Long makes a good base and provides access to the Cai Be floating market. The charming riverside town of Chau Doc is the most beguiling stop in this part of the Mekong Delta, with its fascinating Islamic Cham neighborhoods, its floating fish farms, and the beautiful views of the rice paddies from Sam Mountain. Farther west is Ha Tien, where ferries depart daily to the beautiful—and mostly unspoiled—tropical island gem Phu Quoc.

MY THO

70 km (43 miles) south of Ho Chi Minh City.

The closest Mekong Delta city to Ho Chi Minh City, My Tho is a city with a fascinating history. It was the center of the ancient civilization of Funan from the 1st to 5th centuries AD, before the culture mysteriously disappeared—no one really knows the reason—and it wasn't until the 17th century that the modern city was established, by Chinese refugees fleeing Taiwan (then known as Formosa). During the Vietnam War, My Tho was one of the centers of operations for American and Australian troops. The largest battle in the Mekong Delta was fought in 1972 at Cai Lai, only 20 km (12 miles) outside the city.

Now mostly known as a supplier of fruit and fish, My Tho is considered a day trip from Ho Chi Minh City, and consequently the dining and accommodations options are somewhat basic.

GETTING HERE AND AROUND

Buses arrive here from Ho Chi Minh City and major centers in the Mekong Delta, and Phuong Trang is one of the more comfortable and reliable bus companies that ply this route. The main bus station is Tien Giang, but most buses stop along Highway 1A to pick up and set down passengers. Xe om drivers wait near the set down point on the highway, but if you want a taxi and there are none there, the xe om drivers can summon one for you. For trips to the nearby islands, you can hire a ferry for about 300,000d, but it will be a very touristic tour. My Tho's ferry station is at 830 Thang 4 Street.

ESSENTIALS

Bus Contact Tien Giang Bus Station ⊠ *42 Ap Bac St.* ☎ *0273/385–5429."*

Taxi Contact Mai Linh Taxi ☎ *0273/387–8787.*

EXPLORING

TOP ATTRACTIONS

Ben Tre. A 20-minute ferry ride from My Tho (and then a 10-minute *xe om* ride) is Ben Tre, considered the Mekong Delta's coconut capital. Many Mekong Delta day trips from Ho Chi Minh City stop at Ben Tre, which has many interesting waterways and river islands to explore, as well as several coconut candy factories. ⊠ *Ben Tre.*

Dong Tam Snake Farm (*Trai Rang Dong Tam*). On the road to Vinh Long, 10 km (6 miles) northwest of My Tho, is an old U.S. military compound that lay deserted for years until a northern Vietnamese general decided to take over the land and develop it into a for-profit snake farm and research site for medicinal uses of reptile venom. The 12-hectare farm specializes in cobras, the most dangerous being the king cobras. There's also a bunch of relatively docile pythons and a selection of rather miserable-looking animals—many of them rare—such as monkeys, bears, wildcats, and pangolins, locked in tiny cages. Animal lovers will definitely want to stay away. The restaurant on the farm, which not surprisingly mostly serves snake dishes, is extremely popular with Vietnamese families on weekend day trips. ⊠ *Binh Duc, Chau Thanh* ☎ *0273/385–3204* ⊕ *trairandongtam.com.vn* ▧ *20,000d* ⊗ *Daily 8–5.*

Island of the Coconut Monk (*Ong Dau Dua*). About 2 km (1 mile) from My Tho, on the Mekong River, is Phoenix Island, better known as the Island of the Coconut Monk. A religious sanctuary before the war, the island once had a garish, eclectic complex in a style similar to the Caodai Holy See in Tay Ninh. It was built in the 1940s by a French-educated engineer-turned-monk named Nguyen Thanh Nam, nick-named the Coconut Monk by locals because he reputedly lived for some years on nothing but coconuts. The monk presided over a small community of followers, teaching a religion that combined elements of Buddhism and Christianity. He was imprisoned repeatedly, first by the Saigon regime and later by the Communists for anti-government activities; he died in 1990. All that is left of the monk's utopian dreams are some dragons and gargoyles and columns with mythical creatures wrapped around them.

Phoenix Island is one of My Tho's four islands named after mythical beasts—Dragon (Con Tan Long), Tortoise (Con Qui), and Unicorn (Con Lan) are the other three. Tours from My Tho usually visit all four, stopping at tourist pavilions where coconut candy, local honey, rice wine, and local musicians await. Organizing a visit through a reputable travel agency in Ho Chi Minh City is recommended to avoid the contrived tourist trail followed by the local government–controlled tour companies. If you do take a local tour, be sure to explore the islands beyond the tourist centers by strolling the narrow lanes to see the fruit orchards and get glimpses of local life. Boats leave from Trung Trac Street, next to Mekong tributary.

My Tho Market. This large covered market is an interesting place to explore, especially if you haven't already wandered through a Vietnamese *cho* (market) before. Expect to see the usual Vietnamese wet market offerings of fresh fruit, vegetables, mounds of mysterious greens, meat, dried goods, clothes, shoes, and plastic paraphernalia. Do stop in for a bowl of the local specialty, *hu tieu My Tho* (pork-and-prawn noodle soup). ✉ *Corner of Trung Trac and Vo Tan Sts.*

WORTH NOTING

Vinh Trang Pagoda. Delightfully fanciful, this pagoda built in 1849 features European and Asian design elements and is set within lovely ornamental gardens with bonsai and lotus ponds. Take some time to soak up the tranquil atmosphere of the pagoda, which was built in the shape of the Chinese character for nation, then tour the grounds to see the giant Buddha statues, including a very happy laughing Buddha. ✉ *Nguyen Trung Truc, My Hoa* 🎟 *Free* 🕒 *Daily 9–11:30, 1:30–5.*

WHERE TO EAT

$ VEGETARIAN

🍴 **Bo De Quan.** The setting of this charming vegetarian restaurant, which helps support the nearby Vinh Trang pagoda, is rustic, with basic tables and chairs set up in open-air thatched huts, surrounded by greenery. Service is not the fastest, but the food is truly delicious. Don't be fooled by the English menu that lists meat dishes, this is a strictly vegetarian place and they are made with imitation, soy-based "meats." The house specialty is the vegetarian Thai-style sour-and-spicy hotpot (*lau Thai Lan*); the lotus salad is also a standout dish. [$] *Average main: 50000d* ✉ *69A Nguyen Trung Truc St.* ☎ *0273/397–6469.*

$$ VIETNAMESE

🍴 **Loc Pho.** A garden restaurant with open-air thatched huts, this spot is popular with locals, but can prove quite the adventure for non-Vietnamese-speaking travelers because of the absence of any English on the menu. Recommended dishes include *dau hu* (tofu), *cha gio* (spring rolls), *goi ngo sen* (shrimp and lotus stem salad), *thit heo* (pork), and *com chien hai san* (seafood fried rice). Take along some patience and a sense of fun—and do look at what the locals are eating and point to what looks and smells good to you. [$] *Average main: 100000d* ✉ *922 Tran Hung Dao* ☎ *0273/397–4919* 💳 *No credit cards.*

$ VIETNAMESE

🍴 **My Tho Night Market.** The little night market along the waterfront, just along from Chuong Duong Hotel in front of the floating restaurant, has a selection of food stalls that provide a good point-and-order exercise (not much English is spoken here). Take some time to look at what the locals are eating before settling into a plastic chair for some street food. [$] *Average main: 40000d* ✉ *10 Thang 4* ⏲ *No lunch.*

WHERE TO STAY

$ HOTEL 🏨 **Chuong Duong Hotel.** For those determined to stay in My Tho itself rather than in a homestay, the two-star riverfront Chuong Duong Hotel is one of the better options in town. **Pros:** great central location on the waterfront. **Cons:** little English spoken; rooms are looking worn. [$] *Rooms from: 500000d* ✉ *10D 30 Thang 4* ☎ *0273/387–0875* 🛏 *24 rooms, 2 suites* 🍴 *No meals.*

$$$$ B&B/INN 🏨 **Jardin du Mekong.** Small and charming, this family-run guesthouse has five cute bamboo bungalows set in a lovely garden area, well off the tourist trail, and is an ideal rural retreat for those seeking a glimpse of local life and a taste of excellent home cooking. **Pros:** delicious home-cooked food; truly friendly-family atmosphere. **Cons:** no air-conditioning or fridge in the room; isolated. [$] *Rooms from: 1600000d* ✉ *Cau Song Doc, Ben Tre* ☎ *090/314–9696* 🌐 *gitesmekong.com/en/* 🛏 *5 bungalows* 🍴 *Some meals.*

$$ B&B/INN 🏨 **Mango Home Riverside.** A boutique homestay on the banks of the Ham Luong River, Mango Home Riverside has comfortable air-conditioned thatched bungalows set in a beautiful tropical garden, warm and friendly staff, and very good food. **Pros:** relaxing riverside retreat; staffers are more than happy to suggest activities and tours. **Cons:** isolated. [$] *Rooms from: 710000d* ✉ *My Huan, Ben Tre* ☎ *098/323–2197; Ho Chi Minh City office (English), 096/768–3366 hotline* 🌐 *mangohomeriverside.com* 🛏 *9 rooms* 🍴 *Breakfast.*

VINH LONG

74 km (46 miles) southwest of My Tho, 170 km (105 miles) southwest of Ho Chi Minh City.

The capital of the Vinh Long Province is the transport hub of Vinh Long, a mid-size industrial town with few points of interest. Most of the tourist infrastructure is near the river, which is a short walk from the main market. Vinh Long can be used as a base to visit the Cai Be Floating Market or the town of Sa Dec, 50 km (30 miles) away. Sa Dec is the modern-day home of many flower farmers and the 1920s home of French novelist Marguerite Duras—and the setting of her most famous novel, *The Lover*. The drive from Vinh Long south to Tra Vinh has some very pretty sections.

GETTING HERE AND AROUND

Vinh Long's main bus station is about 4 km (2½ miles) from downtown, with most buses providing a free shuttle service to hotels. The long-haul buses from Ho Chi Minh City stop here while the buses from Can Tho often let passengers off closer to the center of town. The main bus companies that operate out of the Vinh Long bus depot are Phuong Trang (☎ *070/3879–777*) and Thanh Buoi (☎ *08/3833–3999*).

ESSENTIALS

Bus Contact Vinh Long Bus Station ✉ *1E Dinh Tien Hoang, Ving Long* ☎ *0270/823458.*

EXPLORING

Cai Be Floating Market (*Cho Noi Cai Be*). A colorful wholesale market that runs from early in the morning to about 5 pm, this is where you'll see the iconic images of boats big and small loaded with fruit, vegetables, and flowers; with sellers advertising their wares by hoisting samples up the flagpole. Cai Be Floating Market is included on many Mekong Delta tours running out of Ho Chi Minh City. This market is becoming smaller each year as vendors use the new roads and bridges to send their goods directly to Ho Chi Minh City. The floating markets near Can Tho are more interesting. ✉ *Off Cai Be Wharf, Cai Be.*

Huynh Thuy Le Ancient House (*Nha Co Huynh Thuy Le*). Built in 1895 by a wealthy Chinese family and rebuilt in 1917, this house is famous for being the home of Huynh Thuy Le, upon whom French novelist Marguerite Duras based the title character of *The Lover*, a 1984 semi-autobiographical book (*L'Amant* in the original French) about a schoolgirl's love affair with a rich Chinese man. The house was used as a government building for many years, which meant the 1992 film *The Lover* was shot at another colonial house in Can Tho. But it's been restored reasonably faithfully—without the original gold leaf decorations—and it's possible to stay in one of the bedrooms for about $50 a night, including dinner and breakfast. The architecture is quite interesting—French colonial on the outside but ornately Chinese on the inside—with many photographs of the "The Lover," both in real life and as he was portrayed on screen. ✉ *255A Nguyen Hue, Sa Dec* ☎ *0277/377–3937* 🎟 *30,000d* 🕓 *Daily 7:30–5.*

Van Thanh Mieu Pagoda. About 5 km (3 miles) from the Vinh Long Market, this large Chinese Confucian temple was built in the mid-19th century. It's decorated with multicolor dragons and statues of Confucius, which is odd because the monks here practice Buddhism. Added to the original structure is a different style of hall built in honor of a local fighter against colonialism, Phan Tanh Gian, who committed suicide in the 1930s rather than submit to French rule. Often the locals refer to the temple by his name rather than its official title. Although the temple has opening hours posted on the gate, it's often inexplicably closed. ✉ *Tran Phu, Ving Long.*

WHERE TO EAT

$$$ VIETNAMESE

🍴 **Phuong Thuy.** A plain and simple restaurant, associated with the Cuu Long Hotel across the road (which issues guests with tickets to the breakfast buffet), the riverside Phuong Thuy has a range of standard Vietnamese dishes, including hotpot, and a few Western choices. The main drawcards here are the English subtitles on the menu and the great river views, though service can be a bit slow. The staff don't mind if you grab a riverside seat for a few quiet drinks rather than ordering a meal. [$] *Average main: 175000d* ✉ *1 Phan Boi Chau, Ving Long* ☎ *0270/382–4786.*

$ VIETNAMESE 🍴 **Quan Nem Nuong.** An English menu takes care of the language barrier here, allowing non-Vietnamese speakers to tuck into the house specialty, *nem nuong* (grilled pork skewers), served with a platter of fresh herbs, salad items, and rice paper to roll everything together. There are a few other items on the menu but the nem nuong is the star. The interior of the restaurant is simple, with metal tables and folding chairs, and it's open to the street. [$] *Average main: 42000d* ✉ *12 Thang 5, Ving Long* ☎ *0270/382–7122* 💳 *No credit cards.*

$ VIETNAMESE 🍴 **Vinh Long Market.** Make your way through the bustling Ving Long Market to the food section at breakfast or lunchtime and inspect what the locals are eating. Point to what looks good and you will be chowing down on something cheap, authentic, and delicious in no time. One tasty local specialty is *banh uot,* which translates literally as "wet cakes" but in reality is a dish of steamed rice crepes, pickled vegetables, shredded pork, and barbecued pork patties topped with a tangy dressing. The market stalls start packing up at around 4 pm and are usually closed by 5 pm. [$] *Average main: 30000d* ✉ *Nguyen Van Nha, Ving Long* 🕒 *No dinner.*

WHERE TO STAY

$ HOTEL 🏨 **Cuu Long Hotel.** This hotel is the best in town, with a great central location across from the Tien River and a block from the market. **Pros:** great location; very reasonable price. **Cons:** occasional wailing from the karaoke place down the road; housekeeping staff can be very noisy in the corridors. [$] *Rooms from: 580000d* ✉ *2 Thang 5, Vinh Long* ☎ *070/382–3656* 🌐 *www.cuulongtourist.com* 🛏 *48 rooms* 🍽 *Breakfast.*

$$$$ RESORT FAMILY 🏨 **Mekong Riverside Resort and Spa.** A delightful boutique resort on the river, with rooms in thatched bungalows, a pool, a spa, and excellent dining options, this is a great base for exploring the area and there are many walking, cycling, and boat tours on offer. **Pros:** eco-friendly; many on-site activities. **Cons:** isolated; limited outside dining choices. [$] *Rooms from: 2365000d* ✉ *Hoa Qui Ward, Hoa Khanh subdistrict, Cai Be* ☎ *073/392–4466* 🌐 *www.mekongriversideresort.vn* 🛏 *50 rooms* 🍽 *Breakfast.*

CHAU DOC

61 km (38 miles) from Long Xuyen, 245 km (152 miles) west of Ho Chi Minh City.

One of the Mekong Delta's most interesting destinations, Chau Doc is a religiously diverse and picturesque border town with Kinh (Vietnam's ethnic majority), Khmer, Cham, and Chinese communities. The town, on the banks of the Hau Giang River, has a jaunty air, possibly from the *xe loi* (bicycle trailers) that ply the streets.

The riverside promenade, a short walk from the bustling main market, is a pleasant spot to explore, watch the sunset, and catch the local ferry across the river to visit the city's biggest mosque. Sam Mountain (Nui Sam) is also worth a visit, for the interesting temples and the stunning views of the flat rice paddies below. An added bonus of this lovely little town is the friendliness of the locals; the xe loi drivers smile and wave even after you've shaken your head to indicate you don't want a ride.

GETTING HERE AND AROUND
Buses from major centers in the Mekong Delta arrive and depart at Chau Doc's main bus station, on the eastern outskirts of town. It's about seven hours by bus to Ho Chi Minh City and about 3½ hours to Can Tho. The main bus companies operating out of the bus depot are Phuong Trang and Hung Cuong. There are taxis and xe om drivers waiting at the bus depot to take you into town. Most sites within town are a short taxi ride and it's best to use the meter rather than try to negotiate a price. If you're planning a longer trip, including to Sam Mountain, see if your hotel can negotiate a rate for you. (Taxi drivers don't like driving up the mountain because it puts a strain on their engine.) Chau Doc is flat and the traffic is quite mild, making the city easy to traverse by bicycle. The Victoria Chau Doc Hotel and Murray Guesthouse both have free bicycles for guests, which can be rented for quite reasonable rates by nonguests. Xe loi are unique to a few Mekong Delta towns and are quite a fun way to get around, although the seats are quite low. To avoid getting ripped off, ask your hotel to organize a short xe loi tour of the town. It should cost about 50,000d for an hour.

ESSENTIALS
Transportation Contacts Chau Doc Bus Station ✉ *QL 91* ☎ *0296/355–0747* **Mai Linh Taxi** ☎ *0296/392–2266.*

EXPLORING
Floating Fish Farms. You can see some of the floating farms from 30 Thang 4 Park and the Chau Giang ferry terminal, off to the left across the river, but to visit one you need a guide. The fish farms are underneath the floating houses, in underwater pens accessed through the floors. A visit to a floating fish farm is usually on the itinerary of organized tours that come through Chau Doc. If traveling independently, ask your hotel for assistance in organizing a visit. ✉ *Hau Giang River.*

Fodor's Choice ★ **Mubarak Mosque.** One of nine mosques serving An Giang Province's Muslim population, Mubarak Mosque is a short ferry ride from Chau Doc's passenger pier. First built in 1750, the mosque is the spiritual heart of the area's Cham community. Take some time wandering the surrounding streets to view the Khmer-style wooden houses. ✉ *TL953, Chau Doc.*

Sam Mountain (*Nui Sam*). It's possible to walk to the smallish (230 meters) Sam Mountain, 5 km (3 miles) southwest of Chau Doc, although it is a long walk. Or you can get a *xe om* or a taxi to the top of the mountain and walk down (there's a surcharge for navigating the steep bumpy road; make sure you organize a round-trip unless you want to walk back to town, which is a actually a very pleasant stroll).

There are several interesting shrines on the mountain, known as Nui Sam in Vietnamese. The first, at its base, is Tay An Pagoda, originally constructed in 1847 and renovated several times since, with a mix of Vietnamese and Indian architecture. A little way past Tay An Pagoda is Chua Ba Xu (Lady Xu Pagoda), dedicated to a goddess whose origins have been lost in the mists of time and legend. Lady Xu—who may or may not be a feminine version of the Indian god Shiva, a Cham queen, or the Chinese goddess Mazu—is believed to protect Vietnam's borders, and a three-day festival is held in her honor at the start of the rainy season, from the 23rd day of the 4th lunar month each year. Farther along is the Tomb of Thoai Ngoc Hau, an official of the Nguyen dynasty who died in 1829, and his two wives. Hang Pagoda (Cave Pagoda), at the top of 400 steps, has amazing views of the surrounding countryside, the flat rice paddies, and flood plains that stretch out beyond the Cambodian border. ✉ *Off Vong Nui Sam.*

Tra Su Bird Sanctuary. The 845-hectare (2,088-acre) Tra Su bird sanctuary, 25 km (15½ miles) southwest of Chau Doc, is home to more than 70 species of birds, including storks, egrets, and herons. The best time to visit is when the *cajeput* (paperbark) forest is flooded, from July to November. A one-hour exploration by boat includes a motorboat ride and then a peaceful cruise by rowboat through the brilliant green duckweed, lotus flowers, and water lilies. The tour usually includes a stop at a bird-observation tower that is 23 meters (75 feet) high. For most of the year, the sanctuary's narrow 12-km (7½-mile) track can also be explored by bicycle, with rentals available at the boat station. ✉ *Van Giao Commune, Tinh Bien District* 🎟 *Boat tour 75,000d* ⏲ *Daily 6–5.*

WHERE TO EAT

$$$ VIETNAMESE

🍴 **Bassac Restaurant.** The old-world charm of the Victoria Chau Doc Hotel extends to its in-house restaurant, which serves Western and Asian cuisine in a stylish riverfront setting. Take a seat on the terrace to enjoy the sunset (and happy hour at the bar) and the attentive but discreet service. This is the priciest place in town, but the food, the staff, and the river views make it worthwhile. Reservations are recommended because sometimes the restaurant hosts bus tours. [$] *Average main: 250000d* ✉ *Victoria Hotel, 1 Le Loi* ☎ *0296/386–5010* 🌐 *www.victoriahotels.asia.*

$$ VIETNAMESE

🍴 **Lien Phat.** Western tourists will find an English menu (with some very unusual translations) at this basic Vietnamese restaurant, where a range of standard dishes includes the local specialty, *lau mam* (fermented fish hotpot). A big plus is the air-conditioned room, in a town where many places are fan-cooled only. The style is basic, with check table cloths and wooden dining settings inside and plain marble-topped tables on the terrace. [$] *Average main: 145000d* ✉ *To 2A Trung Nu Vuong* ☎ *0296/356–6868.*

$$ VIETNAMESE

🍴 **Mekong Floating Restaurant** (*Nha Hang Be Noi Mekong*). A bit of a tourist novelty, the floating restaurant serves decent Vietnamese food with great river views, and its range of special and set menus offer great value. The specialty is *lau mam* (fermented fish-flavored hotpot), which tastes much better than it smells, and during the rainy season includes the yellow *dien dien* flower. The English menu doesn't list *lau mam* because it's not all that popular with non-Vietnamese people. Ask for it if you dare. [$] *Average main: 140000d* ✉ *443 Le Loi St.* ☎ *0296/355–0838.*

WHERE TO STAY

$$ B&B/INN Fodor's Choice ★ **Murray Guest House.** This family-run contender is fighting well above its price range, with large clean stylish rooms, comfortable beds, well-appointed bathrooms (with solar heated water), and friendly staff. **Pros:** only a short walk from the riverfront and half a block from the ferry terminal; a much-welcome respite from the standard local-style budget hotels and guesthouses. **Cons:** no elevator. [$] *Rooms from: 640000d* ✉ *11–15 Trung Dinh* ☎ *091/221-7448* 🌐 *www.murrayguesthouse.com* 🛏 *10 rooms* 🍴 *Breakfast.*

$$$ HOTEL Fodor's Choice ★ **Nui Sam Lodge.** Halfway up Sam Mountain (Nui Sam in Vietnamese), this collection of charming stone cottages is a relaxing getaway from the bustle of Mekong Delta towns, but close enough to take day trips in and around Chau Doc—and it has stunning views over brilliant green rice paddies and flood plains. **Pros:** wonderful views; peaceful location; family rooms; new spa to open during 2015. **Cons:** the mountainside location and the many stairs make it unsuitable for people with mobility problems; isolated. [$] *Rooms from: 1270000d* ✉ *Vinh Dong I, Nui Sam* ☎ *0296/357-5888* 🌐 *www.victoriahotels.asia* 🛏 *36 rooms* 🍴 *Breakfast.*

$$$$ HOTEL **Victoria Chau Doc Hotel.** The French-colonial style Victoria Chau Doc, with its prime riverfront position, offers a touch of glamour in the Mekong Delta, along with international-standard service and a good restaurant. **Pros:** great central location with views of the river. **Cons:** the hotel, built in 1997, seems a little tired in places. [$] *Rooms from: 3813000d* ✉ *32 Le Loi* ☎ *0296/386-5010* 🌐 *www.victoriahotels.asia* 🛏 *88 rooms, 4 suites* 🍴 *Breakfast.*

HA TIEN

112 km (70 miles) southwest of Chau Doc, 306 km (190 miles) west of Ho Chi Minh City.

Just 8 km (5 miles) from the Cambodian border, Ha Tien has some interesting sights, such as a network of caves that have been converted into makeshift temples with Buddha images and psychedelic background lights. The town's busy waterfront, with its bustling market, is charming. Under Khmer rule Ha Tien was a thriving port, and in the 17th century the Nguyen lords gave it to a Chinese lord, Mac Cuu, as a private, protected fiefdom. For the next 40 years the Khmer, Siamese, and Vietnamese all struggled for control of the port and the trade that would come with it. Ha Tien finally became an outpost of the Vietnamese Lords of Hue in 1780.

GETTING HERE AND AROUND

Buses connect Ha Tien to the provincial capital of Rach Gia and to Chau Doc in nearby An Giang Province, with several services a day to each center. The bus depot is on the outskirts of town and the main bus companies that service the station are Kumho Samco and Phuong Trang. (The road between Ha Tien and Chau Doc is very bumpy, but there are some very pretty views along the coast.) There are also a number of small minibus services that travel to Ca Mau, Vung Tau, Ben Tre, Soc Trang, Tra Vinh, and Can Tho. The ever-present Mai Linh taxi company has a fleet of taxis in Ha Tien, as well as a local company called Ha Tien Taxi. There are usually many taxis waiting at the ferry terminal when the Phu Quoc ferry is due in.

ESSENTIALS

Bus Contacts Ha Tien Bus Station ⊠ *Tao Dan St.* ☎ *0297/395–6072.*

Taxi Contacts Ha Tien Taxi ☎ *0297/385–2569.* **Mai Linh Taxi**
☎ *0297/395–6956.*

EXPLORING

Mac Cuu Tombs (*Linh Temple*). Sometimes referred to as the hill of tombs, this site is a garden cemetery containing the remains of General Mac Cuu and his family. Mac Cuu is credited with establishing Ha Tien in 1670, when the region was part of Cambodia. The family mausoleum, with its traditional Chinese tombs decorated with dragons, phoenixes, tigers, and lions, was built in 1809. There's a small temple dedicated to the family at the base of the complex. ⊠ *Mac Cu.*

Mui Nai Beach. With its pebble-strewn brown sand, Mui Nai, 6 km (4 miles) west of Ha Tien, is definitely not the prettiest beach around, but the sea is calm and shallow and the water is relatively clean so it's a nice place to take a dip. There are deckchairs for rent and shacks selling seafood, and in the late afternoon the locals play volleyball and swim. **Amenities:** food and drink. **Best for:** swimming. ⊠ *4 miles from Ha Tien.*

Thach Dong Cave Pagoda. On the road to the Cambodian border, 5 km (3 miles) northwest of Ha Tien, this atmospheric cave pagoda is in an echoey cavern in a limestone karst, with various chambers holding funerary tablets. The cave is home to a colony of bats (so keep your mouth closed when you look up), and the views from some of the openings across to Cambodia are just stunning. At the base of the mountain there is a small monument shaped like a clenched fist that commemorates the murder of 130 local civilians by the Khmer Rouge in 1978. ⊠ *Off DL80, My Duc.*

WHERE TO EAT

$ ⎯ **Ha Tien Market.** There's a range of street food stalls in the streets surrounding Ha Tien's impressive market, which comprises several buildings, including one marked "*an uong*" ("eat and drink"). $ *Average main: 50000d* ⊠ *Cho Ha Tien* ⊘ *No dinner.*

VIETNAMESE

$$ ⎯ **Oasis Bar.** A plain and simple bar serving a range of drinks, including super-cold beers, Oasis lives up to its name for the wealth of free travel information English owner Andy provides. (There is also a small travel agency inside the bar.) Oasis is the only place in town serving Western food, starting with breakfast, including the full English hot breakfast, and continuing through the day with bar-style meals such as chili con carne, baguettes, and Thai green chicken curry. $ *Average main: 80000d* ⊠ *42 Tuan Phu Dat* ☎ *0297/370–1553* ⊕ *www.oasisbarhatien.com* ⊟ *No credit cards.*

INTERNATIONAL

WHERE TO STAY

$ B&B/INN 🏨 **Bao Anh** (*Nha Nghi Bao Anh*). Close to the market, this guesthouse has large, neat-as-a-pin rooms with not-too-hard beds and bathrooms with shower cubicles rather than the usual Vietnamese splash room. **Pros:** cheap, clean, and comfortable. **Cons:** the language barrier can be frustrating. [$] *Rooms from: 400000d* ✉ *Khu TTTM* ☎ *0297/395–5979* 🛏 *8 rooms* 🍴 *No meals.*

$ HOTEL 🏨 **Hai Phuong Hotel.** This is a pleasant enough option, close to the market, with spacious, clean comfortable rooms, all with windows and private balconies. **Pros:** within walking distance of the market and the riverfront area. **Cons:** slightly tired-looking bathrooms; the language barrier can create problems. [$] *Rooms from: 400000d* ✉ *52 Dang Thuy Tram* ☎ *0297/385–2240* 🛏 *25 rooms, 18 suites* 💳 *No credit cards* 🍴 *No meals.*

$$$$ HOTEL 🏨 **River Hotel.** Ha Tien's only four-star hotel, in a prime location on the river, is understandably proud of counting Vietnamese and Cambodian prime ministers among its guests. **Pros:** a step up from some of the more basic options in the Mekong Delta. **Cons:** limited English requires a degree of patience; slightly sterile feel; expensive for what and where it is. [$] *Rooms from: 1890000d* ✉ *Lo B3, TTTM Tran Hau* ☎ *0297/395–5888* 🌐 *www.riverhotelvn.com* 🛏 *70 rooms, 11 suites* 🍴 *Breakfast.*

PHU QUOC ISLAND

45 km (28 miles) west of Ha Tien in the Gulf of Thailand.

Fodor's Choice ★ The white-sand beaches, turquoise waters, swaying palms, and laid-back feel of this beautiful island in the Gulf of Thailand have made it one of Vietnam's most popular resort destinations. Unfortunately, this means the 48-km- (30-mile-) long tropical island is at risk of being overdeveloped, with many new resorts opening in recent years—each one bigger than the last—and many more under construction.

Despite the grand plans investors have for Phu Quoc, its local charm remains, and well-traveled types say the island reminds them of Bali 30 years ago. There are many deserted beaches that are ideal for exploring by motorbike (or taxi), several of the resorts welcome non-guests to their waterfront restaurants, and the resorts themselves do offer a range of amenities to make for a relaxing tropical island pampering holiday.

Phu Quoc, or Koh Tral as the Cambodians call it, is much closer to Cambodia than it is to Vietnam.

Note: since March 2014, foreign passport holders who arrive on Phu Quoc via an international flight or boat will be eligible for a 30-day visa exemption. The exemption only applies to Phu Quoc, so any onward travel to the Vietnamese mainland requires a visa.

GETTING HERE AND AROUND

Phu Quoc International Airport is 10 km (6 miles) from the main town of Duong Dong. Direct flights arrive regularly from Hanoi, Ho Chi Minh City, Can Tho, Singapore, and Siem Reap in Cambodia. Most resorts have an airport transfer service and taxis and xe om drivers meet scheduled flights. Superdong ferries leave Ha Tien three times a

day (more often in peak periods) for Phu Quoc, arriving at the main passenger port of Bai Vong Port, 15 km (9½ miles) from Duong Dong town. The journey from Ha Tien takes 80 minutes. For ferry times, check the website.

Metered taxis are easy to get in Long Beach and Duong Dong Town, much more difficult to get in the more remote parts of the island. Mai Linh and Sasco have fleets on Phu Quoc. It's possible to negotiate a flat rate for a full day, exploring either the north or the south of the island, for about 650,000d. To do the whole island (not recommended), a flat rate should be about 1 million dong. Most hotels and resorts can quickly and easily organize motorbike rentals. Expect to pay around 200,00d a day for an automatic motorbike (with helmet).

ESSENTIALS

Boat Contact Superdong ✉ *Kim Du, Ha Tien* ☎ *0297/395–5933* ⊕ *superdong. com.vn.*

Taxi Contacts Mai Linh Taxi ✉ *Phu Quoc* ☎ *0297/399–7799.* **Sasco Taxi** ✉ *Phu Quoc* ☎ *0297/399–5599.*

EXPLORING

Coconut Tree Prison (*Nha Lao Cay Dua, Phu Quoc Prison*). Established by the French and used by the Americans as well, the Coconut Tree Prison, also known as Phu Quoc Prison, is a chilling visual reminder of the atrocities the human race is capable of, as well as a stark record of history. Like many other war-related sites in Vietnam, the Coconut Tree Prison uses life-size mannequins to show the horrors committed in the past. The prison is right at the southern end of Phu Quoc, about 5 km (3 miles) north of An Thoi town. ✉ *Nguyen Van Cu, Phu Quoc* ✈ *Free, donations welcome* ⊙ *Daily 8–11:30 and 1:30–5.*

Fish Sauce Factories. Local tours often stop in at one of the very pungent fish sauce factories along the river in Duong Dong town. It's possible to visit without an organized tour, although not much English is spoken at the factories. Try Khai Hoan in Hung Vuong Street (☎ *077/ 3848–555*) and Hung Thanh at Khu Pho 3 (☎ *077/3846–124; www. hungthanhfishsauce.com.vn*). ■ **TIP→ Airlines that fly out of Phu Quoc will not allow fish sauce aboard, but it is possible to buy it at the departure lounge and have it shipped home.** ✉ *Phu Quoc.*

Phu Quoc National Park (*Vuon Quoc Gia Phu Quoc*). Covering most of the northern part of the island, the Phu Quoc National Park comprises mangroves, forest, and wetlands and supports many plant and animal species. It's an interesting place to explore by motorbike, or you could consider hiring a guide through your hotel (the cheaper local tour agents are best avoided or you might have a disappointing experience). The most beautiful parts of the national park are near Ganh Dau Beach in the island's northwest. There's a pretty walking trail about 5 km (3 miles) before Ganh Dau Village. The trail is not signed, so just look for an obvious walking trail about 100 meters after the 5-km (3-mile) Ganh Dau road marker. If you're coming from Ganh Dau, the trail is almost 5 km (3 miles) from town. ✉ *Phu Quoc* ☎ *0297/384–6344* ✈ *Free* ⊙ *24 hrs.*

Su Muon Pagoda. This colorful temple, built in 1932, sits on top of a hill 4 km (2½ miles) east of Duong Dong Town. Access is via 40 stone steps, and the view of the island from the top is stunning. ✉ *Off Tran Hung Dao, Phu Quoc.*

Suoi Tranh. At the end of a 20-minute rainforest walk, you'll reach this picturesque waterfall, which is much more spectacular in the rainy season but still worth visiting in the dry season. There are food and drink vendors and restrooms at the waterfall. ■ **TIP→ Suoi Tranh is popular with bus tours, so arrive early to avoid the crowds.** The entrance fee is used to pay trash collectors, so this site is much cleaner than some others on the island. ✉ *Off TL47, Phu Quoc* ✈ *3,000d* ⊙ *Daily 7–6.*

Vinpearl Land. This vast amusement park in Phu Quoc's north officially opened in November 2014, even though it was only half-completed. When finished, the 17-hectare amusement park, like its sister property in Nha Trang, will include rides, a water park, a 5D movie theater, and an aquarium. ✉ *Ganh Dau Beach, Phu Quoc* ⊕ *www.vinpearlland. com/en/content/vinpearl-land-phu-quoc* ✈ *500,000d* ⊙ *Daily 9–9.*

3

BEACHES

Dai Beach (*Bai Dai*). This beach in Phu Quoc's northwest is what tropical island paradises are all about—fine golden sand and warm turquoise water. A handful of seafood stalls along the beach mean you won't go hungry. The nicest part of the beach is at the southern end, but gaining access can be difficult as heavy trucks (associated with the nearby Vin-Pearl development) have made a mess of the dirt track. **Amenities:** food and drinks. **Best for:** solitude; sunsets; swimming. ⊠ *Bai Dai, Phu Quoc.*

Long Beach (*Bai Truoc*). The golden sand of the generically named Long Beach stretches for nearly 20 km (12 miles) along Phu Quoc's western coast, from just south of Duong Dong Town. This is where most of the island's resorts and restaurants are located, which means some parts of the beach can be quite crowded with sunbathers and swimmers. It's still possible, however, to find deserted stretches of this beach. Cassia Cottage Resort, Long Beach Resort, May House Resort, Paris Beach Resort, Salinda Premium Resort and Spa, and La Veranda all front Long Beach. **Amenities:** food and drink; water sports. **Best for:** sunsets; swimming; walking. ⊠ *Access via side streets off Tran Hung Dao, Phu Quoc.*

Ong Lang Beach (*Bai Ong Lang*). More of a series of coves than one long beach, Ong Lang is still very pretty, with its rocky outcrops and narrow strips of white sand. Mango Bay Resort and Bo Resort both front the beach, so you can follow the signs to these resorts to enjoy wonderful views of the beach from their in-house restaurants. Public access to the beach is slightly tricky as the network of roads in this area aren't named. Head toward Mango Bay Resort and look for the "public beach" signs (in English) just south of the resort. **Amenities:** food and drink. **Best for:** snorkeling; solitude; sunsets; swimming. ⊠ *Phu Quoc.*

Sao Beach (*Bai Sau*). The northern end of Sao Beach is what Phu Quoc is all about: crystal clear water and fine white sand. Make sure you take the third, northernmost entry to the beach—the first two entrances are where the tour buses go, so the beach gets crowded and noisy with Jet Skis buzzing about. To the north of all this activity, you'll find a deserted beach and the elegant Khong Sao Beach Bar, with its cold beer, excellent cocktails, and free showers. During peak season (November to March), the onshore wind blows in some garbage from the fishing vessels, and during this time, the bar staff keep the northern section of the beach much cleaner than the southern stretch. **Amenities:** food and drink; showers. **Best for:** solitude; snorkeling; sunrise; swimming; walking. ⊠ *Phu Quoc.*

Thom Beach (*Bai Thom*). On the northeastern side of the island, about 35 km (22 miles) from Duong Dong Town, is the remote and rocky tree-lined Thom Beach, accessible via a new paved road. There are a few local outlets selling food and drinks near the beach, which you're likely to have to yourself. Beware of spiky sea urchins and jellyfish if taking a dip. **Amenities:** food and drink. **Best for:** solitude; swimming. ⊠ *Phu Quoc.*

WHERE TO EAT

DUONG DONG

$$ CAFÉ ✕**Buddy Ice Cream and Info Café.** Across the road from the marina, this small, neat, and cozy café is a good place to stop for a coffee, ice cream, milk shake, or smoothie, as well as light meals such as salads, burgers, and Vietnamese dishes. It's probably the only place in town where you can get toasted Vegemite-and-cheese sandwiches, reflecting the owner's Australian roots. Famous for its "scoop" on Phu Quoc Island, Buddy, one block from the night market, also acts as a de facto tourist information center. $ *Average main: 80000d* ⊠ *6 Bach Dang, Duong Dong Town, Phu Quoc.*

$$ VIETNAMESE ✕**Dinh Cau Night Market.** For fresh, cooked-before-your eyes seafood, head down to the Duong Dong Night Market. Dining at the street food stalls here, which set up around 6 pm, are a great experience, especially for group dinners. If you're not a seafood fan, never fear—a range of pork, chicken, and beef dishes is also available. $ *Average main: 80000d* ⊠ *Vo Thi Sau, Phu Quoc* ⊘ *No lunch.*

LONG BEACH

$$ INDIAN ✕**Ganesh.** For authentic Northern Indian cuisine, including great tandoor and naan, stop by this little restaurant, with simple style and friendly staff. Portions are generous and the masala tea is very delicious, although service can be on the slow side. $ *Average main: 150000d* ⊠ *97 Tran Hung Dao, Long Beach* ☎ *0297/399–4917* ⊕ *www. ganeshphuquoc.com.*

$$ GERMAN ✕**German B Bar.** Serving up German specialties such as schnitzel, frikadelle, and bratwurst, the open-air bar also does well with burgers, pizza, and lattes. This place is a good spot to relax and enjoy free Wi-Fi and a little taste of Europe. $ *Average main: 120000d* ⊠ *78 Tran Hung Dao, Long Beach* ☎ *0166/465–3830.*

$$$$ TAPAS **Fodor's**Choice ★ ✕**Itaca Resto Lounge.** Superb tapas are served with style in an open-air restaurant with a lovely garden section illuminated by lanterns and candles. Itaca isn't on the beach but the food and the design makes that fact completely forgettable, and provides a welcome break from the resorty-ness of the island. Set up by three Catalan friends in 2012, Itaca's drinks menu is as sophisticated as its food menu, which include mains as well as tapas. The patatas bravas served in a piece of bamboo and the marinated anchovies are highly recommended. $ *Average main: 300000d* ⊠ *125 Tran Hung Dao, Duong Dong Town, Phu Quoc* ☎ *0297/399–2022* ⊕ *itacalounge.com* ⊘ *No lunch.*

$$$$ INTERNATIONAL ✕**Pepper Tree Restaurant.** La Veranda's in-house restaurant provides a full sensory experience, with refined Pacific-rim cuisine, stunning views over the ocean, and elegant French colonial style. One of the priciest options on Phu Quoc, it's well worth it for the service, setting, food, wine list, and sunset views. It's the perfect location for a romantic dinner. $ *Average main: 645000d* ⊠ *La Veranda Resort, Tran Hung Dao, Long Beach, Phu Quoc* ☎ *0297/398–2988* ⊴ *Reservations essential.*

$$ CAFÉ ✕**Rory's Beach Bar.** Cheap and cheerful bar food is available here day and night—think pizza, burgers, paninis, salads, stir-fries, and pasta, served on the beach, on the deck, or beside the boat-shape bar. Hosts

Rory and his wife Yoon preside over the café/bar, which has a genuinely welcoming atmosphere and fabulous sunset views. [$] *Average main: 150000d* ✉ *118/10 Tran Hung Dao, Long Beach, Phu Quoc* 🌐 *www.facebook.com/RorysBarPhuQuoc.*

$$ INTERNATIONAL Fodor's Choice ★ 🍴 **The Spice House.** Cassia Cottage Resort's in-house restaurant has romantic settings: beside a pond filled with water lilies in a manicured tropical garden or right on the beach. The restaurant, which specializes in Vietnamese and international cuisine, uses fresh local produce, prepared with care and a bit of a French flourish. This is a great option for a special evening that won't break the bank. [$] *Average main: 145000d* ✉ *Cassia Cottage, KP 7, Phu Quoc* ☎ *0297/384–8395* 🌐 *www.cassiacottage.com* ✍ *Reservations essential.*

ONG LANG BEACH

$$$ INTERNATIONAL 🍴 **Bo Bar and Restaurant.** Vietnamese and Mediterranean food is served in an open-air pavilion overlooking the turquoise waters in front of the secluded Bo Resort. Finding the resort can be an adventure and then you still need to walk down a hill to the ocean. It's a great spot to watch the sunset, disturbed only by the gentle shushing of the waves. [$] *Average main: 160000d* ✉ *Bo Resort, Ong Lang Beach, Phu Quoc* ☎ *0297/370–2446* 🌐 *boresort.com* ✍ *Reservations essential.*

$$$ INTERNATIONAL 🍴 **On The Rocks.** Mango Bay Resort's in-house restaurant serves excellent Asian and Western fusion cuisine from a wooden deck (with rocks peeking through) over the water. The views of the sunset over the Gulf of Thailand are fantastic, the cocktails delicious, the staff attentive, the music mellow, and the food, including the tapas, is some of the best on the island. [$] *Average main: 240000d* ✉ *Ong Lang Beach, Phu Quoc* ☎ *0297/398–1693* ✍ *Reservations essential.*

$$ VIETNAMESE 🍴 **Sakura.** Overseen by the friendly Mrs. Kiem, this tiny open-air shack on the side of the road serves up some very tasty fare. The house specialty is fish with lemongrass and chili, although the Vietnamese chicken curry and the hotpot are delicious as well. This is a great place to stop, refresh, and have a chat when you're in the Ong Lang Beach area. [$] *Average main: 150000d* ✉ *Ong Lang Beach, Phu Quoc* ☎ *0122/818–3484* 💳 *No credit cards.*

WHERE TO STAY

LONG BEACH

$$$$ RESORT 🏨 **Cassia Cottage Resort.** This beachfront resort has a comfortable yet relaxing ambience, with its pretty little brick cottages, manicured gardens, two swimming pools, and a charming garden restaurant, not to mention the helpful staff. **Pros:** a free cocktail every afternoon for each guest; two pools can help separate families and nonfamilies; a handy little Internet lounge with a well-stocked bookcase. **Cons:** no TV; limited breakfast menu gets boring after a few days. [$] *Rooms from: 4600000d* ✉ *KP7, Long Beach, Phu Quoc* ☎ *0297/384–8395* 🌐 *www.cassiacottage.com* 🛏 *26 rooms, 2 suites* 🍽 *Breakfast.*

$$$$ RESORT Fodor's Choice ★ 🏨 **La Veranda.** Reminiscent of a colonial seaside mansion, with its wide verandas to catch the balmy sea breezes and swaying palms, La Veranda is an immaculately maintained haven of indulgent luxury on a quiet stretch of Long Beach. **Pros:** within walking distance of a range of bars and restaurants. **Cons:** it's easy to get lost in the mazelike system of garden paths; restaurants and bars are pricey. [$] *Rooms from: 4770000d* ✉ *Tran Hung Dao, Long Beach, Phu Quoc* ☎ *0297/398–2988* 🌐 *www.laverandaresorts.com* 🛏 *61 rooms, 9 suites* 🍴 *Breakfast.*

$$$$ RESORT 🏨 **Long Beach Resort.** Designed to resemble a traditional northern Vietnamese village, the two-story stone-and-wood "houses," ponds, gazebos, tiled roofs, landscaped gardens, and quaint curved bridges evoke a whimsical movie set. **Pros:** a very Vietnamese ambiance; free airport transfer included in the room rate. **Cons:** the wood-paneled rooms can seem a bit gloomy; service can be patchy. [$] *Rooms from: 5910000d* ✉ *Group of Households 4, Cua Lap Hamlet, Duong To Commune, Long Beach, Phu Quoc* ☎ *0297/398–1818* 🌐 *www.longbeach-phuquoc.com* 🛏 *66 rooms, 6 suites* 🍴 *Breakfast.*

$$$$ RESORT 🏨 **Mai House Resort.** With cute thatched bungalows set among lush tropical gardens that lead down to a private beach, Mai House Resort is a solid mid-range resort choice on pricey Phu Quoc. **Pros:** laid-back friendly atmosphere; a free cocktail for each guest every afternoon; massages available at the resort's beach-front spa. **Cons:** no TV or phones in the bungalows (but they are air-conditioned); no pool. [$] *Rooms from: 2308000d* ✉ *112/8 Tran Nao, Long Beach, Phu Quoc* ☎ *0297/384–7003* 🌐 *maihousephuquoc.com* 🛏 *31 bungalows* 🍴 *No meals.*

$$$$ RESORT 🏨 **Salinda Premium Resort and Spa.** It may look like a giant shoebox from the street, but inside it's luxurious and elegant, with an emphasis on incorporating natural elements, such as coconut husks, bamboo, lacquer, and wood, into the design. **Pros:** great beachfront location; new resort with eager young staff. **Cons:** very expensive; the sheer size of the main building can make it seem impersonal. [$] *Rooms from: 13158000d* ✉ *Cua Lap Hamlet, Dong To Commune, Long Beach, Phu Quoc* ☎ *0297/399–0011* 🌐 *www.salindaresort.com* 🛏 *106 rooms, 14 villas* 🍴 *Breakfast.*

ONG LANG BEACH

$$$$ RESORT 🏨 **Bo Resort.** With thatched wood-and-stone bungalows set on a hillside with lovely tropical gardens that overlook a bay of clear blue-green water, the focus of Bo Resort is a simple and "authentic" lifestyle right on the beach. **Pros:** gentle and harmonious atmosphere, with only the shush-shush of the waves to disturb you. **Cons:** Ong Lang Beach is quite isolated, 20 minutes from Duong Dong town. [$] *Rooms from: 1700000d* ✉ *Ong Lang Beach, Phu Quoc* ☎ *0297/370–2446* 🌐 *www.boresort.com* 🛏 *17 bungalows* 🍴 *Breakfast.*

$$$$ RESORT 🏨 **Chen Sea Resort and Spa.** Luxurious bungalows and villas overlook a private beach and the beautiful Gulf of Thailand at this polished resort from Thailand's Centara Hotels group, which promises simplicity, refinement, and some unique extras. **Pros:** range of leisure amenities; on-site spa. **Cons:** the resort is isolated, with little within walking distance. [$] *Rooms from: 6640000d* ✉ *Bai Xep, Ong Lang Beach, Phu*

Quoc ☎ *0297/399–5895* 🌐 *www.centarahotelsresorts.com* 🛏 *24 bungalows, 12 villas* 🍴 *No meals.*

$$$ RESORT 🏨 **Freedomland.** Guests rave about the eco-friendly Freedomland experience, with its communal dining, rustic bungalows, jungle setting, and super-chilled vibe. **Pros:** welcoming atmosphere; fantastic Asian-fusion food; back-to-nature experience; family-size bungalows. **Cons:** no air-conditioning, hot water, TV, or Wi-Fi in rooms; a 15-minute walk to the beach; minimum three-night stay in high season, two in low season. [$] *Rooms from: 1500000d* ✉ *Ong Lang Beach, Phu Quoc* ☎ *0122/658–6802* 🌐 *www.freedomlandphuquoc.com* 🛏 *17 bungalows* 🍴 *Breakfast.*

$$$$ RESORT Fodor's Choice ★ 🏨 **Mango Bay Resort.** A collection of rammed-earth and wooden bungalows scattered through a vast stretch of jungle and gardens fronting Ong Lang Beach, this eco-lodge is the perfect location for low-key relaxing interspersed with the many activities on offer. **Pros:** free airport transfers when booking three nights or more; solar-powered hot water; low season rates can be fantastic value. **Cons:** bungalows have no air-conditioning and no TV; the bars and restaurants of Duong Dong Town are 8 km (5 miles) away, about 10 minutes by taxi or motorbike. [$] *Rooms from: 2600000d* ✉ *Ong Lang Beach, Phu Quoc* ☎ *0773/981693* 🌐 *mangobayphuquoc.com* 🛏 *5 rooms, 39 bungalows* 🍴 *Breakfast.*

GANH DAU BEACH

$$$$ RESORT 🏨 **Peppercorn Beach Resort.** This is a relaxed, simple, and secluded hideaway, only a few steps from the ocean, with enough creature comforts to make a longer stay enjoyable. **Pros:** small and exclusive resort; free airport shuttle when booking five nights or more; free use of mountain bikes to explore the nearby fishing village. **Cons:** isolated location means Internet can be slow and electricity cuts out sometimes; not a "resort" resort, so no pool, spa, or deckchairs. [$] *Rooms from: 3900000d* ✉ *To 8, Ap Chuong Vich, Ganh Dau, Phu Quoc* ☎ *0297/398–9567* 🌐 *www.peppercornbeach.com* 🛏 *12 bungalows* 🍴 *Breakfast.*

NIGHTLIFE

Phu Quoc's nightlife centers on the more heavily resorted part of Long Beach. The sprawling nature of Phu Quoc means that most people enjoy their resort facilities at night, rather than heading out.

Drunk'n Monkey. A sports bar with pool table, foosball table, and all kinds of football being broadcast, Drunk'n Monkey is usually a lively choice in high season and quieter in the off-season. The friendly staff add to the relaxed atmosphere, and the pizzas are pretty good, too. ✉ *82 Tran Hung Dao, Long Beach, Phu Quoc* ☎ *090/9259–6055.*

Itaca Resto Lounge. This is a more refined nightlife option, where the guest DJs (lightly) pump up the music after sundown. An excellent choice for an evening sampling Mediterranean wines and liquors or sipping on the bartender's special mojitos. ✉ *125 Tran Hung Dau, Long Beach, Phu Quoc* ☎ *0297/399–2022* 🌐 *itacalounge.com* 🕒 *Closed Mon.*

Fodor's Choice ★ **Rory's Beach Bar.** Relaxed, welcoming, and right on the beach, Rory's is a must-visit when on Phu Quoc for its chilled vibe, cold beers, friendly staff—especially Rory and his wife Yoon—and classic takes on café-bar food. Nighttimes can run late, with bonfires on the beach (weather permitting), foosball games, and general laid-backness. Rory's attracts all types, from families to backpackers to old-timers; expect to hear some interesting conversations at the bar, involving people with an interest in the world and its travelers. ⊠ *118/10 Tran Hung Dao, Long Beach, Phu Quoc* ⏱ *Daily 10 am–midnight (or later).*

SPORTS AND THE OUTDOORS

DIVING AND SNORKELING

Flipper Diving Club. This is one of Phu Quoc's most reputable tour companies, offering snorkeling and scuba diving trips as well as dive training courses. Trips include hotel transfers, lunch, and drinks, and—more importantly—do not include extra stops at tourist shops for the guide to get kickbacks. ⊠ *60 Tran Hung Dao, Phu Quoc* ☎ *0297/399–4924* ⊕ *www.flipperdiving.com* ✉ *Snorkeling tours start at $25, scuba tours start at $74.*

Rainbow Divers. With a seasonal presence on Phu Quoc from October to March each year, Rainbow Divers is a PADI-accredited dive center with daily boat-diving and snorkeling trips, as well as all PADI course offerings. ⊠ *The Rainbow, 11 Tran Hung Dao, Duong Dong, Phu Quoc* ☎ *0913/400–964* ⊕ *www.divevietnam.com.*

GO-KARTING

Bobstar Racing. You can take an exhilarating spin around the 320-meter outdoor go-kart track in a well-maintained Genesis SX1 200cc kart. No drivers' license is required. ⊠ *2 Ong Lang, Phu Quoc* ☎ *093/9391–459* ⊕ *www.bobstarracing.com* ✉ *420,000d for 15 laps.*

GOLF

Vinpearl Golf Club. Phu Quoc's first and only golf course, which opened in late 2014, is a challenging 27-hole course designed by IMG Worldwide, with rolling fairways set among trees. The Nha Trang Course has beautiful sea views, the Phu Quoc Course has views of the jungle, and the Quy Nhon Course has mountain views. The entire course covers more than 100 hectares (247 acres). ⊠ *Ganh Dau, Phu Quoc* ☎ *058/359–0919* ⊕ *vinpearlgolf.com* ✉ *9 holes from 945,000d, 18 holes from 1,575,000d weekdays* ⛳ *Nha Trang Course: 9 holes, 3724 yards, par 36; Phu Quoc Course: 9 holes, 3521 yards, par 36; Quy Nhon Course: 9 holes, 3582 yards, par 36.*

SHOPPING

Dinh Cau Night Market. Setting up just before sunset, the night market is an interesting place to explore and shop for souvenirs, such as shells, handicrafts, and wooden boats. ■ **TIP→ Avoid the pearls, they're low-quality imports, not genuine Phu Quoc pearls.** The main attraction here is the group of seafood stalls near the main entrance, with a staggering array of live and fresh-caught fish and assorted crustaceans, which are cooked to order and eaten local-style at small metal tables. There are also other food options in the market, including vegetarian dishes.

Expect to bargain for souvenirs, but not for food. The jetty nearby and the Dinh Ba pagoda are popular spots for locals to watch the sunset. ⊠ *Vo Thi Sau, Phu Quoc.*

Ngoc Hien Pearl. With its boat-shape showroom, this is considered the best place on the island for genuinely local cultured seawater pearls (rather than imported Chinese freshwater pearls). If you're in the market for pearls, avoid anything offered at the local markets and make your way here. ⊠ *Ap Duong Bao, Phu Quoc* ☏ *0297/398–8999* ⊕ *ngochienpearl.com.*

SOUTH-CENTRAL MEKONG DELTA

The southernmost section of Vietnam is a flat, lush, and watery region, with extensive areas given over to cultivating rice and aquaculture. Can Tho, the main center, is a large riverside town with enough tourist facilities to make for a relaxing stay.

Southeast of Can Tho, on the eastern side of the Bassac River (Song Hau), is the fascinating and pretty little township of Tra Vinh, home to a large population of ethnic Khmers who have built stunning Khmer temples in and around Tra Vinh. South again, over on the western side of the Bassac, lies Soc Trang, another town with a thriving Khmer population.

Ca Mau is capital of Vietnam's southernmost province, and the sole city in the region. It's a sleepy place, with wide streets and rather laid back (for Vietnam) traffic, and is the jumping off point for visits to nearby bird sanctuaries and the Mui Ca Mau National Park.

CAN THO

34 km (21 miles) southwest of Vinh Long, 108 km (67 miles) southwest of My Tho, 170 km (105 miles) southwest of Ho Chi Minh City.

The meeting point of various waterways, Can Tho is the capital of the Mekong Delta and the region's gateway. This bustling hub of activity is connected to other centers in the Mekong Delta by a system of waterways as well as by road. For those seeking a comfortable base from which to explore the delta, Can Tho has a number of elegant accommodations options, as well as several river cruise companies with trips ranging from half-day explorations of the nearby floating markets to multiday cruises through the region.

Can Tho retains a hint of its colonial past as one of the largest French trading ports in Indochina. During the Vietnam War, Can Tho was almost constantly surrounded by hostile Vietcong forces, but the city itself stayed loyal to the Saigon regime and many American and South Vietnamese troops were based here. It was the last city to fall to the North Vietnamese army, on May 1, 1975, a day after the fall of Saigon, as North Vietnamese forces moved south.

3

GETTING HERE AND AROUND

Regular flights from Hanoi, Phu Quoc, and Danang City arrive at the Can Tho International Airport, 9 km (5½ miles) from the city center. VietJet and Vietnam Airlines fly to this airport, which only really becomes international when chartered flights arrive, usually during Tet. A taxi to downtown Can Tho will cost around 100,000d. Hung Vuong Bus Station, north of Can Tho's main tourist area, is a regional hub. Buses arrive and depart here from Ho Chi Minh City's Mien Tay bus depot and most Mekong Delta centers, including Chau Doc, Long Xuyen, Vinh Long, and My Tho. The main bus companies operating from here are Phuong Trang and Thanh Buoi.

Can Tho's traffic is not as chaotic as in Ho Chi Minh City but not as calm as in more laid-back places like Phu Quoc or Con Dao. It's not recommended as a place to try driving a motorbike for the first time in Vietnam. Mai Linh operates a fleet of taxis in Can Tho. A daily fee of about 1,500,500d can be negotiated through the operator.

ESSENTIALS

Bus Contact Hung Vuong Bus Station ✉ *1 Hung Vuong* ☎ *0292/3821–475.*

Taxi Contact Mai Linh Taxi ☎ *0292/382-8282.*

TOURS

Mystic Sampans. The most popular Mystic Sampan cruises are the three-hour breakfast tours to visit either the Phung Hiep or the Cai Rang floating markets. Itineraries include stops at interesting places such as a fish sauce factory, a traditional apothecary, or a rice husking mill. The sampans also do sunset cruises and private tours, and the boats are all designed with safety and passenger comfort in mind. ✉ *144 Hai Ba Trung St.* ☎ *0292/382–9540* ⊕ *transmekong.com* ✆ *From: 890,000d for a 3-hr floating market tour.*

EXPLORING

Fodor's Choice ★ **Binh Thuy Ancient House.** One of the very few remaining examples of 19th-century residences in the Mekong Delta, this house has been designated an official national relic by the Ministry of Culture. Built in 1870, the privately owned house is now managed by the sixth generation of the Duong family. The exterior looks French, but the interior is uniquely Vietnamese, and all five rooms are furnished with antiques. The house appeared briefly in the 1992 film *The Lover*, based on the novel of the same name by French author Marguerite Duras, as the ancestral home of her Chinese lover (the actual home of *The Lover* still exists in Sa Dec but at the time of filming it was being used as a government office). ✉ *26/1A Bui Huu Nghia, Binh Thuy* ☎ *0292/382–6395* ✆ *Free* ⊙ *Daily 8–1, 2–5.*

Fodor's Choice ★ **Cai Rang Floating Market** (*Cho Noi Cai Rang*). A bigger market than Phong Dien and used by many wholesalers, Cai Rang is crowded and noisy (with many tourist boats), but still fascinating. The market, about 6 km (4 miles) or 40 minutes by boat from Can Tho, starts trading at around 4 am, in the dark, and is usually finished by 10 am. It really is worth making a super-early start to watch dawn break over the market.

Coffee and breakfast are included in most floating market tours from Can Tho.

Can Tho Museum. A surprisingly interesting museum, with quite a bit of English signage, the Can Tho Museum has a large collection of artifacts from the local region. Displays illustrate the lives of former Chinese and Khmer occupants, and there's a life-size pagoda and a traditional teahouse. ✉ *1 DL Hoa Binh* ☎ *0292/382–0955* 🎟 *Free* ⏲ *Tues.–Thurs. 8–11, 2–5, weekends 8–11, 6:30–9.*

Munirangsyaram Pagoda. This example of a Khmer Hinayana Buddhist pagoda was built in the 1940s to serve and provide spiritual well-being to Can Tho's Khmer community. Access to the interior is limited nowadays, but the pagoda is an emblem of one of the numerous ethnic groups that live side by side in the Mekong Delta. ✉ *36 Hoa Binh* 🎟 *Free.*

Ong Pagoda. This picturesque 19th-century Chinese temple is inside the Guangzhou Assembly Hall, which is next to the redeveloped Ninh Kieu Pier waterfront park. Ong Temple is dedicated to Chinese military leader Kuang Kung (known as Quan Cong in Vietnam). Many of the decorative features of the temple, completed in 1896, were imported from China. ✉ *32 Hai Ba Trung* ☎ *0292/382–3862* 🎟 *Free* ⏲ *Daily 6–9.*

Phong Dien Floating Market. About 20 km (12 miles) southwest of Can Tho, the Phong Dien is one of the most lively and colorful markets and, as an added bonus, less popular with tourists who usually visit the Cai Rang floating market that's closer to Can Tho. The market is best viewed well before 8 am—preferably before dawn. ✉ *Phong Dien.*

WHERE TO EAT

$$ VIETNAMESE

🍴 **Hotpot Alley.** In a hidden alley about 10 minutes from the riverfront, this collection of little local places is the place to come for delicious hotpot, including *lau vit nau chao* (duck hotpot with pickled tofu and taro), a Can Tho specialty. The surroundings are basic and English is almost nonexistent, but the hotpot is fantastic and finding the place is quite an adventure (as is reading some of the translations on the menu). Note: the alley is too small for cars, so you'll have to walk from the main road. It can be accessed through Hem 142 Mau Than; turn left at the intersection of Hem 1 Ly Tu Trong. [$] *Average main: 75000d* ✉ *Hem 1 Ly Tu Trong* 💳 *No credit cards.*

$$$$ FRENCH

🍴 **L'Escale.** The finest dining in town, on a beautiful rooftop terrace overlooking the Hau River, L'Escale serves a mix of French and Vietnamese dishes, accompanied by an extensive wine list and a jazz soundtrack, along with attentive service. The restaurant, in the Nam Bo Boutique Hotel, serves breakfast, lunch, and dinner, but you can also slide into a seat at the bar and enjoy a drink and the view. ■ **TIP→ Time your visit around 5 pm, when the light on the river is the most magical.** [$] *Average main: 400000d* ✉ *Nam Bo Boutique Hotel, 1 Ngo Quyen, 4th fl.* ☎ *0292/381–9139* 🌐 *nambocantho.com/english/escale.*

$$$ VIETNAMESE

🍴 **Nam Bo Restaurant.** Part of the highly acclaimed Nam Bo Boutique Hotel, this all-day café-restaurant serves a variety of traditional Mekong specialties and European staples in a casual French bistro-style setting. For local fare, try the *lau* (a hotpot served with rice noodles, lean pork, seafood, and a pile of vegetables) or, if you're feeling adventurous, the snake set (*menu de serpent* in French). The stylish, artsy interior is complemented by a superb riverfront setting and free Wi-Fi, making it a pleasant spot for a coffee break. Reservations are recommended at peak times, as large tour groups can arrive en masse. $ *Average main: 175000d* ⊠ *Nam Bo Boutique Hotel, 1 Ngo Quyen, Phuong Tan An, Quan Ninh Kieu* ☎ *0292/382–3908* ⊕ *nambocantho.com/english/ restaurant* ⊰ *Reservations essential.*

$ ✕ **Ninh Kieu Night Market.** There are two parts to the night market, one
VIETNAMESE section selling clothes and tourist items and the other serving food from a variety of mobile stalls, with vendors who are well versed in the point-and-nod style of ordering. Most of the food can be munched while strolling and is more of a snack than a meal, but what's on offer can change from day to day, so it's best to just go and see what is available. Food stalls start appearing at around 6 pm each day. $ *Average main: 50000d* ⊠ *Hai Ba Trung* ⊟ *No credit cards.*

$$$ ✕ **Sao Hom.** In a superb riverside setting inside Can Tho's beautiful old
VIETNAMESE market hall, Sao Hom's friendly staff serves a range of Vietnamese and Western favorites, including the local version of *cha gio* (spring rolls). The service and venue are as relaxed as the river flowing by. Just a short walk from Ninh Kieu pier, Sao Hom is a great place to pause before exploring the local market beyond. $ *Average main: 175000d* ⊠ *Old Market Hall, Hai Ba Trung* ☎ *0292/381–5616* ⊕ *saohom.transmekong. com.*

WHERE TO STAY

$$ ⬚ **Green Village Homestay.** Experience local Mekong Delta life from
B&B/INN the comfort of a simple palm-thatched bamboo hut, surrounded by
Fodor's Choice rice paddies and banana trees, at this small friendly family-run home-
★ stay (which is more of a B&B). **Pros:** super-friendly staff; comfortable yet rustic setting. **Cons:** isolated; no air-conditioning in the rooms. $ *Rooms from: 855000d* ⊠ *Xeo Tre, Khanh Binh* ☎ *094/7224–467* ⮐ *6 rooms* ⦿ *Breakfast.*

$ ⬚ **Hotel Xoai.** A budget option outside of Can Tho's riverfront area,
HOTEL Hotel Xoai is a bright mango-yellow (*xoai* means mango) place that takes care of the basic necessities, providing a clean and comfortable place to sleep. **Pros:** great English spoken; elevator; a range of budget tour options. **Cons:** the small rooms are too small to accommodate a wardrobe so things can get very crowded; need to get a taxi or *xe om* to the riverfront tourist area. $ *Rooms from: 300000d* ⊠ *93 Mau Than* ☎ *0292/383–4283* ⊕ *hotelxoai.com* ⮐ *22 rooms* ⊟ *No credit cards* ⦿ *No meals.*

$$$ ⬚ **Iris Hotel.** Though it's outside the riverfront area, this shiny new inter-
HOTEL national-standard hotel has spacious, modern rooms with slick Western-style bathrooms. **Pros:** nice new rooms at a great price; great views from the rooftop bar; fitness center and massage services. **Cons:** the cheapest rooms have no windows; slight business hotel ambiance; loud music from the bar can be heard on some floors. $ *Rooms from: 1200000d* ⊠ *224 30 Thang 4* ☎ *0292/368–6969* ⊕ *www.irishotelcantho.vn* ⮐ *66 rooms, 6 suites* ⦿ *Breakfast.*

$$$$ ⊞ **Nam Bo Boutique Hotel.** Small and personal, this colonial-style hotel
HOTEL   provides a warm and welcoming retreat, with large elegant suites,
Fodor's Choice   friendly staff, great rooftop breakfasts, and many thoughtful little
★   touches, such as local snacks left on the bed, a welcome cocktail, and
a fruit platter. **Pros:** central location; fabulous river views. **Cons:** when
the party boat is cruising the river, the music can be heard in the rooms,
although the cruise finishes at around 9 pm. $ *Rooms from: 2900000d*
⊠ *1 Ngo Quyen, Tan An* ☎ *0292/381–9139* ⊕ *nambocantho.com* ⇨ *7
suites* ⦿ *Breakfast.*

$$$ ⊞ **Ngyen Shack Homestay.** This is a small family-run operation designed
B&B/INN   to give guests an off-the-beaten-track experience from the home base of
Fodor's Choice   a cute little bamboo shack over the Ong Tim River. **Pros:** lovely friendly
★   atmosphere with hosts who really want to showcase Mekong Delta life.
Cons: steep ladder leading to the bungalows could present problems
for people with mobility issues; no air-conditioning in rooms; isolated
(6 km/4 miles from Can Tho). $ *Rooms from: 1050000d* ⊠ *Ong Tim
Bridge, Thanh My, Cai Rang* ☎ *096/6550–016* ⊕ *www.nguyenshack.
com/cantho* ⇨ *5 rooms* ⦿ *Breakfast.*

$$$$ ⊞ **Victoria Can Tho Resort.** Built in a style befitting French colonial times,
RESORT   the Victoria Can Tho Resort comes replete with teak balustrades, hard-
wood floors, and bamboo ceiling fans. **Pros:** exemplary service; elegant
rooms with all modern conveniences; excellent restaurant. **Cons:** a little
isolated. $ *Rooms from: 3408000d* ⊠ *Cai Khe Ward, Ninh Kieu Dis-
trict* ☎ *0292/381–0111* ⊕ *www.victoriahotels.asia* ⇨ *84 rooms, 8 suites*
⦿ *Breakfast.*

SHOPPING

Old Market Hall. Can Tho's renovated old market, built in 1915, contains
dozens of kiosks selling tourist-oriented items, including handicrafts,
carvings, lanterns, silk items, and food souvenirs. ⊠ *Hai Ba Trung St.*

TRA VINH

*200 km (124 miles) southeast of Ho Chi Minh City, 82 km (51 miles)
from Can Tho.*

Tra Vinh is a pretty little riverside town populated by friendly people,
tall trees, and an amazing proliferation of temples used by the local
Khmer and Chinese communities, as well as the dominant Vietnamese.
In addition to pagodas, there's an eerily beautiful square pond outside
of town, another relic of the Khmer kingdom that once ruled this area.
Making the effort to visit this town, which welcomes few foreign tour-
ists, can be a very rewarding experience.

GETTING HERE AND AROUND

It takes about 4½ hours by bus from Ho Chi Minh City's Mien Tay bus
station to Tra Vinh's bus depot, on the town's southern edge. There are
a couple of local taxi companies in town, including Tra Vinh Taxi and
the silver Taxi Thanh Thuy. Ask your hotel to help call a taxi.

ESSENTIALS

Bus Contact **Tra Vinh Bus Station** ⊠ *559 QL 54* ☎ *0294/384–0324*

HISTORY AND CULTURE OF THE DELTA

Early settlement and ethnic disputes

The region was first mentioned in Chinese scholarly works as a part of the ancient kingdom of Funan. The Funan civilization was influenced by Hindu and Buddhist cultures and flourished between the 1st and 5th centuries AD. The Mekong Delta was settled by the Cham and the Khmer in the 7th century and was annexed by the Khmer civilization based at Angkor between the 9th and 10th centuries. Some Vietnamese settlers lived in the area even under Khmer rule, but with the defeat of the Cham in the late 15th century, more Vietnamese moved south. In the 17th century some of the Chinese fleeing one of the many northern dynastic autocrats appeared in the Mekong Delta. The Tay Son Rebellion in the late 18th century brought even more Vietnamese into the region. Allegiances were based on ethnicity—Cham, Khmer, Vietnamese, and so on—rather than on nationality. And there was feuding: the Khmer believed that over the centuries the Vietnamese had taken away their land, and they wanted it back.

20th-century conflict

French colonialism briefly put a stop to the disputes—and later contributed to them. The French encouraged the Vietnamese and the Chinese, who were much more commercially driven than the Khmer, to continue settling here. As more Vietnamese moved south, more Khmer left. Uncertainty over who would have sovereignty over the Mekong Delta lasted until 1954, when the French bequeathed the area to the new country of South Vietnam. Under Pol Pot's rule in Cambodia, the Khmer again laid claim to the delta as their ancestral land, and there were frequent skirmishes between Khmer Rouge and Vietnamese soldiers along the border.

During the Japanese occupation in the 1940s, colonial French and Vietnamese families fled from farther north to avoid the fighting. But the fighting eventually spread to the Mekong Delta, and these refugees were forced to fan out into the previously uninhabited mangrove swamps, hacking them down as they went.

A modern melting pot

Today the Mekong Delta is still populated by several cultures. The majority of people living in the area are Vietnamese, with the Khmer comprising the second-largest ethnic group. Nearly 2 million Khmer people live in the vicinity of the city of Soc Trang and on the Cambodian border, and the Mekong Delta is still often referred to as Khmer Krom by Cambodians. A small number of Cham also live close to the Cambodian border, but these Cham, unlike their counterparts in the central highlands, are not Hindu but Muslim. Malay and Javanese traders who skirted the coast several hundred years ago converted the southern Cham to Islam. The Cham groups don't really mix with each other. The cultural diversity of the region accounts for the variety of religions practiced: Buddhism, Catholicism, Cao Daism, and Islam. Your travels throughout the delta will take you past examples of their remarkable coexistence.

Taxi Contacts **Taxi Thanh Thuy** ☎ *0294/386–8686.* **Tra Vinh Taxi**
☎ *0294/386–4374.*

EXPLORING

Ang Pagoda (*Angkorajaborey Pagoda*). Originally built in the 10th century, Ang Pagoda has been rebuilt and restored several times. Set in on 4 hectares (10 acres) among ancient trees, the pagoda still retains its beautiful Khmer architecture. Ang Pagoda is 5 km (3 miles) from the center of Tra Vinh, a short walk from Ao Ba Om pond, and right across the road from the Khmer Culture Museum. ⊠ *Off Nguyen Du.*

Ao Ba Om. A relic of the glory days of the Khmer civilization, Ao Ba Om, which poetically translates as "square pond," is now a peaceful and serene body of water surrounded by tall trees. The pond, about 5 km (3 miles) from Tra Vinh, is a nice place to visit in the early morning, when the mists make the area seem even more romantic. Combine your exploration of the the pond with visits to the nearby Ang Pagoda and Khmer Cultural Museum. ⊠ *Off Nugyen Du.*

Hang Pagoda (*Chua Hang, Stork Pagoda, Kompom Chray*). This Khmer temple was built in 1637, and the tall trees on its 2-hectare (5-acre) grounds are home to a small school and hundreds of storks, explaining one of its nicknames—Stork Pagoda. The pagoda, about 5 km (3 miles) from Tra Vinh, is also known as Cave Pagoda because of its cavelike entrance, as well as by its Khmer name of Kompom Chray (banyan tree wharf). It was once also called Bat Pagoda but bombing in 1968 scared the bats away and they've never returned. The monks here are famous for their woodworking skills and the intricate bonsai garden they tend while not studying, praying, and chanting. ■ TIP→ **Hang Pagoda is best visited in the late afternoon when the birds come home to roost, but try not to stand under a tree because the bird droppings come down like rain.** ⊠ *End of Dien Bien Phu.*

Museum of Khmer Culture. Housed in a blocky concrete building across the road from Ang Pagoda, the Khmer Culture Museum reopened in mid-2014 after a two-year renovation. The museum has four exhibition rooms containing re-creations of various aspects of traditional Khmer life, as well as collections of musical instruments and farming tools. All signs are in Vietnamese and Khmer. It's not the most interesting museum, but worth dropping by if you're just across the road anyway. ⊠ *Off Nguyen Du* 🎫 *Free* ☉ *Daily 7–11, 1–5.*

Ong Met Pagoda. A Khmer temple has stood in this spot since 711 and the beautiful complex, also known as Bodhisalaraja, is now the center of Khmer spiritual life in Tra Vinh. A library with unique wooden features was added in 1916. The monks here are quite friendly and sometimes like to practice speaking English with male tourists. ⊠ *50/1 Le Loi.*

Ong Pagoda (*Phuoc Minh Palace*). A centuries-old Chinese pagoda that's undergone a 20th-century renovation, Ong Pagoda, or Phuoc Minh Palace, is an important cultural and spiritual meeting place for Tra Vinh's Chinese community. The interior is shaped like the Chinese character for earth and the exterior represents the character for water, and throughout the pagoda mythical characters abound (some in front of a very pretty patch of artificial lawn). Every year on the 15th day

CLOSE UP

Floating Markets of the Mekong Delta

Before the modern roads and bridges were built, land travel here was difficult, and virtually impossible during the annual flooding season. This reliance on riverine life continues, with waterborne commerce, including several lively floating markets, an everyday occurrence.

Flying the flag of commerce

The unique feature of the Mekong Delta's floating produce markets is how the vendors advertise their wares—by running a sample up the flagpole. This means buyers aren't forced to waste time peering into the dark hulls of boats; if they're in search of pineapples, they just row or chug over to a vessel that's raised one of these fruits aloft. The abundance of the Mekong Delta is most apparent at these floating markets, where boats large and small are laden with coconuts, pineapples, pomelos, flowers, bananas, longans, onions, leafy greens, mangoes, and dragonfruit. Narrow boats, mostly rowed by women, wend their way through the market looking for good deals or offering coffee or food to those boat-bound. In the background, goods are transferred from seller to buyer in the time-honored tradition of throwing things from boat to boat. These markets provide a fascinating glimpse into lives lived aboard relatively small boats.

Visiting a market

A visit to a floating market requires a certain amount of dedication. Their predawn start and early morning finish makes a day trip impossible to do from Ho Chi Minh City, although many travel agents will happily sell you such a tour and ignore your disappointment when you arrive at a virtually deserted stretch of river. The exception is the Cai Be floating market, which, because it's a wholesale market, operates for longer during the day, so it can be worth taking a trip here with one of the Ho Chi Minh City operators. Sadly, though, this market is a shadow of its former self because it's become easier to transport goods from here to Ho Chi Minh City by road. It's still better to access the Cai Be floating market from Vinh Long or Cai Be itself than from Ho Chi Minh City.

Sunrise tours

Most floating markets are best viewed at sunrise, so an overnight stop in Can Tho is advised. Can Tho–based tour companies usually set out on floating market tours between 5 and 7 am. Two of the bigger, livelier markets are close to Can Tho—the Phong Dien and Cai Rang floating markets. Cai Rang is just 6 km (4 miles) from Can Tho's main pier and Phong Dien is 20 km (12 miles) away. It's possible to visit both markets during one morning tour.

of the first lunar month, this colorful pagoda hosts the Nguyen Tieu Festival, which marks the first full moon of the lunar new year. ✉ *44 Dien Binh Phu.*

WHERE TO EAT

$ ✕ **Bun Nuoc Leo.** This basic street food outlet serves a great version of
VIETNAMESE   the local specialty, *bun nuoc leo,* a murky pork noodle soup. Foreign patrons can expect celebrity treatment at this place, with extra plates

of spring rolls, fried prawn cakes, and banana-leaf-wrapped roast pork offered, along with wide smiles. Don't worry—if you don't eat any of the extras, you don't have to pay (but they are very good). $ *Average main: 30000d ⊠ 48 Ly Thuong Kiet ☎ 0294/627–2433 ▭ No credit cards.*

$$$ ✕ **Phuong Hoang Restaurant.** An eccentric tourist restaurant catering to
VIETNAMESE   domestic travelers, Phuong Hoang can be quite the experience, whether you choose to dine in a thatched hut, the fake floating restaurant, or the dining area that's in a giant cement reproduction of a helicopter cabin (minus rotor and skids). The menu offers a range of traditional Vietnamese dishes and a host of local specialties, such as bat, snake, and field mouse. The staff has limited English, but the restaurant does have one English menu, which makes things easier. An abandoned-looking children's playground fronts the complex, but keep walking until you see the huts. $ *Average main: 160000d ⊠ Hwy. 60, just west of Hwy. 52 turnoff ☎ 0294/379–8868 ▭ No credit cards.*

$$ ✕ **Quan An Dong Khoi.** For a truly local dining experience, make your
VIETNAMESE   way to this thatched hut in someone's back garden. The staff speaks no English and there's no English menu, but if you point and order the house specialties you won't go wrong. Try *cha gio hai sang Hong Kong*—seafood spring rolls, with lots of mayonnaise inside—and *lau Dong Khoi*, a regional kimchi–flavored seafood hotpot served with lots of vegetables. The other specialty is *ga quay lu*, a whole roast chicken (served complete with the head and feet), but this takes an hour to prepare. $ *Average main: 130000d ⊠ Dong Khoi ☎ 0294/374–0840 ▭ No credit cards.*

WHERE TO STAY

$ ⊡ **Cuu Long Hotel.** The three-star Cuu Long Hotel is the best place in
HOTEL   town, and it does seem quite fancy compared to the other options. **Pros:** rooms are quite large. **Cons:** the location isn't the best; popular with tour groups. $ *Rooms from: 480000d ⊠ 999 Nguyen Thi Minh Khai ☎ 0294/3862–615 ⇗ 53 rooms* ◎| *No meals.*

$ ⊡ **Thanh Binh 1 Hotel.** Basic but spacious, clean, and functional, with
HOTEL   dark-wood furniture and Vietnamese-style bathrooms, the pastel-blue four-story Thanh Binh 1 Hotel, which opened in 2013, is a good budget choice. **Pros:** cheap and clean. **Cons:** very little English is spoken here. $ *Rooms from: 300000d ⊠ 199 Nguyen Thi Minh Khai St. ☎ 0294/626–6789 ⇗ 38 rooms* ◎| *No meals.*

SOC TRANG

63 km (39 miles) southeast of Can Tho.

Soc Trang is one of the centers of Khmer culture in Vietnam (the others are Tra Vinh in the Mekong Delta and Nha Trang on the south-central coast). The town itself is unremarkable and the dining and accommodations options are limited, but it does have several interesting Khmer temples. This was once a provincial capital of the Angkor Empire, which covered much of Indochina from the 9th to the 15th century. Vietnamese settlers did not appear here until the 17th century; later, in colonial times, they were encouraged to come by the French, who sought to develop agricultural production in the region.

GETTING HERE AND AROUND

If you're in a car coming from Tra Vinh, you will need to backtrack to Can Tho to get to Soc Trang, but if you're traveling by motorbike, there's a motorbike-only river ferry. Buses run regularly from Can Tho to Soc Trang, most continuing on to Ca Mau. Soc Trang Bus Station is in the city's south, but most bus companies set down passengers on the side of the highway on the outskirts of town. Xe om drivers congregate at the bus stopping area, where there's a small stall selling drinks. The main bus companies serving Soc Trang are Phuong Trang and Hoang Vinh. The ever-present Mai Linh taxi company has a fleet in Soc Trang, and there's also a local company, Soc Trang Taxis. Expect to pay around 500,000d to hire a taxi for a day to see the local sights.

ESSENTIALS

Bus Contact Soc Trang Bus Station ✉ *Le Duan* ☎ *0299/362–1777.*

Taxi Contacts Mai Linh Taxi ☎ *0299/386–8868.* **Soc Trang Taxis** ☎ *0299/383–8383.*

EXPLORING

China Bowl Pagoda (*Xa Lon, Chen Kieu and Srolon*). Twelve kilometers (7 miles) outside Soc Trang, in the village of Dai Tan, this is the largest Khmer pagoda and religious school (for novice monks) in the area. The original pagoda, built in 1815, was destroyed during the Vietnam War and was restored in 1969 using China bowls and plates—hence the name. The garden has several thatched huts in which pilgrims can meditate and a lively little market operates in front of the pagoda gates. ✉ *QL1A, Dai Tam, My Xuyen.*

Clay Pagoda (*Dat Set Pagoda, Buu Son Tu*). This is a vibrant Vietnamese temple that was built more than 200 years ago by a Chinese family called Ngo. A descendant, Ngo Kim Tong, who died in 1970, spent 42 years fashioning the pagoda's brightly colored statues, dragons, and gargoyles. Inside are candles so big and so broad—each about 12 meters (40 feet) high and so wide that two people extending their arms around it can barely reach each other—that have been burning continuously for more than 40 years. ✉ *286 Ton Duc Thang.*

Khmer Museum. In a large stucco French-Khmer colonial-style building, originally built as a Khmer school in the 19th century, the museum's collection includes Khmer statues and clothing, antique pots and utensils, and two long and colorful racing boats. During the French-Indochina War the building served as the headquarters for the local French militia, and during the Vietnam War it was a headquarters for American troops. ✉ *23 Nguyen Chi Thanh* ☎ *0299/382–2983* 🎫 *Free* 🕑 *Tues.– Sun. 8–4:30.*

Kleang Pagoda. The beautiful Khmer pagoda and nearby communal longhouse and meditation center are off the road behind graceful palm groves and huge banana trees. The richly worked interior of the pagoda houses extensive gilded wood carvings. Originally constructed in the 16th century, the pagoda was rebuilt in the French-Khmer style at the turn of the 20th century. It's an almost ethereal photo opportunity if you can snap monks posing in the foreground. ⊠ *Nguyen Chi Thanh.*

Matoc Pagoda (*Bat Pagoda, Chua Doi*). Legend has it that about 400 years ago Khmer monks constructed this pagoda, 3 km (2 miles) from Soc Trang, to honor the flying foxes (a type of bat) that live in the surrounding fruit trees. In Buddhism bats are considered sacred and, above all else, lucky. Strangely, the bats don't eat the fruit of the trees on which they live but feed on fruit trees several miles away. The best time to see these nocturnal creatures is dawn or dusk. A fire severely damaged the interior of the temple in 2010 and it took two years for resoration work to be completed. Keep an eye out for the graves of five-hoofed pigs behind the temple; these creatures are believed to be bad luck so are given to the temple to be cared for until their death. ⊠ *Van Ngoc Chinh.*

WHERE TO EAT AND STAY

$ | **✕ Café Que Toi.** Offering very basic Vietnamese café fare, such as stir-
VIETNAMESE | fried noodles, pork and rice, and baguettes, this café associated with the Que Toi Hotel is a place more for satisfying hunger pangs than enjoying fine dining. Like most Vietnamese cafés, it's a place for people to meet, drink coffee, and smoke cigarettes. On the plus side, it has an English menu, which most places in town don't have. $ *Average main: 50000d* ⊠ *278 Phu Loi.*

$ | **▦ Minh Phuong Hotel.** Clean and serviceable, Minh Phuong is a reason-
HOTEL | able choice for one or two nights. **Pros:** reception staff speaks some English. **Cons:** karaoke can be heard in some of the rooms. $ *Rooms from: 280000d* ⊠ *294 Phu Loi* ☎ *079/364–5888* ⊕ *www.hotelminhphuong. com* ⤳ *17 rooms* ▤ *No credit cards* ⦿| *Breakfast.*

$ | **▦ Que Toi Hotel.** The big selling point of the three-star Que Toi Hotel is
HOTEL | its large airy rooms and on-site swimming pool. **Pros:** a dip in the pool can be just the ticket after a long hot day of sightseeing. **Cons:** rooms are a bit plain; can be noisy. $ *Rooms from: 290000d* ⊠ *278 Phu Loi* ☎ *0796/278278, 0793/815815* ⊕ *quetoi.com.vn* ⤳ *50 rooms, 5 suites* ▤ *No credit cards* ⦿| *No meals.*

$ | **▦ Tin Hoa Hotel.** Soc Trang's newest hotel has light and spacious rooms
HOTEL | with pine furniture, fancy wallpaper, silver blackout curtains, and a grand view of the People's Committee building across the road. **Pros:** brand-spanking new, neat and clean. **Cons:** staff speaks very little English. $ *Rooms from: 360000d* ⊠ *50C Phu Loi* ☎ *0299/363–7788* ⊕ *www.tinhoahotel.com* ⤳ *31 rooms* ⦿| *No meals.*

CA MAU

116 km (72 miles) southwest of Soc Trang, 360 km (224 miles) southwest of Ho Chi Minh City.

Ca Mau was once part of the Kingdom of Funan, then the Khmer Empire, and was only ceded back to Vietnamese control in 1757. On the Dai Dong River at the Phung Hiep Canal, some 50 km (31 miles) from the South China Sea, it is the capital of Vietnam's southernmost province. Not many tourists make it this far down into the Mekong Delta, and this shows in the lack of foreigner-friendly infrastructure and English language skills. The lure of sprawling Ca Mau is not the city itself, but the birdlife within the nearby cajeput (paperbark) and mangrove forests, and access to Vietnam's southernmost point within the Mui Ca Mau National Park.

GETTING HERE AND AROUND

Ca Mau Airport is about 3 km (2 miles) from the center of town. Vietnam Aviation Service Company (VASCO) operates one flight a day each way between Ho Chi Minh City and Ca Mau. Expect to pay around 40,000d to get from the airport to the city center in a taxi. Ca Mau is pretty much the end of the line for bus service from Can Tho and Ho Chi Minh City. The main bus companies are Phuong Trang and Kumho Samco, and they drop off at the main bus depot, near the airport on the eastern outskirts of town. Mai Linh taxis operate in Ca Mau and Ca Mau Taxi is also usually pretty reliable.

ESSENTIALS

Bus Contact Ca Mau Bus Station ⊠ *Ly Thuong Kiet* ☎ *0290/383–1723.*

Taxi Contact Ca Mau Taxi ☎ *0290/383–7837.* **Mai Linh Taxi** ☎ *0290/378–7878.*

EXPLORING

Bac Lieu Bird Sanctuary (*Vuon chim Bac Lieu*). In a mangrove forest about 5 km (3 miles) from the township of Bac Lieu is a large bird sanctuary that is home to 46 species of birds, including the endangered painted stork and small king cormorant. An estimated 40,000 birds live here, within a 385-hectare (951-acre) mangrove ecosystem. The best time to visit is when the birds nest during the rainy season between May and October. Time a visit for dawn or dusk, when thousands of birds take to the skies. ⊠ *Cao Van Lau, Bac Lieu* ☎ *0291/383–5991.*

Ca Mau Market. The wet market here is small, but a bustling hive of activity from early in the morning to dusk. Few foreign tourists visit Ca Mau, so expect a lot of attention if you walk through. ⊠ *Phan Chu Trinh.*

City Bird Park (*Lam vien 19/5*). This pretty 18 hectare (45-acre) park is divided into two sections: a large park with walking paths, a lake and an ancient-style house; and a fenced bird sanctuary, which—sadly—contains many caged birds. The park is a popular spot for wedding photos and the bird sanctuary is a great place to watch thousands of birds, including some rare species, coming home to roost in the late afternoon. ⊠ *Corner of Ngo Quyen and So 1 Sts.*

Mui Ca Mau National Park. This 42-hectare (104-acre) mangrove forest, which stretches to Vietnam's southern-most point, was recognized as a UNESCO World Biosphere Reserve in 2009. Ca Mau Cape National Park is home to many rare and endangered birds, animals, and reptiles. The national park is 110 km (68 miles) from Ca Mau City, about two hours by speedboat. No organized tours visit the park (at the time of writing), but it is possible to hire a speed boat to take you there. This should be arranged well in advance of arriving in Ca Mau (preferably from Ho Chi Minh City) and should include the services of an English-speaking guide. Arrangements can be made through Exo Travel (*028/3519–4111; www.exotravel.com*) in Ho Chi Minh City.

✉ *Dat Mui Commune, Ngoc Hien District* ☎ *0290/387–0545* 🌐 *www.vietnamnationalparks.org* 🎟 *10,000d* 🕒 *Daily 7–5.*

U Minh Cajeput Forest. The vast U Minh Cajeput Forest, 35 km (22 miles) from Ca Mau, contains swathes of swampland and pearl-white cajeput trees, also known as melaleuca or paperbark trees. A boat trip through the forest is breathtaking and eerily quiet. There are several "ecotourism" ventures in the forest, primarily in the Vo Voi area, which cater to domestic tourists rather than international visitors. Nevertheless, a visit can be interesting, but it's best organized well before arriving in Ca Mau. ✉ *Khánh Lâm Commune* ☎ *0290/391–0029* 🎟 *10,000d* 🕒 *Daily 7–5.*

WHERE TO EAT AND STAY

$$ VIETNAMESE 🍴 **Huong Viet.** Popular with locals, this restaurant is designed to look like a bamboo village hut, and is a bit of a point-and-order eating adventure for visitors—the menu has no English, only a few photos on each page that vaguely correspond to the dishes listed below. The menu offers seafood, salad, beef, chicken, sparrow (*chim se*), and hotpot. Luckily the prices are so low it doesn't really matter if you mis-order a few dishes. [$] *Average main: 150000d* ✉ *126 Phan Ngoc Hien* ☎ *0290/365–9999* 💳 *No credit cards.*

$$ VIETNAMESE Fodor's Choice ★ 🍴 **Pho Xua.** This is a great find in Ca Mau, with nostalgic style (the name translates as "ancient street"), including quaint little wooden pavilions, a courtyard bonsai garden, and fish ponds. Serving Chinese-influenced dishes as well as Vietnamese cuisine, the menu contains English subtitles, although not much English is spoken by the staff. With its proximity to the ocean, it's no wonder that seafood is the house specialty, but there's also a range of chicken, beef, buffalo, and pork dishes. [$] *Average main: 150000d* ✉ *239 Phan Ngoc Hien, Phuong 9* ☎ *0290/356–6666* 💳 *No credit cards.*

$ HOTEL 🏨 **Anh Nguyet Hotel.** The pick of Ca Mau's hotels, Anh Nguyet has spacious carpeted rooms with all the creature comforts. **Pros:** English language ability of the reception staff; clean and comfortable, which is not guaranteed in this part of the world. **Cons:** on-site karaoke can be loud, as can wedding parties held downstairs. [$] *Rooms from: 490000d* ✉ *207 Phan Ngoc Hien* ☎ *0290/356–7666* 🌐 *www.anhnguyethotel.com* 🛏 *82 rooms, 1 suite* 🍽 *Breakfast.*

$ HOTEL 🏨 **Dong Anh Hotel.** Small and serviceable, with heavy wooden furniture, Vietnamese-style bathrooms, and a central location, this is nevertheless a hotel for Vietnamese businessmen (who tend to smoke a lot). **Pros:** central location, within walking distance of local cafés and food stalls. **Cons:** very little English spoken; can be noisy [$] *Rooms from: 350000d* ✉ *25 Tran Hung Dao* ☎ *0290/356–6777* 🌐 *donganhhotel.com.vn* 🛏 *37 rooms* 🍽 *No meals.*

4

THE SOUTH-CENTRAL
COAST & HIGHLANDS

Updated by
Barbara Adam

Vietnam's South Central Coast and Central Highlands have long seduced travelers with contrasting attractions. The allure of coastal towns, with their long beaches and clear warm waters, is a world away from the region's cool misty highlands, with their pine forests, flower farms, and ethnic minority villages. Traveling by road or rail through this region takes you through stunning scenery: long white beaches; vibrant emerald rice paddies; Dr. Seuss–like dragonfruit farms; eerie salt farms; vivid green rice paddies; rolling hills; beautiful valleys; and many exotic temples.

The fishing village of Phan Thiet and the resort town of Mui Ne are the first major coastal centers when heading north from Ho Chi Minh City. Although near-neighbors, the two towns are vastly different: Phan Thiet is a hive of local activity, with a picturesque fishing fleet and some cheap-and-cheerful seafood joints, while Mui Ne is a strip of resorts fronting a narrow and often windy beach, popular with kitesurfers. Further north is Nha Trang, with its stunning crescent beach, islands, and established tourist infrastructure, including many luxurious five-star resorts, an enticing mix of eateries, and a picturesque new island golf course.

High in the mountains, where the air is crisp and cool, is Dalat, "Le Petite Paris," founded by the French in the early 1900s as an escape from the hot and steamy lowlands of Vietnam. The Central Highlands' biggest city still draws visitors from all over Vietnam—and the rest of the world. They come to enjoy the mountain air, the views, the cool-climate produce, and the French colonial feel the city still retains.

For those seeking adventure and insights into Vietnam's fascinating ethnic minorities, Dalat can be the starting point for a deeper exploration of the Central Highlands, including the scenic Lak Lake, home to Vietnam's elephant hunters (now retired), the coffee capital Buon Ma Thuot, the tiny town of Pleiku where fierce fighting raged during the last war, and the pretty riverside town of Kon Tum, a great base for treks to hill tribe villages.

Between Ho Chi Minh City and Dalat, at the base of the Central Highlands, is the Cat Tien National Park, home to gibbons, sun bears, and many other rare animals and birds. North of Nha Trang, on the coast, lies sleepy Quy Nhon, a destination for those seeking an off-the-beaten-path beach break.

Just outside the coastal town of Quang Ngai lies a sobering reminder of the savage toll war often exacts on the innocent: the Son My Memorial, erected in memory of the victims of the My Lai massacre.

TOP REASONS TO GO

Nha Trang beach break: Nha Trang's stretches of white-sand beaches are ideal for strolling and the warm waters are perfect for swimming, especially near Bai Dai Beach, where a string of food stalls sell the day's catch with a bucket of beer.

Dalat, Le Petite Paris: Head to the former French hill station of Dalat for long walks, a visit to Emperor Bao Dai's summer palace, and fascinating temples.

Mui Ne resort hideaway: Pamper yourself at one of Mui Ne's many five-star resorts, emerging only to view the spectacular colored sand dunes at sunset or try your hand at kite surfing.

Coffee: Buon Ma Thout in the Central Highlands is Vietnam's coffee capital, and fantastic local coffee is available all through the region, from the tiniest roadside shack to the fanciest cafés. The local brew is so strong it's usually served in shot glasses.

Hill Tribes: With a little more time, you can include a trip to the rugged mountainous area around Pleiku and Kon Tum to visit the villages of Vietnam's hill tribes. Head out to Lak Lake where the M'Nong people offer elephant rides on the giant beasts they used to hunt many years ago.

ORIENTATION AND PLANNING

GETTING ORIENTED

The neighboring coastal towns of Pan Thiet and Mui Ne take five to six hours to reach by car from Ho Chi Minh City. Further north along the coast is Nha Trang, a short flight from Ho Chi Minh City and an easy overnight train journey. From Nha Trang, many head farther north toward Hoi An, a trip that can be broken at the small beach town of Quy Nhon or, farther north, the Son My Memorial near Quang Ngai. West of Nha Trang, along windy mountain roads that lead to the cool Central Highlands, is the former French hill station of Dalat and the ethnic minority villages in the remote regions around Buon Ma Thuot, Pleiku, and Kon Tum. It's possible to skip some of the arduous road journeys through this region by flying into Dalat, Buon Ma Thuot, or Pleiku from Ho Chi Minh City or Hanoi.

The Southern Coast. The resort town of Mui Ne is the preferred beach getaway for expats living in Ho Chi Minh City, as well as a destination for thousands of international visitors seeking a beach break. For those interested in local life, Phan Thiet is a great place to explore and people-watch.

Nha Trang. The natural wonders of Nha Trang, which sits between a beautiful bay with warm, clear water studded with islands and green-clad mountains can be enjoyed by swimming, scuba diving, relaxing on the palm-lined beach, or exploring local waterfalls. More indulgent activities can be undertaken at the many resorts that overlook the bay.

The Central Highlands. Dalat, 1,500 meters above sea level, was founded in the early 1900s as a "sanatorium," or health retreat, for the French elite and remains a popular destination for local and international visitors. It is also the gateway to the Central Highlands, home to many ethnic minorities, dense jungle, waterfalls, and picturesque scenery. The towns of Buon Ma Thuot, Pleiku, and Kontum make good bases for exploration.

North of Nha Trang. Heading north from Nha Trang by rail or road takes you past some picturesque scenery, including glimpses of lovely long white beaches, rocky coves, green-clad mountains, and bucolic countryside scenes. Quy Nhon is a quiet seaside town that's a great place to break the long journey between Nha Trang and Hoi An.

PLANNING

WHEN TO GO

The best time to visit Nha Trang is between April and September, during the dry season. It rains frequently in October, and November and can be chilly. With a temperate climate, Dalat is worth visiting any time of the year but provides the most relief from June through August, when the rest of the country is sweltering. Avoid visiting the coastal regions between October and mid-December during monsoon season.

GETTING HERE AND AROUND

AIR TRAVEL

Cam Ranh International Airport is 30 km (18 miles) from Nha Trang, Flights between Nha Trang and Ho Chi Minh City take 45 minutes. There are several flights a day to Dalat's Lien Khuong Airport from Ho Chi Minh City, Hanoi, and Vinh. Buon Ma Thuot is served from Ho Chi Minh City, Hanoi, and Danang, Vinh, and Haiphong. The former U.S. airbase at Pleiku is now the Pleiku Airport, which welcomes several flights a day from Ho Chi Minh City and Hanoi, and one flight a day from Danang. Quy Nhon has direct flights between from Ho Chi Minh City and Hanoi.

Airport Contacts Cam Ranh International Airport ⊠ *Nha Trang* ⊕ *www.nhatrangairport.com* .**Lien Khuong Airport** ⊠ *Lien Khuong, Dalat* ☏ *0263/3843–373* ⊕ *vietnamairport.vn.* **Phu Cat Airport (Quy Nhon)** ⊠ *1 Nguyen Tat Thanh St., Quy Nhon* ☏ *0256/3537–500* ⊕ *vietnamairport.vn*

BUS TRAVEL

Daily buses run between Nha Trang and Ho Chi Minh (with a stop in Mui Ne). The nine-hour trip costs around 200,000d. Several buses head north to Hanoi, with stops in Hoi An and Hue, or inland to Dalat by connecting in Phan Rang. The trip between Nha Trang and Hoi An takes about 10 hours and costs 125,000d. Sleeper buses have bunk beds, but the incessant honking and reckless driving are bound to keep you awake all night. Bus tickets are sold at all tour offices in central Nha Trang. The northern station services towns in the Central Highlands, including Buon Ma Thuot and Quang Ngai. From the southern station, buses depart for major centers throughout Vietnam, including points south to Ho Chi Minh City, north to Hanoi, and west to the Central

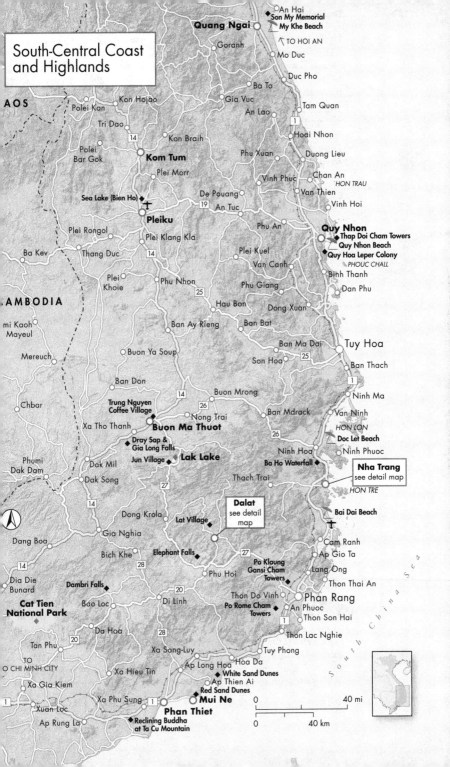

Highlands. Buses also run regularly between Dalat and Ho Chi Minh City, taking seven to nine hours during the daytime and a much speedier (and scarier) six hours by overnight bus. If you opt for an overnight bus, double-check it has sleeper beds rather than seats. A luxury coach between Dalat and Ho Chi Minh City costs 125,000d.

Bus Contacts Mai Linh Express ☎ *0263/3521-111.* **North Nha Trang bus station** ✉ *1 St. 2/4, Nha Trang* ☎ *0258/3838-799.* **Phuong Trang bus company** ✉ *274–276 De Tham, Ho Chi Minh City* ☎ *028/3830-9309* ⊕ *www. futabuslines.com.vn* **South Nha Trang Bus Station** ✉ *58 Ba Thang Hai St., Nha Trang* ☎ *0258/3822-192.***Thanh Buoi bus company** ✉ *266–268 Le Hong Phong St., Ho Chi Minh City* ☎ *028/38308-090* ⊕ *www.thanhbuoi.com.vn.*

CAR TRAVEL

Hiring a private driver will cost you about 1,000,000d per day and is best arranged through your hotel tour desk. Taxis are much easier to organize for mid-range trips, with taxi company operators able to quote set fees for certain routes. For example, the mountainous and winding 140-km (87-mile) journey from Nha Trang to Dalat, which takes about four hours, costs 1,200,000d in a four-seater Mai Linh taxi and 1,635,000d in a seven-seater Mai Linh taxi. From Dalat, Lak Lake is an easy 150-km (93-mile) drive, again along some winding mountain roads, which often provide stunning views of verdant valleys. Lak Lake to Buon Ma Thuot is another easy drive, again through very pretty countryside. Past Buon Ma Thuot, roadworks are ongoing for vast stretches of the road to Pleiku. Once complete, the road should be a breeze to negotiate. Check the status with a taxi company operator.

TRAIN TRAVEL

The Reunification Express runs five times a day between Ho Chi Minh City and Hanoi, stopping at four train stations in the South Central Coast region: Binh Thuan (you can take a taxi from here to Phan Thiet or Mui Ne); Nha Trang; Dieu Tri (10 km [6 miles] from Quy Nhon); and Quang Nghia. From Ho Chi Minh City, the train takes about 3½ hours to Binh Thuan, another four hours to Nha Trang, just under four hours from Nha Trang to Dieu Tri in Quy Nhon, and just under three hours from Dieu Tri to Quang Ngai. A separate twice-daily train service runs between Ho Chi Minh City and Phan Thiet, which takes about 3½ hours and costs around 180,000d. Tickets can be purchased online (⊕ *vietnam-railway.com*) and at train stations, but by far the easiest option is to ask your hotel to arrange tickets, rather than a travel agent. It's best to book several days in advance to ensure you get a comfortable seat or bed (go for soft every time), and there's usually a small fee—44,000d or less—to get your tickets delivered to your hotel.

Golden Express Train. This is a privately owned carriage that attaches to the Reunification Express train on the overnight route between Ho Chi Minh City and Nha Trang. The carriage contains one one-berth VIP cabin (760,000d per person), six four-berth cabins (680,000d per person), and a small restaurant. The Golden Express Train departs Saigon daily at 8:30 pm and arrives in Nha Trang at 5:30 am the following day. In the opposite direction, it leaves Nha Trang at 7 pm and arrives in Ho Chi Minh City at 4 am. ✉ *6th fl., 57–59 Ho Tung Mau, Ho Chi Minh City* ☎ *028/3825–7636* ⊕ *golden-train.com.*

RESTAURANTS

Nha Trang is famous for its seafood, which can be enjoyed local-style, in a noisy shack surrounded by beer-chugging Vietnamese, or in more sophisticated surrounds, in a resortlike setting overlooking the beach. The tourist-oriented town also has numerous international restaurants. Outside of Nha Trang, dining options are more basic; seafood is still the specialty along the coast but in the Central Highlands, the focus is on the locally grown vegetables and free-range village-raised chicken and pork. Local specialties are candied fruit, jam, artichoke tea, and Dalat wine. Beyond Dalat and Nha Trang, only local restaurants exist, and English menus are scarce. Dining choices are humble though tasty, but service standards are definitely local. It's the customer's job to summon service, not the waitstaff's responsibility to be aware of what could be needed.

HOTELS

Accommodation in this region runs the gamut from very basic government-run one-star hotels to international-standard five-star hotels with all the bells and whistles you could possibly imagine. Nha Trang and Mui Ne have, in recent years, experienced a boom in fancy beach resorts, while high up in Dalat, local entrepreneurs have been focusing on smaller boutique properties that take advantage of the area's cooler climate and natural beauty. Outside these centers, the offerings are mixed, with many run-down budget hotels and a surprising number of quirky choices, from traditional long houses to charming new high-quality hotels.

WHAT IT COSTS			
$	$$	$$$	$$$$
Restaurants Under 60,000d	60,000d–150,000d	151,000d–250,000d	over 250,000d
Hotels Under 600,000d	600,000d–900,000d	901,000d–1,500,000d	over 1,500,000d

Prices in the reviews are the average cost of a main course at dinner or, if dinner is not served, at lunch. Prices in the reviews are the lowest cost of a standard double room in high season.

THE SOUTHERN COAST

Heading north of Ho Chi Minh City by road or rail, the first notable stop is the fishing village of Phan Thiet, a thriving local town full of smiling locals who are fascinated by the tourists who do stop by, because many go to straight to the neighboring resort town of Mui Ne. While most international visitors are more interested in the beach, this region is best known among Vietnamese as a prime dragonfruit-growing region.

PHAN THIET

192 km (119 miles) northeast of Ho Chi Minh City.

Phan Thiet is a lively fishing village, divided by the Phan Thiet River, where the colorful feline-eyed fishing fleet is moored. The town has some interesting sights and some excellent people-watching opportunities. It's a great place to see local life in action. Until 1692, the Cham controlled the area, as evidenced by the Cham towers in the area. Many locals are ethnically Cham, descendants of these former rulers.

GETTING HERE AND AROUND

Two daily trains run from Ho Chi Minh City to Phan Thiet, which leaves the main north-south rail line at Binh Thuan. The journey takes four hours and there are many xe om and taxis at the station to take you into Phan Thiet or to the resort town of Mui Ne 25km (15½ miles) away (a 30- to 40-minute drive). It's also possible to take the main Ho Chi Minh City–Hanoi train, alight at Binh Thuan station, and get a taxi or xe om to your destination. Phan Thiet is 16 km (10 miles) from Binh Thuan and Mui Ne is 38 km (24 miles) away.

Note that the travel times advised by many bus companies are wildly inaccurate, without traffic it's about five hours by road from Ho Chi Minh City to Phan Thiet and Mui Ne, not the three hours advertised by some companies. When traffic is bad it can take up to seven hours. Coaches and sleeper buses stop in Mui Ne and then continue north towards Dalat and Nha Trang.

ESSENTIALS

Taxi Contact **Mai Linh Taxi.** This is the most reliable company. ☎ *0252/383–8383* .

Train Contact **Phan Thiet Railway Station** ⊠ *1 Le Duan, Phan Thiet* ☎ *0252/3833–952.*

EXPLORING

TOP ATTRACTIONS

Duc Thang School. Ho Chi Minh himself supposedly taught here in 1910, when he was known as Nguyen That Thanh, as he was making his way down to Saigon, from where he set sail for Paris and other foreign shores. History records Ho Chi Minh as teaching Chinese, Vietnamese, and martial arts to the second class. The school is a beautifully tended and unusual monument, with interesting little placards marking out where "Uncle Ho" rested and read. ⊠ *39 Trung Nhi.*

Reclining Buddha at Ta Cu Mountain (*Chua nui Ta Cu*). The largest reclining Buddha in Southeast Asia is on Ta Cu Mountain, about 28 km (17 miles) southwest of Phan Thiet. The 49-meter-long and 18-meter-high white concrete Buddha is at the top of a large temple complex, past a range of other deieties. Access is via a cable car that provides stunning views of the area and then a long haul up some steep stairs. There are usually plenty of pilgrims praying and lighting incense for all of the deities, including the reclining Buddha (Thich Ca Nhap Niet Ban), depicted as he enters Nirvana and shown with the most serene smile on his face. Several years ago, when renovation work was underway, every visitor to the site was asked to carry two bricks to the top of the complex for general absolution as well as to assist the construction workers. ✉ *Hwy. 1A, Thuan Nam.*

WORTH NOTING

Doi Duong Beach. The narrow Doi Duong Beach, at the end of Nguyen Tat Thanh Street, is not the prettiest in the country, but the locals love it anyway, especially in the early morning and late afternoons, when couples stroll along the paved beachside walkway, families play in the sand, and everyone eats snacks from the many roadside food vendors. **Amenities:** food and drinks. ✉ *Nguyen Tat Thanh.*

Ho Chi Minh Museum. This riverfront museum traces the life of Ho Chi Minh from his humble beginnings to his death in 1969, with displays of objects from his life. Some exhibits relate to the history of Phan Thiet and there are also some preserved specimens of local wildlife and large squid. The museum was built in 1986 on the site of Ho Chi Minh's former home, when he was a teacher at the Duc Thang School across the road. ✉ *39 Trung Nhi* ☎ *0252/3820–574* 🎫 *Free* 🕒 *Tues.–Sat. 7–11, 1:30–4:30* 🕒 *Closed Mon.*

4

Posha Inu Towers. These three crumbling towers, relics from the 8th century when the Cham empire ruled this part of Vietnam, are not the best examples of such ruins—the towers in Nha Trang and Hoi An are more extensive and better preserved even though they pale when compared to the magnificence of Angkor Wat in Cambodia—but still worth spending an hour or so exploring. The towers, in front of a working monastery, are about 7 km (4 miles) east of Phan Thiet on Ong Hoang Hill. ✉ *Ong Hoang Hill (Off Nguyen Thong St.)* 🎫 *10,000d.*

Van Thuy Tu (The Whale Temple). The main attraction at this small temple, built in 1762, is the 22-meter-long whale skeleton. The temple honors the deity of Nam Hai (the whale), who is believed to protect fishermen. There are two sections to the temple, a large room that houses the complete skeleton and a small temple with an interesting and colorful miniature ship and glass-fronted cabinets containing assorted whale bones. ✉ *20A Ngu Ong.*

WHERE TO EAT

$ VIETNAMESE 🍴 **Banh Xeo.** This basic off-street eatery serves up Central Vietnam-style *banh xeo* (sizzling pancakes), which are smaller and not as yellow as their cousins in Ho Chi Minh City. A stack of banh xeo, freshly cooked on the street-side barbecue, is served alongside a basket of herbs. To eat: tear off a bite-size piece of pancake, wrap it in herbs, and dip it into the sauce provided. [$] *Average main: 60000d* ✉ *40 Tuyen Quang* 💳 *No credit cards.*

$ VIETNAMESE 🍴 **Cha Cuon.** This basic spot specializes in roll-your-own fresh spring rolls. One serving includes a plate of various cuts of meat, sliced boiled egg, and Vietnamese sausage, a plate of herbs and cucumber sticks, a plate of fried spring rolls, and a stack of stiff rice paper. Compile, roll, then dip into the tangy dipping sauce provided. [$] *Average main: 60000d* ✉ *9 Tuyen Quang* 💳 *No credit cards.*

$$ VIETNAMESE Fodor's Choice ★ **Quan 49.** A basic seafood eatery (with English and Russian subtitles on the menu) fronting the river, Quan 49 does a great line in barbecued seafood, conch salad, and, when in season, *dong* lizard. The beers are cold, the food is delicious, and the waitstaff aren't scared of dealing with foreigners. A great place for a local-style night out. *Average main: 130000d* *49 Pham Van Dong* *No credit cards.*

WHERE TO STAY

$$$ RESORT **Du Parc Ocean Dunes Resort.** An older property fronting a private beach, Ocean Dunes Resort has everything you're looking for in a resort—ocean views, white beaches, palm trees, beach bar, pool, spacious rooms—and all rooms have private balconies. **Pros:** comfortable rooms with lovely views of the local fishing fleet; pool setup is great of families with kids. **Cons:** showing its age; service standards are local, rather than international; pool closes at 6 pm. *Rooms from: 1368000d* *1 Ton Duc Thang* *0252/3822–393* *www.oceandunesresort.com.vn* *123 rooms* *Breakfast.*

$$$$ RESORT FAMILY **Green Organic Villas.** A tranquil and eco-friendly resort 15 minutes from Phan Thiet, the beachfront Green Organic Villas has only seven private air-conditioned villas, set among palm trees and rolling green lawns, all sumptuously furnished in an Oriental-chic style. **Pros:** discreet and attentive service; very relaxing atmosphere. **Cons:** isolated; dining options limited to the in-house restaurant. *Rooms from: 3075000d* *Thon Tien Phu* *0252/3846–546* *greenorganicvillas.com* *7 rooms* *Breakfast.*

$ HOTEL **Truong Thinh Hotel.** A basic hotel in street with many local eateries, the appeal of Truong Thinh Hotel is not the karaoke bar that's popular with locals but the sidewalk coffee shop, Pet Coffee, featuring the owner's pet lizards. **Pros:** easy on the wallet; central location. **Cons:** can get noisy when the karaoke fires up or the hotel is full of domestic travelers. *Rooms from: 320000d* *26–28 Tuyen Quang* *www.truongthinhhotel.com.vn* *16 rooms* *No credit cards.*

$$$$ RESORT **Victoria Phan Thiet Beach Resort & Spa.** With thatched bungalows set in seven hectares of lush gardens a stone's throw from the beach, Victoria Phan Thiet Beach Resort & Spa has all the requirements for a relaxing resort holiday, including two swimming pools, a kids' club, tennis, badminton and volleyball courts, and an excellent in-house spa. **Pros:** great facilities, including pétanque, billiards, and free use of bicycles to explore Phan Thiet and surrounds. **Cons:** food and beverage prices are much higher than outside the resort; as one of the older Mui Ne Resorts, the age of the property does show in places. *Rooms from: 5900000d* *Km 9 Phu Hai, Mui Ne* *0252/3813–000* *www.victoriahotels.asia* *57 bungalows* *Breakfast.*

MUI NE

225 km (140 miles) east of Ho Chi Minh City, 25 km (16 miles) east of Phan Thiet.

Twenty years ago, Mui Ne was nothing but a deserted road running along an equally deserted beach. Now there's a 15-km (9-mile) stretch of resorts, restaurants, and souvenir shops. There is not much to the town, which is usually not a problem for those planning to hole up in a luxurious resort and enjoy the amenities—massages, dips in the pool, local seafood, and cocktails on the beach. Despite the difficulty of getting to this narrow (and windy) beach and the relative dearth of worthwhile sights, international tourists, including hordes of Russians, flock here. In recent years, Mui Ne has also become an international destination for kitesurfers, who converge during the windy season from November to April.

GETTING HERE AND AROUND

Mui Ne is an arduous six-hour-plus bus journey from Ho Chi Minh City. The train is a more comfortable option; a four-hour journey will get you to Phan Thiet Station, 25 km (16 miles) from Mui Ne. The final leg is easy to do by taxi, and many taxi drivers await the arrival of the daily train. Try to choose a Mai Linh taxi.

EXPLORING

Red Sand Dunes. The red sand dunes are the closest dunes to the tourist strip of Mui Ne and a lovely spot to watch the sun rise or set, despite the trash scattered around. Children offer plastic mats for rent so tourists can slide down the dunes, an activity that can be a lot of fun, albeit hot, sweaty, and sandy fun. Mat hire should be around 20,000d for an hour; expect to get pestered for a tip afterward. ✉ *706B (off Vo Nguyen Giap St.), Mui Ne.*

White Sand Dunes. These stunning desertlike soft white sand dunes are best seen at sunrise. Even if dawn isn't your thing, it's best to get there very early to enjoy the dunes in the peace before the noisy quad bikes start buzzing around. The vendors who rent out the quad bikes can be very pushy and you need to beware of the "guides" who jump on the back of your quad, who will demand a hefty tip at the end of the trip. The dunes are about an hour's bumpy drive from Mui Ne's main tourist area. ✉ *Haa Thang, Mui Ne.*

WHERE TO EAT

$$$ INTERNATIONAL

🍴 **Breeze Restaurant and Bar.** With one of the best views in Mui Ne from high on a hill, away from the main tourist strip, this restaurant serves a range of Western dishes, including great local seafood. Use of the pool in the surrounding resort is free for guests who order food or drinks at Breeze. [$] *Average main: 160000d* ✉ *Mui Ne Hills Resort, 69 Nguyen Dinh Chieu, Mui Ne* ☎ *0252/3741–682* 🌐 *www.muinehills.com/index.php/en/breeze-restaurant-a-bar* ✍ *Reservations essential.*

$$$ VIETNAMESE

🍴 **Cay Bang.** An unpretentious two-story local joint that specializes in seafood, this is the place to try local specialties such as devil-face fish (*ca bo hom*) and a raw fish "salad" that you wrap with rice paper and herbs and dip in a tasty sauce. The menu is in English, although the servers speak very little. Expect Vietnamese-style service, which can seem rude if you're not used to it. And dishes will be served as they're cooked—there's no concept of "starters" and "mains" here. [$] *Average main: 220000d* ✉ *2–4 Nguyen Dinh Chieu, Mui Ne* ☎ *0252/3847–009.*

$$$$ ASIAN FUSION

🍴 **Cham Garden Restaurant.** Most romantic when candle-lit in the evenings, the small fine dining restaurant inside the boutique Cham Villas Resort adds an extra touch of class to a visit to Mui Ne. Overseen by a German chef, the kitchen prepares a range of Vietnamese and International dishes, including a nashi pear–and–shrimp cocktail, beef-and-prawn skewers, and spicy lemongrass beef served with fried *thien ly* flowers. $ *Average main: 365000d* ✉ *Cham Villas Resort, 32 Nguyen Dinh Chieu, Mui Ne* ☎ *0252/3741–234* ⚓ *Reservations essential.*

$$$
RUSSIAN
✗ **Drugoe Mesto.** Not as sordid as the name suggests, Drugoe Mesto is a groovy café-bar with a shisha lounge section that serves Russian and European cuisine and a fine range of desserts. The terrace is a nice spot to enjoy the sea views and a glass of wine. $ *Average main: 200000d* ✉ *106 Nguyen Dinh Chieu, Mui Ne* ☎ *0123/722–4147.*

$$$
VIETNAMESE
✗ **LongSon.** For a break from Mui Ne's main tourist strip, head over to LongSon, 5 km (3 miles) out of town, for traditional Vietnamese cuisine in an open-air thatched restaurant looking out through the gardens to a secluded beach. The specialty is barbecued locally caught seafood and if you want to make a day of it, there are deckchairs, showers just off the beach, and cold beer and cocktails at the Pirate Beach Bar. ■ TIP→ The cheapest way to get to LongSon is by local bus; bus number one stops right outside the resort. $ *Average main: 200000d* ✉ *St. 706, Hon Rom, Mui Ne* ☎ *0252/383–6055* ⊕ *longsonmuine.com.*

$$
CAFÉ
✗ **Pogo Bar and Grill.** This is a friendly beach bar that does an all-day breakfast, salads, sandwiches, pasta, and a range of main meals. At night the music is cranked up so the backpacker brigade can party until late into the night. $ *Average main: 110000d* ✉ *138 Nguyen Dinh Chieu, Mui Ne* ☎ *093/801–8414.*

$$$
GERMAN
✗ **Ratinger Lowe.** Once the in-house restaurant at the Cham Villa resort, Ratinger Lowe's traditional German fare became so popular the eatery had to move to larger premises next door. The chef, who has been officially named the Phan Thiet culinary ambassador of his hometown of Ratingen to Phan Thiet, overseas a menu featuring *burgunderbraten* (roast beef), bratwurst, wiener schnitzel, and *kaiserschmarrn* (fluffy pancake chunks), as well as a small selection of international and Vietnamese dishes, served in charming rustic decor. $ *Average main: 200000d* ✉ *32 Nguyen Dinh Chieu, Mui Ne* ☎ *0252/374–1234* ⊕ *www.ratinger-loewe.com.*

$$$
INTERNATIONAL
Fodor's Choice
★
✗ **Sandals.** Inside Mia Resort in a high-ceilinged Bali-style pavilion overlooking the beach and the South China Sea, Sandals is considered one of Mui Ne's best dining options, with well-presented Western and Asian fusion dishes, fabulous cocktails, a reasonable wine list, excellent Italian-style coffee, and professional wait staff. The setting is superb, inviting guests to linger a little bit longer, something the staff don't mind at all. $ *Average main: 240000d* ✉ *Mia Resort, 24 Nguyen Dinh Chieu, Mui Ne* ☎ *0252/3847–440* ⊕ *www.miamuine.com/dine.*

$$
INDIAN
✗ **Shree Ganesh.** Serving delicious North Indian and tandoori dishes and excellent naan bread, Shree Ganesh offers a sometimes-welcome break from Vietnamese cuisine in its homey but basic restaurant in the heart of Mui Ne's tourist strip. The curries are highly recommended and there's also a range of vegetarian options. $ *Average main: 140000d* ✉ *57 Nguyen Dihn Chieu, Mui Ne* ☎ *0252/3741–330.*

$
MIDDLE EASTERN
✗ **Sindbad.** Fresh, tasty, and quite fabulous kebabs, salads, and dips: Sindbad's menu is short and sweet but everything on it is top-quality.

The restaurant is tiny, the staff friendly, and the service quick. It's just the ticket for a cheap and cheerful meal, and they also deliver. [$] *Average main: 60000d* ✉ *233 Nguyen Dinh Chieu, Mui Ne* ☎ *016/999–15245* 🌐 *www.sindbad.vn.*

WHERE TO STAY

$$$ RESORT 🏨 **Ananda Resort.** One of the more basic options on Mui Ne's main tourist strip, the beachfront Ananda Resort has clean, simple thatched rooms and bungalows, a swimming pool, a private stretch of beach, and an in-house restaurant that has great views and reasonably priced versions of Western and Vietnamese dishes. **Pros:** excellent location; right on the beach. **Cons:** service and amenities not as slick as some of the pricier resorts in Mui Ne. [$] *Rooms from: 990000d* ✉ *48 Nguyen Dinh Chieu, Mui Ne* ☎ *0252/3741–692* 🌐 *www.ananda.vn* 🛏 *27 rooms* 🍴 *Breakfast.*

$$$$ RESORT 🏨 **Anantara Mui Ne Resort and Spa.** Refined luxury and attentive welcoming service are the hallmarks of the Antara Mui Ne Resort and Spa, a beachfront resort with beautifully landscaped grounds, a stunning infinity pool with a swim-up bar, and an on-site spa. **Pros:** stunning setting; staff really do go the extra mile. **Cons:** a fairly long walk to the central part of the strip. [$] *Rooms from: 3585000d* ✉ *Km 10, Mui Ne* ☎ *0252/3741–888* 🌐 *mui-ne.anantara.com* 🛏 *70 rooms, 20 villas* 🍴 *Breakfast.*

$$$$ RESORT 🏨 **Cham Villas.** This is a luxurious private paradise on the beach, with thatched-roof bungalows and villas set in a lush 1-hectare garden of coconut trees, orchids, tropical plants, and Cham-style sculptures. **Pros:** charming setting; central location; villas have private patios with daybeds. **Cons:** one of the pricier options in Mui Ne. [$] *Rooms from: 3600000d* ✉ *32 Nguyen Dinh Chieu, Mui Ne* ☎ *0252/3741–234* 🌐 *www.chamvillas.com* 🛏 *15 rooms, 6 suites* 🍴 *Breakfast.*

$$$$ RESORT FAMILY 🏨 **Coco Beach Resort.** The first resort in Mui Ne, Coco Beach is still one of the best; daytimes here are for relaxing on a lounger on the private white-sand beach, rocking in a hammock under a tree, utilizing the beachside massage pavilion, and enjoying one of the three on-site restaurants. **Pros:** kids' swimming pool and small play area make it ideal for families with young children; central location. **Cons:** the swimming pool is small. [$] *Rooms from: 3655000d* ✉ *58 Nguyen Dinh Chieu, Mui Ne* ☎ *0252/3847–111* 🌐 *cocobeach.net* 🛏 *34 rooms* 🍴 *Breakfast.*

$$$$ RESORT 🏨 **Full Moon Village.** Twenty minutes west of the main Mui Ne tourist strip is the tranquil Full Moon Village, a collection of spacious, elegantly furnished one-, two-, and three-bedroom bungalows. **Pros:** a regular shuttle bus runs into Mui Ne proper; water sports available. **Cons:** isolated. [$] *Rooms from: 2365000d* ✉ *Suoi Nuoc Beach, Mui Ne* ☎ *0252/3836–099* 🌐 *www.fullmoon-village.com* 🛏 *16 villas* 🍴 *Breakfast.*

$$$$ RESORT 🏨 **Grace Boutique Resort.** A family-run three-story resort on the beach, Grace Boutique Resort has comfortable clean rooms, a small infinity pool, a beautiful tropical garden, and an on-site restaurant with a terrace overlooking the South China Sea. **Pros:** reasonably priced; very helpful staff. **Cons:** pool is small; no on-site spa. [$] *Rooms from:*

1700000d ✉ 144A Nguyen Dinh Chieu, Mui Ne ☎ 0252/374–3357 🌐 graceboutiqueresort.com ⇨ 14 rooms 🍴 Breakfast.

$$$$ RESORT FAMILY Fodor's Choice ★ 🏨 **Mia Resort Mui Ne.** A classy-yet-relaxed luxury resort in tropical gardens fronting the beach, Mia Resort Mui Ne has contemporary rooms with high ceilings and wooden floors, all with their own private terrace. **Pros:** central location, within walking distance to cafés and restuarants; free bicycles for guests to explore the local area. **Cons:** pricey; extra beds not available in standard rooms. [$] *Rooms from: 2760000d ✉ 24 Nguyen Dinh Chieu, Mui Ne ☎ 0252/3847–440 🌐 www.miamuine.com ⇨ 31 rooms 🍴 Breakfast.*

$$$ RESORT 🏨 **Mui Ne Village and Kitesurf.** About 20 minutes from Mui Ne's main tourist strip with its own stretch of private beach, the Mui Ne Village Resort is a haven for lovers of water sports and those looking for a reasonably priced beach break. **Pros:** one of the cheaper options; nice pool. **Cons:** isolated; a fair amount of trash washes up on the beach; service can be lackluster. [$] *Rooms from: 1010000d ✉ Suoi Nuoc, Mui Ne 🌐 www.stox-office.com/muine-village-english.html ⇨ 68 rooms 🍴 No meals.*

$$$$ RESORT FAMILY 🏨 **Shades Resort Mui Ne.** Run by a New Zealand couple, this small and friendly resort is homey with spacious and stylish accommodation options—studio rooms or self-contained apartments with private gardens. **Pros:** central location; great beachfront setting; wonderful service. **Cons:** limited breakfast choices; small pool. [$] *Rooms from: 1620000d ✉ 98A Nguyen Dinh Chieu, Mui Ne ☎ 0252/3743–236 🌐 shadesmuine.com ⇨ 4 rooms, 7 apartments 🍴 Breakfast.*

$$$$ RESORT 🏨 **Victoria Phan Thiet Beach Resort & Spa.** With thatched bungalows set in 7 hectares of lush gardens a stone's throw from the beach, Victoria Phan Thiet Beach Resort & Spa has all the requirements for a relaxing resort holiday, including two swimming pools, a kids' club, tennis, badminton and volleyball courts, and an excellent in-house spa. **Pros:** great facilities, including pétanque, billiards, and free use of bicycles to explore Phan Thiet and surrounds. **Cons:** food and beverage prices are much higher than outside the resort; as one of the older Mui Ne Resorts, the age of the property does show in places. [$] *Rooms from: 5900000d ✉ Km 9 Phu Hai, Mui Ne ☎ 0252/3813–000 🌐 www.victoriahotels.asia ⇨ 57 bungalows 🍴 Breakfast.*

$$$$ RESORT 🏨 **Villa Aria Mui Ne.** One of the newest places on the Mui Ne strip, Villa Aria's lush gardens make the resort feel secluded even though it's in the middle of the tourist area. **Pros:** central location; caring staff; boutique feel. **Cons:** limited breakfast choices. [$] *Rooms from: 3225000d ✉ 60A Nguyen Dinh Chieu, Mui Ne ☎ 0252/3741–660 🌐 www.villaariamuine.com ⇨ 23 rooms, 1 suite 🍴 Breakfast.*

NIGHTLIFE

Mui Ne nightlife is dominated by the party-hard backpacker crowd and fun-loving super-fit kitesurfers. Few refined options exist, with most visitors content to frequent the bar of their resort.

Jibes Beach Club. After a day on the water, kitesurfers head to Jibes to discuss their exploits over sunset drinks (which can last until hours after the sun goes down). Nonkitesurfers are most welcome at this relaxed beachfront bar that doubles as the headquarters for the Jibes kitesurfing school. ✉ *Full Moon Resort, 84–90 Nguyen Dinh Chieu* ☎ *0252/3847–008* ⊕ *www.windsurf-vietnam.com/index.php/management-team/85.*

Pogo Bar and Grill. This open-air beachfront bar is popular among back-packers for its laid-back daytime vibe and nighttime party atmosphere, pumped up by the resident DJ. Reasonably priced food is available, including an all-day breakfast. ✉ *138 Nguyen Dinh Chieu, Mui Ne* ☎ *093/8018–414.*

Sankara. Offering pool-side beachfront relaxation during the day, Sankara pumps up the music for nighttime partying. The elegant restaurant/bar regularly hosts foam parties, which are popular with younger travelers. ✉ *78 Nguyen Dinh Chieu, Mui Ne* ☎ *0252/3741–122.*

SPORTS AND THE OUTDOORS
GOLF
Sea Links Golf and Country Club. Designed by Ron Fream, set on sand dunes 80 meters above sea level, Sea Links Golf and Country Club is a beautiful but challenging course stretched over 7,700 yards, with undulating fairways, many water hazards, and strong winds for part of the year. Fees start at 1,350,000d for 18 holes on weekdays. ✉ *Km 9 Nguyen Thong* ☎ *0252/3741–741* ⊕ *www.sealinkscity.com.* ⅄ *18 holes, 7,700 yards, par 72.*

WATER SPORTS
C2Sky. This purpose-built kitesurfing center operates out of two beach-front locations in Mui Ne—Sunshine Beach Resort at 82 Nguyen Dinh Chieu and Seahorse Resort at Spa at 16 Nguyen Dinh Chieu—to make the most of prevailing conditions. The kite school offers private lessons with IKO-certified instructors for beginner to advanced level, as well as kitesurfing gear rental and storage. ✉ *Sunshine Beach Resort, 82 Nguyen Dinh Chieu, Mui Ne* ☎ *01279/002–251* ⊕ *www.c2skykitecenter.com.*

Jibes. The experienced international instructors at Jibes offer lessons in windsurfing, kitesurfing, surfing, and sailing, with all the equipment, including kayaks, stand-up paddleboards, and a beach catamaran for hire. The oldest kitesurfing school in Mui Ne (and the first in Vietnam), Jibes has a strong focus on safety and making water sports as enjoyable as possible. ✉ *Full Moon Resort, 84–90 Nguyen Dinh Chieu, Mui Ne* ☎ *0252/3847–008* ⊕ *www.windsurf-vietnam.com/index.php/management-team/85.*

Manta Sail Training Center. Vietnam's first and only official sailing school, Manta Sail Training Center offers sailing instruction for all levels, from introductory to advanced as well as race training. The courses are hands-on, with a focus on safety and good seamanship, as well as having fun. Sailing instruction starts at $60/hour/person and boat hire starts at $40/hour. Wakeboarding and stand-up paddleboarding are also available and there's budget accommodations on-site for those who just can't tear themselves away. ✉ *108 Huynh Thuc Khang, Mui Ne* ☎ *0908/8400–108* ⊕ *mantasailing.org.*

Windchimes Kitesurf. Set on a wide section of beach, which makes kite-boarding takeoff and landing safer, Windchimes offers kitesurfing, windsurfing, surfing, and stand-up paddleboarding lessons, as well as equipment hire. The beach boys are helpful and very safety-conscious and there's even an on-site Jet Ski just in case anyone needs rescuing. ⊠ *Saigon Mui Ne Resort, 56 Nguyen Dinh Chieu, Mui Ne* ☎ *090/9720–017* ⊕ *www.windsurfing-vietnam.com.*

NHA TRANG

250 km (155 miles) northeast of Mui Ne.

Home to some of Vietnam's best beaches and dive sites, the coastal city of Nha Trang is a magnet for those seeking sunshine and underwater adventure. Backdropped by mountains, white sandy coves shelter lovely bays and distant islands. The capital of Khanh Hoa province, Nha Trang lacks the culture found in neighboring areas but still has a few temples and such to remind you that you're in Vietnam. But don't be surprised to find signs written in Russian—more than 10,000 Russians come here each month. Now is the time to visit Nha Trang; Bai Dai Beach is slated for development, and by 2018 it won't be so pristine. The beach is the main draw here, and most people either come to bask in the sun or dive at nearby islands. Major sites can be seen in a single day, but plan to tack on another day or two for island-hopping, scuba diving, or a visit to neighboring waterfalls and villages.

GETTING HERE AND AROUND

The traffic is bearable (by Vietnam's standards) in Nha Trang, but driving is not recommended. To get from Cam Ranh airport to the town center you can take a bus, or a cab will cost 350,000d. Most hotels also offer a more expensive airport pick up. The best way to get around town is by foot or taxi. Mai Linh also offers a minibus service between Nha Trang and major towns running north and south. If you are staying outside of town near Bai Dai Beach, plan to spend about 320,000d for a one-way trip from Nha Trang to your hotel. Transportation between the airport and central Nha Trang should cost around 400,000d for the 45-minute drive.

Nha Trang also has local public buses running six routes in the city. This can be a cheap and fun way to get around, if you have someone who can tell you which route to take. The main bus companies in Nha Trang are Phuong Trang, Mai Linh, and Khanh Hoa.

ESSENTIALS

Taxi and Minibus Contacts Mai Linh Taxi and Minibus ⊠ *98B/9 Tran Phu St.* ☎ *0258/3838–3838* ⊕ *www.mailinh.vn* **Vinasun Taxi** ☎ *0258/3827–2727.*

Train Contacts Nha Trang Railway Station ⊠ *17 Thai Nguyen* ☎ *0258/822–113.*

VISITOR INFORMATION **Nha Trang Live.** Although not an official tourism office, Nha Trang Live has free city maps and information about the area. ⊠ *Intersection of Thong Nhat and 2 Thang 4, 12A Nguyen Truong To* ☎ *058/350–0025* ⊕ *www.nhatranglive.com.*

100 Egg
Mud Bath **10**

Ba Ho Waterfall...**3**

Doc Let Beach **4**

Hon Chong
Promontory **1**

I-Resort **6**

Long Son
Pagoda **8**

Nha Trang
Beach **9**

North Beach **7**

Po Nagar Cham
Towers **2**

Thap Ba Hot
Spring Center **5**

Vinpearl Land ...**11**

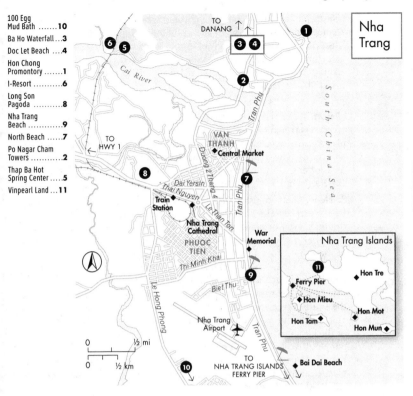

TOURS

Smiling Easy Rider. The reliable and honest Mr. Duc is Nha Trang's Smiling Easy Rider, a knowledgeable and cheery guy who can arrange motorbike tours of Nha Trang and surrounds or longer multiday trips throughout Central Vietnam down to Ho Chi Minh City. A former fisherman, Mr. Duc taught himself English (and invested in a high-powered motorbike) so he could become an easy rider. He can arrange other drivers from his network of freelance easy riders to cater for couples or groups or he can act as an escort and guide for those who want to ride their own motorbikes. ☎ *093/5774–426* ⊕ *vietnam-smiling-easyrider.com.*

EXPLORING

Nha Trang can easily be explored in a single day, and most of the sites are a short taxi ride away. Start the day with culture at the Po Nagar Towers and Long Son Pagoda, followed by a tour of traditional villages and rice paddies near Cai River. By midafternoon, you'll be ready for a swim or snorkel at one of Nha Trang's beautiful beaches. Watch the sunset at the trendy Sailing Club, the best spot to sink your toes into the sand while sipping a cocktail. If you've got the time, use Nha Trang as a base to explore neighboring hot springs, mud baths, and waterfalls. No visit to Nha Trang is complete without a boat trip to the surrounding scenic islands, such as Mieu Island (home to a quirky aquarium), Hon Mun (Ebony Island), and Hon Tam (Silkworm Island). Boat trips can be arranged through local hotels and travel agencies, and the waters around Mun Island are a popular stop on snorkeling and diving trips from Nha Trang.

TOP ATTRACTIONS

I-Resort. While the mud baths are the main attraction at I-Resort, there are also warm mineral pools, mineral water spas, waterfalls, and a kid's play area, all set within landscaped grounds northwest of the main tourist area of Nha Trang. Some of the massages and mud bath package deals offer good value and include a "light bite" that's really a full meal. ⊠ *I Resort* ☎ *0258/3838–838* ⊕ *www.i-resort.vn* ⊙ *Daily 7 am–8 pm.*

Po Nagar Cham Towers (*Thap Ba [Tower of the Lady]*). Perched on Cu Lao hillside overlooking the Cai River, the four remaining towers of an original seven or eight are reminiscent of those found at Angkor Wat and offer a glimpse of the Champa Kingdom, who built the complex in the 8th century to praise their deity. The largest tower of the four stretches 23 meters (75 feet) high and contains a statue in honor of Goddess Ponagar, praised for her knowledge of agriculture and civilization. The center tower was built for Cri Cambhu, the god of fertility, and the south tower commemorates the god of success, Ganesh, recognizable by the human body and elephant head. The northwest tower is of the god Shiva. Visitors must cover knees and shoulders to enter the temple. If you happen to be in Nha Trang on the 20th to 23rd day of the third lunar month, you can catch the Po Nagar Festival that takes place near the ancient towers. ⊠ *2 Thang 4, at end of Xom Bong Bridge* 🖅 *20,000d* ⊙ *Daily 6–6.*

Vinpearl Land. This vast amusement park on Hon Tre Island is accessed by cable car with stunning views back over Nha Trang. Allocate a full day to explore the amusement park and take your swimsuit because the complex is vast and includes a water park, rides, an electronic games arcade, dolphin and seal shows, an aquarium, and many shopping and dining options (the most varied food options are close to the water park). This is an excellent value for money and a truly fun day out for kids of all ages. ⊠ *Hon Tre Island* ⊕ *vinpearl.com* 🖅 *550,000d.*

WORTH NOTING

100 Egg Mud Bath (*Tan Bun Cham Trung*). Nha Trang's newest mud bath complex, 100 Egg Mud Bath is named after the dinky egg-shape private bathing capsules that each accommodate two to three people. There are larger tubs for groups and a range of hot and cold water pools, as well as saunas and steam rooms. The 100 Egg Mud Bath complex, which has a dining area, is 20 minutes from the main tourist center but well worth allocating half a day for an unusual—and very messy— take on pampering. ⊠ *Nguyen That Thanh, Phuoc Trung, Phuoc Dong* ☎ *0258/3711–733* ⊕ *www.tambuntramtrung.vn* ⊙ *Daily 8–7.*

Ba Ho Waterfall. A stop often included in countryside motorbike tours, Ba Ho Waterfall is not the most impressive waterfall around but the journey there can be quite an adventure. The entrance to the waterfalls is at the end of a long and bumpy dirt track, and the waterfalls themselves are at the end of long hike and short climb over large rocks (that requires sturdy shoes). You need a swim to cool off once you get there—if you don't mind the local fish nibbling at your feet. ⊠ *Ninh Ich, Ninh Hoa.*

Hon Chong Promontory. On the same side of the river as the Po Nagar Cham Towers, this promontory provides good views of the coastline and the surrounding islands and is a great spot to watch the sunset. Climb up for a view of Nha Trang and its islands. If you look northwest you can see Fairy Mountain (Nui Co Tien), said to resemble a reclining fairy. To get here from the Po Nagar ruins, head north on 2 Thang 4 Street and take a right on Nguyen Dinh Chieu Street. ⊠ *Nguyen Dinh Chieu* ✚ *About ¾ km (½ miles) from intersection of Nguyen Dinh Chieu and 2 Thang 4 Sts.* 🕑 *10,000d* ⊙ *Daily 8–4.*

Islands. No visit to Nha Trang is complete without a boat trip to the surrounding scenic islands, such as Mieu Island (Tri Nguyen Island), Mun Island, and Tam Island. Boat trips can be arranged through local hotels and travel agencies or directly at the port on the south end of town. Both Mieu and Tam islands have bungalows where you can spend a quiet night away from the bustle of Nha Trang. ⊠ *Nha Trang.*

Long Son Pagoda (*Chua Long Song*). Climb the 150 steps, breaking halfway to view the 80-meter-long (262-foot) white statue of sleeping Buddha. At the top of the hill, visit the Long Son Pagoda and sitting Buddha. This site is free to the public—watch out for the hecklers and scammers asking for miscellaneous fees and the pushy ladies selling fans. The panoramic views of rice fields and the city below are absolutely breathtaking. ⊠ *Thai Nguyen.*

Thap Ba Hot Spring Center. If your idea of relaxation involves soaking in a mineral mud bath, head to Thap Ba Hot Spring Center, on the northern outskirts of Nha Trang, 7 km (4½ miles) from the tourist area. In addition to mud baths there are hot mineral pools and a mineral swimming pool. You can choose to soak solo, with a partner, or in a group. ⊠ *15 Ngoc Son, Ngoc Son* ☎ *0258/3835–345* ⊕ *www.thapbahotspring.com. vn* ⊙ *Daily 7–5:30.*

BEACHES

Fodor'sChoice **Bai Dai Beach** (*Long Beach*). Located 20 km (12½ miles) south of Nha
★ Trang near Mia Resort, this beach is definitely worth a visit sooner rather than later. Right now, Bai Dai Beach, meaning "Long Beach," is a favorite with locals, but beginning in 2018, 39 luxury resorts will be going up along this pristine stretch in the hopes of turning it into the next Cancún. On weekends, hordes of beachgoers gather at the seafood shacks for cold beers and the morning catch. The crystal clear water is shallow far past the shore, making this an ideal swimming spot. Jet Skis, surfboards, rafts, and kayaks are available for rent, and nearly every shack offers chairs, toilets, and showers with any food or drink purchase. This is one of the few spots where surfers can find waves through April. Bai Dai Beach continues 25 km (15½ miles) south to Cam Ranh Airport. ■**TIP**➜ The best section is on the north end at the

protected bay. **Amenities:** food and drink; showers; toilets; water sports. **Best for:** surfing; swimming; walking. ✉ *5 min south of Mia Resort, 3 Khuc Thua Du, Phuong Phuoc Long.*

Doc Let Beach. About 45 km (25 miles) north of Nha Trang is the picture-postcard Doc Let Beach, a beautiful 10-km (6 miles) stretch of casuarina-lined fine white sand and crystal blue water that welcomes few tourists. It's a great location for a laid-back beachy day trip from Nha Trang or Some Days of Silence Resort and Spa. It will take about an hour to get here from Nha Trang by taxi. **Amenities:** food and drink; water sports. **Best for:** walking; swimming; sunsets. ✉ *Bai Doc Let, Con Dao.*

Nha Trang Beach (*Tourist Beach*). Located near downtown Nha Trang, Nha Trang Beach is more commonly known as "Tourist Beach," because travelers gather on this bustling stretch that starts north near the Sheraton Hotel and ends 5 km (3 miles) south at Bao Dai Villas. Plenty of amenities are available at the trendy Sailing Club, or you can simply bask in the sun on an open patch of sand and buy snacks from a passing vendor. This is the most centrally located beach, meaning it can get crowded on sunny weekends. Divers and snorkelers won't find much marine life here, since this beach is best for swimming, walking, or kayaking. To see clown fish, scorpionfish, and moray eels, it is better to organize a dive at the Sailing Club to the protected island of Hon Mun. The beach is not patrolled but authorities do raise red flags when conditions are unsafe. **Amenities:** food and drink; showers; toilets. **Best for:** partiers; swimming; walking. ✉ *72–74 Tran Phu St., between Sheraton Hotel and Bao Dai Villas.*

North Beach. Starting at the bridge near the Sheraton Hotel and running 30 km (18 miles) north beyond Nha Trang city are several beautiful beaches that together are commonly referred to as "North Beach." The most picturesque stretch of beach can be found past Ninh Hoa City, where shallow waters and powdery sand beckon swimmers and sunbathers alike. A handful of surfers paddle to the point break that whips up decent waves between October and April. Amenities are offered to those who buy food or drinks at neighboring properties such as Paradise Resort or White Sand Doclet Resort. **Amenities:** food and drink; toilets. **Best for:** surfing, swimming; walking. ✉ *26–28 Tran Phu, north of Sheraton Resort.*

WHERE TO EAT

$$$ VIETNAMESE

🍴 **Galangal.** Authentic Vietnamese cuisine, including street food dishes, are served in a charming, relatively up-market atmosphere. The street food is cooked along the sides of the restaurant, giving the place a lively edge. It's a tasty and safe option for those who are wary of real street food, or groups seeking a mixture of street food and restaurant fare. Tasting menus are available for those struck by indecision. [$] *Average main: 200000d* ✉ *1A Biet Thu* 🌐 *galangal.com.vn* 💳 *No credit cards.*

$$$ ITALIAN

🍴 **Good Morning Vietnam.** Serving traditional Italian cuisine in a rustic setting, Good Morning Vietnam is a Nha Trang institution popular for its thin-crust pizzas and friendly service. Head upstairs for air-conditioning or dine downstairs in the open-air section that looks out onto one of Nha Trang's busiest tourist streets. $ *Average main: 160000d* ✉ *19b Biet Thu* ☎ *0258/3522–071* ⊕ *www.goodmorningviet.com.*

$$
VIETNAMESE

✕ **Lac Canh.** Join the locals at this popular and sometimes rowdy barbecue and hotpot joint that becomes quite smoky when the serious table-top barbecuing gets underway. The decor is very plain, the food is cheap and delicious, and the management is savvy enough to have an English menu. $ *Average main: 150000d* ✉ *44 Nguyen Binh Khiem* ☎ *0258/3821–391* ▭ *No credit cards.*

$$
VIETNAMESE
Fodor's Choice
★

✕ **Lanterns.** Fantastic service, a pleasant setting, and authentic Southern Vietnamese dishes are what make Lanterns one of Nha Trang's most popular restaurants. Adorning the open-air dining room (the retractable roof closes on rainy days) are orange paper lanterns that match the traditional dress of the endearing wait staff. The six-course prix fixe is remarkably inexpensive, or you can opt for such house favorites as slow-cooked shrimp, beef served in a clay pot, or whole red snapper grilled on a bed of coal and then wrapped in foil to capture the flavor. Vegetarians have a designated menu, and there is an on-site cooking school for those who want to learn the secrets of the kitchen. $ *Average main: 89000d* ✉ *34/6 Nguyen Thien Thuat St.* ☎ *0258/2471–674* ⊕ *www.lanternsvietnam.com* ◷ *Daily 7 am–10:30 pm.*

$$$
BISTRO

✕ **Le Petit Bistro.** Bypass the bar for a table on the quaint garden patio, where imported pâté, Camembert, and Brie are served with a platter of cold cuts. Pricey by Vietnam standards, the menu includes French favorites like roasted duck, cordon bleu, and *filet de boeuf,* each served with a side of creamy au gratin potatoes. Only those who speak French will be able to hobnob with the talented chef-owner, Claude Durand, who frequently mingles with guests. Wine connoisseurs will enjoy the adjacent *boutique du vin,* the main distributor of blends to Nha Trang's hotels and restaurants. $ *Average main: 200000d* ✉ *26D Tran Quang Khai* ☎ *0258/352–7201.*

$$$
INTERNATIONAL

✕ **Louisiane Brewhouse.** A laid-back beach bar—with its own pool and sunbeds—that serves a selection of craft beer, as well as International, Vietnamese, and Japanese cuisine, Louisiane Brewhouse has a bit of something for everyone, including live music in the evenings. ■ TIP➔ **Beer connoisseurs should ask about the brewery tours.** $ *Average main: 160000d* ✉ *29 Tran Phu* ☎ *0258/3521–948* ⊕ *www. louisianebrewhouse.com.vn.*

$$
VIETNAMESE

✕ **Nha Trang Xua.** For a taste of authentic Vietnam, head 6 km (4 miles) outside the city center to this 300-year-old house surrounded by rice paddies and lotus ponds. Brick pathways lined with clay pots and antique scooters lead to low picnic tables under a thatched palm leaf roof. The menu, handwritten on cardboard, features fish barbecued in bamboo, banana flower salad, crispy prawn pancakes, and Asian spinach soup with basil-seasoned rice. For a unique dessert, try the white rice and mung beans in coconut sauce. Don't expect too much in the way of customer service because the staff doesn't speak a word of English. ■ TIP➔ **This place is difficult to find on your own, so if you plan to arrive by taxi or motorbike, make sure you have exact directions.** $ *Average main: 120000d* ✉ *6 km (4 miles) from downtown Nha Trang, Thai*

Thong, Vinh Thai ⊕ *Left at light past Cau Dua Bridge, over railroad tracks, and right at Vinh Thai School, then follow signs to Nha Trang Xua Restaurant* ☎ *0258/389–6700* ▭ *No credit cards.*

$$$
FRENCH

✕ **Refuge.** At this tiny log cabin replica, you're greeted by French owner Pierre Dimitri and his Vietnamese wife, Thien, who have created a menu highlighting the best of both their worlds. Portions are plentiful and most dishes—like the tender crocodile or frog legs—are heavy on the cream. If you aren't bursting at the seams after the main entrée, try the chocolate mousse, made with 75% cocoa. It pairs nicely with *La Grolle*, a coffee liquor seasoned with cinnamon and orange. This French Alp tradition is served in a wooden "friendship bowl" with eight drinking spouts for parties to share. $ *Average main: 160000d* ✉ *01L Hung Vuong, Quant Tran* ☎ *0258/352–7897* ▭ *No credit cards* ☾ *Closed June.*

$$$
INTERNATIONAL

✕ **Sailing Club.** Whether you're looking for some seaside relaxation, great meals, or a thumping party, the Sailing Club has you covered with its prime beachfront location and three restaurants (Vietnamese, Indian, and Mediterranean), which magically morph into Nha Trang's hippest club in the evenings. Daytime options include coffee and/or cocktails while lounging on a four-poster bed near the lotus pond or on a deck chair on the beach; the more upright options including dining, playing pool, or hanging out on a swing, all with with a spectacular view of the South China Sea. Dive trips can be booked at the associated dive shop. $ *Average main: 220000d* ✉ *72–74 Tran Phu St., Con Dao* ☎ *0258/3524–628* ⊕ *www.sailingclubvietnam.com.*

$$$$
BARBECUE

✕ **Sandals.** For the most romantic dining experience in Nha Trang, reserve a table for two at this beachfront barbecue restaurant just a stone's throw from the water—you can even sink your toes into the sand. Tiki torches and lanterns surround your private table; nearby, a chef prepares fresh lobster, squid, scallops, lamb, and chicken on a fiery grill. Expect to get a little messy, as most seafood dishes require peeling and prying with your fingers. Private dining on the sand is not available on windy or rainy days, and must be booked two hours in advance. Isolated from the main Sandals dining room, this is a true VIP experience. $ *Average main: 2000000d* ✉ *Mia Resort, Bai Dong, Cam Hai Dong, Cam Lam* ☎ *0258/398–9666* ⊕ *www.mianhatrang. com* ◈ *Reservations essential.*

$$
MEXICAN
Fodor's Choice
★

✕ **The Shack Vietnam.** The Shack is a beachfront restaurant and surf club serving up delicious fresh seafood, some of which can be barbecued at your table, as well as much-raved-about Mexican food and Western options such as burgers. The Shack is down a dirt track, about 21 km (13 miles) south of Nha Trang's main tourist area. It's worth planning to spend some time here, enjoying the views of the spectacular Bai Dai Beach, a few drinks, a nap in a hammock or, if you are so inclined, you can rent a surf board or a stand-up paddle board (October to April). Bring your swimsuit. $ *Average main: 140000d* ✉ *Bai Dai Beach* ⊕ *www.shackvietnam.com* ▭ *No credit cards.*

WHERE TO STAY

There is no shortage of resorts in Nha Trang, but only a select few offer a beachfront location with unobstructed views. If you plan on enjoying local sites, restaurants, and bars, stay close to the action near the center of town. For something a bit more private, choose one of the more remote resorts that offer daily shuttle service into Nha Trang.

$$$$
RESORT
FAMILY
Fodor's Choice
★

Amiana Resort. One of the newest properties in Nha Trang, this luxurious and private beach retreat has elegant villas, each with its own private terrace, outdoor bathroom, and hand-crafted furniture. **Pros:** quality amenities, including the salt water and fresh water outdoor pools (with life guards on duty); pool bar; free shuttle bus to the main tourist strip. **Cons:** 15 minutes from downtown Nha Trang. $ *Rooms from:* 4945000d ⊠ *Pham Van Dong* ☎ 0258/3553–333 ⊕ *www.amianaresort. com* ↩ *94 rooms, 19 apartments* ⍟ *Breakfast.*

$$$$
RESORT
FAMILY
Fodor's Choice
★

Evason Ana Mandara. A secluded beachfront oasis with excellent facilities, but within walking distance of Nha Trang's main tourist strip, this resort has the best of both worlds, delivering the high service standards and quality amenities that make for a genuinely relaxing stay. **Pros:** large rooms; central location; kids' club. **Cons:** restaurants are somewhat pricey. $ *Rooms from:* 4494000d ⊠ *Tran Phu* ☎ 058/352–2222 ⊕ *www.sixsenses.com* ↩ *74 rooms* ⍟ *Breakfast.*

$$$$
HOTEL
FAMILY

Intercontinental Nha Trang. A luxurious high-rise across the road from the beach, the Intercontinental has fabulous views of the South China Sea, professional attentive staff, and just about every modern convenience you could possible need, including a 24-hour fitness center, kids' club, on-site spa, and a leafy pool deck overlooking the ocean. **Pros:** great central location; well-appointed bathrooms. **Cons:** the large size and high-rise nature of the hotel can make it seem slightly sterile. $ *Rooms from:* 2880000d ⊠ *32–34 Tran Phu* ☎ 0258/3887–777 ⊕ *www.ihg.com* ↩ *279 rooms* ⍟ *Breakfast.*

$$
B&B/INN

La Paloma. A Spanish-looking family-run guesthouse with a carefully tended gardens surrounding a pool, La Paloma has simple spacious rooms with Vietnamese-style bathrooms, and a sweet little breakfast area. **Pros:** affordable and friendly; pool; close to Po Nagar and two of Nha Trang's three mud baths. **Cons:** beds are quite hard; no phone in the room; 3 km (2 miles) from the main Nha Trang tourist strip. $ *Rooms from:* 746000d ⊠ *1 Hon Chong* ☎ 0258/3831–216 ⊕ *www. lapaloma-nhatrang.com* ↩ *19 rooms* ⍟ *Breakfast.*

$$$$
RESORT
Fodor's Choice
★

Mia Resort. Thirty minutes south of Nha Trang, this immaculate resort of flat-roof villas is chiseled into cliffs that shelter a private bay and infinity pool that melds into the sea. **Pros:** free movies on demand; private beach; one-bedroom condos are an excellent value. **Cons:** far from central Nha Trang; hotel is often fully booked. $ *Rooms from:* 4720000d ⊠ *Bai Dong, Cam Hai Dong, Cam Lam* ☎ 0258/398–9666 ⊕ *www.mianhatrang.com* ↩ *18 condos, 28 villas, 2 suites* ⍟ *Breakfast.*

$$$$
HOTEL

Novotel Nha Trang. An international-standard high-rise hotel, the Novotel has airy spacious rooms, each with its own balcony with great views of Nha Trang Bay, as well as courteous, well-trained staff and a private section of beach across the road. **Pros:** central location, close to main tourist area; room rate includes access to private beach across the road from the hotel, with sun-lounge. **Cons:** not right on the beach. [$] *Rooms from: 2850000d* ✉ *50 Tran Phu* ☎ *0258/6256-900* 🌐 *www.accorhotels.com* 🛏 *152 rooms, 2 suites* 🍴 *No meals.*

$$$$ HOTEL FAMILY 🏨 **Sheraton Nha Trang Hotel & Spa.** The 30-story Sheraton Nha Trang has a wellness and relaxation focus, which is aided by the stunning views of Nha Trang's famous crescent bay, resortlike infinity pool on the sixth floor, state-of-the-art fitness center, kids' club, and on-site cooking school. **Pros:** central location, close to restaurants and shops; excellent in-house dining options. **Cons:** across the road from the beach, rather than on the beach. [$] *Rooms from: 4327000d* ✉ *26–28 Tran Phu* ☎ *0258/3880–000* 🌐 *www.sheratonnhatrang.com* 🛏 *217 rooms, 63 suites* 🍴 *Breakfast.*

$$$$ RESORT 🏨 **Six Senses Ninh Van Bay.** On a white sandy beach, backed by towering mountains, Six Senses Ninh Van Bay has 58 villas, each with two rooms, a garden terrace, private pool, and ocean views. **Pros:** stunning beach; excellent restaurant (open, by appointment, to nonguests). **Cons:** expensive food and drinks; 20 minutes from Nha Trang; can be accessed only by boat. [$] *Rooms from: 12006000d* ✉ *Ninh Van Bay, Ninh Hoa* ☎ *0258/352–4268* 🌐 *www.sixsenses.com* 🛏 *58 villas* 🍴 *Breakfast.*

$$$$ RESORT 🏨 **Some Days of Silence Resort and Spa.** Promising a peaceful retreat from everyday life, this boutique property has just nine bungalows, all with soothing views of the garden or the ocean. **Pros:** friendly staff; excellent in-house restaurant. **Cons:** isolated; limited dining options outside the resort; sometimes quite a bit of trash washes up on the nearby beach. [$] *Rooms from: 2365000d* ✉ *Dong Hai, Ninh Hoa - Hon Khoi, Doc Let Beach* ☎ *0258/3670–952* 🌐 *www.somedaysresort.com* 🛏 *9 bungalows* 🍴 *Breakfast.*

$$$ RESORT 🏨 **Whale Island Resort** (*L'Ile de la Baleine*). This tranquil beachfront eco-lodge in Van Phong Bay, about two hours north of Nha Trang, has basic but comfortable fan-cooled bamboo bungalows set among coconut palms. **Pros:** a great getaway from everything, with just enough activities to keep boredom at bay. **Cons:** no air-conditioning; set meals are compulsory; bugs and geckos are part and parcel of island life in the tropics. [$] *Rooms from: 1070000d* ✉ *2 Me Linh* ☎ *0258/3840–501* 🌐 *www.iledelabaleine.com* 🛏 *19 rooms, 14 beach bungalows* 🍴 *Multiple meal plans.*

SPORTS AND THE OUTDOORS

Just 45 minutes by boat from Nha Trang, the island of Hon Mun is considered the best dive destination in the South China Sea. Further north at Van Phuong Bay is the more spectacular Whale Island, where Jacque Cousteau conducted his first Vietnamese explorations. Nha Trang has all kinds of water-related activities, including snorkeling, Jet Skiing, scuba diving, and boating. You can rent equipment through most hotels or operators right on the beach.

BOATING AND DIVING

Buffalo Safari Tours. Specializing in tours for cruise ship visitors, Buffalo Safari Tours offers personalized day and half-day tours of Nha Trang and surrounds, including river and island tours. This is a more upmarket option for those wanting to avoid the party boat tour crowds. ☎ *0167/820–865* ⊕ *www.buffalosafaritours.com.*

Funky Monkey Tours. For a fun and cheap day trip, join one of Funky Monkey's daily boat trip tours, which includes snorkeling, lunch, entertainment by the Funky Monkey Boy Band, and access to the floating bar. Note: the tour price doesn't include entry fees to two of the islands or the Tri Nguyen Aquarium. Funky Monkey has a range of other day tours, including city, river, and fishing tours. ✉ *75A Hung Vuong* ☎ *0258/3522–426* ⊕ *funkymonkeytour.com.*

Rainbow Divers. Although Nha Trang's streets are lined with dive shops, Rainbow Divers is the only one to receive the prestigious PADI Five Star National Geographic Dive Center Award, given for the shop's progressive environmental practices. Dives start at $90 and take place at 7 am daily. The team here also offers instructor courses, trips to Whale Island, and snorkeling packages ($25) that include equipment and lunch. The outfit is open year-round but the best diving is from March to October. ✉ *90A Hung Vuong* ☎ *0258/352–4351* ⊕ *www.divevietnam.com.*

Sailing Club Divers. This five-star dive center offers snorkeling tours, scuba-diving courses, and diving packages to Hon Mun Island. Trips take place daily 8–2, and start at $50 for a two-tank dive and $20 for snorkeling tours. ✉ *72–74 Tran Phu* ☎ *258/352–2788* ⊕ *www. sailingclubdivers.com.*

GOLF

VinPearl Golf Club. This 18-hole par 71 championship course, designed by IMG, is part of the Vinpearl complex on Hon Tre Island, accessible by (free) speedboat and a shuttle across the island. Every hole has spectacular views of Nha Trang Bay, with water in play on most holes. Practice facilities include a 300-yard driving range and an all-grass teeing area. ✉ *Hon Tre Island* ☎ *0258/3590–919* ⊕ *vinpearlgolf.com* 🏌 *9 holes from 945,000d, 18 holes from 1,575,000d on weekdays* 🏌 *18 holes, 6787 yards, par 71.*

SHOPPING

Dam and Xom Moi Markets. Test your bartering skills at the local markets, where you can find everything from clothing and food to souvenirs and electronics. With its knockoff brands and cheap trinkets, Dam Market caters to tourists, while Xom Moi is more for locals who come for the fresh produce and dried goods. Xom Moi is at 49 Ngo Gia Tu Street. Dam Market is on the corner of Hai Ba Trung and Phan Boi Chau. Both are open daily 6–6. ✉ *Xom Moi, 49 Ngo Gia Tu St.*

Nha Trang Center. The area's only shopping mall includes a bowling alley, movie theater, grocery store, and more than 100 brand-name shops that sell everything from clothing and jewelry to souvenirs and sunglasses. The top floor has a food court for those looking for a quick bite while bargain shopping. ✉ *20 Tran Phu St.* ☎ *0258/222–6259* ⊕ *www. nhatrangcenter.com.*

XQ Dalat Historical Village. Located across from the main beach, this village replica has several galleries showcasing hand-embroidered works from Nha Trang, Hanoi, Danang, Hue, and Ho Chi Minh City. Even if you don't plan to buy anything, it's worth taking a peek at the on-site seamstresses as they guide their needles through cloth to create impressive works of art that resemble paintings. ✉ *64 Tran Phu* ☎ *0258/352–6579* ⊕ *www.tranhtheuxq.com.*

THE CENTRAL HIGHLANDS

Part of the southern end of the Truong Son range, Vietnam's Central Highlands are a landscape of mountains, clear streams, dense forests, and gushing waterfalls spread over the provinces of Lam Dong, Dac Lac, Gia Lai, and Kon Tum. The area also includes the towns of Buon Ma Thout, Pleiku, and Kon Tum. With the increasing development of coffee, pepper, tea plantations, and rice farms, the region has become an important agricultural center. his is one of the

> **A VIEW WORTH STOPPING FOR**
>
> About 43 km (27 miles) southeast of Dalat, on the way to Nha Trang, along Highway 20, the Ngoan Muc Pass affords superb views of the surrounding lush countryside and, on a clear day, the Pacific Ocean in the distance, some 55 km (34 miles) away.

few parts of the country where it is cool enough to wear a sweater, even in summer. Vietnam's hill tribes have long been the primary inhabitants of the central highlands, but in the last decades the region has seen significant settlement by lowland Vietnamese. A large population of these hill tribes, also known as Montagnards from the French for "mountain people," inhabits the difficult-to-reach western part of the Central Highlands. Some of the tribes have lived in Vietnam for thousands of years; others came from neighboring Thailand several centuries ago. These tribes of largely nomadic farmers, who live an isolated existence, are culturally and linguistically distinct from each other and from the ethnic Vietnamese who make up the majority of the country's population.

Cat Tien National Park, which spans the lowlands and the start of the Truong Son mountain range, lies almost midway between Ho Chi Minh City and the mountain town of Dalat. This is the principal town of the southern Central Highlands region. It has an abundance of natural beauty and a good measure of kitschy tourist development targeted at the domestic market.

CAT TIEN NATIONAL PARK

150 km (93 miles) northwest of Ho Chi Minh City, 175 km (109 miles) southwest of Dalat.

This vast park, recognized as a UNESCO biosphere reserve, includes jungle, swampland, lakes, rivers, and hills, all of which are home to a multitude of exotic flora and fauna.

GETTING HERE AND AROUND

Cat Tien National Park is three hours by road from Ho Chi Minh City. Buses that ply the Ho Chi Minh City–Dalat route, including Phuong Trang, stop at the Tan Phu Post Office. From here, it takes 45 minutes by xe om or car to traverse the 24 km (15 miles) to the national park. If you prebook a room at the national park's hotel, you can also organize a private car pickup from the Tan Phu Post Office for 640,000d return. The national park office offers transportation around the park, as well as boat and bicycle hire. There are several accommodations outside the park that offer transfers to the park, as well as tours and other activities within the park.

EXPLORING

Cat Tien National Park. The 72,000-hectare ruggedly beautiful Cat Tien National Park, one of six biosphere reserves recognized by UNESCO in Vietnam, is home to hundreds of species of plants, birds, animals, and reptiles, including several species of endangered monkeys, Asian elephants, sun bears, and gaur. (Sadly, Vietnam's last Javan rhino was shot in the park by poachers in 2010.) The national park office has cars, bicycles, and boats available for hire and guests staying at the National Park's hotel can book early morning gibbon treks for 1,050,000d per person. The price includes breakfast at one of the two restaurants inside the park and a tour of the gibbon rehabilitation center. Accommodation within the park is basic, with small double rooms starting at 680,000d. There are nicer accommodation options outside the park, which can also arrange jungle excursions for you. ✉ *Nam Cat Tien, Tan Phu, Dong Nai* ☎ *0251/3669–228* 🌐 *www.namcattien.vn.*

Dambri Falls. The biggest waterfall in Lam Dong Province, the thundering Dambri Falls are 130 km (80 miles) southwest of Dalat and 19 km (12 miles) from the village of Bao Loc, near Cat Tien National Park. Like most of the falls in the area, they are surrounded by tasteless local "eco" tourism development, including trinket shops and a mini roller coaster. The 70-meter-high falls are still impressive, whether viewed from the paths in front of the waterfall, or from behind. According to local legend, the waterfalls are the tears of a girl called Bri who cried as she sat and waited for her love to return from the forest. The boy, Kdam, never did and when Bri died, her body turned to stone but her tears kept flowing. ■ **TIP→ Avoid Dambri Falls on weekends and public holidays when it's very crowded.** ✉ *Ly Thai Tho, Bao Loc* 🎟 *50,000d* 🕑 *Daily 7–5.*

WHERE TO EAT AND STAY

$ B&B/INN 🏨 **Green Hope Lodge.** Across the river from the national park, the family-owned Green Hope Lodge has basic but comfortable bungalows with mosquito nets (essential), spacious clean bathrooms, communal dining, and a range of tours and excursions in the park and surrounding villages. **Pros:** peaceful and rustic setting; charming staff. **Cons:** a 10-minute walk to the pier to cross the river to the national park; no other dining options nearby. [$] *Rooms from: 537000d* ✉ *Hamlet 4, Cat Tien Ward, Tan Phu, Dong Nai* ☎ *0251/3669–919* 🌐 *greenhopelodge.com* 🛏 *7 rooms* 🍴 *Breakfast.*

$ B&B/INN FAMILY Fodor's Choice ★ **Ta Lai Longhouse.** This traditional bamboo longhouse is a great base for adventurous travelers to experience all that Cat Tien National Park has to offer, as well as local village life. **Pros:** authentic local experience; wonderful staff; Wi-Fi. **Cons:** communal sleeping means little privacy. [$] *Rooms from: 450000d* ✉ *Ta Lai Village, Dong Nai* ☎ *097/4160–827* 🌐 *talai-adventure.vn* 🛏 *1 longhouse, which sleeps up to 30 people* 🍴 *Breakfast.*

DALAT

308 km (191 miles) north of Ho Chi Minh City, 205 km (127 miles) southwest of Nha Trang.

With its mini–Eiffel Tower and colonial architecture, the mountain resort of Dalat bears a vague resemblance to a French town. Its temperate climate and cool misty mornings provide a welcome respite from Vietnam's tropical heat. Kitsch is a Dalat specialty, in the form of swan-shape paddleboats, tacky souvenirs, and tourist attractions designed to be backdrops for photo ops. It's a favorite destination for Vietnamese honeymooners. Named for the "River of the Lat Tribe," after the native Lat people, Dalat was "discovered" in 1892 by Dr. Alexandre Yersin (1863–1943), a protégé of scientist Louis Pasteur. It quickly became a vacation spot for Europeans eager to escape the infernal heat of the coastal plains, the big cities, and the Mekong Delta. During the Vietnam War the city was a favored nonpartisan resting spot for both high-ranking North and South Vietnamese officers, before it capitulated to the North Vietnamese on April 3, 1975.

Dalat's prime sight is its market, an interesting place to poke around day or night, and the city also has a number of interesting temples that are worth exploring. For golfers, an 18-hole golf course originally set up by Emperor Bao Dai is now known as one of the best in the region.

GETTING HERE AND AROUND

Lien Khuong Airport is about 28 km (17 miles) from Dalat. Try to negotiate a taxi fare of around 300,000d to get to Dalat rather than using the meter. An airport bus, which meets every flight, also runs to Le Thi Hong Gam Street in Dalat. Tickets are 40,000d.

Dalat's main depot, 3 km (2 miles) south of the central market, is serviced regularly by buses from Ho Chi Minh City, Nha Trang, and Mui Ne, as well as points north. Hiring a taxi for full day to see the sights of Dalat city should cost around 400,000d.

ESSENTIALS

Taxi Contacts Mai Linh taxis (☎ *063/3511–111*), Da Lat taxis (☎ *063/3556–655*).

TOURS

Dalat Backpacker Easyrider. This is a well-regarded outfitter that offers motorbike tours around Dalat and longer multiday trips that can take you through the Central Highlands to Hoi An, Nha Trang, Ho Chi Minh City, or even right down to the Mekong Delta or north to Hanoi. ✉ *7/2 Hai Thuong St* 🌐 *easyridertours.vn.*

Dalat Easy Rider. This outfit may or may not be the original Dalat Easy Rider group, so many Dalat-based motorbike touring companies make the claim. The truth is that most of the original easy riders have retired so there are no real originals out there anymore. This company, whatever its origins, is reliable and professional, but like any tour, your enjoyment hinges on how you relate to your guide. So do visit the Easy Rider headquarters and have a chat with potential drivers to make sure you get along. Dalat Easy Riders offer one-day countryside tours around Dalat for very reasonable prices. Longer tours, either as pillion passengers or self-driving with an easy rider guide, can be arranged at good prices. You can email to negotiate prices, and you will be required to pay a deposit via Western Union. ✉ *70 Phan Dinh Phung, Dalat* ✎ *vndalateasyriders@yahoo.com* ⊕ *dalat-easyrider.com.*

Groovy Gecko Tours. Trekking, biking, rock climbing, canyoning, cycling—take your pick of athletic and adventurous tours with this fun and professional tour company that offers day tours as well as multiday trips from Dalat around the Central Highlands. ✉ *65 Truong Cong Dinh* ☎ *0263/3836–836* ⊕ *www.groovygeckotours.net.*

Phat Tire Ventures. This safety-conscious, fun-loving Dalat-based adventure tour company offers trekking, canyoning, cycling, and mountain-biking day and multiday trips, including cycling tours from Dalat down the mountain to either Nha Trang, Mui Ne, or Hoi An. Phat Tire also has a lakeside ropes course that's mainly used for team-building activities and school trips. ✉ *109 Nguyen Van Troi* ☎ *0263/3829–422* ⊕ *www.ptv-vietnam.com.*

EXPLORING

TOP ATTRACTIONS

Bao Dai's Summer Palace (*Dinh III*). A yellow cement structure built in 1933, Bao Dai's Summer Palace, on the south side of Xuan Huong Lake, is a wonderfully preserved example of modernist architecture. The palace houses the original 1930s French furnishings of Emperor Bao Dai, the last emperor of the Nguyen dynasty, who ruled from 1926 to 1945 with the support of the French. With hundreds of visitors tramping through each week, the palace is showing its age. If you manage to avoid a big tour group, it's possible to find a quiet spot that feels like it's been suspended in time. For a kitsch souvenir, you can can have your photo taken wearing a traditional royal getup. ✉ *1 Trieu Viet Vuong* ☎ *063/3540–213* 🎫 *15,000d* ☉ *Daily 7 am–5 pm.*

Central Market. Originally built in 1929 and rebuilt in 1937 after a fire, the central market is the heart of Dalat. Locals and tourists come to the indoor-outdoor market to buy and sell fruit, vegetables, and local specialties such as dried fruit, fruit candy, flowers, mulberry wine, and jam. The main part of the two-story market is open from before dawn until nightfall. At sundown, a food town springs up outside the market and down the steps beside it. The specialty is *banh trang Dalat*, almost like a pizza on rice paper, barbecued, rolled up, and wrapped in a piece of newspaper. ✉ *4 Nguyen Thi Minh Khai.*

Crémaillère Railway (*Ga Da Lat*). In 1933, 30 years after work started, a 105-km (65-mile) cog railway line was completed, linking Dalat to

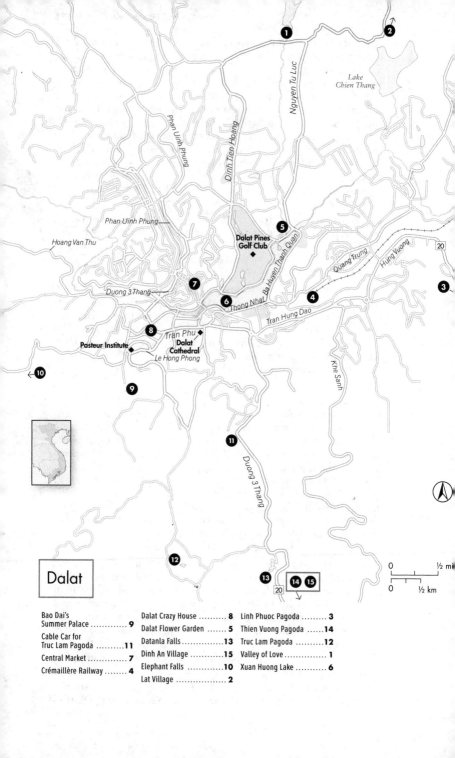

Lake
Chien Thang

Nguyen Tu Luc

Phan Uinh Phung

Dinh Tien Hoang

Hoang Van Thu

Phan Uinh Phung

**Dalat Pines
Golf Club**

Quang Trung

Hung Vuong

20

Duong 3 Thang

Thong Nhat

Ba Huyen Thanh Quan

Tran Hung Dao

Khe Sanh

Pasteur Institute

Tran Phu

**Dalat
Cathedral**

Le Hong Phong

Duong 3 Thang

0   ½ mi
0   ½ km

20

Dalat

Bao Dai's
Summer Palace **9**

Cable Car for
Truc Lam Pagoda **11**

Central Market **7**

Crémaillère Railway **4**

Dalat Crazy House **8**

Dalat Flower Garden **5**

Datanla Falls **13**

Dinh An Village **15**

Elephant Falls **10**

Lat Village **2**

Linh Phuoc Pagoda **3**

Thien Vuong Pagoda **14**

Truc Lam Pagoda **12**

Valley of Love **1**

Xuan Huong Lake **6**

Nha Trang and Saigon. The line was closed in 1969 and the track ripped up sometime after the war ended in 1975. Twenty years later, a 7-km (4-mile) section of the track was restored and the art deco railway station renovated. Now it's possible to take the train (which now uses diesel traction) to the village of Trai Mat, home to the Linh Phuoc Pagoda. The round-trip takes two hours, although actually catching the train can prove tricky. It only departs once 10 people have bought tickets so it's best to get your hotel to call ahead to check the state of play. The railway station itself is architecturally interesting, with the three roofs representing the peaks of Lang Biang mountain while also paying tribute to the high pointed roofs of traditional Central Highlands communal houses. Vietnam's last steam locomotive sits at the station, serving as a basic coffee shop. The station and the locomotive are popular with wedding photographers, especially during the wedding "season" that runs from November to January. ⊠ *1 Quang Trung* ☎ *0263/3834–409* ✉ *Free to visit train station. Train tickets are 106,000d for non-Vietnamese.*

4

FAMILY **Dalat Crazy House** (*Biet thu Hang Nga*). This psychedelic flight of architectural whimsy will probably be the wackiest thing you see in Vietnam, which is saying something, given the local penchant for quirkiness. Free-form stairs and tunnels wend their way through multistory Dr. Seuss–like concrete trees that contain 10 hotel rooms, unexpected sitting areas, and concrete animals. Its owner and designer, Dr. Dang Viet Nga, who studied architecture in Russia, built the structure to remind people of the importance of nature and the environment. Work on the crazy house is ongoing, and is not expected to be completed until 2020. ⚠ **Some of the staircases are very steep and the railings quite low. People who are unsteady on their feet or in charge of small children should be very careful.** ⊠ *1 Huynh Thuc Khang* ☎ *0263/3822–070* ⊕ *www.crazyhouse. vn* ✉ *45,000d* ☽ *Daily 7 am–8 pm.*

Xuan Huong Lake (*Ho Xuan Huong*). Circumscribed by a walking path, Xuan Huong Lake is a hub of leisurely activity, including swan-shape paddleboats. Although there's traffic nearby, the lake provides a pleasant place to walk and bike. The dam-generated lake takes its name from à 17th-century Vietnamese poet known for her daring attacks on the hypocrisy of social conventions and the foibles of scholars, monks, mandarins, feudal lords, and kings. ⊠ *Tran Quoc Toan.*

WORTH NOTING

Dalat Flower Garden (*Vuon Hoa Dalat*). The Dalat Flower Garden, on the northeast side of Xuan Huong Lake, contains 300 species of native and exotic flowers, including roses, hydrangeas, fuschias, and mimosa. The colors are particularly vibrant in the late afternoon, as the light turns golden ahead of sunset. In January and February, around the time of Tet (the lunar new year), a wide variety of *hoa lan* (orchids) are in full bloom. ⊠ *2 Phu Dong Thien Vuong* ☎ *0263/3553–545* ✉ *30,000d* ☽ *Daily 6–6.*

Datanla Falls (*Thac Datanla*). One of Dalat's more easily accessible waterfalls, Datanla Falls is 5 km (3 miles) south of the city. The entrance is near the top of the falls and an easy 15-minute walk takes you down to the bottom. The more adventurous can reach the bottom via a mini-roller coaster (45,000d per person). ⊠ *Deo Prenn* 🔊 *10,000d.*

Dinh An Village (Chicken Village). A K'Ho ethnic minority village, Dinh An has found itself on the tourist radar mainly because of its proximity to the highway and its giant concrete chicken. The village itself is quite spread out, with most families involved in small-scale farming of vegetables and flowers. The villagers don't wear their traditional dress, which disappoints some visitors, but keep in mind that they receive minimal benefit from tourists trooping through. There's a couple of small handicraft shops and a tiny grocery store across from the chicken statue. ang Dinh An Village is 9 km (5½ miles) from the airport and could be visited en route to Dalat rather than by making the 18-km (11-mile) trip from Dalat. The village is often included in easy rider tours, and is only really worth visiting as one stop on a day-long exploration of the countryside surrounding Dalat. ⊠ *Dinh An.*

Elephant Falls (*Thac Voi*). About 30 km (19 miles) southwest of Dalat, these 30-meter-high waterfalls (one large and several smaller falls) are a popular stop on easy rider countryside tours. The mossy path down to the viewing area can be treacherous in the rainy season and challenging in the dry season, but once there, the views are impressive. It takes about 45 minutes to get the falls, which are just outside the village of Nam Ban. There's a coffee shop and handicraft shop at the waterfalls. Take the time to check out the textiles woven on-site by Ms. Inra Anh and her family, from the K'Ho ethnic minority. Also wander next door to the Linh An Pagoda, a peaceful working temple with hydrangeas and pine trees in the garden and a giant Happy Buddha (which doubles as a storage shed for garden supplies) out the back. The pagoda is closed for lunch from noon to 1:30. ⊠ *Off DT725.*

Lat Village. About 12 km (7½ miles) north of Dalat, at the base of Langbian Mountain, is Lat Village, home to the Lat minority group for which Dalat is named. The village is a popular stop on guided tours, with tour guides pointing out traditional farming and weaving techniques and the village's handicraft shops. It's not a very edifying site and those with an interest in Vietnam's ethnic minorities should venture farther afield, to Lak Lake and Kon Tum, for a more authentic experience. ⊠ *Lat Village.*

Linh Phuoc Pagoda (*Chua Ve Trai*). The gaudy Linh Phuoc Pagoda is in Trai Mat, a village 7 km (4 miles) northeast of Dalat accessible by road or the tourist train. Completed in 1952, the colorful pagoda is known for the inlaid pieces of broken glass throughout and the 49-meter-long dragon made from 12,000 beer bottles, as well as for its bell and 36-meter-high bell tower. This is an amazing piece of architecture worth exploring even by those suffering temple fatigue. ⊠ *120 Tu Phuoc, Trai Mat Village.*

Thien Vuong Pagoda (*Chua Tao Thien Voung*). The Chinese Thien Voung Pagoda, southeast of town, sits atop a steep mountain with great views of the surrounding area. The pagoda was built in 1958 by the Chaozhou Chinese congregation. Three large, Hong Kong–made gilded sandalwood sculptures dominate the pagoda in the third of the three buildings, and peaceful gardens surround the complex. ✉ *Mimosa St.* 🎟 *Free* ⏲ *Daily 9–4.*

Truc Lam Pagoda. This peaceful Zen Buddhist pagoda, about 5 km (3 miles) from central Dalat, sits on top of Phuong Hoang Hill, and the best way to get here is via cable car (70,000d return). The 24-hectare complex is relatively new, completed only in 1994, and includes a working monastery in a section that's closed to the public, as well as a meditation center. The public areas include a ceremonial hall, bell tower, and beautiful flower garden. The pagoda is next to Tuyen Lam Lake and the 15-minute stroll down to shore is pleasant.

To organize a visit to the meditation center, women should call the nuns on (☎ *063/3830–558*), and men should speak to the monks (☎ *063/3827–565*). Day visits are relatively easy to arrange, although every guest needs to be approved by the Grand Master so you may need a separate visit to gain approval. Longer stays are possible but require some complicated paperwork. The monks and nuns can explain the steps involved. ✉ *Cable Car station, Ba Thang Thu* ☎ *0263/382–7565.*

4

FAMILY **Valley of Love** (*Thung Lung Tinh Yeu*). A superb example of how Dalat won its reputation as a kitschy destination, the Valley of Love is a pseudo theme park popular with honeymooning Vietnamese couples for photographs with "cute" man-made backdrops. Set in a valley that leads down to a lake, the park can keep younger kids entertained for quite a while, with fairground rides, a miniature train, swan-shaped pedal boats, and carriages drawn by very skinny horses. Older kids might enjoy paintball and jeep rides. The main attraction for adults is not the views but the people-watching opportunities. ✉ *7 Mai Anh Dao* ☎ *0263/3554–311* 🌐 *thunglungtinhyeu.vn* 🎟 *30,000d* ⏲ *Daily 7:30–5.*

WHERE TO EAT

$ CAFÉ 🍴 **Bicycle Up Cafe, Bar and Store.** A cute and quirky little coffee shop serving a range of drinks, including beer, cakes, ice cream, and yogurt, Bicycle Up is a great place to rest and recharge with a book (check out the homemade book light fittings), a coffee, or a fruit smoothie while listening to mellow jazz. This quiet refuge is perfect for a rainy day. [$] *Average main: 50000d* ✉ *82 Truong Cong Dinh* ☎ *0263/3700–177* 💳 *No credit cards.*

$ VIETNAMESE 🍴 **Dalat Night Market.** Sampling a fresh *banh trang,* aka Dalat pizza, from one of the night market street vendors is a must—a great snack to sustain you while you explore all that the night market has to offer. *Banh trang* is a circle of rice paper, brushed with an egg and dried prawn mixture, barbecued on an open brazier, folded, and wrapped in a square of newspaper. There are many banh trang sellers at the top of the stairs next to the market. Along the stairs and at the base of the staircase are more food vendors, offering a range of soups, *chao* (rice porridge), and barbecued chicken feet. [$] *Average main: 40000d* ✉ *Near Dalat Central Market.*

$$ CAFÉ 🍴 **Dalat Train Cafe.** A quaint little café in a restored 1910 French train carriage that's now parked in lovely grounds next to a small guesthouse, this place serves up a selection of Western and Vietnamese dishes and a ton of charm. For trainspotters wanting to get a double train fix,

the café and its friendly staff are an easy walk along a main road and down a narrow local road from the old Dalat Railway Station. $ *Average main: 100000d ✉ Villa #3, 1 Quang Trung ✚ From Xuan Huong Lake, take first left after old Dalat Railway Station* ☎ 0263/3816–365 ⊕ *www.dalattrainvilla.com.*

$$
VIETNAMESE

✕ **Goc Ha Thanh.** This is a cheap-and-cheerful eatery serving up slightly Westernized versions of Vietnamese fare from a cute little place a short walk from the Central Market. The service can be a bit slow, but the food is reliably delicious and reasonably priced. Try the spring rolls (worth ordering for the presentation alone), the vegetable curry, and the Dalat salad. $ *Average main: 100000d ✉ 53 Truong Cong Dinh* ☎ 0263/3553–369.

$$
VEGETARIAN

✕ **Hoa Sen.** This is the pick of Dalat's many vegan places, with a focus on fresh local produce rather than mock meat (although that's on the menu, too), served up in a bright, airy space with wooden furniture. Hoa Sen is very popular with locals for a good reason: the food is delicious. Try the tom yum soup, banana leaf salad, and the hotpot. $ *Average main: 90000d ✉ 62 Phan Dinh Phung* ☎ 0263/3567–999.

$$$$
FRENCH
Fodor's Choice
★

✕ **Le Cafe de la Poste.** Part of the Du Parc Hotel across the road, Le Cafe de la Poste is housed in a former French colonial department store with wooden floorboards, intimate window booths, and outdoor seating under umbrellas (which is a great vantage point for watching the city wake up in the morning). The menu offers a range of French and Asian dishes and the set lunch menu offers great value. $ *Average main: 600000d ✉ 12 Tran Phu* ☎ 0263/3825–444.

$$$$
FRENCH

✕ **Le Rabelais.** Allow yourself to be transported to a French country estate, complete with chandeliers, period furniture, starched linens, gleaming silverware, flawless service, and fine French cuisine. With an extensive wine list and gentle live piano music, this is the place for a romantic—albeit expensive—evening in a superb setting. Le Rabelais also does lunch and a sumptuous high tea: colonial-era opulence at its finest. $ *Average main: 1500000d ✉ Dalat Palace Luxury Hotel, 2 Tran Phu* ☎ 0263/3825–444 ⊕ *www.dalatresorts.com* ⚑ *Reservations essential.*

$
VIETNAMESE

✕ **Nem Nuong Ba Hung.** This plain but pleasant local eatery serves only one dish: *nem nuong* (barbecued pork skewers), with a range of edible accoutrements that are rolled up and dunked in a delicious dipping sauce. $ *Average main: 40000d ✉ 254 Phan Dinh Phung* ☎ 0263/3824–344.

$$
INTERNATIONAL

✕ **News And New Art Cafe.** Tacky to some, quaint to others, the News and New Art Café is one of the many tourist-oriented eateries in Dalat, serving a range of Vietnamese and international dishes. The unique selling point of this café is the artwork of owner Vo Trinh Bien, famous for his ink and red wine finger painting technique. Every now and again Mr. Bien will paint for his customers. $ *Average main: 100000d ✉ 70 Truong Cong Dinh* ☎ 0263/3510–089 ▭ *No credit cards.*

$
VIETNAMESE

✕ **Pho Hieu.** This basic streetside eatery is insanely popular with locals for its steaming bowls of beef *pho*, with a dessert chaser of local yogurt. Pull up a plastic chair and find out why the Vietnamese love this place.

💲 *Average main: 35000d* ✉ *23 Tang Bat Ho* ☎ *0263/383–0580* ▭ *No credit cards.*

$$$
VIETNAMESE
✕ **Thanh Thuy Blue Water Restaurant.** A stylish lakeside location for coffee, cocktails, or a meal, either on the deck under one of the purple umbrellas or inside, Thanh Thuy has an extensive menu (in English) of Vietnamese, Szechuan, and Vietnamese twists on Western dishes. Prices are quite high for Vietnam but there's no better view in town. The service can seem slow if you're not used to the local style of flagging a water down when you need one, rather than waiting for service. 💲 *Average main: 240000d* ✉ *2 Nguyen Thai Hoc* ☎ *0263/3531–668* ▭ *No credit cards.*

WHERE TO STAY

$$$$
RESORT
Fodor's Choice
★
🏨 **Ana Mandara Villas Dalat Resort & Spa.** This charming resort, on a hill 5 km (3 miles) from downtown Dalat, comprises 17 French colonial villas restored to capture the elegance of a former age, albeit with every modern convenience, including a spa for pampering. **Pros:** heated swimming pool; great breakfast and dining options; impeccable service. **Cons:** 10 minutes by taxi from all the downtown action. 💲 *Rooms from: 2400000d* ✉ *Le Lai* ☎ *0263/355–5888* ⊕ *anamandara-resort. com* ⇆ *48 rooms, 24 suites* ⏺️ *Breakfast.*

$$$$
RESORT
🏨 **Binh An Village.** A misty mountain paradise near Tuyen Lam lake, about 20 minutes outside of Dalat, Binh An Village is a boutique resort that pays tribute to Dalat's French and hill tribe heritage in its design and decor. **Pros:** free shuttle into Dalat; use of kayaks. **Cons:** isolated. 💲 *Rooms from: 4277000d* ✉ *Tuyen Lam Lake* ☎ *0263/3800–999* ⊕ *www.binhanvillage.com* ⇆ *16 rooms, 10 suites* ⏺️ *Breakfast.*

$
HOTEL
🏨 **Camellia Hotel.** A new player in the budget niche in Dalat, the Camellia Hotel is wowing even nonbudget travelers with its clean, comfortable, spacious rooms, welcoming staff, homemade peanut butter and strawberry jam, and basement recreation area with pool table and PlayStation. **Pros:** great price; friendly and helpful staff. **Cons:** slightly outside the action of central Dalat; decor is a bit spartan. 💲 *Rooms from: 252000d* ✉ *56 Le Thanh Ton* ☎ *0263/3819–279* ⇆ *15 rooms, 2 dorms* ⏺️ *Breakfast.*

$$
HOTEL
🏨 **Dalat Crazy House.** Each of the 10 rooms has its own offbeat theme at this small guesthouse, which is also a tourist attraction in its own right, but beware: the Dalat Crazy House has the kitsch factor turned up so high it's almost off the scale. **Pros:** a unique experience; makes for an unusual travel tale. **Cons:** tourists knock on the doors of the hotel rooms and peer in the windows from 8:30 am to 7 pm when the attraction is open to the public; not suitable for anyone with vertigo. 💲 *Rooms from: 750000d* ✉ *3 Huynh Thuc Khang* ☎ *0263/3822–070* ⊕ *www.crazyhouse.vn* ⇆ *10 rooms* ⏺️ *No meals.*

$$$$
HOTEL
🏨 **Dalat Palace Luxury Hotel.** Retaining the splendor and charm of a bygone age with 15-foot ceilings, ornate fireplaces, artworks, beautiful manicured grounds, library, and spacious rooms with claw-foot bathtubs and original moldings, this historic property oozes old-world charm, matched by world-class service. **Pros:** central location with great views over the lake; genuine link to history. **Cons:** as you would expect in a property of this age, things malfunction from time to time.

$ Rooms from: 4400000d ⊠ 2 Tran Phu ☎ 0263/3825–444 ⊕ www.dalatresorts.com ⮎ 48 rooms ⭢◉⭠ Breakfast.

$ 🏨 **Dalat Train Villa.** A boutique guesthouse in a restored French colonial
B&B/INN villa built in 1935, the Dalat Train Villa is associated with the Dalat Train Cafe, which is on the grounds. **Pros:** very intimate property, with only four rooms. **Cons:** standard rooms are on the small side; ground floor rooms can be noisy if guests are staying in the rooms above. $ Rooms from: 500000d ⊠ 1 Quang Trung, Villa #3 ☎ 0263/3816–365 ⊕ www.dalattrainvilla.com ⮎ 4 rooms ⭢◉⭠ Breakfast.

$$$ 🏨 **Du Parc Hotel Dalat.** Built in 1932 to take the overflow from the popu-
HOTEL lar Langbian Palace Hotel (now the Dalat Palace Luxury Hotel), the art deco–style Du Parc Hotel Dalat is full of character, from the original metal-cage elevator and the ornate staircase in the lobby to the hardwood floors in the rooms. **Pros:** charming old-world feel at very reasonable prices. **Cons:** small rooms; no air-conditioning; breakfast is served across the road. $ Rooms from: 1400000d ⊠ 7 Tran Phu ☎ 0263/3825–777 ⊕ www.dalatresorts.com ⮎ 140 rooms ⭢◉⭠ Breakfast.

$$ 🏨 **Terrasse des Roses.** This romantic boutique hotel, on a hill 3 km (2
HOTEL miles) from downtown Dalat, is one of the city's best-kept secrets. **Pros:** the peaceful atmosphere is most conducive to relaxing; incredibly helpful staff. **Cons:** breakfast is modest; Wi-Fi can be patchy in the rooms. $ Rooms from: 890000d ⊠ 35 Cao Ba Quat ☎ 0263/3565–279 ⊕ www.terrassedesroses-villa.com ⮎ 8 rooms, 1 suite ⭢◉⭠ Breakfast.

$$ 🏨 **Villa Vista Highlands Home.** The standout feature of this small B&B
B&B/INN with fancifully ornate French decor and stunning panoramic views of
Fodor's Choice Dalat is the attentive and welcoming hosts, Australian Tim and his
★ Vietnamese wife Huong, who are happy to share their love of cooking, music, and Dalat with their guests. **Pros:** intimate, friendly atmosphere. **Cons:** outside the main tourist district. $ Rooms from: 860000d ⊠ Ngo Thi Sy ☎ 0263/3512–468 ⮎ 4 rooms ⭢◉⭠ Breakfast.

$ 🏨 **Zen Café & Villas.** A very intimate place to stay, the family-run Zen Café
B&B/INN and Villas only has three rooms, but all are comfortable and tastefully decorated in a simple French colonial style. **Pros:** lovely homey atmosphere; staff can help with local tourist information, including bookings. **Cons:** not in the heart of Dalat. $ Rooms from: 520000d ⊠ Pham Hong Thai ☎ 0263/5949–311 ⊕ en.zencafedalat.com/guestrooms ⮎ 3 rooms ⭢◉⭠ No meals.

$$$ 🏨 **Zen Valley Dalat.** Zen is a small and tranquil family-owned resort
B&B/INN with lovely views of the valley, large comfortable rooms with modern bathrooms, and an excellent in-house restaurant. **Pros:** personalized service **Cons:** outside the city center. $ Rooms from: 1175000d ⊠ 38 Khe San ☎ 099/4799–518 ⊕ www.zenvalleydalat.com ⮎ 7 rooms, 4 bungalows ⭢◉⭠ Breakfast.

NIGHTLIFE AND PERFORMING ARTS

Dalat's groovy cafés are ideal for quiet reflective evenings, and there's also some newish bars featuring live music. These bars close relatively early here and those wishing to kick on are limited to the karaoke joints, where little English is spoken.

Fodor's Choice **Escape Bar.** Under the same management as V Cafe, Escape Bar has a
★ great live band that plays mostly rock and roll covers every night from

9 pm. The bar attracts a mixture of friendly locals and tourists and visiting musicians are usually welcome to jam with the band. This is the liveliest place in town, usually kicking on until midnight. ⊠ *Basement of Muong Thanh (Blue Moon) Hotel, 4 Phan Boi Chau* ☎ *0263/3578–888* ⊕ *www.vcafedalatvietnam.com.*

V Cafe. This is a cool little café that features surprisingly good live acoustic music every evening from 7:30 to 9 pm and a range of Western and Vietnamese comfort foods. If you're lucky, the owner will join a jam session. ⊠ *1/1 Bui Thi Xuan* ☎ *0263/3520–215* ⊕ *www.vcafedalatvietnam.com.*

SPORTS AND THE OUTDOORS

Dalat offers many activities to appeal to outdoorsy types, including the novelty swan-shape paddleboats that are available to rent on Xuan Huong Lake. Bicycles, including tandem "love bicycles" and mountain bikes, can be rented along the main street, but do check the size of the bikes before you commit to hiring one, as some of them are very small. A number of adventure tour operators cover trekking, cycling, canyoning, and more. *See listings under Essentials for more.*

GOLF

Dalat Pines Golf Club. The pristine and historic Dalat Pines Golf Club has an 18-hole championship course overlooking Xuan Huong Lake. Built in the 1930s with just six holes after Emperor Bao Dai encountered golf on a trip to France, the course was abandoned in 1945 and languished for nine years until a group of investors rebuilt it as an eight-hole course (with one sponsor per hole). he original clubhouse, built in 1956, is still in use today. A full practice facility complements the golf course and clubhouse, with a 290-yard grass driving range, a putting green, and practice bunkers. ⊠ *Phu Dong Thien Vuong* ☎ *0263/3821–201* ⊕ *www.vietnamgolfresorts.com/dalatpalacegolfclub* 🏌 *9 holes from 1,400,000d, 18 holes from 2,200,000d on weekdays, less for Dalat Palace and Du Parc guests.* 🏌 *18 holes, 7009 yards, par 72.*

LAK LAKE

150 km (93 miles) north of Dalat.

Lak Lake, set among picturesque rolling hills, is still an off-the-beaten-path destination, even though the last Emperor of Vietnam, Bao Dai, saw fit to build a summer house overlooking the lake, which doubles in size in the rainy season. There's a laid-back feel to the lake shore, where most visitors end up, with elephants awaiting passengers or strolling slowly around the lake and through the M'nong settlement of Jun Village. Elephant rides, treks, and homestays can also be organized through Duc Mai Coffee, and their helpful website ⊕ *laklaketravel.com.*

GETTING HERE AND AROUND

Lak Lake is 154 km (96 miles) from Dalat. It's possible to rent a taxi for the day to visit the lake and return to Dalat. Expect to pay around 2,000,000d in a four-seater or 2,500,000d in a seven-seater for a round trip lasting less than 11 hours. Local buses to Lak Lake run regularly between Lak Lake and Buon Ma Thuot's North Coach Station. (☎ *050/876–785*).

EXPLORING

Gong Shows. At the Van Long Motel, gong shows are performed by people from nearby ethnic minority villages. The 45-minute shows, which need to be organized in advance, usually involve dancing and rice wine, and cost about $50, a fee usually split by a group of people. ✉ *N3Y Jut, Buon Le, Lien Son* ☎ *0262/3585–659* 🌐 *www.dulichvanlong.com.*

Jun Village. A small community of about 30 ethnic M'Nong households on the shores of Lak Lake, Jun Village is an interesting place for a stroll to see the traditional bamboo and wood longhouses and the more modern concrete versions, most with a collection of pot-bellied pigs, chickens, dogs, and children running around or napping nearby. There are two restaurants on the lakefront, both serving cheap Vietnamese fare, as well as some handicraft shops selling baskets, weaving, windchimes, and other knickknacks. It's possible to organize a stay in one of the longhouses in Jun Village through Duc Mai Coffee, but this can be an uncomfortable experience if you're not traveling with a guide. ✉ *Buon Jun, Lien Son.*

WHERE TO EAT AND STAY

$$ VIETNAMESE 🍴 **Duc Mai Coffee.** A favored haunt on easy rider tours, Duc Mai Coffee is more of a restaurant than a café, with a unique feature—there's no menu. Diners are expected to "order whatever they want" an hour before they eat, which can be a challenge if you don't know basic Vietnamese Central Highlands cuisine. A recommended feastlike order, eaten at simple metal tables, would be *thit heo nuong xien* (barbecued pork on skewers), *rau mong xao toi* (stir-fried morning glory with garlic), *rau xao* (stir-fried vegetables), *nam tam bot chien* (battered mushrooms), *canh ca chua* (sour fish soup with tomato), *com trang* (white rice), and omelet. The food will be simple but delicious and, if you don't have your own, an easy rider tour guide will probably step in to assist at some point. This place also serves as a center for lake activites. [$] *Average main: 100000d* ✉ *69 Y Jut, Buon Jun* ☎ *0262/3586–280* 🌐 *laklaketravel.com* 💳 *No credit cards.*

$$ HOTEL 🏨 **Bao Dai Villa.** This seven-room villa, a former royal residence, used to serve as a vacation residence of Bao Dai, the last emperor of Vietnam. **Pros:** many photographs of Vietnamese royalty; coffee shop and restaurant on-site. **Cons:** villa rooms are quite basic; even the King Room has quite tragic "modern" decor. [$] *Rooms from: 660000d* ✉ *Dinh Bao Dai, Lien Son* ☎ *0262/3586–184* 🌐 *www.daklaktourist.com.vn* 🛏 *7 rooms* 💳 *No credit cards* 🍽 *Breakfast.*

$ HOTEL Fodor's Choice ★ 🏨 **Van Long Motel.** This neat-as-a-pin new hotel across the road from Lak Lake is a pretty slick operation for this part of the world, with large, clean, and comfortable (albeit basic) rooms with roomy Vietnamese-style bathrooms (shower-and-toilet combination with no screen or curtain), a perfectly acceptable in-house restaurant, and an interesting range of entertainment options, including elephant rides (at about $35/hour) and gong shows. **Pros:** great location, right next door to Jun Village and across the road from the lake. **Cons:** walls are thin so you can hear quite a bit of what's going on in the adjoining room. [$] *Rooms from: 250000d* ✉ *N3Y Jut, Buon Le, Lien Son* ☎ *0500/3585–659* 🌐 *www.dulichvanlong.com* 🛏 *8 rooms, 1 10-bed longhouse* 🍴 *No meals.*

BUON MA THUOT

50 km (31 miles) north of Lak Lake.

Central Highlands towns are good bases from which to stage trips to the ethnic minority villages and jungles of the hinterland. Buon Ma Thuot, the capital of the Central Highlands and Vietnam's coffee capital, is a vibrant bustling town with a population of about 300,000 people. It was once the administrative and economic center of the region and its central location gave it strategic importance during the Vietnam War. Traveling here, and onward to Pleiku and Kon Tum, can be fairly rough going because of long driving distances and limited facilities, but they are great places to escape the tourist trail and meet some of Vietnam's 54 recognized ethnic minorities. An exploration of this area will take you past coffee plantations and should include regular stops at local cafés, where the strong coffee is served in shot glasses.

4

GETTING HERE AND AROUND

Nonstop flights to Buon Ma Thuot are available from Ho Chi Minh City, Danang, Vinh, and Hanoi. Buses arrive several times a day from Ho Chi Minh City, Nha Trang, Danang, Pleiku, Quy Nhon, and Hanoi. Mai Linh operate a fleet of taxis in Buon Ma Thuot (☎ *0500/3819–819*).

TOURS

Vietnam Highland Travel. The friendly and knowledgeable team at Vietnam Highland Travel operates tours around the Central Highlands, including the regions surrounding Pleiku and Kon Tum, many of which include trekking and homestays at ethnic minority villages. ✉ *24 Ly Thuong Kiet St., Buon Ma Thuot* ☎ *0500/3855–009* 🌐 *vietnamhighlandtravel.com* 🎟 *From: $87.*

EXPLORING

Dak Lak Museum (*Bao Tang tỉnh Daklak*). This museum, which opened in late 2011, pays tribute to local ethnic minority people with its overall design and displays, which include artifacts from the 44 ethnic minority groups who live in Dak Lak Province. Exhibits are signed in Vietnamese, English, French, and Ede. ✉ *12 Le Duan St., Buon Ma Thuot* ☎ *0262/6253–636* 🌐 *daklakmuseum.org.vn* 🎟 *20,000d.*

Dray Sap and Gia Long Falls (*Thac Dray Sap*). These pretty waterfalls, 32 km (20 miles) southwest of Buon Ma Thuot, are a good place to break the journey from Lak Lake to Buon Ma Thuot. Trails lead to the bottom of the falls, where it's possible to take a dip in the slightly murky green water. ✉ *Dak Sur, Dak Nong* 🎟 *30,000d.*

Trung Nguyen Coffee Village (*Lang Ca Phe Trung Nguyen*). This tourist site, owned by the Trung Nguyen coffee behemoth, Vietnam's answer to Starbucks, is essentially a giant coffee shop with a beautiful replica "ancient house" at the front. There's a museum at the rear of the property, showcasing coffee paraphernalia from around the world. A gift shop at the front of the property sells a selection of coffees, including weasel coffee that goes for $50 per 225-gram box. ✉ *222 Ly Thai To, Buon Ma Thuot* ☎ *0500/6511–168* 🌐 *www.trungnguyen.com.vn* 🎟 *20,000d* 🕘 *Museum daily 7–5.*

Victory Monument (*Tuong dai Chien thang Buon Ma Thuot*). This monument, in the center of Buon Ma Thuot's biggest roundabout, honors the day the town was "liberated" by the North Vietnam army (the losing side would say that Buon Ma Thuot "fell") on March 10, 1975. The provincial administrative center was the first domino to fall as the northern army pushed south toward Ho Chi Minh City, which was liberated only a few weeks later, on April 30, marking the end of the Vietnam-American War. The monument features a replica tank and fighters with suitably victorious raised arms and guns. There's no need to make a special trip to the monument, you'll probably pass it as you enter the town. ✉ *Center of roundabout at Le Duan, Phan Chu Trinh, and Nguyen Tat Thanh Sts., Buon Ma Thuot.*

WHERE TO EAT

$ VIETNAMESE Fodor's Choice ★

🍴 **Nem Viet.** This is a basic metal-tables-and-chairs joint that's open to the street, serving up a delicious version of *nem nuong* (barbecued pork) served with platters of rice paper, herbs, pickled vegetables, fried wonton wrappers (for crunch), fresh rice noodles, sliced green banana, and star fruit, which are rolled together and dipped into a pork-and-peanut sauce. This is a Central Highlands specialty that's best washed down with a cold beer. [$] *Average main: 35000d* ✉ *14–16 Ly Thuong Kiet, Buon Ma Thuot* ☎ *0262/3818–464* 💳 *No credit cards.*

$$ VIETNAMESE

🍴 **Quan Vu.** This very popular local "jungle food" joint serves a range of barbecue and hotpot dishes, which are a great way to warm up on a cool Buon Ma Thuot evening. No English is spoken, but pictures on the menu and on the walls can assist with ordering. The specialty is "jungle" pork (*heo rung*), perhaps better known as wild boar, as well as other "jungle" animals, including *nai* (deer), *tho* (rabbit), *ech* (frog), *vit* (duck), and *chim bo* (pigeon). One of the tastiest ways to try the house specialty, which is offered seven ways, is *heo rung nuong* (barbecued jungle pig). [$] *Average main: 80000d* ✉ *102/8 Nguyen Cong Tru, Buon Ma Thuot* ☎ *0262/3860–190* 💳 *No credit cards.*

$ CAFÉ Fodor's Choice ★

🍴 **Rider Café.** This is a motorbike-themed drinks-only café that is worth a visit for the decor, which includes vintage and high-powered motorbikes as well as super-cute motorbike-coffee tables. The locally grown coffee is strong, thick, and tasty, served in cups so small they can be dealt with in just two sips. Try the *ca phe sua nong* (hot coffee with sweet milk), which is served atop a tealight-powered warmer. [$] *Average main: 20000d* ✉ *127 Nguyen Cong Tru, Buon Mat Thuot* ☎ *090/5397–947* 💳 *No credit cards.*

$$ VIETNAMESE

🍴 **Trung Nguyen Coffee Village** (*Lang Ca Phe Trung Nguyen*). The standout feature of what is essentially a giant café is the beautiful replica open-air ancient house, of a type that would have housed royalty in Imperial times, which serves Vietnamese dishes, such as *bo kho* (beef stew) and *bo luk lak* (shaking beef). The menu also includes a variety of coffees, as well as cake and ice cream. Try a coffee in the ancient house, in the "cave" section, reached via concrete stepping stones over a pond, or on the deck overlooking the gardens. $ *Average main: 90000d* ⊠ *222 Ly Thai To, Buon Ma Thuot* ☎ *0500/6511–168* ⊕ *www.trungnguyen. com.vn.*

WHERE TO STAY

$$
HOTEL
Fodor's Choice
★

🏨 **Coffee Tour Resort.** Part of the Trung Nguyen coffee empire, Coffee Tour Resort is a cute boutique hotel a little more than 2 km (1 mile) from the center of Buon Ma Thuot with lovely grounds, an on-site restaurant, and clean modern rooms (with fluffy bathrobes in the wardrobes). **Pros:** the friendly receptionist Ms. Hoa speaks excellent English; very restful ambience. **Cons:** a long walk from downtown Buon Ma Thuot; no elevator access to second- and third-floor rooms. $ *Rooms from: 700000d* ⊠ *149–153 Ly Thai To, Buon Ma Thuot* ☎ *0262/3575– 575* ⊕ *www.coffeetour.com.vn/Khachsan* ⇥ *33 rooms* ⦿| *Breakfast.*

$
HOTEL

🏨 **Damsan Hotel.** This three-star hotel is one of the finer options in town because rooms are comfortable, clean, and spacious, with decor accents in the form of textiles from local ethnic minorities. **Pros:** central location, walking distance to the Victory Monument; very reasonable price. **Cons:** showing its age (it opened in 1997). $ *Rooms from: 500000d* ⊠ *212–214 Nguyen Cong Tru, Buon Ma Thuot* ☎ *0262/385–1234* ⊕ *www.damsanhotel.com.vn* ⇥ *70 rooms* ⦿| *Breakfast.*

$
HOTEL

🏨 **Eden Hotel.** Clean and comfortable rooms, friendly English-speaking staff, and a central location in a café-lined street make the unpretentious Eden Hotel popular with budget travelers. **Pros:** cheap price; fridges in rooms; helpful staff. **Cons:** the beds are very firm; the noise from the karaoke place next door can be disturbing. $ *Rooms from: 300000d* ⊠ *228 Nguyen Cong Tru, Buon Ma Thuot* ☎ *0500/3840–055* ⊕ *www. edenhotelbmt.com.vn* ⇥ *54 rooms* ▭ *No credit cards* ⦿| *No meals.*

PLEIKU

180 km (112 miles) north of Buon Ma Thuot, 140 km (87 miles) west of Quy Nhon.

Pleiku, the capital of Gia Lai province, is smaller and less colorful than its neighbor Kon Tum, but it makes a practical base in this forested and mountainous region. Much of this area served as a major battleground during the Vietnam War.

GETTING HERE AND AROUND

Flights arrive at Pleiku Airport from Ho Chi Minh City, Hanoi, and Danang. The airport is about 5 km (3 miles) north of central Pleiku. Buses arrive daily in Pleiku from all over Vietnam, including Ho Chi Minh City, Hanoi, Dalat, and Nha Trang. It's an uncomfortable 12 hours from Ho Chi Minh City and 24 from Hanoi, but only 6 hours from Dalat and 1 hour and 40 minutes from Kon Tum. Taxis are the best way to get around town. Mai Linh operates a fleet in Pleiku ☎ *059/585–858*

TOURS

Gia Lai Eco-Tourist. This local outfit can help arrange trekking and tours of the Central Highlands ethnic minority villages with an English-speaking guide (Ms. Nga is highly recommended). Tours can start with airport pickup in Pleiku or Buon Ma Thuot, or even from further afield, such as Nha Trang or Hoi An. The company can also arrange car (and driver) hire. Hill-tribe treks start at about $100 per person per day, including transport, accommodation, guide, and some meals. ✉ *82 Huong Vuong St., Pleiku* ☎ *0269/3760–898* 🌐 *www.gialaiecotourist.com.*

EXPLORING

Sea Lake (Bien Ho) (*Bien Ho, T'Nung, Ea Nueng*). About 6 km (4 miles) north of downtown Pleiku, Sea Lake is a flooded crater of an extinct volcano. A pine tree–lined road leads to a viewing area, which includes an aging gazebo that looks over the freshwater lake. Locals say the lake is at its best in the early morning when covered in fog that looks like strips of silk. ✉ *Access road is off Ton Duc Thang St., Pleiku* 🎫 *Free.*

WHERE TO STAY

$$$$ HOTEL 🏨 **HAGL Hotel.** A slick high-rise right on Pleiku's main traffic circle, this is the only four-star option in town. **Pros:** decent bar and restaurant; gym; tennis court. **Cons:** mountain-view rooms also overlook the traffic circle; traffic noise. [$] *Rooms from: 1161000d* ✉ *1 Phu Dong, Pleiku* ☎ *0269/371–8459* 🌐 *www.haglhotelpleiku.vn* 🛏 *115 rooms, 2 suites* 🍴 *Breakfast.*

$ HOTEL 🏨 **Tre Xanh Hotel.** This three-star business hotel close to the central market has large clean rooms and reasonable bathrooms, making it a good choice for budget travelers looking for a place to crash in Pleiku. **Pros:** central location; cheap rates. **Cons:** not much English; noise from the in-house karaoke venue can be heard in some rooms. [$] *Rooms from: 350000d* ✉ *18 Lei Lai, Pleiku* ☎ *0269/371–5787* 🌐 *trexanhhotel.vn* 🛏 *120 rooms* 🍴 *Breakfast.*

KON TUM

50 km (31 miles) north of Pleiku, 50 km (30 miles) west of Quy Nhon.

The best base for exploring the region, Kon Tum is a sleepy, relatively undiscovered gem on the banks of the Dakbla River, surrounded by interesting ethnic minority villages. The Bahnar and Jarai, two of the largest hill-tribe groups in the area, possess a fascinating culture with traditions that stretch back for centuries. You can join them in drinking the *ruou can* (rice wine) for which this region is famous. Of particular cultural interest are the wood carvings made by the Bahnar tribe (who have villages within walking distance of Kon Tum) to adorn the graves of their departed. The strong animistic beliefs of the Jarai tribe are expressed through traditional musical instruments, such as the wind flute and gongs with which they produce ethereal and entrancing hymns.

GETTING HERE AND AROUND

The easiest way to get to Kon Tum is to fly into Pleiku airport and get a taxi or a private car for the one-hour drive. You can usually organize a private car (and driver) when you book your hotel in Kon Tum, otherwise just take a Mai Linh taxi from the rank at the Pleiku airport (☎ 059/585–858). By bus, it's 1 hour and 40 minutes from Pleiku to Kon Tum. Getting to Kon Tum from anywhere by bus is arduous. It's 11 to

13 hours from Ho Chi Minh City, 8 hours from Nha Trang, and 20 to 24 hours from Hanoi.

TOURS

Fodor'sChoice ★ **Highlands Eco Tours.** A well-regarded local tour company with guides that speak English, French, and several hill-tribe languages, Highlands Eco Tours offers cycling, trekking, boating, and adventure tours as well as tours of the hill tribe village around Kon Tum and farther afield. ⊠ *15 Ho Tung Mau, Kon Tum* ☏ *0260/3912–788* ⊕ *www.vietnamhighlands. com.*

EXPLORING

Konklor Suspension Bridge. This bridge, about 2 km (1 mile) from downtown Kon Tum, spans the Dakbla River. The 292-meter bridge was completed in 1994, making it easier for people in Konklor village to get to town. If you're really lucky, you may see a "traffic jam" caused by a bullock cart crossing the bridge. Don't miss the rong house on the left side of the northern bank of the river. ⊠ *Tran Hung Dao St., Konklor Village, Kon Tum.*

Kon Tum Seminary. Another picturesque wooden building, the three-story Kon Tum's Catholic seminary was completed in 1934. It contains a small minorities museum that shows the history of Christianity and conversion in the region, as well as exhibits from local hill tribes. ⊠ *146 Tran Hung Dao, Kon Tum* ☏ *0260/3862–372* ⊆ *Free* ☉ *Mon.–Sat. 8–11, 2–4.*

Fodor'sChoice ★ **Rong Houses.** Each ethnic minority village in the region has its own rong house, which serves as a community hall. These tall stilted structures, with long pitched roofs, often thatched, are where meetings, weddings, and other community activities take place. The size of the rong house is an indication of how wealthy the village is—and the roofs can be as high as 30 meters! The Bahnar people usually build their rong houses from wood and bamboo, with wooden stilts, while the Jarai people use corrugated iron for the roof and concrete for the supporting pillars. There are a few rong houses within easy reach of Kon Tum, including two near the suspension bridge in Konklor Village. ⊠ *Kon Tum.*

Wooden Church (*Nha Tho Go; Kon Tum Cathedral; Our Lady of the Immaculate Conception Cathedral*). This church, completed in 1918, combines Roman and Bahnar architectural styles in a unique and beautiful building with wide verandas. The church is usually open, so you can go inside and admire the stained-glass windows that light up the airy interior. There's an orphanage behind the church that welcomes visitors and some interesting workshops in the grounds. Masses are held at the church on Saturday at 5:30 pm and on Sunday at 6 am, 7:45 am, and 5:30 pm. ⊠ *Nguyen Hue, Kon Tum.*

WHERE TO EAT AND STAY

$$ ✕ **Eva Cafe.** A beautiful, restful garden café, filled with carvings and
VIETNAMESE sculptures, this is the place to come for excellent coffee, egg coffee (a Hanoi specialty of whipped egg yolk and coffee), fruit shakes, and simple Vietnamese fare. The English-speaking owner, Mr. An, is a fountain of knowledge about the local area and is available to lead multiday treks or tours through nearby ethnic minority villages. He charges $60 per

person ($70 for solo travelers) for a two-day, one-night trek, including transport, lunch, and a gong show. [$] *Average main: 70000d* ✉ *1 Phan Chu Trinh, Kon Tum* ☎ *0260/3862–944* 💳 *No credit cards.*

$ CAFÉ Fodor's Choice ★ 🍴 **Indochine Coffee.** This stunning café was designed by international-award-winning Vietnamese architect Vo Trong Nghia, who specializes in structures made completely out of bamboo. Part of the Indochine Hotel, it's a local drinks-and-ice cream spot overlooking the Dakbla River, with soaring inverted cone-shape bamboo columns and many peaceful fish ponds. [$] *Average main: 15000d* ✉ *30 Bach Dang, Kon Tum* 🌐 *www.indochinehotel.vn* 💳 *No credit cards.*

$$ HOTEL 🏨 **Indochine Hotel (Kon Tum).** Billing itself as an international-standard three-star property, the eight-story Indochine Hotel has a commanding position overlooking the Dakbla River and surrounding countryside. **Pros:** central location; offers a pickup service from Pleiku Airport, starting from 590,000d; welcome flowers and fruit are a nice touch. **Cons:** some parts of the hotel are looking a bit tired. [$] *Rooms from: 753000d* ✉ *30 Bach Dang, Kon Tum* ☎ *0260/3863–335* 🌐 *www.indochinehotel.vn* 🛏 *61 rooms, 2 suites.*

$ HOTEL Fodor's Choice ★ 🏨 **Konklor Hotel.** An easy 2.5-km (1.6-mile) bicycle or motorbike ride from downtown Kon Tum, this charming family-run operation in Konklor Village has clean, spacious rooms with roomy private bathrooms in a series of bungalows, each a few steps from the central lounge area and restaurant, where you can have breakfast, lunch, and dinner at very reasonable prices. **Pros:** motorbikes and bikes available for hire; it's a short walk to Kon Tum's suspension bridge and two Bahnar rong houses; great value for money. **Cons:** a long walk from downtown Kon Tum. [$] *Rooms from: 336000d* ✉ *155 Bac Kan, Kon Tum* ☎ *093/5016–210* 🌐 *konklorhotel.vn* 🛏 *25 rooms* 🍽 *No meals.*

$ HOTEL 🏨 **Thinh Vuong Hotel.** In a quiet tree-lined street just off the main drag, the family-run Thinh Vuong Hotel has clean spacious rooms and a friendly owner, Ms. Yen, who speaks English and is on-site most of the time. **Pros:** many cafés and local eating places nearby; helpful staff; an elevator. **Cons:** breakfast not included in room rate. [$] *Rooms from: 250000d* ✉ *16B Nguyen Trai, Kon Tum* ☎ *0260/3914–729* 🛏 *30 rooms* 💳 *No credit cards* 🍽 *No meals.*

NORTH OF NHA TRANG

The portion of the south-central coast between Nha Trang and Hoi An is an area with few tourist attractions but often breathtaking scenery and seemingly endless white-sand beaches. If you're traveling by car between the two cities, Quy Nhon is a worthwhile place to overnight. You can break the next day's journey at the poignant Son My Memorial, built in remembrance of the brutal My Lai massacre of between 347 and 504 unarmed villagers by American soldiers in March 1968.

QUY NHON

222 km (138 miles) north of Nha Trang, 296 km (184 miles) south of Hoi An.

Once the Cham capital of Vijaya, Quy Nhon is an undiscovered seaside gem, located midway between Nha Trang and Hoi An. The laid-back atmosphere is perfect for those interested in exploring a town with no heavy industry and locals who aren't jaded by tourism.

GETTING HERE AND AROUND

The airport is about 30 km (19 miles) northwest of the main tourist area of Quy Nhon. Mai Linh and Phuong Trang buses run between Nha Trang and Quy Nhon (and onward to Danang/Hoi An). From Nha Trang it takes about six hours and there are some spectacular views along the way, though trip can be quite nerve-wracking. Thuan Thao bus company runs one bus a day from Quy Nhon to Dalat and it's also possible to catch a minibus from Pleiku. The Reunification Express, which runs five times a day between Ho Chi Minh City and Hanoi, stops at Dieu Tri Train Station, which is about 10 km (6 miles) west of the main tourist area of Quy Nhon. The town is well-serviced by taxis and most hotels will assist with motorbike rentals.

EXPLORING

Quy Hoa Leper Colony. An unlikely tourist attraction, this village, just behind the beautiful Quy Hoa Beach, is an interesting place to explore. Most of the lepers are quite elderly now, and it's their descendants that populate the village, some of whom work in a small clothing factory or as crab fishermen. The residents are quite friendly and don't seem to mind foreigners wandering around. The village and its hospital is well-known among Vietnamese because one of the country's most famous poets, Han Mac Tu, died there in 1940 after contracting leprosy at age 38. The cemetery is interesting and quite colorful. ⊠ *Quy Hoa.*

Quy Nhon Beach. This white-sand beach is a long crescent dotted with basket boats that runs along An Duong Vuong Street. Local fishing boats are often moored just offshore, which unfortunately means there's often quite a bit of trash on the beach. You can walk to the southern end of the beach, then up and over a headland to get to the more secluded but rocky Queen's Beach and then farther on to the Quy Hoa leper colony. Allocate half a day for this hike—it's a good 6 km (4 miles) or so. **Amenities:** food and drinks. **Good for:** walks; sunset; sunrise. ⊠ *An Duong Vuong St., Quy Nhon.*

Thap Doi Cham Towers. These restored Cham towers, built some time between the 11th and 13th centuries, are some of the most easily accessible in southern Vietnam, set in a little park that's a popular meeting place for locals. The twin towers, with their intricate carvings of mythical animals, are considered unusual relics of the Cham empire because most other towers were built in clusters of three. ⊠ *Thap Doi.*

WHERE TO EAT

$ ✕ **Com Sau Thu.** One of the most popular *com binh danh* (canteens) in

VIETNAMESE town, Com Sau Thu has been making locals happy with their cheap and cheerful fare for more than 10 years. (The husband and wife Sau and Thu now have three shops, but locals agree the original one at this address remains the best.) The daily options are displayed in a glass case at the front of the restaurant, so you can just point to a range of dishes and then take a seat. Vietnamese people usually order one meat dish, one or two vegetable dishes, and a soup, and all are placed in the middle of the table and shared. There's no need to order rice because it comes automatically. $ *Average main: 60000d* ⊠ *121 Tran Cao Van* ☎ *098/445–1714* ▤ *No credit cards.*

$
VIETNAMESE
Fodor's Choice
★

✕ **Ngo Van So Street.** Qui Nhon's "eating street" has a range of little local places serving Central Vietnamese-style *banh xeo* (sizzling pancake) and *banh canh ca* (peppery fish noodle soup). Make your way to the top of the street and amble around to peruse the options. The *banh xeo* at 12 Ngo Van So are particularly recommended; tear off a small piece of pancake, wrap it in rice paper with herbs and cucumber slices, and dip it into the tasty sauce. $ *Average main: 50000d* ⊠ *Ngo Van So* ▤ *No credit cards.*

WHERE TO STAY

$$$$
RESORT
Fodor's Choice
★

⌂ **Avani Quy Nhon Resort & Spa.** Ideal for a get-away-from-it-all break, this luxury hideaway (one of Vietnam's best-kept secrets) has comfortable, spacious rooms, all with private balconies overlooking the South China Sea. **Pros:** excellent massages at the in-house spa; superb dining options; attentive staff. **Cons:** isolated, a one-hour drive from Phu Cat Airport and 20 minutes south of Quy Nhon. $ *Rooms from: 2967000d* ⊠ *Ghenh Rang, Bai Dai Beach* ☎ *056/384–0132* ⊕ *www.avanihotels. com/quynhon* ⇄ *41 rooms, 21 suites* ▮◎▮ *Breakfast.*

$
B&B/INN
Fodor's Choice
★

⌂ **Life's A Beach.** Two British guys opened this rustic beachfront homestay in November 2014 after falling in love with the small fishing village of Bai Xep, one of Vietnam's hidden delights. **Pros:** beachfront location; genuinely welcoming hosts; many opportunities to interact with locals. **Cons:** occasional power cuts and water shortages; cots and high chairs not available; 10 km (6 miles) outside of Quy Nhon. $ *Rooms from: 550000d* ⊠ *Bãi Xếp, Quy Nhon* ☎ *016/2993–3117* ⊕ *lifesabeachvietnam.com* ⇄ *4 rooms, 1 treehouse, 2 bamboo beach houses, 1 dormitory* ▮◎▮ *Breakfast.*

$$
HOTEL

⌂ **Seagull Hotel** (*Khach San Hai Au*). An older place that's trying hard to keep up with the times, the Seagull Hotel's main selling points are its beachfront location, the great views from the beachside rooms, all of which have balconies, and the pool. **Pros:** location; price; fitness center. **Cons:** some rooms have a stale carpet smell. $ *Rooms from: 860000d* ⊠ *489 An Dương Vương, Quy Nhon* ☎ *0256/3846–377* ⇄ *170 rooms* ▮◎▮ *Breakfast.*

QUANG NGAI

174 km (108 miles) north of Quy Nhon.

This unremarkable town is worth stopping at only in order to visit to the Son My Memorial.

GETTING HERE AND AROUND

Quang Ngai is a stop on the Reunification Express train. Taxis are the best way of getting around town.

The My Lai Massacre

My Lai, a sleepy hamlet about 14 km (9 miles) east of the city of Quang Ngai in the Son My district, is a site infamous for the worst atrocity carried out by American forces during the war in Vietnam. On the morning of March 16, 1968, U.S. troops entered the Son My area (including My Lai, Thuan-Yen, and other hamlets) and massacred hundreds of Vietnamese civilians—mostly women and children—in an act that has come to symbolize the often-senseless brutality that accompanied the conflict in Vietnam. Although the full truth concerning the events of My Lai remains shrouded in controversy, what is known is that the area around Son My was considered by the U.S. military to be a stronghold of the Vietcong and that some American soldiers had been killed and wounded in the area in the days preceding March 16, 1968. (A note on the term Vietcong: Vietcong is used to refer to the opposition movement in the South because it is the term that is probably the most familiar, though the history of this term is a complex one.)

In response, three platoons under Charlie Company exacted a terrible revenge that included pillaging, rape, and mass executions of civilians. The killing and destruction, which occurred under the at least tacit approval of higher officers, took place over a number of hours, during which time the soldiers took a break for lunch before resuming their criminal acts.

Hundreds of Vietnamese civilians died; the only reported American casualty was a U.S. soldier who shot himself in the foot in order to avoid partici-pating in the atrocities. Although a cover-up of the events of My Lai was attempted, several participants went public; the resulting scandal contrib-uted to the deterioration of American support for the war in Vietnam. Only one man, Lieutenant William Calley, who led Charlie Company's 1st Platoon—responsible for some of the worst atrocities—was ever convicted for the crimes that took place at My Lai. After serving three years of his sentence, Lieutenant Calley was paroled in 1974.

ESSENTIALS

Taxi Contact Mai Linh taxi company ☎ *055/3838–3838.*

Train Contact **Quang Ngai Train Station** ✉ *Tran Quoc Toan St., Quang Ngai* ☎ *255/382-0280.*

EXPLORING

My Khe Beach. About 15 km (9 miles) from Quang Ngai town, just past the My Son Memorial, lies the pretty casurina-lined beach of My Khe. The accommodation offerings here are fairly dire, so it's best to plan to visit the beach, dine at one of the seafood shacks along the beach, and continue north to Hoi An or south to Quy Nhon to stay the night. **Amenities:** food and drinks. ✉ *Highway 24B, Quang Nghia.*

Son My Memorial and Museum (My Lai). The Son My Memorial is dedicated to the victims of the massacre at My Lai and lies about 10 km (6 miles) east of National Highway 1A, just north of the town of Quang Ngai. The memorial itself is in the former hamlet of Thuan-Yen, where many of the worst crimes occurred. The village, which was burned down after the attacks, has been re-created to look as it did immediately after the massacre, with the paths between the rice paddies containing the footprints of the victims and their booted attackers, giving a chilling sense of the frenzy of killing that occurred. The nearby museum recounts the events of the day in vivid detail, with explanations in English and very graphic color photographs of some of the victims. English-speaking guides are available at the museum. In striking contrast to the terrible events that took place here, the memorial and the museum are located in a quiet and pastoral area. To get to the memorial, you can take public bus number 3 from Quang Ngai bus station, or you can hire a taxi in Quang Ngai. Expect to pay around 220,000d each way for the taxi ride and it's probably best that you ask the taxi driver to wait at the memorial. ⊠ *Tinh Khe, Son Tinh, Quang Ngai, My Lai* ☎ *0255/3843–222* 🎫 *14,000d* 🕐 *Weekdays 8–11:30, 1–4:30.*

WHERE TO EAT AND STAY

$

HOTEL

🏨 **Central Hotel.** The run-down hotel, which claims to be four-star, is probably the best option in town, which isn't saying much. **Pros:** central location. **Cons:** dated property; noise of traffic filters into the rooms; limited English skills. 💲 *Rooms from: 400000d* ⊠ *1 Le Loi, Quang Ngai* ⊕ *centralhotel.com.vn* 🛏 *85 rooms* 🍽 *Breakfast.*

Louisiane Brewhouse. A laid-back place to chill, drink craft beer, and soak in the beach views during the day, the Louisiane Brewhouse perks up at night, with live music and beach views. ⊠ *29 Tran Phu, Nha Trang* ☎ *0258/3521–948* ⊕ *www.louisianebrewhouse.com.vn.*

THE CENTRAL COAST

Updated by
Caroline Mills

Vietnam's long, lovely Central Coast has iconic sandy beaches, ancient Cham ruins, and fascinating royal tombs and pagodas. The highlights of the region are Hoi An and Hue, two of the country's most interesting and hospitable cities, but a visit to the central provinces isn't complete without a few days spent exploring inland, around the incredible karst formations and caves of Phong Nha Khe Be National Park.

As you travel around this region, expect to catch glimpses of the emerald-green South China Sea and scenes of traditional Vietnamese rural life as they have appeared for centuries. The age-old rhythm of planting and harvesting continues undisturbed, and you'll see families drying their rice in their front yards only inches from the road against a stunning backdrop: the dramatic peaks of the Truong Son Mountains cascading into the sea. The culinary curious will love Hoi An, an enigmatic but hip coastal town full of old-world charm, with some of the best street food and restaurants in the region. Originally a port trading village, it is incredibly well preserved. Amble around 200-year-old homes incorporating architectural elements from traditional Chinese, Vietnamese, and Japanese styles, reflecting those who populated Hoi An over the centuries. This is also Central Vietnam's gateway to diverse mountainous countryside, home to hill tribes.

Hugging the coastline north of Hoi An is 30 km (19 miles) of tropical white sandy beaches lined with some of the most luxurious beach hotels in the country, and three international golf courses. Just inland, the spectacular Marble Mountain range creates a beautiful backdrop for golf-loving escapists.

A little farther north is Danang, once an important U.S. Air Force base during the Vietnam War. Today it is the country's fastest growing city, with an international dining scene, stunning beaches, great street food, vibrant nightlife, and the region's gateway airport.

Once the capital of Vietnam and the home of its emperors, Hue, north of Danang, was once largely in ruins, the consequence of both French attacks in the late 19th century and American bombings during the Vietnam War. Only during the past decade have efforts been made to restore Hue's imperial architecture. Today the Imperial City continues to attract visitors with the grandeur of its royal past. From here it's a three-hour drive north across the DMZ, a must for military buffs only, to the limestone mountain, caves, and grottoes of Phong Nha Kha Be National Park, a bucket-list destination for adventurists and home to the biggest cave on the planet, Han Son Doong.

TOP REASONS TO GO

Hoi An: Discover the charm of Hoi An's Old Quarter with its historic sites, traditional architecture, flavorful cuisine, and lantern-strewn streets.

Tee-off on Vietnam's new golf coast: Soak in the splendid scenery while working on your handicap on three of Vietnam's award-winning golf courses, all within easy reach of Danang.

Tomb explorations: Pay tribute to past emperors by visiting the tombs scattered throughout Hue and beyond.

Take to the trails: Rub shoulders with a Co-Tu Hill Tribe King and overnight in Bho Hoong village, in a beautifully appointed stilt house deep in the jungle, a thrilling motorbike or jeep ride from Hoi An or Hue.

Adventure beyond the cave: Phong Nha is one of the most spectacular limestone regions in Southeast Asia. Explore untamed jungle, climb steep karst mountains, and sleep under a thousand stars.

5

ORIENTATION AND PLANNING

GETTING ORIENTED

The Annamite Mountain range that marks the border between Vietnam and Laos hugs the Central Coast, and it's relatively easy to travel around. South are the flatlands of Hoi An, an ancient port town surrounded by rice fields and organic farms, which are fed by tributaries of the Thu Bon River, carving the landscape into tiny rural islands out to the East Sea and the marine protected Cham Island archipelago. An hour away to Hoi An's east the Champa kingdom of My Son lies in the valley of the Truong Son Mountains, which continue all the way north, bordering the coastal city of Danang, a 40-minute drive from Hoi An. Farther north, the two-hour journey to Hue takes you through the mountain ranges of Bach Ma through sweeping, low-lying countryside and onward, to the karst mountain region of Phong Nha, a four-hour drive from Hue.

Hoi An. Fast gaining status as Vietnam's culinary capital, the atmospheric river town of Hoi An is quite rightly one of Vietnam's top destinations. The big draw here is the Old Town Quarter, a lantern-lit labyrinth of ancient Indochine architecture, trader's houses, and temples, a short bike ride through rural countryside from Hoi An's other major draw—its beaches.

Danang and Around. Two miles from Central Vietnam's main airport is Danang City, a buzzy urban sprawl of skyscrapers and colonial architecture with a vibrant dining and nightlife scene. The luxury beach resorts along the city's coastline are the main attraction, along with the Marble Mountains.

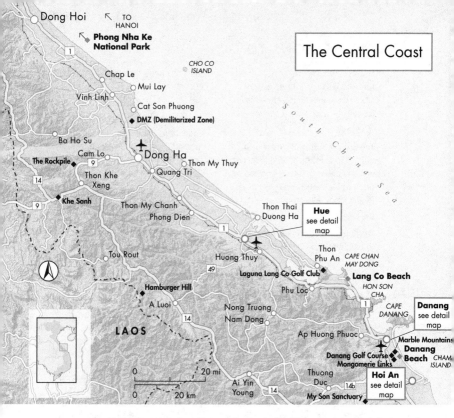

Hue. The one-time Imperial Capital of Vietnam is the place to slow down and take in the country's regal past. Explore the Citadel, Imperial Palace, museums, and emperors' tombs, and take a cruise on the Perfume River. For a more rural vibe, a short drive through fishing villages and lagoons takes you to undeveloped beaches lined with seafood shacks.

Phong Nha Ke Bang National Park. Hang Son Doong is the world's largest cave, but it's just one of many in this spectacular park, where a vast network of underground caves, awesome jungle scenery, and fascinating history form the perfect backdrop for outdoor adventure.

PLANNING

WHEN TO GO

The Central Coast has four distinct seasons. The monsoon season that begins in October and ends in January is plagued by some of Vietnam's worst and most unpredictable weather, and typhoons are not unheard of during this time. The low-lying coastal towns of Hoi An, Danang, Hue, and the mountain valleys of Phong Nha are particularly prone to flooding during October and November, but good warning systems and protocols are in place and in most instances, this need not affect your trip. The cooler months of spring, which begins in February and ends in April, are generally dry and are a good time to travel if you want to avoid the intense heat and humidity of the summer months from April to July, which are the best months to visit if you are planning a beach holiday. During autumn, from August to September, humidity reaches its peak and thunderstorms roll in off the mountains most evenings, while the days are usually sunny and hot. Like the rest of the country, the area comes alive during Tet, the celebration of the lunar New Year, which takes place in January or February. Due to long national holidays, this can be a difficult time of the year to travel. Tet Trung Thu, which takes place in August or September, is a far more tourist-friendly event, celebrated on a huge scale in the central town of Hoi An.

GETTING HERE AND AROUND

AIR TRAVEL

Danang airport (serving Danang and Hoi An) has fast become Vietnam's third international airport, and makes for a great hub from which to hop between popular destinations within Vietnam. Few international flights service Danang, the most popular are direct services to Siem Reap, Kuala Lumpur, Tokyo, and Singapore. Although new destinations are slowly being added, most connect north in Hanoi or south in Ho Chi Minh, both a 70-minute flight from Danang.

Hue's Phu Bai Airport serves as a popular hub for flights into central Vietnam, although few international flights offer transport here. Most connect north in Hanoi (1 hour) or south in Ho Chi Minh (70 minutes). Phu Bai Airport is 20 minutes from central Hue.

Dong Hoi airport is the closest gateway to Phong Nha National Park and Vietnam Airlines run scheduled flights from Hanoi (1 hour, 25 minutes) and Ho Chi Minh City (1 hour, 40 minutes) several times a week. The airport is 43 km (26 miles), or a one-hour journey, from Phong Nha.

Airport Contacts Danang Airport ✉ *3 km west of Danang city center, Danang* ☎ *0236/3823–391* ⊕ *www.danangairportonline.com.* **Dong Hoi Airport** ✉ *AH14, Loc Ninh, Quang Binh Province* ☎ *0232/810–878* ⊕ *www.vietnamairport.vn.* **Phu Bai Airport** ✉ *Huong Thuy, Hue* ☎ *0234/3861–131.*

BUS TRAVEL

To reach Hoi An from the Danang airport, catch the yellow Bus #1 at the roundabout where Dien Bien Phu and Nguyen Tri Phuong meet (a 10-minute walk). Buses run daily from 6 am to 6 pm, leaving for Hoi An every 20 minutes and terminate an hour later at Hoi An's main bus station on Le Hong Phong Street, a 15-minute walk from the Old Town. Tourist minibus services run directly from the airport and train station. These cost approximately 80,000d and can be arranged at the information counter upon arrival.

Tour buses north to Hue take about 3½ hours, overnight buses south to Nha Trang take 10 to 12 hours, while tour buses north to Phong Nha take eight or nine hours. There are also Open Tour buses available for the route between Hoi An and Hue that include stops at Marble Mountain and Lang Co Beach. These take about five hours.

Hue's Phu Bai Airport runs a regular shuttle bus service into the city. The 15-km (9-mile) trip takes about 25 minutes and costs 30,000d. Only prearranged, private minibuses run the route between Dong Hoi airport and Phong Nha and the nearest public bus station is Nam Ly, which is just over 10 km (6 miles) away in the wrong direction, so it's best to book transfers through your hotel. Prices start at 125,000d.

Local buses ply the route between Danang's central bus station and Le Hong Phong Street in Hoi An, a couple of kilometers outside of the Old Town. Buses leave every 30 minutes from 5:30 am until 5:50 pm, taking approximately 45 minutes from door to door. Expect to pay extra for luggage.

Tour companies like Hanh Café and Sinh Café offer long-distance bus service to and from northern and southern provinces.

BUS CONTACTS **Danang Central Bus Station** ⊠ *201 Ton Duc Thang, 2½ km (1½ miles) north of junction with Hwy. 1A, Danang* ☎ *0236/376–7679.*

Dong Hoi Bus Station. Nam Ly bus station is 1 km (¼ mile) up the road from Dong Hoi's central bus station (walk up Tran Hung Dao for 50 meters and you'll see a sign post on the right). There is only one bus a day to Phong Nha and it departs at 2 pm, costing approximately 40,000d. The return bus departs Phong Nha at 8 am, so unless you plan on staying overnight, you'll need to make other transportation arrangements for your return journey. ⊠ *Nam Ly, To Huu, Dong Hoi, Quang Binh Province* ☎ *0232/3822–018.*

Hanh Café. A cheap and safe bet for organizing onward travel from Hoi An, this café has helpful staff who speak English. Unlike many bus companies, this fleet of air-conditioned minibuses and sleeper buses are well maintained. Hotel pickup and drop-off can be arranged and will generally work out to be far cheaper than organizing a taxi or *xe om* (motorbike taxi) at either end. ⊠ *2 Thai Phien St., Hoi An* ☎ *0235/386–4609* ⊕ *hanhcafe.vn.*

Sinh Café. One of the longest-running tourist bus services in Hoi An, offering twice-daily services south to Nha Trang or north to Hue, this is a great option if you want to take in a few popular attractions en route to break up the journey. However, it's worth bearing in mind these stops are arranged around whichever place pays the most commission. Sinh Café also provides the option of a multistop open ticket for travel throughout the country. ⊠ *587 Hai Ba Trung St., Hoi An* ☎ *0235/386–3948* ⊕ *www.sinhcafe.com.*

CAR TRAVEL

There are still very few car rental companies and due to poor road conditions, insane traffic, and few parking options, it's best just to hire a private car and driver. The coastal road linking Danang and Hoi An is manageable and takes about 40 minutes to drive 28 km (17½ miles) and should cost no more than 500,000d by taxi. From Hoi An to Hue the most direct route takes you through the Hai Van tunnel, the 140-km (87-mile) journey takes 2½ hours and costs around 1,200,000d by private car. An alternative and more scenic route takes you along coastal roads and over the Hai Van Pass, with a few stops to enjoy the view. This 160-km (99-mile) mountainous drive takes upward of four hours and costs 1,700,000d. The 227-km (141-mile) route from Hue to Phong Nha offers spectacular scenery and outside of rush hour the journey can be done in just over four hours, although during the rainy season, already poor road conditions around the national park area are prone to flooding and mudslides, which can add a good hour onto the journey time. A private car and driver costs starts at 2,000,000d.

MOTORBIKE TRAVEL

Riding by motorbike in Vietnam can be frightening at times, but if you're going to try it, Hoi An is the best place to enter the motorbike mayhem because traffic is minimal, especially in the surrounding countryside. Rates start at 100,000d per day and include two helmets. Failure to wear one will result in a hefty fine. Keep in mind that the pedestrian-only Old Town bans motorbikes most of the day and that road conditions vary, especially during the rainy season, when riding can be treacherous. For regularly serviced bikes and reliable service go to Mrs. Hao at Tran Cao Van, opposite the Phouc An Hotel. *For important information on motorbike rental as a foreigner, see Travel Smart.*

TRAIN TRAVEL

Danang's railway station serves as the main access point to Hoi An, a 40-minute drive from the Old Town. In startling contrast to the larger city train stations, Danang is easy to navigate, clean, and well-serviced with a tourist helpdesk manned by English speaking staff. As a stop between Ho Chi Minh and Hanoi, Hue's train station is near the river on the east side of Le Loi. If you're short on time (and money), overnight trains are a good way to travel while you sleep. Express trains are recognizable by the SE prefix. Local trains, which are much slower and cheaper, have the TN prefix. Trains between Hoi Chi Minh and Hue cost about 1,260,000d and take 18½ hours. Those between Hue and Hanoi cost around 887,000d and take 14 hours. There are also daily connections between Danang and Hanoi, with a stop in Hue and Dong Hoi.

The train ride between Danang and Hue is like passing through a postcard; it's one of most scenic train coastal train routes in the country, taking in the Hai Van Pass, Son Tra Peninsula, Lang Co beach, and the jungle-clad mountains of Bach Ma National Park. Crossing mountainous landscape, the route gives way to patches of emerald and blue, where rice fields meet lagoons and bays. The public TN train takes four to five hours and includes stops at the smaller coastal stations including Lang Co, while the more expensive Reunification Express (SE trains) take 2½ hours. The later costs roughly 300,000d and is offered four times daily. The SE trains also continue on to Dong Hoi—the main station for Phong Nha Ke Bang National Park. The journey from Danang takes 6 to 7 hours, or 4 to 5 hours from Hue.

Hue's train station is conveniently located 1 km (½ mile) from the city center and serves as the central transit point for the country-long Reunification line, with daily services to Ha Noi (13 hours), Nha Trang (12 hours), and Ho Chi Minh City (20 hours). A licensed taxi (look out for the green Mai Linh cars) to centrally located hotels should cost no more than 50,000d.

TRAIN
CONTACTS **Hue Train Station** ☒ *On right bank at southwest end of Le Loi St.*

Lang Co Train Station ☒ *Lang Co* ☎ *0236/3821–175.*

RESTAURANTS

The Central Coast is known for its outstanding cuisine, with Hoi An now considered a culinary destination in its own right, full of trendy restaurants, cooking schools, and hipster cafés alongside the lively street food scene in Old Town. For Vietnam's fastest growing city, Danang, the future of the dining scene looks bright; recent years have seen an influx of design-savvy restauranteurs, inspiring bartenders, and top international chefs. While lacking in international options, Hue's imperial cuisine is as richly diverse as the city's past, and equally as interesting. Bun bo (a lemongrass and chili infused beef and pork noodle soup) originated here as did the "kingly table," a sociable, family-style dining experience where tables are loaded and food is shared tapas style.

HOTELS

The Central Coast is home to some of the most luxurious resorts and hotels in the country, with the highest concentration found in Hoi An and Danang. Small hotels and guesthouses (which are more commonly known locally as homestays) have also upped their game. For five-star experiences you'll find your money goes a lot further in Hue, where luxury hotels and resorts are, for the most part, located just outside of the city. As long-stay beach vacations become more fashionable, coastal areas that were once considered remote have started to develop.

For expanded reviews, facilities, and current deals, visit Fodors.com.

WHAT IT COSTS			
$	$$	$$$	$$$$
Restaurants	Under 60,000d	60,000d–150,000d	151,000d–250,000d	over 250,000d
Hotels	Under 600,000d	600,000d–900,000d	901,000d–1,500,000d	over 1,500,000d

Prices in the reviews are the average cost of a main course at dinner or, if dinner is not served, at lunch. Prices in the reviews are the lowest cost of a standard double room in high season.

TOURS

Handspan. One of the oldest and most respected tour operators in Vietnam, Handspan offers a wide range of tours and package holidays, and staff members are a great source for travel information on the region. Tours on offer are varied, well priced, and child friendly with great off-track options, licensed English-speaking guides, and high-quality transport. ☒ *Hanoi* ☎ *024/3926–2828 head office* ⊕ *www.handspan.com.*

Hoi An Express. Offering everything from visas to interpreters and chauffeur-driven cars to countrywide travel, Hoi An Express excels in customer service and competitive pricing. Tours on offer range from countryside bike rides in Hoi An on vintage Vespas to street food tours in Danang's liveliest night markets, with chauffeur-driven cars starting at 1,300,000d per day. ✉ *57 Tran Phu, Hoi An* ☎ *0235/391–9293.*

Trails of Indochina. This company provides a choice of vehicles, responsible drivers and private tour guides in and around the central region. From 1,200,000d per day. ✉ *Hue* ☎ *0234/383–6525* ⊕ *www. trailsofindochina.com.*

HOI AN

More than 500 km (310 miles) north of Nha Trang.

From the lantern-strewn streets of Old Town to the farmers shouldering their harvest in balanced baskets, the scenes of Hoi An capture what every traveler imagines Vietnam to be. It is the country's "must-see" destination, delivering culture, cuisine, history, and charm with the added bonus of a beach just minutes from the town center. The moment you arrive in Hoi An, you can't help but exhale, realizing that this quaint town has an endearing quality that spans from the colorful food markets to the friendly locals who somehow work their way into your heart without even trying.

This enchanting town defies the insidious pace of modernization. Preserved in pristine condition are its 18th-century houses, pagodas, and assembly halls built by early Fujian, Canton, Chaozhou, and Hainan-Chinese communities. The many galleries selling the works of local artists and artisans and the numerous cafés lend a strong bohemian feel. Hoi An has great cuisine and is probably the most tourist-friendly town in the country, with English being widely spoken. The whole town can easily be navigated on foot in a half a day, but plan to spend more time in Hoi An than you think you'll need, because it's easy to fall in love with the place. Just outside of town is the pleasant An Bang Beach, which you reach by taking a 5-km (3-mile) ride through a picturesque slice of rural Vietnam. Also nearby are the My Son Cham ruins, which evoke the ancient history of this region and the coral-encircled Cham Islands that provide spectacular diving alongside some of the most under-developed beaches in Vietnam.

GETTING HERE AND AROUND

The closest airport to Hoi An is the one in Danang, 30 km (19 miles) north. The only way to get to Hoi An from Danang airport is by minibus or car, which takes about 40 minutes. The trip to Hoi An costs 108,000d–431,000, depending on the number of passengers, and is a very scenic coastal drive through small towns and rice paddies. You can rent a car with a driver from Danang or from any travel agency in Hoi An.

Hoi An has two bus stations, one on Hung Vuong and a second on the corner of Le Hong Phong for public buses servicing north and south routes. Taxis line Thu Bon River to the south of the Hoi An Peninsula. They can also be found outside most hotels or parked on Le Loi Street in Old Town. The going rate is about 1,000d per kilometer. Bikes can be hired for around 20,000d per day from many hotels and independent bike hire stalls found throughout the town and surrounding streets.

TOURS

FAMILY

Fodor's Choice
★

Eat Hoi An Street-Food Tour. Boost your culinary credentials and learn to pull up a plastic stool like a pro on this four-hour walking street-food tour, accompanied by local foodie Mr. Phuoc. It's a meandering stroll through the alleyways and markets of the Old Town, allowing ample time to graze at Hoi An's tastiest stalls, while learning about condiments, culture, and the history of the cuisine with plenty of fun interaction with the vendors. Tour prices start at $35 and run daily from 2 pm, finishing with sunset drinks by the river. ✉ *37 Phan Chu Trinh* ☎ *0905/411–184* ⊕ *www.eathoian.com.*

Hoi An Photo Tour. Learn the basics of composition, shutter speed, and light exposure while capturing images of farmers in rice fields during a sunrise or sunset tour to local villages. Tours are led by Pieter Janssen, a talented photographer who has an easy way with locals and students, making his tours as fun as they are diverse. The workshop includes boat transportation, coffee, and bikes for exploration. Tours start at $35 and are suitable for all levels. ☎ *988/705–755* ⊕ *www. hoianphotowalks.com.*

Trails of Indochina. The custom package-tour itineraries offered by Trails of Indochina range from Hoi An's historic sites to culinary tours through the Central Market. Fees include luxury transportation and knowledgeable English-speaking guides. ☎ *028/384–41005 in Ho Chi Minh City, 234/383–6525 in Hue* ⊕ *www.trailsofindochina.com.*

FAMILY

Vietnam Vespa Adventures. One of the big names in Saigon, Vietnam Vespa Adventures offers a full range of vintage Vespa tours exploring the islands, countryside, and beaches of Hoi An, along with a hugely popular street-food night cruise through the lantern-lit streets lining the Old Town. Prices start at 1,400,000d for an all-inclusive guided tour and can be booked from the company's centrally located office and restaurant, Café Zoom. ✉ *134 Tran Cao Van* ☎ *0907/722–681* ⊕ *vietnamvespaadventures.com.*

VISITOR INFORMATION

Hoi An Tourism Office, the state-run travel agency on Phan Chau Trinh, organizes tours following several different itineraries of the city, as well as excursions to the Marble Mountains and My Son. Staff members speak perfect English and provide excellent service.

VISITOR
INFORMATION

Hoi An Ancient Town Entrance Ticket. Every person over the age of 16 (children go free) is required to buy a ticket to enter Old Town, though each ticket (despite being printed with the words "valid for 24 hours") is valid for the duration of your stay. You need to show it each time you enter, so keep it handy. The ticket has six tear-off coupons. One gives you access to the hour-long traditional performances held daily at the Folklore Museum on riverside Bach Dang Street, near the Central Market. The others are for entrance to your choice of 5 of the 21 ticket-only sites in Old Town. Eighty percent of the ticket proceeds go directly back into Old Town renovations and paying the guides and families who open their private homes to visitors. ✉ *78 Le Loi* ☎ *0235/3915–454* ⊕ *www.hoianworldheritage.org.vn.*

Hoi An History

Hoi An, or Faifo as it was called in previous centuries, is a composite of many foreign influences. From the 2nd to 10th century AD, the city was under the control of the Kingdom of Champa and was an important port town. During the 14th and 15th centuries, the Cham and the Vietnamese fought for control of Hoi An, and as a consequence the city ceased to be a trading center. Peace between the Cham and the Vietnamese in the 16th century once again made possible the accommodation of ships from all over Asia and Europe, bringing merchants in search of silk, porcelain, lacquer, and medicinal herbs. During the Tay Son Rebellion in the 1770s, Hoi An was severely damaged by fighting.

After a speedy reconstruction the town managed to sustain a two-century tenure as a major international port town where Chinese, Japanese, Dutch, and Portuguese merchants came to trade. During the off-season, seafaring merchants set up shop, and foreigners' colonies began to develop along Hoi An's riverfront. To this day, ethnic Chinese, who settled early in Hoi An, make up a significant portion of the population.

The French arrived in the late 1800s and made Hoi An an administrative post. They even built a rail line to Danang (then called Tourane). By this time, the Thu Bon River, which connected Hoi An to the sea, had begun to fill up with silt, making navigation almost impossible. Danang gradually eclipsed Hoi An as the major port town in the area.

Hoi An Office of Tourist Services. The official government-run tourist information office, located on the main resort bus drop-off point on the outskirts of Old Town, is the place to go for free maps, brochures, and information on Old Town and surrounds. The office shares its space with the local cinema, in a kitschy, Soviet-modernist building that is completely out of tune with the surrounding architecture. It's a great example of the postwar construction that would have replaced most of the ancient architecture of Old Town had things turned out differently. ⊠ *47–51 Phan Chau Trinh St.* ☎ *0235/391–6961* ⊕ *www. quangnamtourism.com.vn.*

EXPLORING

Most of the UNESCO World Heritage Sites—as well as restaurants and boutiques—are located in the Old Town, which can be explored in half a day. The Old Town is strictly reserved for pedestrians and bicycles, with motorbike access limited to a few hours each day. With ancient structures on almost every corner, it's the perfect place for a leisurely stroll. You can get a map from your hotel or from the local tourist office.

TOP ATTRACTIONS

An Hoi Night Lantern Market. As dusk falls, the area directly opposite the walking bridge connecting the Old Town to An Hoi Peninsula is lit by what seems to be a thousand silk lanterns, spilling out from little

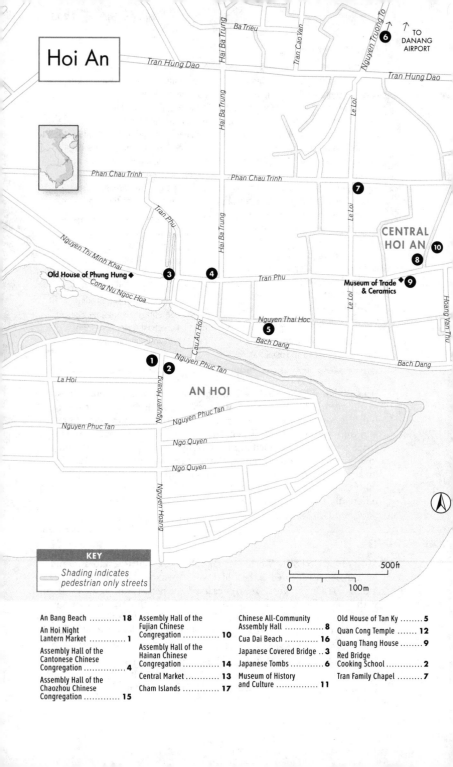

Hoi An

TO DANANG AIRPORT

CENTRAL HOI AN

Old House of Phung Hung ◆

Museum of Trade ◆
& Ceramics

AN HOI

KEY

Shading indicates
pedestrian only streets

0   500ft

0   100m

An Bang Beach **18**

An Hoi Night
Lantern Market **1**

Assembly Hall of the
Cantonese Chinese
Congregation **4**

Assembly Hall of the
Chaozhou Chinese
Congregation **15**

Assembly Hall of the
Fujian Chinese
Congregation **10**

Assembly Hall of the
Hainan Chinese
Congregation **14**

Central Market **13**

Cham Islands **17**

Chinese All-Community
Assembly Hall **8**

Cua Dai Beach **16**

Japanese Covered Bridge .. **3**

Japanese Tombs **6**

Museum of History
and Culture **11**

Old House of Tan Ky **5**

Quan Cong Temple **12**

Quang Thang House **9**

Red Bridge
Cooking School **2**

Tran Family Chapel **7**

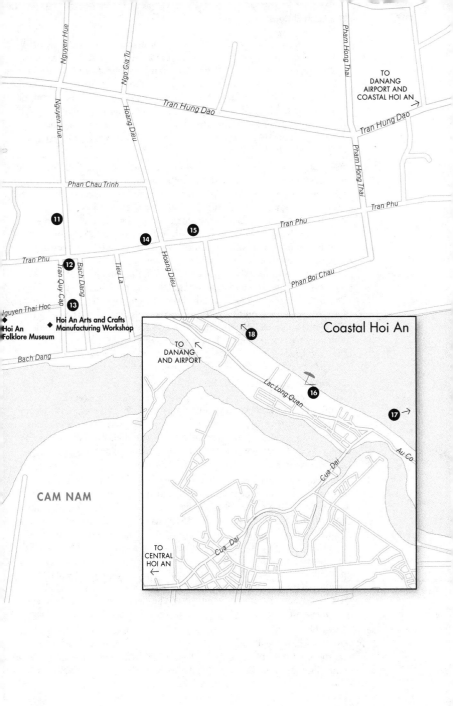

wooden chalets that wouldn't look out of place at a European Christmas market. In the daytime you can come here to watch the lanterns being crafted from wafts of silk and bamboo, but it's not until night when the lantern sellers are joined by a whole host of mobile craft, jewelry, and souvenir stalls, that this area really comes alive. The night market has the biggest selection of lanterns in town and you can even design your own, and while the stalls in between are not particularly notable, you can pick up cute little trinkets for very reasonable prices. ⊠ *Nguyen Phuc Chu, An Hoi.*

Assembly Halls. As part of their cultural tradition, the Chinese built assembly halls as a place for future generations to gather after they migrated to new countries. Once a major Southeast Asian trading port, Hoi An is home to five such halls that date back to the 16th and 17th centuries, however, exact dates for the buildings are unclear from historic records as most have been subjected to newer 18th- and 19th-century improvements. Recognizable by their Chinese architecture, the assembly halls generally feature ornate gates, main halls, altar rooms, and statues and murals in honor of gods and goddesses. Four of Hoi An's assembly halls—Fujian, Hainan, Cantonese, Chinese—are on Tran Phu Street near the river. The Chaozhou assembly hall is in the French Quarter, a short stroll east of Old Town on Nguyen Duy Hieu. Among them, the Fujian Hall, Phuc Kien, is considered the most prominent. Entrance to each Assembly Hall is one coupon from the five included in the Old Town ticket. ⊠ *Tran Phu St., near Chuc Thanh Pagoda* 🖃 *Included in 120,000d tourist-office ticket* ⊙ *Daily 8–5.*

Central Market. This is one of the most enjoyable fresh markets in Vietnam, covering a large area, snaking its way around the French Colonial food hall, Cho Hoi An, down to the river on Bach Dang, with feeder lanes sprouting off down mossy side alleys. The merchants are friendly and a large selection of merchandise is available, but barter hard to strike a good deal—expect to come in at the midway point and haggle upward to around a third off the start price.

The stalls that surround the market are lined with fruit and flower sellers, while the small local shops opposite specialize in bamboo baskets and household wares; this is the best place to pick up the pretty blue-and-white china popular in Hoi An. The fish market down by the river is best avoided during the pungent hours of midday; the best time to visit for ambience and photos is just before sunrise as the conical-hatted traders descend upon fishing boats laden with colorful fish, squid, and giant prawns. ■TIP➔ **Made famous by Anthony Bourdain, Phuong Banh Mi has a small stall here serving quite possibly the best banh mi in Vietnam. To find it walk 50 meters around the outside of Cho Hoi An, to the left of the well.** ⊠ *Intersection of Tran Quy Cap and Tran Phu Sts.* ⊙ *Daily 6–dusk.*

Fodor's Choice
★

Cham Islands (*Cu Lau Cham*). The Hoi An coast is flanked by eight small, coral-fringed islands featuring beautiful seascapes, deserted white sandy beaches, and some of the best microdiving sites in central Vietnam. Despite their beauty, the islands have never been developed for tourism, and it wasn't until their 2009 designation as a World Biosphere reserve by UNESCO that anyone took any interest. Those that did were dive companies, limiting visitors to just a couple of dives. From April to September, daily junk and speedboat services run the 18-km (11-mile) route between Cua Dai dock and Hon Lau Island, where you can arrange a homestay or camp on two of the main island beaches, though few visitors do, which makes it one of the most tranquil respites from the touristy beaches of Hoi An and also one of the most beautiful places to watch the sunset from your own private beach. Activities available include snorkeling, diving, swimming, camping, fishing, and trekking. ■ TIP→ **Local tour offices and hotels can arrange island tours. For camping visit Cham Island Divers or the Blue Coral Diving offices on Nguyen Thai Hoc Street in Hoi An.** ✛ *Daily boat services run from Cua Dai Harbour to Hon Lau Port.*

Chuc Thanh Pagoda and Phuoc Lam Pagoda. Head north on Nguyen Tru-ong To Street for approximately 1 km (½ mile) to the end, turn left, and follow the path until you reach Chuc Thanh Pagoda, the oldest pagoda in Hoi An. Founded in 1454 by Minh Hai, a Chinese Buddhist monk, the pagoda contains several ancient religious objects, including several bells and gongs made of both stone and wood. On the way back, stop at the Phuoc Lam Pagoda, built in the mid-17th century. Note the interesting Chinese architecture and the large collection of ceramics on its roof. ▨ *Free* ☉ *Daily 8–5.*

Hoi An Lantern Festival. Every month on the 1st and 14th day of the lunar calender, Hoi An closes Old Town to traffic, switches off its lights, and hosts the beautiful Lantern Festival. Domestic travelers flock to the streets, and temples and pagodas open their doors for ancestral worship. Most people choose to while away the evening watching the festivities from a restaurant balcony, but to really get the best experience you need to tackle the crowds head on and mingle with the locals at street level. Festivities start at sunset and this is a particularly ambient time to visit the candle-lit pagodas (which are free to enter on full moon) and take in the street entertainment, pop-up poetry reading groups, and musicians. As darkness falls, approach the small river boats that line Bach Dang and arrange for a half-hour cruise finishing up on An Hoi, where a short stroll on quieter streets lined with restaurants leads you to the glowing night lantern market where you can pick up souvenirs and grab a taxi back to your hotel.

Fodor'sChoice
★ **Japanese Covered Bridge.** On the west end of Tran Phu, Hoi An's most celebrated icon was built in 1593 by Japanese merchants to connect the Japanese quarter with the Chinese neighborhood on the other side of the river. This unique city symbol has been rebuilt several times since, but still retains the original ornate roofing, arched frame, and small temple housed inside. Legends surround the functions of the bridge, the most popular being that it was built to disable a disaster-causing dragon, with the small altar inside dedicated to the worship of Bac De Tran Vu, a northern God in charge of wind and rain. The pair of spirit dogs on the east side of the bridge are thought to be protective deities, placed on altar stones to exorcise bad blessings. If you look closely you'll notice they are different sizes: a boy and a girl. Some say the monkeys here represent Japanese emperors. What is not widely known is that the

monkeys are copies carved by the carpenters of Kim Bong Village; the original pair were swept away during a flood and washed up beyond repair 20 years later. ⊠ *West end of Tran Phu St.* ⌧ *One of 5 sites on the 120,000d Hoi An Ancient Town Entrance Ticket.*

Japanese Tombs. Erected in the 1600s, these are the few remaining tombs of Hoi An's old Japanese community. Although the tombs—tombstones, really—are not nearly as grand as those in Hue, it's worth the trek if only to see the "suburbs" of Hoi An. En route you'll encounter families sitting in their front yards and field workers harvesting rice. Buried in the first tomb along the dirt path—clearly visible in the front yard of a family home—is a Japanese merchant named Masai. About another 1,500 feet ahead is the most famous of Hoi An's Japanese tombs, the burial place of a Japanese merchant named Yajirobei, who died in 1647. Perched right in the middle of a working rice field, his tomb has an almost supernatural feel. The main tombs are are easily accessible by bicycle, just head along Hai Ba Trung Street and go north of Old Town. To find the tombs your eyes peeled for the white-and-yellow signs positioned along the right side of the road. (Cars are not recommended because the tombs are at the end of narrow, rugged paths.) ■TIP→ Continue 5 km (3 miles) to the end of Hai Ba Trung for a refreshing dip and lunch at one of the bohemian seaside shacks on An Bang beach. ⊠ *North of Old Town, Hai Ba Trung.*

Museum of History and Culture. This small museum—housed in just one large room—provides a small insight into Hoi An's history and culture. On display are ancient bowls, cups, and other ceramics, many of them archaeological artifacts dating back to the Cham. A collection of traditional Chinese objects includes pagoda bells and the "watchful eyes" placed above doorways for protection. Information is scant, so you are likely to leave underwhelmed and none the wiser, but the old black-and-white photos of 20th-century Hoi An make for an interesting comparison to the town today. The connecting door to the back of Quang Ong Temple provides a little more interest. ⊠ *7 Nguyen Hue St.* ⌧ *Included in 120,000d tourist-office ticket* ⊙ *Daily 8–5:30.*

Fodor's Choice ★ **Old House of Tan Ky.** One of the oldest and best-preserved private houses in Hoi An, this structure has remained largely unchanged in the 200 years since it was built. Seven generations of the Tan Ky family have lived here. The house incorporates both Chinese and Japanese styles. Chinese poetry is engraved in mother-of-pearl on the walls, each character formed in the shape of birds in various stages of flight. Look up into the eaves and you will see symbols of dragons, fruit, crossed sabers, and silk intricately carved into the wooden framework. The back door was constructed to open onto the river so that waterborne goods could be easily transported into the house; look out for the marks etched in to the wall recording the height of the annual flood waters. ⊠ *101 Nguyen Thai Hoc St.* ⌧ *Included in 120,000d tourist-office ticket* ⊙ *Daily 8– noon, 2–5.*

Red Bridge Cooking School. Learn the secrets of Vietnamese cuisine at this cooking school located beside Thu Bon River. Half- and full-day cooking classes are available and include a market tour, boat transportation, and either lunch or dinner. Courses range from $19–50 and commence at Hai Café in Old Town where they also run evening cooking classes daily (111 Tran Phu Street). ■TIP→ Take your bathing suit and grab a hammock by the pool, complimentary access is offered to all diners and students. ⊠ *Thon 4, Cam Thanh, 2 km (1 mile) outside of Hoi An* ☎ *0235/393–3222* ⊕ *www.visithoian.com.*

WORTH NOTING

Quan Cong Temple. Founded in 1653 by the Chinese community, this rather impressive temple is dedicated to Quan Cong, a revered general of the Chinese Han dynasty. The temple is divided into three parts. The entrance leads through a large garden to the temple, where the main altar is, along with a gilt-and-paper-maché statue of the general standing between two life-size, jolly-looking horses. Quan Cong lends itself to contemplation and meditation, and you get a real sense of that in the rear courtyard, gazing up at the unicorns and dragons perching on the colorful ceramic tiled roof or watching the small school of fish that happily dart around in the pond out front. The carp, symbolic of patience in Chinese mythology, is displayed throughout. ⊠ *Corner of Nguyen Hue, near Central Market, 24 Tran Phu St.* ☒ *Included in 120,000d tourist-office ticket* ⊙ *Daily 8–5.*

Quang Thang House. One of Hoi An's ancient family homes, Quang Thang was built about 300 years ago by the current owners' Chinese ancestors. This house has some beautiful wood carvings featuring peacocks and flowers on the walls of the rooms that surround the mossy courtyard. These were sculpted by the craftsmen from the Kim Bong carpentry village, who are renowned for their intricate craftmanship of the Hue garden houses. It's a beautiful and very well-preserved example of a traders house, popular with large tour groups. ■TIP→ If Quang Thang House is busy, wait it out with a coffee at Lantern Town restaurant across the road. ⊠ *77 Tran Phu St.* ☒ *Included in 120,000d tourist-office ticket* ⊙ *Daily 8–5* ⊙ *Closed daily noon–2.*

Tran Family Chapel. This elegantly designed house was built in 1802 by Tran Tu Nhuc, a 19th-century Mandarin and Chinese ambassador as a place of worship for the Tran family's deceased ancestors. It's packed full of interesting antiquities and in the morning, light floods down through a glass tile in the roof, illuminating the family altar that stands behind three sliding doors; the left for men and the right for women. The central door is opened only at Tet and other festivals, for deceased ancestors to return home; an architectural design common for older residential houses throughout the country.

The altar houses a box with pictures and names of dead relatives, a 250-year-old book that records the Tran family history, and a bowl of Chinese coins representing yin and yang—toss one for good luck. Tours are given in English by members of the Tran family. ⊠ *21 Le Loi St.* ☒ *Included in 120,000d tourist-office ticket* ⊙ *Daily 8–5.*

BEACHES

FAMILY
Fodor's Choice
★

An Bang Beach. The locals' favorite beach, An Bang is one of the few remaining public beaches on the long Hoi An–Danang coastline. Locals flock here for sunrise swimming and sunset family picnics, leaving this lovely stretch of beach almost deserted during the day. A row of palm-thatched restaurants border the clean sandy beach offering free use of beach loungers and umbrellas if you buy food or drinks. Competition is fierce and staff can be pushy. Development has been minimal, with only a few homestays and holiday cottages, but plans for two large resorts at either end of the beach are set to change this over the next few years. **Amenities:** food and drink; showers; surfboard hire. **Best for:** swimming; sunsets; families; surfing; walking. ✉ *Hai Ba Trung, 5 km east of Hoi An, An Bang.*

Cua Dai Beach. Ten minutes from the Old Town is Hoi An's main public beach, where clear water and warm surf beckon tourists and locals alike. Recently the coastline has been subject to erosion and the shore to the right of the intersection at the end of Cua Dai Road has been sectioned off and replaced by an ugly iron coastal defense wall. Resorts have all been heavily affected because beach frontage has been lost and the views from what were once idyllic beach-facing villas and pools are now of rocky sea defense walls.

Despite this, the public beach area to the north has retained much of its sand and the beach is clean. It's the perfect spot to escape the sweltering humidity of Old Town during the hottest months. Walking beach vendors can be a problem, heckling people to buy fresh fruit and crafts, but most are easily rebuffed with a firm "no thank-you." A line of food shacks sell fresh fish, squid, and shellfish, and offer amenities. Bikes can be rented for about 22,000d per day; Jet Skis start at 648,000d. ■ **TIP→** If Cua Dai Beach is crowded, walk or bike 3 km (2 miles) north to An Bang beach. **Amenities:** food and drink; free parking; toilets; showers; water sports. **Best for:** surfing; swimming; walking. ✉ *Cua Dai Beach.*

Ha My Beach. A little ways outside of Hoi An, this peaceful beach, located midway between the award-winning Nam Hai and Le Belhamy resorts is the best place to head to escape the hawkers and crowds that frequent the more famous Cua Dai. With just a few incredibly good seafood restaurants, and a couple of loungers and umbrellas, this regularly cleaned, gently shelving beach offers great swimming conditions, a chilled-out atmosphere, and plenty of space for children to run around safely. **Amenities:** showers; toilets; food and drink; free parking. **Best for:** swimming; walking; solitude; sunset. ✉ *6 km (3½ miles) north of An Bang along Danang coastal road, Dien Duong Village, Cam An.*

WHERE TO EAT

OLD TOWN

$$
VIETNAMESE
Fodor's Choice
★

✕ **Ancient Faifo.** Fusing art, music, history, and cuisine, this 19th-century house in Hoi An's Old Quarter has been beautifully restored and offers silver service at remarkable prices. Slightly overshadowed by the setting, the menu is Vietnamese-meets-modern cuisine with such dishes as bean sprout dumplings, mango and lotus salad, caramelized pork, and wok-fried ancient noodles. The four-course set menu is probably the best deal. Enjoy a cocktail on the garden patio and then request a table on the small balcony overlooking the lantern-strewn street. There's live jazz nightly from 7 pm to 8 pm, except on weekends, when traditional music is played. $ *Average main: 325000d* ⊠ *66 Nguyen Thai Hoc St.* ☏ *0235/391–7444* ⊕ *www.ancientfaifo.com.vn* ☉ *Daily 7 am–10 pm.*

$$
VIETNAMESE
FAMILY

✕ **Ba Le Well.** Local families who come in droves to this popular no-frills diner make out-of-town visitors feel warmly welcome, even if they occasionally giggle at your attempts to master the fiddlesome art of rolling the perfect *banh xeo.*The time to dine here is early evening. There's no menu, just pull up a stool and within minutes you'll be presented with pork skewers, crispy pancakes stuffed with bean sprouts, deep-fried shrimp spring rolls, rice paper, various herby greens, a satay-style dip, and a confusing array of condiments. Once your table is groaning, you'll be offered instructions by the lady of the house. Say yes and pay attention, particularly with the final rice paper preparation. There's an art here that'll save you from being the chosen entertainment for the evening. ■ TIP→ **Go hungry, portions are large, but the 100,000d set price is not.** $ *Average main: 100000d* ⊠ *Cut down alleyway near Le Loi end of Phan Chau Trinh, 45/51 Ba Le Well* ☏ *0235/3864–443.*

$
VIETNAMESE
Fodor's Choice
★

✕ **Banh Mi Phuong.** Ms. Phuong serves from a simple little take-away counter, next door to a bakery on the edge of Old Town. When famed foodie Anthony Bourdain visited, he declared the banh mi served here to be quite possibly the best in Vietnam; and he might just be right. What you get here is a symphony in a sandwich, and though both her menu and popularity have grown, she's still serving up the same secret family recipes and silence-inducing sandwiches. Bourdain's banh mi deluxe is a pork feast consisting of a mouth-meltingly slow-roasted five-spiced fillet, a rich peppery pate, a handful of herbs, pickled vegetables, and finished off with a generous scoop of mayonnaise, smoked chili sauce, and messy fried egg. ■ TIP→ **Phuong also has vegetarian alternatives; ask for banh mi chay.** $ *Average main: 30000d* ⊠ *2B Phan Chau Trinh* ▭ *No credit cards.*

$$$
CAFÉ
FAMILY
Fodor's Choice
★

✕ **Cocobox.** Part organic farm shop, part juice bar, this trendy hipster hangout on Le Loi also serves sandwiches, snacks, coffee, and cold-pressed juices that come in little jam jars. Run by Swedish expat Jan and his Vietnamese partner, the uniquely styled old traders house has become Hoi An's coolest place to escape; expats form lineups at the rustic bar made from reclaimed shutters for take-away smoothies, while visitors eye-up the healthy snacks served to those lucky enough to have bagged one of the few too-cool-for-school bar stools. ■ TIP→ **Try the delicious hot chocolate with coconut milk.** $ *Average main: 150000d* ⊠ *94 Le Loi* ☏ *0235/3862–000* ⊕ *www.cocoboxvietnam.com* ☉ *Closes at 8 pm.*

$$$
VIETNAMESE
Fodor's Choice
★

✕ **Green Mango.** Standards have been set high in this beautifully restored wooden traders house, one of the most opulent in Old Town. The fine-dining menu is a fusion of French cooking techniques and local ingredients, curated by Chef Hai whose sister restaurant in Ha Noi was recognised by the Miele Guide as "One of Asia's Finest." Downstairs, the lounge bar serves top-shelf single malts, classic cocktails, and boutique beers. The balconied upper level is reserved for romantic dining, the decadent surroundings reflecting the food. Try the *pho hai san,* a spicy, creamy seafood noodle soup, the Thai red curry, or imported steak. $ *Average main: 150000d* ⊠ *54 Nguyen Thai Hoc* ☎ *0235/392–9918* ⊕ *www.greenmango.vn.*

$$
VEGETARIAN
Fodor'sChoice
★

✕ **Little Menu.** For simple, authentic, great-value dining, few places come close to the extraordinarily good Little Menu. On the main thoroughfare into the Old Town, this is an unfussy but undoubtedly lovely 19th-century family home, where local artwork hangs from crumbling yellow walls and seating takes second place to a huge open kitchen. The street-facing patio is the place to sit here, with great views across to an ornate community temple. Order the *mi quang,* a Quang Nam specialty of flat noodles, organic herbs, and a choice of beef or pork in broth. $ *Average main: 70000d* ⊠ *12 Le Loi* ☎ *0235/3939–568* ⊕ *www.thelittlemenu.com.*

$$$
ASIAN FUSION

✕ **Mango Mango.** A spinoff of the original Mango Rooms in Old Town, this Vietnamese fusion restaurant is located along the river directly across from the Japanese Covered Bridge. Owner-chef Duc has created an innovative menu of modern-Asian-meets-the-world, inspired from his 20-plus years of travels abroad. He goes to the local market to find ingredients like giant prawns, which he bathes in a sauce of white wine, passionfruit, and bitter chocolate. Many of the dishes stay true to classic Vietnamese cuisine such as the spring rolls, crusted duck, and fried rice wrapped in banana leaves. $ *Average main: 300000d* ⊠ *45 Nguyen Phuc Chu* ☎ *0235/3911–863* ⊕ *www.mangorooms.com.*

$$
VIETNAMESE
FAMILY
Fodor'sChoice
★

✕ **The Market Restaurant and Cooking School.** For an introduction to regional fare, without the shock of a street food stall, this buzzy, upscale food hall, owned by local celebrity chef Ms. Vy, attracts a steady stream of enthusiastic foodies keen to take a culinary tour of Hoi An's gastronomic classics. The menu here is visual, and diners are invited to wander among the various food stations where traditional dishes like *cau lao* noodles, banh mi, and savory country pancakes are made to order, to be devoured on simple bench seating arranged in the central courtyard. It's a clever concept encouraging diner interaction, with ad-hoc cooking demonstrations thrown in for good measure—maybe that's just to encourage you to sign up for one of Ms. Vy's cooking classes, but it adds a bit of theater to the occasion, and makes the very unstreet prices here more palatable. ■ TIP→ **The fixed-price all-you-can-eat breakfast buffet is well worth shelving the bikini diet for, and don't forget to take a peek at the Weird and Wonderful stall.** $ *Average main: 140000d* ⊠ *3 Nguyen Hoang, An Hoi* ☎ *0235/3926–926* ⊕ *msvy-tastevietnam.com.*

$$
VIETNAMESE

✕ **Miss Ly Cafeteria.** The vivacious Miss Ly was one of the first cooks in town to open her humble, market-edge cafeteria to the trickle of travelers astute enough to have put Hoi An on their itinerary almost 20 years ago. Two decades later, and Ly is still in the kitchen pouring her heart and soul into each dish served. Her *Hoi An wontons,* crispy rice-flour shells with a pocket of minced pork and shrimp, dressed with a fruity, Chinese-style sweet-and-sour salsa, are some of the best in town. This is also the best place to sample Hoi An's two most famous dishes:

White Rose, steamed pork-and-shrimp dumplings served with a fragrant chili dip; and *cao lau,* chewy udon-like noodles with a thick five-spice gravy, pork, bean sprouts, and greens. $ *Average main: 100000d* ✉ *22 Nguyen Hue St.* ☎ *0235/3861–603.*

$$
CAFÉ
✕ **Reaching Out Teahouse.** Amid the bustle of Hoi An is this peaceful teahouse where the quiet is partly due to the fact that the staff have hearing and speech impediments. The profound silence is almost healing, as the graceful team communicates by using wooden blocks inscribed with words (in English). Low wooden tables in the main teahouse offer street views, while those in the back garden are more secluded. For a little pick-me-up, try the fresh coffee and cakes. This fair-trade business also has a neighboring craft shop that sells high-quality Vietnamese souvenirs hand crafted by artisans with disabilities. $ *Average main: 80000d* ✉ *131 Tran Phu* ☎ *0235/391–0168.*

$$
VIETNAMESE
✕ **Streets Restaurant.** Help young locals while you dine at this Old Town restaurant heavy on vegetarian options. Street youth are given the opportunity to refine their hospitality skills during an 18-month training program here through the nonprofit organization Streets International, which employs orphaned and disadvantaged Vietnamese teens, many of whom go on to work at five-star restaurants and hotels. The food is good, so you're not giving up taste for charity. Dishes include thick noodles with pork, crispy rice pancakes, and caramelized eggplant and tofu served in a clay pot. Those with a sweet tooth should save room for the coconut parfait with grilled pineapple and ice cream. The kitchen closes at 9:30. $ *Average main: 150000d* ✉ *17 Le Loi* ☎ *0235/391–1948* ⊕ *www.streetsinternational.org* ⊘ *Closed Sun.*

ON THE BEACH

$$
VIETNAMESE
✕ **Bia Hoi Pho Co.** Before Pho Co opened, the options for fresh beer in Hoi An were limited to below-par tourist restaurants or getting down and dirty in a noisy, often toiletless local boys' beer shop on the outskirts of town. Not that that's a bad thing, but those that have sampled the amber homebrew will understand that a toilet nearby and a good menu of beer snacks to soak up the booze is essential. Pho Co, a lively bia hoi hall near the beach on Cua Dai, provides both, with the added bonus of surprisingly tuneful background music. The local way is to order your bia by the tower and graze through the grill menu of baby pork ribs, fresh seafood (the fish here is incredible), and chicken wings. ■ TIP➔ **Check for live music events on weekends.** $ *Average main: 70000d* ✉ *On road opposite beach, 31 Lac Long Quan* ☎ *0935/330–851* ▭ *No credit cards.*

$$$
ITALIAN
✕ **Luna D'Autunno.** Clay-oven pizza, pasta, antipasti plates, and fine wines, all sourced from Italy, can be enjoyed on a tropically planted beachfront garden, or, on wintery days, holed up in a cozy corner by the kitchen. The sesame-coated tuna with salad, Pecorino cheese, and olives are to die for, as are the Italian homemade desserts. $ *Average main: 160000d* ✉ *6 Cam An, An Bang* ☎ *01659/470–374* ⊕ *www.lunadautunno.vn.*

$ SEAFOOD 🍴 **Ngoc Mai.** Expect a warm welcome from the family (all three generations of them and their dog) when you arrive at this simple seafood shack on the beach between Le Belhamy and the Nam Hai. Locals flood here for sunset and weekend family parties for the restaurant's delicious fresh seafood, ordered by the kilo from the oxygenated buckets at the entrance and charcoal-grilled by grandma on a rickety old metal barbeque out back. The menu (or buckets) change daily, depending on the Ha My fishermen catch that day. If you are lucky there will be oysters, grilled clams, salt-and-pepper *muc* (squid), or snapper grilled in a banana leaf. ■ **TIP→ Drinks rarely come cold, but the ice here is made from filtered water.** [$] *Average main: 50000d* ✉ *Turn left just after Le Belhamy resort and follow road down to beach. Ngoc Mai is 1st restaurant on right, Ha My* 💳 *No credit cards.*

$$ ASIAN FUSION FAMILY Fodor's Choice ★ 🍴 **Soul Kitchen.** The most social spot on the beach, Soul Kitchen attracts a year-round mix of expats and visitors, with frequent live music and open mike events. During the day the shady grass frontage, pool table, and board games keep kids entertained, leaving parents free to relax in raised cabanas with a Vietnamese-French menu, wine list, and cold draft Tiger beer. Standouts are the mixed fish carpaccio or beef bourguignon served with freshly baked bread, and for children, the crispy fried chicken, carbonara pasta, or Vietnamese fried rice. ■ **TIP→ Every Sunday, rain or shine, Soul hosts a live music event from 4 to 10 pm.** [$] *Average main: 100000d* ✉ *Far left at beach intersection, An Bang* 🌐 *www.soulkitchen.sitew.com.*

$$ VIETNAMESE 🍴 **White Sail.** Decked with private cabanas, a castaway bar, and dining area built almost entirely from local materials and wood washed up during the 2013 typhoon, this shabby chic beach restaurant serves up a winning menu of exemplary Hoi An cuisine. Start with the delicious crispy wontons with a tropical tomato and mango salsa or tempura calamari, then move on to the caramelized pork in claypot or try the catch of the day grilled fresh in a banana leaf. Sunsets are served with an international wine list or a tropical cocktail, and the beers are the coldest served on the beach. ■ **TIP→ Dining and drinking guests are invited to use the cabanas and loungers on the beach for free.** [$] *Average main: 70000d* ✉ *Left at beach intersection, An Bang* ☎ *0905/356–177* 💳 *No credit cards.*

WHERE TO STAY

OLD TOWN

$$$$ HOTEL FAMILY Fodor's Choice ★ 🏨 **Alma Courtyard.** The younger, hipper sister to the award-winning Fusion Maia, the spa-focused Alma Courtyard offers contemporary, luxe stays with a focus on wellness, just a 10-minute stroll from Old Town. **Pros:** the biggest spa in Vietnam; impecable service; the exotic herbal-infused cocktail menu; heated pool. **Cons:** street-facing rooms are noisy (a few overlook a nightclub); out-of-town location. [$] *Rooms from: 3199102d* ✉ *326 Ly Thuong Kiet* ☎ *0235/3666–111* 🌐 *www.almacourtyardhoian.com* 🛏 *145 rooms* 🍽 *Breakfast.*

$$$$ ⊞ **Anantara Hoi An Resort.** Situated in three-story buildings, rooms here
RESORT have an apartment-like feel, with small living areas and three stairs
leading to king-size beds. **Pros:** great location near Old Town; helpful staff; comfortable beds. **Cons:** thin walls; daybed patios lack privacy; flood-prone area. $ *Rooms from: 3800000d* ⊠ *1 Pham Hong
Thai St.* ☏ *0235/391–4555* ⊕ *www.hoi-an.anantara.com* ⇝ *94 rooms*
⎮◎⎮ *Breakfast.*

$$$ ⊞ **Ancient House Resort.** Tucked away in a tropical garden, this thin-
HOTEL walled hotel pays tribute to Vietnamese culture with its rice paper fac-
tory and a 200-year-old house, where fifth-generation family members
still live today. **Pros:** great breakfast; local charm; available tours to
Marble Mountains. **Cons:** no elevator; tall bathtubs are awkward for
exiting; mosquitoes in common areas. $ *Rooms from: 1515000d* ⊠ *377
Cua Dai Rd.* ☏ *0235/392–3377* ⊕ *www.ancienthouseresort.com* ⇝ *52
rooms* ⎮◎⎮ *Breakfast.*

$$$$ ⊞ **Hoi An Chic.** Surrounded by rice fields and duck ponds and a short
HOTEL jeep ride from town and beach, this eco-chic countryside pad is a perfect
romantic bolthole without the heavy price tag of an Old Town address.
Pros: quiet; views; romantic; complimentary jeep transportation. **Cons:**
mosquitoes; distance to restaurants/beach; pool needs more shade.
$ *Rooms from: 2205000d* ⊠ *Lane way off Cua Dai Rd, Nguyen Trai*
☏ *0235/3926–799* ⊕ *www.hoianchic.com* ⇝ *17 rooms* ⎮◎⎮ *Breakfast.*

$$$ ⊞ **Hoi An Riverside Resort and Spa.** Midway between the town of Hoi
RESORT An and Cua Dai Beach, the Hoi An Riverside Resort may be the most
FAMILY peaceful accommodation in Vietnam. **Pros:** free transport to town and
beach; spectacular views; quiet; pool. **Cons:** distance from restaurants;
mosquitos. $ *Rooms from: 1435000d* ⊠ *3 km (2 miles) from Hoi An
Town, 175 Cua Dai* ☏ *0235/3864–800* ⊕ *www.hoianriverresort.com*
⇝ *63 rooms* ⎮◎⎮ *Breakfast.*

$ ⊞ **Moon Homestay.** This budget homestay on the outskirts of town offers
B&B/INN fantastic accommodations, incredible service, and exceptional tailoring
on-site, without the hassle of endless fittings in town. **Pros:** great value;
Savile Row–quality on-site tailoring; free bikes; free cooking classes;
great local restaurants nearby. **Cons:** 15-minute walk to Old Town;
5 km (3 miles) from the beach. $ *Rooms from: 580000d* ⊠ *157 Ly
Thai To* ☏ *0235/392–4535* ⊕ *www.moonhomestay.com* ⇝ *5 rooms*
⎮◎⎮ *Breakfast.*

$$ ⊞ **Muca Resort.** Laid-back, intimate, and set amid lush tropical gardens,
RESORT the Muca sits on the river's edge under the shade of coconut trees, just
4 km (2 miles) from Old Town and the beach. **Pros:** tranquil, riverside
setting; great value; on-site spa. **Cons:** unwalkable distance to beach or
town; mosquitos; light sleepers should be aware that village community
announcements sometimes start up at 5 am. $ *Rooms from: 760000d*
⊠ *115–117 Alley, Cua Dai* ☏ *0235/3930–222* ⊕ *www.mucahoian.com*
⇝ *36 rooms* ⎮◎⎮ *Breakfast.*

$ ⊞ **Vaia Boutique.** If you have come to Hoi An to shop, the fashion-savvy
HOTEL Vaia Boutique, a well-located, cheap but chic mini-hotel owned by
tailor giants Yaly (staying here gets you a massive 30% off at any of
their shops in the Old Town), is an excellent choice. **Pros:** great value

5

and location; minimalist design; free bikes; tailor shop discounts. **Cons:** street-facing rooms can be noisy; limited facilities. $ *Rooms from: 590000d* ✉ *489 Cua Dai* ☎ *0235/3916–499* ⊕ *www.vaiahotel.com* ↳ *18 rooms* ⦿ *Breakfast.*

$$$
HOTEL
Fodor'sChoice
★

🏨 **Vinh Hung Heritage Hotel.** Made famous for providing Michael Caine with a dressing room (the decadent suite 206) during the filming of *The Quiet American*, this charming 200-year-old timber merchant house has the best address in the city; right in the heart of the Old Town. **Pros:** complimentary use of sister hotel's (the Vinh Hung Resort) pool; the central Old Town location; welcoming staff. **Cons:** Heritage suites with front-facing balconies are noisy; dark rooms. ■ **TIP→ Cars are banned from the Old Town area, so arrange ahead for luggage transfers.** $ *Rooms from: 1710000d* ✉ *143 Tran Phu St.* ☎ *0235/3861–621* ⊕ *www.vinhhungheritagehotel.com* ↳ *6 rooms* ⦿ *Breakfast.*

$$
HOTEL

🏨 **Vinh Hung Library Hotel.** The sweeping city views from the roof-top pool are a bonus for travelers in search of a great-value base close to the Old Town. **Pros:** pool; library; ambience; excellent tours. **Cons:** standard rooms have no windows; ground floor rooms can be noisy at times. $ *Rooms from: 894000d* ✉ *96 Ba Trieu* ☎ *0235/3916–277* ⊕ *www.vinhhung3hotel.com* ↳ *24 rooms* ⦿ *Breakfast.*

ON THE BEACH

$$$$
B&B/INN
FAMILY

🏨 **An Bang Seaside Village.** These family-friendly residences, scattered among a tropical fruit grove 4 km (2½ miles) from Old Town combine luxurious living with quirky An Bang beach style. **Pros:** beach location; near bars and restaurants; great for kids. **Cons:** no pool; village life starts early; books up quickly. $ *Rooms from: 1659000d* ✉ *An Bang* ☎ *090/6660309* ⊕ *www.anbangseasidevillage.com* ↳ *7 houses* ▤ *No credit cards* ⦿ *Breakfast.*

$$$$
RENTAL

🏨 **Be's Cottage.** Get as close as possible to village life in a stylishly designed, cozy one-bedroom "fisher house," tucked away in a lush tropical garden filled with fruit trees and flowers, a stone's throw from the beach. **Pros:** great value; good for families with small kids; close to beach restaurants and bars. **Cons:** neighborhood roosters set early morning alarms; 6 km (4 miles) from town. $ *Rooms from: 2200000d* ✉ *Left at beach intersection, An Bang* ⊕ *www.hoianbeachbungalows. com* ↳ *1 room* ▤ *No credit cards* ⦿ *No meals.*

$$$$
RESORT

🏨 **Hoi An Beach Resort.** The best feature of Hoi An's oldest beach resort is its riverside setting, and river views somewhat make up for the lack of beach (in 2014, after major renovations at the resort, rapid coastal erosion took the last of the beach). **Pros:** some rooms have river views; impeccable service; lovely pool area overlooking the river. **Cons:** you have to cross a busy road to get to what's left of the beach; restaurant is average. $ *Rooms from: 2325000d* ✉ *Cua Dai Beach, 01 Cua Dai St.* ☎ *0235/392–7011* ⊕ *www.hoianbeachresort.com.vn* ↳ *121 rooms* ⦿ *Breakfast.*

$$$$
RESORT

🏨 **Hoi An Boutique Resort.** For beach villa stays, the colonial-style Boutique Resort located on the sandy coastal stretch between Cua Dai and An Bang Beach is one of the most decadent in town. **Pros:** free transfers to Hoi An; beautiful beach; good local restaurants nearby. **Cons:**

expensive; books up well in advance. [$] *Rooms from: 2600920d* ✉ *Cua Dai* ☎ *0235/393–9111* 🌐 *www.boutiquehoianresort.com* 🛏 *82 rooms* 🍴 *Breakfast.*

$$$$ RESORT FAMILY Fodor's Choice ★ 🏨 **The Nam Hai.** Located on a pristine beach, this all-villa resort has 100 villas, ranging in size from one to five rooms. **Pros:** one of Vietnam's best hotels; excellent service; superb restaurant and spa. **Cons:** 15 minutes from Old Town Hoi An; minimum three-night stay during holidays; expensive resort. [$] *Rooms from: 15572000d* ✉ *Hamlet 1 Dien Duong Village, Dient Ban District* ☎ *0235/394–0000* 🌐 *www.ghmhotels.com* 🛏 *100 villas* 🍴 *Breakfast.*

$$$$ RESORT FAMILY 🏨 **Victoria Hoi An Resort.** Public spaces at this popular, family-friendly resort are well positioned to take in the panoramic coastal view and all rooms come luxuriously appointed, with beautiful bathrooms and traditional Asian furnishings. **Pros:** kids' club, complimentary shuttle service to and from Old Town; large pool; good on-site dining. **Cons:** riverview rooms are road-facing, which can be noisy; coastal erosion means limited beach frontage. [$] *Rooms from: 3392000d* ✉ *Cua Dai Beach* ☎ *0235/392–7040* 🌐 *www.victoriahotels.asia* 🛏 *109 rooms* 🍴 *Breakfast.*

5

NIGHTLIFE AND PERFORMING ARTS

NIGHTLIFE

The energy of the town fades by 11 pm, leaving only a handful of bars and restaurants catering to night owls under the light of their lanterns. The few spots that remain open in the Old Town usually close by midnight leaving few options other than a few late-night backpacker venues across the river on An Hoi peninsula.

Before & Now. A resident DJ, pool table, and 6–9 pm happy hours pull in the backpacker crowds late into the night at this lively bar in Old Town. Cheerfully grungy street art plasters the walls surrounding the dayglow bar and DJ station, where service can be slow and conversation almost impossible. Quieter, more ambient surrounds can be found upstairs in the sofa-strewn lounge bar. ✉ *51 Le Loi* ☎ *235/3910–599.*

Cham Island Dive Bar. Great cocktails and live music are the reason people come here, which is a shame as the excellent Italian menu and shady rear courtyard make for some of the calmest lunchtime dining in the center. Slightly more upscale than the brimming-with-backpackers Before & Now, The Dive Bar is favorite hangout for expats and travelers looking for a more chilled vibe. **TIP→ There is also a tour desk for information on dive trips out to the Cham Islands.** ✉ *88 Nguyen Thai Hoc* ☎ *0235/3910–782.*

Mango Rooms. This restaurant-lounge-bar makes an array of refreshing cocktails with—you guessed it—mangoes. This place is often chock-a-block with expats and tourists, especially during the 5–7 happy hour. Bypass the front busy dining room for a low table beside the river. It's best at sunset. ✉ *111 Nguyen Thai Hoc* ☎ *0235/391–0839* 🌐 *www.mangorooms.com* 🕒 *Daily 8 am–midnight.*

Fodor's Choice
★

Q Bar. Arguably the hippest bar in Hoi An, with the best cocktail menu (try the salted plum mojito), the Q Bar on Nguyen Thai Hoc is all ambient lighting and metropolitan glamour, in one of Hoi An's most beautifully restored wooden pillared trader houses. Generous sunset happy hours (4–7 pm) are a nice time to take a seat on the terrace and relax with soothing jazz, or to watch the black-and-white movies projected onto the shutters of the shop opposite. There's an excellent tapas menu with limited options but generous portions. ⊠ *94 Nguyen Thai Hoc* ☎ *0235/391–1964* ⊘ *11 am–midnight.*

White Marble Wine Bar. One of the few nightlife spots in the heart of Old Town, this corner wine bar has cocktails, beer, spirits, and quality wines by the glass. The cheese platter and various tapas pair well with a chilled sauvignon blanc on a hot day. Grab a table on the top floor for views of the Thu Bon River. ⊠ *98 Le Loi St.* ☎ *0235/391–1862* ⊕ *www. visithoian.com/whitemarble/index.html.*

PERFORMING ARTS

FAMILY **Hoi An Arts and Crafts Manufacturing Workshop.** One of the local attractions offered through the Heritage Pass, this 200-year-old house has 30-minute musical performances at 10:15 and 3:15 daily. In the workshop, talented artisans craft lanterns, carve wood, shape pottery, and embroider silks, all of which can be purchased on-site. Tickets are available on the corner of Bach Dang and Chau Thuong Van beside the Japanese Covered Bridge. ■ TIP➔ **Hour-long craft workshops run daily (bookable onsite), and are great for kids.** ⊠ *9 Nguyen Thai Hoc St.* ☎ *120,000d.*

SPORTS AND THE OUTDOORS ·

BICYCLING

Most hotels in Hoi An offer complimentary bicycles, or you can hire one for roughly 20,000d–40,000d per day. For a low-impact, highly scenic workout, rent a bicycle and ride 20 minutes from the center of town to An Bang Beach, a splendid place to catch a breeze and relax in the sun. To get to An Bang, ride 5 km (3 miles) northeast of the town center along Hai Ba Trung Street, all the way to the beach. If you are feeling really energetic, turn right at the An Bang beach intersection and follow the road out to the Victoria Hoi An Resort and continue on it until you arrive at Cua Dai lighthouse where a small dirt road to the right leads through a picturesque small village.

Active Adventures Vietnam. This countrywide tour company specializes in Hoi An and has an expansive menu of off-track activities and adrenaline-fueled adventure tours. Mountain biking, trekking, kayaking, and rappelling into the depths of Hell's Cave in the Marble Mountains are just some of the options. ⊠ *111 Ba Trieu* ☎ *0235/3929–455* ⊕ *www. activeadventures-vietnam.com* ⊘ *8–6.*

FAMILY **Hoi An Cycling.** If ricocheting between rocks and potholes on two wheels built for city shopping inspires less than comfortable thoughts, Hoi An Cycling offers international branded, full-suspension mountain bikes for rent, as well as helmets. Offtrack tours include a rather challenging 80-km (50-mile) loop to the top of the Son Tra Peninsula north of

Danang. More relaxed itineraries take in the countryside and waterways closer to home, with the option to return to an action-packed cooking class guided by Vietnam's Masterchef runner-up, Chef Hung. ✉ *27 Le Quy Don* ☎ *0919/882–783* ⊕ *www.hoiancycling.com.*

BOATING

Exploring this 15th-century trading port by boat on the Thu Bon River, once used to transport goods along the old Marine Silk Road, is a highlight of a visit to Hoi An. Depending on the type of boat you hire, fees range from 30,000d for a rowboat to 100,000d for an hour-long sunset cruise to a fishing village. There are plenty of riverfront sailors along Bach Dang Street, but be sure to negotiate the price in advance. Short bike ferries across to the neighboring Cam Kim Island, home to the Kim Bong Carpentry Village, and some stunning rural bike rides, run every 10 minutes from the market end of Bach Dang Street and cost around 10,000d each way. Half- and full-day boat tours to either Danang or Son My can be arranged through Rose Travel Service.

Rose Travel Service. Safety comes first with this Hoi An tour company. Its fleet of transport options are not only good value, but are also maintained to international standards. Transportation options include speed boats, luxury spa fishing boats, retro jeeps, and air-conditioned cars and minibuses. This company is particularly recommended for half-day boat trips from Hoi An. ✉ *37–39 Ly Thai To* ☎ *0235/3917–567* ⊕ *www.rosetravelservice.com.*

KAYAKING, SURFING, AND SUP

Hoi An's watersports are governed by the weather. From March to September the tranquil sea, river waterways, and tiny tributaries are perfect for idle sunset paddling, while observing the flow of local life on the water. A few companies based on the An Hoi peninsula provide both kayak rentals and tours. Stand-up paddle and surfboard rentals, classes, and tours can be organized throughout the year.

FAMILY **Hoi An Kayak Center.** Based out of a small riverside arts and crafts café on the An Hoi Penninsula, Hoi An Kayak Center arrange a whole host of kayak and canoe adventure tours designed to get you close to nature and far from the crowded streets of Hoi An. Tours are offered for every level of paddler and include instruction, safety equipment, and trained guides to help unravel the mysteries of life on the river. Kayaks of all sizes can also be rented outside of tour hours from as little as 200,000d for two hours. ✉ *Nam Tran Art Craft Village and Cafe, 125 Ngo Quyen* ☎ *0905/056–640* ⊕ *www.hoiankayak.com.*

SUP Monkey. Hoi An's first stand-up paddleboarding and surf company, SUP Monkey, offer lessons, board rentals, and completely unique tours. They offer a range of routes to suit all levels, from an easy sunrise coastal paddle from the beautiful Ha My to An Bang beach as well as paddles through the rapids on a full-day adventure north of Danang. ☎ *0126/917–1937* ✐ *craigryan66@gmail.com* ⊕ *www.supmonkey.net.*

5

SCUBA DIVING AND SNORKELING

Having gained UNESCO recognition as a global biosphere reserve in 2000, the seven islets that make up the Cham Islands just 25 nautical miles off the Hoi An coast are home to more than 165 hectares of coral reefs and some 947 aquatic species. The scenic underwater landscape is rich in macro life, making it a popular spot for underwater photographers, scuba diving, snorkeling, and swimming. Scuba diving, as well as PADI-certified courses, are available during the dry season that runs from April through September, with prices starting at as little as 1,000,000d for a fun dive to more than 7,000,000d for a three-day open-water course. Snorkeling trips are widely available, with most speedboats running the route over to the islands and offering the use of equipment and a short reef stop. However, due to overcrowding and the lax safety measures applied by speedboat staff, it is better to tag along with one of the dive companies where all-inclusive prices for snorkel day trips start at 800,000d.

Blue Coral Diving. This professional five-star IDC diving outfit offers snorkel and scuba-diving daytrips to the Cham Islands that include stops at two dive sites and a seafood buffet lunch on the beach. PADI certification courses are available for all levels with prices starting at 1,000,000d for a one-tank fun dive, and underwater photography equipment is available to rent. The main office is on Nguyen Thai Hoc in the center of Old Town, where the outfitter also sells a small range of diving and snorkeling equipment. ⊠ *77 Nguyen Thai Hoc* ☎ *0235/6279–297* ⊕ *www.divehoian.com* ☞ *Hoi An's diving season runs Apr.–Sept.*

FAMILY **Cham Island Diving.** "No troubles, make bubbles" is the mantra for this friendly PADI dive center with more than 12 years of experience under its belt. Slickly professional, the outfitter offers daily boat and speedboat transfers over to the coral-fringed Cham Islands, taking breaks along the way at the various dive and snorkel sites. All levels are catered to. ■**TIP→** For seriously good sunsets, book an overnight camping trip with a seafood barbeque on the incredible Cham Island Beach. ⊠ *88 Nguyen Thai Hoc* ☎ *0235/3910–782* ⊕ *www.vietnamscubadiving.com.*

YOGA

Hoi An Yoga. Salute the sun as it rises over emerald-green rice fields from a palm-thatched cabana on the outskirts of Old Town. Hoi An Yoga is run by British yoga instructor Stephanie, who specializes in remedial yoga. Classes run twice daily from two idyllic locations with evening classes and reiki held in a private candlelit studio. She also offers private classes, yoga for kids, prenatal yoga, and yoga retreats. ⊠ *Vong Nhi Hamlet* ☎ *0168/874–1406* ⊕ *www.hoianyoga.com.*

SHOPPING

As the garment capital of Vietnam, Hoi An is the place to have a clone of your favorite designer outfit tailored while you vacation. From suits and dresses to jackets and shoes, whichever items you fantasize about can be made reality. Simply show the masters a photo of your desired item, select the fabric, get fitted, and violà, it's yours—and usually within 48 hours. If time is not your friend, head to the designer boutique–lined Nguyen Thai Hoc, where you'll find off-the-peg fashion, boho arts, and unique souvenirs. Beyond fashion, wander over the bridge to Hoi An's Japanese Quarter, where cheap rental prices have proved a honeypot for Hoi An's most bohemian local artists. Of all Hoi An's bespoke crafts, the one trade that slips under the radar is the talented jewelers (reputed to be some of Asia's best) scattered throughout the outskirts of town. They can melt down and revamp an old heirloom or fashion something new from a photo or a scribbled design.

CLOTHING AND SHOES

avAna. This off-the-peg, edgy fashion boutique stocks everything a fashionista could wish for and won't find anywhere else in Vietnam. The seasonal collections of clothes and accessories are designed by the two in-house flamboyant, expat designers Ava and Anna, and crafted by Hoi An weavers, tailors, and leathermakers. ■ TIP→ **If you love the design, but don't like the color you can choose from a bespoke selection of fabric and they'll run up a one-off design tailored to your taste.** ✉ *57 Le Loi* ☎ *0235/391–1611* ⊕ *www.hoiandesign.com.*

Hot Chili. This funky little traders house on Nguyen Thai Hoc stocks a truly Hoi An–inspired collection of casual resort- and swimwear. Designs are a collaboration between Australian swimwear designer and artist Jenny and her screen-printer husband John. Each fashion-forward piece is professionally printed and stitched in Vietnam. ■ TIP→ **Don't miss the fabulous tropically inspired homewear collection.** ✉ *67 Nguyen Thai Hoc* ☎ *0235/392–9553* ⊕ *www.hotchilifashion.com.*

Lana Tailor. While the city at large has garnered a reputation for its custom-made suits, Lana Tailor stands out among Hoi An's dozens of tailors because of its stylish selections and guarantee. Choose from a showroom of in-vogue dresses, suits, jackets, and skirts, and if you don't find what you're looking for, just show them a photo of it online and they'll make it within 24 hours. Choose from fabrics including leather, cotton, cashmere, and wool. Only pay once you are completely satisfied with the final product. Tailored dresses range from $45 to $85 in U.S. dollars, while suits cost between $79 and $200. Items can be shipped internationally for an additional fee. ✉ *90 Le Loi St.* ☎ *0235/392–9559* ⊕ *lanatailorhoian.blogspot.com* ☼ *Daily 9 am–10 pm.*

Metiseko. This small boutique near the Japanese Covered Bridge sells eco-chic clothing and accessories made from organic cotton and high-end silk. Metiseko also sell quilts, children's clothing, and home decor, all with lovely prints and fabrics. There is a second location at 86 Nguyen Thai Hoc Street. ✉ *3 Chau Thuong Van, Minh An, near the Japanese Bridge* ☎ *0235/392–9278* ⊕ *www.metiseko.com* ☼ *9 am– 9:30 pm.*

Mr. Xe. Feel GQ-worthy with a custom suit from this leading men's tailor, where jackets, suits, and coats are all made within 24 hours. Materials and fabrics are a cut above the other shops in Hoi An, and somehow the flamboyant Mr. Xe manages to get you a perfect fit on the first attempt—maybe because he and his staff are meticulous with measurements. A three-piece suit will set you back around $150; it's okay to haggle for the price. ✉ *71 Nguyen Thai Hoc St.* ☎ *0235/391–0388* ⊕ *www.mrxehoian.com.*

FAMILY
Fodor'sChoice
★

Ô collective. A consortium of Vietnam's most contemporary designers all under one roof, the Ô is the Vietnamese word for umbrella. This fashion-savvy boutique on the trendy Nguyen Thai Hoc sells everything from funky propaganda art posters and Saigon Kitsch trinkets, to funky cushion art, luxury resort wear, and bohemian fashions. ■ TIP➔ **Kids can be entertained in the make-your-own monster workshop.** ✉ *85 Nguyen Thai Hoc.*

Than Thien Friendly Shop. If it's custom shoes you're after, this is Hoi An's top destination for leather boots and sandals. After you select your design and material, the staff will take your measurements and have the item tailored within 24–72 hours. Then they will deliver it to your hotel or ship it directly to your home. Their motto is "No Like. No Pay," which they back up with a 30-day money-back guarantee. ✉ *18 Tran Phu St.* ☎ *0935/211–382* ⊕ *www.friendlyshophoian.com.*

Yaly Couture. From leather boots and silk scarves to high-fashion dresses and corporate suits, Yaly Couture can re-create practically any designer item within two days. Dresses start at $35, while suits cost $65 and up. It is one of the most professional and ethical tailoring businesses in town, with the largest selection of high-quality fabrics. ✉ *47 Nguyen Thai Hoc* ☎ *0235/221–2474* ⊕ *www.yalycouture.com* ☾ *Daily 8–9:30.*

FOOD

Cho Hoi An (Central Market Food Hall). Wander through the labyrinth of vendors serving up freshly prepared Hoi An specialties including *cao lau*—a regional dish made with noodles, pork, and greens that can only be found in Hoi An—alongside a good range of other Vietnamese favourites like pho, *banh zeo* (savory pancakes), and bun bo hue. This is where the locals shop, so expect a lot of activity in some cramped quarters, especially if you arrive for early-bird specials. Once you've chosen your stall you are welcome to order dishes and fruit juices from other vendors who will bring them to your table without worry as prices are fixed and displayed, and the food vendors follow strict food hygiene rules, making this one of the best spots to sample a vast array of dishes normally only available on the street. ■ TIP➔ **Wander past the vendors to find market stalls packed with local spices, coffee, the famous Quang Nam Chili jam, and cooking utensils, but be prepared to barter hard with the friendly, but business-savvy stallholders in this area of the market.** ✉ *Tran Phu.*

GIFTS AND JEWELRY

Lotus Jewellery. Choose from a stunning range of high-quality jewelry designs, handcrafted locally by Quang Nam's finest artisans. Take your pick from a selection of intricate Vietnam inspired pendants, earrings, bracelets, and rings, or tailor your own personal design from a selection of jade, turquoise, opal, amethyst, citrine, blue topaz, or freshwater pearls. Lotus has a second Old Town store at 53A Le Loi Street. ■ TIP➔ **They can also reset and remold jewelry bought from home.** ✉ *82 Tran Phu* ☎ *0235/391–1664* ⊕ *www.lotusjewellery-hoian.com.*

Tôhe. This great little charity-run gift shop provides creative classes and education scholarships for disabled and disadvantaged kids in Hoi An. On offer are an ever-changing rainbow of fabric bags, wallets, passport holders, and other bits and pieces screen-printed with the joyful masterpieces created in class. ✉ *95 Bach Dang* ☎ *976/496–456* ⊕ *www. tohe.vn.*

DANANG AND AROUND

The 30-km (18-mile) coast north of Hoi An consists of one long casuarina- and palm-fringed white sandy beach. The most popular stretch is the beautiful Non Nuoc beach area, which lies at the midway point between Hoi An and Danang, close to world-class golf courses and Marble Mountains. Approximately 10 km (6 miles) farther north is a local favorite, My Khe beach, which runs parallel to the city and connects Danang and the coastal route north to the Son Tra Peninsula.

Once a sleepy port city, Danang has undergone a huge transformation. Five iconic bridges have been built connecting the city in the west to picture-postcard beaches, 3 km (1¾ miles) to the east. Dazzling, modernist hotels, lofty skyscrapers, and gourmet restaurants have sprung up alongside the Han River, creating a dramatic new skyline. It's a stark contrast against the crumbling facades of old colonial villas and tree-lined boulevards that are all that remain of the Danang of old.

But for those eager to delve into the heady nightlife of Vietnam's fastest growing city and to explore nearby sights Lang Co and Ba Na Hills, as well as the nearby beaches, Danang is worthy of at least a couple of days, especially if you take up residence in one of the luxury resorts that line the coast.

MARBLE MOUNTAINS

19 km (12 miles) north of Hoi An, 11 km (7 miles) southwest of Danang.

Five beautiful limestone peaks, known as the Marble Mountains, rise above the beach north of Hoi An and south of Danang. Over the centuries the *dong* (caves) in the Thuy Son Peak have been turned into temples and shrines. The first to use them were the Cham, who converted them into Hindu shrines. The Buddhists have since taken over, adorned, sanctified, and inhabited them.

The climb up the path leading to the various cave-pagodas is not particularly strenuous, unless attempted in the middle of a hot, sunny day, when it is preferable to take the 30,000d elevator that takes you two-thirds of the way to the top.

GETTING HERE AND AROUND

The Marble Mountains are easily accessed by taxi from either Hoi An or Danang. Onward journeys are catered to by a taxi rank at the base of the mountains. An alternative would be to hire a private car and driver for half a day and include a seafood lunch at Ha My beach a few kilometers further south, just past the Nam Hai Resort. Hoi An

Express offers this service for approximately 600,000d. Day tours to Hoi An generally stop here, but it's rare that you will be accompanied by a guide. For more information and to make sure you don't miss anything, ask for the 15,000d map at the ticket office.

EXPLORING

Linh Ong Pagoda. After entering through Ong Chon Gate, the main entrance of the Marble Mountains, you'll see the Linh Ong Pagoda, a Buddhist shrine inside a cave, filled with a large collection of Buddha statues. The hole at the top of the cave filters in an ethereal sort of natural light. ⊠ *Off Hwy. 1* 🖾 *Included in 15,000d entrance ticket to Marble Mountains.*

FAMILY **Marble Mountains** (*Ngu Hanh Son*). Tourists come to these five mountains to see ancient pagodas, Buddhist sanctuaries, sacred caves, spectacular views of the eastern beaches, and villages where artisans carve marble sculptures. Each of the primarily limestone formations are named after the five elements—*kim* (metal), *moc* (wood), *hoa* (fire), *thuy* (water), and *tho* (earth). At Thuy Son Mountain, you can explore several 17th-century pagodas and caves by climbing 156 steps from the base—or take a glass elevator that eliminates a third of the steps in the initial climb, transporting you straight to the foot of Linh Ong Pagoda. Bring plenty of water and take your time, as the steps can be slippery after it rains. It is common to be hassled by locals in Non Nuoc Village who live solely on the production of their stone statues, jewelry, and artwork. Entrance to the Marble Mountains (with elevator access) costs around 30,000d. ■ TIP→ Phat Tire Ventures run rappelling and rock-climbing half-day trips for all ages return transportation to Hoi An. ⊠ *14 km (7 miles) southeast of Da Nang City, Ngu Hanh Son District, Danang* 🖾 *15,000d; elevator ride 15,000d each way.*

Tam Thai Tu Pagoda. Along the main path through the Marble Mountains you'll come the Tam Thai Tu Pagoda, where monks still live. The path then leads to a spectacular view of the mountains and the surrounding countryside. ⊠ *Off Hwy. 1* 🖾 *Free, but donation may be requested at pagodas.*

DANANG

30 km (19 miles) north of Hoi An, 972 km (603 miles) north of Ho Chi Minh City, 108 km (67 miles) south of Hue.

Danang became a significant port city at the end of the 19th century, when silt filled up the Thu Bon River and eliminated neighboring Hoi An's access to the sea. The ancient Kingdom of Champa existed in the region from the 2nd to the 17th centuries, but Cham domination was significantly weakened by the Viet and Khmer in the 15th century; the last Cham king fled to Cambodia in 1820. Then in 1888, the French gained control of Danang (which they called Tourane), taking it by force from Emperor Gia Long—he had promised it to them in exchange for their help but had reneged on his agreement. In its heyday, during the first half of the 20th century, the city was second only to Saigon as Vietnam's most cosmopolitan center. During the Vietnam War, Danang was the first place U.S. Marines landed in March 1965, and it

CHAM ARTIFACTS OF THE CENTRAL COAST

Despite nearly 12 centuries of ascendancy over a large swath of what is present-day Vietnam, very few records remain confirming the existence of the Kingdom of Champa. Because this area served as the seat of the Kingdom of Champa from the 2nd to the 15th century, it has the greatest concentration of Cham art and architecture in the country. You can savor the glories of Champa at the excellent Cham Museum in Danang. Exploring the grand remnants of the Imperial City of Hue and the magnificent Imperial Tombs will introduce you to the history of Vietnam's emperors. In Hoi An, the well-preserved houses and pagodas have hardly changed in the last 200 years, giving you a sense of 17th- and 18th-century Vietnamese life. Hoi An's streets are also lined with art galleries, small shops selling all kinds of artifacts, tailors, and small cafés.

subsequently became home to a large U.S. Air Force base. Only 200 km (124 miles) south of the DMZ, the city was an ideal location for launching bombing missions. The influx of army personnel brought enormous growth, numerous refugees, and all kinds of entertainment, including movie theaters, bars, and prostitution. Soldiers would take time off at the nearby R&R resort of China Beach. By March 1975, Danang was in a state of total chaos as people tried to escape the fast-encroaching North Vietnamese army and had to fight for space on any boat or plane leaving the city. Today there are remnants of the American presence in the city, as well as vestiges of the French in the wide avenues and old villas. Despite extensive modern development, the city itself lacks many conventional sightseeing spots and vacationers could easily tick off Danang's Cham Museum, churches, pagodas, and Han Market in less than a day.

GETTING HERE AND AROUND

Situated only 5 km (3 miles) from the city, Danang airport is well serviced by taxis, but the Mai Linh group is the most reliable. Look for the green-and-white taxis, and make sure the meter is reset at the beginning of your trip. The bus and train stations offer good services, with fares starting at 14,000d.

Danang is an easy city to navigate as many attractions are clustered close to the riverside. Most visitors stay on the beachfront and rely on taxis, though one of Danang's more pleasant and traditional forms of transportation is the three-wheeled bicycle taxi. These rickshaw-like tourist attractions (cyclos) cost about 100,000d per hour allow you to soak in the city at a leisurely pace. Be sure to negotiate the rate in advance. Only experienced riders should consider renting a motorbike in Danang.

Taxi Contact Mai Linh Taxi ☎ *0236/352–5252* ⊕ *www.mailinh.vn.*

Train Contact Danang Train Station ✉ *202 Hai Phong St.* ☎ *0236/382–3810* ⊗ *Ticket office 3–7:30.*

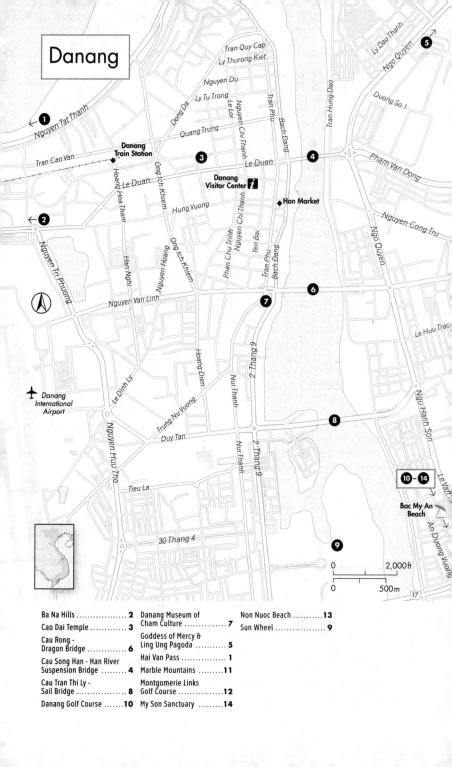

Danang

Nguyen Tat Thanh — **1**

Tran Cao Van

Danang Train Station

Le Duan

Danang Visitor Center 🛈

♦ Han Market

Ba Na Hills — **2**

Nguyen Van Linh

6

7

8

Danang International Airport ✈

9

10 – 14

Bac My An Beach

0	2,000ft
0	500m

17

Ba Na Hills **2**

Cao Dai Temple **3**

Cau Rong -
Dragon Bridge **6**

Cau Song Han - Han River
Suspension Bridge **4**

Cau Tran Thi Ly -
Sail Bridge **8**

Danang Golf Course **10**

Danang Museum of
Cham Culture **7**

Goddess of Mercy &
Ling Ung Pagoda **5**

Hai Van Pass **1**

Marble Mountains **11**

Montgomerie Links
Golf Course **12**

My Son Sanctuary **14**

Non Nuoc Beach **13**

Sun Wheel **9**

TOURS

FAMILY **Danang Unplugged.** Few companies can compete with the city-insider tours run by this outfit, whose tours focus on Danang and the surrounding area. The licensed guides are all Danang locals passionate about sharing the secrets of their city, be it an all-encompassing city sightseeing tour, a night-time street-food cruise, or a tailored tour of the surrounding area from the back of a motorbike or American Jeep. Luxury services include a private spa boat transfer to neighboring Hoi An, romantic beach/country picnics, and a fleet of private transport and guide options. ☎ *0906/555–903* ⊕ *www.danangunplugged.com.*

Hoi An Express. For information on Danang and a full list of available tours using Danang as the start point, visit Hoi An Express's tour office in the Hagl Plaza. Alongside jeep, culture, city shopping, and food tours, Hoi An Express also offer competively priced chauffeur-driven cars, with rates starting at 600,000d for half a day. ✉ *Hagl Plaza, 1 Nguyen Van Linh, Hai Chau District* ☎ *0236/222–3344* ⊕ *www. hoianexpress.com.*

VISITOR INFORMATION

Danang Visitor Center. A great place to come for maps and information on Danang and the surrounding area, the visitor center has helpful staff who speak English. A wide range of tours are also available. They also have small information centers located within the domestic and international arrivals hall at Danang airport, where you can collect free maps and guides of the city. ✉ *32A Phan Dinh Phung, Hai Chau District* ☎ *0236/3550–111* ⊕ *www.danangtourism.gov.vn* ☼ *Daily 8 am–7 pm.*

EXPLORING

TOP ATTRACTIONS

FAMILY **Ba Na Hills.** A former French Hill station left abandoned until after the war, Ba Na is a local favorite, nicknamed "Da Lat, in Da Nang." Accessible via the world's longest single-track cable car (5,801 meters), traversing above jungle and waterfalls, Ba Na presents remarkable views across to the East Sea. At the top is a kitsch, fairground-themed park with a roller coaster, bumper cars, and a very entertaining wax museum—all popular with kids. To skip it, exit the cable car and walk straight ahead for more spectacular mountain views, and take the smaller cable car down to the second, more spiritual level where you can either take a funicular or hike up the mountain to visit the temples and pagodas that line the route. If you have the energy, climb the 17-story tower inside the statue of Buddha Guanyin—the largest in the country at 67 by 35 meters (the equivalent of a 30-story building). The site to save until last is tucked away behind the Shakamuni Buddha statue: the Debay wine cellar, which was tunneled into the mountain in the 1920s by the former French residents. Inside is a large (thankfully cool) fully stocked bar and the chance to do a little wine tasting. ✉ *42 km (26 miles) west of Danang* ☎ *0905/766–777* ⊕ *www.banahills.com.vn* 🎫 *500,000d* ☼ *7:30 am–9:30 pm.*

Cao Dai Temple. Touted as the largest of its kind in Central Vietnam, the colorful Cao Dai Temple lies 1 km (½ mile) west of the Song Han swing bridge, on the Bach Dang side of the Han river, and is a peaceful spot to escape the madness of the city. Built in 1920, the impressive temple is still in use today and serves as a place of worship for approximately 50,000 followers. During the day visitors are welcomed to tour the gardens, temple, and a small building behind that holds a display of historic artifacts and statues of popular saints. The main temple is sparsely furnished and beyond the impressive divine eye that towers from behind the altar, most visitors are left unimpressed. But venture up the staircase at the entrance and you'll be treated to a beautiful view of the city that spans all the way across to the East Sea. ⊠ *63 Hai Phong* ☞ *Prayers are held 4 times daily at 5:30 am, 11:30 am, 5:30 pm, and 11:30 pm.*

Danang Museum of Cham Culture. On display at the Cham Museum, founded by the French in 1919, are artifacts from the Kingdom of Champa, which ruled this region for more than 1,000 years. Exhibits are arranged chronologically, reflecting the changing seats of power in the kingdom. The highly sensual, innovative, and expressive works from Tra Kieu's reign (7th century) and that of My Son (8th–9th centuries), and the abundant sandstone carvings of the god Shiva, testify to the prosperity of the Kingdom of Champa. The Cham adopted many elements of Indian art and Sanskrit as their sacred language. Note the Cham Buddha depicted on a throne in an imperial pose, with his feet flat on the ground, in contrast to the traditional image of Buddha seated in the lotus position. The symbol of fertility, Uroja (meaning "woman's breast"), which you will also see throughout the museum, reveals the esteem afforded women in Cham culture.

The central **Tra Kieu Altar** in the Tra Kieu Room—in the middle gallery, opposite the entrance and across the courtyard—illustrates in relief-sculpture part of the Hindu *Ramayana* epic story. This is the museum's best-preserved relief. English-speaking guides can lead you on tours of the Cham Museum, but make sure your potential guide is truly knowledgeable about the museum's contents first. ⊠ *Intersection of Tran Phu and Le Dinh Duong Sts., 02, 2 Thang 9 St.* ☎ *0236/347–0114* ⊕ *www. chammuseum.danang.com.vn* ✉ *40,000d* ☉ *Daily 7–5:30.*

Fodor's Choice
★

Goddess Of Mercy and Linh Ung Pagoda. Vietnam's largest Goddess of Mercy statue dominates the coastal skyline in a similar way to Rio de Janeiro's Christ the Redeemer; on a clear day you can see her silhouette from coastal Hoi An, 40 km (30 miles) away. The 17-story, 70-meter statue stands on Son Tra Peninsula in the grounds of Linh Ung Pagoda, one of the most significant destinations for Buddhists in the area. The views from here on a clear day are stunning. Equally charming is the journey along the winding coastal road leading to the peak of Son Tra, nicknamed "Monkey Mountain" by U.S. troops stationed there during the war, due to the mischievous monkeys that hang out in the jungle cliffs. The best way to get here is to hire a car and driver (or a motorbike for more experienced riders). The whole trip should take no more than a couple of hours, but it's well worth making a day of it and incorporating a seafood lunch and swim in one of the secluded coves below, followed by a stop at Bai Tien, a small fishing port town littered with crumbling French military remains including pillboxes, a lighthouse, and a small graveyard—the final resting point for many French soldiers defeated by the Vietnamese during their short-lived occupation of Danang during the first Indochine war. ✉ *574D Ong Ich Khiem, Son Tra District* 🎫 *Free.*

My Son Sanctuary. About 70 km (43 miles) southwest of Danang, or 45 km (28 miles) due west of Hoi An, are the My Son Cham ruins: former temples and towers dedicated to kings and deities, particularly Shiva, who was considered the founder of the Kingdom of Champa. Construction first began in the 4th century under the order of the Cham king Bhadresvara and continued until the 13th century. With more than 70 brick structures, of which some 20 remain in recognizable form today, My Son was the most important religious and architectural center of the Kingdom of Champa and was declared a UNSECO World Heritage Site in 1999. Although extensively damaged during World War II and the Vietnam War, extensive conservation work has ensured that the My Son complex still displays vestiges of its former glory. An interesting small museum and performance stage that hosts ad-hoc Aspara dance and music performances is located at the entrance. ■ TIP→ **The best tours incorporate a visit to the Danang Museum of Cham Sculpture. From Hoi An it's possible to take a boat tour to the ruins.** ⊕ *www.mysonsanctuary.com* 🎫 *100,000d* ◷ *6:30 am–4:30 pm.*

WORTH NOTING

Danang Bridges. For all the skyscrapers and modern architectural landmarks that now grace the city skyline, it's the bridges that have become the pride of Danang. As the sun sets, crowds gather along riverside Bach Dang Street to watch the spectacle as the four bridges are illuminated by thousands of LED lights that flow through the color spectrum. Farthest north is the colorful Thuan Phuoc bridge that connects the district of Son Tra to the city, the largest suspension bridge in Vietnam. Next to that is the Han Song Bridge, which holds the title of Vietnam's first swing bridge; every morning between 1 and 4 am the bridge is closed to traffic as it swings on its axis to allow large ships to pass along the Han River. At the heart is the most impressive of them all, the Dragon Bridge (*Cau Rong*) a national symbol of power, nobility, and good fortune, highlighting the city's growth. Every Saturday and Sunday at 9 pm the six-lane highway connecting the city to the beach resorts on the east side of Danang closes to traffic and huge crowds take their place to watch the dragon spout plumes of fire and water. The bridge farthest north, the Tran Thi Ly Bridge, has a 145-meter-high central mast that holds a striking sail, which, when illuminated, can be seen from the beaches of Hoi An. ✉ *Bach Dang.*

Hai Van Pass. For adrenaline-filled road adventures, jungle-clad mountains, hairpin bends, and incredible views, you can't top the ex-military feeder road, known as the Hai Van Pass. Although cyclists have tried it, it's advisable to take a motorbike (experienced riders only) or driver to take on the winding incline to the pillboxes at the pass's peak, where you can stop for photos. After, you can descend toward the lagoon on the Lang Co side where you can pull up a plastic chair for delicious seafood at one of the stilted restaurants, before returning via the Hai

Van Tunnel. ✉ *Head north out of Danang on old QL1A (Nguyen Tat Thanh St.).*

FAMILY **Sun Wheel.** For the best panoramic views of the city and the coastline beyond, forget the expensive skybars and instead head to the Sun Wheel in city central Asia Park. Scaling 110 meters (it's the 10th biggest in the world) and designed by famous U.S architect Bill Bensley, a ride on the Sun Wheel is a great way to get to grips with the geography of Vietnam's fastest growing city. ■ TIP→ **If you are in Danang on either a Friday or Saturday night, time your ride to coincide with the fire-breathing display at the Dragon Bridge at 9 pm.** ✉ *Asia Park ⊹ The Sun Wheel is 4 km (2 miles) from Cham Museum. Continue south along 2 Thang 9 for 4 km (2 miles) and take signposted left-hand street (toward river). Best way to get here is by taxi as it's a long and uninteresting walk.* 🎫 *50,000d* ⊙ *5 pm–11 pm.*

BEACHES

Non Nuoc Beach (*Truong Sa*). Just 14 km (9 miles) from either Danang or Hoi An lies Non Nuoc beach, a stunning stretch of white sandy beach, overlooking the Son Tra Peninsula to the north and the stately Marble Mountains to the west. Once a popular fishing beach, the area has now become the exotic, private playground of some of the finest beach resorts in the area, leaving the surrounding pockets of beachland fenced off for future development. You can see why it's such a sought after area (it even has two international golf courses)—the deserted white-sand beaches seem to go on forever and the sea is clean and perfect for swimming during the long dry season that runs from April to September. **Amenities:** food and drink; lifeguards; showers; toilets; water sports. **Best for:** solitude; sunrise; sunset; surfing; swimming; walking. ✉ *Truong Sa.*

WHERE TO EAT

Like everything in Danang, the city's culinary scene has been taken up a notch or 10 in the last few years. This is mostly thanks to an influx of talented chefs from Hanoi and Ho Chi Minh, who have established the international-standard bars and restaurants that line riverside Bach Dang on Han River's west bank, and neighboring Tran Phu, a scene that is slowly stretching out over to the east banks of the river. For fresh seafood, head to My Khe Beach or stay inland near Han Market where locals come for sizzling *be thui* (grilled veal). Authentic and affordable fare can be found on the avenues skirting Tran Phu, Dong Da, and Hai Phong streets.

$$ ╳ **Banjiro.** Don't be shocked when you walk through the door of Ban-
JAPANESE jiro to find the kimono clad staff yelling in Japanese; it's the way they
Fodor's Choice do it in Japan, and the same goes for the food. Try the omakase set, a
★ piling plate of sashimi that includes blue lobster, tuna, and salmon, or authentic chicken or beef yakitori and sushi. Wash it all down with a carafe or two of sake, brewed in Hue. ■ TIP→ **If the lively atmosphere is too much, reserve a private tatami room in advance.** 💲 *Average main: 80000d* ✉ *23 Nguyen Chi Thanh* ☎ *0236/3849–880* ⊕ *www.banjiro. net* ▭ *No credit cards* ⊙ *Last orders at 9 pm.*

$$ **Bread of Life.** There's nothing fancy about this charity-run diner, just
DINER   excellent Western food at cheap prices and heartwarming service. Set
up as a charity for the deaf in 2005, Bread of Life remains a constant
favorite among expats and visitors. Most come for the cause, but return
for bacon and egg burritos, full English, or American breakfasts; there's
also 17 different burgers, pizza, pasta, and a good selection of vegetar-
ian options, including a delicious baked vegetable pasta. $ *Average
main: 79000d* ⊠ *4 Dong Da* ☎ *0236/3565–185* ⊕ *breadoflifedanang.
com.*

$$$$ **La Maison 1888.** As one of Vietnam's leading fine-dining experiences,
FRENCH   this restaurant resembles an antique French mansion with dining areas
Fodor'sChoice   themed around members of a fictitious aristocratic family. Visit Le Bou-
★   doir de Madam with a pearl-strewn vanity and brass bed on display,
or the Accountant's room with vintage cash registers and chandeliers
made of invoices. The aesthetics have earned La Maison a spot among
the World's Top Ten Designed Restaurants in *Architectual Digest,* and
the cuisine of three-Michelin-star Chef Michel Roux only adds to the
illustrious status. Served on fine china under silver domes are ballon-
tine of salmon, foie gras terrine, scallops with tamarind, and beef fillet
with thyme sauce. The cheese cart with imported French selections is
to die for, but it's the soufflé with passionfruit that will leave you in
ecstasy. $ *Average main: 950000d* ⊠ *Intercontinental Danang Sun Pen-
insula Resort, Bai Bac, Son Tra Peninsula* ☎ *0236/393–8888* ⊕ *danang.
intercontinental.com/la-maison-1888* ⌂ *Reservations essential.*

$$ **Limoncello Italian Restaurant.** If the soft Mediterranean decor doesn't
ITALIAN   grab you on first sight, the scent of good old-fashioned Italian cook-
ing will. Suitably passionate Italian chef Philippo cooks up traditional
dishes like only mamma would. Try the buratta, the seafood spaghetti,
or one of the thin crust pizzas, but don't miss the chocolate mousse.
Warm service and the fantastic wine menu (the house rule is that to
enjoy wine with a meal is as natural as breathing) are more reasons to
linger. $ *Average main: 120000d* ⊠ *187 Tran Phu* ☎ *0236/3561–064*
⊕ *www.limoncellovn.com.*

$$ **Luna Pub.** Danang's hippest hangout, this industrial-style, open-
ITALIAN   fronted warehouse pub-restaurant wouldn't look out of place in New
Fodor'sChoice   York City. The ever-changing menu of authentic Italian fare includes
★   specials such as risotto alla Milanese, pizza, pasta, and steaks. It makes
for a great place to escape the midday sun in the cool industrial sur-
rounds. Come evening, the rustic brick walls and gas station–themed
bar make for a different experience altogether, as the DJ cranks up the
music from the decks in the cab of Luna's central feature—a huge red
truck. A vibrant crowd parties until late, indulging in house shooters
by the yard, imported beers, and cocktails. $ *Average main: 170000d*
⊠ *9A Tran Phu* ☎ *0236/3898–939* ⊕ *www.lunadautunno.vn.*

$$$$ **Murphy's Steakhouse.** An upmarket Irish bar with a gourmet menu of
STEAKHOUSE   imported American steaks and gastropub favorites, Murphy's has all
the right ingredients: delicious food, an excellent host, great service,
and an airy two-story dining area. Top menu items are the ribeye and
lamb shank accompanied by a potato side of your choice as well as

garlic-and-herb vegetables. It's pricey, but servings are large and the quality is outstanding. [$] *Average main: 300000d* ✉ *B4 4 Truong Sa* ☎ *0935/311–202* 🌐 *www.murphys-danang.com* ⏲ *No lunch.*

$$ VIETNAMESE Fodor's Choice ★ 🍴 **Nuong Da Thang.** If you needed any more convincing of Danang's up-and-coming restaurant scene, you'll find it in this cool, two-story shrine to industrial design, just west of the Dragon Bridge. Opened in 2014, Nuong Da Thang is the Vietnamese sister restaurant to the Waterfront on Bach Dang, but the Vietnamese cuisine here is on another level, transforming classic Vietnamese staples and giving them a more modern edge; it's some of the best food available in the city. Ask for a tower of draft beer, or a bottle of wine from the well-priced international wine list, and order food tapas style. The roasted pork in clay pot, fish in banana leaf, and grilled pork ribs will have you ordering seconds. [$] *Average main: 80000d* ✉ *Lo 01, 02 B2, 4 Nguyen Van Linh* ☎ *0236/358–4858.*

$$$ AMERICAN 🍴 **Red Sky Bar and Restaurant.** Don't be fooled by the street view. The (red) sky's the limit at this trendy restaurant with some of the best western food in Vietnam. Start with the salmon tartar followed by homemade spaghetti carbonara. Straight from the grill are perfectly cooked mango chicken and Zurich tenderloin with mushroom and potatoes. For desert, try the passionfruit soufflé or panna cotta with pineapple and coconut ice cream. During happy hour (5–7), you can roll the dice for a chance at free drinks. [$] *Average main: 200000d* ✉ *248 Tran Phu St., 1 block from Han River* ☎ *0236/389–4895* ⏲ *Closed daily 2–5 pm.*

$$$ MODERN AUSTRALIAN 🍴 **Waterfront Danang.** With a menu that fuses Australian, Mediterranean, and Asian elements, this chic riverfront restaurant is the place to see and be seen in Danang. Chalkboard menus profile wines of the week, adding to the metropolitan vibe with its cement walls, plank floors, and live DJ. Start off with the Waterfront Money Bags (fried prawns wrapped in rice paper) or the fried calamari with caper remoulade sauce. The Australian hamburger topped with Emmental cheese is almost too big to get your mouth around, but it's well worth the effort. The menu also features a selection of salads and homemade pasta dishes. ■ **TIP→ Reserve a coveted table on the upstairs patio—the best place to sip a martini at sunset.** [$] *Average main: 180000d* ✉ *150–152 Bach Dang* ☎ *0236/384–3373* 🌐 *www.waterfrontdanang.com.*

WHERE TO STAY

Danang's luxury resorts are located on the coast outside the city center. These beachfront properties are the best option for exploring nearby attractions while still getting a taste of the urban life at city restaurants and night spots. If you are set on staying in the city, there are plenty of business hotels (with good weekend discounts) lining the river along Bach Dang Street on the west bank. More affordable lodging can be found one block south on Tran Phu Street or east in the quieter section of town.

If you plan on visiting the Son Tra peninsula, Marble Mountains, golf courses, or nearby Hoi An, you're better off staying at a beachfront resort and branching off from there. The added benefit is that you won't have to deal with city traffic when accessing attractions outside the center.

$$$ HOTEL Fodor's Choice ★ 🏨 **Brilliant Hotel.** Luxurious rooms, central location, fantastic staff, and spectacular river views make this the most appropriately named hotel in Danang. **Pros:** good discounts; soundproofed rooms; Sothys spa. **Cons:** small pool. [$] *Rooms from: 1400000d* ✉ *162 Bach Dang* ☎ *0236/3222–998* 🌐 *www.brillianthotel.vn* 🛏 *102 rooms* 🍴 *Breakfast.*

$ HOTEL FAMILY 🏨 **Dai A Hotel.** The family rooms in this centrally located city hotel, just a short stroll from riverfront attractions and Han Market, rate as some of the best in the district for those on a budget. **Pros:** excellent restaurant; friendly staff; room service. **Cons:** very firm mattresses; lower-floor rooms can be noisy. [$] *Rooms from: 556000d* ✉ *51 Yen Bai* ☎ *0236/3827–532* 🌐 *www.daiahotel.com.vn* 🛏 *34* 🍴 *Breakfast.*

$$$$ RESORT Fodor's Choice ★ 🏨 **InterContinental Danang Sun Peninsula Resort.** Ocean views await at this enchanting resort that is nestled on rain-forest slopes and is accessed by a funicular train that descends to a private bay on the Son Tra Peninsula. **Pros:** excellent French restaurant; complimentary water sports; great-value Sunday brunch; daily shuttle to Danang and Hoi An. **Cons:** remote location; pricey food and drinks; property is poorly lit at night. [$] *Rooms from: 7596010d* ✉ *Bai Bac, Sontra Peninsula* ☎ *0236/393–8888* 🌐 *www.danang.intercontinental.com* 🛏 *197 rooms, 22 suites* 🍴 *Breakfast.*

$$$$ HOTEL 🏨 **Novotel Danang Premier.** Attracting a mainly business class crowd, the 36-story Novotel towers over the river on central Bach Dang street. **Pros:** skybar; convienent location; complimentary shuttle bus to the airport and beach. **Cons:** slow Wi-Fi; small pool; poor staff service; small rooms. [$] *Rooms from: 3179006d* ✉ *36 Bach Dang* ☎ *0236/3929–999* 🌐 *www.novotel-danang-premier.com* 🛏 *323 rooms* 🍴 *Breakfast.*

$$$ HOTEL 🏨 **Sanouva Danang Hotel.** Four blocks west of Bach Dang, the Sanouva is a stylish city retreat offering contemporary Asian design, good service, and business-class facilities at competitive prices. **Pros:** good weekend discounts; well-equipped gym; walking distance from most sites; free bicycles. **Cons:** rooms on low-level floors can be noisy; restaurant a bit hit-and-miss. [$] *Rooms from: 980000d* ✉ *68 Phan Chau Trinh* ☎ *0236/3823–468* 🛏 *77 rooms* 🍴 *Breakfast.*

NIGHTLIFE

Sky36 Novotel Danang. Taking cocktail culture to new levels, the 36th floor of the Novotel to be precise, Sky36 is a glitzy, glam, neon hangout with fantastic views. Floor-to-ceiling windows on three sides give way to sparkly city views. The high-energy nightclub is a great place to strike some moves. Be warned though, it's pricey, although the cocktails are good and there's a dress code of sorts—smart casual. Although a peek at the dance floor might leave you questioning whether that is

5

actually enforced. ⊠ *36 Bach Dang* ☎ *0236/3227–777* ⊕ *www.sky36. vn* ⊗ *6 pm–2 am* ⌒ *Dress code: Smart casual.*

Soho Danang. The riverside Soho is a weekend magnet for expats and local trendies. Home to the largest disco ball in the city, strong cocktails, and imported drafts on tap, it's a great place to hang out and let off some steam. Those in the know head here early for Thai food with a view on the breezy top-floor terrace overlooking moonlit cityscapes—a perfect prelude to hitting the bar. ⊠ *46 Tran Hung Dao* ☎ *0236/3945– 759* ⊗ *5:30 pm–1 am.*

SHOPPING

Strangely, for a city as dynamic as Danang, the shopping here is still mostly based around the local market tradition. A recent influx of modern stores, fashion boutiques, and designer clothes shops that cater mainly to the Asian market can be found along the roads surrounding the large grocery shopping mall, the Big C, on Hung Vuong. Fabric shops and tailors in the upper level of Han Market on Bach Dang can make clothes for you cheaply and quickly. Shirts and pants should cost less than 324,000d apiece and the quality of craftsmanship is generally better than you would find in neighboring Hoi An.

Han Market. Located right in the center of the city, this sprawling local Vietnamese market is a good place to head if you want to sample some good old-fashioned Danang specialties. Although some might be put off by the food courts proximity to the meat section, you can feel safe in the knowledge that the food served here is as market fresh as it comes. Dishes to try are *mi quang* (noodles with pork, shrimp, and a light broth) or *com hen* (baby clams and rice). Venture upstairs for fabric, clothes, and homewares. ⊠ *Entrances at Bach Dang, Hung Vuong, and Tran Phu Sts., Bach Dang.*

DANANG BEACH

Nicknamed "China Beach" by U.S. and Australian troops during the war, Danang beach stretches for over 30 km (18 miles), and encompasses several smaller beaches, including My Khe, which runs parallel to Danang City and Bac My An. To the north, scores of glitzy Vietnamese seafood restaurants and karaoke bars act as a magnet for nouveau-riche Vietnamese and visiting businessmen. Amble south and you hit rows of humble seafood shacks and Danang's public beach, a wide, white sandy stretch that is almost always deserted during the daytime. Accommodations along My Khe were once limited to dilapidated government-run hotels, but as with the rest of the city, huge redevelopment is in progress and luxury resorts are quickly popping up in their place. To the south of My Khe, Bac My An has the highest concentration of luxury beach resorts in the area (as well as the city's first casino resort). The tranquil, palm-fringed beaches here attract an international crowd and offer wraparound views of the bay. At the Marble Mountains is Non Nuoc, a quaint sculpture village that spills out onto 4 km (2 miles) of breathtaking beaches, luxury resorts, and golf courses.

GETTING HERE AND AROUND

Most city hotels provide free transfers to and from the beach, or you can cover the 3–5 km (2–3 miles) from the city center to the beach by metered taxi, which should cost approximately 70,000d. For a xe om (motorbike taxi), expect to pay no more than 40,000d and be sure to wear a helmet.

BEACHES

Bac My An Beach. Bac My An is a small, gently sloping, white sandy stretch of beach located 7 km (4 miles) east of Danang, just south of My Khe. Sadly, ongoing resort development (of which most appears to be at a standstill) means that this beautiful stretch of beach is only accessible by walking the 5 km (3 miles) south from My Khe or north of Non Nuoc along the beach. **Amenities:** food and drink. **Best for:** walking; swimming; solitude; sunrise. ⊠ *Bac My An Ward.*

Danang Beach. This 30-km (18½ miles) stretch starts at My Khe beach, which runs from the foot of the Hai Van Pass to the north, and ends at Non Nuoc beach near the Marble Mountains to the south. In the middle, south of the Furama Resort, lies Bac My An, the R&R resort spot for U.S. soldiers during the war. Five-star resorts now line the pristine and quiet sandy stretches south of My Khe, leaving only a handful of beaches accessible to the public.

Activity here is limited to lazing on the sand and enjoying some of the region's freshest seafood at the small restaurants that line the beach road. It's best to come between April and August, when the water is placid. Waves can be very large at other times—in fact, the first international surfing competition in Vietnam was held here, in December 1993. **Amenities:** food and drink; toilets; parking. **Best for:** swimming; surfing; walking.

My Khe Beach (*China Beach*). Among the 30 km (18½ miles) of Da Nang's coastline is the city's most popular beach, commonly known as "China Beach." After the arrival of American soldiers in 1965, it became popular with GIs who came here over their holidays. Sandwiched between Monkey Mountain and the nearby Marble Mountains, My Khe Beach is home to several international resorts, including the Pullman, Al La Carte ,and Furama resort. It has fine white sand and warm water, and is surprisingly clean and isolated on weekdays. Beachfront vendors sell coastal specialties like shrimp, crab, and fish. There are palapa umbrellas and restrooms, and it's one of the few beaches with lifeguards on duty year-round. Rip currents and waves mean this is not a swimmer-friendly beach. **Amenities:** food and drink; toilets; lifeguards; water sports. **Best for:** surfing; walking. ⊠ *3 km (2 miles) southeast of Da Nang City.*

WHERE TO STAY

MY KHE

$$$$
HOTEL **Al La Carte.** The hippest address on the beach boulevard, Al La Carte embodies its name perfectly—guests pay a base rate for their room and customize their experience from an all-encompassing menu, only paying for the things they use. **Pros:** beach; reasonably priced dining; near local restaurants; great kids' activities. **Cons:** pool area can get

busy and the area around it is slippery when wet. $ *Rooms from: 2100000d* ✉ *Nguyen Vo Giap, Son Tra District* ☎ *0236/3959–555* ⊕ *www.alacarteliving.com* ⥱ *202 rooms* ᵀ⊙ᴵ *No meals.*

$$ **Frangipani Boutique Hotel.** A fanciful French villa, with wraparound
HOTEL   balconies, Hamptons-style decor, and a talented chef for very reasonable prices—it's surprising what can be found when you cast your net a few blocks back from the beach. **Pros:** great dining at cheap prices; friendly service; near beach and city; quiet. **Cons:** distance from the city; small lobby pool. $ *Rooms from: 750000d* ✉ *8 Nguyen Huu Thong, Ngu Hanh Son District* ☎ *0236/3938–268* ⥱ *12 rooms* ᵀ⊙ᴵ *Breakfast.*

$$$$ **Fusion Maia.** At Asia's first all-inclusive spa resorts, included treat-
RESORT   ments range from body scrubs and facials to manicures and two-hour
Fodor's Choice   pampering sessions arranged by your personal "Fusionista" (lifestyle
★   guru). **Pros:** emphasis on health and relaxation; all spa treatments included in room rate; kids' spa and play area. **Cons:** pool can get congested; some spa treatments are hit or miss; pricey restaurant. $ *Rooms from: 9074700d* ✉ *Truong Sa St., Khue My Ward, Ngu Hanh Son District* ☎ *0236/396–7999* ⊕ *www.fusionmaiadanang.com* ⥱ *87 rooms* ᵀ⊙ᴵ *Breakfast.*

BAC MY AN BEACH

$$$$ **Pullman Danang Beach Resort.** Supremely comfortable rooms and beach
RESORT   bungalows are elegant with little touches of local art dotted about, and they come with bathrooms suitable for the most serious groomers, plus lounges and balconies with sea views. **Pros:** beach; free transfers to Danang, Hoi An, and the golf clubs nearby; plenty of kids' activities; staff are not afraid of offering a free upgrade. **Cons:** seasonal sea swimming—the water can get rough in the winter months; expensive spa. $ *Rooms from: 4206935d* ✉ *Vo Nguyen Giap St., Ngu Hanh Son District* ☎ *0236/395–8888* ⊕ *www.pullman-danang.com* ⥱ *187 rooms.*

NON NUOC BEACH

$$$$ **Hyatt Regency.** Right in the middle of the coastal strip between Hoi An
RESORT   and Danang, the fabulous Hyatt Regency is the perfect beach compromise for those that can't decide between the two cities (both are within a 25-minute drive). **Pros:** beautiful beach; on-site bakery; complimentary shuttles to Danang, Hoi An, Marble Mountains, and nearby golf courses. **Cons:** expensive; club upgrade downgrades your breakfast; impersonal. $ *Rooms from: 4391990d* ✉ *Truong Sa St., Ngu Hanh Son District* ☎ *0236/3981–234* ⊕ *www.danang.regency.hyatt.com* ⥱ *193 rooms, 95 apartments, 27 villas* ᵀ⊙ᴵ *Breakfast.*

$$$$ **Ocean Villas.** Sitting at the midway point between Hoi An and Dan-
RENTAL   ang, between a beach and a golf course designed by Greg Norman,
FAMILY   the state-of-the-art pool villas, beach, and facilities at Ocean offer the perfect compromise for any golfing widow. **Pros:** good for families; beautiful beach; modern; two international golf courses nearby. **Cons:** isolated (unless you like golf); lacking in local flavor. $ *Rooms from: 5670000d* ✉ *Truong Sa, Non Nuoc Beach* ☎ *0236/396–709* ⊕ *www.oceanvillas.com.vn* ⥱ *40 villas* ᵀ⊙ᴵ *Breakfast.*

SPORTS AND THE OUTDOORS

Short of hiring a Jet Ski, surfboard, or bodyboard from one of the large resorts, water sports are fairly limited along Danang's coastal stretch. This isn't a bad thing when you take into consideration the strong rip tides and undercurrents that are common in the area. Lifeguard stations are set up at both public and private resort beaches, as these are the safest areas for swimming. Danang, however, is home to two of Vietnam's finest golf courses.

Danang Golf Course. Located midway along the coastal road between Danang and Hoi An, this is an 18-hole links course designed by Greg Norman with a 3,000-square-meter grass tee area, a 1,600-square-meter chipping/putting green, two practice bunkers, and a driving range. Packages are on offer for every level (and age) including lessons and video analysis of your swing. Golf packages and transfers are available from nearby resorts, or you can stay at Danang Golf Course's beach resort the Ocean Villas. ⊠ *Ngu Hanh Son District* ☎ *0236/3958–111* ⊕ *www.dananggolfclub.com* ✆ *3,400,000d* ⛳ *18 holes, par 72* ☉ *7 am–7:30 pm.*

Mongomerie Links Golf Course. Colin Montgomerie designed this magnificent 18-hole golf course that links the bordering Marble Mountains to the East Sea with sweeping fairways and ocean views. Its facilities include a well-equipped sheltered driving range, pro shop, and par 5 clubhouse overlooking the 18th hole. There is also a PGA golf academy that caters to players of all ages and abilities. ■ TIP➔ **Look out for sunset driving range specials.** ⊠ *Dien Ngoc Commune* ☎ *0235/394–1942* ⊕ *www.montgomerielinks.com* ✆ *From1,500,000d* ⛳ *18 holes, par 72, daily 7 am–7:30 pm .*

LANG CO BEACH

35 km (22 miles) north of Danang, 73 km (45 miles) south of Hue.

In the dry season that runs from April through to August, Lang Co makes for an oasis from the modern construction along the Danang coastline with pristine, white sandy beaches and tranquil lagoons lined with oyster shacks and seafood stalls. The quickest route from Danang takes you through the Hai Van tunnel and knocks a good hour off the journey, while the most scenic involves a sometimes hair-raising drive on a winding mountain road—but it's worth the effort for the spectacular views from the **Hai Van Pass** (Deo Hai Van). The panoramic view of the East Sea and Truong Son Mountain range is unparalleled in Vietnam. (If you look closely, you can make out the Marble Mountains in the distance beyond Danang.)

GETTING HERE AND AROUND

Transport options are plentiful, but the cheapest (and most uncomfortable) is to get the 20,000d public bus from the central bus station on Hai Phong Street in Danang, which operates on a rather haphazard schedule with the bus departing only when full. For a more comfortable, air-conditioned service, opt for one of the 50,000d tourist buses heading for Hue with a stop at Lang Co Beach. Both of these services take you through the tunnel, so you'll miss out on the views. Lang Co train station is just 3 km (2 miles) from the beach and four public trains a day (trains TN7 and TN9) serve the coastal route from Danang. The journey takes just under two hours at a cost of 25,000d. Taxis and xe oms (motorbike taxis) are available at the station, although the walk through the friendly fishing village to the beach is worthwhile. Unless you ask otherwise, a taxi will take you the most direct route along the highway and through the Hai Van tunnel. This 20-km (12-mile) journey takes just 35 minutes and costs under 400,000d. Although this isn't the most scenic route, it makes the attractions of Danang easily accessible if you plan to base yourself in Lang Co. Only the most confident motorbike drivers should consider taking on the pass, but if you do, hire a geared bike and check the brakes and headlights work before you set off.

For the spectacular and sometimes hair-raising drive along the Hai Van Pass, you will need to hire a private car and driver, as very few taxi drivers will volunteer to take on the hairpin bends. This should cost upward of 600,000d and will include a stop at the old army lookout at the peak. Try Lang Co Taxis (☎ *0905/098–515*).

EXPLORING

FAMILY Fodor's Choice ★ **Laguna Lang Co Golf Club.** Rolling rice fields, natural streams, a beautiful beachfront, and impressive rock formations are just some of the landscapes that make up the 18-hole Nick Faldo championship golf course and driving range. Located 35 km (22 miles) north of Danang or 30 km (19 miles) south of Hue, the course is an easy commute for those not staying in the area, though for those in search of a golfing vacation, the Angsana and Banyan Tree share the same beach cove. ■ **TIP→ Nongolfers might want to use Angsana and Banyan Tree resorts' spa, restaurants, kids' club, pools, and beach.**

✉ *Cu Du Village, Lang Co, Phu Loc District, Hue* ☎ *0234/3695–880* 🌐 *www.lagunalangco.com.*

BEACHES

FAMILY **Lang Co Beach.** A convenient stopover on the trip from Hue to Danang, Lang Co is an idyllic hamlet on a peninsula jutting out into the South China Sea. Lang Co Beach is a good place to have lunch and spend the day, and for the true sun worshipper, it's absolutely worth considering if you plan a couple of nights of beach indulgence at the Banyan Tree or its budget friendly little sister, Angsana. Take the turn off Highway 1 at the sign for the Lang Co Beach Resort; this will lead you to the long, sandy beach. **Amenities:** food and drink. **Best for:** sunsets; walks; swimming. ✉ *Lang Co.*

WHERE TO EAT AND STAY

$$$$ RESORT FAMILY 🏨 **Angsana Lang Co.** On a 3-km (2-mile) sandy beach, hugged by the Truong Son mountain range, this resort offers golf, quad bikes, watersports, a kids' club, and a beach club, and despite daily excursions to Hue and Hoi An, it's easy to see why most guests don't venture off the property. **Pros:** great for families; 18-hole Nick Faldo–designed golf course; idyllic beach. **Cons:** building work is almost continuous; expensive tours. [$] *Rooms from: 4020000d* ✉ *Lang Co, Loc Vinh, Phu Loc*

District, Hue ☎ *0234/3695–881* ✉ *laguna@lagunalangco.com* 🌐 *www.angsana.com* 🛏 *229 rooms* 🍴 *Breakfast.*

$$$$ RESORT Fodor's Choice ★ 🏨 **Banyan Tree.** About as paradisal as it gets, the incredibly romantic Banyan Tree is the ultimate beach stop midway between Danang and Hue, with fabulous villas, azure ocean views, a tranquil lagoon, and a wraparound mountain backdrop. **Pros:** 18-hole Nick Faldo–designed golf course; lagoon spa; the food and views from Thai restaurant Saffron. **Cons:** remote; expensive on-site dining; better for summer stays; lagoon villa gardens lack privacy. [$] *Rooms from: 12000000d* ✉ *Cu Du Village, Lang Co* ☎ *0234/3695–888* 🌐 *www.banyantree.com* 🛏 *49 rooms* 🍴 *Breakfast.*

$ RESORT 🏨 **Lang Co Beach Resort.** This has the feel of a state-owned hotel, which it is, though the facilities and beach location are first rate. **Pros:** beach; huge discounted rates for weekday stays; large villas. **Cons:** can be noisy; thin walls. [$] *Rooms from: 450000d* ✉ *Off Hwy. 1, 1A Quoc Lo, Hue* ☎ *0234/3873–555* ✉ *langco@dng.vnn.vn* 🛏 *84 rooms* 🍴 *Breakfast.*

$$$$ RESORT Fodor's Choice ★ 🏨 **Vedana Lagoon and Spa.** Situated on a peaceful lagoon on the outskirts of Hue, this 75-acre luxury resort was the first property to offer over-the-water villas in Vietnam. **Pros:** one of Vietnam's most peaceful properties; enormous beds; private pools in the mountainside villas; free tai chi and yoga classes. **Cons:** 45-minute drive to Hue; mosquitoes at dusk: islolated. [$] *Rooms from: 2409400d* ✉ *Zone 1, Phu Loc Town, Lang Co* ☎ *0234/368–1688* 🌐 *www.vedanalagoon.com* 🛏 *29* 🍴 *Breakfast.*

HUE

73 km (45 miles) north of Lang Co, 240 km (149 miles) south of Phong Nha Ke Bang National Park.

Fodor's Choice ★ Hue (pronounced hway), 13 km (8 miles) inland from the South China Sea in the foothills of the Annamite Mountains (Truong Son Mountains), stands as a reminder of Vietnam's imperial past. The seat of 13 Nguyen-dynasty emperors between 1802 and 1945, Hue was once Vietnam's splendid Imperial City. Although it was devastated by the French in the 19th century and again in the 20th (as well as enduring much suffering because of its close proximity to the DMZ), the monument-speckled former capital has a war-ravaged beauty. One can still imagine its former splendor, despite gaping holes in its silhouette. Hue is a UNESCO World Heritage Site, and the city's gems are slowly being restored. Although much of the Imperial City was reduced to rubble, many sections still exist, and Hue's main draw continues to be the remnants of its glorious past. Today tourists keep the city thriving, drawn by the ancient Citadel, mausoleums, pagodas, and palaces. Winding through this historic capital is Perfume River (Song Huong), overshadowed by the walled Forbidden City on its north bank. Built under Emperor Gia Long in 1805, this fortress covers 5 km (3 miles) of Hue's waterfront. Equally appealing are the tombs scattered throughout the city, including the Khai Dinh mausoleum that stands out from the pack due to its detailed mosaic work. With so many attractions, Hue should not be rushed. Avoid visiting Hue during the worst of the rainy season, between November and late December.

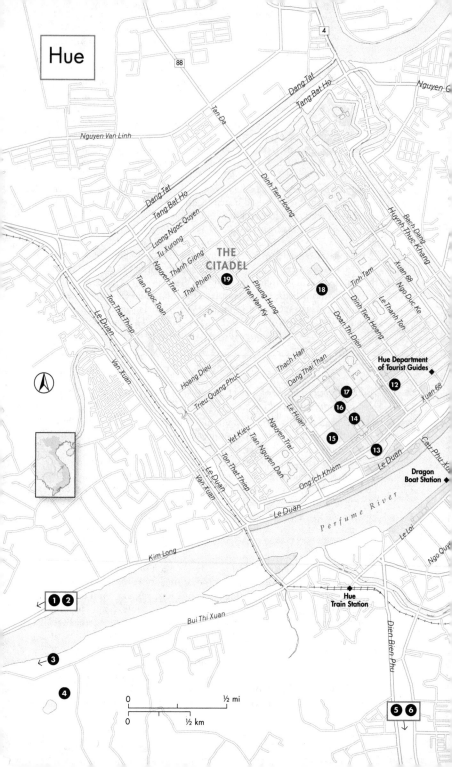

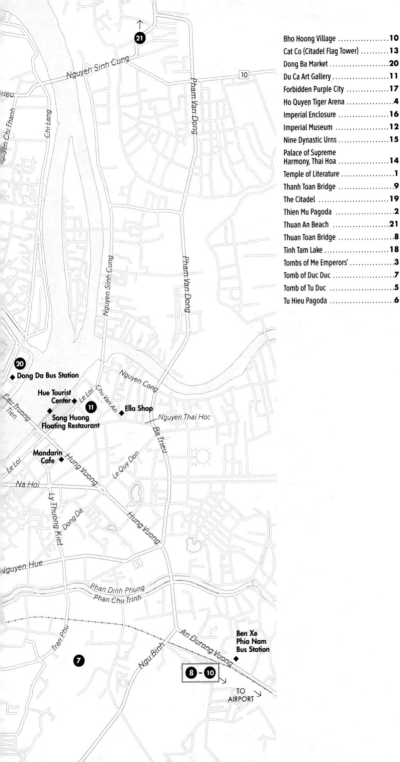

Bho Hoong Village **10**
Cat Co (Citadel Flag Tower) **13**
Dong Ba Market **20**
Du Ca Art Gallery **11**
Forbidden Purple City **17**
Ho Quyen Tiger Arena **4**
Imperial Enclosure **16**
Imperial Museum **12**
Nine Dynastic Urns **15**
Palace of Supreme
Harmony, Thai Hoa **14**
Temple of Literature **1**
Thanh Toan Bridge **9**
The Citadel **19**
Thien Mu Pagoda **2**
Thuan An Beach **21**
Thuan Toan Bridge **8**
Tinh Tam Lake **18**
Tombs of Me Emperors' **3**
Tomb of Duc Duc **7**
Tomb of Tu Duc **5**
Tu Hieu Pagoda **6**

Although initially daunting, Hue can easily be navigated once you get your basic bearings. The Citadel lines the northern banks of the Perfume River, the main landmark of Hue. Four bridges connect the north to the south, where you'll find the train station and the city's newer hotels and restaurants. The south banks also house the backpacker district near Le Loi ("Side Street 66") and Pham Ngu Lao streets. Most hotels outside this city center have free shuttle service to Chu Van An Street, which runs parallel to Pham Ngu Lao. This is the city's highest concentration of restaurants, shops, and budget properties. The best way to explore the tombs and pagodas on the outskirts of Hue is with a private tour, which includes transportation and a guide, as you are likely to get lost using the less-than-detailed maps available from the tourist offices.

GETTING HERE AND AROUND

Travelers reach Hue with air connections from Hanoi or Ho Chi Minh City, or via a three-hour drive from Danang. Tour company Sinh Café runs sleeper buses twice daily between Ho Chi Minh City and Hanoi, with a stop in Hue. Public buses from major cities arrive at An Cuu Station from the south and An Hoa Station from the north. There's no shortage of taxis in Hue, but make sure you hail the green Mai Linh cabs. Rates start at 14,000d.

The most pleasant way to explore Hue is by bicycle, which can be hired for 20,000d a day from hotels and guesthouses. Adventurous travelers might enjoy exploring by cyclo (three-wheeled bike taxi) or xe om (motorbike taxi). Rates vary, so don't be afraid to negotiate.

ESSENTIALS

Bus Contact **An Hoa Bus Station** (*Northern Bus Station*). ⊠ *Huong So, Hanoi, Vietnam* ☎ *084–54/352–2716*

TOURS

Hue Dragon Boat Station. A visit to Hue is not complete without a boat trip down Perfume River. Dozens of dragon boats line up near the bridge on Le Loi Street. A one- to two-hour sunset trip should cost no more than 200,000d, but plan to negotiate to get this rate. Snacks and souvenirs are available for purchase onboard. The nonstop route will take you toward Thien Mu Pagoda and past the markets before returning to the starting point. Several different packages are available, including guided tours. There's a second Dragon Boat station farther north along Le Loi Street, next door to Huong Giang Hotel.

⊠ *Toa Kham landing, 5 Le Loi.*

FAMILY **Mandarin Cafe Tours.** Tomb fatigue is a real thing in Hue, and unless you have a particular passion for Vietnam's imperial history, it tends to set in around tomb two, especially for kids. Mandarin Cafe is one of the few tour gigs in Hue that addresses this by offering a selection of tours that involve escaping the walled citadel and introducing you to Hue's less-visited villages, culture, and people. One of the highlights is a scenic journey into the countryside visiting the villages of the conical hat makers, imperial jewelers, and embroidery, lace, brass, and woodsculpting craftspeople. You can get involved with the crafting, interact with the artisans, and shop at wholesale prices. ■TIP→ Mandarin Cafe's owner, Mr. Cu, also has a fantastic DIY walking tour available for download from his

INLAND ADVENTURES

To escape the crowds (and tombs) for a different experience altogether, head southwest by jeep or motorbike from Hue toward the Ho Chi Minh Trail and the incredibly beautiful jungle-clad mountain borders of Laos. The scenery is mind blowing, taking you past jungle, waterfalls, and ethnic minority villages along the way. Once you've hit the A Shau Valley, your options are either to head back to Hue or to make a couple of days of it continuing south to Hoi An including a stay in the remote Ca Tu village of Bho Hoong, where beautiful bungalows on stilts perch over a stunning river valley. Or you could head northeast to Phong Nha, taking in the military sites via Khe San. Hoi An Motorbike Adventures cover both routes with pickup and drop-off in both Hue and Hoi An.

website. ✉ *24 Tran Cao Van* ☎ *0234/382–1281* ⊕ *www.mrcumandarin. com.*

Trails of Indochina. As the most reputable tour company in Vietnam, Trails of Indochina offers custom tours to Hue's main attractions and has highly experienced English-speaking guides. ✉ *21/1 Ngo Gia Tu St., Vinh Ninh Ward, Hanoi* ☎ *0234/383–6525* ⊕ *www.trailsofindochina. com.*

VISITOR INFORMATION

Hue Department of Tourist Guides. Hue Department of Tourist Guides offers the best online information for up-to-date pricing (ticket prices are reviewed annually) and events planned throughout the year in the city. It's also a handy reference when preplanning which tombs would be best to visit during your stay, as it states clearly the dates and locations of current restoration work. The center also has a small tourist office where you can buy discounted tickets for three or more sites, book tours, or arrange knowledgable guides; it's a far safer bet than hiring someone through your guesthouse or off the street. Its office in Hue is inside the office of Hue Monuments Conservation Center. ✉ *23 Tong Duy Tan* ☎ *0234/351–3818* ⊕ *www.hueworldheritage.org.vn.*

Hue Tourist Information Office. There are many tourist information offices throughout Hue, but this is the official one and the best place to find a decent map of Hue and the surrounding tombs. The staff are multilingual and very helpful at organizing tours, transportation, and onward travel plans. ✉ *45–47 Le Loi* ☎ *0989/177–686* ☉ *Daily 9 am–10 pm.*

EXPLORING

TOP ATTRACTIONS

FAMILY **Bho Hoong Village.** Tours to the ethnic minority villages east of Hue take you out into the jungle-clad Truong Son mountains bordering the Ho Chi Minh Trail. Equidistant from Hue and Hoi An, Bho Hoong Village is a small valley hamlet of the ethnic hill tribe, the Co Tu. Unlike many of the more popular ethnic villages along the trail, Bho Hoong and the surrounding area have retained their charm. It's a spiritual, timeless place, rich in flora, fauna, stunning landscapes, and culture. In the heart of the village, a circle of rong houses have been carefully restored to offer luxurious overnight stays with the Co To as your hosts, cooking up delicious organic meals and allowing visitors a glimpse into their lives. On-site activities include tribal dance performances, trekking or mountain biking to the nearby hot springs, crossbow shooting, and craft tours of nearby villages. Or you can just kick back in a hammock on the river deck, enjoying a slice of Vietnam few get to experience. ⊠ *Nr Prao* ☎ *0905/101–930* ✐ *info@activeadventures-vietnam.com* ⊕ *www. bhohoongbungalows.com.*

Fodor's Choice **The Citadel.** If there is only one site you visit in Hue, make sure this is it.
★ Constructed in 1804 under the rule of Emperor Gia Long, this fortress is sheltered by an outer wall spanning 10 km (6 miles). Marking its entry are the Nine Holy Cannons and a flag that stands 37 meters (121 feet) high, the tallest in the country. Inside the sprawling complex are temples, ruins, shops, and galleries paying tribute to the past. Somewhat of an eyesore are the scaffoldings of sections still being restored from the severe damage caused during the 1947 and 1968 battles. Just beyond the main gate is the Supreme Harmony House, where the emperor addressed officials. Approximately 90% of this main building is still original, including the two unicorns at the base of the throne, symbolizing loyalty. In the Resting House to the left of the courtyard, bullet holes on the front steps leave traces of a battle during the American (Vietnam) War. ⊠ *North Bank, near the flag tower* ☒ *150,000d* ☾ *Daily 7–5* ☞ *Discounted tickets for multiple sites available at ticket office.*

Forbidden Purple City (*Tu Cam Thanh*). Built at the beginning of the 19th century, the Forbidden Purple City, inside the **Imperial City,** was almost entirely destroyed during the Vietnam War; now it's slowly being restored to its former glory. The gateway is ornately adorned with ceramic mosaics, which lead through to a lavish red-lacquered walkway with gilded panels showcasing intricate paintings. It's not quite finished, but it's almost more interesting when you can compare the new with the old.

In its glory days the Forbidden Purple City housed members of the Imperial family and the concubines and eunuchs who served them. Anyone else who entered was executed. After the 1968 Tet Offensive, only the **Royal Theater** on the right-hand side and the intimate and partially restored Royal Library behind it remained intact. ⊠ *In Imperial City* ☒ *105,000d admission to Imperial City includes Forbidden Purple City* ☾ *Daily 7–5.*

Imperial Enclosure (*Hoang Thanh*). The Imperial City, also known as the Imperial Enclosure, was once a complex of palaces and pavilions where civil and religious ceremonies took place. Inside it was the **Forbidden Purple City,** where the royal family lived. Now the Imperial City has buried the few remnants of its past glory beneath the sporadic vegetation that has taken over the ruins, but restoration work is in progress and the site still conveys a sense of splendor. There are four gateways into the enclosure: the **Gate of Peace** (Cua Hoa Binh), **the Gate of Humanity** (Cua Hien Nhan), the **Gate of Virtue** (Cua Chuong Duc), and the **South Gate** (Ngo Mon). You can only get to the Imperial City after you have entered the citadel. ⊠ *Inside citadel* ⊞ *105,000d* ⊙ *Daily 7–5.*

Imperial Museum. The reason to visit this museum is to see the beautiful wooden structure that houses the antiques, rather than the displays themselves. Built in 1845, the small garden house is an architectural wonder, with walls inscribed with Vietnamese poetry and ceilings festooned with beautiful carvings. Inside there are miscellaneous royal knickknacks, such as wooden incense boxes, many inlaid with mother-of-pearl, plus statues, old weapons, and jewelry. Unfortunately, the whole experience is let down by lackluster guides and limited information available. ⊠ *3 Le Truc* ⊞ *Included in 105,000d citadel ticket* ⊙ *Daily 7–noon and 1:30–5.*

Nine Dynastic Urns (*Cuu Dinh O The-Mieu*). Each of these urns, weighing approximately 5,000 pounds and cast in 1835, is dedicated to a ruler of the Nguyen dynasty. The central urn, the most elaborately decorated of the nine, features Emperor Gia Long, the founder of this dynasty. Nature motifs cover the urns, including the sun and moon, rivers and mountains, and one or two bullet pocks. Many of the designs are Chinese in origin, dating back 4,000 years. ⊠ *Southwest corner of Imperial City* ⊞ *105,000d admission to Imperial City includes Nine Urns* ⊙ *Daily 7–6.*

Palace of Supreme Harmony, Thai Hoa (*Thai Hoa Dien*). This richly decorated wooden palace painted gold and red was constructed in 1803. In its imperial glory in the 19th century, it was where the emperor held special events, ceremonies, and festivals for the new moon. This is also where the emperor received dignitaries. Throngs of mandarins paid their respects to his highness while he sat on his elevated throne. Now the palace houses a gift shop where 10,000d will get you an imperial tune from the authentically outfitted minstrels. ⊠ *In Imperial City* ⊞ *55,000d admission to Imperial City includes Palace of Supreme Harmony* ⊙ *Daily 7–5.*

Temple of Literature (*Thai Binh Lau*). The Royal Library, a wooden structure east of the Forbidden Purple City on a field of grass and rubble, is one of the few largely intact buildings in the Imperial City. The delicately carved architecture has survived, although there are no books or other library-like objects left. ⊠ *In Imperial City* ⊞ *55,000d admission to Imperial City includes Royal Library* ⊙ *Daily 7–5.*

Thanh Toan Bridge. Resembling Hoi An's Japanese Bridge, this covered walkway was built in 1771 as a shrine to Japanese local Tran Thi Dao, who bequeathed her life savings for its construction. Childless and without a family, she offered her funds to the Thanh Toan Village for a new bridge to connect townspeople on both sides of the canal. Following her death, several emperors set up altars in her honor, which are still used by villagers who come to show their respect. Located 8 km (5 miles) outside Hue, this bridge is reached by way of the peaceful countryside, making it a pleasant escape from the bustling city. On the far side of the bridge is a small museum displaying ancient farming equipment.

■ TIP→ **If you visit independently, park your bike at the market 100 meters from the bridge.** ✉ *Thuy Thanh Commune, 8 km (5 miles) east of Hue, Huong Thuy District* ☞ *Free.*

Thien Mu Pagoda. Overlooking the Perfume River, this pagoda constructed in 1601 under Lord Nguyen Hoang has impressive Buddha statues, a seven-tiered monument, a bronze bell, and a marble turtle dating back to 1715. Take note of the engraved graffiti covering the turtle's shell, most of which dates back to the 1950s, when refugees from northern Vietnam inscribed notes of their whereabouts. As Hue's oldest pagoda, this structure still functions as a monastery and is perched on a hill above the river at the narrowest point in Vietnam. Housed inside the grounds is the Austin car once belonging to Buddhist Monk, Thich Quang Duc, who lit himself on fire in protest of the war. If you desire, Trails of Indochina will organize time for you to interact with a monk. The best way to reach this official symbol of Hue is by dragon boat down the Perfume River. ✉ *3½ km (2 miles) west of Phu Xuan Bridge, Ha Khe Hill* ☞ *80,000d* ☉ *Daily 7–5.*

Tombs of the Emperors. South of Hue along the Perfume River, these scattered tombs—the ego-boosting mausoleums erected by emperors in the late 1800s and early 1900s—can easily be explored in a day, although it's likely you'll burnout from tomb-overload by your second site because visually and historically they are a lot to absorb. The most impressive one is the **Tomb of Khai Dinh**, due to its ornate architecture reflecting Buddhist imagery. Between 1920 and 1931, the tomb was built with money from a 30% tax increase forced on the people. To construct the final mosaics surrounding the tomb, fine china and ceramics were broken into pieces. Take note of the dragon eyes made from champagne bottles, and the flower petals made from silver spoons. To this day, many Hue locals refuse to visit the shine of this former leader who took advantage of his people. The most respected emperor was **Thieu Tri**, remembered for his compassion for the people, evidenced by his unornamented 1848 tomb. If you plan to see the **Tomb of Tu Duc**, Thieu Tri's son, allow plenty of time to explore the grounds, which once housed 50 buildings in a sprawling lakefront compound. The **Tomb of Gia Long** is 20 km (12½ miles) outside the city, which means you're likely to have the place entirely to yourself. ✉ *South of Hue* ☞ *From 20,000d to 100,000d per tomb. Discounted packages available for multiple tomb touring at Citadel Ticket Office* ☉ *Daily 7–5.*

WORTH NOTING

Cot Co (Citadel Flag Tower) (*Cot Co*). This 120-foot structure, Vietnam's tallest flagpole, is one of the symbols of Hue. It was originally built in 1809 to serve as the Imperial Palace's central observation post. Like much of Hue, it has a history of being destroyed. The Flag Tower was toppled during a typhoon in 1904, rebuilt in 1915, destroyed again in 1947, and rebuilt anew in 1949. When the North Vietnamese occupied the city during the Tet Offensive of 1968, the National Liberation Front flag flew from the Flag Tower. The interior is closed to the public. ✉ *In front of 23 Thang 8 St., facing Ngo Mon Gate.*

Hue History

By the 15th century, the Vietnamese had successfully captured the city from the Cham and renamed it Phu Xuan. In 1558 the city became the capital of a region ruled by Lord Nguyen Hoang, which established control of South Vietnam by the Nguyen lords. During this time, two warring factions—the Nguyen lords, who controlled South Vietnam, and the Trinh lords, who controlled North Vietnam—were fighting for control of the whole country.

Hue becomes the capital

With the Tay Son Rebellion in the 18th century, the Nguyen lords were temporarily defeated. Led by the sons of a wealthy merchant, the Tay Son rebels were acting on a general sentiment of discontent with both Nguyen and Trinh rule. The Tay Son emperor, Quang Trung, was installed in Hue from 1786 to 1802, until the ousted Lord Nguyen Anh returned with French backing. At the same time, Nguyen Anh captured Hanoi from the Tay Son rebels, who had defeated the Trinh and the Chinese-backed Ly dynasty based in the northern capital. In 1802, Nguyen Anh anointed himself Emperor Gia Long and made Hue the capital of a newly united Vietnam.

Establishing an architectural identity

Twelve Nguyen-dynasty emperors followed him to the throne until 1945, and their impressive tombs, Imperial City, and pagodas are reminders of the important role the city once played.

It was under Emperor Gia Long's rule that the city's architectural identity was established, and the prospect of French colonial rule in Vietnam initiated. With guidance, ironically, from the French architect Olivier de Puymanel, Gia Long designed and built the city's surrounding fortress in the style of the Forbidden City in Beijing. The result is a fairly modern structure that looks centuries old. Enclosed within the thick walls of the Chinese-style citadel is the Imperial City (Hoang Thanh), where all matters of state took place and which was off limits to all but mandarins and the royal family. Within the Imperial City was the Forbidden Purple City (Tu Cam Thanh), where the emperor and his family lived; very little of it remains today.

In 1885, after repeated disagreements between the French and the emperors of Hue, the French pillaged the Royal Court, burned the Royal Library, and replaced Emperor Ham Nghi with the more docile Emperor Dong Khanh.

Modern destruction

It was the Tet Offensive of 1968, however, that really destroyed large parts of the Imperial City. During one of the fiercest battles of the Vietnam War, the North Vietnamese army occupied the city for 25 days, flying its flag in defiance and massacring thousands of supposed South Vietnamese sympathizers. The South Vietnamese and the Americans moved in to recapture the city with a massive land and air attack and in doing so further destroyed many of Hue's architectural landmarks. Overall, more than 10,000 people died in the fighting, many of them civilians.

5

FAMILY   **Thuan An Beach.** For now, Thaun An Beach, which lies out on a peninsula 14 km (8 miles) from central Hue, has only one beach resort, leaving an unspoiled, long sandy stretch of coconut- and casaurina-tree-lined beach all but empty. In the summer months the tranquil turquiose sea and gentle breeze make for the most idyllic break from the city, while in winter it makes for wildly romantic walks, with scatterings of family temples, fishing villages, and Vietnam's largest lagoon to explore. **Amenities:** food and drink. **Best for:** walking; swimming; sunsets. ⊠ *Thuan An Ward.*

Tinh Tam Lake (*Ho Tinh Tam*). For much of the year Tinh Tam Lake is hardly worth the bother, but during the spring and summer months this little lake in the citadel comes alive with lotus flowers that cover it entirely. Do as the emperors once did and walk across one of the bridges to the island for a brief respite. The best way to see it (and find it) is by asking your driver to include it in a cyclo tour of the citadel. ⊠ *Dinh Tien Hoang and Tinh Tam Sts.*

Tomb of Dong Khanh. Perhaps the most frequently restored of all the tombs in Hue, the Tomb of Dong Khanh, a despised puppet emperor of the Nguyen Dynasty who died during the French rule at the age of 24, took over 35 years and four kings to build. The architectural result is a unique fusion of traditional imperial Vietnamese and colonial design, which makes it well worth a visit.

The tomb was built around Dong Khahn's final resting place, Ngung Hy Temple, an elaborate triple temple complex typical of the citadel. Look for the well preserved laquer art and Chinese calligraphy that adorn the walls, and the 24 Chinese illustrations featuring the 24 filial sons and daughters taken from the Chinese story Nhi Thap Tu Hieu. The surrounding area, in stark contrast, is the colonial styled graveyard that was constructed between 1916 and 1923. Notice the unsual brick and terracotta-tiled central Stele Pavillion and stained-glass windows. ⊠ *Northeast of Tu Duc on right side of river; follow road that leads to Tomb of Tu Duc about ½ km (⅓ mile) around corner* 🎫 *40,000d* ☉ *Daily 7:30–5:30.*

Tomb of Duc Duc. This partially renovated tomb has a story that beats any soap opera. It begins with the death of Emperor Tu Duc in 1883, when Duc Duc (one of three of Tu Duc's adopted sons) was controversially declared his successor. Duc Duc's reign of the Nguyen Dynasty was to last only three days before he was stripped of his title and incarcerated. The reasons for this are unclear, but it is believed that the three regents responsible for the appointment of Duc Duc, feared that he would strip them of the power they had enjoyed under the weak rule of Tu Duc. In modern history, Duc Duc is considered the first of a long line of "puppet emperors" whose short reign was thought to have been controlled by French colonialists.

Duc Duc's tomb is one of the smallest of the Nguyen Dynasty and was heavily bombed during the war, but having escaped the ambitious renovations of many others, the site retains an enigmatic charm. ⊠ *2 km (1 mile) from Le Loi St. on right bank of river* 🎫 *Free* ☉ *Daily 7–5.*

Fodor's Choice ★ **Tomb of Khai Dinh.** An unbelievable concoction of glitzy Vietnamese and French colonial elements, the Tomb of Khai Dinh, completed in 1931, is a contender for Hue's most impressive mausoleum. Khai Dinh became emperor in 1916 at the age of 31 and died in 1925. The entrance is guarded by a row of impressive stone elephants and imperial soldiers. A climb up a steep flights of steps, flanked by dragons, takes you to a surprisingly colorful tomb heavily decorated with tile mosaics. Scenes from the four seasons welcome you into the main building. It's best to visit this tomb by car, since it's not directly on the river. ■ TIP➡ **Climb to the top for some incredible views of the countryside and nearby Bach Ma Park.** ⊠ *About 16 km (10 miles) south of Hue and about 1½ km (1 mile) inland on right bank of Perfume River* 🎫 *100,000d* ⊙ *Daily 8–5.*

Tomb of Minh Mang. A Hue classic, the Tomb of Minh Mang, emperor from 1791 to 1841, was completed in 1843 by his successor. His tomb is one of the most palatial, with numerous pavilions and courtyards in a beautiful pine forest. The burial site is modeled after the Ming tombs in Beijing. Sculptures of mandarins, elephants, and lions line the route to the burial site. Though the most far flung of all the Hue tombs, Minh Mang is one of the few to have escaped any attempts of restoration. The mountainous backdrop and crumbling structure, make it one of the most eerie, yet beautiful tombs to visit. ■ TIP➡ **Most motorbike guides will tell you it's closed, rather than drive all the way out there—ignore them and go.** ⊠ *About 11 km (7 miles) south of Hue and 1½ km (1 mile) inland on left bank of Perfume River* 🎫 *100,000d* ⊙ *Daily 8–5.*

FAMILY

Fodor's Choice ★ **Tomb of Tu Duc.** The Tomb of Tu Duc, one of Hue's most visited tombs, has its own lake and pine forest, and is easily accessed by bike. Built in 1867 by thousands of laborers, the tomb was once the second residence of Tu Duc, emperor from 1848 to 1883. Despite having more than 100 wives and numerous concubines, but (strangely) no children, Tu Duc somehow found the time to escape here to relax and write poetry. Further along is Hoa Khiem Temple where Tu Duc and the Empress Hoang Le were worshipped. It's not all that impressive, but look closely at the thrones, the larger of the two belonged to the emperor's wife; it gives you an idea of how tiny he was. Behind is an old theater, now home to a vast wardrobe of imperial dress and some interesting props for photo opportunities. One of Tu Duc's favorite spots was the Xung Khiem Pavilion on the pond filled with lotus blossoms. ⊠ *About 6 km (3 miles) south of Hue on right bank of Perfume River* 🎫 *100,000d* ⊙ *Daily 8–5.*

Tu Hieu Pagoda. One of Hue's most beautiful and peaceful pagodas is accessed via a jungle-like path off the road, past a crescent-shape pool. Built in 1843, the temple houses a large gold Buddha and a second temple dedicated to Cong Duc. It's a good place for quiet meditation. The monks live in simple rooms off to the side and hold services several times a day. ⊠ *About 5 km (2 miles) south of Hue on way to Tu Duc Tomb* 🎫 *Free* ⊙ *Daily 8–5.*

5

WHERE TO EAT

Leaning on Hue's history, the city's traditional cuisine incorporates the art of food carving, at royal dinners fit for a king. It's customary for restaurants to serve dishes with intricately designed flowers, dragons, and fish carved from carrots and other vegetables. To maximize this cultural experience, dine at one of Hue's many restaurants that offer royal dinners, including traditional music and dance.

$ ✕ **Am Phu.** A favorite with locals, Am Phu ("hell restaurant"), has been
VIETNAMESE in operation for more than 80 years, serving excellent Vietnamese cuisine. It's famous locally for *com am phu,* a colorful rice, pork, shrimp, and herb specialty dish—the seven colors of this dish represent the first seven steps of Buddha. This isn't a tourist spot; everyone eats together at large tables covered with red plastic tablecloths. Although there are no prices listed on the menu, most dishes cost less than 60,000d depending on how large a serving is requested. $ *Average main: 60000d* ⊠ *35 Nguyen Thai Hoc St.* ☎ *0234/3825–259* ▭ *No credit cards.*

$$$$ ✕ **Ancient Hue Restaurant.** This 200-seat restaurant is located within the
VIETNAMESE walls of the Phu Mong Garden House, which dates back to the 1800s. Blending cultural heritage and fine cuisine, it pays tribute to the last carving artists in Hue. The restaurant is famous for vividly re-creating the authentic cuisines of Hue's royalty. Each dish is beautifully presented with vegetables sculpted into shapes of plants and animals. The menu highlights local specialties like banana blossom salad, *banh beo* (steamed rice flour with shrimp flakes), and *banh khoai* (fried rice pancakes stuffed with shrimp, pork, and bean sprouts). The opulent art gallery in the ancient wooden house to the left doubles as a lounge bar, perfect for predinner drinks. Expect an experience more than a meal with the Royal Court Dinner, a six-course dinner with traditional music and dance. ■TIP➔ **A vegetable carving course is available upon request. They also offer cooking classes, which include a boat trip to the riverside markets.** $ *Average main: 320000d* ⊠ *4/4/8 La. 35 Pham Thi Lien St., Kim Long* ☎ *0234/359–0356* ⊕ *www.ancienthue.com.vn.*

$ ✕ **Banh Beo Ba Cu.** Don't be put off by the grungy interior of this restau-
VIETNAMESE rant. The quality of the decor is in inverse proportion to the quality of the food. This favorite among locals serves only eight dishes, all specialties of the region. The price of 10,000d per dish should allow you to try them all—if you're hungry enough. Particularly memorable is the *banh uot thit nuong* (grilled meat rolled in rice paper). $ *Average main: 10000d* ⊠ *107 Nguyen Hue St.* ☎ *0234/3832–895* ▭ *No credit cards.*

$$ ✕ **Beach Bar Hue.** This inspired little beach club 15 km (10 miles) from
VIETNAMESE Hue has shady beach cabanas, hammocks, and a large cobalt-blue
FAMILY fishing boat that serves as the bar. It's a laid-back place, with a simple Vietnamese seafood menu, where you feel a world away from the annoyances of the city. They make it easy to stay with a few huts housing dorm-style accommodations. ■TIP➔ **The Beach Bar is on private land, and you pay 100,000d to enter (which is refundable against food and drink orders).** $ *Average main: 100000d* ⊠ *Thuan An, Xuan An* ☎ *0234/3984–757* ⊕ *www.beachbarhue.com.*

$ ✕ **Bun Bo Hue.** This very downscale sidewalk food stall close to the center
VIETNAMESE of Hue serves some of the best *bun bo Hue,* the Hue noodle specialty

made with beef and pork. This is the only dish served, and the stall is open from 2 pm until all the food is all gone. A good-size bowl costs 25,000d. [$] *Average main: 25000d* ✉ *Next door to Risotto, Nguyen Cong Tru.*

$$ VIETNAMESE 🍴 **Confetti Restaurant and Art Gallery.** Located in the tourist area just south of Perfume River, this quaint yet kitschy restaurant is decorated from top to bottom in pink, along with paintings by local artist Hoang Phong. But it's the exceptional service, traditional Hue dishes, and good value that draw in repeat customers each night. Local specialties include fried pancakes, noodle soup with seafood, rice flour in banana leaves, and grilled pork in a clay pot. Most dishes are served with lotus-seed fried rice. The eight-course set menu is less than $10 and concludes with a sweet mango soup. ■ **TIP→ Request a table on the more private second floor.** [$] *Average main: 75000d* ✉ *01 Chu Van An St., Hue 054* ☎ *0234/382–4148.*

$$$ VIETNAMESE 🍴 **Huong Giang Hotel Restaurant.** From the windows of this spacious third-floor restaurant you can take in great views of the Perfume River. Large portions of very solid Vietnamese food and Western dishes, such as chicken and French fries, are served. The service is excellent; the only downside is the occasional large tour group that takes over the place. Make a reservation if you want a seat by the window. For a little extra, you can have a "royal meal," for which you dress in court clothes provided by the restaurant and are individually attended to by waitstaff in period costume. [$] *Average main: 180000d* ✉ *51 Le Loi St.* ☎ *0234/3822–122* 🌐 *www.huonggianghotel.com.vn.*

$ VIETNAMESE 🍴 **Lac Thien.** This busy little café is one of the oldest in Hue. On a busy corner by the side of the river, it specializes in just one dish: *banh khoai*, crispy pancakes stuffed with bean sprouts, shrimp, and little mounds of pork, served up with side plates of mixed herby salad and a spicy peanut sauce. To eat, cut them in half, wrap them in herbs and then rice paper, and dip. The shady seats on the sidewalk are perfectly positioned for watching life go by. [$] *Average main: 40000d* ✉ *6 Dinh Tien Hoang* ☎ *0234/352–7348* 💳 *No credit cards.*

$$$$ FRENCH FUSION 🍴 **Le Perfume.** Inside the historical La Residence Hotel, this fine-dining and pricey restaurant rivals anything you might find in Paris. The French fusion degustation menu (which must be requested eight hours in advance) features six exquisite courses, ranging from smoked duck carpaccio to beef tenderloin with rosemary. The Vietnamese chef La Thua An spent 30 years in French Polynesia perfecting his culinary skills, which are now reflected in such dishes as panfried frog legs with truffle potatoes and pumpkin coulis with vanilla and champagne sabayon. International wines are paired with each course, including an impressive dessert of molten chocolate with red hibiscus coulis served under a crystallized sugar dome. [$] *Average main: 500000d* ✉ *5 Le Loi St.* ☎ *0234/383–7475* 🌐 *www.la-residence-hue.com* ✍ *Reservations essential.*

$$$ FRENCH FUSION Fodor's Choice ★ 🍴 **Les Jardins De La Carambole.** Neighboring the historic Citadel, this French-Vietnamese restaurant is fashioned after a colonial villa with green shutters, arched doorways, tile floors, antiques dating back to 1915, and artwork depicting pastoral scenes. Slightly pricey by local

standards, the enormous menu features green mango salad, fresh spring rolls, beef in banana leaves, and grilled sea bass with a Mediterranean sauce, as well as sandwiches, pasta, and pizza. The goat cheese and prosciutto platter is superb, as is the roasted chicken in a white wine sauce. The Chinese emblem embroidered on staff uniforms and napkins is a wish for prosperity and longevity. The restaurant has a second location renowned for its Italian menu in the backpackers' district at 19 Pham Ngu Lao Street. Ⓢ *Average main: 180000d* ✉ *32 Dang Tran Con, Hue 8454* ☎ *0234/354–8815* ⊕ *www.lesjardinsdelacarambole.com.*

$ ✕ **Quan Cam Bun Bo Hue.** No visit to Hue is complete without sam-
VIETNAMESE pling the city's most famous breakfast dish, *bun bo hue*, a glorious lemongrass-and-chili infused beef broth, served with slippery round noodles, beef, pork shank, and a fistfull of fragrant herbs. It's not unlike fiery northern *pho*, and is best slurped from specialty kitchens; the best in Hue is Quan Cam, a tiny family-run noodle shop on Tran Cao Van Street. Ⓢ *Average main: 30000d* ✉ *3 streets back from Saigon Morin Hotel on Le Loi St., 38 Tran Cao Van* ▭ *No credit cards.*

$$ ✕ **Risotto.** The Italian menu at this decent little cafeteria, situated near
ITALIAN the dragon boat dock on the far end of Le Loi, is one of the best in the city—and the cheapest, too. Think plates piled high with herby olive oil–drizzled beef carpaccio, al dente creamy risotto, and real Italian pizza, each coming in at under 100,000d a pop. Nothing is served quickly (everything on the menu is made fresh to order), but the location amid bustling street food hawkers makes it a great spot to kick back and people watch. Ⓢ *Average main: 80000d* ✉ *14 Nguyen Cong Tru* ☎ *0932/413–313* ▭ *No credit cards.*

$$ ✕ **Shiva Shakti Indian.** There are times when only a good old-fashioned
INDIAN curry will do, and the talented Indian chefs here make some of the best. Highlights of the menu include anything from their tandoor oven, soft buttery naan, mixed vegetable or meat grilled dishes, and tikka. For vegetarians the channa masala and paneer dishes come in belt-slackening-sized servings, and for upset stomachs, the honey lassi is a great cure. Ⓢ *Average main: 90000d* ✉ *27 Vo Thi Sau* ☎ *0234/3935–627* ⊕ *www.ganeshhue.com.*

$$ ✕ **Tropical Garden.** Outstanding Western, Asian, and regional dishes are
VIETNAMESE on the menu at the Tropical Garden. House specialties include grilled shrimp and tropical fried rice, which you can enjoy in the pretty courtyard while local musicians perform Hue folk songs. There's a large garden area, and the interior is air-conditioned in the hot summer months. Ⓢ *Average main: 120000d* ✉ *27 Chu Van An St.* ☎ *0234/3847–143.*

WHERE TO STAY

Most of Hue's upscale, full-service hotels are on Le Loi Street near Perfume River. Close to the sites, these properties are your best bet for service with a view. A few mid-range hotels are clustered around the area between Trang Tien and Phu Xuan bridges, the main access bridges to the citadel. Hotels of all sizes have travel services and can arrange boat tours to the tombs and pagodas as well as guided tours in and around Hue.

$$$$
RESORT
FAMILY
Fodor's Choice
★
☆ **Ana Mandara Hue Beach Resort.** Hue's most beautiful luxury resort, perched on one of the best beaches in the region (you can see it just beyond the infinity pool as you check in), has sumptuous rooms with indochine styling, imperial silks elegantly draped over oversize beds, and colossal bathrooms housing roll-top tubs. **Pros:** on the beach; free daily transfers to Hue; great discounted spa packages; family-friendly. **Cons:** seasonal, it's not quite as idyllic during the monsoon months; remote location. $ *Rooms from: 2800000d* ⊠ *15 km (9 miles) east of Hue, Thuan An Town* ☎ *0234/3983–333* ⊕ *www.anamandarahue-resort.com* ⥃ *78 rooms* ⭘ *Breakfast.*

$$$$
HOTEL
FAMILY
☆ **Best Western Premier Indochine Palace.** The tallest building in Hue and one of its most luxurious hotels, this 17-story property blends modern Vietnamese with colonial elegance to avoid the chain-hotel effect. **Pros:** live music nightly; attentive English-speaking staff; excellent beds and showers. **Cons:** open bathroom design lacks privacy; 20-minute walk to closest sites. $ *Rooms from: 2100000d* ⊠ *105A Hung Vuong St., Hue 47000* ☎ *0234/393–6666* ⊕ *www.bwp-indochinepalace.com* ⥃ *222 rooms* ⭘ *Breakfast.*

$
HOTEL
☆ **Duy Tan Hotel.** Despite its large and semigrand appearance, this hotel functions as a glorified minihotel. **Pros:** value; service; location. **Cons:** popular with tour groups; firm mattresses; uninspiring design. $ *Rooms from: 500000d* ⊠ *12 Hung Vuong St.* ☎ *0234/3825–001* ⊕ *www.duytanhotel.com.vn* ⥃ *138 rooms* ⭘ *Breakfast.*

$$$
HOTEL
☆ **Eldora Hotel.** Aspiring starlets will love the Moulin Rouge stylings of this grandiose hotel in central Hue—it's all ooh-la-la French elegance with a bohemian twist. **Pros:** close to all the city attractions; pool; very good value. **Cons:** some ongoing construction in the area; the best breakfast choices go quickly. $ *Rooms from: 1300000d* ⊠ *60 Ben Nghe* ☎ *0234/3866–666* ⊕ *www.eldorahotel.com* ⥃ *81 rooms* ⭘ *Breakfast.*

$$
RESORT
☆ **Huong Giang Hotel.** Although not the swankiest, this huge riverside property offers all the benefits of resort facilities, a central location, and pool, all at low prices, while the helpful staff make this one of the most pleasant placed to stay in Hue. **Pros:** exceptional travel office; rooftop bar with panoramic views; good restaurant. **Cons:** newer, front-facing rooms overlook the hotel's karaoke bar; popular with tour groups. $ *Rooms from: 800000d* ⊠ *51 Le Loi St.* ☎ *0234/3822–122* ⊕ *www.huonggianghotel.com.vn* ⥃ *165 rooms* ⭘ *Breakfast.*

$
HOTEL
FAMILY
☆ **Jade Hotel.** You don't have to wander far from the action to discover some great budget options, and Jade Hotel is Hue's best: a bijou, boutique colonial villa with eight art deco inspired rooms. **Pros:** a five-minute walk from restaurants; cheap transfers; coffee- and tea-making facilities in-room. **Cons:** rooms at the front overlook Hue's biggest sports stadium; standard rooms are dark with tiny showers. $ *Rooms from: 300000d* ⊠ *17 Nguyen Thai Hoc* ☎ *0234/3938–849* ⊕ *www.jadehotelhue.com* ⥃ *8 rooms* ⭘ *Breakfast.*

$$$$
HOTEL
Fodor's Choice
★
☆ **La Residence Hotel and Spa.** Built in the 1930s, this swanky hotel near the river (a French-colonial mansion and two newer wings) is recognized for its service as well as its art deco, jazzy panache. **Pros:** central location; excellent service; river views: tour service. **Cons:** not child friendly; newer rooms are small. $ *Rooms from: 3559368d* ⊠ *5 Le Loi*

5

St. ☎ *0234/383–7475* 🛏 *115 rooms, 7 suites* 🕒 *www.la-residence-hue.com* 🍴 *Breakfast.*

$$ HOTEL 🏨 **New Star Hotel.** What the rooms here lack in style, they make up for with comfort, but the reason to stay here is the giant outside pool, a rarity at such a well-priced city-center location. **Pros:** pool; walking distance to restaurants, bars; great balcony views from deluxe rooms. **Cons:** staff don't speak much English; lackluster breakfast. [$] *Rooms from: 750000d* ✉ *36 Chu Van An St.* ☎ *0234/3946–555* 🌐 *www.newstarhuehotel.com* 🛏 *49 rooms* 🍴 *Breakfast.*

$$$$ RESORT Fodor's Choice ★ 🏨 **Pilgrimage Village.** Reminiscent of a rural Vietnamese village, this peaceful property has artisan shops lining a brick pathway that lead to spacious villas with hardwood floors, private balconies, and marble bathtubs framed with river stones. **Pros:** wonderful breakfast buffet; enormous swimming pool; complimentary yoga, tai chi, and shuttle service. **Cons:** pricey cocktails; odd shuttle schedule; poor lighting; popular with tour groups. [$] *Rooms from: 3766500d* ✉ *130 Minh Mang Rd., Hue 8454* ☎ *0234/388–5461* 🌐 *www.pilgrimagevillage.com* 🛏 *99 rooms* 🍴 *Breakfast.*

$$ B&B/INN 🏨 **Tam Tinh Vien Homestay.** Artful wooden garden house accommodations in a little oasis on the edge of the city, Tam Thin makes for a wonderfully relaxing base. **Pros:** quiet, relaxing getaway; great tours; bicycles; good local restaurants nearby. **Cons:** 5 km (3 miles) from the citadel; small; no TVs. [$] *Rooms from: 760000d* ✉ *Long Ho Ha village, Huong Tra* ☎ *0234/519–990* 🌐 *www.huehomestay.wevina* 🛏 *2 rooms* 💳 *No credit cards* 🍴 *Breakfast.*

$ B&B/INN 🏨 **Thanh Thien (Friendly) Hotel.** A couple of streets removed from the late-night goings-on of Pham Ngu Lao, the peaceful, luxurious Thanh Thien has rooms that offer outstanding value for money. **Pros:** Wi-Fi; flatscreen TVs; customer service; close to dragon boat station. **Cons:** breakfast choices are limited; bikes in poor condition. [$] *Rooms from: 400000d* ✉ *10 Nguyen Cong Tru* ☎ *0234/3834–666* ✉ *thanthienhuehotel@gmail.com* 🌐 *www.thanthienhotel.com.vn* 🛏 *30 rooms* 🍴 *Breakfast.*

$$ RESORT 🏨 **Vedana Lagoon Resort and Spa.** Situated on a peaceful lagoon halfway between Danang and Hue, this 75-acre luxury resort is the only property to offer over-the-water villas in Vietnam. **Pros:** one of Vietnam's most peaceful properties; enormous beds; free tai chi and yoga classes. **Cons:** staff speaks minimal English; 45-minute drive to Hue; mosquitoes at dusk. [$] *Rooms from: 2709200d* ✉ *Zone 1, Phu Loc Town, Phu Loc District* ☎ *084–54/368–1688* 🌐 *www.vedanalagoon.com* 🛏 *30 villas* 🍴 *Breakfast.*

NIGHTLIFE

Nightlife centers on the lively backpacker district near Le Loi and Pham Ngu Lao streets. During Happy Hour, this south-bank bar scene has 25-cent beers, which can be borderline dangerous, considering the amount of tourist traffic on the block. For something a bit more local, a string of local beer joints line Dong Da near Le Hong Phong Street. If you are looking for a quiet cocktail with a view in more refined environs, head for the upscale hotels on the south bank of the river.

Brown Eyes. If the street promoters with flyers don't grab your attention, the blaring sound system with pumping bass certainly will. There's a dance floor, pool table, and happy hour that generally lasts all day. This expat and backpacker hangout is small and crowded, but the cool air-conditioning and garden patio make it bearable. ⊠ *56 Chu Van An* ☎ *0234/382–7494.*

DMZ Bar. Located in the heart of the tourist zone, this hopping spot is Hue's longest running bar. Cheap eats are overshadowed by the atmosphere and drinks that are ridiculously cheap during happy hour, offered three times daily. This backpacker's hangout is where everyone comes to dance the night away to loud and outdated hits. For a drink with a view, head upstairs to the balcony overlooking the bustling avenue. It's tradition for patrons to add some graffiti to the wall before leaving. ⊠ *60 Le Loi St.* ☎ *0234/382–3414.*

Dragon Boat Night Cruise. A culturally enlightening way to spend an evening in Hue is to take a night cruise on the Huong River. Boats with musical groups performing traditional Hue folk songs can be rented through most tourist agencies or directly at the river next to the Hoang Giang Hotel at the northern end of Le Loi Street. If you still have the energy after a day of visiting Hue's tombs and pagodas, don't miss this enchanting experience. ⊠ *Le Loi St.*

Song Huong Floating Restaurant. Although the thought of dining in a giant illuminated lotus flower might not be high on your travel agenda, the Song Huong makes for a good spot for some light entertainment and romantic river views. While the menu here is overambitious in content and price, if you stick to the basic Vietnamese dishes or an evening cocktail, it makes for an easy way to pass a few hours in the evening. ■ TIP→ **For the best views and to avoid the tour groups, take a table upstairs.** ⊠ *3 Le Loi* ☎ *0234/3823–738* ⊕ *www.nhahangnoisonghuong. com.*

SHOPPING

Shoppers have plenty of options, from lacquer paintings and calligraphic artwork to painted silk and handmade ceramics. For a local keepsake, conical bamboo hats are available at souvenir shops and markets throughout Hue, the original birthplace of these national symbols. For military paraphernalia, wood carvings and replicas of antique compasses and teapots, you are better off swerving around the pop-up stands lining the park near the boat station, and heading to some of the smaller shops on the northern end of Le Loi. If you didn't get your designer fix in Hoi An, your best bet for tailor-made clothing is in the backpacker's district on Chu Van An Street.

Dong Da Market. Hue's main market, Dong Da, situated north of the citadel just beyond the central Hue bus station, is the place to go for street food, souvenirs, clothing, and knockoff brands. It's enormous and packed to the rafters, so it can feel cramped and hot, especially near the food stalls in the center. Unlike many other local markets in the central region, this one comes alive as the sun goes down, when crowds descend for dinner and a line of bia hoi stalls set up parallel to the river. Bargaining is expected at the market stalls. ⊠ *Tran Hung Dao St., north of Tran Tien Bridge* ⊘ *6 am–10 pm.*

Du Ca Art Gallery. Blending traditional with avant-garde, artist Phan Trinh offers a large collection of lacquer paintings that can be shipped to your home. The gallery showcases abstract works depicting scenes throughout Vietnam. As one of the country's most celebrated artists, Trinh has exhibited worldwide for more than two decades. For additional modern works, head next door to New Space Art Foundation. ⊠ *24 Pham Ngu Lao St.* ☏ *0234/382–5287.*

Ella Shop. Silks scarves and traditional Vietnamese dresses, known as *ao dai*, are available at this fashion boutique. In addition to traditional and modern styles, Ella's offers custom-made clothing tailored within 72 hours. Smaller items like jewelry, handbags, and leather wallets are also for sale. ⊠ *39 Chu Van An St.* ☏ *0234/3893–9495* ⊕ *www.ellaviet.com.*

PHONG NHA KE BANG NATIONAL PARK

240 km (149 miles) north of Hue, 53 km (32 miles) north of Dong Hoi.

Fodor's Choice ★ Part of the Annamite Mountain Range on the northwest Central Coast, Phong Nha Ke Bang National Park was listed as a World Heritage Site in 2003. Covering more than 800 km (497 miles), it's thought to be one of the most distinctive examples of karst landforms in Southeast Asia, with more than 300 caves and grottoes including Son Doong, the world's largest cave, only discovered in 2009. The park is incredibly beautiful and tourism is (to date) being managed with sustainability in mind. It's a great family destination and although the caves are the main draw, there are plenty of adventurous activities including bike trails, kayaking, mountain climbing, and trekking on offer. For a small taster of Phong Nha, allow at least two full days and remember to account for travel time. If you're pushed for time, forget about traveling independently and book a tour.

The best months to visit for trekking and caving are March, April, and May, before the draining humidity of summer kicks in. From the end of September, Phong Nha can get very wet with the chance of typhoons. Some services wind down during October and November as caves can flood, and roads become thick with mud, making it difficult to get around.

GETTING HERE AND AROUND
Dong Hoi's airport is 46 km (28 miles) east of Phong Nha Town. Taxis meet all incoming flights, but it's a good idea to pre-arrange transfers with your hotel.

Direct transport options are limited to either a private car or tour bus. All other options terminate in Dong Hoi, which has just one public bus transfer a day covering the 47-km (29-mile) onward journey to the national park town. The easiest start point for Phong Nha is Hue. Local buses leave from the northern bus terminal near Dong Ba Market (look for the small bus with a sign for Phuc Vu and ask the driver for Phong Nha) at 10:30 am and occasionally again at 1 pm. A far more reliable, direct service is offered by most tour offices in Hue's backpacker district at the northern end of Le Loi Street. If taking a private car from either Danang or Hoi An, note that the highways further north are not in good condition and travel can be painfully slow. From Hue the 226-km (140-mile) journey takes around four hours and will cost upwards of 2,000,000d. The Vinh Moc Tunnels make for a good midway stop to stretch your legs and should not add too much time to the journey.

By far the best way to get to Dong Hoi (you'll need to arrange onward transport to Phong Nha) is by train. The scenic coastal route takes you through some of the most breathtaking landscapes, from the jungle-clad cliffs and ocean views from Danang, through the rice fields and rural villages surrounding Hue, and onwards past the giant karst formations that announce your arrival to beautiful Quang Binh Province. Danang, a 30-minute taxi ride, is the closest train station to Hoi An. From Danang there are several express (SE) trains available daily via Hue (three hours) and then on to Dong Ha (three hours). To avoid turning up in Dong Hoi in the small hours of the morning, the best trains are the SE2 leaving Danang at 12:46 pm and Hue at 3:31 pm, or the 12:13 pm SE4 from Danang (4:47 from Hue).

ESSENTIALS

Train Contact **Dong Hoi Train Station** ⊠ *Subregional 4, Tieu Khu 4, Dong Hoi, Quang Binh Province* ☎ *0232/3820–558.*

Money Matters Credit cards and dollars are rarely accepted at any of the businesses in Phong Nha and the only ATM (near the tourism office) is infrequently filled, so bring enough money to cover your costs. The alternative is less-than-favorable exchange rates in some of the larger hotels or a trip to Dong Hoi for an ATM.

TOURS

FAMILY **Mandarin Cafe Tours.** Tomb fatigue is a real thing in Hue, and unless you have a particular passion for Vietnam's imperial history, it tends to set in around tomb two; especially for kids. Mandarin Cafe is one of the few tour gigs in Hue that addresses this by offering a selection of tours that involve escaping the walled citadel and introducing you to Hue's less-visited villages, culture, and people. One of the highlights is a scenic journey into the countryside visiting the villages of the conical hat makers, imperial jewellers, and embroidery, lace, brass, and wood-sculpting craftspeople. You can get involved with the crafting, interact with the artisans, and shop at wholesale prices. ■TIP➔ Mandarin Cafe's owner, Mr. Cu, also has a fantastic DIY walking tour available for download from his website. ⊠ *24 Tran Cao Van, Hue* ☎ *0234/382–1281* ⊕ *www. mrcumandarin.com.*

Fodor'sChoice **Oxalis.** The best place to head for tours, Oxalis is the most professional ★ outfit in town. The company has specialized in adventure caving tours since 2011, and focuses on sustainability. The impressive team includes Howard and Deb Limbert from the British Cave Research Association, the couple that helped to put Phong Nha on the map and later, to discover Hang Son Doong, with the help of Oxalis porter Ho Khanh. Oxalis is the first and only tour company to have gained permission to take a small number of cave enthusiasts to explore the world's biggest cave on a seven-day adventure tour. Tours range from full-day trekking, swimming, and climbing out to Tu Lan, to two-, three-, four-, and five-day treks assisted by a support team of guides and porters. ■ TIP→ A must-do is the two-day Hang En Cave Adventure that includes a night camping out in one of the cave's biggest chambers. ⊠ *Son Trach office, Phong Nha Commune, Phong Nha, Quang Binh Province* ☎ *0232/3677–678* ⊕ *www.oxalis.com.vn.*

Phong Nha Ke Bang Tourism Services. In Phong Nha town, the government-run Phong Nha Ke-Bang Tourism Office provides excellent information and has a very informative website with some of the best maps of the area. ⊠ *Son Trach, Bo Trach, Phong Nha, Quang Binh Province* ☎ *0232/3677–021* ⊕ *www.phongnhakebang.vn.*

Quang Binh Tourism. With so many bucket-list-warranting activities available at Phong Nha, it's best to do as much preplanning (and booking) before you arrive as possible. Quang Binh's main tourist information center runs from an office in Dong Hoi, and is good for activities throughout the province, including information on Phong Nha and hotels in the area. Their website makes for a good planning resource, providing a decent map of the area and up-to-date information on news and events. ⊠ *1 Me Suot, Quang Binh Province* ☎ *0232/3822–018* ⊕ *www.quangbinhtourism.vn.*

EXPLORING

Phong Nha town is tiny and easily manageable on foot. To explore farther afield, you'll need a mountain bike. For independent touring, Phong Nha cave is accessed by dragon boat via the small boat station in the center of town. For tickets go to the nearby tourism center. Visitors are now allowed to enter the national park, but you must stick to the roads unless you have a guide.

Fodor's Choice
★

Hang Son Doong. This cave was discovered in 2009 by a British Cave Research team led by Howard and Deb Limbert and guided by the "King of the Caves" Ho Khanh. Hang Son Doong has been distinguished as the largest cave in the world—a 747 could fit in its largest chamber. A lucky few (the government only releases a handful of visitors permits a year) can now take thrilling seven-day trek through remote ethnic villages and deep jungle, and across rivers before exploring the entire length of this otherworldly cave, passing enormous stalagmites and fossil passageways to the "Great Wall of Vietnam" and beyond. ■ TIP→ You'll need to have a good level of fitness and get in early to book. Tours are released by Oxalis in November and sell out very quickly. ⊠ *Son Trach, Phong Nha, Quang Binh Province* ☎ *0232/3677–678* ⊕ *www. oxalis.com.vn.*

FAMILY
Fodor's Choice
★

Paradise Cave. The must-see Paradise Cave opened to the public in 2011 and is one of the most beautiful park caves you can visit on a day trip. Tours and transport can be arranged from the Tourism Center in town, but if you are feeling energetic you can cycle there along the stunning 16-km (10-mile) Nuoc Mooc Spring Eco Trail within the National Park (tickets are available at the entrance gate). The scenic trail takes you all the way to Paradise Cave, where there is another ticket booth. It's a long trek from here to the cave entrance, but an electric golf cart is available to whisk you to the stairs (all 500 of them) that lead up to the cave entrance, where more stairs lead you down into the cave's magnificent chambers linked by a wooden walkway that winds around majestic rock formations deep into the belly of the cave. To get to Paradise, follow the road through town past the Phong Nha ticket office. Continue on that road for 16 km (10 miles) until you reach the intersection where you take a right at a huge billboard. ✉ *Phong Nha, Quang Binh Province* 🎟 *Nuoc Mooc Spring Eco Trail: 50,000d; Paradise Cave: 120,000d.*

FAMILY **Phong Nha Cave.** Up until the discovery of Son Doong, the beautiful Phong Nha Cave was the national park's most famous treasure. It's the park's easiest cave to navigate and there really is no need to visit it with a guide. Buy tickets from the Tourism Center in the village and pick up a dragon boat from the boat station nearby. The boat takes you on a picturesque journey along the Son River right into the giant river cave, where you disembark to explore 1,500 meters inside, viewing the most splendid formations, stalagmites, and stalactites, enchantingly lit in a rainbow of colors. ✉ *Son Trach* 🎟 *80,000d.*

5

WHERE TO EAT

$$ ASIAN 🍴 **Cavern Pub and Restaurant.** The karst mountain views from this friendly pub on the edge of town are enough to make you return, and the beers are usually cold. There's free Wi-Fi, good music, vegetarian menu options, and a great English-speaking host. The atmosphere is chilled and in the colder winter months, you can sit around the open bonfire in the yard to keep warm. ■ **TIP→ You can book tours and onward travel here, but do read the small print.** [$] *Average main: 80000d* ✉ *Near boat station, Son Trach* ☎ *0232/3677–677.*

$ VIETNAMESE 🍴 **De Nui.** This basic, but popular restaurant with cheerful red table-cloths has just one thing on the menu, goat, served in multiple styles—aromatic, slow-cooked curry, charcoal-roasted, or in a warming winter hotpot with sides of rice. The restaurant is about 300 meters down from the Catholic church on the edge of town. [$] *Average main: 60000d* ✉ *Son Trach* 💳 *No credit cards.*

$$$ VIETNAMESE Fodor's Choice ★ 🍴 **The Pub With Cold Beer.** At the midway point of one of the most incredible (and strenuous) 22-km (13½-mile) bicycle loops in the Bong Valley, with views over rice fields and the river, The Pub With Cold Beer has not just beer, but also hammocks, a pool table, and, in season, tubes on which you can float down the river. It's a beautiful spot to unwind for a few hours, which is just as well, since that's how long your chicken lunch is going to take, once you've chosen your live bird. Chef Nguyet also offers free cooking classes, showing you how to prepare her famous peanut sauce and how to barbeque a chicken on an open fire in the hut out the back. [$] *Average main: 180000d* ✉ *Rte. maps available from Phong Nha Farmstay, Easy Tiger, and Pepper House (where you can also catch a boat)* 💳 *No credit cards.*

$ VIETNAMESE 🍴 **Trang and Nhung.** The sign outside says "The best spitroast pork and noodle shop in the world (probably)" and if the pork belly they serve is anything to go by, the claim is justified. It's a local joint with plastic chairs and an enormous grill out front and it's easy to find if you follow your nose from the small boat station in town. The menu is simple and cheap with delicious pork-stuffed *banh mi* sandwiches coming in at 40,000d. The stars of the show (surprise) are the spit-roasted pork and the *bun bo hue* (beef noodle soup). [$] *Average main: 40000d* ✉ *Town center, near boat station to Paradise Caves, Son Trach* 💳 *No credit cards.*

$ VIETNAMESE 🍴 **Vung Hue Restaurant.** Having taken the boat out to Paradise Cave it might have crossed your mind what exactly those people were doing fishing riverweed out of the water with giant chopsticks. Wander up the road to the north from the boat station and you'll find three restaurants that will uncover the mystery (we'll leave that for you to discover). The best and fairest-priced of them all is Ving Hue, which sells top-quality local-style Vietnamese food (they even have an English menu, with fixed prices) and fresh river fish that you can pick live from the buckets out the back and choose how you'd like it cooked—charcoal-grilled in lemongrass and chili with a side of fried greens, with garlic and rice on the side, is a good choice. [$] *Average main: 40000d* ✉ *Heading north from boat station, Ving Hue is middle restaurant* 💳 *No credit cards.*

$ VIETNAMESE 🍴 **Wild Boar Eco Farm.** A couple of kilometers downstream from The Pub With Cold Bear, this rustic jungle hut is run by local tour operator Captain Chung. The scenery is awe-inspiring—swinging hammocks overlook the wilderness and Chung's prize collection of free-range Euro-Asian wild boar. Chung serves traditional jungle dishes including a very good pork dish, cooked in bamboo shoots and served with rice and a choice of fresh vegetables fried with garlic. Chung operates an on-call boat service from Pepper House. The farm is 11 km (7 miles) from town. Ask for a map from The Farmstay, Easy Tiger, Pepper House, or Ho Khanh. [$] *Average main: 50000d* ✉ *Phong Nha, Quang Binh Province* ☎ *01/891–5538* 💳 *No credit cards.*

WHERE TO STAY

$$ B&B/INN FAMILY Fodor's Choice ★ 🏨 **Ho Khanh's Homestay.** On the banks of the Son River, on the edge of Phong Nha town, this ornately carved wooden traditional homestay provides family-friendly lodgings, hosted by Mr. Ho Khanh, the original discoverer of the world's biggest cave.**Pros:** quiet, riverside location; a short walk to bars and restaurants; perhaps the most knowledgable guide in the province; free bikes. **Cons:** shared bathroom in cheaper rooms; mosquitoes; gets booked up weeks in advance. [$] *Rooms from: 800000d* ✉ *Near Phong Nha tourism center, Son Trach* ☎ *0916/794–506* 🌐 *www.phong-nha-homestay.com* 🛏 *3 rooms* 🍽 *Breakfast.*

$$$ B&B/INN Fodor's Choice ★ 🏨 **Pepper House.** For romantic retreats it would be hard to find anything as charming as the four enchanting French colonial eco-villas at Pepper House, set amid a pepper plantation, 6 km (4 miles) from town. **Pros:** idyllic location; impeccable service; great tours; boat service. **Cons:** mosquitoes; isolated location; no family accommodations. [$] *Rooms from: 1600000d* ✉ *Just off HCM Hwy., 6 km (4 miles) south of Phong Nha* ☎ *0918/915–538* ✍ *info@pepperhouse-homestay.com* 🛏 *4 rooms* 🍽 *Breakfast.*

$$ B&B/INN FAMILY **Phong Nha Farmstay.** This small, but stylish, family-run colonial villa, a short distance from the national park, is probably the best deal to be had in town. **Pros:** complimentary Jeep or Ural motorbike transfers to town; live music and movie nights; great Western/Vietnamese restaurant; fantastic tours; free bikes. **Cons:** remote; mosquitoes; difficult to find. [$] *Rooms from: 700000d* ✉ *1 km east of Ho Chi Minh Rd., 9 km (5 miles) from town center* ☎ *0232/367–5135* ✍ *phongnhafarmstay@gmail.com* 🌐 *www.phong-nha-cave.com* 🛏 *17 rooms* 🍴 *Breakfast.*

$$ HOTEL **Phong Nha Lake House Resort.** Sheltered in the mountain valleys of Lai Chau, overlooking the beautiful lake Dong Suon, the Lake House makes for an idyllic base within easy reach of Phong Nha Ke Bang National Park. **Pros:** genuinely friendly staff; great food (and wine menu); incredible views; lake swimming. **Cons:** remote; steps down to the lake side bungalows a little steep; mosquitoes. [$] *Rooms from: 800000d* ✉ *Khuongha, Hung Trach, Bo Trach* ☎ *0232/367–5999* 🛏 *8 rooms* 🌐 *phongnhalakehouse.com* 🍴 *Breakfast.*

5

NIGHTLIFE

Phong Nha is on the up, with a couple of places in town now serving cold beer (it's a new thing) and a resident Filipino band performing ad-hoc live music evenings at a few choice addresses.

Jungle Bar. The popular Jungle Bar takes up the whole ground floor of backpacker hotel Easy Tiger, in the center of Phong Nha town. Great staff, live music, a decent menu, and cold Huda beer makes this the best spot in town. Hangover-inducing happy hours kick off with gin and tonic from 5 to 6 pm and change hourly to beer, rum, and then vodka. Those who indulge tend to return in the morning for a full English breakfast to aid their recovery. ■ **TIP→ Come here and speak to owner Hai for maps, information, and tour advice.** ✉ *Center of Phong Nha Town, Son Trach* ☎ *0975/920–844* 🌐 *www.easytigerhostel.com.*

SPORTS AND THE OUTDOORS

BIKING AND MOTORBIKING

The roads in the park and surrounds are in terrible condition and although motorbikes are available to rent from many places in town, unless you are an experienced rider, it's inadvisable to tackle them on your own. Experienced riders can hire everything from a standard Japanese scooter to a Russian Ural from Phong Nha Farmstay, where excellent motorbike tours are also available that take you through remote villages, incredible karst landscapes, and waterfalls that you would not find on your own.

Easy Tiger. In the town center, this backpacker hostel rents mountain bikes and motorbikes and has maps with great DIY routes in the area. One of the best loops from town is the Nuoc Mooc Spring Eco Trail, which takes you through dramatic scenery and some equally dramatic inclines. ✉ *Son Trach* ☎ *0232/3677–844* ✍ *easytigerphongnha@gmail.com* 🌐 *www.easytigerhostel.com.*

FAMILY **Phong Nha Adventure Cycling With Private Shi.** For thrills and maybe the odd spill, local villager and tour guide Private Shi runs a professional mountain bike adventure tour company, exploring the trails, villages, and waterholes of Phong Nha Ke Bang National Park. The tours range from a 20-km (12-mile) village ride to a thigh-burning 70-km (43-mile) adventure trail along the Ho Chi Minh Trail, through rice and peanut fields, war remnants, and river crossings in an old B52 boat. Private Shi is an exceptional guide. ⊠ *Phong Nha, Quang Binh Province* ☎ *0985/555–827* ⊕ *www.phongnhacycling.jimdo.com.*

HALONG BAY AND NORTH-CENTRAL VIETNAM

Updated
by Duncan
Forgan

There can be no disguising the stature of Halong Bay among Vietnam's tourist draws. The UNESCO World Heritage–listed seascape, a mind-blowing collection of limestone karsts that loom jaggedly from the emerald waters of the Gulf of Tonkin, is justifiably famous and is a key part of an itinerary for most visitors to the country. Many luxurious cruise boats ply the seas, and spending at least one night on the bay is a must. East of Halong Bay, Bai Tu Long Bay shares similar scenery with its near neighbor, but sees far less tourist traffic. Cat Ba Island is the biggest island in the area and offers stirring jungle scenery as well as some wonderful beaches.

These coastal attractions are far from the only highlights in the area east and immediately south of Hanoi. Although missing the dramatic impact of the mountains of the far north, the sprawling Red River delta, the leafy port town of Haiphong, and the spectacular inland karst scenery at Ninh Binh are worthy additions to any schedule.

Even though the region has borne the brunt of centuries of war—first Chinese invaders, then French colonialists, the Americans, and once again the Chinese—and bomb craters still pockmark the Red River delta, much of this area of Vietnam has maintained its beauty.

The Red River delta is the most densely populated area of Vietnam, with more than 1,000 people per square mile, compared with approximately 400 per square mile in the Mekong Delta. Extreme weather patterns—too much rain and too many damaging storms in the wet season; too little rain in the dry season—make living off the land more difficult than in the south.

Haiphong is more prosperous. Once the sleepy second cousin to the booming port of Saigon (now Ho Chi Minh City), Haiphong is emerging as more than just Vietnam's second-largest port. The city is awakening to the prospect of both tourism and the rapid development of import-export channels. Tree-lined boulevards, expansive green parks, and impressive—if a little shopworn—French colonial architecture fill the downtown. To the north of the city center, 10,000-ton freighters unload containers bound for Hanoi and load up with Vietnamese exports.

Farther northeast, natural beauty and nationalized industry share the spotlight. In Quang Ninh Province an ever-expanding coal-mining industry is counterbalanced by the scenic splendor of forested peaks and Halong and Bai Tu Long bays.

TOP REASONS TO GO

Views from the water: Cruise among thousands of limestone karsts and deserted islands where sandy coves, hidden caves, and floating villages abound.

Exploring Cat Ba Island: At this national park the endangered langur monkey finds refuge among lakes, waterfalls, and limestone cliffs that are now prized territory for rock-climbers.

Luxury at sea: You don't have to spend the earth to enjoy a Halong

Bay cruise, but the ever-growing selection of sumptuous vessels with top-class amenities that ply the waters make it worth splashing a few dollars more on the experience.

Laid-back café culture: Haiphong may not get the same press as other major Vietnamese hubs, but the city's tree-lined boulevards and colonial-era architecture are easily appreciated from one of its many friendly coffee shops.

Around 100 km (62 miles) south of Hanoi, the provincial town of Ninh Binh is the gateway to more quintessentially Vietnamese karst scenery. Although there's a steady trickle of foreign tourists, local visitors are the primary market. Attractions here include the grottoes of Trang An and Tam Coc as well as the nation's biggest pagoda.

ORIENTATION AND PLANNING

GETTING ORIENTED

One of the most appealing aspects of this part of Vietnam is how easy it is to get to all the major points of interest from Hanoi. Although the 3½-hour journey from the capital to Halong Bay may seem like an inconvenience, it is a mere trifle in a Vietnamese context. Likewise, Haiphong and Ninh Binh are an easy hop from the big city, with plenty of comfortable and convenient transportation services operating the routes. In fact, if your time is very limited, you can even take in a selection of attractions in a (long) day trip from Hanoi. However, such is the visual manna on offer, a few days to absorb the area's splendor is far preferable.

Ninh Binh and Nearby. A short trip (around 100 km or 62 miles) south of Hanoi, the provincial city of Ninh Binh is pleasant enough, but it is the quintessentially Vietnamese limestone karst scenery surrounding the city that puts it on the tourist map. Dive headlong into the landscape while getting rowed along lazy rivers and through intricate cave systems.

Haiphong. Overlooked by many visitors, Haiphong is well worth a day or two of anyone's time. Although it is one of Vietnam's most important ports and an industrial center, the city's tree-lined boulevards, colonial architecture, and excellent transportation links with Hanoi make it a fine addition to a travel itinerary.

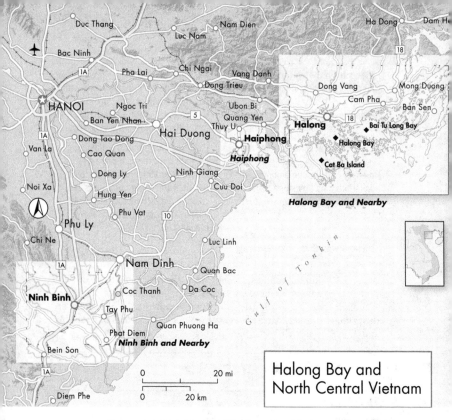

Halong Bay and Nearby

Halong Bay and Nearby. The karst-studded seascape of Halong Bay (around four hours by road from Hanoi) is one of the world's most arresting sights and a trip here is an absolute must if you are in northern Vietnam. Farther east, Bai Tu Long Bay showcases virtually the same visual splendor, but welcomes a fraction of the tourists. Cat Ba Island is a rugged, jungle-clad paradise that has become a favored center for adventure sports.

PLANNING

WHEN TO GO

Around Halong Bay, the season runs from early summer to mid-autumn. From July to September beware of tropical typhoons; flooding in Haiphong and Hanoi is common during these storms. The capital is hot and extremely humid in summer, which makes it a popular time for residents to head for the hills or the coast.

During Tet, the lunar new year, you'll find northern Vietnam cold and drizzly but extremely festive. If you're coming during this time, make flight and hotel reservations very early. Also understand that many tour operations, such as trips to Halong Bay, are limited or suspended during this period.

GETTING HERE AND AROUND

AIR TRAVEL

Vietnam Airlines, Jetstar Pacific, and VietJet Air all offer daily flights to Haiphong's Cat Bi Airport from Ho Chi Minh City. VietJet Air has four daily flights; Vietnam Airlines has three; Jetstar Pacific has two. Vietnam Airlines operates a daily service to Haiphong from Danang.

BOAT AND FERRY TRAVEL

There is no boat service from Hanoi to Haiphong, but ferries, high-speed boats, and hydrofoils link many of the coastal destinations. However, with roads much improved these days, most travelers find it more convenient to go overland when possible.

Unless you're a guest of the Vietnamese military, the only way on and off Cat Ba Island is by boat or hydrofoil. There is a ferry service from Halong City to Cat Ba, but the more common route is from Haiphong.

Ferry Contact Mekong Hoang Yen ⊠ *6 Cu Chinh Lan St., Haiphong* ☎ *0225/384–1009*

BUS TRAVEL

Frequent buses travel from Hanoi to Haiphong, Ninh Binh, and other points in the area. Highly recommended companies operating the route include Hai Au, which is widely held to have the best service and cleanest buses. Buses depart from Gia Lam bus station near Hanoi's Old Quarter and take around 2½ hours to complete the journey to Haiphong's Niem Nghia bus station. The fare is about 85,000d each way and there are 11 buses each day. For those traveling from Hanoi to Cat Ba Island, Hoang Long Bus Company offers an all-in package that includes the cost of the ferry crossing from Haiphong. Tickets for this service cost around 240,000d each way.

Bus Contacts Hai Au Bus Company ⊠ *16 Ton Duc Thang St., Haiphong* ☎ *091/229–6088* ⊕ *www.haiaubus.vn.* **Hoang Long Bus Company** ⊠ *Luong Yen Bus Station, 1 Nguyen Khoai St., Hanoi* ☎ *024/3987–7225.*

CAR TRAVEL

Renting a car and driver from one of the many travel agencies and tour-ist cafés in Hanoi or going with an organized tour by minivan are the easiest ways to get around the northeast. The condition of the roads in the area has improved significantly over the last few years, making travel much more comfortable than it once was.

Infrastructure is also improving. For instance, a new Hanoi to Haiphong highway is scheduled to open at the end of 2015. This will ease the traf-fic burden on Highway 5, one of the most overloaded stretches of road in the north. Until the new road is officially opened, riding to Haiphong by motorbike is not recommended. Renting an air-conditioned car with a driver for a day's drive to Haiphong and back to Hanoi will run from 1,200,000 to 1,500,000 and will take about two hours each way. Of note on your way are the half-dozen pagodas set back in the rice fields along Highway 5. Cars or minivans traveling on to Halong Bay from Haiphong must cross the Cam River by ferry at Binh Station (Ben Binh), at the north end of Cu Chinh Lan Street. Access is easiest from Ben Binh

Street, one block east. Ferries leave every 10 or 15 minutes. Passenger tickets cost about 5,000d, more for cars.

Halong Bay is a 3½-hour drive from Hanoi. Your driver will most likely head east on Highway 5. Halfway to Haiphong, just before the city of Hai Duong, you'll turn left onto Highway 18. Although crowded, the road has one of the better surfaces in the north and the journey is rarely anything less than smooth. Renting an air-conditioned car with driver from Hanoi costs between 2,400,000d and 2,600,000d for a two-day, one-night trip to Halong, including all car and driver expenses. If it's not the weekend, or if it's in the dead of winter or heat of summer, bargain hard—you can usually get a better deal.

TRAIN TRAVEL

Four trains per day (from 6 am to early evening) leave Hanoi bound for Haiphong from one of two stations: Hanoi Railway Station (Ga Hanoi) and Long Bien Station. Tickets for all trains can be purchased at the Hanoi Railway Station, but you must ask at the ticket booth whether your train leaves from there or from Long Bien Station. The cost is 90,000d for travel in a soft sleeper carriage and 115,000d for travel in an air-conditioned soft sleeper carriage. The unspectacular trip takes just over two hours. There are two stations in Haiphong. The first, Thuong Li Railway Station, is west of the city. You should detrain at the Haiphong Railway Station, which is the end of the line on the Hanoi route.

Train Station Haiphong Railway Station ⊠ *75 Luong Khanh Thien St., Ngo Quyen, Haiphong* ☏ *0225/920025.* **Vietnam Railway System** ⊠ *Hanoi* ☏ *090/461–9926* ⊕ *vietnam-railway.com.*

TOURS

Traveling independently is not particularly difficult in Vietnam. However, the presence of several reputable tour operators that specialize in itineraries in the north of Vietnam supplies succor and security for those who prefer to leave the legwork to others. Whether it's flight tickets, hotel reservations, or luxurious multiday voyages out on the pristine waters of Halong Bay, these specialists major in making life easy for travelers.

Fodor's Choice ★ **Backyard Travel.** The consultants here pride themselves on their insider knowledge of Asia, and their Vietnam itineraries deviate from the tried and tested to offer something a little different for the adventurous traveler. In northwest Vietnam, tours include a three-day, two-night cruise around Bai Tu Long Bay. ⊕ *www.backyardtravel.com* ✉ *Bai Tu Long cruise from 8,880,000d.*

Handspan Travel. One of the most respected tour operators in Vietnam, Handspan can organize everything from luxurious cruises on Halong Bay to more offbeat adventures such as bike tours and kayaking itineraries. ⊠ *78 Ma May St., Hanoi* ☏ *024/3926–2828* ⊕ *www.handspan. com* ✉ *2-night Halong Explorer and Kayak Discovery Tour from 5,656,000d.*

Tonkin Travel. Founded by two native Hanoian women in 2002, Tonkin Travel has built a formidable reputation in the intervening years. In common with the other top operators in Vietnam, Tonkin is as comfortable directing tourists to the main sights and attractions in the country as it is designing more imaginative bespoke itineraries to off-the-beaten-track destinations around Lan Ha Bay, Ninh Binh, and Bai Tu Long Bay. ✉ *164 Xuan Dieu St., Hanoi* ☎ *024/3719–1184* ⊕ *www.tonkintravel. com* ✆ *Halong Bay/Ninh Binh/Mai Chau tour (4 days/3 nights) from 11,300,000d.*

RESTAURANTS

With the emerald waters of the Gulf of Tonkin lapping the coastline, fresh seafood is the undoubted star in this part of northern Vietnam. In fact, the Vietnamese set great store by the ritual of plucking a delicious morsel out of a giant tank and having it prepared for them—and so should you. Delicious fruits of the ocean can be found all the way along the coast, purveyed in venues ranging from simple family-run establishments to more ostentatious (and expensive) options. Aside from seafood, there are some solid Vietnamese restaurants in the region serving specialties including *thit de* (goat meat) and other local favorites. Larger cities such as Haiphong have a growing selection of international restaurants with Indian, American, and Mexican among the cuisines available.

HOTELS

If it's the height of luxury you're after, you probably won't find it in many places outside Hanoi in the north of Vietnam. However, the pre-tourism days of mainly dank and dingy accommodations are long gone and even less vaunted destinations tend to have at least one highly acceptable hotel. Clean and friendly (if a little low on character) family-run hotels are the norm, but more luxury and individuality are creeping in as tourist flow increases.

For expanded reviews, facilities, and current deals, visit Fodors.com.

WHAT IT COSTS				
	$	$$	$$$	$$$$
Restaurants	Under 60,000d	60,000d–150,000d	151,000d–250,000d	over 250,000d
Hotels	Under 600,000d	600,000d–900,000d	901,000d –1.5 million d	over 1.5 million d

Prices in the reviews are the average cost of a main course at dinner or, if dinner is not served, at lunch. Prices in the reviews are the lowest cost of a standard double room in high season including tax.

NINH BINH AND NEARBY

An easy trip from Hanoi, Ninh Binh Province is one of the undoubted stars of Vietnam. The karst scenery that surrounds the provincial capital, Ninh Binh town, is some of the country's loveliest, and Cuc Phuong National Park makes up for its relative shortage of wildlife with lush peaks and peaceful lakes. Not only does the area have beautiful scenery, it also offers intriguing cultural sights such as Hoa Lu, the country's first capital, and Phat Diem Cathedral, its most distinctive—and arguably

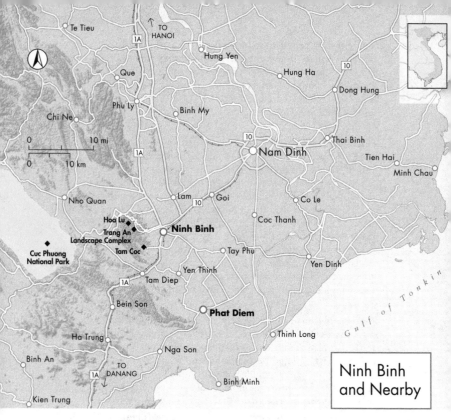

most storied—Catholic church. The area's accessibility has its draw-backs, however. It is a huge favorite with domestic travelers, so that many of its main attractions are overrun, and hard-sell tactics are not uncommon at places such as Tam Coc.

NINH BINH

94 km (58 miles) south of Hanoi.

Pleasant enough in itself, but a largely unremarkable provincial capital on the main road between Hanoi and Hue, Ninh Binh is notable for being within easy striking distance of some of Vietnam's most stunning limestone karst scenery. With its easy transportation links to destinations both north and south, it makes a perfectly amenable base from which to explore the surrounding splendor. Much of the area to the west comes within the UNESCO World Heritage Site of Trang An Landscape Complex, including a series of caves accessible by boat and the fascinating remains of Vietnam's first capital, Hoa Lu, 12 km (7½ miles) northwest of town. Just to the south of Trang An are the more famous Tam Coc caves.

GETTING HERE AND AROUND

There are regular buses, leaving every 15 minutes or so, from Hanoi's southern Giap Bat bus terminal to Ninh Binh. A one-way journey takes between 1½ and 2½ hours, depending on the traffic, and the fare is 80,000d. Ninh Binh is a regular station on the north-south train route. The fare for a one-way journey from Hanoi is 45,000d and the trip takes 2½ hours. Taxis can be chartered for the journey from Hanoi and cost 1,448,000d from the city center.

If you are approaching from the opposite direction, an open tour bus from Hue to Hanoi can drop you off in Ninh Binh by request. This is a service offered by various tour companies including The Sinh Tourist, one of the longest-running operators in the country. The buses leave Hue at 5 pm and the journey takes around 10 hours, meaning an extremely early arrival in Ninh Binh. A one-way ticket costs 400,000d. There are three trains daily from Hue to Ninh Binh. They leave Hue at 5:39 am, 1:36 am, and 9:33 pm and take approximately 12 hours. A one-way fare for a comfortable soft sleeper is 916,115d.

Most hotels can organize a motorbike and driver to take you round the sights. These should cost around 325,000d for the day.

TOURS

The Sinh Tourist. A day trip from Hanoi by minibus will take you to the Tam Coc caves for a rowboat tour in the morning and to Hoa Lu in the afternoon. The outfitter also offers three-day tours for a more in-depth exploration of the area. ✉ *66 Hang Than St., Hanoi* ☎ *024/3836–4212* ⊕ *www.sinhtourist.vn* ✉ *Day trips from 554,000d.*

EXPLORING

Hoa Lu. This is an interesting excursion on a number of different levels. Significantly, it was the first capital of independent Vietnam, and equally arresting is its stirring location amid the karst scenery that distinguishes Ninh Binh Province. Both the stunning natural surroundings of limestone outcrops and meandering streams and Hoa Lu's status as a former seat of power make for a worthy addition to any travel itinerary.

The **Dinh Tien Hoang Temple** at Hoa Lu honors the emperor who established the capital here. The musty, dimly lit back chamber here houses statues of the king and his three sons. The main hall has been heavily restored, and much of the wood construction visible today is from renovations done in the 17th century. In the temple courtyard stands a meter-high (3-foot) sculpture made of stone. The dragon lying atop it is meant to symbolize the king sleeping, while unicorns stand guard on each side to protect him. To the left of the temple is a small structure containing three stone stelae inscribed with the king's blessings and details about various restorations. In 1696, the entire temple compound was shifted from its original northward orientation, the direction of evil according to Taoist belief, to face the more auspicious east, In 1898, Emperor Nguyen Thanh Thai had the temple raised 0.6 meters (2 feet) as a gesture of respect to Dinh Tien Hoang. The entire walled in compound was designed in the shape of the Chinese character meaning "country."

The **Le Dai Hanh Temple** is named after the general who became the first emperor of the dynasty in 980. The back chamber here houses ornate wooden statues of Le Dai Hanh, his son Tri Trung, and one of his five wives, Duong Van Nga, arguably the most interesting of the three figures. Upon the emperor's death, Duong Van Nga beseeched the head military mandarin of the time to prevent Chinese invaders from entering the country. She promised that she'd take away the rule of her six-year-old son and put it in the mandarin's hands, marrying him if he succeeded. When the mandarin repelled the Chinese, she made good on both promises. Her lifetime saw her become the wife of two kings, as well as the mother of two kings—the only woman with such a distinction in Vietnamese history. Depending on the angle from which you view her statue, her face will appear to reflect one of three feelings: seriousness over her daily affairs, sadness for the death of her husbands, and a half smile of satisfaction after the military mandarin defeated the invading Chinese forces and reinstalled her as queen. ⊠ *Hoa Lu, Ninh Binh Province* ✉ *100,000d* ⊙ *Daily 8–5.*

Tam Coc. A short bus or car ride away from Ninh Binh (drivers and tour group operators know exactly where to go) is a trio of caves accessible by a traditional boat ride down the Hoang Long River, a peaceful stream that winds through rice paddies after cutting its path through the steep cliffs around nearby Hoa Lu. Village women row you the 2 km (1 mile) through Tam Coc, a series of three caves, one of which has a cement plaque on its far side commemorating Nguyen Cong Cay, a Vietnamese weapons maker who lived in Hoa Lu from 1947 to 1950 and plotted with other resisters against the French. At the far end of the boat ride, other women in similar boats are waiting to sell you soft drinks, bananas, and even embroidery. It's a hard sell and somewhat ruins the idyllic moment. Another cave, Bich Dong, can also be reached by boat; you can disembark to visit the 17th-century pagoda here. ⊠ *Ninh Binh Province* ✉ *Boat trips 110,000d, or 140,000d for 2 passengers* ⊙ *Daily 7–3:30.*

Fodor's Choice ★ **Trang An Landscape Complex.** Closer to Ninh Binh city than Tam Coc, UNESCO World Heritage–listed Trang An offers a very similar experience to its more famous near neighbor. Although it is very popular with Vietnamese tourists, most visitors find it less crowded and more hassle-free than Tam Coc. Boat trips leave from the garish main office and take around 2½ hours. The journey by row-boat takes you through nine caves, some of which are very low and twisting, and along beautiful waterways lined with limestone karst. The landscape is of high historic and archaeological importance. Several pagodas can be visited on the boat tours, while the highest altitude caves dotted around the area have archeological traces of human activity dating back almost 30,000 years. Unfortunately, it is not yet possible for visitors to access these higher altitude caves. ⊠ *Ninh Binh* ✉ *150,000d.*

WHERE TO EAT

$$
ECLECTIC
✕ **Chookie's.** As is the case in many restaurants in Vietnam that cater predominantly to travelers, the menu at Chookie's runs the culinary gamut. Vietnamese specialties such as spring rolls and hearty noodle soups are all present and correct and of a decent standard. However,

CLOSE UP

Vietnam's First Capital

After three decades of internal strife following the expulsion of the Chinese by Ngo Quyen in 938, Dinh Bo Linh, also known as Dinh Tien Hoang, unified the country. (A colorful festival on the 12th day of the third lunar month commemorates this successful reunification.) The new king moved the capital to Hoa Lu, in a valley whose maze of narrow streams and inhospitable limestone outcroppings served as natural protection for the fledgling nation; he had numerous fortifications built around his citadel in order to avert another Chinese invasion, and word quickly spread of his ruthless treatment of prisoners. (The king reportedly fed enemies to tigers and then boiled their bones in ceremonial urns.) Despite such tactics, the Dinh dynasty was short-lived; bodyguards assassinated Dinh Tien Hoang in 979. The killers were discovered and put to death, and General Le Dai Hanh ascended to the throne, establishing the Early Le dynasty. Upon Le Dai Hanh's death in 1009, Ly Thai To became the first king of the Ly dynasty and moved the capital to Thang Long, the site of present-day Hanoi.

6

it is the authentic and well-priced Western food that stands out. The house burger is substantial, and imaginative options such as a chickpea wrap showcase the effort that is on display here. Extra touches such as genuine Heinz tomato ketchup and ultra-friendly service enhance the experience further. $ *Average main: 65000d* ⊠ *17 Luong Van Tuy St.* ☎ *094/483–6026* ▭ *No credit cards* ⊘ *Closed Tues. No lunch.*

$$

VIETNAMESE

✕ **Trung Tuyet.** You won't eat the best Vietnamese food of your life here by any means, but for solid local fare there are few better places in Ninh Binh. Classics such as pho are just adequate, but vegetarian dishes like morning glory fried with garlic, and the restaurant's roast offerings are of an exacting standard. Expect a friendly welcome, giant portions, and low prices. $ *Average main: 60000d* ⊠ *14 Hoang Hoa Tham St.* ☎ *097/366–5186* ▭ *No credit cards.*

WHERE TO STAY

$$$$

RESORT

Fodor's Choice

★

▦ **Emeralda Resort.** The most prestigious address in Ninh Binh Province, this plush resort luxuriates in a bucolic location on the outskirts of the city. **Pros:** the marvelous outdoor swimming pool is the highlight of a very alluring selection of leisure facilities. **Cons:** the restaurants are rather expensive and there are no other options nearby. $ *Rooms from: 2300000d* ⊠ *Van Long Reserve, Gia Vien District* ☎ *0229/365–8246* ⊕ *www.emeraldaresort.com* ⇱ *172 rooms* ⚭ *Breakfast.*

$

B&B/INN

▦ **Ngoc Anh Hotel.** Another of Ninh Binh's small family-run hotels, this is a friendly and well-run option that prides itself on its service. **Pros:** friendly and attentive service. **Cons:** rooms are a little on the small side. $ *Rooms from: 361675d* ⊠ *36 Luong Van Tuy St.* ☎ *0229/388–3768* ⇱ *10 rooms* ⚭ *Breakfast.*

$$$$
HOTEL
Fodor'sChoice
★

⌖ **Ninh Binh Legend Hotel.** The closest thing to a luxury option in Ninh Binh city, this sparkling hotel doesn't disappoint. **Pros:** giant beds. **Cons:** by Ninh Binh standards, it is a little out of the way. ⓢ *Rooms from: 1893576d* ⊠ *Ly Thai To, Tien Dong Zone* ☎ *0229/389–9880* ⊕ *www.ninhbinhlegendhotel.com* ⇥ *108 rooms* ⊙| *Breakfast.*

$$$$
B&B/INN
Fodor'sChoice
★

⌖ **Tam Coc Garden Resort.** A boutique retreat in the heart of the beautiful Ninh Binh countryside, this is a great place to get away from it all. **Pros:** the location is heartbreakingly beautiful. **Cons:** ceramic bathtubs cool down hot water rather too quickly. ⓢ *Rooms from: 2450000d* ⊠ *Hai Nham Hamlet, Hoa Lu District* ☎ *096/603–2555* ⇥ *8 rooms* ⊙| *Breakfast.*

$$
HOTEL
Fodor'sChoice
★

⌖ **Vancouver Hotel.** It is all about the welcome at this smart, family-owned hotel, overseen by manager David, who studied in Canada—hence the hotel's name—and whose English is near impeccable. **Pros:** manager has fantastic knowledge and impeccable English. **Cons:** breakfast is a little plain for the price of the room. ⓢ *Rooms from: 829725d* ⊠ *75 Luong Van Tuy St.* ☎ *0229/389–3270* ⊕ *www.thevancouverhotel.com* ⇥ *4 rooms, 1 suite* ⊙| *Breakfast.*

PHAT DIEM

30 km (19 miles) from Ninh Binh, 121 km (75 miles) southeast of Hanoi.

Phat Diem's hulking cathedral is prominent among Vietnam's religious buildings. Unique both for its vast dimensions and also an architectural mélange that incorporates both European and Sino-Vietnamese influences, it is a formidable sight and also possesses a fascinating backstory. Although the cathedral is undoubtedly the main selling point of the area, there are other points of interest, including a covered bridge dating from the late 19th century.

GETTING HERE AND AROUND

Phat Diem is incorporated into many tour itineraries from Hanoi and Ninh Binh, but not all tours that go to Hoa Lu stop here, so check before you book. Most travelers who visit the cathedral independently choose to do so by renting a motorcycle in Ninh Binh. The cathedral is in the town of Kim Son, which is an easy ride. Motorcycle rental from a hotel costs around 200,000d per day. It is easy to charter a taxi from Ninh Binh, and the fare should cost approximately 600,000d for a round-trip. You can also hire and car and driver, which shouldn't cost more than 1,080,000d for the round-trip (although finding a driver prepared to get you there for the 5 am Mass might not be easy).

EXPLORING

Fodor'sChoice
★

Phat Diem Cathedral. All churches in the area pale in comparison to the massive complex known as Phat Diem Cathedral, built in 1891 in Kim Son village, which was one of the first landfalls of Portuguese missionaries in the 16th century. The cathedral, a hulking edifice made of stone and hardwood, was designed by a Vietnamese priest named Father Sau, who died the same year the cathedral was completed. He is now interred in the narrow courtyard behind the bell tower, which was immortalized by Graham Greene in a description of a battle that took place here between French and Vietnamese forces in *The Quiet American.* The third floor of this tower supports a two-ton bronze bell that purportedly can be heard from 10 km (6 miles) away. The cathedral is flanked on both sides by four small chapels, all built in the late 19th century and dedicated to various saints. The prayer hall is a wooden marvel; almost the entire interior is made of Vietnamese ironwood, with 48 massive pillars supporting arched ceiling beams in what is truly an artist's loving creation. The curved eaves are a nod to Sino-Vietnamese architecture, but the crosses and saints (all sitting in the lotus position) reflect the fervor of the 150,000-strong congregation. Many of Phat Diem's Catholics fled to the south in 1954, when Vietnam was divided. A great deal of restoration work has been done on the complex, which was bombed heavily by American B-52s in 1972.

Catholicism has experienced a comeback in these parts, and because a more liberal tone has been adopted toward religion by Hanoi, Sunday Mass is now extremely popular. Services are held at 5 and 9 am, and by 10 everyone's already out in the fields. On holidays such as Christmas and Easter, expect crowds of 10,000 or more. ⊠ *Kim Son.*

CUC PHUONG NATIONAL PARK

6

40 km (25 miles) from Ninh Binh, 130 km (81 miles) southwest of Hanoi.

The first national park in Vietnam and still one of its most important, Cuc Phuong is a refuge for diverse animal and plant life and an idyllic place to spend a couple of days. Hiking is major draw and there numerous trails that cut through the forest. Ornithologists flock here to catch a glimpse of silver pheasants and red-collared woodpeckers among other species. In the early part of the last decade the Ho Chi Minh Highway was rerouted through the park, cutting off some 150 hectares (371 acres) from the main area of the park. The construction of the road has aided connectivity, but environmentalists maintain it has also harmed the biodiversity of the park.

GETTING HERE AND AROUND

It is relatively straightforward to travel here from Hanoi. Most of the reputable tour operators such as Handspan, Exo Travel, and Buffalo Tours run trips here. If you are traveling under your own steam, there's a regular bus from Hanoi to the park that departs Giap Bat station daily at 3 pm. The return bus to Hanoi leaves at 9 am and the journey takes around three hours. From Ninh Binh, the best option is to rent a motorbike or to engage the services of a motorbike and a driver for the journey.

EXPLORING

Fodor'sChoice **Cuc Phuong National Park.** Established in 1962 by President Ho Chi Minh
★ as Vietnam's first national park, Cuc Phuong consists of 220 square km (85 square miles) of heavily forested subtropical lowlands sheltering 97 mammal species, including nine species of civet, a kind of barking deer called the muntjac, as well as the extremely rare Delacour's langur. Approximately 300 bird species and 53 types of reptiles and amphibians live here as well, along with nearly 2,000 species of flora.

The low-key Endangered Primate Rescue Center, which can be visited with staff accompaniment, focuses its rescue efforts on channels of illegal trade, then tries to establish populations in captivity. Although Cuc Phuong's habitat would seem to be the perfect place to see Vietnam's wildlife in full splendor, mammal- and bird-watching are sadly not particularly successful pastimes in the park. Despite Cuc Phuong's status as a protected preserve, the primary forest habitat has been heavily denuded during the past few decades, and officials believe the park's wildlife numbers are dwindling due to increased hunting and high tourism pressures, which have led to the creation of in-park facilities, hiking trails, and paved roads.

Despite the misfortunes of northern Vietnam's animals, Cuc Phuong is quite beautiful. In April it's particularly lovely, with swarms of butterflies. Dozens of miles of trails lead to such highlights as cascading Giao Thuy waterfall, a 1,000-year-old tree, and Con Moong Cave—the "cave of early man"—where evidence of prehistoric humans has been discovered. Longer hikes lead to some Muong villages. Many trails are well marked, but exploring this thick forest would be foolish without a guide. Be sure to bring lots of mosquito repellent, especially if you plan to stay the night. ☎ *0229/384–8006 park headquarters* 🌐 *www.cucphuongtourism.com* 🎫 *40,000d.*

WHERE TO EAT AND STAY

You can overnight in one of three areas in the park: the park headquarters, Mac Lake just 2 km beyond the main gates, or Bong, a tiny village 20 km (12 miles) into the park. If you plan on staying overnight, you may wish to consider going on a weekday, as Cuc Phuong's proximity to Hanoi makes it a favorite weekend retreat among Vietnamese student groups. Bong, secluded as it is, occasionally fills with a boisterous crowd of 100 to 200 students. Culinary refinement is not a feature of the national park, but visitors can fill up on adequate fare at the restaurants attached to the accommodations sites within the park.

$$ B&B/INN 🏨 **In Bong.** Two stand-alone bungalows, beside a large, algae-green pool, are equipped with en suite bathrooms, air-conditioning, and hot water. [$] *Rooms from: 170000d* ✉ *Bong* ☎ *0229/384–8006* 🌐 *www.cucphuongtourism.com* 🛏 *10 rooms* 💳 *No credit cards* 🍴 *No meals.*

$ B&B/INN 🏨 **Mac Lake.** The bungalows at Mac Lake are possibly the nicest in the park with good facilities including hot water and en suite bathrooms complementing the idyllic surroundings. **Pros:** beautiful location. **Cons:** things can get noisy on weekends when young Hanoians descend upon the area; no hot water in the stilt house. [$] *Rooms from: 570000d* ✉ *Cuc Phuong National Park* ☎ *0229/384–8088* 🌐 *www.cucphuongtourism.com* 🛏 *4 rooms* 💳 *No credit cards* 🍴 *No meals.*

$ B&B/INN 🏨 **Park headquarters.** Tour operators usually guide people to the facilities at park headquarters, which now has a wide range of rooms, from those within detached bungalows and basic accommodations in a large stilt house to deluxe rooms with amenities such as television, air-conditioning, and hot water. **Pros:** most luxurious accommodations within the national park. **Cons:** it's a tour group favorite, so is frequently busy. [$] *Rooms from: 148925d* ✉ *Cuc Phuong National Park, Ninh Binh* ☎ *0229/384–8006* 🌐 *www.cucphuongtourism.com* 🛏 *16 rooms* 🍴 *No meals.*

HAIPHONG

103 km (64 miles) east of Hanoi.

Vietnam's third-largest city, with a population of more than 1.8 million, has been a hub of industrial activity for the last century and one of the most significant seaports since the Tran dynasty's rule (1225–1400). Haiphong's reputation as a dingy industrial port is by no means justified. This is indeed the largest and busiest port in the north, and container trucks rumble through town on the way to Highway 5 and Hanoi. But the port itself is on the northern edge of the city and hugs the Cam River, away from the heart of the city. As you cross the Lac Long Bridge into the city center, you leave the dusty, industrial outskirts and slip into a quaint, clean downtown. Here huge banyan trees and blossoming magnolias line wide boulevards, and Vietnamese play badminton in the stately Central Square (Quang Truong). Walking through the city center feels like stepping into a time warp: portraits of revolutionary heroes, especially Ho Chi Minh, hang elegantly from the eaves of buildings; socialist realist propaganda posters announce the latest health-awareness campaign; and swarms of bicycles fill the streets.

Today you are most likely to use Haiphong as a transfer point to destinations like Cat Ba and Halong Bay. Here you can catch a cyclo to the port, and take the first boat out. If you have time, however, settle into an enjoyable two-day stay in Haiphong before moving farther afield. Some say it is what Hanoi was like not too long ago: a sleepy northern city with less traffic and less nightlife, but bursting with potential. It's very easy to navigate central Haiphong. Sidewalks on the main boulevards are wide, and the parks and gardens provide ample room to roam. If you've come to Haiphong by car and plan on a day of leisurely sightseeing, have the driver park at a hotel and then go for a long walk.

GETTING HERE AND AROUND

There are daily direct flights from Ho Chi Minh City and Danang to Haiphong. The airport is an easy 5-km (3-mile) journey from Haiphong. You probably won't need to take a taxi except to get from the airport or train station to your hotel, or to the ferry landing. Taxi companies have figured this out, and plenty wait outside the airport, train stations, and at the ferry landing.

Seeing downtown Haiphong by bike is almost idyllic and many of the city's hotels have their own supply of bikes, which can be rented for around 108,000d per day.

Haiphong cyclos are large enough for two Westerners, and you can find them just about anywhere you go. They're great during the calm of midday or later in the evening when the streets are empty; riding one in the hectic and slow evening rush hour is not advised. Rates are negotiable, but with some bargaining you can usually talk cyclo riders down to around 50,000d per hour.

Taxi Contact Mai Linh Taxi ☎ *0225/3829-8888.*

VISITOR INFORMATION

Haiphong Tourism Office ✉ *18 Minh Khai St.* ☎ *0225/382-2616* ⊕ *www. haiphongtourism.gov.vn.*

An Bien Park **5**

Du Hang Pagoda ..**7**

Haiphong
Cathedral
(Nha Ton Lon) **4**

Haiphong
Museum **2**

Haiphong Opera
House **3**

Navy Museum **1**

Nghe Temple **6**

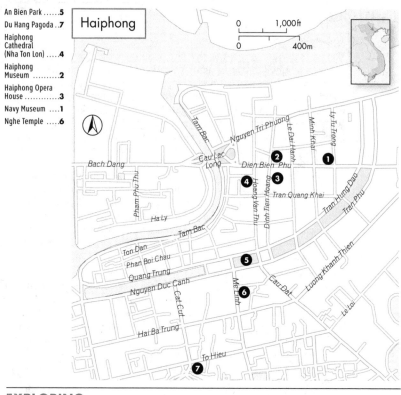

EXPLORING

TOP ATTRACTIONS

Du Hang Pagoda. Some beautiful pagodas stand in the southern and eastern districts of the city, and this is the most impressive and moving of all. The 300-year-old temple is a good example of traditional Vietnamese architecture, with a gate and three buildings surrounding a stone courtyard crowded with flowers, statues, and bonsai plants. In front and to the right of the compound is a round pond with lotus flowers encircled by white statues of the Buddha and scholars. One of the 10 monks who live here may be chanting his daily prayers and tapping on a round wooden drum in the richly gilded main sanctuary. Occasionally in the afternoons, the senior monk holds one-on-one healing sessions with the sick. Hundreds of Buddhists fill the courtyard on Buddhist holy days, the 1st and 15th of every lunar month. To get here follow Cat Cut Street south until you hit Chua Hang Street. After a few alleyways you'll see the pagoda set back on the left. ⌧ *Off Chua Hang St.* 🚆 *Free* ⊙ *Daily 7 am–10 pm.*

Haiphong Cathedral (*Nha Tho Lon, Queen of the Rosary Cathedral*). Haiphong's pagodas are tucked into the city's alleyways or off in the suburbs; no major religious structures except the city's main Catholic cathedral stand out in the middle of town. The cathedral was built in

1880 by missionaries from Spain; regular Masses are still held. ⊠ *46 Hoang Van Thu St.* 🎫 *Free.*

Haiphong Opera House (*Nha Hat Thanh Pho*). One of the most beautiful buildings in Haiphong, the Opera House, built by the French in 1907, has all the exterior designs of a classic, except for its coat of splendidly pink paint. Once the site of lavish French and Vietnamese productions, the 400-seat theater was taken over by the Vietminh following World War II. President Ho Chi Minh addressed the world's youth from the steps in June 1946, and a huge likeness of him, visible from hundreds of yards away, hangs above the wooden front doors, making this feel eerily like the focal point of the city. In a way it is; the Haiphong People's Committee now holds its major meetings and assemblies here. Stage productions and concerts do take place, but they're rare. If you're not attending a show, you need written permission from the authorities to step inside. ⊠ *Between Hoang Van Thu and Dinh Tien Hoang Sts.* ☎ *0225/3745–5763*

WORTH NOTING

FAMILY **An Bien Park.** Shady and green, this park is the site of early morning tai chi classes, while at night strolling couples compete with roller skaters, and locals sit at sidewalk stalls drinking fruit shakes and eating sweets. Near the southwestern edge stands a massive statue of local heroine Le Chan, and there's a colorful daily **Flower Market.** Kids enjoy the playground and amusement rides in the attached **Children's Park.** ⊠ *Tran Phu and Tran Hung Dao Sts.*

Haiphong Museum (*Bao Tang Thanh Pho Hai Phong*). In the heart of the city, a huge shuttered French villa with creaky wooden staircases, musty corners, and occasionally rotating ceiling fans houses this museum—an underrated gem of a building that rivals the Opera House in "pinkness." Although it attempts to cover all of the history, geography, archaeology, agriculture, and wildlife of the region (the stuffed owl with a rodent in its claws is rather macabre), the museum's main focus is on Vietnam's struggle for independence from various forces. Little is in English, so bring a good guide or be prepared to do some guesswork. ⊠ *66 Dien Bien Phu St.* 🎫 *5,000d* ⊙ *Weekdays 8–12:30, 2–4; also 7:30–9:30 Wed. and Sun.*

Navy Museum. As might be expected of a city whose name means "sea defense," much of Haiphong's more intriguing history is documented in the Navy Museum. Here you can see the Bach Dang stakes—the sharp wooden poles driven into the riverbed that impaled Kublai Khan's boats in 1288. A room dedicated to the Vietnam War houses a (presumably deactivated) MK-52 mine pulled from the waters of Haiphong Harbor in 1973, the lighthouse lantern that warned of impending bombing raids, and the anti-aircraft gun that brought down a dozen American planes. ⊠ *38 Dien Bien Phu St.* 🎫 *Free* ⊙ *Tues., Thurs., and Sat. 8 am–11 am.*

Nghe Temple (*Den Nghe*). This temple is dedicated to Le Chan, a heroic peasant woman who helped organize the popular revolt against the Chinese that was led by the two Trung sisters in AD 40. Later Le Chan helped lay the foundation for the city of Haiphong. Ceramic reliefs at the top of the front wall depict the Trung sisters in royal carriages. Two huge red-and-gold wooden carriages (built in 1916), similar to those used by the Trung sisters and by royalty, are on display. Ancestral altars and chapels are to the right, through the courtyard. ✉ *Corner of Me Linh and Le Chan Sts.* 🎟 *Free* ⏲ *Daily 7–11:30, 1–10.*

WHERE TO EAT

For a city of 1.8 million people, Haiphong doesn't have many upscale restaurants. That said, the once sleepy port has been sharpening up its culinary act in recent times and a range of alternative options spanning everything from Indian to Pan-Asian fusion cuisine now bolsters the city's indigenous restaurants. Local seafood is excellent and cheap, however, and available at any number of small, nondescript, family-run establishments. Just follow the crowds and remember the adage that "busier is better." Restaurants specializing in fish cluster around the north end of Rau Bridge (Cau Rau), a few miles from the city center on the road south to the nearby beach town of Do Son.

$$ VIETNAMESE

🍴 **Big Man.** In a town not noted as a culinary hotspot, this popular venue offers decent enough options, but it's really less about the food here than the convivial atmosphere, fueled by the house-brewed German-type beers. The light pilsner is popular with the local crowd, but the pick of the drops in the view of many is the velvety dark beer. While the beer is probably the star attraction here, the kitchen does a satisfactory job in supplying ballast to soak up all the alcohol. Adventurous eaters might want to try out the multitude of "interesting"-sounding dishes featuring obscure wildlife. More sensible souls will probably stick to the ocean-fresh seafood and Vietnamese rice and vegetable dishes. [$] *Average main: 100000d* ✉ *7 Tran Hung Dao St.* ☎ *0225/381–0257* 💳 *No credit cards.*

$$$ INDIAN Fodor's Choice ★

🍴 **Indian Kitchen.** Vietnam may not be as well endowed with Indian restaurants as near-neighbor Thailand, but the handful of eateries specializing in spicy cuisine from the subcontinent do a sterling job. This little venue doesn't let the side down. From the ornate Sanskrit-style lettering on the door to a menu balanced well between meat and vegetarian options, the restaurant is as authentic as they come. Curries are fiery, but not overpowering, grilled meats are juicy and smoky, and the breads are crisp and moist. [$] *Average main: 160000d* ✉ *22 Minh Khai St.* ☎ *0225/384–2558.*

$$$ STEAKHOUSE Fodor's Choice ★

🍴 **Phono Box.** While Hanoi and Ho Chi Minh City are increasingly replete with bohemian bistros, it is rare to find such a venue in provincial cities such as Haiphong. That's why Phono Box, with its imaginative menu and laid-back jazz soundtrack, stands out. The food here may not reinvent the wheel, but set menus that encompass everything from juicy steaks to fresh, imaginative salads are a world away from the standard Vietnamese fare available elsewhere in the city. The owners here are self-styled bon vivants and the extensive wine list and impressive collection of vinyl records reflect their tastes. [$] *Average main: 250000d* ✉ *79 Dien Bien Phu St.* ☎ *090/435–7212.*

Haiphong History

EARLY HISTORY

With its old-time aura, Haiphong feels very Vietnamese compared to the country's other big conurbations, and appropriately so, because the port city has played a key role in the nation's tumultuous history. Because of its strategic coastal location, it has witnessed the coming and going of many foreign invaders. The Bach Dang River, on the outskirts of the city, was the site of one of Vietnam's greatest victories against its old foe China when, in 1288, Kublai Khan's 300,000-man army and navy were soundly trumped by the Vietnamese, under the command of Tran Hung Dao.

20TH-CENTURY CONFLICTS

Six centuries later, the French settled into Haiphong and began turning it into a major industrial and shipping center. Later, following the German occupation of France during World War II, the Japanese muscled in, and began redirecting valuable Vietnamese exports to Japan. Once again in control of the port city after the war, the French bombed Haiphong over a bizarre customs dispute, killing up to 1,000 Vietnamese civilians and precipitating the eight-year war between the Vietminh and the French.

Haiphong figured prominently in the war against the Americans as well and, because of its strategic location on the northeast coast, the city was frequently bombed during the conflict. President Richard Nixon ordered the mining of Haiphong Harbor in May 1972, and during the holiday season that same year, the city suffered particularly devastating attacks, which became known as the Christmas bombings. The following year, as part of the agreement between the U.S. government and Vietnam in the Paris peace talks of 1973, the U.S. Navy was asked to help clear the mines.

CHINESE EXODUS

In 1979, following conflicts between Vietnam and China, as many as 100,000 ethnic Chinese, who had lived for generations in the Haiphong area, piled into barely seaworthy boats and fled from what they expected to be deadly reprisals by their Vietnamese neighbors. In fact, few acts of retribution took place, but the damage had been done. And because the departing Chinese represented a large section of the city's merchant class, Haiphong has struggled to gain back the economic power lost as a result of their departure.

Its history may be littered with contentious incidents, but there's little sign of disharmony in modern Haiphong, and the most prominent remnant of foreign interlopers is the graceful French architecture that's sprinkled throughout the city center.

6

$$ \times **Texas BBQ.** If it's hearty Western comfort food you are after, there is
AMERICAN no better place in Haiphong. The focus here, unsurprisingly, is on calorific and cholesterol-heavy Tex-Mex food. All the staples you would expect, such as chicken wings, tacos, ribs, and nachos, are present and correct. To please everyone, a few European favorites like fish-and-chips and some Vietnamese dishes are also featured on the extensive menu. ⓢ *Average main: 100000d* ⊠ *22H Minh Khai St.* ☎ *0225/382–2689.*

WHERE TO STAY

Although its hotel portfolio cannot compare to that of Hanoi or Ho Chi Minh City, Haiphong has a pretty handy selection of accommodations nowadays. Family-run hotels rub shoulders with a smattering of international brands as well as some more unique boutique-style options, meaning that there is variety across the price spectrum. If you're shopping around for hotels in person, ask to see the room before you hand over your cash. Room standards are generally pretty decent, but you may find that some have a better view or amenities than others in the same price bracket. Also keep in mind that almost none of the rates are written in stone—meaning you may be able to make a deal.

$$$$ HOTEL Fodor's Choice ★ 🏨 **AVANI Haiphong Harbour View Hotel.** With its French colonial architecture and smart, well-appointed rooms, this hotel is Haiphong's one-and-only luxury lodging choice. **Pros:** beautiful architecture and smart rooms contribute to overall salubrious atmosphere. **Cons:** not much in the way of harbor views. [$] *Rooms from: 5403850d* ✉ *4 Tran Phu St.* ☎ *0225/382–7827/8* 🌐 *www.avanihotels.com* 🛏 *127 rooms* 🍴 *Breakfast.*

$$$ HOTEL 🏨 **Lac Long Hotel.** Some lapses in style aside, this centrally located hotel is a very solid option—in the heart of Haiphong, within easy walking distance of the city's main attractions, and not far from the ferry for Cat Ba Island. **Pros:** there's a greal feeling of space in the giant rooms. **Cons:** garish interior design may not be to everybody's taste [$] *Rooms from: 1090000d* ✉ *83 Bach Dang St.* ☎ *0225/382–0777* 🌐 *www.laclonghotel.vn* 🛏 *28 rooms, 2 suites* 🍴 *Breakfast.*

$$$$ HOTEL Fodor's Choice ★ 🏨 **Nam Cuong Hotel.** With clean and spacious rooms, a rooftop restaurant and pool, and a glorious light-filled atrium stretching the entire length of the building, this is clearly the best locally run hotel in Haiphong. **Pros:** thoughtful trimmings add to overall feeling of luxury. **Cons:** gym in need of an upgrade. [$] *Rooms from: 1800000d* ✉ *47 Lach Tray St.* ☎ *0225/382–8555, 0225/382–8222* 🌐 *namcuonghaiphonghotel.com.vn* 🛏 *74 rooms, 2 suites* 🍴 *Breakfast.*

$$$ HOTEL 🏨 **Seastars Hotel.** This imposing new hotel is an archetypal Vietnamese business hotel, and though aesthetes won't go for the garish decoration throughout, it's convenient for exploring and has some good amenities. **Pros:** great rooftop bar. **Cons:** highway outside can mean noisy traffic intrusion. [$] *Rooms from: 1500000d* ✉ *1/3A Le Hong Phong St., Ngo Quyen, Haiphong* ☎ *0225/355–6998* 🌐 *www.seastarshotel.vn* 🛏 *90 rooms* 🍴 *Breakfast.*

$$$$ RESORT Fodor's Choice ★ 🏨 **Song Gia Resort.** In the same complex as the Korean-owned Song Gia Golf and Country Club, this plush new property, 13 km (8 miles) outside Haiphong, is ideal for golfers and those looking to get away from it all. **Pros:** a luxurious haven for golfers. **Cons:** not the place to come if you want to learn more about Vietnam. [$] *Rooms from: 3940685d* ✉ *Luu Kiem St.* ☎ *0225/363–3333* 🌐 *www.songgia.com* 🛏 *60 rooms* 🍴 *Breakfast.*

NIGHTLIFE

It may never be regarded as a party town, but Haiphong has some more than adequate options for letting your hair down. A smattering of smart café-bars caters to an upwardly mobile, youthful market, with regular live music adding to the conviviality. For a more local experience, Haiphong is blessed with numerous bia hoi venues, where gallons of low-price, pilsner-style beer are consumed on a nightly basis. Also fun (if only the once) are the city's nightclubs and karaoke venues, where pumping house music and enthusiastic crooning are the order of the day.

Haiphong Club. This dark club hosts live music—predominantly of the rock variety, but genres such as classical and flamenco get a look in, too. ⊠ *17 Tran Quang Khai St.* ☎ *0225/382–2603* ⊕ *haiphongclub.com.vn.*

Julie's Bar. The favored hangout spot for Haiphong's expat contingent, Julie's is a lively and convivial place for a few drinks. Drinks are slightly more expensive than in some of the more local venues, but a lively selection of music and a friendly crowd make this one of the best evening options in the city. ⊠ *22C Minh Khai St.* ☎ *098/906–2990.*

Maxim's Bar. A café by day and a bar by night, this venue has live pop and rock music from 9 pm each evening. ⊠ *51B Dien Bien Phu St.* ☎ *0225/382–2934.*

Fodor's Choice ★ **Saigon Café.** This is Haiphong's version of the corner pub, and it's popular with locals, expats, and travelers alike. ⊠ *107 Dien Bien Phu St.* ☎ *0225/382–2195.*

HALONG BAY AND AROUND

A visit to the north is not complete without a trip to Halong Bay, where placid waters give way to more than 3,000 limestone karsts and wind-sculpted limestone formations that jut from foggy lagoons. Dotting the bay are tiny islands bordered by white sandy coves and hidden caves, adding to the majestic landscape of this UNESCO World Heritage Site. Adding to this naturalist's dream is the biodiversity of islets, grottos, and Cat Ba Island National Park. The bay, however, shows tourism's impact: the clearing of mangrove forests to make way for jetties and piers, marine life threatened by game fishing, and garbage from passenger boats and fishing villages washed up on the shores.

Beyond its geological uniqueness are activities like hiking, kayaking, rock climbing, or exploring one of the many floating villages where fishermen bring in their daily catch. The downside to all this allure is the large number of unlicensed boats it draws to the bay each day.

Boat trips out onto the bay are the main tourism stock in trade farther north, but a more multifaceted side of the area can be experienced at Cat Ba Island. The largest island in Halong Bay, Cat Ba is very much its own entity. Its national park offers incredible biodiversity, with more than a thousand species of plants having been recorded here. Animal life is slightly thinner on the ground, but alert visitors may spy inhabitants such as the endangered golden-headed langur, wild boar, deer, civets,

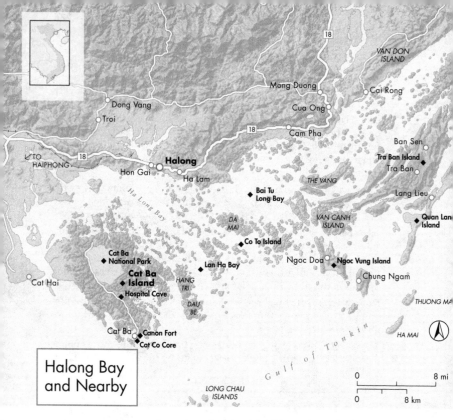

Halong Bay and Nearby

and several species of squirrel. Trekking through the wilderness is a highlight with a number of fascinating trails to follow.

Cat Ba Island has also become a firm favorite with the adventure sports set. Indeed, along with Railay Beach in Thailand, it is recognized as one of the top spots in the region for rock climbing. Other outdoor pursuits include sailing and kayaking around the karsts. Although Halong Bay has arguably been tainted by over-exposure, Bai Tu Long Bay farther east toward China, retains all the majesty of Vietnam's premier bucket-list natural attraction but sees a fraction of the traffic of its immediate neighbor to the west. Here, visitors will find islands of substantial size with deserted beaches and untamed jungle.

HALONG BAY

55 km (34 miles) northeast of Haiphong, 175 km (109 miles) east of Hanoi.

Fodor's Choice ★ Halong Bay's 3,000 islands of dolomite and limestone cover a 1,500-square-km (580-square-mile) area, extending across the Gulf of Tonkin nearly to the Chinese border. According to legend, this breathtaking land- and seascape was formed by a giant dragon that came barreling out of the mountains toward the ocean—hence the name

(Halong translates into "descent of the dragon"). Geologists are more likely to attribute the formations to sedimentary limestone that formed here between 300 and 500 million years ago, in the Paleozoic Era. Over millions of years water receded and exposed the limestone to wind, rain, and tidal erosion.

Today the limestone formations are exposed to hordes of tourists—but don't let that discourage you. Hundreds of fishing trawlers and tour boats share space on these crystal waters, yet there seems to be room for everyone. Most people use the main population center, **Halong City,** as a base from which to venture into the bay. Although it's now officially one municipality, Halong City was, until 1996, two separate towns: Bai Chay is now Halong City West, where Halong Road winds its way around the coast and past the lifeless central beach; Hon Gai is the grimier Halong City East, where a coal transportation depot dominates the center of town and covers nearby roads and buildings with a sooty film. Locals still refer to the towns by their old names, but they are now inexorably lassoed together by a bridge. Boat trips through Halong Bay are the main attraction. Little of the majesty of this region can be found in the city, so head out onto the water and start exploring. Countless 10- and 30-foot fishing boats have been converted into Halong Bay's formidable tourist-boat fleet. Hotels or travel agencies in Halong City or Hanoi can arrange boat trips for you (often they are part of organized tours from Hanoi). It is still possible to go down to the wharf and bargain yourself onto a boat for the day, but you are likely to be charged (sometimes significantly) more than you would pay for a prebooked tour, so this is not advised. Self-sufficient travelers have fallen victim to the old bait-and-switch: they've arranged a next-day boat tour with local fishermen, only to be told in no uncertain terms the following morning that they could not board their chosen boat, but they could take a different one for quite a bit more money. You may have no choice in the end. Usually travel agencies, however, have their tried-and-true favorites.

GETTING HERE AND AROUND

The most common way to reach Halong Bay is by taking a four-hour shuttle bus from Hanoi's Old Quarter. However, it is possible to reach Halong Bay directly from Hanoi's main airport by hiring a private transfer. Since most boats depart from the dock at noon, only passengers with early arrival times into Hanoi Airport should pursue this method. All shuttles to Halong Bay depart from Hanoi at around 8 am. They stop midway at art galleries that double as rest stops, where restrooms, shops, and restaurants are available. Passengers are finally dropped off at Halong City's bustling port between 11:30 and 12:30 daily.

AIR TRAVEL There are now two ways to fly directly from Hanoi to Halong Bay. The most exciting—and accessible—way of transferring is via a new seaplane service launched last year by Hai Au Aviation. Travelers are flown from Hanoi's Noi Bai Airport to Tuan Chau Marina in Halong City in a Cessna Grand Caravan seaplane. The flight takes just 30 minutes and costs $280 per person for a one-way flight. Round-trip tickets cost $500 per person; it's also possible to tag on an extra 15-minute scenic tour over Halong Bay for an additional $110. Another way of flying direct is by private helicopter between Hanoi's Gia Lam Airport and Halong's heliport on General Giap Hill. Round-trip tickets cost between $1,260 and $7,689 per person, depending on the number of passengers and the category of helicopter that is chartered. Cat Bi Airport in Haiphong has daily flights to and from Ho Chi Minh City and one per day to and from Danang. By 2015, this domestic airport is slated to expand and receive international flights.

Air Travel Contacts Hai Au Aviation ✉ *70–72 Ba Trieu St., Hoan Kiem District, Hanoi* ☎ *024/3926–3148* ⊕ *www.seaplanes.vn.* **Luxury Travel Vietnam** ✉ *Halong Bay* ☎ *024/3927–4120* ⊕ *www.luxurytravelvietnam.com.* **Northern Airport Flight Service Company** ✉ *Gia Lam Airport, 173 Pho Truong Chinh St., Hanoi* ☎ *024/3827–4409.*

BOAT TRAVEL Take your pick from more than 500 boat operators that cruise Halong Bay. Standards vary from cheap "get 'em in, get 'em out" passenger boats to high-end luxury vessels that aim to make relaxing your main priority. Package tours usually include round-trip transportation from Hanoi, with bay excursions like kayaking, cave tours, and island expeditions. Overnight trips include the above, plus meals, a private cabin, a visit to floating villages, and a day at Cat Ba Island (two-night tours only). If you are paying less than 2,158,000d for a two-night, three-day trip, then expect some dodgy services. *For package tours, see Exploring.*

Day trips to Halong Bay are extremely rushed and should only be booked if time is limited. Ranging from about 648,000d for budget tours to about 1,726,000d for higher-end ones, these day trips are rather exhausting considering the four-hour drive from Hanoi. For those short on time and money, it's possible to take a ferry from Halong City to Cat Ba Island for 130,000d. This will give you a glimpse of the landscape and an afternoon on the island before returning to Haiphong City by hydrofoil.

Boat Travel Contact Au Lac Quang Ninh Company ✉ *Tuan Chau Ward, Halong City* ☎ *0203/247–3668* ⊕ *www.tuanchau-halong.com.vn.*

BUS TRAVEL Buses depart for Halong Bay from Hanoi's Gia Lam Bus Station. The four-hour ride costs 91,000d. Most boat tours include shuttle service to/from Halong Bay with an 8 am pickup at your hotel and noon drop-off at Halong City port. A number of public shuttles depart from Hanoi's Old Quarter, offering round-trip transportation for about 216,000d.

CAR TRAVEL Like elsewhere in Vietnam, although the law is changing and international driving permits will be accepted, the details are still under discussion, and certain restrictions may be applied to foreign drivers. Check the situation before considering renting a vehicle. Hiring a private car or taxi should cost about 1,200,000d—1,500,000d from Hanoi to Halong Bay (four hours). Round-trip shuttle service is generally included for overnight cruise passengers, or it might be tacked on for an added fee.

Car Travel Contact Vietnam Transfer Service ✉ *Ha Thanh Plaza, Thai Thinh St., Suite 801, Dong Da District, Hanoi* ☎ *046/286–1019* ⊕ *www. vietnamtransferservice.com.*

Halong Bay Safety Tips

When visiting Halong Bay, make sure your operator follows safety regulations (including life jackets) and provides experienced guides and admission to designated sites. It wasn't until 2013 that safety regulations were somewhat enforced on Halong Bay. You get what you pay for, so choose your cruise operator wisely, including opting for higher-end operators that have stringent safety standards and that insist passengers wear life jackets during bay activities. Incidentally, the increased number of boats on the water led to a rise in boat collisions and in late 2012, the government issued a ruling that all Halong boats were to be painted white in an effort to decrease the number of accidents. Another thing to keep in mind is that most land-based activities require some level of fitness. Access to caves and coves have slippery stone steps devoid of guardrails. Wear suitable footwear when exploring the area, especially on island trails that are narrow and somewhat arduous.

TAXI TRAVEL A taxi from Cat Bi International Airport in Haiphong to Halong Bay takes 2½ hours and costs about 863,000d. A metered taxi from Hanoi to Halong Bay will cost at least 2,159,000d.

TRAIN TRAVEL Several daily trains run from Hanoi to Haiphong. The two- to three-hour train ride costs 90,000d–135,000d. From the Haiphong Ferry Terminal, passengers can catch a hydrofoil to Cat Ba Island.

EXPLORING

So much to sail, so little time . . . Halong Bay is a destination not to be rushed; you need several days to do it justice. Day cruises will only whet your appetite, and an overnight trip will simply get you in the zone moments before it's over. If your schedule allows, opt for a two-night, three-day trip to properly explore the waters. Halong's "must sees" include a visit to a floating village, kayaking, caving, and a day at Cat Ba Island. The eons of erosion have left countless nooks and crannies to explore: secluded half-moon beaches lie at the base of steep untouched forest canopies, and grottoes of all shapes and sizes—some well tramped, others virtually unknown—are open jaws of stalactites and stalagmites. One of the largest and most visited is the **Grotto of the Wooden Stakes** (Hang Dau Go), claimed to be the 13th-century storage spot for the stakes that General Tran Hung Dao planted in the Bach Dang River in order to repel the invasion of Kublai Khan. This cavernous grotto has three distinct chambers and is reached by climbing 90 steps. Another quite popular destination in the bay is the **Grotto of Bewilderment** (Sung Sot), a stalagmite cave, estimated to be 1 million years old, with 29 chambers inside.

The best way to hit all destinations is through a reputable tour company.

Fodor's Choice **Heritage Line.** This company operates two cruise boats on Halong Bay. ★ The most luxurious of the two is the 12-passenger *Violet,* which parades the waters in royal Indochine-style by combining classical French design with Vietnamese allure. It offers tours from one to three nights, and destinations include Tien Ong Cave, the Cua Van fishing village, and Ti Top Island. Each of its six suites has a private balcony, Jacuzzi tub, hardwood floors, ornate furnishings, and a flat-screen TV. Set menus and à la carte cuisine are included in the rate, and there's also a gym, sauna, library, sundeck, and spa on board.

The 30-passenger *Sunset* also offers a one-day excursion, subject to availability (check in advance), which explores the southern part of Halong Bay to Cat Ba Island. A restaurant on board serves brunch shortly after passengers embark. The highlight of the voyage is Cat Ba Island, where passengers can explore small coves, fishing villages, mangrove forests, limestone cliffs, and the main town.

Both vessels offer tai chi, cooking workshops, and spa treatments as part of the on-board activities. ✉ *22 Slot C, Cai Dam, Garden Villa, Bai Chay, Halong Bay* ☎ *0203/351–2446* ⊕ *www.heritage-line.com.*

WHERE TO EAT

Halong City, the launching point for Halong Bay, is not the place to come for fine cuisine, or any cuisine for that matter. In fact, you're better off suppressing your appetite until you dine aboard ship. However, there's a string of mediocre restaurants on Ha Long Road, just west from Vuon Dao Road. If you want to try something local, tu hai is a shellfish specialty from Van Don Island. Other Halong dishes include dried shrimp, steamed cuttlefish, sea snails, and gat gu (steamed pancake made from rice flour).

$$
SEAFOOD

✕ **BMC Hai Au Restaurant.** Halong City is no gourmet destination, but this place, opposite Bai Chay tourist port, is one of the best of the city's options for fresh seafood. As is commonplace at such venues across Vietnam, morsels from the ocean are grilled, fried, or steamed according to your taste. Big spenders go for the lobster, but you may be just as happy with shimmeringly fresh squid, scallops, and snapper. A lively atmosphere and friendly wait staff add to the conviviality. $ *Average main: 80000d* ✉ *Group 4, Block 5 Bai Chay* ☎ *0203/384–5065.*

$$$
VIETNAMESE

✕ **Co Ngu Restaurant.** Catering toward tour groups, this gaudy restaurant resembles an imperial palace and has lovely views over Halong Bay. The menu features fresh seafood and local specialties like *Tu Hai*, a shellfish unique to the region; it's famous for its shark fin soup. Other exotic (and daring) dishes include jellyfish salad, steamed pork, seafood tofu, and sautéed sea cucumber. Options from the Western menu range from grilled salmon and cheeseburgers to spaghetti marinara and BLTs. The staff speaks very little English, but the menu has handy pictures of the food meaning that ordering is easy enough with a little perseverance. Although this is one of the better restaurants in Halong City, it pales in comparison to what you might find elsewhere in Vietnam. $ *Average main: 159000d* ✉ *Block C2, Luxury Villa Zone, Halong Rd., Bai Chay* ☎ *0203/351–1363* ⊕ *www.halongcongu.com.*

WHERE TO STAY

Most visitors who choose to overnight here do so in Halong City West. The larger hotels, some of which are listed below, are slightly less tacky than the average downtown minihotel, and many offer a 50% discount in the steamy summer months.

$$$$ HOTEL **Halong Plaza Hotel.** A glass-fronted entryway looks out onto the bay from the spacious front lobby at this modern luxury hotel close to the ferry landing. **Pros:** tremendous views of Halong Bay. **Cons:** fittings and interiors need some TLC. [$] *Rooms from: 1533000d* ✉ *8 Halong Rd.* ☎ *0203/384–5810* 🌐 *www.halongplaza.com* 🛏 *187 rooms, 13 suites* 🍴 *Breakfast.*

$$$ HOTEL **Heritage Halong.** Fronting a nondescript stretch of beach, this eight-story international hotel soaks up much of the local package-tour business, but don't be put off—it's a decent option with a range of amenities and great views from the upper floors. **Pros:** leisure facilities are a major bonus. **Cons:** tour group favorite; has a rather tired feel. [$] *Rooms from: 1200000d* ✉ *88 Halong Rd.* ☎ *0203/384–6888* 🌐 *heritagehalonghotel.com.vn* 🛏 *101 rooms* 🍴 *Breakfast.*

$$$$ HOTEL Fodor's Choice ★ **Novotel Halong Bay.** Still the only international hotel brand in Halong City, the Novotel does a sterling, if unflashy, job, and as it's on Bai Chay Beach, it offers a stunning outlook over Halong Bay from many of its guest rooms, most of which come with a balcony. **Pros:** balconies make ideal alfresco vantage points to enjoy the stunning sea views. **Cons:** interiors could use a refresh. [$] *Rooms from: 2874825d* ✉ *160 Halong Rd.* ☎ *033/384–8108* 🌐 *www.novotelhalong.com.vn* 🛏 *225 rooms* 🍴 *Breakfast.*

NIGHTLIFE

Halong City has a surprisingly active nightlife, but it is not what you would call sophisticated. Rather questionable-looking karaoke bars are popular with locals and visiting Chinese, Korean, and Japanese, and loud nightspots for the younger demographic. Also popular are the city's legion of *bia hoi* venues where cheap beer and food keep the spirits high.

Queen VOSA. This bar/club has something of a split personality. The lower levels are relatively subdued with classical music performances held on a regular basis. The higher up you go the rowdier it gets, and the fifth floor resounds to the familiar strains of throbbing dance beats. ✉ *70 Le Thanh Ton* ☎ *0203/382–6193.*

Top Disco. One of Halong City's most popular nightspots, this is the place to go to dance into the night to thumping house and techno tunes. Occasional live music reveals a more sophisticated side to the venue. ✉ *Halong Rd., Bai Chay* ☎ *0203/384–6000.*

SPORTS AND THE OUTDOORS

The most popular sporting activity in Halong City—aside from playing or watching football—is kayaking on Halong Bay. Most of the better hotels can organize an itinerary for you. Alternatively, the best approach is to book a specialized tour from one of the respected tour operators, such as The Sinh Tourist, in Hanoi.

The Sinh Tourist. This long-established tour operator can arrange dedicated one-day kayaking tours of Halong Bay. The tours leave from Hanoi early in the morning, but if you are staying in Halong City you can join a group at around midday. Itineraries take guests out to islets and caves within easy striking distance of Halong City. The tour includes a seafood lunch. ✉ *52 Luong Ngoc Quyen St., Hanoi* ☎ *024/3926–1568* 🌐 *www.thesinhtourist.vn* 🎫 *From 854,000d.*

CAT BA ISLAND

At the southern end of Halong Bay, 30 km (19 miles) east of Haiphong by boat.

Fodor's Choice ★ One of Halong Bay's most remarkable formations is Cat Ba Island, 420 square km (162 square miles) of wildly steep spines of mountains, narrow valleys and waterfalls, lush wetlands, golden beaches, and one of Vietnam's most beautiful national parks, which protects about two-thirds of the island. The sea life in much of the surrounding inshore waters is also protected. Included in these ecosystems are tropical evergreen forests, 15 kinds of mammals (including wild boars and hedgehogs), 200 species of fish, 21 species of birds, and 640 species of plants. Don't expect to see many wild mammals, however, such as the endangered langur monkeys that supposedly swing from the trees.

In 1938 a French archaeologist found traces of an ancient fishing culture on the island dating from the end of the Neolithic Era. Human bones alleged to be 6,000 years old were also found. More recently, during the Vietnam War, American bombers targeted the military and naval station here, causing numerous casualties and forcing hospitals to set up in nearby caves on the island to avoid the bombings. An ethnic Chinese community numbering about 10,000 settled on Cat Ba over the years, only to leave en masse in 1979 after Chinese troops invaded Vietnam in the brief but bloody border war of that year. The ethnic Chinese, or Hoa, sailed in dinghies to Hong Kong and other Asian ports, many dying along the way. Few ethnic Chinese have returned to Cat Ba.

Today the population of more than 20,000 continues to subsist on fishing and rice and fruit cultivation, but tourism is quickly becoming Cat Ba's primary cash crop. The beaches, particularly the lovely curved stretch of sand just over the hillside from the southeast corner of the wharf, are infinitely nicer than most of the others in Northern Vietnam. Walk off your seafood dinner by heading to the nearest beach, where you can sip iced coffee and watch the shooting stars. Splendid caves, just off the road to the national park, are great for exploring. Hiking through Cat Ba can be strenuous: the mountain ridges are steep, trails are poorly marked, and roads are narrow, making blind crests somewhat dangerous. Talk to your hotel manager or one of the many local tour operators about the best hiking trails for your level. A hike through the park—through the tropical forest to a rocky peak overlooking much of the island—is best undertaken with a guide. The park is also a favorite spot for Vietnamese tourists, many of whom seem to be able to scale the slippery rocks in stiletto heels.

GETTING HERE AND AROUND

Unless you're a guest of the Vietnamese military, the only way on and off Cat Ba Island is by boat or hydrofoil. There is a ferry service from Halong City to Cat Ba, but the more common route is from Haiphong. Several companies operate the route between Haiphong's Binh Station (Ben Binh) and Cat Ba town and departure times are liberally scattered throughout the day meaning that missing a crossing needn't be a disaster. Note, however, that services are reduced significantly during the off-season winter months. Fares vary according to each company, the most reputable of whom include Hadeco, Hoang Long, and Mekong Hoang Yen, but range from 110,000d to 240,000d. Crossing times vary from one to two hours depending on the speed and condition of the vessel. Hadeco also offers bus-boat package from Halong City, costing around 300,000d one way; buy tickets from their office in Halong City's Luong Yen Bus Station.

Just about any of the hotels can arrange for car or minibus tours of the island and rides to the national park. You can also get to the park on your own (rent a motorbike, or take a motorbike taxi) and hire a guide there. But it's much easier to go along on one of the tours, where the park and guide fees are prepaid and a hike is mapped out. Tour packages usually include minibus transportation to the national park, where a guide leads a hike through it, down to Viet Hai village, and over to a bay where a boat is waiting to bring you back to town. This runs about $217,000 per person, with lunch included. Or you can head down to the wharf and arrange for a boat yourself—just make sure they know what you're asking and you know what they're offering. Rates are negotiable, so be sure to bargain.

Boat Contacts Hadeco Speed Boat ☒ *Ben Binh Pier, Haiphong* ☏ *0225/382–2333* ⊕ *www.hadeco.vn.* **Hydrofoil Transfers** ☒ *Ben Binh Pier, Haiphong.*

EXPLORING

Cannon Fort. A French-era fort that was also used during the defense of Haiphong during the war with the United States, this hilltop landmark is also notable for offering some of the best views on Cat Ba Island. A motorbike taxi can take you most of the way up the hill from Cat Ba Town. From there it is a steep 20-minute walk to the top. The effort is worth it for a sweeping vista that captures the karst-studded landscape in all its glory. ☒ *Cat Ba Town* 🎫 *50,000d* 🕐 *Daily 7–7.*

Fodor'sChoice
★ **Cat Ba National Park.** Covering about 263 square km (164 square miles) of Cat Ba Island, this national park is home to 32 species of mammals, including the endangered langur monkey, which live among the jungle terrain and freshwater lakes. Within its tropical rain forest are 78 species of birds and 20 species of reptiles. In addition to impressive beaches and mangroves, within its boundaries are two historical caves once used as clinics during the Vietnam War. Active travelers can tackle the reserve by hiking the demanding (yet rewarding) 18-km (11-mile) Cang Viet Hai Trail across the park. For a striking vista of the surrounding scenery, the view from the park's observation tower is hard to beat. Be warned, though, the climb up metal ladders and cliffs is not for the faint of heart. The park is about 30 minutes from Cat Ba Town. ☒ *Trung Trang, Cat Ba Island, Halong Bay* ☏ *0225/3121–6350* 🎫 *30,000d.*

Fishing Villages. Many overnight boat tours will take you to see one or more of the four floating villages on Halong Bay, where 1,600 locals make a living by fishing the mystical waters. If they're not fishing or fixing their nets for the next big catch, they may be passing the time swinging on hammocks—or even rowing toward your cruise boat to sell you groceries and souvenirs in a floating "store." These impressive fishing villages have their own schools, wooden shacks, and grocery stores that stay afloat by Styrofoam platforms wrapped in waterproof tarps. ✉ *Halong Bay*.

Fodor's Choice
★
Hospital Cave. One of the most intriguing sights on Cat Ba Island, Hospital Cave served as a bomb-proof medical facility during the American War. It also provided well-hidden refuge for Viet Cong leaders and fighters during the conflict. Like Cu Chi Tunnels in the south and Vinh Moc Tunnels near Dong Ha, Hospital Cave is a prime example of the Communists' engineering ingenuity. Built between 1963 and 1965, the three-story facility is a labyrinth of dim chambers. Guides operate from outside the cave, which is around 10 km (6 miles) north of Cat Ba Town, and will show you around the 17 rooms and point out notable features such as the old operating theater and a natural cavern that was used as a movie theater. ✉ *Cat Ba Town* 🎫 *20,000d* ⊙ *Daily 7–4*.

Fodor's Choice
★
Lan Ha Bay. Although it is technically and geologically an extension of Halong Bay, the 300 or so karst islands of Lan Ha Bay feel somewhat removed from tourist traffic. Lying south and east of Cat Ba Town, they are too distant for most of the tour boats that leave from Halong City to reach. Therefore visitors here, mostly on itineraries arranged in Cat Ba Town, can enjoy the sense of peace and isolation that Halong Bay has arguably lost. Sailing and kayaking are popular activities here. Lan Ha Bay also possesses several idyllic beaches such as Hai Pai Beach (also known as Tiger Beach), where it is possible to camp out for the night. ✉ *Cat Ba Town*.

BEACHES

Cat Co Cove. The island's beaches are among the best in North Vietnam and the three stretches of sand at Cat Co Cove are justifiably popular with Vietnamese tourists and other sun-worshippers. Of the three beaches, the one at Cat Co 2 is prettiest with limestone cliffs backing golden sand. Here, you will find Cat Ba Beach Resort, one of the island's more luxurious lodgings. The other two beaches are less crowded, but there tends to be more debris and trash in the water. Cat Co is an easy 15-minute walk from Cat Ba Town. **Amenities:** food and drink; parking; toilets. **Best for:** swimming; sunset. ✉ *Cat Ba Town*.

WHERE TO EAT

In recent years, Cat Ba Island has evolved into one of the top tourist destinations in Northern Vietnam. Unfortunately, that progress has not been reflected in its restaurant sector, which remains resolutely mediocre. Identikit menus that cover all the culinary bases are standard, so don't expect much in the way of gastronomic flair. For a more local experience, join the hordes of Vietnamese tourists and dine at one of the floating restaurants on the harbor. These garish neon-lighted venues tend to close and reopen under another name on a regular basis and specialize in fresh seafood.

$$
VIETNAMESE
✗ **Bamboo Café.** This is a decent Vietnamese all-rounder with an alluring seafront location. Most visitors to Cat Ba Town find that, with a couple of exceptions, most of the restaurants tread a very similar path. Certainly there's nothing particularly adventurous about this option with the menu encompassing such tried-and-true staples as crab spring rolls and seafood fried rice. Nevertheless, the bamboo-clad interior

gives the venue a certain rickety charm and the service is undoubtedly friendly. Experienced Cat Ba–watchers swear that the beer here is the coldest in town. $ *Average main: 80000d* ⊠ *St. 1/4* ☎ *0225/388–7552.*

$$$
INTERNATIONAL

✕ **Green Mango.** A little something for everyone appears to be the pervading ethos at this place, the most sophisticated dining option in Cat Ba Town. Running the gamut between a generous handful of cuisines, including Vietnamese, Mexican, Thai, Italian, and Indian, the menu revels in eclecticism. Such a scattershot approach can be a cause for concern at some venues, but the kitchen staff at Green Mango are nothing if not versatile. The food here won't be winning any gongs for culinary sophistication, but dishes are generally well executed. An extensive list of cocktails and wine further up the ante. $ *Average main: 151000d* ⊠ *231 St. D1–4* ☎ *0225/388–7151* ⊕ *www.greenmango.vn.*

$$$
VIETNAMESE

✕ **Le Pont.** The secret to having a good meal at this Cat Ba restaurant is ordering what is local and fresh. Pass on the steak and order instead whole fish, prawns, squid, or the house specialty: seafood hotpot. This Vietnamese version of fondue comes with fresh vegetables, noodles, and every type of seafood imaginable—simply drop them into a pot of boiling broth at your table. The spring rolls are delicious and pair well with the cliff-side view over the bay. This is the best place to come for a cocktail at sunset or an ice coffee on a hot summer day. If you're here past dark, you can enjoy Le Pont's attached dance club that's popular with locals. $ *Average main: 209400d* ⊠ *Near Beach 3* ☎ *092/800–6879* ⊕ *www.lepontcatba.com.*

$$
CAFÉ

✕ **My Way Coffee.** They don't do the coffee here my way or your way—they do it their way, and it's all the better for it. Indeed, the rich and chocolatey brew on offer here has earned this small venue a reputation for doing the finest cup of joe on Cat Ba Island. Try the traditional Vietnamese *ca phe* or one of the restaurant's iced frappuccinos. Unsurprisingly, the food pales in comparison to the drinks. Nevertheless, the standard Cat Ba blend of western and Vietnamese favorites seems to keep the customers happy, and it's open 24 hours. $ *Average main: 60000d* ⊠ *192 Cang Ca St.* ☎ *098/209–3138* ▭ *No credit cards.*

$$
SEAFOOD

✕ **Phuong Phuong.** One of the most consistently well reviewed restaurants on the Cat Ba Town waterfront, this is a reliably good option. While there's a wide range of dishes on offer (in common with practically every other dining venue here), fresh seafood is the undoubted star of the show. Morsels such as squid, clams, scallops, and oysters are cooked to order, as are glistening fish fresh from the ocean. The rest of the menu takes in the usual greatest hits of Vietnam (pho, spring rolls, and so on) and a smattering of European offerings. $ *Average main: 70000d* ⊠ *232 St. 1/4* ☎ *0225/388–8254.*

WHERE TO STAY

CAT BA TOWN

$$
HOTEL

▨ **Cat Ba Palace Hotel.** You may not get much in the way of trimmings here, but rooms are spacious and spotlessly clean, and it's an easy walk from the ferry port, in an extremely convenient location in the center of town. **Pros:** a stone's throw from everything. **Cons:** Wi-Fi reception can be somewhat spotty. $ *Rooms from: 667000d* ⊠ *180 Nui Ngoc St.* ☎ *0225/369–6030* ⊕ *www.catbapalace.com* ⇗ *14 rooms, 6 suites* ⏍ *Breakfast.*

$ HOTEL **Duc Tuan Hotel and Restaurant.** With good-value rooms and stunning views of the ocean from its more elevated floors, this is as fine an option as any in Cat Ba Town. **Pros:** impeccable service spearheaded by manager Mr. Tuan. **Cons:** bathrooms are on the basic side. [$] *Rooms from: 300398d* ✉ *210 Rd. 1/4* ☎ *0225/388–8783* 🛏 *16 rooms* 🍴 *Breakfast.*

$ HOTEL **Gieng Ngoc Hotel.** With a prime location on the seafront and many rooms with ocean-facing balconies, this is one of the better options in Cat Ba Town. **Pros:** ocean-facing balconies are pleasant. **Cons:** in-house karaoke can cause a ruckus. [$] *Rooms from: 300509d* ✉ *Rd. 1/4* ☎ *031/388–8243* 🌐 *www.giengngochotel.com.vn* 🛏 *70 rooms* 🍴 *Breakfast.*

CAT BA BEACHES AND ISLANDS

$$$$ RESORT **Cat Ba Island Resort and Spa.** The oldest of Cat Ba Island's luxury lodgings, this resort could probably do with a bit of TLC, but it still has many advantages—not least its location right next to Cat Co 1 beach. **Pros:** stunning beachside location. **Cons:** entire resort needs a freshening up. [$] *Rooms from: 1501992d* ✉ *Cat Co 1 Beach* ☎ *0225/368–8686* 🌐 *www.catbaislandresort-spa.com* 🛏 *165 rooms* 🍴 *Breakfast.*

$$$$ RESORT **Sunrise Resort.** Seductively located on Cat Co 3 beach, this is an ideal place to unwind for a couple of days, with high levels of comfort and extras like complimentary fruit baskets and bottled water. **Pros:** lush grounds add to an atmosphere of bucolic abundance. **Cons:** overpriced for what you get overall. [$] *Rooms from: 1969279d* ✉ *Cat Co 3 Beach* ☎ *0225/388–7360* 🌐 *www.catbasunriseresort.com* 🛏 *39 rooms* 🍴 *Breakfast.*

$ HOTEL Fodor's Choice ★ **Whisper of Nature.** In the small village of Viet Hai, on the eastern side of the island, these simple concrete-and-thatch bungalows are the very definition of a getaway, and the surrounding landscape of rice fields and the nearby seascape of Lan Ha Bay are as enticing as they come. **Pros:** secluded hideaway amidst beautiful nature. **Cons:** not entirely without karaoke sessions, which can be loud, but they are only occasional. [$] *Rooms from: 319515d* ✉ *Viet Hai Village* ☎ *0225/388–8615* 🌐 *www.vietbungalow.com* 🛏 *8 rooms* 🍴 *Breakfast.*

NIGHTLIFE

Flightless Bird. Owned by an expatriate from New Zealand, this cozy venue is Cat Ba Island's number-one Western watering hole. Like many bars of its ilk, it contents itself in doing the simple things well. The beer is cold, there's a large screen television for sporting events, and the kitchen serves up hearty snacks like stone-baked pizzas. ✉ *189 St. 1/4* ☎ *0225/388–8517.*

Noble House. Bars in Cat Ba Town have a habit of disappearing or reemerging under a new moniker. Noble House, therefore, has earned its status as something of a stalwart. Drinks are cheap, there are diversions such as foosball and pool, and the outlook over the ocean is stunning. ✉ *Cat Ba Town* ☎ *0225/388–8363* 🌐 *thenoblehousecatba.wordpress.com* ⏲ *Daily 10 am–2 am.*

Oasis Bar. Nobody could ever call Cat Ba Town's nightlife sophisticated, but it can be fun. Nowhere is this more evident than at the Oasis Bar, where owner Miss Blue and her staff preside over a mixed crowd of travelers. Drinks are very reasonably priced and the food does an acceptable job of soaking them up. There's a pool table, and karaoke is available for those who fancy strutting their vocal stuff. ⊠ *228 St. 1/4* ☎ *098/270–4659.*

A major factor in Cat Ba Island's emergence as a traveler favorite is the sheer variety of outdoor activities on offer. From trekking through the vivid-green jungle in Cat Ba National Park to kayaking among the karsts on Lan Ha Bay, the island has adventures to suit a range of tastes. Rock climbing is a particularly popular pursuit, and there are numerous routes up and down the limestone outcrops. These routes vary in grades of difficulty, making Cat Ba as suitable for beginners as it is for expert climbers.

Fodor'sChoice
★
Asia Outdoors. Based on Cat Ba Island, this adventure company, formerly known as Slo Pony, specializes in rock climbing, kayaking, and hiking tours. ⊠ *Cat Ba Island* ☎ *0225/368–8450* ⊕ *www.asiaoutdoors. com.vn.*

Fodor'sChoice
★
Blue Swimmer Sailing. Sailing, biking, and kayaking tours are available through this Cat Ba–based tour operator. It also offers overnight eco-junks that are geared more toward budget-conscious travelers. ⊠ *Ben Beo Pier, Cat Ba Island, Halong Bay* ☎ *0225/368–8237* ⊕ *www.blueswimmersailing.com* ✍ *Full day activities: kayaking from 257,000d; guided mountain biking from 427,000d; skippered chartered junk from 2,575,000d.*

BAI TU LONG BAY

202 km (125 miles) east of Hanoi, 56 km (34 miles) east of Halong Bay.

The limestone outcrops that rise out of the waters of Bai Tu Long Bay are perhaps not as lofty as the ones at Halong, but the two seascapes are virtually interchangeable and you would need to be a seriously obsessed karst aficionado to notice the difference. Clearly apparent, however, is the relative lack of tourists here, in comparison with its more famous next-door neighbor. The submerged limestone plateau, the geological phenomenon that gave rise to the scenic splendor in this part of the Gulf of Tonkin, continues all the way to the Chinese border and Bai Tu Long Bay is the easternmost extension of the chain. Having neglected it for years, tour operators are beginning to cash in on the bay's awesome potential. Nevertheless, development is in still in its infancy, which means largely unpolluted waters and a wealth of unexplored islands, caves, and immaculate sandy coves. Despite the area's undoubted beauty, here are some clouds on the horizon. Boat traffic may not be as heavy as it is in Halong Bay, but garbage from trawlers and from mainland Vietnam and China is a common and unsightly blight. For the most part, however, Bai Tu Long Bay, and islands such as Quan Lan, Tra Ban, and Van Don, offer a laid-back alternative to Halong Bay that makes traveling the extra distance from Hanoi worthwhile.

The life of Ho Chi Minh

EARLY YEARS

Ho Chi Minh (literally, "bringer of light") is the final and most memorable pseudonym in a series of more than 50 that Vietnam's intrepid leader, originally named Nguyen Sinh Cung, acquired during the course of his remarkable life. Born in 1890 in the central Vietnamese province of Nghe An, Ho received traditional French schooling and became a teacher. However, he inherited from his father (who abandoned the family early on) a wanderlust that became fueled by a lifelong obsession with Vietnamese independence.

YEARS ABROAD

In 1911 Ho signed on to the crew of a French freighter; two years later a stint aboard another French ship took him to the United States, where he settled for a year in Brooklyn, New York, and found work as a laborer. Ho then left for London, where he became an assistant pastry chef. He mastered several languages—among them English, French, German, Russian, Cantonese, and Japanese. He moved to Paris for six years and became increasingly active in Socialist, Communist, and Nationalist movements. After helping to found the French Communist Party, Ho left for Moscow in 1924. It soon became clear that to foment a successful workers' revolution in Vietnam, he would have to dedicate himself to organizing his countrymen. By the end of the 1920s, several poorly organized revolts had incited aggressive French retaliation, which was only compounded by economic depression. In 1930, while based in Hong Kong, Ho consolidated a number of rebellious factions under the umbrella of the Indochinese Communist Party. However, it was not until 1941—after escaping arrest in Hong Kong, forging documentation "proving" his death, shuttling between China and the Soviet Union, and disguising himself as a Chinese journalist—that he was able to sneak back into Vietnam.

LEADERSHIP IN VIETNAM

Shortly thereafter Ho founded the Vietminh Independence League. In July 1945, U.S. OSS officers met with Ho; impressed with Ho's operation, they agreed to supply him with arms. In August, Ho called for a general uprising, known as the August Revolution. Ho proclaimed himself president of the Democratic Republic of Vietnam in the north. The following year, Ho, in order to rid northern Vietnam of Chinese troops, agreed to an accord with the French: Vietnam would be a "free state" within the French Union and 25,000 French troops would be stationed there. Tensions between the Vietminh and the French escalated, however, and soon led to the French-Indochina War. By 1950 the United States was supplying military aid to the French, and Ho's government was recognized by the Soviet Union and China. The French-Indochina War ended in 1954 with the Vietminh's defeat of the French at Dien Bien Phu. American involvement in Vietnam escalated rapidly.

Ho died of natural causes during the Vietnam War in September 1969 at the age of 79. From his embalmed body in the Ho Chi Minh Mausoleum to his portrait on Vietnamese currency, he is still very present in Vietnamese life.

GETTING HERE AND AROUND

Frequent buses run between Halong City and Cai Rong bus station. The journey takes around 1½ hours and costs about 10,100d. Boat charters to the outlying islands and onto the bay can be organized from Cai Rong Pier. Costs vary depending on bargaining skills, but expect to pay at least 150,000d per hour. Daily ferries link Cai Rong with islands such as Quan Lan, Tra Ban, and Ngoc Vung. One-way fares range from 40,000d to 70,000d. There's also a faster speedboat servicing Co To that departs from Cai Rong at 7 am daily (155,000d).

EXPLORING

Co To Island. Although it is the farthest inhabited island from the mainland in the Bai Tu Long archipelago, Co To is fast becoming the area's rising star. Good facilities including hotels and restaurants complement natural attractions that include sandy beaches and some impressive peaks.

Ngoc Vung Island. Skirting the boundary of Halong and Bai Tu Long bays, Ngoc Vung boasts dramatic limestone cliffs. There's also a very attractive sandy beach with some basic beach huts on its southern shore.

Quan Lan Island. Sunseekers disappointed by Northern Vietnam's relative lack of good beaches will find succor at the beautiful stretch of sand at Minh Chau beach on the northeastern coast of Quan Lan. Be warned, however, the water is too chilly for most during the winter months while the summer months see a mass influx of Vietnamese tourists. Other points of interest on the island include a 200-year-old pagoda in Quan Lan Town. Beyond beach-bumming, the main activities here include forest walks and leisurely cycling along the island's quiet byways.

Tra Ban Island. The largest island in Bai Tu Long Bay is also one of its wildest and most undeveloped. Thick jungle blankets the southern part of the island, while the offshore karsts are among the most impressive in the entire region. There's very little in the way of accommodations on the island beyond a few basic beach huts, so plan for a day trip rather than an overnight stay.

Van Don Island. The largest island in the Bai Tu Long archipelago is also its most populated and developed. Linked to the mainland by a series of bridges, the island mainly serves as a jumping off point for the smaller, more idyllic, destinations in the area. Cai Rong, the main town, is a bustling port with some acceptable accommodations options. There's not much else to see on Van Don, but the outlook to the offshore karst formations from Bai Dai (long beach) on the southern side of the island is stunning. The Vietnamese government has big plans for Van Don, with a special Economic Zone with an international airport in the pipeline.

WHERE TO EAT AND STAY

Neither Cai Rong nor the outlying islands have much in the way of outstanding restaurants. Nevertheless, the Minh Chau Beach Resort on Quan Lan Island and Co To Lodge on Co To Island have very acceptable dining options. Elsewhere in the archipelago, simple eateries serve up fresh seafood to a predominantly Vietnamese crowd.

$$ ✕ **Jellyfish Restaurant.** Attached to the Coto Lodge Hotel, this surprisingly chic restaurant does a reasonable line in Vietnamese favorites.

VIETNAMESE

For a really special dining experience, however, guests should prebook for an outdoor seafood feast on the beach. With twinkling lanterns and comfortable cushions creating a winning ambience, it is the most romantic way to dine in this part of Vietnam. $ *Average main: 150000d* ✉ *Coto Lodge Hotel, Co To Town* ☎ *097/878–1423* ⊕ *www.cotolodge. com* ⊟ *No credit cards* ⊙ *Daily7 am–10 pm.*

$$$ ✕ **Palm Garden Restaurant.** Attached to the Minh Chau Beach Resort,
SEAFOOD   this amiable and attractive dining space specializes in local seafood. If a decent measure of a restaurant can be made by its popularity with the natives, this venue comes up trumps. The lush gardenlike dining area is regularly packed with locals and visiting Vietnamese eager to get their share of fresh oysters, lobster, and crab. $ *Average main: 200000d* ✉ *Minh Chau* ☎ *0203/399–5016* ⊙ *Daily 7 am–10 pm.*

$ ⌂ **Co To Lodge.** Several new lodging options have opened on Co To
HOTEL   Island in the last few years and this is one of the best. **Pros:** forward-thinking management in tune with Western tastes. **Cons:** rooms a little on the small side. $ *Rooms from: 400000d* ✉ *Co To Island Centre, Co To Town* ☎ *097/878–1423* ⊕ *www.cotolodge.com* ⇦ *13 rooms* ⦿| *Breakfast.*

$$$$ ⌂ **Minh Chau Beach Resort.** One of the best options in the Bai Tu Long
RESORT   area, this low-key resort enjoys a prime beachside location. **Pros:** right by the beach. **Cons:** expensive. $ *Rooms from: 2100000d* ✉ *Quan Lan Island* ☎ *090/408–1868* ⊕ *www.dulichminhchau.com* ⇦ *26 rooms* ⦿| *Breakfast.*

HANOI

Updated
by Duncan
Forgan

Hanoi marked its 1,000-year anniversary amidst much fanfare back in 2010, and although Western fashions, music, and food have long since elbowed their way into the once-impenetrable north, the city maintains a strong sense of identity. It's a fascinating mix of old and new Vietnam, with Chinese and French influences, ancient culture, colonial architecture, broad tree-lined boulevards, and beautiful lakes.

Full of things to see, from the architecture of the Old Quarter and the French Quarter to Ho Chi Minh's Mausoleum and the Temple of Literature, the Vietnamese capital lends itself to leisurely exploration. The city is home to one of Asia's stronger indigenous culinary traditions, with earthy markets and a rambunctious street-food culture, but also boasts a stellar range of international dining options. Hanoi is also very affordable by urban Asian standards, with the majority of hotels and restaurants offering plenty of value.

Hanoians have increasing amounts of disposable income, and the city continues to modernize at a breakneck pace. The predominant sound at an intersection was once the delicate ring of bicycle bells. Today motorcycles and cars, including luxury models such as BMWs and Bentleys, are taxing the city's antiquated road system. Like their counterparts in Ho Chi Minh City, the youth of Hanoi express themselves through an eclectic range of influences ranging from skateboard culture and envelope-pushing contemporary art to high living and luxury labels. Nonetheless, Hanoi remains a refined city of academics, artists, diplomats—and contradictions. Timeless tableaus of "Old Asia" are easy to spot. Emerge early and you'll find old timers practicing tai chi moves down by the banks of mist-shrouded Hoan Kiem Lake. Nearby, beret-wearing grandfathers stroke their wispy beards as they contemplate their next chess move over a cup of full-bodied Vietnamese coffee. Those looking for a city preserved in aspic won't find it in this urbane, confounding metropolis.

ORIENTATION AND PLANNING

GETTING ORIENTED

Hanoi is a sprawling city, but the main areas of interest to visitors are all conveniently congregated within easy reach of each other. The city's most famous neighborhood, the Old Quarter, is laid out as a warrenlike maze north of Hoan Kiem Lake. Further south, the cacophonous streets and narrow shophouses yield to the tree-lined avenues and stately villas of the French Quarter. Immediately west of the Old Quarter is Ba

TOP REASONS TO GO

Embark on a cultural odyssey: Delve into the thriving art scene at one of the city's contemporary galleries or at a museum highlighting Vietnam's rich culture and history.

Take it to the streets: Wander the narrow streets of Hanoi's Old Quarter, where cafés, bars, shops, and street vendors spill onto the sidewalks.

Go on a gastronomic adventure: Appease your palate in a melting pot of meals, ranging from pho food carts with plastic stools to fancy French restaurants offering the ultimate in refined service.

Seek out the revolutionary: Eye-catching propaganda art displayed in public and in small galleries to banner attractions such as Ho Chi Minh's mausoleum brings Hanoi's revolutionary past to life.

Check out hip Hanoi: From arty bars, where intellectual discourse flows as freely as red wine, to cutting-edge live music venues, the capital continues to stake its claim to being Vietnam's most febrile cultural hub.

Dinh District, home to Hanoi's most important cultural and historical monuments. West Lake is a short ride northwest from here. Getting around on foot can be tiring, so if you intend to stick within the Old Quarter or elsewhere in Hoan Kiem District, break up your walks with a cyclo (pedicab) ride or two. Otherwise consider taking taxis, or if you're feeling a little more adventurous, hop on the back of a *xe om* (motorcycle taxi). Keep in mind that many streets bear different names in different sections.

The Old Quarter. The logical starting point for most visitors, this ancient enclave bursts with amenities and attractions. After 1,000 years one of Hanoi's main centers of commerce, the narrow streets are still alive with shops, markets, bars, and a plethora of people-watching opportunities.

The French Quarter. The wide avenues and graceful villas of the area south and southwest of Hoan Kiem Lake present an alluring change of pace after the frenetic hubbub of the Old Quarter. The area, large swathes of which were the old French Quarter, is much easier to navigate too, and the numerous restaurants and cafés make convenient refueling stations during a walking tour of its main sights.

Ho Chi Minh Mausoleum and Around. Ba Dinh District is home to a variety of historic sights, both ancient and more contemporary. Ho Chi Minh's monolithic mausoleum dominates Ba Dinh Square, while the One Pillar Pagoda and Temple of Literature are venerable relics of the Ly Dynasty.

West Lake. Hanoi's most westernized and upscale area, West Lake is home to some of the best of the city's dining and lodging options. Hidden enclaves showcase an easier going side to Hanoi life.

PLANNING

WHEN TO GO

In terms of weather, the ideal time to visit Hanoi is between October (with temperatures averaging 80 degrees Fahrenheit) and mid-December (with temperatures ranging from the upper 60s to mid-70s), when the heat and humidity are not so oppressive. But be prepared for cold snaps and chilly nights. The brief spring from March to April is also a pleasant time. From January to March a layer of clammy mist—the infamous *mua phun*—hovers over Hanoi. The city begins its summer swelter in May and sweats through August, when the monsoons bring heavy downpours and sudden flooding. This continues until late September, so if you choose to brave the elements at this time, bring rubber footwear and rain pants or buy them in Hanoi because you could be in it up to your knees. Temperatures range from the mid-70s to the high 90s.

FESTIVALS AND EVENTS

JANUARY— **Tet.** Late January to early February is a good time to visit if you want
FEBRUARY to breathe in the excitement of Tet, the lunar new year, a movable date based on the Chinese lunar calendar. In preparation for Vietnam's largest festival, the Old Quarter comes alive with floor-to-ceiling displays of moon cakes, red banners, joss sticks, and red envelopes for giving lucky money (*mung tuoi*) to children. Beware: when Tet does arrive, many shops and restaurants close for up to a week—although some restaurants have discovered the financial benefits of staying open. If you're planning to conduct any business, this is definitely not the time to do it.

SPRING **Pilgrimage to the Perfume Pagoda.** February and March are the months to join the mass Buddhist pilgrimage to the Perfume Pagoda, but be prepared to deal with serious crowds—many thousands each day—if you make the trip during this peak season. Smaller religious festivals take place at Hanoi's temples and outlying villages in March and April. Because all Vietnamese festivals follow the lunar calendar, check online or with your tour operator for exact dates.

PLANNING YOUR TIME
IF YOU HAVE TWO DAYS

If you'll just be passing through, your time would be best spent exploring the Old Quarter and visiting the Ho Chi Minh Mausoleum and the adjacent museum. Since your time is limited, do as the Vietnamese do and start at the crack of dawn. Make your way down to the northern shore of **Hoan Kiem Lake** and look on as the Vietnamese limber up with tai chi routines and other exercises. You'll need some sustenance for a busy day so head to nearby Pho Thin for a warming bowl of Vietnam's de facto national dish. After breakfast, take a couple of hours to wander around the narrow streets of the **Old Quarter**. The sheer volume of traffic can make strolling hazardous, but it is worth the perilous progress to experience the sights and sounds of the area. After grabbing lunch at either a smart, contemporary café such as Joma or Hanoi Social Club, or on the street, make your way to **Ba Dinh District** for a pilgrimage to Ho Chi Minh's mausoleum where the body of the venerated former leader of Vietnam remains on display. To find out more about his life and work, head to the nearby Ho Chi Minh Museum, which celebrates both the man and the onward march of revolutionary socialism. For dinner, head to one of **West Lake's** many contemporary restaurants before going back to the Old Quarter to end a busy day with some *bia hoi*, Vietnam's legendarily cheap beer. After an action-packed first day you can afford to take things slightly easier on day two. After breakfast and some potent Vietnamese coffee, make your way to the **French Quarter**, stroll the shady tree-lined avenues and admire the lovely colonial architecture. Lunch on Vietnamese street food in a palatial setting at **Quan Ngon** then make your way back to Ba Dinh District, this time focusing on ancient relics such as the One Pillar Pagoda and the Temple of Literature. For another quintessentially Hanoian experience, take in an evening show at the water puppet theater before treating yourself to a fine-dining dinner at the Sofitel Legend Metropole Hotel.

IF YOU HAVE FIVE DAYS

Five days gives you time to spread your wings beyond the obvious sights. After following the two-day itinerary, the remainder of your time can then be devoted to really exploring Hanoi's myriad nooks and crannies. Those with an interest in architecture will find it both fascinating and instructive to take one of the **walking tours** organized by companies such as Hidden Hanoi. These guided explorations delve deep beyond the surface and can provide invaluable insight to everything from the unique "tube houses" in the Old Quarter to the European (and especially Gallic) influences at play in the French Quarter. Another Hanoi highlight that few short-stay visitors really have the time to get to grips with is the city's mind-blowing **street food culture**. For a comprehensive insight try one of the itineraries run by Hanoi Street Food Tours. Cultural sights beyond the big-hitters, meanwhile, include the fascinating Vietnam Museum of Ethnology and a growing number of contemporary art spaces. While taking it easy may seem contrary to the restless spirit of the city, there's a lot to be said for slowing down to a more leisurely pace. Enjoy the view over **Hoan Kiem Lake** from an upstairs coffee shop and spend your evening holed up in left-field drinking dens such as Cama ATK or Tadioto. If you have a day left to spare, leave the city and take a trip out to the Perfume Pagoda, a complex of Buddhist temples that is one of Vietnam's most famous pilgrimage sites.

GETTING HERE AND AROUND

AIR TRAVEL

Noi Bai International Airport lies about 35 km (22 miles) north of the city. Several improvements have been made to the airport in recent years to bring it up to international standards. The existing Terminal 1 has been extended to encompass a new hall with a capacity for 3 million extra passengers per year. The most significant addition to the airport, however, is the new Terminal 2, which was inaugurated at the beginning of 2015. The new terminal will provide capacity for 10 million passengers per year.

The somewhat arduous journey between the airport and downtown Hanoi, meanwhile, has been shortened by the new Nhat Tan–Noi Bai Highway, routed over the new Nhat Tan Bridge, both of which opened in January 2015.

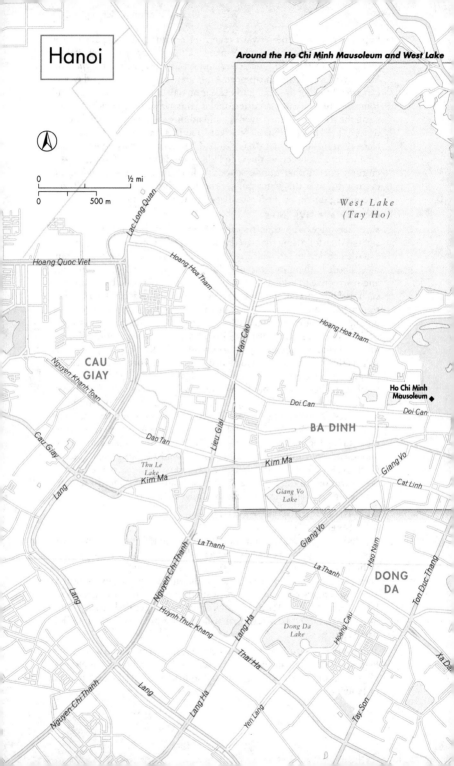

Hanoi

Around the Ho Chi Minh Mausoleum and West Lake

West Lake
(Tay Ho)

0 — ½ mi
0 — 500 m

Lac Long Quan

Hoang Quoc Viet

Hoang Hoa Tham

Van Cao

Hoang Hoa Tham

CAU GIAY

Nguyen Khanh Toan

Ho Chi Minh Mausoleum ◆

Doi Can

Doi Can

BA DINH

Dao Tan

Lieu Giai

Cau Giay

Thu Le Lake

Kim Ma

Kim Ma

Giang Vo

Cat Linh

Lang

Giang Vo Lake

La Thanh

Giang Vo

Hao Nam

Ton Duc Thang

Nguyen Chi Thanh

La Thanh

DONG DA

Lang

Huynh Thuc Khang

Lang Ha

Dong Da Lake

Hoang Cau

Xa Da

Thai Ha

Nguyen Chi Thanh

Lang

Lang Ha

Yen Lang

Tay Son

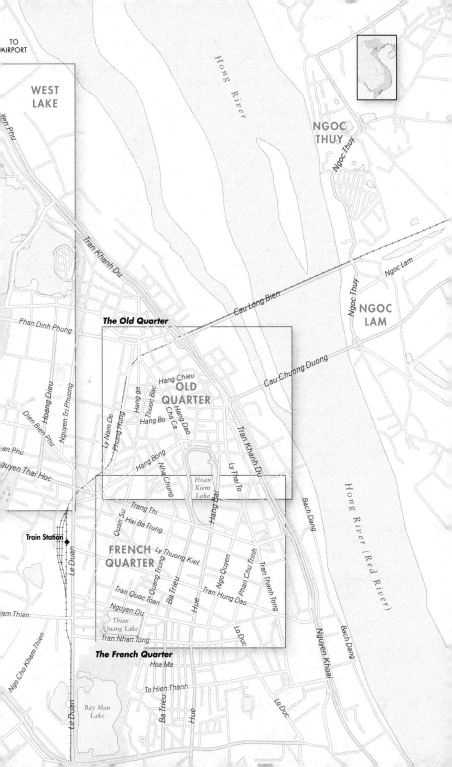

International airlines fly into Hanoi from other parts of Asia and also from European hubs such as Frankfurt, Paris, and London. As of this writing, there are no direct flights from North America, but there are plenty of connecting services via cities such as Beijing, Seoul, and Tokyo.

Domestic destinations served from Hanoi include Danang, Dien Bien Phu, Ho Chi Minh City, Hue, Phu Quoc, and Nha Trang.

AIRPORT TRANSFERS Vietnam Airlines has an airport shuttle located just outside the Noi Bai arrival terminal. It departs once it is full (approximately every 45 minutes) and will take you to the Vietnam Airlines office on Quang Trung in central Hanoi. It's a bit of an uncomfortable ride, but the 44,000d per person fee is the most direct and economical way to travel to/from the Noi Bai airport. Look for the logo on the side of the minivan.

Just outside the Noi Bai airport terminal (to the right as you exit) are Jetstar buses that travel to Hanoi's city center. With periodic stops, they head south along the dyke road, recognizable by a mosaic that is 4 km long (2½ miles), which holds the Guinness World Record for being the longest mural of its kind. Jetstar charges 40,000d per sector and goes as far south as the Opera House. Tickets can be purchased on the bus.

A number of taxi companies operate the route between Noi Bai Airport and Hanoi city center. The largest of these is Noi Bai Taxi, which has its own parking lot at the airport. All these companies offer a fixed price fare for the route. For a four-seat taxi the price between Noi Bai and the Old Quarter is 250,000d. The bigger the vehicle, the higher the price.

Airport Contacts **Noi Bai International Airport** ⊠ *Phu Minh* ☎ *024/3886–5047* ⊕ *en.vietnamairport.vn.*

Airport Transfer Contacts **Noi Bai Taxi** ☎ *098/698–2356* ⊕ *www.noibaitaxi. com.* **Vietnam Airlines bus** ☎ *024/3832–0320* ⊕ *www.vietnamairlines.com.*

BIKE TRAVEL

Bikes can be rented from establishments such as café–rental store Hanoi Bicycle Collective who have a selection of mountain and city bikes. Prices range from 50,000d per half-day to 100,000d for the full day. You can get the tires pumped up at just about any street corner for 1,000d per tire. Traffic is so congested in the Old Quarter, however, that walking is advisable.

Fodor's Choice ★ **Hanoi Bicycle Collective.** While nobody would call frenetic Hanoi a cyclist's paradise, the Hanoi Bicycle Collective is doing its best to encourage the use of pedal power. As well as serving as a retail space, with several brands of bike on offer, the outlet has set itself up to become a hub of cycling life, commuting, social activity, and fitness. ⊠ *29 Nhat Chieu, Tay Ho District* ☎ *024/3718–3156* ⊕ *www.thbc.vn.*

BUS TRAVEL

Bus travel in Vietnam has improved immeasurably in recent times. Aside from in remote, rural destinations, public buses are generally fairly clean and comfortable. Four major bus stations—none of which are in the center of town—serve the capital, in addition to a few express minibus services. Giai Bat Bus Station (Ben Xe Giai Bat) serves most southern routes, including Vinh, Hue, and ultimately Ho Chi Minh City. It's 7 km (4 miles) south of the Hanoi Railway Station, on Giai Phong Street, opposite the Giap Rat Railway Station. Gia Lam Bus Station (Ben Xe Gia Lam) provides services to points east to destinations such as Lang Son and Haiphong. It's best to buy your ticket ahead of time. The station is across the Red River and just beyond the tollbooth, 100 yards off Nguyen Van Cu Street on Ben Xe Street. My Dinh Bus Station services routes north and is located in Cua Giay District in the north of the city. Yen Nghia Bus Station, meanwhile, services points west of Hanoi.

Bus Contacts Giai Bat Bus Station ⊠ *Km 6, Giai Phong St., Hoang Mai* ☎ *024/3864–1467* **Gia Lam Bus Station** ⊠ *9 Ngo Gia Kham St., Long Bien* ☎ *024/3827–1529.* **Hoang Long Bus Company** ⊠ *1 Nguyen Khoai* ☎ *024/3987–7225.*

CAR TRAVEL

As Hanoi is the largest city and tourist center in northern Vietnam and a major international gateway, few Western visitors actually arrive here by car. Those who do are usually coming from Ho Chi Minh City via Highway 1 or from Danang or Hue after flying there from Ho Chi Minh City. A much more common method is to tour the south by land, by car or train from Ho Chi Minh City to Hue and then fly from there to Hanoi.

It's quite easy to arrange leaving Hanoi by car for side trips. There are any number of reputable international and local rental companies that will hire you a car and driver. You can count on paying around 1,500,000d per day in the city for an air-conditioned sedan and a driver. Expect to pay 2,000,000d or more per day for a minivan. You can arrange for a pickup at your hotel, although a deposit—usually 50% of the fare and some form of identification, such as a photocopy of your passport—is often expected. There is no need for you to leave your passport with the agency renting you the car.

CYCLO TRAVEL

Traffic in Hanoi is notorious for its chaotic mix of cars, buses, motorcycles, and bicycle rickshaws, known as cyclos.

The traditional way to explore Hanoi's Old Quarter is by cyclo. You'll feel like royalty (or maybe a bit conspicuous) as you're pedaled around the bustling city on a padded tricycle. Rates start at 100,000d per hour. Tipping is not required or even expected, but giving your driver 10,000d is a nice gesture.

TAXI AND MOTORBIKE TAXI TRAVEL

There are several options for getting around, but taxis are generally the safest and most efficient, although a bit more expensive. Taxi scams are not uncommon, but can usually be avoided by riding only with a trusted taxi company—Mai Linh and Hanoi Taxi are two of the capital's most reputable companies.

Taxis tend to congregate at the northwest corner of Hoan Kiem Lake, on Trieu Viet Vuong Street, and outside most major hotels. You can also call for a cab, as all taxi dispatchers speak English.

Motorbike taxis, known as xe om, are another way to get around the city—if you're brave. Although the traffic may look a little daunting, drivers know how to navigate the traffic.

If you decide to rent a motorbike yourself and drive around the city, keep in mind that the traffic *is* busy, loud, and crazy. Although the streets may be less intimidating in Hanoi than in Ho Chi Minh City, the consensus is that drivers are worse. And visitors are paying the price: Vietnam's number-one cause of injuries and death among foreigners is accidents involving a motorcycle. You can purchase helmets at various outlets for between 200,000d and 1,200,000d. Don't become a Vietnam traffic statistic—wear one.

That said, most hotels and many tour and travel agencies will find you a bike and throw in a helmet with few questions asked. Prices start at around 150,000d per day. A deposit is usually required, as is a passport or a photocopy, and you usually sign a short-term contract (be sure you're aware of the stipulated value of the bike in the contract). And speaking of contracts, you would be wise to consult your insurance policy; many companies refuse to cover motorcycle drivers or riders.

Taxi ContactsHanoi Taxi ☎ *024/3853-5353* **Mai Linh Taxi** ☎ *024/3833-3333.*

TRAIN TRAVEL

The ticket office at the main Hanoi train station, Ga Hanoi, is open 5 am–6:10 am and 7 am–11pm. You'll find a special counter where foreigners buy tickets, and some of the schedules are even in English. Another, smaller train station, across the tracks from the main one, services northern routes; the foreign booking agents at the main station will direct you.

Trains leave four times daily for Ho Chi Minh City (soft berth 1,371,000d–1,473,000d, 41 hours), but only one is an express (32 hours). The express makes stops at most major cities, including Vinh, Hue, Danang, and Nha Trang. Purchase a day in advance if you want to ensure a seat. Other destinations include Lao Cai (soft sleeper 315,000d; three times daily; 10 hours) and Haiphong (90,000d; seven times daily; two hours).

Train Contact Ga Hanoi ✉ *120 Le Duan, Hoan Kiem District* ☎ *024/3825-3949.*

TOURS

Reputable tour operators based in Hanoi provide detailed itineraries (often tailor-made to individual requirements), visitor information, transportation and hotel bookings, car and bus rentals, guided tours, private tour guides, and visa extensions. These companies can organize everything from an extended itinerary in Northern Vietnam to shorter excursions to nearby highlights such as Ninh Binh, Halong Bay, Mai Chau, and Sapa. Types of tours, meanwhile, range from adventure to luxury and cultural tourism. Within Hanoi itself, these companies as well as a growing number of boutique operators run by local and foreign enthusiasts, can organize specialty excursions such as detailed investigations into the city's amazing street food culture, its markets, and its architectural heritage.

CONTACTS **Buffalo Tours.** Started in 1994 by Tran Trong Kien, then a medical student, Buffalo Tours is one of the pioneers of adventure travel in Vietnam. The company puts an emphasis on responsible, low-impact travel and has a reputation for creating imaginative intineraries for clients.

It can tailor a trip to all tastes, whether it is luxury or something more rustic. ✉ *70–72 Ba Trieu St., Hoan Kiem District* ☎ *024/3926–3425* ⊕ *www.buffalotours.com.*

Handspan Travel. Whether it is a cultural tour of Vietnam's stunning mountainous far north or a sumptuous couple of days cruising the karsts on a luxury junk, Handspan can arrange a trip to suit. Known for its commitment to responsible tourism, the company also employs some of the most skilled and knowledgable guides in the country. ✉ *78 Ma May St., Hoan Kiem District, Hoan Kiem District* ☎ *024/3926–2828* ⊕ *www.handspan.com.*

Fodor's Choice ★ **Hanoi Street Food Tour.** There are now numerous ways to experience the glories of Hanoi's rich street-food culture, but this is one of the most respected food tour companies. Stroll through hidden alleyways and sample the pick of local specialties. Tours start at $20 per person based on a group of 10 people; solo tours cost $40 per person. ✉ *76 Hang Bac St., Hoan Kiem District* ☎ *096/696–0188* ⊕ *www.hanoistreetfood.com.*

Fodor's Choice ★ **Hidden Hanoi.** Although Hanoi is firmly established as a destination on the Southeast Asian tourist map, there remains a wealth to discover. And, as the name suggests, this exemplary operator is the outfit to guide you around them. As well as cooking classes that cover some of the lesser known dishes in the city's culinary ouvre, the company can take guests on walking tours with an emphasis on education. Other highlights include informal Vietnamese lessons, the ideal tool for haggling at a local market or negotiating a taxi fare. ✉ *147 Nghi Tam, Tay Ho District* ☎ *091/225–4045* ⊕ *www.hiddenhanoi.com.vn.*

ESSENTIALS

MONEY MATTERS ATMs—many in international banks—are easy to find throughout Hanoi. U.S. dollars are the preferred currency of exchange, but other major currencies are easy to change at banks, exchange kiosks, and hotels.

Vendors or small businesses in the countryside surrounding Hanoi will frequently not have change for a 500,000d note (a common denomination issued at ATMs). Make sure you have plenty of small change on hand. Credit card transactions often involve additional surcharges, usually around 3%.

VISITOR INFORMATION

The privately run Tourist Information Center can arrange tours, and is a good resource for maps.

Contact Tourist Information Center ✉ *7 Dinh Tien Hoang, Hoan Kiem District* ☎ *024/3936–3369* ⊕ *www.ticvietnam.com.*

EXPLORING

Hanoi is divided into four main districts, or *quan.*

The **Hoan Kiem District,** named after the lake at its center, stretches from the railway tracks to the Red River, north of Nguyen Du Street, and is the hub of all local and tourist activity. Just north of the lake is the **Old Quarter**, a charming cluster of ancient streets. South of the lake you'll find the modern city center, part of the **French Quarter**, which houses grand colonial-style villas that have been converted into hotels and offices; the best examples of French-era architecture are around Dien Bien Phu and Le Hong Phong streets, where embassies line the road.

The **Ba Dinh District** includes the zoo, the **Ho Chi Minh Mausoleum,** and other big attractions such as the Temple of Literature and the One Pillar Pagoda. Northwest of both Ba Dinh and Hoan Kiem is picturesque **West Lake** with its wide range of dining venues, bars, and luxury hotels.

Outside these main four districts are other areas of interest. The **Hai Ba Trung District,** which covers the southeast part of Hanoi and largely encompasses the French Quarter, is a calm, elegant residential area; the primary attraction here is Lenin Park, in the northwest corner of the district.

THE OLD QUARTER

Hoan Kiem Lake, Long Bien Bridge, a former city rampart, and a citadel wall surround the oldest part of Hanoi. The area was unified under Chinese rule, when ramparts were built to encircle the city. When Vietnam gained its independence from China in the 11th century, King Ly Thai To built his palace here, and the area developed as a crafts center. Artisans were attracted from all over the northern part of the country and formed cooperative living and working situations based on specialized trades and village affiliation. In the 13th century the various crafts—silversmiths, metalworkers, potters, carpenters, and so on—organized themselves into official guilds.

This area is referred to as the 36 Streets (Pho Co), though there are actually nearly 70. To this day the streets are still named after the crafts practiced by the original guilds, and they maintain their individual character despite the encroachment of more modern lifestyles. Note the slim buildings called "tunnel" or "tube" houses—with narrow frontage but deceiving depth—that combine workshops and living quarters. They were built this way because each business was taxed according to the width of its storefront. In addition to the specialty shops you'll still find here, each street has religious structures reflecting the beliefs of the village from which its original guilds came. Some are temples dedicated to the patron saint of a particular craft. Hang Bong and Hang Dao, for example, each have five of these pagodas and small temples. Many are open to the public and provide welcome relief from the intensity of the streets.

TOP ATTRACTIONS

Fodor'sChoice
★
Bia Hoi Corner. For some in-your-face Vietnamese chaos, venture into Hanoi's lively Old Quarter, home to cheap eats, authentic cuisine, and the *bia hoi* corner, where fresh beer is less than 20 cents a pint. The hub of this brew haven is at the intersection of Luong Ngoc Quyen and Ta Hien streets, where you pull up a mini plastic chair and sit to watch Hanoi in action. ⊠ *Near Hoan Kiem Lake, Hoan Kiem District.*

Dong Xuan Market. Once conveniently accessible by riverboat, this market, the oldest and largest in the city, has seen trading with the whole

Bia Hoi Corner ... **3**

Dong Xuan Market **1**

Hang Bac Street **5**

Hang Dao Street **7**

Hang Gai Street **8**

Hang Ma Street **2**

Hang Quat Street **6**

Hoan Kiem Lake **10**

Memorial House **4**

Ngoc Son Temple **9**

St Joseph's Cathedral **11**

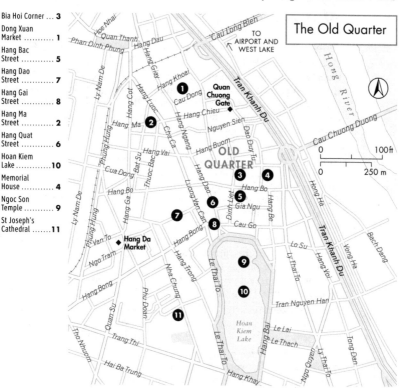

The Old Quarter

of Southeast Asia. The huge structure was destroyed by a massive fire in 1994. The fire displaced 3,000 workers, caused millions of dollars in damage and losses, and took five human lives, not to mention the lives of thousands of exotic and endangered animals. The market reopened in December 1996 and today looks more like a concrete shopping mall, but continues to sell all manner of local and foreign goods. In truth, the standard of what's on offer is variable. Clothes and other miscellanea are of the cheap, Chinese-produced variety. Nevertheless, the atmosphere is buzzing and very much local, making this an authentic market experience. ⊠ *Dong Xuan and Hang Chieu Sts., Hoan Kiem District* ☉ *Daily 6 am–9 pm.*

Hoan Kiem Lake. This lake is linked to the legend of Emperor Le Loi, who is believed to have received a magical sword from the gods, which he in turn used to repel Chinese invaders. Afterward a giant turtle reclaimed the sword for the gods from Le Loi as he boated on Hoan Kiem Lake, which derives its name ("returned sword") from the story. The sword-lifting turtle is commemorated by the lake's distinctive Turtle Tower. Ngoc Son Temple on the island at the lake's north end is a tribute to Vietnam's defeat of Mongolian forces in the 13th century. The temple can be reached by way of a lovely red bridge. History aside, the park serves as an important part of daily life for locals in the Old Quarter and is a pleasant place for people-watching or taking a break from exploring the city. Bordering the water are park benches, small cafés, and a 30-minute walking trail that loops the lake. ⊠ *Hoan Kiem District.*

WORTH NOTING

Hang Bac Street. Silversmiths and money changers once dominated this street, which still has a wide selection of jewelry shops. The Dong Cac jewelers' guild was established here in 1428, and it later erected a temple (now gone) in tribute to three 6th-century brothers whose skills, learned from the Chinese, made them the patron saints of Vietnamese jewelry. ⊠ *Hang Bac St.*

Hang Dao Street. Since the 15th century, when it was one of the original silk-trading centers, Hang Dao Street has been known for its textiles. It first specialized in lovely pink silk, always in particular demand because the color symbolizes the Vietnamese lunar new year. By the 18th century the street had branched out into a whole spectrum of colors. When the French colonized Vietnam, Hang Dao Street became the center for all traffic in silk, with massive biweekly trade fairs. Indians who settled here at the turn of the 20th century introduced textiles from the West, and today shops on this street sell ready-made clothing in addition to bolts of silk. In recent years, however, much of the silk trade action has moved to nearby Hang Gai. ⊠ *Hang Dao, Hoan Kiem District.*

Hang Gai Street. The Street of Hemp now sells a variety of goods, including ready-made silk, lovely embroidery, and silver products. With plenty of art galleries, crafts stores, and souvenirs, this is a popular spot for tourists. ⊠ *Hang Gai, Hoan Kiem District.*

Hang Ma Street. Here you can find delicate *ma,* paper replicas of material possessions made to be burned in tribute to one's ancestors. These days Honda motorbikes are sold alongside merchandise such as imported party decorations. ⊠ *Hang Ma St., Hoan Kiem District.*

Hang Quat Street. Shops along the Street of Fans sell a stunning selection of religious paraphernalia, including beautiful funeral and festival flags, porcelain Buddhas, and lacquered Chinese poem boards. Giant plane trees shade the street, which is bookended by Strawberry Temple (Den Dau) and a traditional wooden house honoring Vietnamese soldiers (Nha Tuong Niem Liet Si). Shooting off the street is Tich To, an alley bursting with bright, lacquered water puppets, rattan and bamboo baskets, porcelain and ceramics. If you can pull your attention away from all the eye-grabbing street-level sights, you'll discover the time-worn facades of several French colonial teahouses. ⊠ *Hang Quat St., Hoan Kiem District.*

Memorial House (*Ngoi Nha*). On the southern edge of the Old Quarter's Rattan Street stands a Chinese-style house built at the end of the 19th century. A rich dark-wood facade fronts a sparsely decorated interior. Exquisitely carved chairs, bureaus, and tea tables decorate the second floor, where a balcony overlooks a courtyard festooned with Chinese lanterns. A Chinese family that sold traditional medicines on the ground floor originally occupied this house until they resettled in 1954 in southern Vietnam, along with many other Chinese living in the Old Quarter. It's hard to imagine that from 1954 until 1999, when a cooperative venture between the local government and a group of architects from Toulouse, France turned the house into a museum, five families shared this small space. ⊠ *87 Ma May St., Hoan Kiem District* ☎ *024/3926–0585* ⌂ *5,000d* ⊗ *Daily 8:30–5.*

Ngoc Son Temple (*Den Ngoc Son*). On Jade Island in Hoan Kiem Lake, this quiet 18th-century shrine, whose name means "jade mountain," is one of Hanoi's most picturesque temples. This shrine is dedicated to 13th-century military hero Tran Hung Dao, the scholar Van Xuong, and to Nguyen Van Sieu, a Confucian master who assumed responsibility for repairs made to the temple and the surrounding areas in 1864. He helped build both Pen Tower (Thap But), a 30-foot stone structure whose tip resembles a brush, and the nearby rock hollowed in the shape of a peach, known as the Writing Pad (Dai Nghien). To get to the temple, walk through Three-Passage Gate (Tam Quan) and across the Flood of Morning Sunlight Bridge (Huc). The island temple opens onto a small courtyard where old men, oblivious to visitors, play spirited games of *danh co tuong,* or Chinese chess. In the pagoda's anteroom is a 6-foot-long stuffed tortoise that locals pulled from Hoan Kiem Lake in 1968. ⊠ *Dinh Tien Hoang, Hoan Kiem District* ⌂ *20,000d* ⊗ *Daily 8 am–5:30 pm, later for festivals and on 1st and 15th days of every lunar month.*

St. Joseph's Cathedral (*Nha Tho Lon*). The imposing square towers of this cathedral rise up from a small square near Hoan Kiem Lake on the edge of the Old Quarter. French missionaries built the cathedral in the late 19th century and celebrated the first Mass here on Christmas Day 1886. It feels as though nothing has changed since then—the liturgy has not been modernized since the cathedral was built. The small but beautiful panes of stained glass were created in Paris in 1906. Also of note is the ornate altar, with its high gilded side walls. The government closed down the cathedral in 1975, but when it reopened 10 years later the number of returning devotees was substantial. ⊠ *40 Nha Chung St., Hoan Kiem District* ⊗ *Main gate 5 am–noon, 2–7:30.*

THE FRENCH QUARTER

To the French must go the credit of thoroughly transforming this once-swampy southern suburb of Hanoi. In order to reflect the grandeur and aesthetic befitting the capital of their protectorate (the French called it Tonkin, from the Vietnamese *Dong Kinh,* or Eastern Capital), French developers rebuilt much of southern Hanoi from the ground up. The wide tree-lined boulevards combine with the majesty of Parisian-style villas and the shuttered elegance of government buildings to form a handsome seat of colonial power. The French are long gone, of course, and for decades Hanoians lacked the affluence to renovate or further build on the architectural contributions of the colonialists. Villas fell into disrepair, and only those buildings appropriated for state offices were even moderately maintained. This part of the city is caught in a 1920s and 1930s time warp.

Although much of the French Quarter's appeal lies in its grand but aging architecture, the area is now a leading diplomatic and commercial

Ambassador's
Pagoda **7**

Hanoi Opera
House **3**

Hoa Lo Prison **6**

Museum of
History **2**

Museum of the
Vietnamese
Revolution **1**

Tran Hung Dao
Street **5**

Vietnam Women's
Museum **4**

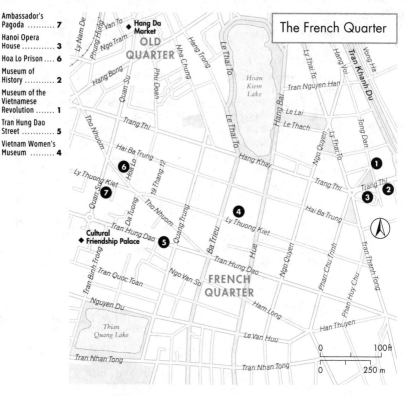

The French Quarter

section of the city. As you walk through this airy, surprisingly green district, note the considerable international presence here: several embassies occupy renovated villas or compounds in the grid of avenues south of Hoan Kiem Lake, and modern office buildings have begun to shadow the streets of this lovely part of town.

TOP ATTRACTIONS

Fodor's Choice ★ **Hanoi Opera House.** One of colonial Hanoi's most iconic edifices, the Hanoi Opera House was built by the French in the first decade of the 20th century as an Indochinese twin to Paris's largest opera house. Today it hosts traditional and modern performances by Vietnamese and international musicians and dancers and is home to the Vietnamese National Opera and Ballet. Public tours are not offered—only ticket-holding guests can enjoy the ornate architecture inside. You'll find an English-language performance schedule on the website www.ticketvn.com. Shows begin at 8 pm, and tickets generally start at around 200,000d. ⊠ *1 Trang Tien, Hoan Kiem District* ☎ *024/993–0113* ⊕ *hanoioperahouse.org.vn.*

Fodor's Choice ★ **Hoa Lo Prison.** Originally built by French colonizers to house Vietnamese political prisoners, Hoa Lo prison later held American prisoners of war and was called the "Hanoi Hilton," a name given in sarcasm because the conditions were actually quite miserable. In the 1990s more than half of the prison was demolished; the gatehouse was converted into a museum that highlights the cruelty of the occupying French but white-washes prisoner treatment during the American War, as the Vietnam War is known locally. ✉ *1 Pho Hoa Lo, Tran Hung Dao, Hoan Kiem District* ☎ *024/3824–06358* 💵 *20,000d* ⏰ *Daily 8–11:30, 2–4:30.*

WORTH NOTING

Ambassador's Pagoda (*Chua Quan Su*). This stately prayer house once served the many ambassadors who called on the Le kings. A hall named Quan Su was built in the 15th century to receive these guests, mostly Buddhists, and a pagoda was built for them in which they could comfortably worship. The hall burned to the ground, but the pagoda was saved. The Ambassador's Pagoda escaped destruction a second time, as it was the only pagoda not burned or ransacked in the final chaotic days of Le Dynasty. This pagoda sees more action than most in town, as it serves as headquarters for the Vietnam Buddhist Association. Government elites often make official visits to the pagoda, and people commonly hold "send-off" ceremonies here for the souls of family members who have recently died. The pagoda is also in part dedicated to a monk who is said to have saved King Ly Than Tong from his deathbed, so many older women come here to pray for good health. Dozens of young monks reside on the south side of the complex and study in the classrooms directly behind the pagoda. ✉ *73 Quan Su St., Hoan Kiem District* ☎ *024/3825–2427* 💵 *Free* ⏰ *Daily 7:30–11:30, 1:30–5:30.*

Museum of History (*Bao Tang Lich Su*). Opened in 1932 by the French, this building has served in its present capacity since 1958, when it was turned it over to Hanoi authorities. The ground floor houses treasures from early history, particularly Vietnam's Bronze Age. Of special interest are the Ngoc Lu bronze drums, vestiges of this period some 3,000 years ago that have become enduring national Vietnamese symbols. Tools from the Paleolithic Age are on display, as are ceramics from the Ly and Tran dynasties. Painstakingly elaborate but somewhat corny dioramas depict various Vietnamese victories over hostile invaders. Upstairs, exhibits focus on more modern Vietnamese culture. Standouts include 18th- to 20th-century bronze bells and *khanh*gongs (crescent-shape, decorative gongs); Nguyen-dynasty lacquered thrones, altars, and "parallel sentence" boards (Chinese calligraphy on lacquered wood carved into shapes of cucumbers, melons, and banana leaves); and an entire wing devoted to 7th- to 13th-century Champa stone carvings.

As you explore the museum, be sure to consult the English-language brochure you are given with the purchase of your entrance ticket, as the information it contains about the exhibits is nearly the only information on hand. Displays provide little explanatory text, even in Vietnamese, and English-language translation is lacking. It's possible to arrange in advance for one of four English-speaking museum guides. ✉ *1 Trang Tien St., Hoan Kiem District* ☎ *024/3825–2853* ⊕ *www.baotanglichsu. vn* 💵 *20,000d* ⏰ *Tues.–Sun. 8–noon, 1:30–5.*

Fodor's Choice ★ **Museum of the Vietnamese Revolution** (*Bao Tang Cach Mang*). Built in 1926 to house the French tax office, this cavernous museum opened its doors in 1959 and now has 29 halls, individual rooms that focus on specific events or periods in Vietnam's arduous road to independence. The focus naturally lands on the country's efforts against French colonialism, Japanese fascism, and American imperialism. The photographs from the August 1945 Revolution are particularly interesting. History buffs may do better here than at the Museum of History, just across the street: just about all the exhibits here have English and French commentary, so a few hours of exploration can be a great learning experience. ⊠ *25 Tong Dan, Hoan Kiem District* ☎ *024/3825–4151* ▢ *20,000d* ⊗ *Daily 8–noon, 1:30–5* ⊗ *Closed 1st Mon. of every month.*

Tran Hung Dao Street. Once called rue Gambetta, Tran Hung Dao Street is now named after the revered Vietnamese warrior who repulsed Kublai Khan's Mongol hordes three times between 1257 and 1288. This long, tree-lined boulevard is the southern border of the French Quarter and a marked example of the stateliness with which the French imbued these east–west streets. Several diplomatic missions line the boulevard; among them, fittingly, is the massive French embassy (No. 57), which takes up an entire city block. ⊠ *Hai Ba Trung District.*

Vietnam Women's Museum. Founded in 1987, this informative museum focuses on the cultural and historical aspects of Vietnamese women across 54 ethnic community groups. The three main exhibits highlight the themes of fashion, war, and family life, and the female gender role as it pertains to customs and tradition. History is told through videos, photographs, and well-presented displays of Vietnamese women in times of peace and war. The museum also covers areas of marriage, customs, and birth. There is an interesting section honoring the modern plight of the street vendor. Signage is in English, French, and Vietnamese. ⊠ *36 Ly Thuong Kiet St., Hoan Kiem District* ☎ *024/3825–9936* ⊕ *www. baotangphunu.org.vn* ▢ *30,000d.*

THE HO CHI MINH MAUSOLEUM AND NEARBY

This once-forested area west of the citadel, which is still a military base, is an expansive and refreshingly tranquil district, where stalwart buildings and monuments seem to revel in the glories of Ho Chi Minh and the Communist cause. As you travel northwest on Dien Bien Phu Street, you'll leave the tightly woven fabric of the Old Quarter behind and find yourself surrounded by sweeping French-era villas and massive ocher-color government buildings, most of which are protected from the sun by a phalanx of tall tamarind trees. Many of these villas house the embassies of socialist (or once-socialist) nations that have stood fast by Vietnam during the last few decades. Scattered among these gems are occasional anomalies of Soviet-era architecture.

Several important sights, including the final resting place of Ho Chi Minh and his former home, are close to Ba Dinh Square, where the beloved leader read his Declaration of Independence in 1945. The One-Pillar Pagoda, the underrated Fine Arts Museum, the Army Museum, and the famed Temple of Literature are within easy walking distance of the square.

If you're coming here from the French Quarter, ask a cyclo or taxi driver to take you from Hoan Kiem Lake to the Ho Chi Minh Mausoleum, in Ba Dinh District.

TOP ATTRACTIONS

Fodor's Choice ★ **Fine Arts Museum** (*Bao Tang My Thuat*). Silk paintings, folk art, sculptures, artifacts, and lacquer works are among the works of art at this museum neighboring the Temple of Literature. You can see traditional paintings depicting village scenes as well as socialist-inspired works following the Vietnam War. The full collection of Cham and Buddhist art is housed in two separate buildings with signage in Vietnamese and English. ⌧ *66 Nguyen Thai Hoc St., Ba Dinh District* ☎ *024/3823–3084* ⊕ *www.vnfam.vn* ⌧ *30,000d* ⊗ *Daily 8:30–5.*

Fodor's Choice ★ **Ho Chi Minh Mausoleum.** Ho Chi Minh may have opposed the idea of being preserved and displayed in state after his death, but his wishes to be cremated were ignored for this Vietnamese interpretation of Lenin's mausoleum. The structure's choice of location on Ba Dinh Square was a natural one—it was here where Ho declared the founding of the Democratic Republic of Vietnam in 1945. Visits to the mausoleum are expected to be quiet and respectful—skirts and shorts are forbidden, as is photography. Checking and claiming bags at the entrance can be slow, so pack lightly if possible. Lines can wind up to 2 km long, so be prepared to wait. Hours are limited to 8 am–11 am and it is closed to the public on Monday and Friday; it's also closed September through November when Ho's remains receive maintenance work. ⌧ *Ba Dinh Sq., Ba Dinh District* ☎ *024/828–9465.*

Ho Chi Minh's Residence (*Nha Bac Ho*). Just beyond Ho Chi Minh's Mausoleum is the modest wooden home where the revolutionary leader chose to live during his reign, from 1954 until his death in 1969. The lovely parklike setting offers a glimpse into the humble existence of this former ruler. Well-manicured gardens lead to a small pond where Ho Chi Minh used to clap his hands to beckon the fish for feeding time. A simple clap is enough to make these carp go wild in anticipation. Bordering the pond is the simple residence on stilts where Ho Chi Minh lived. Several rooms and his three classic cars are sectioned off for viewing. The opulent Presidential Palace, at the site's entrance, can only be viewed from the exterior; it now operates as a government building. The bomb shelter to the right of Ho Chi Minh's home is also closed to the public. ⌧ *Hung Vuong, Ba Dinh District* ⌧ *25,000d* ⊗ *Daily 7:30–11, 1:30–4.*

Fodor's Choice ★ **Temple of Literature** (*Van Mieu*). The Temple of Literature, or Van Mieu, is a treasure trove of Vietnamese architecture and a monument to the importance of education and Confucianism to Vietnam's national identity. Loosely modeled on the temple at Confucius's hometown in China, the nearly 1,000-year-old compound features five manicured courtyards surrounded by the Lake of Literature. Highlights of the Temple of Literature include giant stone turtles, the Constellation of Literature pavilion (a symbol of modern Hanoi), and the Imperial Academy—Vietnam's first university—which was founded in 1076. It is tradition for students to touch the stone turtles for luck, so don't be surprised to find this

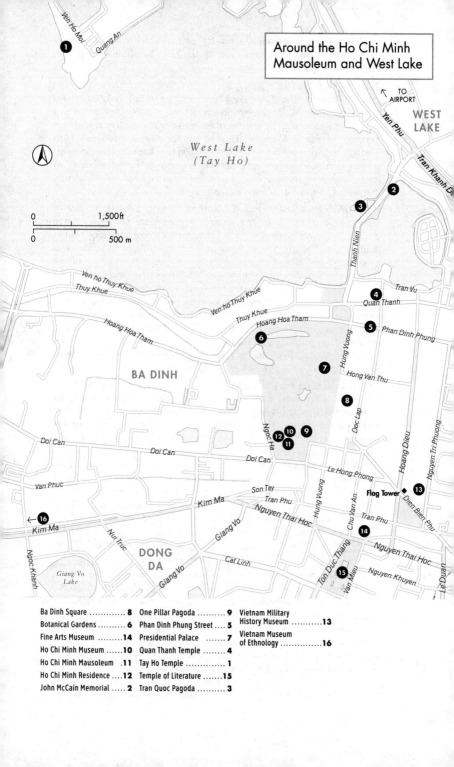

Around the Ho Chi Minh Mausoleum and West Lake

WEST LAKE

↖ TO AIRPORT

West Lake (Tay Ho)

0 ——— 1,500ft
0 ——— 500 m

BA DINH

DONG DA

Giang Vo Lake

Flag Tower

Ba Dinh Square **8**
Botanical Gardens **6**
Fine Arts Museum **14**
Ho Chi Minh Museum **10**
Ho Chi Minh Mausoleum ..**11**
Ho Chi Minh Residence **12**
John McCain Memorial **2**

One Pillar Pagoda **9**
Phan Dinh Phung Street **5**
Presidential Palace **7**
Quan Thanh Temple **4**
Tay Ho Temple **1**
Temple of Literature **15**
Tran Quoc Pagoda **3**

Vietnam Military
History Museum **13**
Vietnam Museum
of Ethnology **16**

place packed with graduates in traditional dress. Go with a tour guide since few signs are in English. ⊠ *58 Quoc Tu Giam, Dong Da District* ☎ *024/3845–2917* 🖃 *20,000d* ⏱ *Tues.–Sat., 7:30–11:30, 1:30–4:30.*

FAMILY

Fodor's Choice ★

Vietnam Museum of Ethnology. Showcasing the cultural heritage of 54 ethnic groups in Vietnam, this museum has an indoor exhibition with a large collection of photographs and artifacts, including clothing, jewelry, tools, weapons, instruments, and items related to religious beliefs and wedding and funeral ceremonies. Behind the main building is an outdoor exhibit space with winding pathways that lead to 18 replicas of lifesize tombs, boats, and traditional Vietnamese homes, including the impressive *Nha Rong Bana* Communal House reachable by a log ladder with chiseled steps. A free water puppet show is presented twice daily. ⊠ *Nguyen Van Huyen Rd., Nghia Do, Cau Giay* ☎ *024/3756– 2193* ⊕ *www.vme.org.vn* 🖃 *40,000d; guided tour 100,000d* ⏱ *Daily 8:30–5:30* ⏱ *Closed Mon.*

WORTH NOTING

Vietnam Military History Museum (*Bao Tang Quan Doi*). Although not as provocative as its Ho Chi Minh City counterpart, the Army Museum is nonetheless an intriguing example of Vietnam's continuing obsession with publicizing its past military exploits. At the southern edge of what was once the Thang Long citadel, which housed the imperial city, the museum buildings were once used as French military barracks. In the courtyard of the museum, Chinese- and Soviet-made weaponry— including MiG fighters, antiaircraft guns, and what is said to be the tank that smashed through the gates of the Presidential Palace in Saigon on April 30, 1975—surround the wreckage of an American B-52 and F-4 fighter jet shot down over Hanoi. Other, far-less-arresting displays include depictions of the Trung sisters' revolt against Chinese overlords in AD 40, sound-and-light shows highlighting battles and troop movements during the wars against the French and Americans, bicycles known as steel horses that were used on the Ho Chi Minh Trail, captured French and American firearms and uniforms, field maps and tables of major attacks, and the dreaded pungee sticks.

Adjacent to the museum is the Hanoi Flag Pillar, a 100-foot tapered hexagonal guard tower atop a three-tier square base. Built in 1812, the pillar escaped destruction by the French when they leveled much of the citadel; instead they used the tower as an observation and communication station—much like the Vietnamese military before them. The intricate fan- and flower-shape holes allow light into the tower, which has a crisp red-and-yellow Vietnamese flag fluttering from its flagpole. ⊠ *28 Dien Bien Phu St., Ba Dinh District* ☎ *024/3823–4264* ⊕ *www. btlsqsvn.org.vn* 🖃 *30,000d* ⏱ *Tues.–Sun. 8–11:30, 1–4:30.*

Ba Dinh Square. Dien Bien Phu Street comes to an end at the minimally landscaped Ba Dinh Square, in the center of which flutters Hanoi's largest Vietnamese flag. This is where half a million northern Vietnamese gathered to hear Uncle Ho's Declaration of Independence on September 2, 1945, and where, after Ho's death in 1969 (also on September 2), another 100,000 Hanoians gathered to pay homage. On the west side

7

of the square is the mausoleum itself, a cold and squat cubicle that's nonetheless arresting in its simplicity and grandeur.

Across the square from the mausoleum and slightly to the left is the Ba Dinh Meeting Hall, the four-story headquarters of the Communist Party and the site where the National Assembly convenes. Across the square and to the right, where Dien Bien Phu Street meets the square, stands the huge and graceful Ministry of Foreign Affairs. Directly opposite the mausoleum and at the end of short Bac Son Road is the monument to Vietnam's revolutionary martyrs. A palm- and willow-shaded mansion to the right of the monument is the home of former minister of defense General Vo Nguyen Giap, who orchestrated the siege at Dien Bien Phu in 1954. ✉ *Ba Dinh Sq., Ba Dinh District.*

Botanical Gardens (*Vuon Bach Thao*). This 50-acre park behind the Presidential Palace was designed by French landscape engineers in 1890. After defeating the French in Hanoi in late 1954, the state rebuilt the gardens and opened the grounds and its extensive network of trails to the public. Athletes in search of exercise congregate here for pickup soccer games, badminton, tai chi, and jogging. Lovers looking for seclusion head to the sculpture garden on the east side of the park, or cross the bridge to an island in the middle of the tree-shaded, preternaturally green lake. ✉ *Hoang Hoa Tham St.* 🎫 *2,000d.*

Fodor's Choice
★

Ho Chi Minh Museum (*Bao Tang Ho Chi Minh*). With English commentary on the sometimes bizarre exhibits, this museum is a must-see on the Uncle Ho circuit. A collection of manifestos, military orders, correspondence, and photographs from the Communist Party's early days to the present are mixed with historical exhibits covering Vietnam's revolutionary history, the fight against fascism, Ho's revolutionary world movement, and Vietnam's struggle against imperialism. ✉ *3 Ngoc Ha St.(also accessible from Chua Mot Cot St.), Ba Dinh District* 📞 *024/3846–3752* 🎫 *25,000d* 🕐 *Tues.–Thurs. and weekends, 8–11, 1:30–4.*

One-Pillar Pagoda (*Chua Mot Cot*). The French destroyed this temple on their way out in 1954. It was reconstructed by the incoming government and still commemorates the legend of Emperor Ly Thai Tong. It is said that the childless emperor dreamed that Quan Am, the Buddhist goddess of mercy and compassion, seated on a lotus flower, handed him a baby boy. Sure enough, he soon met and married a peasant woman who bore him a male heir, and in 1049 he constructed this monument in appreciation. The distinctive single pillar is meant to represent the stalk of the lotus flower, a sacred Vietnamese symbol of purity. The pillar was originally a single large tree trunk; today it's made of more durable cement. An ornate curved roof covers the tiny 10-square-foot pagoda, which rises out of a square pond. Steps leading to the pagoda from the south side of the pond are usually blocked off, but if there aren't too many people around, a monk may invite you into this miniature prayer room.

Just a few yards from the One-Pillar Pagoda is Dien Huu Pagoda, a delightful but often-overlooked temple enclosing a bonsai-filled courtyard. A tall and colorful gate opens out onto the path leading to the

Ho Chi Minh Museum, but the entrance is opposite the steps to the One-Pillar Pagoda. ⊠ *Ong Ich Kiem St., Ba Dinh District* 🗋 *25,000d* ⊙ *Daily7:30–11, 2–4* ⊙ *Closed Mon. and Fri. afternoon.*

Presidential Palace (*Phu Chu Tich*). This imposing three-story palace just north of the Ho Chi Minh Mausoleum testifies to France's dedication to architectural elegance in Indochina. Constructed from 1900 to 1906, the bright, mustard-yellow building served as the living and working quarters of Indochina's governors-general. When Ho Chi Minh returned to Hanoi after the defeat of the French in 1954, he refused to live in the palace itself but chose the more modest quarters of the palace electrician. He did, however, offer use of the palace to distinguished guests during their visits to the capital. Today the building is used for formal international receptions and other important government meetings. You can view the structure from the outside but cannot enter the palace. Surrounding the building are extensive gardens and orchards, as well as the famed Mango Alley, the 300-foot pathway from the palace to Ho Chi Minh's stilt house. ⊠ *Huong Vuong St., Ba Dinh District.*

WEST LAKE

About 3 km (2 miles) northwest of Hoan Kiem Lake is West Lake (Ho Tay), a body of water that's steeped in legend. It is said that a giant golden calf from China followed the peals of a monk's bronze bell to this spot. When the ringing stopped, the calf lost its direction and kept walking in circles, creating the basin of West Lake. Like Hoan Kiem's tortoise, the calf is said still to dwell in the lake. If so, it likely feeds on the snails that are considered a local delicacy.

7

West Lake's wealth of history takes a more tangible form in the temples and war memorials that line its shores. Development is changing the face of the shore, however, as luxury hotels and high-rent villas eat away at the land of traditional flower villages like Nghi Tam, where wealthy expatriates seclude themselves behind walls of bougainvillea.

The lake itself is a weekend boating spot for Vietnamese families, who paddle around the murky waters in boats shaped like ducks, swans, and dragons, or in rubber dinghies for rent on Thanh Nien Street. Afterward they stop in one of the floating restaurants for snails boiled in lemon leaves or *banh tom* (deep-fried shrimp cakes). You can also rent boat houses made of bamboo for an afternoon of fishing (although eating what you catch is not recommended). The causeway can be traversed in about 20 minutes, but allow for an hour or more if you want to peek around the temples. Allow even more time if you want to rent a paddleboat from the quay on the Truc Bach side. The walk along Phan Dinh Phung Street to the water tower is another 15 to 25 minutes.

TOP ATTRACTIONS

Phan Dinh Phung Street. This beautiful shaded avenue leads past sprawling French villas and Chinese mandarin mansions (many occupied by long-serving party members) as well as the gracious but seldom-used **Gothic North Door Cathedral** (Cua Bac), at the corner of Phan Dinh Phung and Nguyen Bieu streets. The large wheel of stained glass at the cathedral is reminiscent of Renaissance-era artwork in Europe and is

Hanoi History

CITY OF THE ASCENDING DRAGON

Hanoi residents are known for their civic pride. And it is little wonder given the long and storied history of their city. The city dates to the 7th century, when Chinese Sui dynasty settlers occupied the area and set up a capital called Tong Binh. In 1010 King Ly Thai To is said to have seen a golden dragon ascending from Hoan Kiem Lake. He relocated his capital to the shores of the lake and named his new city Thang Long, or "City of the Ascending Dragon." During the 11th century the old citadel was built, and 36 villages, each with its own specialized vocation, sprang up to service the royal court. This is the origin of the 36 streets that define the city's Old Quarter.

FRENCH CAPITAL

In the late 1800s, the French began to exert influence in Vietnam. The colonialists set up the protectorate of Annam in 1883–84, which meant the Hue royalty held the reins but only under the auspices of French rule. In the following years the French set up its administration and used Hanoi as the Eastern Capital of French Indochina.

In 1954 the French were defeated by the Vietminh at Dien Bien Phu, and France, Britain, the United States, and the Soviet Union decided at the Geneva Accords to divide the country at the 17th parallel. From 1954 until 1975, Hanoi served as the capital of the Democratic Republic of Vietnam, or North Vietnam, from which Ho Chi Minh initiated his struggle to reunify the country.

The decades after 1975 were a tough time for Hanoians and everyone else.

Natural disasters and international isolation led to near mass starvation. Then in 1986 the government proclaimed *doi moi,* the move to a market economy.

CAPITALISM IN THE CAPITAL

In the intervening 30 years the Vietnamese have learned the ways of capitalism quickly. In the 1990s Hanoi welcomed billions of dollars of foreign investment and the many international visitors eager to see this city (and nation) in the midst of renewal. One clear milestone for Vietnam was the normalization of trade relations with the United States in 2001 after years of negotiation. These market freedoms have led to a huge growth in privately run businesses such as hotels, restaurants, tour agencies, and other ventures.

The move to a market-based system hasn't been plain sailing. Vietnam's economy overheated massively in the years leading up to 2008 when the global financial crash decimated growth. Things have stabilized somewhat, but doubts remain as to how effectively the ruling party can manage reform. And as congestion increases and the government embarks on ever more ambitious building plans, the question of how Hanoi will preserve its ancient heritage remains unanswered.

enchanting from the inside; try the large front doors or ask around for a caretaker to let you in. Another option is to come on Sunday at 10 am for an English-language service. On the right side of the street stand the tall ramparts of the **citadel**, the military compound that once protected the Imperial Palace of Thang Long. In a surprising move, army officials in 1999 opened to the public Nguyen Tri Phuong Street, which runs straight through this once secretive space. ⊠ *Phan Dinh Phung St., Ba Dinh District.*

Fodor'sChoice **Tran Quoc Pagoda** (*Chua Tran Quoc*). Hanoi's oldest temple dates from ★ the 6th century, when King Ly Nam De had a pagoda, named Khai Quoc, built on the bank of the Red River. More than a thousand years later excessive erosion of the riverbank caused King Le Kinh Tong to move the pagoda to Goldfish Islet (Ca Vang) on West Lake and rename it Tran Quoc. This modest temple is noted for its stelae dating from 1639, which recount the history of the pagoda and its move from the Red River. There are also lovely brick stupas adjacent to the main temple. Tran Quoc is an active monastery where resident monks in brown robes hold daily services. Architecturally distinct from other Hanoi pagodas, Tran Quoc maintains a visitor's hall in front and various statues, including a gilded wooden depiction of Shakyamuni Buddha. In the main courtyard is a giant pink-and-green planter holding a bodhi tree, purportedly a cutting from the original bodhi tree beneath which the Buddha reached his enlightenment. The bodhi was a gift from former Indian president Razendia Prasat, who visited the pagoda in 1959. ⊠ *Thanh Nien St., Tay Ho District* 🖃 *Free* ☉ *Daily 8–4:30.*

WORTH NOTING

John McCain Memorial. This small memorial between West Lake and Truc Bach Lake marks the capture of one of the Vietnam War's most famous American POWs. On October 26, 1967, Navy lieutenant commander John McCain's jet fighter was shot down, sending him parachuting into Truc Bach Lake. Suffering from badly broken bones and severe beatings, he was imprisoned in the "Hanoi Hilton" and other North Vietnamese prisons for more than five years. He went on to become an Arizona senator and a vocal advocate of reconciliation between the United States and his former captors. The underwhelming red-sandstone memorial features a bound and suspended prisoner with his head hanging low and the letters U.S.A.F. (the memorial is incorrectly labeled, as McCain belonged to the Navy and not the Air Force). ⊠ *Thanh Nien St., Tay Ho District.*

Quan Thanh Temple (*Chua Quan Thanh or Tran Vu Quan*). A large black bronze statue of the Taoist god Tran Vu is housed here, protected on either side by wooden statues of civil and military mandarins. Built by King Ly Thai To in the 11th century, this much-made-over temple was once known as the Temple of the Grand Buddha; its present name translates into "Holy Mandarin Temple." An important collection of 17th-century poems can be seen in the shrine room. On the right side of this room is an altar dedicated to Trum Trong, the master bronze caster who oversaw the construction of Tran Vu's statue. Note the red, gold-stitched boots in the center of the shrine room; although such boots customarily appear in temples with figures of civil and military mandarins, Emperor Thanh Thai presented them in a vein of humor to Tran Vu's shoeless statue. Above the ornamental main gate is a 1677 replica of the bronze bell that supposedly lured the West Lake's legendary golden calf from China. Huge mango and longan trees drape over the courtyard, keeping the temple and its environs cool and somewhat dark, even in midday. Two mounted stone elephants, symbols of loyalty, flank the entrance here. ⊠ *Quan Thanh St., Ba Dinh District* 🖅 *5,000d donation* ⊘ *Daily 24 hrs.*

Tay Ho Temple. Phu Tay Ho, a temple dedicated to a 17th-century princess named Lieu Hanh, more popularly known here as Thanh Mau (Mother of the Nation), is attractive for its gigantic banyan trees and the view from across West Lake's eastern shore. In the middle chamber of the main prayer hall is a subaltar containing the statue of a holy tiger that protects Lieu Hanh, who is visible through the wooden slats of a locked separating wall inside the back chamber. In a second worship hall, women come to pray to another national mother figure, Nhi Thuong Ngan, for happiness and luck in motherhood and marriage. Two prayer stupas in the shady courtyard are dedicated to the guardian spirits of young boys and girls, Lau Cau and Lau Co, respectively. In spring and summer, you can sometimes catch locals treading water as far as 200 yards from the lakeside wall of the temple, fully clothed and with their conical hats glinting in the sun as they manipulate long pole-nets to collect snails from the bottom of the lake. A taxi is the easiest way to get here. ⊠ *At end of Pho Phu Tay Ho St., directly off Dang Thai Mai St., Tay Ho District* 🖅 *Free* ⊘ *Daily 24 hrs.*

WHERE TO EAT

From curbside feasts on Lilliputian plastic chairs to superb fine dining, Hanoi's restaurant scene has something for everyone. Locals are fiercely proud of their street food culture and this is where the essence of Hanoi's food scene can be discovered. Signature northern dishes include bun cha (vermicelli with minced pork burgers), banh cuon (steamed rice rolls stuffed with minced pork, mushrooms, and shallots), and the ubiquitous pho, Vietnam's nominal national dish, which comes in chicken and beef varieties. These classics represent just a tantalizing taste of what is on offer in the city. And with a seemingly endless array of vendors slaving over hot grills, simmering alchemy in large pots or doling out pillow-soft steamed buns from a ramshackle cart, opportunities to eat like a local are limitless. In the past, Hanoi's restaurant sector has suffered in comparison to its Kingly street dining scene. That has changed significantly over the past decade or so. There is now an eclectic selection of interesting (and often excellent) eating spots that run the gamut from simple French bistros and laid-back cafés to opulent venues for multicourse blowouts and cutting-edge options that would not be out of place in the world's major gastronomic hubs.

Use the coordinates (✛ A1) at the end of each listing to locate a site on the cooresponding map.

	WHAT IT COSTS			
	$	$$	$$$	$$$$
Restaurants	Under 70,000d	70,000d –270,000d	271,000d –400,000d	over 400,000d

Prices in the reviews are the average cost of a main course at dinner or, if dinner is not served, at lunch.

THE OLD QUARTER

$ VIETNAMESE Fodor's Choice ★ 🍴 **Banh Cuon Gia Truyen.** This is a reliable and popular spot to sample one of Hanoi's indigenous classics: *banh cuon,* steamed rice rolls stuffed with ground pork and chopped wood-ear mushrooms. Less a restaurant, more a hole-in-the-wall with a few tables and chairs strewn around, this venue compensates for its lack of sophistication with giant-size portions of the delicate rolls. Watch the resident cooks painstakingly roll out their sheets of rice noodle and spoon on the filling and feel your mouth start to water. [$] *Average main: 40000d* ✉ *14 Hang Ga* 💳 *No credit cards* ✥ *F4.*

$ VIETNAMESE Fodor's Choice ★ 🍴 **Bun Bo Nam Bo.** Like all the best restaurants purveying local favorites, this place specializes in one thing and one thing only. In this case, the delicious dish in question is, as the name suggests, *bun bo nam bo.* Although it translates as "southern-style rice noodles with beef," this mixture of rice vermicelli, grilled beef, shredded lettuce, sliced cucumber, fried shallots, bean sprouts, cilantro, and chopped peanuts is more commonly found in Hanoi. This venue is spotlessly clean and, despite its popularity with tourists, is still very much the real deal. Be sure to mix the concoction thoroughly with your chopsticks to experience the alchemy created by the small serving of broth at the base of the bowl. [$] *Average main: 40000d* ✉ *76 Hang Dieu St.* ☎ *024/3923-0701* 🌐 *www.bunbonambo.com* ✥ *F4.*

$$$ FRENCH 🍴 **Café des Arts Millenium.** Successor to the Hanoi classic, the renovated Café des Arts remains popular with the city's French expatriates. Once homey in feel, the makeover has brought about a radical change with chic leather seats replacing the old wooden chairs and monochrome prints lining the walls. The menu, too, has been significantly spruced up. The emphasis is still on French cuisine, but ambitious creations such as duet of lobster and Canadian scallop with vanilla bean jus are favored over bistro staples. A variety of set menus run the gamut from a good value prix-fixe lunch for 250,000d to more opulent evening affairs. [$] *Average main: 330000d* ✉ *11A Ngo Bao Khanh, Hoan Kiem District* ☎ *024/3828–7207* 🌐 *www.cafe-des-arts.com* ✥ *F4.*

$ CAFÉ 🍴 **Cafe Pho Co.** Once referred to as the "secret café" by those in the know, this café overlooking Hoan Kiem Lake has become more popular in recent years. Despite the crowds, the ambience remains appealing. Customers enter through a silk shop that leads to an antique-bedecked courtyard. From here, it is a climb up steep, winding staircases to a platform overlooking the lake. There's not much in the way of food, but the coffee is excellent. Try the *ca phe trung da,* coffee topped with a beaten egg white. [$] *Average main: 40000d* ✉ *11 Hang Gai* ✥ *F4.*

7

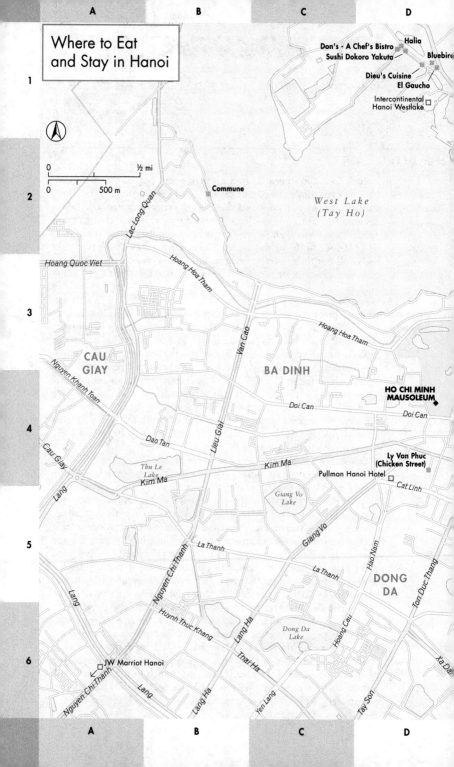

Where to Eat and Stay in Hanoi

Don's – A Chef's Bistro
Sushi Dokoro Yakuta
Halia
Bluebird
Dieu's Cuisine
El Gaucho
Intercontinental Hanoi Westlake

½ mi
0
500 m

Commune

West Lake (Tay Ho)

Lac Long Quan

Hoang Quoc Viet

Hoang Hoa Tham

Hoang Hoa Tham

CAU GIAY

BA DINH

Van Cao

Nguyen Khanh Toan

HO CHI MINH MAUSOLEUM ◆

Doi Can

Doi Can

Dao Tan

Lieu Giai

Ly Van Phuc (Chicken Street)

Kim Ma

Pullman Hanoi Hotel

Cat Linh

Thu Le Lake

Cau Giay

Kim Ma

Lang

Giang Vo Lake

La Thanh

Giang Vo

Hao Nam

DONG DA

La Thanh

Nguyen Chi Thanh

Huynh Thuc Khang

Lang Ha

Hoang Cau

Ton Duc Thang

Lang

Dong Da Lake

JW Marriot Hanoi

Nguyen Chi Thanh

Lang

Lang Ha

Thai Ha

Yen Lang

Tay Son

Xa Dan

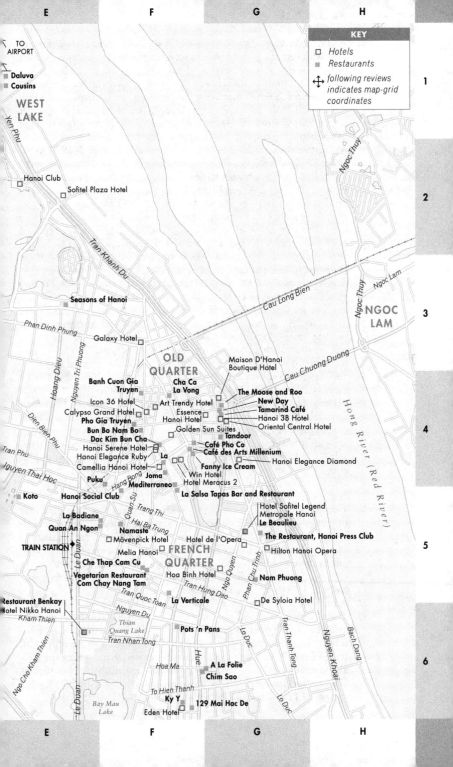

$$
VIETNAMESE

✕ Cha Ca La Vong. This century-old restaurant doesn't always score high with visitors, possibly due to sometimes gruff service and a simple menu, but it is still considered a "must dine" location in Hanoi. It is famous for its grilled snakehead fish served with vegetables, rice vermicelli, and a fish-based dipping sauce. Seasoned with turmeric and dill, the flavorful fish is smothered in shrimp paste and cooked in a skillet over a charcoal burner. Health junkies might not like the fact that the fish is bathed in oil, but this is what makes it a favorite among locals. Ⓢ *Average main: 170000d* ⊠ *14 Pho Cha Ca* ☎ *024/3825–3929* ✛ *F4.*

$
VIETNAMESE
Fodor's Choice
★

✕ Dac Kim Bun Cha. After shopping on Hang Bac Street, consider lunching at this Old Quarter institution. The tiny first floor is used for food preparation, but staff members will lead you up the winding tiled stairs until enough empty plastic stools can be found for your party. You may be planted cozily among other customers. Ordering shouldn't be hard. The restaurant serves only two delicious dishes: *bun cha* (grilled pork patties with rice noodles) come with heaping plates of herbs and lettuce; as a side, try the huge pork- and crab-filled spring rolls. Wash both down with *bia lanh* (cold beer) or *tra da* (iced Vietnamese tea). Ⓢ *Average main: 50000d* ⊠ *1 Hang Manh St., Hoan Kiem District* ⊟ *No credit cards* ✛ *F4.*

$$
CAFÉ

✕ Fanny Ice Cream. This café dishes up the best ice cream in town. The offerings, all made with natural ingredients and no preservatives, include unique local flavors like young rice or tamarind, along with old favorites such as coffee, rum raisin, and coconut. Try the refreshing lemon or, if you're determined to sin, a double scoop of raspberry and dark, wickedly rich chocolate. Ⓢ *Average main: 100000d* ⊠ *51 Ly Thuong Kiet* ☎ *024/3734–5719* ⊟ *No credit cards* ✛ *F4.*

$$
CAFÉ

✕ Hanoi Social Club. The main draw here is the convivial, bohemian atmosphere. Housed in a stunning 1920s French colonial villa in a quiet part of the Old Quarter, the café is rustic and warm, with original tiles, wooden furnishings, and high ceilings. While the simple menu of pastas, salads, and wraps can be hit or miss, the coffee is on the money. An adequate list of wine and beers and regular left-field events make the café a decent bet in the evenings, too. Ⓢ *Average main: 120000d* ⊠ *6 Hoi Vu St., Tay Ho District* ☎ *024/3938–2117* ✛ *F5.*

$$
CAFÉ

✕ Joma. This chain of cool cafés started in Laos and now has four branches in Hanoi, all serving the same selection of soups, sandwiches, and delicious bakery items. A favorite with local creatives and expats who have the freedom to work without an office, the various branches of Joma offer an inviting slice of modern café culture in sophisticated surroundings. Ⓢ *Average main: 150000d* ⊠ *22 Ly Quoc Su* ☎ *024/3938–1619* ⊕ *www.joma.biz* ✛ *F4.*

$$
VIETNAMESE

✕ La. This cozy venue near St Joseph's Cathedral in the Old Quarter does simple bistro food well. International and Vietnamese menus are available and it pays to mix between the two and order a number of things. The restaurant makes a bright impression with friendly staff, fresh-cooked bread, and a small but effective wine list setting the amiable tone. Mains don't push the culinary envelope, but dishes such as clay pot pork and grilled duck breast are more than acceptable. Ⓢ *Average main: 150000d* ⊠ *25 Ly Quoc Su* ☎ *024/3928–8933* ✛ *F4.*

$$ ✕ **La Salsa Tapas Bar and Restaurant.** Nibble on small servings of ceviche, zesty meatballs, and marinated mushrooms or choose an entree of
SPANISH
warm duck salad, panfried salmon, or lamb tenderloin. If you're not in the mood to see and be seen, avoid the cozy downstairs bar and hide out in the quieter upstairs dining room. To wash down your meal, try some of La Salsa's Spanish wines or the house sangria, which is made according to a secret family recipe. Ⓢ *Average main: 250000d* ✉ *25 Nha Tho St., Hoan Kiem District* ☎ *024/3828–9052* ⊕ *www.lasalsahanoi.com* ✛ *F5.*

$$ ✕ **Mediterraneo.** Delicious, reasonably priced Italian food is served in
ITALIAN
the bright, California-like atmosphere of this central eatery. Along with exemplary *bruschetta* (toasted bread with olive oil and various toppings) and homemade pastas, the Italian hosts serve excellent cappuccinos, Napoli-style thin-crust pizzas cooked in a wood-burning oven, and interesting homemade grappas—try licorice or peach. Ⓢ *Average main: 250000d* ✉ *23 Nha Tho St., Hoan Kiem District* ☎ *024/3826–6288* ✛ *F4.*

$$ ✕ **The Moose and Roo.** Run by two long-term expats—one Canadian,
BRITISH
one Australian—this gastropub has become a big favorite for its well-
Fodor's Choice
executed comfort food. While many of Hanoi's Western menus are
★
pretty prosaic, there is some genuine flair on display here. Dishes such as braised short rib with truffle mash, baby onions, and carrots wouldn't be out of place in this upscale bistro. Simpler options such as the chicken wings, burgers, and pies also hit the spot. With a decent list of wines and beers to accompany the comfort food, this is a convivial refuge for homesick Westerners in the bustling heart of Hanoi. Ⓢ *Average main: 160000d* ✉ *42 Ma May, Hoan Kiem District* ☎ *024/3200–1289* ✛ *G4.*

$$ ✕ **New Day.** Popular with tourists and native Hanoians alike, this is one
VIETNAMESE
of the few restaurants in the Old Quarter that manages to unite the two demographics. There is an à la carte menu as well as set menus, but locals usually prefer to go for the "popular" dishes, which involves pointing at steaming vats containing things such as eggplants with salt, fried pork ribs, and Chinese braised pork. The food is freshly cooked and regularly replenished, and is reliably delicious whichever way you order. Ⓢ *Average main: 80000d* ✉ *72 Ma May* ☎ *024/3828–0315* ⊕ *www.newdayrestaurant.com* ✛ *G4.*

$ ✕ **Pho Gia Truyen (Pho Bat Dan).** Of the countless venues dishing out ver-
VIETNAMESE
sions of Vietnam's de facto national breakfast dish, this is one of the
Fodor's Choice
best. When it comes to street food, Hanoians don't go in for much
★
ostentation and the eating area here is decidedly prosaic; just a few communal tables under a couple of bare lightbulbs. What matters is the expertly judged broth, the light rice noodles, and the delicious meat, which is peeled in strips from hulking slabs of brisket then dunked in the broth for seconds to cook. Don't worry too much about identifying the restaurant, you'll recognize it from the long lines of people waiting outside. Ⓢ *Average main: 30000d* ✉ *49 Bat Dan St.* ▭ *No credit cards* ☉ *Daily 7 am–10 am* ✛ *F4.*

$$ ✕ **Puku.** Open around the clock, Puku is nothing if not convenient. The
CAFÉ
international fare served won't have gourmands forming an orderly queue, but the quality is decent. While night owls appreciate the

7

generous opening hours, the restaurant's forte is probably its breakfast options, which include a full range of eggs (Benedict, florentine, royale) and a hearty full English. Occasional live music and movies add to the venue's appeal. [$] *Average main: 150000d* ✉ *16/18 Tong Duy Tan St.* ☎ *024/3938–1745* ✥ *F4.*

$$ VEGETARIAN 🍴 **Tamarind Cafe.** This restaurant serves creative, international vegetarian fare such as Zen pasta (stir-fried with vegetables in a sweet soy sauce) and Taiwanese *popiah,* sweet crepes with various fillings. The fresh fruit juices and blends—particularly the "Sapa spice tickler" (pineapple, carrot, ginger, and lemon juice)—are refreshing. Weekday evenings the Tamarind hosts live entertainment such as salsa-dancing lessons and jazz. [$] *Average main: 150000d* ✉ *80 Ma May St., Hoan Kiem District* ☎ *024/3926–0580* ✥ *G4.*

$$ INDIAN 🍴 **Tandoor.** This small Indian restaurant makes up for its lackluster setting with a wonderful yet inexpensive menu. Food is prepared fresh, with hand-ground spices. You can't go wrong with anything here, but fluffy garlic nan bread, tender chicken masala, and eggplant curry are particularly good. The fish tikka in red sauce and the chicken kebab marinated in yogurt are also sensational. Service is very friendly, although it can become chaotic at dinnertime. The restaurant delivers. [$] *Average main: 200000d* ✉ *24 Hang Be St., Hoan Kiem District* ☎ *024/3824–5359* ✥ *G4.*

THE FRENCH QUARTER

$$ CAFÉ 🍴 **129 Mai Hac De.** Locals and visitors flock to this closet-size café to perch on knee-high stools and sip smooth, creamy fruit shakes. The basic café menu lists pastries, baked potatoes, some rather mediocre rice and noodle dishes, and a selection of excellent grilled sandwiches. The star of the show is arguably the English breakfast, which is regarded by lovers of British stodge as being one of the finest fry-ups in all of Hanoi. Even if you crave something a bit lighter this is still a fine place to stop for a snack and some perhaps much-needed caffeine after a tour of Lenin Park. [$] *Average main: 100000d* ✉ *129 Mai Hac De St., Hai Ba Trung District* ☎ *024/3821–6342* 💳 *No credit cards* ✥ *F6.*

$$ BISTRO 🍴 **A La Folie.** There are few bells and whistles to this homey little French bistro, just well-executed Gallic bistro fare. Owned by a French couple, the restaurant specializes in hearty, rustic fare. Expect generous terrines, charcuterie plates, and gloriously stinky and oozy cheese galore. In addition to an à la carte selection, there are two fair-priced set menus. The wine list, meanwhile, is also French-focused with bottles starting at a very reasonable 600,000d. [$] *Average main: 240000d* ✉ *63 Ngo Hue, Hai Ba Trung District* ☎ *024/3976–1667* ✥ *G6.*

$ VIETNAMESE 🍴 **Che Thap Cam Cu.** This hole-in-the-wall serves only one thing, *che:* a sweet green bean concoction that is part drink, part pudding. Especially popular with Vietnamese women, che is a typical treat on sultry summer afternoons. A number of imitators have sprung up following the success of this old Hanoi institution. Walk to the end of the alley and look for the shop on your left. [$] *Average main: 20000d* ✉ *72G Tran Hung Dao St., Hoan Kiem District* 💳 *No credit cards* ✥ *F5.*

$$ ✕ **Chim Sao.** For an authentic Vietnamese dining experience in a classy,
VIETNAMESE arty setting this is a fine bet. On a quiet street, Chim Sao is a favorite
Fodor's Choice with Hanoi's bohemian crowd who come here to talk about weighty
★ topics while wolfing down traditional dishes from the north of Vietnam. An emphasis is put on the cuisine of the mountainous regions north of Hanoi with plenty of smoked pork and cured meats such as sausage and preserved pork ear in salt. Vegetarians are amply catered for with a wide selection of salads, vegetable dishes, and tofu creations. Ⓢ *Average main: 130000d* ✉ *65 Ngo Hue St., Hai Ba Trung District* ☎ *024/3976–0633* ⊕ *www.chimsao.com* ✛ *F6.*

$$ ✕ **Ky Y.** The Japanese equivalent of your friendly neighborhood diner,
JAPANESE this cozy restaurant is always packed with Japanese businesspeople and expats in the know. Astonishingly low prices encourage overindulgence in sushi or sashimi; the lunch specials are a steal at less than 150,000d. Seating is at low, take-your-shoes-off tables in small private rooms or at a long polished bar on the ground floor. Ⓢ *Average main: 160000d* ✉ *166 Trieu Viet Vuong St., Hai Ba Trung District* ☎ *024/3978–1386* ✛ *F6.*

$$$$ ✕ **La Badiane.** Bringing fine French cuisine to the heart of Hanoi, Chef
FRENCH Benjamin Rascalou, who trained at several prestigious restaurants in
Fodor's Choice Paris, has created an inspired menu of crab remoulade, foie gras ter-
★ rine, and smoked salmon with eggplant crumble in Gorgonzola sauce. Main entrées, such as the candied duck or sesame-encrusted shrimp, will set you back more than most restaurants in Hanoi will, but the flavors are worth the splurge. Those who order the six-course degustation are treated to a trio of desserts and a complimentary bottle of champagne. The open-air courtyard is delightful, and the ambience is classy and sophisticated without being overly pretentious. Fans of beef carpaccio must try it here, as it is dribbled with pistachio oil and fig syrup. Ⓢ *Average main: 481620d* ✉ *10 Nam Ngu* ☎ *024/3942–4509* ⊕ *www.labadiane-hanoi.com* ☽ *Closed Sun.* ✛ *F5*

$$$$ ✕ **La Verticale.** French chef Didier Corlou is a big food personality in
FRENCH FUSION Hanoi and his signature restaurant showcases his skills to alchemic effect. Fusing Gallic flair with Vietnamese ingredients and methods, his approach makes for a unique fine-dining experience. Not everything works. Sometimes Corlou's vivid imagination makes for slightly prissy presentation and flavor combinations that don't quite come off. When dishes are good, however, they are very good indeed. The upstairs dining room can feel a little formal, but service is unpretentious, friendly, and welcoming. Ⓢ *Average main: 650000d* ✉ *19 Ngo Van So, Hai Ba Trung District* ☎ *024/944–6317* ⊕ *www.verticale-hanoi.com* ✛ *F5.*

$$$$ ✕ **Le Beaulieu.** For old-school French fine dining, the Metropole's stal-
FRENCH wart flagship restaurant sets the tone. If it is innovation you are after, there are more creative menus in Hanoi, many of which have been created by French chefs. However, for complex and creamy sauces as well as classics such as foie gras and côte de boeuf, this is the place. The spacious dining room doesn't lend itself particularly well to intimacy, but an extensive wine list and expert service heighten the allure. Ⓢ *Average main: 850000d* ✉ *15 Ngo Quyen, Hai Ba Trung District* ☎ *024/3826–6919* ⊕ *www.sofitel-legend.com* ✛ *G5.*

7

$$ INDIAN Fodor's Choice ★ 🍴 **Namaste.** Be transported to the subcontinent at this authentic Indian restaurant, where the owners import herbs and spices directly from India. Specializing in both northern and southern cuisine, the menu highlights curries, hot and spicy soups, and vegetarian and rice dishes. Flat breads like paratha and naan are cooked in a genuine clay tandoor oven, and the impressive cone-shape dosa pancake stands 2 feet tall. The kebabs, ranging from chicken and fish to prawn or vegetarian, are grilled to perfection with spices and lime. [$] *Average main: 209400d* ✉ *46 Ngo Thuom* ☎ *024/3935–2400* 🌐 *www.namastehanoi.com* 🕒 *Closed 2:30–6 pm* ✥ *F5.*

$$ VIETNAMESE 🍴 **Nam Phuong.** Aimed more at tourists than at a local clientele, this restaurant in a nicely renovated French villa provides a good introduction to Vietnamese cuisine. Just bear in mind that portions of the tasty and beautifully presented dishes, such as beef in coconut milk, can be disappointingly small. But the experience of dining here is lovely, with musicians playing traditional Vietnamese instruments and waitstaff dressed in traditional outfits. [$] *Average main: 200000d* ✉ *19 Phan Chu Trinh St.* ☎ *024/3824–0926* 🌐 *www.namphuong-restaurant.com* ✥ *G5.*

$$$ VIETNAMESE 🍴 **Pots 'n Pans.** This well-frequented spot presents traditional Vietnamese flavors in new ways to produce an experience that is both local to the region yet altogether distinctive. Dishes such as braised duck leg in spiced shiitake mushroom jus with lemongrass duck sausage, and vegetarian cannelloni served with cassia-scented potato puree and a Southern-style curry sauce, are just the tip of the creative iceberg. The fine cuisine is complemented by a well-stocked wine bar and excellent desserts. It's a splurge by Hanoi standards—but worth it. [$] *Average main: 300000d* ✉ *57 Bui Thi Xuan St., Hai Ba Trung District* ☎ *024/39440204* 🌐 *www.potsnpans.vn* ✥ *F6.*

$$ VIETNAMESE Fodor's Choice ★ 🍴 **Quan An Ngon.** Well known among Hanoi locals and expats for its lively atmosphere and unparalleled variety of street food, this noted eatery has specialties from northern, central, and southern Vietnam. The restaurant has additional branches in Ho Chi Minh City and elsewhere in Hanoi at 34 Phan Dinh Phung and at 25T2 Hoang Dao Thuy Street. It's almost as popular for the old courtyard setting as for the great food. Spring rolls, green papaya salads, barbecued seafood, pho, and dozens of other dishes provide diners a stellar opportunity to explore one of Asia's most popular cuisines. To top it all off, prices are extremely reasonable. [$] *Average main: 120000d* ✉ *18 Phan Boi Chau St.* ☎ *024/3734–9777* 🌐 *www.ngonhanoi.com.vn* ✥ *F5.*

$$$$ JAPANESE Fodor's Choice ★ 🍴 **Restaurant Benkay.** High prices match the high standards at this elegant hotel restaurant. The traditional Japanese interior is as delicately understated as the service, and the food will transport you straight to Tokyo. Set lunches, such as breaded pork or chicken, start at just 250,000d, although once here it's all too tempting to go for the five-course *kaiseki* menu of seafood specialties or the divine sushi dinner. Be forewarned that portions are small. [$] *Average main: 750000d* ✉ *Hotel Nikko Hanoi, 84 Tran Nhan Tong St., Hai Ba Trung District* ☎ *024/3822–3535* ✥ *E6.*

$$$$ ECLECTIC 🍴 **The Restaurant, Hanoi Press Club.** An exceptional assortment of fine wines, cigars, and single-malt Scotch complements the fine international

cuisine at this semiformal restaurant where Hanoi's movers and shakers gather. Chef Guillaume Guertin prepares the finest ingredients with French techniques. The peppered and smoked duckling breast is blissful. The grilled beef tenderloin with cabernet sauvignon essence and sauteéd chicken breast with proscuitto are also standouts. An outside deck area is more casual. $ *Average main: 450000d* ⊠ *Hanoi Press Club, 59A Ly Thai To St., 3rd fl.* ☎ *024/3934–0888* ⊕ *www.hanoi-pressclub.com* ⌂ *Reservations essential* ✢ *G5.*

$$

VEGETARIAN

✕ **Vegetarian Restaurant Com Chay Nang Tam.** Unusual vegetarian dishes, many prepared to resemble meat, are served in a dimly lighted villa. The warm corn squares are a pleasing starter, and the "ginger fish," made of tofu, is a good main course. Indeed, so realistic are the approximations of fish and meats such as pork and beef that you may begin to question the restaurant's vegetarian credentials. Fear not, however, this venue has been catering to satisfied customers for decades. The restaurant has limited seating, so reservations are recommended, especially for larger parties. $ *Average main: 170000d* ⊠ *79A Tran Hung Dao St.* ☎ *024/3942–4140* ✢ *F5.*

THE HO CHI MINH MAUSOLEUM AND NEARBY

$$

ECLECTIC

Fodor's Choice

★

✕ **Koto.** The flavors here—from honey prawns to bamboo beef—are bold and brilliant, and the menu is a mix of creative dishes like fish cakes, five-spice duck, Thai salad, and glazed ribs. If you like spring rolls, try the sampler with this Vietnamese staple prepared several different ways. The fact that Koto (an acronym for "know one, teach one") is a charity-restaurant that benefits street youth, is just the icing on the mango cheesecake. Located across from the Temple of Literature, this place can get packed, especially on the third floor dominated by tour groups. $ *Average main: 120000d* ⊠ *59 Van Mieu, across from Van Mieu Temple of Literature, Ba Dinh District* ☎ *024/3747–0337* ⊕ *www.koto.com.au* ✢ *E5.*

$$

VIETNAMESE

✕ **Ly Van Phuc (Chicken Street).** Colloquially known as "Chicken Street," this is the place to come for delicious barbecued poultry. Visitors may not be overly enamored by the sight of chicken parts marinating in open buckets, but horror stories about upset stomachs are surprisingly rare. The street is lined with vendors working near-identical alchemy with a limited menu of grilled chicken wings and feet, sweet potatoes, and bread that's been brushed with honey before being toasted on the grill. The resulting dish is served up with chili sauce and pickled cucumbers in sweet vinegar and washed down with icy bottles of local beer. The grills go into action around sundown and stay burning until after midnight. $ *Average main: 80000d* ⊠ *Ly Van Phuc, Ba Dinh District* ▭ *No credit cards* ✢ *D4.*

WEST LAKE

$$$

WINE BAR

Fodor's Choice

★

✕ **Bluebird.** High-quality, well-prepared food and a well chosen and reasonably priced selection of wine are the watchwords at this West Lake favorite. The menu bears strong Italian influences, but runs the gamut from American-style options like giant rack of ribs to such left-field creations as Peruvian ceviche. The kitchen staff manage to stay on point despite the scattershot approach and dishes are beautifully presented. The upstairs dining room is a pleasant space, but for a truly intimate experience request the private dining table in the restaurant's basement. [$] *Average main: 280000d* ✉ *7 Xuan Dieu St., Tay Ho District* ☎ *024/3722–4165* 🌐 *bluebirdrestaurant.com.vn* ✥ *D1.*

$$ INTERNATIONAL Fodor's Choice ★ 🍴 **Commune.** Branded as a "collaborative office and enterprise hub," this think-tank café has a little bit of everything—early breakfasts and coffee, a diverse international menu perfect for all-day noshing, some of the best drinks in Hanoi, and on weekends a hefty Hangover Special, complete with a Bloody Mary and strong coffee. The menu includes homemade granola, salads, sandwiches, bangers and mash, and plenty of vegetarian and gluten-free options. Commune is also one of the best vantage points for gazing out at West Lake. [$] *Average main: 100000d* ✉ *201 Trich Sai St. (Thuy Khue), Tay Ho District* ☎ *024/6684–7903* 🌐 *www.communehanoi.com* 💳 *No credit cards* ✥ *B2.*

$$ FRENCH 🍴 **Cousins.** The outdoor area of this French-influenced, lakeside venue is an ideal place for some very romantic dining, especially on less humid evenings. Indoor things are equally convivial with stripped pine tables and wooden furniture creating an almost Scandinavian ambience. The food is a mixed bag of French, Italian, and Vietnamese dishes. Not all of the offerings live up to expectations, but dishes such as oxtail gnocchi and the charcuterie board are very good indeed. [$] *Average main: 250000d* ✉ *3 Quang Ba, Tay Ho District* ☎ *012/3867–0098* ✥ *E1.*

$$ ISRAELI Fodor's Choice ★ 🍴 **Daluva.** With an imaginative menu that covers Middle Eastern, Vietnamese, and American cuisines, Daluva is a cool, contemporary spot. Israeli Shay Lubin has established himself as one of Hanoi's best chefs during his extended stay in the city and his flair is reflected in the menu here. The restaurant bills itself as a Middle Eastern gastropub and dishes such as Arab flatbread with ground beef, spices, and pine nuts, and Tunisian fish stew reflect the chef's origins. For many diners, however, it is perfectly executed comfort food favorites like a giant burger and a Philly cheesesteak that keeps them coming back for more. [$] *Average main: 225000d* ✉ *33 To Ngoc Van St., Tay Ho District* ☎ *024/3718–5831* 🌐 *www.daluva.com* ✥ *E1.*

$$ VIETNAMESE 🍴 **Dieu's Cuisine.** Good wine, fresh Vietnamese cuisine, a romantic lakeside setting, and friendly service have helped Dieu's Cuisine build a loyal clientele since the restaurant opened in 2011. The menu is strong on meat dishes, including grilled pork loin in clam sauce, and fried chicken with lemongrass and chili, plus there's a good selection of spring rolls and stir-fry dishes. Vegetarians and omnivores wanting to eat light will find plenty of options. Alfresco dining is pleasant most of the year, but the air-conditioned dining space upstairs comes in handy when it's hot and humid. Reservations are recommended during peak dining times. [$] *Average main: 140000d* ✉ *25 Xuan Dieu, Tay Ho District* ☎ *098/734–6843* 💳 *No credit cards* 🕒 *Closed Mon.* ✥ *D1*

$$$ ECLECTIC Fodor's Choice ★ 🍴 **Don's - A Chef's Bistro.** The only venue in Vietnam to make it to the most recent list of Asia's 50 best restaurants, Don's is fully deserving of its exalted reputation. The impressive menu ranges from authentic international specialties and an oyster bar to sophisticated fusion

dishes. Canadian chef Don Berger eschews culinary frills to deliver food that places an emphasis on local produce and top-quality imports. No-nonsense options such as pasta and risotto, steaks and grilled meats, and wood-fired pizzas don't push the envelope, but deliver brilliantly within their parameters. The location overlooking West Lake, meanwhile, is effortlessly romantic. $ *Average main: 300000d* ✉ *16 Quang An Rd., Tay Ho District* ☎ *024/719–2828* ⊕ *www.donsbistro.com* ✛ *D1.*

$$$$
STEAKHOUSE
Fodor'sChoice
★

✕ **El Gaucho.** The West Lake branch of a chain of Argentinian steakhouses with outlets in Ho Chi Minh City and Bangkok, El Gaucho Hanoi serves up exemplary (if expensive) slabs of meat. Steaks are the specialty, and there's nothing to fault about the ones here. A variety of cuts are imported from the United States and Australia. Sides range from comfort options such as macaroni-and-cheese and creamed spinach to healthier choices, including arugula salad and corn on the cob. There's also a decent range of chicken, fish, and vegetarian dishes. $ *Average main: 900000d* ✉ *99 Xuan Dieu St., Tay Ho District* ☎ *024/3718–6991* ⊕ *www.elgaucho.asia* ✛ *D1.*

$$$$
ASIAN FUSION
Fodor'sChoice
★

✕ **Halia.** A unique marriage of European cooking styles and Southeast Asian flavors, Halia is one of the more notable establishments in Hanoi's constantly expanding fine-dining scene. Some of the more inspired items served here include chili-crab spaghetti, tamarind spiced pork ribs, and frozen ginger-nougat parfait. The three-course lunch menu (240,000d) is served between 11 am and 2 pm and highlights such dishes as beef teriyaki spaghetti and ravioli of mushroom ragout. Decor is modern and airy with fine outlooks over the lake. $ *Average main: 450000d* ✉ *29 Xuan Dieu, Tay Ho District* ☎ *024/3946–0121* ⊕ *www.thehalia.com* ⊘ *Closed Sun.* ✛ *D1*

$$
VIETNAMESE

✕ **Seasons of Hanoi.** French elegance meets Vietnamese charm in a beautifully restored villa dating from 1902, which is filled with antiques from Indochina. The coconut-and-lemongrass chicken curry is a rich choice, as is the divine eggplant cooked in a clay pot. Sunday brunch is popular and the spacious setting makes the restaurant a very popular choice with big groups. $ *Average main: 200000d* ✉ *95B Quan Thanh St., Ba Dinh District* ☎ *024/3835–5444* ⊕ *www.seasonsofhanoi.com.vn* ✛ *E3.*

$$
JAPANESE

✕ **Sushi Dokoro Yutaka.** This West Lake institution serves some of the best Japanese food in Hanoi. The city has a sizeable community of Japanese expats, which means that this venue is reliably packed with homesick salary men looking to sample an authentic taste of home. Westerners also flock to the restaurant to sample its inexpensive lunch sets and bento boxes as well as sophisticated evening dining. Sushi and sashimi are particularly good, but the extensive menu features everything from *yakitori* (grilled skewers) to *sukiyaki* (hotpot). $ *Average main: 250000d* ✉ *95 Xuan Dieu, Tay Ho District* ☎ *024/3718–6344* ✛ *D1.*

7

WHERE TO STAY

If there is one thing Hanoi is not short of it is places to stay. In the Old Quarter, small family-run hotels rule the roost. While many of these remain fairly basic affairs, there has been real movement in the mid- to high-end sector. Many of the more salubrious establishments bill themselves as "boutique hotels." For Westerners used to this sobriquet being used in relation to individualist, design-led options, the term may feel like a misnomer given the relative uniformity of most of what is on offer. Nevertheless, with opulent marble-clad lobbies coupled with excellent, personal service and smart and luxurious bedrooms, there is little to fault about many of these places. Outside the Old Quarter, some of the biggest international hotel brands have made their mark. The leafy avenues of the area south of Hoan Kiem Lake shelter some sterling lodgings, including the city's undisputed grande dame, the Sofitel Legend Metropole. West Lake, Ba Dinh, and even some outlying areas such as Tu Liem, an enclave mooted as the city's new Central Business District, are also home to some excellent international-standard options. *For expanded reviews, visit Fodors.com.*

Use the coordinates (✛ A1) at the end of each listing to locate a site on the cooresponding map.

WHAT IT COSTS				
	$	$$	$$$	$$$$
Hotels	Under 750,000d	750,000d –1,000,000d	1,100,000d –2,500,000d	over 2,500,000d

Prices in the reviews are the lowest cost of a standard double room in high season.

THE OLD QUARTER

$$　**Art Trendy Hotel.** In one of the quieter Old Quarter streets, this small
HOTEL but lovely option provides a peaceful refuge from the bustle found
Fodor'sChoice elsewhere. **Pros:** fantastic views from upper level rooms; attentive ser-
★ vice. **Cons:** breakfast is on the simple side. $ *Rooms from: 832056d* ⊠ *6A Hang But, Hoan Kiem District* ☎ *024/3923–4293* ⊕ *www. arttrendyhotel.com* ⥌ *25 rooms* ⦿*| Breakfast* ✛ *F4.*

$$　**Calypso Grand Hotel.** Another of the Old Quarter's "boutique" options,
HOTEL this small hotel offers a fair quotient of refinement for a relatively low price. **Pros:** free airport pickup a major bonus. **Cons:** some guests may balk at the color schemes. $ *Rooms from: 960300d* ⊠ *27A Cua Dong, Hoan Kiem District* ☎ *024/3923–4070* ⊕ *www.calypsograndhotel.com* ⥌ *17 rooms* ⦿*| Breakfast* ✛ *F4.*

$　**Camellia Hanoi Hotel.** This well-run, well-maintained hotel in the
HOTEL thick of the Old Quarter has clean, bright rooms and friendly staff. **Pros:** high standards; great street life. **Cons:** decor is a little garish. $ *Rooms from: 400000d* ⊠ *12C Chan Cam St., Hoan Kiem District* ☎ *024/3828–5936* ⊕ *www.camelliahanoihotel.com* ⥌ *17 rooms* ⦿*| Breakfast* ✛ *F4.*

$$$ B&B/INN Fodor's Choice ★ **Essence Hanoi Hotel.** Great location, elegantly simple rooms with a Vietnamese touch, and an obsession with service are the hallmarks of this property, which, despite its small size, offers most of the services of a five-star hotel. **Pros:** rental laptops with free Wi-Fi; helpful travel desk. **Cons:** rooms without windows are a little gloomy. [$] *Rooms from: 1100000d* ✉ *22 Ta Hien St., Hoan Kiem District* ☎ *024/3935–2485* 🌐 *www.essencehanoihotel.com* 🛏 *14 rooms, 6 suites* 🍴 *Breakfast* ✣ *G4.*

$$ HOTEL **Golden Sun Suites.** Conveniently located a stone's throw from Hoan Kiem Lake, the newest addition to the family-run Golden Sun chain is within easy walking distance of major attractions in the area. **Pros:** excellent customer service; regularly replenished fresh flowers. **Cons:** some rooms are compact. [$] *Rooms from: 1173425d* ✉ *35 Hang Quat, Hoan Kiem District* ☎ *024/3938–7066* 🌐 *www.goldensunhotel.com* 🛏 *35 rooms* 🍴 *Breakfast* ✣ *F4.*

$ HOTEL Fodor's Choice ★ **Hanoi 3B Hotel.** Located on busy Ma May, this spot perhaps doesn't enjoy the same sense of seclusion of some of its nearby competitors, but offers serious bang for your buck in the Old Quarter. **Pros:** palatial lodgings at prices a serf can afford; huge rooms. **Cons:** Ma May is one of the Old Quarter's noisier streets. [$] *Rooms from: 448035d* ✉ *99 Ma May St., Hoan Kiem District* ☎ *024/3926–2285* 🌐 *www.hanoi3bhotel.com* 🛏 *38 rooms* 🍴 *Breakfast* ✣ *G4.*

$$$ HOTEL Fodor's Choice ★ **Hanoi Elegance Diamond.** This 12-story property, the newest addition to the Hanoi Elegance chain, is the tallest building in the area, offering spectacular river and city views from top-level rooms. **Pros:** rooms have personal laptops; free Wi-Fi; suites offer sweet value. **Cons:** rooms next to the restaurant can be a little noisy. [$] *Rooms from: 1465800d* ✉ *32 Lo Su St., Hoan Kiem District* ☎ *024/3935–1632* 🌐 *www.hanoielegancehotel.com* 🛏 *34 rooms* 🍴 *Breakfast* ✣ *G4.*

$$ B&B/INN **Hanoi Elegance Ruby.** One of the better-known names among the growing number of boutique hotels in Vietnam's capital, Hanoi Elegance Ruby gets high marks for location, service, and value; from the moment you step foot in the lobby, the staff will make you feel like you're a VIP. **Pros:** specatcular breakfasts; dedicated staff. **Cons:** rooms are small. [$] *Rooms from: 1050000d* ✉ *3 Yen Thai St., Hoan Kiem District* ☎ *024/3938–0963* 🌐 *www.hanoielegancehotel.com* 🛏 *19 rooms, 7 suites* 🍴 *Breakfast* ✣ *F4.*

$$ HOTEL **Hanoi Serene Hotel.** Serene might not be a word you would immediately associate with busy Hanoi, but the young and attentive staff here go out of their way to ensure a peaceful and stress-free stay in the city. **Pros:** free use of computers; breakfast is included. **Cons:** tucked away location can be hard for taxis to find. [$] *Rooms from: 960300d* ✉ *10C Yen Thai St., Hoan Kiem District* ☎ *024/3938–2416* 🌐 *www.hanoiserenehotel.com* 🛏 *32 rooms* 🍴 *Breakfast* ✣ *F4.*

$$$ HOTEL **Hotel Meracus 2.** The sister property of one of the most respected small hotels in the Old Quarter is even more impressive than the original—the service and decor has been spruced up to make it one of the standout options in a part of the city that doesn't lack for good hotels. **Pros:** laptops and a daily newspaper are provided; fresh flowers. **Cons:** windowless rooms are far less desirable than ones with a view. [$] *Rooms from:*

1365440d ✉ *32 Hang Trong St., Hoan Kiem District* ☎ *024/3938–2526* 🌐 *www.meracushotels.com* 🛏 *22 rooms* 🍴 *Breakfast* ✣ *F4.*

$ HOTEL 🏨 **Icon 36 Hotel.** Tucked away down a quiet street at the western edge of the Old Quarter, this hotel offers spotless value for money. **Pros:** great quality for the price. **Cons:** downstairs bar is dingy. [$] *Rooms from: 597380d* ✉ *35–37 Bat Su St., Hoan Kiem District* ☎ *024/3923–3735* 🌐 *www.icon36hotel.com* 🛏 *41 rooms* 🍴 *Breakfast* ✣ *F4.*

$$$$ HOTEL 🏨 **Maison d'Hanoi Boutique Hotel.** Nestled on a street that is quiet (by Hanoi's standards), this cozy boutique hotel—a spinoff of its sister property, Maison Hanova—has an ideal location for exploring Hanoi's Old Quarter and Hoan Kiem Lake. **Pros:** prime amenities; lovely piano bar and restaurant. **Cons:** bustling public areas can be a little noisy. [$] *Rooms from: 5580000d* ✉ *35–37 Ma May St., Hoan Kiem District* ☎ *024/3923–4999* 🌐 *www.maisondhanoi.com* 🛏 *36 rooms, 6 suites* 🍴 *breakfast* ✣ *G4.*

$$ HOTEL Fodor's Choice ★ 🏨 **Oriental Central Hotel.** Perhaps more luxurious than others in the area, the lodgings combine the height of comfort with elegant and classy design. **Pros:** stylish design makes this a true boutique gem. **Cons:** mattresses are slightly hard. [$] *Rooms from: 853400d* ✉ *39 Hang Bac St., Hoan Kiem District* ☎ *024/3935–1117* 🌐 *www.orientalcentralhotel.com* 🛏 *25 rooms* 🍴 *Breakfast* ✣ *G4.*

$ HOTEL 🏨 **Win Hotel.** Immaculate and homey all at once, the Win is just off Le Thai To Street, a short skip from Hoan Kiem Lake, and next to the famous Café Nhan, which is the size of a mansion and famous for its avocado shakes and rocket-fuel coffee. **Pros:** rooms are airier than many Hanoi hotels. **Cons:** floor tiles can be a little chilly in the colder months. [$] *Rooms from: 532625d* ✉ *34 Hang Hanh St., Hoan Kiem District* ☎ *024/3828–7371* 🌐 *www.win-hotel-hanoi.com* 🛏 *8 rooms* 🍴 *Breakfast* ✣ *F4.*

THE FRENCH QUARTER

$$$ HOTEL 🏨 **De Syloia Hotel.** A true French Quarter boutique hotel, the French colonial–style De Syloia is small but fashionable, with wooden furniture, large beds, and cream-color linens in the well-appointed and well-maintained rooms. **Pros:** friendly, attentive staff. **Cons:** restaurant is average; rooms book out quickly. [$] *Rooms from: 1390000d* ✉ *17A Trang Hung Dao St., Hoan Kiem District* ☎ *024/3824–5346* 🌐 *www.desyloia.com* 🛏 *33 rooms* 🍴 *Breakfast* ✣ *G5.*

$$$ HOTEL 🏨 **Eden Hotel.** Bright rooms at this top-rated hotel near Thuyen Quang Lake have all of the conveniences—carpeted floors, carved-wood furniture, big baths, and extras such as flat-screen televisions and classy wall hangings. **Pros:** rooftop pool, spa; sauna. **Cons:** hotel has been known to overcharge for airport transfers. [$] *Rooms from: 1700000d* ✉ *22 Doan Tran Nghiep, Hoan Kiem District* ☎ *024/3974–8622* 🌐 *www.edenhotel.com.vn* 🛏 *60 rooms* 🍴 *Breakfast* ✣ *F6.*

$$$ HOTEL 🏨 **Hilton Hanoi Opera.** A stone's throw from the Hanoi Opera House, this was arguably the city's top hotel for many years and is still a solid bet today, offering easy access to the French Quarter, while Hanoi's old quarter and modern central business district are also nearby. **Pros:** some rooms have views of the Opera House; excellent restaurant.

Cons: rooms and common areas are a little dated. [$] *Rooms from: 2500700d* ✉ *1 Le Thanh Tong St., Hoan Kiem District* ☎ *024/3933–0500* ⊕ *www3.hilton.com* ⇔ *255 rooms, 14 suites* ❙◎❙ *Breakfast* ✛ *G5.*

$$$$ ⊡ **Hotel Nikko Hanoi.** With its sleek and airy lobby affording a peek
HOTEL   into a tiny Japanese garden, this 15-story hotel is a shining example of understated Japanese elegance. **Pros:** corner suites are highly desirable; excellent food including Sunday dim sum. **Cons:** not exactly in the thick of the action. [$] *Rooms from: 3000000d* ✉ *84 Tran Nhan Tong St., Hai Ba Trung District* ☎ *024/3822–3535* ⊕ *www.hotelnikkohanoi.com.vn* ⇔ *257 rooms* ❙◎❙ *Breakfast* ✛ *E6.*

$$$$ ⊡ **Hotel Sofitel Legend Metropole Hanoi.** A classic Asian colonial-era hotel
HOTEL   in the same league as the Peninsula in Hong Kong and Singapore's
Fodor's Choice   Raffles Hotel, the Metropole is Hanoi's most storied accommodation,
★   offering world-class service in a historic building nestled in the French Quarter across from the Hanoi Opera House. **Pros:** one of Hanoi's most inviting swimming pools; daily tours to the hotel's wartime bomb shelter. **Cons:** newer rooms are pleasant but lack period charm. [$] *Rooms from: 6877865d* ✉ *15 Ngo Quyen St., Hoan Kiem District* ☎ *024/3826–6919* ⊕ *www.sofitel-legend.com/hanoi/* ⇔ *342 rooms, 22 suites* ❙◎❙ *No meals* ✛ *F4.*

$$$ ⊡ **Melia Hanoi.** A solid option for those who appreciate chain-hotel
HOTEL   facilities at highly reasonable prices, there are always discounts worth bargaining for here. **Pros:** attractive outdoor pool and well-maintained fitness facilities; discounts available. **Cons:** it's not Hanoi's most charming hotel. [$] *Rooms from: 2300000d* ✉ *44B Ly Thuong Kiet St., Hoan Kiem District* ☎ *024/3934–3343* ⊕ *www.melia.com* ⇔ *308 rooms* ❙◎❙ *Breakfast* ✛ *F5.*

$$$ ⊡ **Movenpick Hotel.** This well-run Swiss chain is popular with business
HOTEL   travelers, and the pleasant rooms and efficient service are certainly a cut above the average. **Pros:** state-of-the-art gym; spa and sauna facilities. **Cons:** no pool, which is unusual for such an upscale name. [$] *Rooms from: 2553000d* ✉ *83A Ly Thuong Kiet St., Hoan Kiem District* ☎ *024/3822–2800 024* ⇔ *154 rooms* ❙◎❙ *Breakfast* ✛ *F5.*

THE HO CHI MINH MAUSOLEUM AND NEARBY

$$$ ⊡ **Pullman Hanoi Hotel.** An impressive green glass–fronted facade and
HOTEL   attentive and professional service are indicative of the elevated ambitions of this smart business hotel. **Pros:** excellent buffet breakfast is a cut above; smart fitness facilities; outdoor pool. **Cons:** rooms are not overly large. [$] *Rooms from: 1981000d* ✉ *40 Cat Linh St., Ba Dinh District* ☎ *024/3733–0688 024* ⊕ *www.pullmanhotels.com* ⇔ *242 rooms* ❙◎❙ *Breakfast* ✛ *D4.*

WEST LAKE

$$$ ⊡ **Hanoi Club.** Well-appointed rooms at this swanky sports club afford
HOTEL   spectacular sunset views over West Lake and include the use of the club's plush facilities. **Pros:** lakeside setting; plenty of sports facilities. **Cons:** restaurant is on the chintzy side. [$] *Rooms from: 1216000d* ✉ *76 Yen Phu St., Tay Ho District* ☎ *024/3823–8115* ⊕ *www.thehanoiclub.com* ⇔ *63 rooms* ❙◎❙ *Breakfast* ✛ *E2.*

$$$$ HOTEL FAMILY **Intercontinental Hanoi Westlake.** In a tranquil setting, over-the-water pavilions house spacious rooms with balconies and great views of West Lake and Hanoi, helping guests feel removed from the urban bustle of the city center, even though the hotel is only a couple of miles from the Old Quarter and Hoan Kiem Lake. **Pros:** large pool; well-stocked gym. **Cons:** spa not up to the level you would expect at this price point. [$] *Rooms from: 3245700d* ✉ *1A Nghi Tam, Tay Ho District* ☎ *024/6270–8888* 🌐 *www.intercontinental.com/hanoi* 🛏 *377 rooms* 🍴 *Breakfast* ✥ *D1.*

$$$ HOTEL Fodor's Choice ★ **Sofitel Plaza Hotel.** Stunning views of Truc Bach and West Lake and a central location are two of the highlights of this luxury hotel, but the standout is the indoor heated swimming pool with a view over the neighboring lakes and a retractable roof for year-round swimming. **Pros:** club floor benefits are extremely attractive; great restaurants. **Cons:** rooftop bar needs a little attention. [$] *Rooms from: 2343000d* ✉ *1 Thanh Nien St., Ba Dinh District* ☎ *024/3823–8888* 🌐 *www.sofitel.com* 🛏 *273 rooms* 🍴 *Breakfast* ✥ *E2.*

GREATER HANOI

$$$$ HOTEL Fodor's Choice ★ **JW Marriot Hanoi.** Although located a fair distance from the thick of the action, in an area mooted as the city's new main business district, Marriott's first Hanoi property still makes a worthwhile base. **Pros:** the best hotel dining in the city; delightfully landscaped grounds, with a lake. **Cons:** out of the way. [$] *Rooms from: 2900000d* ✉ *8 Do Duc Duc, Tu Liem* ☎ *024/3833–5588* 🌐 *www.marriot.com* 🛏 *395 rooms* 🍴 *Breakfast* ✥ *A6.*

NIGHTLIFE AND PERFORMING ARTS

NIGHTLIFE

Hanoi has enough bars and clubs to keep you busy. They range from low-key drinking venues and more salubrious venues with extensive wine lists to raucous places where loud house music and cheap drinks keep dancers on the floor. Because many ventures are short-lived—Hanoi's nightclubs are curiously prone to electrical fires and other mysterious disasters—it is wise to call ahead when possible. For something a bit more casual, head to one of the cafés or bars in Old Quarter, where rooftop lounges, cocktail bars, and the popular Bia Hoi beer corner cluster about in a historical setting. Upscale hotels tend to have swanky bars of their own with live jazz to accompany a dry martini. For a mellow vibe and drinks with a view, you can go to waterfront bars near West Lake. Head into town early for happy hour since most joints close by midnight.

OLD QUARTER

BARS AND PUBS

Highway 4. This is a fine place to go for a drink, a snack, and some travel advice. This stylish bar specializes in Vietnamese rice wine, which is used in traditional medicines. The liquor, sold under the restaurant's own Son Thinh brand, is quite strong, so you should avoid drinking it on an empty stomach. As much of a restaurant as it is a bar, the country-style food here acts as ideal ballast to counteract the drink. ⊠ *5 Hang Tre St., Hoan Kiem District* ☎ *024/3926–4200.*

Mao's Red Lounge. Bars come and go down on the Ta Hien strip in the heart of the Old Quarter, but Mao's is a perennial favorite. Grungy, but friendly, the bar is frequented by a mixed crowd of locals, travelers, and expatriates. ⊠ *7 Ta Hien St., Hoan Kiem District* ☎ *024/3926–3104.*

Nola Café. Down a hidden alley in Old Quarter, this quirky, three-tiered Hanoi hot spot has a rooftop terrace popular with travelers and expats. Antiques blend with funky decor to give it plenty of character and charm. The music is borderline too-loud-for-conversation, but the eclectic playlist certainly draws in a crowd. Choose from a variety of coffees, teas, and cocktails. ⊠ *Alley 89 Ma May* ☎ *094/248–7605.*

Polite Pub. One of the original expat hangouts in Hanoi, this welcoming venue still attracts a decent crowd on a nightly basis. On weekends, the place is often packed from 9 pm to midnight as sports fans crowd around its screens. ⊠ *5 Ngo Bao Khanh St., Hoan Kiem District* ☎ *024/3825–0959.*

DANCE CLUBS

Hanoi EDM. The letters stand for Electronic Dance Music and that's the order of the day at this throbbing venue. Closing times in Hanoi can rely on the whims of the authorities, but this place generally stays open until the wee hours. ⊠ *46 Cuong Duong Do St., Hoan Kiem District* ☎ *098/658–4965.*

Phuc Tan. Hanoi is not a nightlife hub, but if you are looking for unreconstructed late-night fun then this is the place to go. Inside things are smoky, hot, and sweaty, but there's fresh air on the outside terrace and a river close by. ⊠ *51 Tu Gian Phuc Tan St.* ☎ *091/590–7785.*

FRENCH QUARTER

BARS AND PUBS

Fodor's Choice ★ **Binh Minh's Jazz Club.** Minh's Jazz Club is owned by one of Hanoi's best-known jazz musicians, Quyen Van Minh. Live jazz performed by both foreign and local musicians, including Minh's son, are the big draws here. ⊠ *1 Trang Tien, Hoan Kiem District* ☎ *024/3933–6555.*

Fodor's Choice ★ **CAMA ATK.** One of the hippest venues in Hanoi, this speakeasy-style venue combines effortless conviviality with an excellent cocktail list. Regular events run the gamut from live bands to no-holds-barred DJ nights where the playlist veers from electro to '50s rock and roll. ⊠ *73 Mai Hac De, Hai Ba Trung District* ⊕ *www.cama-atk.com.*

Press Club. The drinking venues at the Press Club combine plush couches, unobtrusive staff, and a menu of fancy (and expensive) cocktails and Cuban cigars. On Friday evenings the attached terrace hosts an after-work happy hour popular with Hanoi's expats. ✉ *59A Ly Thai To St., Hoan Kiem District* ☎ *024/3934–0888.*

Rooftop Bar. Hanoi is not generally an obviously flashy city, but this is one of the few places in town where a bit of glitz is part of the fun. Expect great views across the city, sleek decor, and classy (but expensive) drinks. ✉ *19th fl., Pacific Place, 83B Ly Thuong Kiet St., Ba Dinh District* ☎ *091/370–6966* ⊕ *www.therooftop.vn.*

Fodor's Choice ★ **Tadioto.** Owned and operated by journalist and raconteur Nguyen Qui Duc, this Hanoi institution is now in its fourth incarnation near the Opera House. Expect a bohemian crowd, an eclectic music policy, and a great selection of wine. ✉ *24 Tong Dan, Hoan Kiem District* ☎ *024/6680–9124* ⊕ *www.tadioto.com.*

HO CHI MINH MAUSOLEUM AND AROUND
BARS AND PUBS

Fodor's Choice ★ **Bar Betta.** This hip spot attracts a mixed crowd of trendy Vietnamese kids and expats. The venue has a retro chic feel and drinks—especially the house Old Fashioned—are considered to be among the best in the city. ✉ *34C Cao Ba Quat, Ba Dinh District* ☎ *024/734–9134.*

WEST LAKE
BARS AND PUBS

Hanoi Rock City. With a spacious outdoor bar downstairs and a large and fully soundproofed indoor area upstairs, this is Hanoi's premier alternative music venue. The emphasis is on live music, but there are also regular DJ events. ✉ *27/52 To Ngoc Van, Tay Ho District* ☎ *016/3316–6170* ⊕ *www.hanoirockcity.com.*

Madake. One of Hanoi's new breed of hip bars, this spot near West Lake offers regular live music and a relaxed vibe. ✉ *81 Xuan Dieu, Tay Ho District* ☎ *024/6276–6665.*

R&R Tavern. A Hanoi institution, R&R Tavern reopened in its current location near West Lake in 2012. The hippy-friendly pub has an all-American menu of nachos and burgers, draft beer, darts, and Grateful Dead classics as well as regular live music. ✉ *256 Nghi Tam St., Tay Ho District* ☎ *24/6295–8215* ⊕ *www.rockandrolltavern.com.*

PERFORMING ARTS

In its musical theaters and diverse nightlife, Hanoi's cultural allure comes alive when the sun goes down. Productions showcasing traditional music and theater are a great way to delve into the spirit of Vietnam. With the multimillion-dollar restoration of the Opera House in the late 1990s, Hanoi's performing-arts scene reemerged. The imposing French-built arts palace hosts Vietnam's top traditional musicians and pop stars as well as the occasional Western performer. Elsewhere in the city, you can catch a performance of Vietnamese folk opera, traditional music, or enchanting water puppetry. If you want a peek at the results of years of Eastern European physical training, head to the circus at the northern edge of Lenin Park for Vietnam's version of the Cirque du Soleil.

To find out about upcoming cultural events, pick up a copy of *The Word,* a useful arts and entertainment monthly available at many venues, hotels, and bars.

CIRCUS

Fodor's Choice ★ **Vietnam Central Circus** (*Rap Xiec*). Vietnam Central Circus was founded in the 1950s in the mountains, along with the Communist Party. Besides an evening of guaranteed entertainment—the elephants and monkeys are accompanied by the antics of 160 human performers—the circus arena itself is also a sight to see, with its distinctive 1,500-seat, round-top building. In winter, bring a jacket. The two-hour shows take place weekends and sometimes during the week. ⊠ *67–69 Tran Nhan Tong St.* ☎ *024/3941–2064* ⊕ *www.vietnamcircus.com.*

FILM

Fodor's Choice ★ **Cinematheque.** Run by movie buffs, this is the best (only) place in Hanoi to catch up with the best in arthouse cinema. It is run as a membership organization, but nonmembers are welcome to attend screenings for a very reasonable fee of 60,000d. ⊠ *22A Hai Ba Trung, Hai Ba Trung District* ☎ *024/936–2648.*

L'Espace. Operated by Institut Francais de Hanoi, L'Espace regularly screens world cinema as well as hosting an eclectic selection of cultural events. ⊠ *24 Trang Tien, Hoan Kiem District* ☎ *024/3936–2164* ⊕ *www.ifhanoi-lespace.com.*

Megastar Cinema. Located at the flashy Vincom Center, this multiplex screens the latest Hollywood releases as well as Vietnamese movies and the occasional left-field curveball. ⊠ *191 Ba Trieu* ☎ *024/3974–3333* ⊕ *www.megastar.vn.*

THEATER AND OPERA

Hanoi's performing-arts legacy is impressive. As in Europe, the emperors often kept acting guilds and musicians in or around the Imperial Palace. Roving drama and musical troupes entertained citizens in the countryside. The arrival of the French and the 20th century saw an explosion of theater culture in the capital, the lingering remnants of which can be experienced at a handful of small drama houses that host troupes performing traditional folk arts.

Tuong is a classical art form developed in central Vietnam. It uses very few stage props, and the actors must conform to age-old rules of behavior concerning their specific characters. Content usually focuses on Vietnamese legends, and music is minimal. The northern folk art known as *cheo* is more of a "people's opera," incorporating both comic and tragic elements. Music and singing are prominent, as cheo developed into a loud and lively art form in order to outdo the noise and distractions of the marketplace, where it was originally performed.

Cai luong, the "renovated opera" that emerged in the early 20th century, is more similar to Western dramas and operas than the other styles. Music and singing are an important feature of these performances. Although cai luong is a southern creation, the form has endeared itself to Hanoians. The Hanoi theaters listed below stage productions; none prints schedules in English, so call or drop by the theater to see if there's something on for an evening when you're in town.

Golden Bell Show. This popular cultural show encompasses a wide variety of traditional Vietnamese folk and dance forms. Shows take place every Saturday evening at 8 pm and take audiences on a journey across the country from the steamy southern Delta to the mountainous north with its minority tribe traditions. Expect colorful costumes and enthusiastic performers. ⊠ *72 Hang Bac St., Hoan Kiem District* ☎ *098/830–7272* ⊕ *www.goldenbellshow.vn.*

Hanoi Cheo Theater. This tiny, simple drama house seats 50 people. Cheo operas and traditional music concerts are usually staged on Friday and Saturday evenings at 8 pm, but call or stop by to confirm. Cheo is a form of satirical music theater. This theater will arrange special performances for groups of 10 or more. ⊠ *15 Nguyen Dinh Chieu St., Ba Dinh District* ☎ *024/3943–7361.*

Hanoi Opera House (*Nha Hat Lon*). Hanoi Opera House, whose Vietnamese name translates into "House Sing Big," is worth a visit no matter what happens to be showing. This beautifully restored French building hosts regular classical music concerts, ballets, and Western and Vietnamese operas, plus a variety of singers. Check out the venue's website for details on upcoming shows. ⊠ *1 Trang Tien St., Hoan Kiem District* ☎ *024/3993–0113* ⊕ *www.hanoioperahouse.org.vn.*

Thang Long Ca Tru Theater. Not to be confused with the Thang Long Water Puppet Theater, this venue, a historical house in Hanoi's Old Quarter, offers a musical performance focused on traditional Ca Tru ceremonial singing. The hour-long shows take place three times per week on Tuesday, Thursday, and Saturday. During the 20-minute intermission, guests are invited to try out the instruments and enjoy complimentary tea and cakes. By day you can tour the home. ⊠ *87 Ma May, Hoan Kiem District* ☎ *01/223–266–897* ⊕ *www.catruthanglong.com* 🎫 *210,000d* ⊙ *Tues., Thurs., and Sun. from 8 pm.*

Vietnam National Tuong Theatre. Rivaling the musical aspect of the famed Water Puppet Theater, but sans the water puppets, this remarkable show blends acting, music, comedy, and storytelling in an hour-long performance. This version of a Chinese opera comprises five acts, and there is English translation between each segment. Performances are Monday and Thursday evenings at 6:30 pm. ⊠ *51 Duong Thanh, Mai Dich; Cau Giay* ☎ *091/3322–932* ⊕ *www.vietnamtuongtheatre.com* 🎫 *150,000d.*

Youth Theater (*Nha Hat Tuoi Tre*). Youth Theater, a 650-seat facility, is one of the larger theaters in the city and focuses mainly on contemporary drama, although music and dance are sometimes performed. About a dozen foreign theater groups perform here annually. ⊠ *11 Ngo Thi Nham St., Hoan Kiem District* ☎ *024/3943–0820* ⊕ *www.nhahattuoitre.vn.*

TRADITIONAL MUSIC

As many of Vietnam's dramatic performances are closely linked with the strains of Vietnamese music, there are very few concerts of exclusively traditional music in the city. Your best bet is to see a water-puppet performance or go to the theater to watch cheo, tuong, or cai luong.

If you happen across an old man or woman on the street who's playing a one-stringed instrument in an impromptu fashion, consider yourself extremely lucky.

WATER PUPPETRY

The thousand-year-old art of *roi nuoc*, or water puppetry, is unique to northern Vietnam and easily ranks as one of Southeast Asia's most beautiful and complex art forms. Long considered an art of the common people, water puppetry gained acceptance at royal celebrations and was often performed for reigning emperors and kings. Water puppetry is performed on—and under, in particular—a small pond whose surface conceals the flurry of activity beneath it. Through the near-magical use of bamboo rods and a system of pulleys and levers, master puppeteers stand waist deep at the back of the pond (usually behind a curtain) and make their lacquered marionettes literally walk on water. Shows usually depict scenes from rural life and Vietnamese legend, and the experience is positively delightful.

National Puppet Theater. National Puppet Theater holds water-puppet shows that are more in the vein of village performances, harking back to the days when water puppets were used as political commentary right under the noses of bad kings or provincial French rulers. Traveling water-puppet theaters traditionally relayed information from village to village. You may find that you are as much of the show as the puppets. Performances take place daily at 5 pm. ✉ *361 Truong Chinh St., Dong Da District* ☎ *024/3563–0242* ⊕ *www.vietnampuppetry.com.*

Fodor's Choice
★
Thang Long Water Puppet Theater. As one of Hanoi's top tourist attractions, this entertaining performance gives you insight into Vietnam's history and traditions through water puppetry storytelling, three musicians, and interlude commentaries. Somewhat humorous and endearing at times, puppets are guided through the water by puppeteers hidden behind a stage. The hour-long show, which takes place five times a day (six on Sundays), highlights the folklore and culture of this ancient civilization. Puppet theater is not for the cynical and disenchanted traveler, so come with an open mind. Flashing cameras and video recorders can be extremely distracting. ✉ *57B Dinh Tien Hoang, Hoan Kiem District* ☎ *024/3824–9494* ⊕ *www. thanglongwaterpuppet.org* 🎫 *100,000d.*

SPORTS AND THE OUTDOORS

Sports have been an integral and institutionalized part of the Hanoi educational system for years. Many resources are still committed to the study and improvement of martial arts such as tae kwon do and *wushu*, two disciplines in which Vietnam is world renowned. Ping-Pong and badminton are also determinedly pursued.

BIKING

Fodor's Choice ★   **Hanoi Bicycle Collective.** While nobody would call frenetic Hanoi a cyclist's paradise, the Hanoi Bicycle Collective is doing its best to encourage the use of pedal power. As well as serving as a retail space, with several brands of bike on offer, the outlet has set itself up to become a hub of cycling life, commuting, social activity, and fitness. ⊠ *29 Nhat Chieu, Tay Ho District* ☎ *024/3718–3156* ⊕ *www.thbc.vn.*

BOATING

Paddleboating and sculling are voguish forms of boating in Hanoi. You can rent dragon-shape paddleboats on **Truc Bach Lake** at a few spots, one on the southwest corner of the lake and another on the causeway. Thien Quang Lake, just north of Lenin Park, also has paddleboats for rent. Go to the **Student Culture Center** (Nha Van Hoa Hoc Sinh Sinh Vien) on the small island that is connected by bridge to Tran Nhan Tong Street. Boats are 20,000d to 40,000d per half hour. The newer plastic boats are more expensive than the rusting metal hulks.

BOWLING

Bowling is a popular activity for Vietnam's trendy young urbanites. If your image of bowling includes folks in matching shirts, you're in for a surprise: pumping music, lights, and attached bars add a little extra excitement to this wholesome pursuit. Call ahead to reserve a lane.

Hanoi Starbowl Centre. Hanoi Starbowl Centre, housed in a trendy shopping mall, has 30 lanes of high-tech bowling fun for between 20,000d and 40,000d depending on the day and the time. ⊠ *2 Pham Ngoc Thach St., Dong Da District* ☎ *024/3574–1614.*

Trung Tam Cosmos Bowling Centre. This hopping spot charges 30,000d per game. ⊠ *8B Ngoc Khanh St., Ba Dinh District* ☎ *024/3831–6868.*

GOLF

King's Island Golf and Country Club. King's Island Golf and Country Club is a gorgeous course surrounded by the beautiful Tan Vien Mountain. Golf in Vietnam is not cheap, however, and caddy fees add an extra 630,000d. Renting clubs will set you back another 1,050,000d. You reach the club via a scenic boat trip across a reservoir. ⊠ *Dong Mo, about 45 km (28 miles) west of Hanoi, Son Tay town, Ha Tay Province* ☎ *024/3368–6555* ⊕ *www.kingsislandgolf.com* 🏌 *Weekdays 2,190,000d for guests, weekends 3,290,000d* 🏌 *36 holes, 6454/7100 yards, par 72.*

SOCCER

Hang Day Stadium. No sport captures the attention and hearts of the Vietnamese quite like soccer. The national V League packs them in at the 22,000-seat capacity Hang Day Stadium. The season runs roughly from January to August, and when the Hanoi teams play here, the stadium is rocking. Nearly every Vietnamese bar in town has a soccer schedule, and with a bit of gesturing and pointing you should be able to figure out whether or not a huge match is going to be played while you're in town. ✉ *Trinh Hoai Duc* ☎ *024/3734–4922.*

SHOPPING

Whether they're selling clothing, pottery, silks, or souvenirs, shops in Hanoi can do some serious damage to your spending account. Tackle your wish list in Old Quarter, where 40 colonial streets offer every type of product imaginable, and then some. This fashion hub is a good place to find silk dresses and skirts, and if you can't find what you're looking for, a local tailor will certainly offer to create something for you. Hanoi is a good place to pick up a traditional ao dai, as many local women still wear these fitted silk tunics that drape over elegant pants. Throughout the city are galleries and shops selling ceramics, lacquer and silk paintings, and traditional embroidery.

Souvenir shops are easy to come by, with the best ones located in Old Quarter and near the Temple of Literature. When buying art in Vietnam, be careful of fakes. Paintings by Vietnam's most famous painters—Bui Xuan Phai, Nguyen Tu Nghiem, and Le Thiet Cuong—are the most widely copied. Serious art collectors should consult the well-respected high-end galleries.

It's possible to have clothes made to order with enough time—one day to three weeks, depending on what you want made and the tailor's schedule. You may also need to return a couple of times to have the clothes fitted.

THE OLD QUARTER

ART

Apricot Gallery. Even if you have no intention of shelling out thousands of dollars for a painting, this beautiful gallery is still worth visiting. It's a great introduction to modern Vietnamese art as it displays works by the country's most famous contemporary artists. ✉ *40B Hang Bong St., Hoan Kiem District* ☎ *024/3828–8965* ⊕ *www.apricot-artvietnam. com.*

Fodor'sChoice ★ **Mai Gallery.** Mai Gallery, which is down an alley, is run by the daughter of Vietnam's leading art critic, Duong Tuong. It is largely a showcase for Hanoi painters and is very popular with serious collectors. ✉ *113 Hang Bong St., Hoan Kiem District* ☎ *024/3938–0568* ⊕ *www.maigallery-vietnam.com.*

Fodor'sChoice ★ **Salon Natasha.** Salon Natasha, the avant-garde hub of Hanoi's art scene, is run by a Russian expatriate and her husband, artist Vu Dan Tan. It exhibits and sells some of the most provocative art in Vietnam today. Natasha, a respected and trusted art dealer, sells painted vases and unframed oil paintings by well-known artists at reasonable prices. ✉ *30 Hang Bong St., Hoan Kiem District* ☎ *024/3826–1387.*

CLOTHING AND ACCESSORIES

Ginkgo. Established in Ho Chi Minh City in 2007, Ginkgo has become one of Vietnam's most respected clothing brands. The emphasis is on print T-shirts, some made with organic cotton, that showcase eclectic aspects of Vietnamese culture. ⊠ *44 Hang Be, Hoan Kiem District* ☎ *024/3926–4769* ⊕ *www.ginkgo-vietnam.com.*

Kelly Bui. One of Vietnam's best known clothing stores and designer labels, Kelly Bui specializes in daring and contemporary creations for women. ⊠ *2D Ly Quoc Su, Hoan Kiem District* ☎ *024/3928–9663* ⊕ *www.kellybui.vn.*

Fodor'sChoice ★ **Magonn.** Mixing retro and modern stylings to create items that are fresh and unique, Magonn has become one of Vietnam's leading female fashion brands with several branches throughout Hanoi and Ho Chi Minh City. ⊠ *19 Ma May St., Hai Ba Trung District* ☎ *024/3935–1811* ⊕ *www.magonn.com.*

EMBROIDERY

Kana. There's a little something for every size and taste here, though the large selection of embroidered handbags are particularly eye-catching. Other products available include dresses, skirts, knitwear, swimwear, shoes, wallets, and bags. ⊠ *41 Hang Trong* ☎ *024/3928–6208* ⊕ *www. kana.com.vn.*

Fodor'sChoice ★ **Tan My Design.** Tan My is the most famous embroidery shop in Hanoi. Employees from Thuong Tin Province, which is known for its rich embroidery tradition, adorn tablecloths, silk clothing, and wall hangings with intricate designs. Ready-made work depicts everything from traditional Vietnamese floral patterns and dragon designs to scenes from Western fairy tales, or you can custom-order. ⊠ *61 Hang Gai St., Hoan Kiem District* ☎ *024/3938–1154* ⊕ *www.tanmydesign.com.*

HANDICRAFTS

Green Palm Gallery (*Green Palm Gallery*). This gallery and shop sells boxes and figurines made of silver. The owner was an art critic in a previous life, speaks good English, and is very reputable. ⊠ *39 Hang Gai St., Hoan Kiem District* ☎ *024/91321–8496.*

Fodor'sChoice ★ **Indigenous.** As the name suggests, this outlet specializes in quirky ethnic-style gifts. Also available is fair-trade coffee and tea from Vietnam's provinces. ⊠ *36 Au Trieu, Hoan Kiem District.*

Quang's Ceramics. This huge shop in the Old Quarter sells colorful crockery and ceramic lamps made in the nearby pottery village of Bat Trang. ⊠ *63 Hang Trong, Hoan Kiem District, Hoan Kiem District* ☎ *024/3928–6349* ⊕ *www.quangceramic.com.*

HOUSEWARES AND FURNISHINGS

La Casa Vietnam. This boutique is filled with stylish, Italian-designed and locally made housewares, including beautiful wooden bowls and trays, mirrors, ceramics, candlesticks, and boxes. ⊠ *51 Xuan Dieu St., Tay Ho District* ☎ *024/3718–4084* ⊕ *www.lacasavietnam.com.vn.*

Mosaique. Custom-designed mosaics, Japanese paper lamps, place settings, aromatherapy items, bedding, and some jewelry and clothing make nice gifts. ✉ *427 Dong Kim Nguu St., Hai Ba Trung District* ☎ *024/3971–3797* ⊕ *www.mosaiquedecoration.com.*

Van Loi Oriental Style. The accent is on traditional wood-carved Chinese furniture here. The collection of classic furniture is based on antique designs with graceful horseshoe chairs and hand-carved cabinets among the items stocked. ✉ *87 Hang Gai St.* ☎ *024/3828–6758* ⊕ *www.vanloi.com.*

MARKETS

Hom Market (*Cho Hom*). This is one of the biggest and most crowded markets in town. Upstairs is a Western-style market with air-conditioning, and downstairs is a Vietnamese-style open market. If you need plastic tubs, candles, or padded bras, this is the place to go. ✉ *Pho Hue and Tran Xuan Soan Sts., Hai Ba Trung District.*

FRENCH QUARTER

ART

Red Moon Gallery. Emerging and established Vietnamese artists are showcased at this small gallery. Artworks are presented with a certificate of authenticity as well as a copy of the artist's biography. ✉ *38 Trang Tien, Hoan Kiem District* ☎ *024/3934–2531* ⊕ *www.redmoongallery.net.*

CLOTHING AND ACCESSORIES

Cao Minh. With branches in Hanoi and Ho Chi Minh City, the tailors here are very well respected and their services are engaged by top executives as well as foreign clients. ✉ *250 Hang Bong, Hoan Kiem District* ☎ *024/3939–3595* ⊕ *www.caominh.com.*

Fodor'sChoice ★ **Ipa-Nima.** This is the place to get beautifully designed, funky, and fashionable handbags made of rattan, brocade, crochet, beads, and all kinds of other materials. It also sells original jewelry and accessories such as cuff links. The brand has gone international in recent years and celebrity fans are said to include actress Jamie Lee Curtis and Hillary Clinton. ✉ *34 Han Thuyen, Hoan Kiem District* ☎ *024/3928–7616* ⊕ *www. ipa-nima.com.*

Luala Milano. This super-chic luxury fashion boutique stocks a decent selection of world-renowned labels such as Canali, Azzedine, Carolina Herrera, and Dolce & Gabbana. ✉ *61 Ly Thai To St., Hai Ba Trung District* ☎ *024/3936–9899* ⊕ *www.lualamilano.com.*

Metiseko Hanoi. This fashion boutique in Hanoi's Old Quarter has several locations throughout Vietnam and is gaining fame for its poetic prints and eco-chic clothing. From dresses and shirts to pants and tops, selections feature lovely prints and fabrics like high-end silks and 100% organic cotton. Designed by the shop's French owner, the clothing is fashionable yet comfortable. The shop also sells household goods and accessories. ✉ *71 Hang Gai* ☎ *024/3935–2645* ⊕ *www. metiseko.com.*

Vo Viet Chung. Regarded as one of Vietnam's leading designers, Vo Viet Chung's elegant creations have been showcased at fashion events worldwide. Although his designs are primarily feminine, he is equally adept at catering for gentlemen. ⊠ *106 Mai Hac De, Hai Ba Trung District* ☎ *024/3974–7973* ⊕ *www.vovietchung.com.*

HO CHI MINH MAUSOLEUM AND AROUND

ART

Nguyen Art Gallery. This prestigious gallery stocks original and quality paintings as well as sculptures. The focus is on young and emerging artists from Vietnam. Art can be viewed and ordered online and shipped worldwide. ⊠ *31 Van Mieu St.* ☎ *024/3747–6001* ⊕ *www. nguyenartgallery.com.*

CLOTHING AND ACCESSORIES

Khai Silk. Wth branches, boutiques, as well as a string of restaurants part of its nationwide empire, this is arguably Vietnam's leading silk business. In Hanoi, you'll find fine silk blouses, sweaters, scarves, lingerie, sheets, and more. Linen is also available, as are men's clothes. ⊠ *113 Hang Gai St., Hoan Kiem District* ☎ *024/3828–6198* ⊕ *www. khaisilkcorp.com.*

HANDICRAFTS

Craft-Link. This nonprofit organization benefits local artisans by selling their handmade crafts—such as textiles, bags, scarves, clothing, and trinkets—at fair-market prices. Items are of high quality and prices are reasonable. The back room on the first floor has a designated section of handbags and silk purses. ⊠ *43 Van Mieu, near Temple of Literature* ☎ *024/3733–6101* ⊕ *www.craftlink.com.vn.*

HOUSEWARES AND FURNISHINGS

DOME. Well-designed, modern home furnishings—linens, furniture, lamps, candles, and more—are for sale here. Simple, curved designs in wrought iron are a signature style, one you'll see in restaurants and hotels throughout town. ⊠ *10 Yen The St., Ba Dinh District* ☎ *024/3843–6036* ⊕ *www.dome.com.vn.*

WEST LAKE

ART

54 Traditions Gallery. Vietnam's amazing ethnodiversity is highlighted at this gallery/antique emporium. Craft works and cultural antiques obtained from the 54 ethnic groups in Vietnam are spread over four floors. A shipping service is available. ⊠ *30 Hang Bun, Tay Ho District* ☎ *024/3715–0194* ⊕ *www.54traditions.com.vn.*

Art Vietnam Gallery. To really appreciate Hanoi's art scene this is the ideal place to start. Gallery director Suzanne Lecht is one of the leading experts on Vietnamese art and she can lead you on studio tours and advise you on major purchases. The gallery is long established, but has recently moved to a bright new space in an up-and-coming arty enclave. ⊠ *24 Ly Quoc Su, Hoan Kiem District* ☎ *024/3928–5190* ⊕ *www.artvietnamgallery.com.*

BOOKS

Fodor's Choice ★ **Bookworm.** Owned by avid reader Hoang Van Truong, this is by some distance Hanoi's best bookshop. There's more than 10,000 books in stock and Truong and his learned team speaks excellent English. ⊠ *44 Chau Long, Tay Ho District* ☎ *024/3715–3711* ⊕ *www.bookwormhanoi.com.*

CLOTHING AND ACCESSORIES

Fodor's Choice ★ **Chula Fashion Showroom.** This fashion boutique is Hanoi's best clothing store for finding a blend of classic and modern fashions, including European- and Asian-inspired dresses, jackets, skirts, and gorgeous silk garments. Each item is perfectly tailored by Spanish owners Laura and Diego. The couple designs with unique patterns, materials, and embroidery, meaning that no two items are ever the same. The Chula website gives a glimpse into their innovative style. ⊠ *6 Ven Ho Tay, enter by 396 Lac Long Quan* ☎ *090/425–8960* ⊕ *www.chulafashion.com.*

Fodor's Choice ★ **George's Fashion Boutique.** Established by two former English teachers, this boutique in the expatriate enclave of West Lake caters to larger Western figures. Although the focus is on women's fashion, the shop also stocks homewares, accessories, and gifts. ⊠ *36 To Ngoc Van St., Tay Ho District* ☎ *024/3718–6233* ⊕ *www.georgeshanoi.com.*

MARKETS

Long Bien Market. Long Bien Market really kicks off at around 3 to 4 am and is worth seeing after a late night on the town. All of the produce from north of Hanoi lands here before being distributed throughout the city. Just follow the crowds on the streets adjacent to the bridge ramp to witness the intense buying and selling of the freshest produce in town. ⊠ *Hang Dau St. near Long Bien Bridge, Hoan Kiem District.*

Quang Ba Flower Market. Earlier risers and victims of jet lag will enjoy this flower market that opens at 2 am and continues until just past sunrise. It's the floral hub for wholesalers who arrive with bundles of roses and chrysanthemums tethered to their bikes and mopeds. Even if you aren't in the market for flowers, this place is oozing with photo opportunities. ⊠ *Au Co St., Tay H, near West Lake.*

GREATER HANOI

HANDICRAFTS

FAMILY
Fodor's Choice ★ **Bat Trang Ceramic Village.** At this traditional pottery-making village just outside Hanoi you can purchase ceramics made by local artisans or participate in a pottery-making workshop. Everything from pots and plates to masks and jugs are sold at the dozens of shops lining the streets. It's the best place to buy a teapot or traditional Vietnamese coffeemaker. A stroll through the village is a welcome escape from the city, and children can pay a small fee to make their own ceramic souvenirs. Most impressive is watching the locals hand paint their latest creations. ⊠ *II Humlet Bat Trang Village, 10 km (6 miles) outside Hanoi* ☎ *043/874–0501* ⊕ *www.gomsubattrang.com.*

SIDE TRIPS FROM HANOI

Although Hanoi is the cultural hub of northern Vietnam, much of the city's history and many of its legends and traditions are rooted in the region surrounding the capital. Citadels, temples, art guilds, and festival focal points ring the city, and a few hours' drive in any direction will bring you to points of interest ranging from pagodas to idyllic valleys and national parks.

Tours organized by Hanoi's tourist cafés and tour operators cover all of the sights and are the most time-efficient way to see this region. Tourist café tours are less expensive than those run by travel agencies. If a group tour isn't available to the site you want, arrange a private car and driver for the day. A good example is the "Suburbs of Hanoi" tour: this full-day trip goes to the silk-making village of Ha Dong, the Bat Trang pottery village, a snake farm in Gia Lam across the Red River, and the village of Dong Ho, where the ancient folk art of wood-block printing is still practiced. The trip averages 1,500,000d for an air-conditioned car and driver for the whole day. An English-speaking guide costs from 640,350d to 843,800d per day.

Another great way of escaping the city and seeing some of its most interesting immediate outlying areas is by taking a day or a half-day cycling tour. Most of the best tour operators can arrange an itinerary that typically takes in the villages along the Red River and Bat Trang before looping back to the Old Quarter via West Lake and Ba Dinh District.

For history, religion, and a bit of hiking, head west to the Thay and Tay Phuong pagodas. Combine a trip here with Co Loa Citadel, and you've got a full day of exploring. Go with a group tour or rent a private car with a driver for between 1,500,000d and 2,000,000d for the trip.

CO LOA CITADEL

15 km (9 miles) north of Hanoi.

Less than 30 minutes north of Hanoi is a series of large earthen ramparts that used to protect one of the country's earliest capitals from Chinese invaders. Co Loa, or "snail," so named for the spiral-shape protective walls and moats that resembled the design of a nautilus, was built by An Duong Vuong more than 2,000 years ago and remains one of northern Vietnam's important historical relics.

GETTING HERE AND AROUND

You should be able to hire a car with driver for about 1,500,000d to go from Hanoi to Co Loa Citadel as well as the Thay and Tay Phuong pagodas. A round-trip and a visit to Co Loa alone takes about two hours. Tourist cafés and tour operators can arrange minivan tours to the three sites if there is enough interest. This trip takes about two-thirds of a day, depending on how long you linger at the sites.

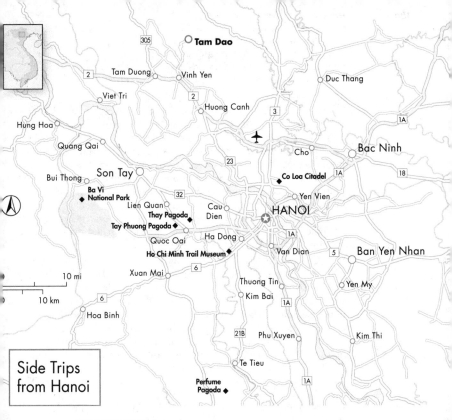

Side Trips
from Hanoi

EXPLORING

Co Loa Citadel. The first fortified citadel in Vietnamese history (dating back to the 3rd century) and a one-time capital of the country, Co Loa is worth visiting for those with an interest in the nation's backstory. Only three of the original earthen ramparts are extant today. You can explore the site of the ancient imperial palace and nearby, under an old banyan tree, is Ba Chua, a pretty temple. A large and colorful festival on the sixth day of Tet, the lunar new year, celebrates King An Vuong Duong, now considered the guardian spirit of Co Loa. This is a popular destination for school groups, which can sometimes transform the normally serene temples into playgrounds reverberating with the laughter and chatting of hundreds of children. Don't be surprised, either, if the kindly priests and caretakers in each building you visit persistently request extra money from you. ⊠ *Co Loa Citadel, Hanoi* ⊠ *30,000d.*

THAY PAGODA AND TAY PHUONG PAGODA

40 km (25 miles) southwest of Hanoi in Hay Tay Province.

These two lovely pagodas can be combined with the Co Loa Citadel to make an enjoyable day trip from Hanoi.

GETTING HERE AND AROUND

Trips organized by tourist cafés and tour operators usually cover the admission fees for these sites. It's easy to combine a trip to these two pagodas with a visit to Co Loa Citadel, north of Hanoi.

EXPLORING

Tay Phuong Pagoda. The Tay Phuong Pagoda, or Western Pagoda, comprises three sanctuaries built into Cau Lau Mountain and surrounded by a square enclosure. Each ancient wooden structure is separated by a small pool of water that reflects an eerie soothing light into the temples. Begun in the 3rd century, the pagoda was rebuilt in the 9th century and expanded to its present size under the Tay Son dynasty in 1794. The centuries-old curved rooftops are particularly noteworthy, as are the masterpieces of wood sculpture: more than six dozen figures carved from jackfruit wood. The pagoda's rafters are elaborately carved with bas-reliefs of dragons and lotuses, and ceramic animal statues grace the rooftops. ⊠ *Ha Tay Province* ☜ *5,000d.*

Thay Pagoda. The Thay Pagoda, or Master's Pagoda, is named in honor of Tu Dao Hanh, a 12th-century monk. The grounds of the four main sanctuaries here ring shrill with the chirping of cicadas and are lush with fruit trees and a giant frangipani said to be 700 years old. In the upper pagoda (Chua Thuong) a statue of Master Hanh sits in the foreground of a large central altar that supports the statues of 18 arhats, monks who have reached enlightenment. The altar to the left of this holds Ly Nhan Tong, a king who was the supposed reincarnation of Tu Dao Hanh. Stone steps adjacent to the pagoda lead farther up the mountain to various shrines and temples and lovely vista points. The Thay Pagoda is the site of one of two ancient water-puppetry stages remaining in Vietnam. Constructed during the 15th century, this small stage sits on stilts in the middle of a pond and was used during elaborate pagoda ceremonies and royal visits. Water-puppetry shows still take place here, particularly on the annual festival of the pagoda, which is from the 5th through the 7th days of the third lunar month. ⊠ *Ha Tay Province* ☜ *5,000d.*

TAM DAO HILL STATION

85 km (53 miles) northwest of Hanoi in Vinh Phuc Province.

Up in the clouds, the damp hill station of Tam Dao feels like the mountain town that time forgot—almost. In 1907 French developers scaled the rugged 4,590-foot peaks (there are three of them) north of Hanoi and decided the cool weather of a nearby mountain retreat could serve the French well. The result was a graceful town of elegant villas surrounded by lush vegetation and sweeping views of the valley below. Since the French left in 1954, however, little grace has been bestowed on Tam Dao, whose chalet charm took a decided turn for the worse when Soviet-era architecture announced itself in the form of a monstrously square 40-room hotel. Most villas, and the town church, have fallen into disrepair, although a few developers remain confident that Tam Dao could be resuscitated as a tourist resort; they've bought up some crumbling lodges and have begun to build.

GETTING HERE AND AROUND

Buses to the town of Vinh Yen near Tam Dao run from Gia Lam bus station in Hanoi (40,000d, one hour). From there, the easiest way to get to Tam Dao is to charter a xe om (motorbike taxi) for the 24-km journey to the national park. The ride should cost no more than 100,000d. Hiring a car and driver for the day from Hanoi will cost about 1,090,500d.

EXPLORING

Tam Dao Hill Station. Tam Dao's main attraction lies in its elevation and subsequent cool temperatures: it's a nice way to beat the heat of Hanoi, and the hiking is fair. Don't expect much in the way of information on trails, however, unless you have organized a tour with one of the better Hanoi tour operators. Few people, even locals, realize that Tam Dao and the surrounding peaks are in a national park, which may be one reason why logging and poaching remain a problem for the area (most of the restaurants here list supposedly protected animals on their menus). But for the most part, a hike up to the radio transmitter above the town is a walk into dense jungle. Small Buddhist temples line the concrete steps up to the tower, and a spring bubbles up from beneath the underbrush and splays out into a small waterfall. If you're spending the night up in these mountains, bring a sweater and some rain gear. People have been known to ride mountain bikes up to Tam Dao and spend the night, but the climb is extreme (a 10% gradient over long stretches). Less-active riders put their bikes in minivans on the way up and then career down the extremely winding and dangerous—but ultimately exhilarating—route to the base of the mountain.

7

WHERE TO EAT AND STAY

$$$ RESORT 🏨 **Belvedere Resort.** Like many resorts in North Vietnam, the Belvedere combines trappings of luxury with the odd lapse in taste. **Pros:** terrace café is a lovely spot; outdoor pool; tennis courts; pool table. **Cons:** severe mark up on average restaurant food. [$] *Rooms from: 1601000d* ✉ *Hamlet 2, Tam Dao* ☎ *0211/382–4149* 🌐 *www.belvedereresort.com.vn* 🛏 *48 rooms* 🍴 *Breakfast.*

$$$ HOTEL 🏨 **Mela Hotel.** Some rooms at this semi-luxurious villa on the town's outskirts have views of the valley, while the passable restaurant, which serves Asian and Western food, seems to be the only one in Tam Dao that doesn't have endangered (or soon-to-be-endangered) animals on the menu. **Pros:** views of the valley; bird-watching guides and hikes into the surrounding countryside can be arranged. **Cons:** needs refurbishment. [$] *Rooms from: 1210000d* ✉ *Near path to Tam Dao Waterfall, Tam Dao* ☎ *0211/3824–321* 🛏 *25 rooms* 🍴 *Breakfast.*

HO CHI MINH TRAIL MUSEUM AND THE PERFUME PAGODA

15 km (9 miles) and 60 km (37 miles) south of Hanoi, respectively.

One of Hanoi's less visited historic sights, perhaps due to its distance from the city center, the Ho Chi Minh Trail Museum delivers an interesting insight to the effort and determination that went into maintaining the famous supply route from the Communist north to Vietcong strongholds in the American-backed south of Vietnam. The Perfume Pagoda, meanwhile, offers interesting shrines and a romantic river journey. This trip can also be combined with a visit to the mummies in the Dau Pagoda.

GETTING HERE AND AROUND

Day trips from Hanoi to the Perfume Pagoda, leaving at about 6:30 am, are available from any number of tour operators, as well as from tourist cafés. These tours run around 800,000d per person, including all transport and entrance fees. You can also rent a car for about 1,500,000d, and a guide for 650,000d. Most tours from Hanoi skip the Ho Chi Minh Trail Museum, meaning that to combine the two attractions you'll need to rent a vehicle.

EXPLORING

Dau Pagoda. This 11th-century pagoda from the Ly dynasty houses Vietnam's two most famous mummies. In 1639 the Buddhist monks Vu Khac Minh and Vu Khac Truong locked themselves in a private room to meditate, instructing their disciples not to disturb them for 100 days. On the 100th day, their disciples entered the room to find both monks seated in a lotus position, perfectly preserved in death. The monks' bodies were covered in a thin but durable red lacquer. What makes these mummies unique is that they still have all their bones and organs.

Dau Pagoda contains several other noteworthy artifacts, including a giant bronze bell built in 1801, a bronze book detailing the pagoda's construction, several stone stelae dating to the 17th century, and six altars for the worship of 18 *arhats* (enlightened monks). The pagoda, which was partially destroyed by French forces in 1947, consists of five halls, an accessible (just barely) bell tower, and a small walking garden full of jackfruit and longan trees, birds of paradise, and a temple dedicated to local deities. Rice fields and ponds surround the pagoda, and you'll pass duck farmers and lotus vendors near the grove-shaded road that leads to the entrance.

The pagoda is less than an hour's ride south of Hanoi. Take a taxi or hire a private car to get here, and keep an eye peeled for a sign directing you to turn right off Highway 6 toward the pagoda. ⌂ *Hwy. 6, 24 km (15 miles) south of Hanoi, Gia Phuc hamlet, Ha Tay Province* ⌂ *Free* ⏰ *Daily dawn–dusk.*

Ho Chi Minh Trail Museum. The elaborate network of paths of the Ho Chi Minh Trail was used by North Vietnam to transport supplies to Vietcong strongholds in South Vietnam during the Vietnam War. The Ho Chi Minh Trail Museum (Bao Tang Duong Mon Ho Chi Minh) provides color on the trail, one of the war's most riveting symbols of dedication and perseverance. Displays are heavy on photojournalism from the period. There's also an extensive collection of captured American ordnance and military equipment as well as personal artifacts such as helmets, IDs, and uniforms. This museum lies some distance outside of Hanoi and can be hard to find (it is in the village of Ba La just a kilometer or so past the turn off to the Perfume Pagoda) so it's best if you hire a taxi or car and driver. ⌂ *Hwy. 6, Ha Tay Province* ☎ *024/34382–0889* ⌂ *40,000d* ⏰ *Tues.–Sat. 7:30–11, 1:30–2:30* ⏰ *Closed Sun. and Mon.*

Perfume Pagoda. Considered Vietnam's most important Buddhist site, the Perfume Pagoda (Chua Huong) is the largest of a cluster of shrines carved into the limestone of the Huong Tich Mountains. In late spring the trails leading up to the shrines are clogged with thousands making their pilgrimage to pray to Quan Am, the goddess of mercy and compassion.

According to a Vietnamized version of the Chinese legend, Quan Am was a young wife falsely accused of trying to kill her newlywed husband. Thrown out of her mother-in-law's house, she took refuge in a monastery, posing as a monk. A reckless girl one day blamed her pregnancy on the monk, not knowing he was a she. Without a word of self-defense, the vilified monk took the child in and raised him. Only after Quan Am died did villagers discover her silent sacrifice. In the past, pilgrims came to the grottoes to pray for Quan Am's help in bearing sons and in fighting unjust accusations.

From the shores of the Yen River, you are ferried to the site, 4 km (2½ miles) away, on sampans that seem to be made of flimsy aluminum. It's a spectacular ride through the flooded valley, past boats laden with fruit and farmers at work in their fields. You'll be let off at Chua Tien Chu. From there, follow a stone path uphill to the various pagodas and shrines. Three kilometers (2 miles) later you'll reach the Perfume Pagoda. A steep set of stairs takes you inside the impressive cavern, where gilded Buddhas and bodhisattvas sit nestled in rocky recesses. The air is misty from incense and the cooking fires of the Buddhist monks who tend the shrines.

In early spring, from just after Tet to the middle of the second lunar month, thousands of Buddhists make their pilgrimage to the Perfume Pagoda. This is an intense—and sometimes stressful—time to visit as the crowds of Vietnamese faithful clog the Yen River with extra boats and make navigating the slippery stairs more of an exercise in caution than a journey of discovery. The atmosphere at this time of year is positively electric with thousands of Buddhists crowding into the cavern to leave offerings, catch a droplet of water from a holy stalactite, or buy Buddhist trinkets and mementos from the dozens of stall owners. Note that the climb up to the pagoda can be rough going, especially when it's muddy, and that local operators sometimes lead the climb at a very fast pace. ⊠ *Huong Son, My Duc, Hanoi* 📞 *90,000d* ⊗ *Daily.*

BA VI NATIONAL PARK

65 km (41 miles) west of Hanoi.

With the triple-peaked Ba Vi Mountain as its towering centerpiece, this former French hill station is a popular weekend excursion for Hanoians. The park shelters several rare and endangered plants as well as plentiful birdlife. The highpoint (literally) of the park is a temple dedicated to Ho Chi Minh that sits at the mountain's summit.

GETTING HERE AND AROUND

Ba Vi National Park is a fair distance from Hanoi and is not commonly on the radar of most tour operators. Therefore, to get there the best option is to rent a vehicle in Hanoi for one or two days, depending on whether you want to overnight. A car with a driver starts around 1,500,000d per day. Another cheaper way of visiting is to come here on motorbike. Bikes can be rented from any number of hotels, rental firms, and tourist cafés and start from 250,000d per day.

EXPLORING

Fodor'sChoice
★

Ba Vi National Park. Magnificent and (especially on one of the frequent foggy days) moody, Ba Vi offers a convenient natural refuge from the bustle of Hanoi. The national park is dominated by the triple-peaked Ba Vi Mountain, once a French hill station. The reserve around the mountain, meanwhile, boasts plentiful plant and bird life and is ideal for hiking. The most popular walk in the area is the climb to the mountain's summit, which is a strenuous ascent up 1,229 steps through the trees. A temple dedicated to Ho Chi Minh sits at the mountain's summit. Due to its proximity to the capital, Ba Vi is one of Vietnam's most visited protected areas and numbers can be high on weekends and during holiday periods. ⊠ *Ba Vi National Park, Tan Linh Commune* ☎ *024/3388–1082* ⊕ *www.vuonquocgiabavi.com.vn* ✉ *20,000d.*

WHERE TO STAY

$$$
RESORT

🏨 **Tan Da Spa Resort.** The sterling setting and some comfortable touches mean that this remains a good-value option for a little bit of luxury on a sojurn to Ba Vi National Park. **Pros:** stilt houses add a touch of traditional charm. **Cons:** service is willing but erratic; high-end doesn't necessarily mean top class. $ *Rooms from: 1500000d* ⊠ *Tan Linh Commune, Ba Vi District, Hanoi* ⊕ *www.tandasparesort.com.vn* 🛏 *80 rooms* ⎮◎⎮ *Breakfast.*

THE NORTHWEST

staggering beauty and ethnic diversity are per-
most evident in the Northwest, where dozens of ethnic-
minority groups as well as the Kinh, the ethnic majority,
inhabit the imposing highlands. Physically and culturally
removed from Hanoi, many communities in the remote
region exist today as they have for generations, harvesting
terraced rice fields or practicing slash-and-burn agriculture
on the rocky hillsides. This region of imposing mountains
bore witness to French ignominy at the battle of Dien Bien
Phu, a crucial factor in the end of colonial rule in Indochina,
which at the same time nurtured Ho Chi Minh's revolution.

The mountain town of Sapa is a star attraction for both domestic and international tourists, and with the new highway cutting journey times from Hanoi by more than a half, the popularity of the former French hill station is set to increase. A large part of Sapa's appeal lies in its proximity to some of the most compelling sights in the region. It is the jumping-off point for expeditions into the nearby Hoang Lien Mountains, dubbed the Tonkinese Alps by the French. Preeminent among these mist-shrouded peaks is Fansipan, Vietnam's tallest summit at 3,143 meters (10,308 feet). If the arduous hike up Fansipan doesn't appeal, numerous less demanding treks can be arranged from Sapa to nearby hill tribe villages and through the bucolic surrounding scenery. Northeast of Sapa, the town of Bac Ha has a pleasant climate and one of the liveliest weekly Sunday markets in the region. From Sapa it is a glorious motorbike, car, or bus journey over the Tram Ton Pass, Vietnam's highest stretch of tarmac, to Lai Chau. This area has undergone a massive transformation. The former town of Lai Chau was flooded during construction of the Song Da Reservoir and is now known as Muong Lay. The new town of Lai Chau, formerly known as Tam Duong, has little of interest for travelers beyond the beautiful surrounding scenery and a diverting hill-tribe market.

Once considered something of an outpost, Dien Bien Phu has grown significantly since becoming a provincial capital in 2004. There are daily flights from Hanoi, and the presence of the nearby Tay Trang-Sop border crossing ensures a steady flow of tourist traffic. Beyond the historic and military sights, the main draw for visitors is the opportunity for trekking in the area. Surrounding villages make convenient hopping-off points for hikes into the hinterland. With flights from Hanoi making Dien Bien Phu simple to reach, it is perhaps the quickest and most convenient way of immersing yourself in the wondrous scenery. Southeast of Dien Bien Phu lies Son La Province, which is one of Vietnam's most ethnically diverse regions, home to more than 30 minorities including

TOP REASONS TO GO

Conquer Vietnam's highest peak: Standing proud at 3,142 meters (10,308 feet), Mount Fansipan is no pussycat. The two-day hike to the summit can be wet and arduous, but if you get lucky with the weather you'll have the best vista in the country.

Tackle the Northwest Loop by motorbike: Vietnam has its fair share of classic road trips, but none are more epic than the so-called Northwest Loop from Hanoi to Sapa and back via Dien Bien Phu. Soak up the scenery and enjoy meeting a mosaic of minority groups.

Travel your tastebuds in Sapa: Beyond Hanoi and Ho Chi Minh City, few destinations in Vietnam can claim as much culinary variety as Sapa. Feast on contemporary takes on hill-tribe cuisine, decadent French cakes, and even pizza.

Bicycle around minority villages in Mai Chau Valley: Hardcore exploration it is not, but the flat floor of the Mai Chau valley is ideal territory for using pedal power to propel yourself between traditional White Thai villages, buying expertly woven garments and souvenirs along the way.

Brush up on some history in Dien Bien Phu: Scene of one of the greatest victories in Vietnamese military history, the sleepy Muong Thanh Valley abounds with significant sights. Bone up at Dien Bien Phu Museum before visiting evocative remnants of conflict in the area.

Black Thai, Meo, Muong, and White Thai. Farther southeast still is the Mai Chau Valley, an area that has boomed in popularity with tourists over the last few years. Homestays with the White Thai minority in the area are a fascinating way of experiencing traditional life, and the flat floor of the valley makes it a perfect place to explore by bicycle.

A booming business of selling handicrafts, clothing, and textiles to tourists has sprung up in many communities of the Northwest, particularly around Sapa. Increased contact between these ethnic minorities and tourists has created a flurry of interest in their cultures and lives, but has also cost them some privacy. One unfortunate casualty, for instance, has been the near disappearance of authentic Saturday-night "love markets," where young Red Dao men and women in search of a spouse or lover would pair off for an evening of socializing and possible romance. In Sapa there is a sanitized version of this every Saturday evening, but the real deal takes place only very rarely in the more remote areas of the north.

Traveling around this region often takes a long time and changing weather can make some roads quite dangerous, or even impassable. In the mountains, heavily traveled routes are paved but are still in poor condition and though the scenery is spellbinding, travel can be physically exhausting. But it's a rewarding challenge to cover the region by car, from Hanoi to Sapa to Lai Chau to Dien Bien Phu to Son La then back to Hanoi. If you can handle five or more days on rutted mountain roads, this route is adventurous and allows for some great exploring.

ORIENTATION AND PLANNING

GETTING ORIENTED

A little planning goes a long way when visiting this region. The preferred entry point for exploring the area is undoubtedly Sapa and the traditional way of getting to the former French hill station was by overnight train from Hanoi to the border city of Lao Cai and then onward by bus. Now, however, with the opening of the Noi Bai-Lao Cai highway, in September 2014, a bus journey from Hanoi to Lao Cai takes a mere 3½ hours, making travel by road the quickest option. For travelers heading directly to Dien Bien Phu, the main airport there has daily connections with Hanoi and flying is a much better option than the marathon bus journey between Dien Bien Phu and the capital, which has been known to take up to 13 hours. By far the best way of experiencing the region in all its grandeur is via the Northwest Loop. This grand tour, which takes at least a week to do properly, kicks off in Hanoi before checking in at Sapa then turning southwest to Lai Chau and Dien Bien Phu. From there the route heads back to the capital via Son La and Mai Chau.

Sapa and Nearby. Although much of the Northwest remains remote and undeveloped, Sapa is the region's undisputed tourism star. Idyllically located high among the mountains, yet less than an hour's drive from the transportation hub of Lao Cai, Sapa feels accessible yet suitably sanctuary-like. The bustling town center has plentiful hotels, restaurants, and shops, yet a short distance away, the rhythms of traditional mountain life beat on as they have for centuries.

Dien Bien Phu and Nearby. Its main claim to fame is as the site of one of the most significant military victories in Vietnamese history, but there's more to Dien Bien Phu than just echoes of the past. In the Muong Thanh valley, not far from the border with Laos, the town enjoys a rarefied position amid some archetypically gorgeous highland scenery, perfect for hiking.

PLANNING

WHEN TO GO

The best time to tour the northern highlands is from late August to mid-December, after the summer monsoons have abated and any mudslides are likely to have been cleared.

Northwest Vietnam has a clearly defined winter, with a cold and clammy mist settling in for a few months starting in January. January and February are quite cold in the mountains, and Mount Fansipan, is occasionally dusted with snow. If you're heading into the highlands in winter and intend to do some trekking, come prepared: a light sweater, a waterproof jacket, a wool hat, long johns, and some insulated hiking boots should keep you warm.

There are also various microclimates in the Northwest. Sapa, for example, is the coldest place in Vietnam on average, with mist and cloud

regularly making visibility an issue and lowering temperatures even further. Just over the Tram Ton Pass, however, the area around Lai Chau experiences much clearer weather. The best time to visit Sapa is in spring and early summer (approximately March to May) and in the fall (September to November), the latter being the ideal time to see the area's rice terraces in their full verdant glory. The climate in Bac Ha is noticeably sunnier and warmer than in Sapa, making it a plausible alternative base in the region. There are not as many festivals in Dien Bien Phu as there are in the towns farther north, but you might want to time your visit to coincide with the biennial Dien Bien Phu Festival, which takes place on May 7th. The festival commemorates the battle of Dien Bien Phu, but also encompasses a host of other events and activities.

FESTIVALS

During winter, after the turn of the lunar new year, the minority tribes of the area celebrate a colorful array of festivals. Special events at this time include the Nhan Song and Nao Song Festival, celebrated by the Red Dao, and the Gau Tao Festival, marked by the H'mong ethnic group. Both festivals and others in the Sapa area are centered upon themes of regeneration and longevity.

Gau Tao Festival. A H'mong festival where members of the mountain communities ask for happiness and longevity, Gau Tao is celebrated early in the lunar year. Following a blessing by a H'mong holy man, the festival is marked by a series of lively traditional games and competitions. ⊠ *Sapa.*

Nhan Song and Nao Song Festival. Celebrating the coming of spring, and held in the first lunar month every year, this festival is celebrated by the Red Dao people in the village of Giang Ta Chai. People of the village indulge in a range of ceremonies with the purpose of raising awareness of deforestation. The village leader, also the forest protector, will announce regulations about deforestation that the people have to obey. ⊠ *Giang Ta Chai.*

During Tet, the lunar new year, you'll find northern Vietnam cold and drizzly but extremely festive. If you're coming during this time, make plane and hotel reservations very early.

GETTING HERE AND AROUND
AIR TRAVEL

Twice-daily Vietnam Airlines flights connect Hanoi to Dien Bien Phu; the one-way fare starts at around 1,000,000d. Consider flying to Dien Bien Phu and returning to Hanoi via some form of ground transportation, either down Highway 6 or up to Sapa and down Route 70 and back to the capital on the Noi Bai-Lao Cai Expressway. Talk with one of the travel agencies or tourist cafés in Hanoi to see if they have contacts that can book you a one-way trip back to the capital. They may insist, however, that you pay for the mileage for the driver's return to Dien Bien Phu or Son La.

BIKE TRAVEL

If you've got the legs, lungs, and equipment, mountain biking is a formidable but fantastic way to experience the steep mountain ranges of Hoa Binh Province. Most people who do the Hoa Binh–Mai Chau route find alternative transportation to the provincial capital of Hoa Binh, such as an early morning public bus. Bus drivers will strap bikes to the top of their vehicles for a nominal payment of around 10,000d. From there it's about 100 km (62 miles) up and down two major sets of mountains. Hardy bikers reach Mai Chau by evening, exhausted. Slower riders can spend the night in a home in one of many roadside villages. The Hanoi Bicycle Collective rent out a variety of bikes from simple runarounds to more advanced models capable of negotiating the steep mountain roads of northern Vietnam.

Bike Contact Hanoi Bicycle Collective. ✉ *29 Nhat Chieu* ☎ *024/3718–8246* ⊕ *www.thbc.vn* ✉ *Bike rental from 100,000d per day.*

CAR TRAVEL

A sedan is a perfectly viable way to get around much of the Northwest. You can rent a car and driver in dozens of spots in Hanoi, and you'll be able to book a two-day, one-night car trip to Sapa for about 2,000,000d, all driver's expenses included. A longer excursion in a four-wheel-drive vehicle is more expensive: the going rate for the popular six-day, five-night excursion through the Northwest (Hanoi–Mai Chau–Son La–Dien Bien Phu–Sapa–Hanoi) in a Toyota Innova (with a driver) is 8,000,000d. A host of rental companies in Hanoi will provide modern four-wheel-drive vehicles for such an itinerary. Popular models include Mercedes, Toyota, Ford, and Hyundai.

Set aside at least five days to visit Dien Bien Phu from Hanoi: two days traveling each way and one full day to see what you came for—although the remarkable scenery makes the trip as interesting as the history of the place. If you're coming from Mai Chau and Son La, the natural next step is to continue clockwise: through Lai Chau, on to Sapa, and then back to Hanoi. The Dien Bien Phu–Sapa road has been much upgraded and is narrow, but in good condition. It is a beautiful stretch and, although the round-trip adds a day or two to your journey, it's much more interesting than simply retracing your outward route.

The 35-km (22-mile) stretch of road from Sapa north to the border town of Lao Cai is in good condition. If time is limited, you may prefer to go directly to Sapa, bypassing Dien Bien Phu, Son La, and Mai Chau, and heading up and down Route 70 and the main Noi Bai-Lao Cai Expressway.

Cars with drivers can be hired from travel agencies, car rental firms, and tourist cafés in Hanoi. Try Hoa Mai Tour, who can rent everything from a compact four-seater car to a Landcruiser and even a bus, with a selection of top-of-the-range modern models. The Hung Thanh Company also has a broad range of new vehicles ranging from smaller cars to Landcruisers and minibuses.

Car Contacts Hoa Mai Tour ✉ *9 La. 92, Nguyen Khanh Toan St., 2nd fl., Hanoi* ☎ *024/3633–7614* ⊕ *www.hoamaitour.com.* **Hung Thanh Company** ✉ *287 Tran Khat Chan, Hanoi* ☎ *024/3633–7575* ⊕ *www.hungthanhtravel.vn.*

8

MOTORCYCLE TRAVEL

The Northwest, with its visual splendor and patchwork of ethnic minorities, has become a hotly favored destination for exploration by motorbike, although the roads are not of the highest of standard. Traveling as part of a group is the best and safest option.

The Hanoi–Dien Bien Phu–Sapa route is only for adventurous motorcyclists. These roads are very remote, and adequate emergency care is virtually nonexistent. Wear a helmet, take a sheet of important words and phrases (such as the Vietnamese expression for "My clutch is broken"), and go with someone else. You'll need reasonable clearance and maneuverability, however, so doubling up on one bike is not recommended. Also, be prepared to get wet in mud puddles, although at some larger washout spots enterprising locals set up ferry services on small boats for motorcycles. If you drive a motorbike from Hanoi to Mai Chau, pay extra attention on the mountain roads—the trucks that run this route are notoriously stingy when it comes to giving adequate room to two-wheelers.

Several companies specializing in motorbike tours of the north operate from Hanoi. They can supply well-maintained bikes ranging from classic to modern models and offer expert advice on worthwhile diversions and how to tackle the roads. Rental bikes vary in price, depending on the model, but start from around 214,000d per day. For beginners, however, a better option would be to join one of the group tours these companies offer, providing strength in numbers and guide expertise.

TOURS

Fodor's Choice
★

Cuong's Motorbike Adventures. A founder member of Hanoi's Minsk Club, Cuong has been synonymous with motorbiking in northern Vietnam for more than a decade. A skilled mechanic who has provided support to high-profile Western television shows filmed in Vietnam, Cuong knows everything there is to know about bike maintenance. He and his team are also expertly versed in the best routes to take in the North. As well as group and individual tours, Cuong has a broad range of bikes for rent and is an invaluable resource for anyone looking to hit the road on two wheels. Cuong also runs tours in classic U.S. Army M151 MUTT jeeps. ✉ 46 Gia Ngu St., Hanoi ☎ 091/876–3515 ⊕ www.cuongs-motorbike-adventure.com ✍ 125cc from 214,000d per day, including helmet.

Motorbike Tour Expert. Founded by three Hanoian motorbike nuts, this operation is well versed in the routes and lore of the northern mountains. The Japanese bikes they use for their tours are of the highest quality, and guides are well trained and skilled at getting guests out of a tight spot should their machine malfunction. Tour itineraries range from bite-size options to more epic voyages into magnificent landscapes. ✉ 226 Nghi Tam St., Tay Ho District, Hanoi ☎ 097/988–4588 ⊕ www.hanoimotorcycletour.com ✍ Tours start at 1,280,000d per day per person based on group of 5.

TRAIN TRAVEL

If you don't want to lose the best part of a day driving to Sapa, take the overnight train from Hanoi to Lao Cai. The most comfortable trip is on Friday night, when you get a soft sleeper in a four-person compartment on the "luxury" train. The one-way ticket costs 600,000d. Trains leave

Hanoi train station at 9:15 pm, 9:50 pm, and 8:25 pm, and take 11 hours. On weekends there's an additional service that departs at 7 pm. The easiest way to buy tickets is through a Hanoi travel agency, but the Vietnam Railways System website is an ultra-handy online resource that lets you study timetables for every route in Vietnam, including the Hanoi–Lao Cai service. Tickets booked online can be delivered to your hotel or picked up at the departure train station.

Don't lose your ticket after boarding the train. You need to present it to the station guards in Lao Cai when arriving at the station and again when departing the station upon returning to Hanoi. You can purchase your round-trip ticket in Sapa (and check train and bus schedules) at the tourist office in the center of town. Hotels in Sapa can book a round trip in a private soft-sleeper carriage.

Minibuses waiting at the Lao Cai train station can take you the 35 km (22 miles) to Sapa for 28,000d. The buses leave when full and usually drop you in the town center. From Sapa buses return to the Lao Cai train station twice daily, at 6:30 am and 2 pm, but you can join with other travelers and share a bus or a taxi that will leave at the time you want. If you'd like to combine a one-way train to Sapa with a return to Hanoi by car, you can arrange that in Sapa at one of the tour agencies dotting the main roads.

Train Contact Vietnam Railways System ☎ 090/461–9926 ⊕ www.vietnam-railway.com.

MONEY MATTERS

There are several ATMs in Sapa and in major towns such as Lao Cai and Dien Bien Phu. Make sure you stock up on cash if you are taking an extended trip outside these hubs, as ATMs are nonexistent in more remote areas.

RESTAURANTS

With the exception of Sapa, with its range of international and Vietnamese options, dining in the Northwest is often more of a necessity than a delight. The mountains provide little gratification for gourmands. Life has traditionally been extremely difficult up in these high passes, and culinary flair has rarely been at the top of the agenda. Consequently, most of the restaurants in the area purvey very similar, basic fare. Expect plenty of boiled chicken and grilled meat (mostly pork) accompanied by rice and vegetables such as corn, cassava, and greens. Don't expect much in the way of fragrant herbs or delicious marinades. Here, the staple flavoring agent is pungent fish sauce, often augmented with a boiled egg, which is mashed up and stirred into the salty condiment. Atmosphere and aesthetics are also low on the list of priorities, so you're likely to dine around stainless steel tables under unforgiving strip lighting.

One "pleasure" that you most likely will be unable to avoid while traveling through the highlands is rice wine, or *ruou* (pronounced *zee-oo*). Distilled locally, ruou is everywhere and is used as a welcoming drink. It is also drunk at lunch; before, during, and after dinner; while gathering with friends; when meeting with officials; at small and large celebrations; and as a good-luck send-off. Refusing it outright is difficult, stopping once you've started is nearly impossible, and getting sick from drinking too much is easy.

A communal twist on the ruou standard is *ruou can* (straw-rice wine), which is consumed by up to a dozen people at the same time through bamboo straws stuck into an earthenware jar. First half-filled with manioc and rice husks, the jar is sealed tight and left to ferment for 17 days. On the day of consumption, a water-sugar mixture is added. The sweet, slightly fetid alcohol is downed at weddings and other major celebrations—such as a couple of foreigners stepping into a remote village. It's beneficial that ruou can is more diluted than its bottled brother, which can be anywhere from 60 to 110 proof.

HOTELS

The lodging situation in the Northwest has improved immeasurably in recent years. Established tourist destinations like Sapa have added several enticing new options to their hotel portfolio, and even the budget hotels have good amenities such as free Wi-Fi, hot water, and satellite television. The situation is also much changed in the smaller towns and cities in the region, with several family-run minihotels doing a decent, if unflashy, job. In more remote areas, such as ethnic-minority villages, you may have to share a mat or roll-away mattress in the living room of a host family—with a bathroom that's a curtained shack next to a well where you draw your own water. Don't write off such an experience, however; many of the stilt houses in ethnic-minority villages are exquisitely built, cool, and comfortable, and you may find the owners to be your most gracious hosts. In fact, in Mai Chau in particular, a homestay with a local family has become an integral part of the tourist experience.

For expanded reviews, visit Fodors.com

WHAT IT COSTS			
$	$$	$$$	$$$$
Restaurants	Under 60,000d	60,000d –150,000d	151,000d –250,000d	over 250,000d
Hotels	Under 600,000d	600,000d –900,000d	901,000d –1,500,000d	over 1,500,000d

Prices in the reviews are the average cost of a main course at dinner or, if dinner is not served, at lunch. Prices in the reviews are the lowest cost of a standard double room in high season.

TOURS

Travel agencies and tourist cafés in Hanoi, such as Exo Travel and Handspan, can organize a variety of trips to the Northwest. One of the most popular is an overnight or two-night excursion to Mai Chau. On the very popular Mai Chau tour, you generally stay at the White Thai village where most of the homestays and guesthouses operate. Prices for this tour vary, but generally cost between 2,600,000d and 5,000,000d for the two-night version. Several tour operators conduct one- to seven-day hiking trips to Mount Fansipan and other areas around Sapa. The

CLOSE UP

Hiking in the Northwest

One of the best ways to experience northern Vietnam is by tackling the trails that lead out of the towns and into more remote areas of the highlands. These footpaths lead through more pristine terrain than you would be able to see from the back seat of a Landcruiser. Villages throughout the mountains are connected by trails, and it may not be long before someone produces a publication documenting and mapping a network of the best hiking trails in the north. Until then, however, your best bet is to pick up local maps when you arrive at a destination or to arrange a trekking itinerary with a reputable tour agency either in Hanoi or in Sapa.

The best of these operators have researched the hikes with knowledgeable locals and are pretty familiar with the needs and preferences of Western travelers. Dozens of trails lead out of the hillside town of Sapa, for instance, and into H'mong villages. Minority peoples have a vast knowledge of local routes. Indeed, most of the tour outfits that operate in the area employ local guides from the hill-tribe villages. You can strike out independently, but communication may be a problem. A decent guide becomes essential if you intend on trekking to the top of Mount Fansipan, Vietnam's highest peak.

Fansipan trip costs around 1,300,000d for one person in a group trip of 15 people, getting correspondingly more expensive the fewer the hikers. The price includes food, tents, and tours of remote mountain villages.

CONTACTS **Handspan Travel.** A range of touring experiences are offered, including homestays combined with trekking, bicycle tours, and an eight-day north loop trip. Prices include accommodations, meals, transportation, English-speaking guides, and admission fees. ✉ *78 Ma May St., Sapa* ☎ *024/3926–2828* ⊕ *www.handspan.com* ✉ *From: 3,310,000d.*

SAPA AND NEARBY

The northernmost section of the Northwest Loop is also its most accessible and user-friendly. Rising majestically above this part of the Northwest is Mount Fansipan, Vietnam's tallest peak. In its shadow lies the bustling hill town of Sapa, the tourist center of the Northwest, where Dao and H'mong women converge at the local market to buy, sell, and trade.

Near Sapa, the unhurried town of Bac Ha makes a plausible alternative base in the area. It is famous for its Sunday market and has a growing choice of acceptable lodgings.

SAPA

350 km (217 miles) northwest of Hanoi.

Ringed by the majestic Tonkinese Alps, Sapa is an enchanting hill town that has become the undisputed tourist capital of the Northwest. Make the journey here and you'll be rewarded with a glimpse of some of

Vietnam's most breathtaking mountain scenery and the opportunity to discover its mosaic of ethnic-minority cultures. Overlooking a verdant valley of rice terraces, the town enjoys an outstanding location and a cool, fresh climate. It was this, and the surrounding beauty, that prompted the French to establish a hill station here in 1922.

Today, Sapa attracts an even more international crowd, who come for its selection of restaurants, hotels, and pampering options, complemented by bustling markets that strike a mostly pleasant balance between unashamed tourism and earthier local character. The mountains and hill-tribe villages outside the town are magnets for well-equipped hikers.

Sapa's popularity has created increasing demand for accommodations, and the hotel building boom that continues unchecked has resulted in parts of the town transforming into a mess of ill-conceived concrete architecture. It has also attracted the persistent presence of H'mong and Dao traders, looking to offload handicrafts and trinkets, which can prove extremely tiresome after a few hours. For the moment, though, these are minor quibbles that are easy to overlook when you're tucking into a gourmet meal or gazing in wonder as the mist rises to reveal the timeless, beguiling landscapes.

GETTING HERE AND AROUND

The inauguration of the new Noi Bai-Lao Cai Expressway in September 2014 has made travel by road the easiest and fastest way to get to Sapa. The new highway has cut journey times between Hanoi and the border town of Lao Cai from seven hours to four hours by car and a little longer by bus. Several bus companies service the route. Buses leave from Hanoi's My Dinh Bus Station to Lao Cai Bus Station and the journey takes around 5½ hours. Ticket prices for the one-way journey start at around 250,000d. Sapa Express also operates a direct service from Hanoi to Sapa. It leaves from Hanoi's Old Quarter at 6:30 am and arrives in Sapa at 12:30 pm. The one-way fare is 378,000d. The new road has also made car rental from Hanoi much more attractive with a number of rental firms offering cars with drivers.

Despite the ease of road travel, the overnight train from Hanoi to Lao Cai remains a popular way to get to Sapa. The most comfortable trip is on Friday night, when you get a soft sleeper in a four-person compartment on the "luxury" train. The one-way ticket costs about 600,000d. Trains leave Hanoi train station at 9:15 pm, 9:50 pm, and 8:25 pm and take 11 hours. On weekends there's an additional service that departs at 7 pm. The easiest way to buy tickets is through a Hanoi travel agency.

Minibuses waiting at the Lao Cai train station can take you the 35 km (22 miles) to Sapa for 28,000. The buses leave when full and usually drop you in the town center. From Sapa buses return to the Lao Cai train station twice daily, at 6:30 am and 2 pm, but you can join with other travelers and share a bus or a taxi that will leave at the time you want. If you'd like to combine a one-way train to Sapa with a return to Hanoi by car, you can arrange that in Sapa at one of the tour agencies dotting the main roads.

Privately run buses operate between Sapa and Dien Bien Phu. The journey takes approximately eight hours and one-way tickets cost around 300,000d.

Transportation Contacts Sapa Express ⊠ *12 Ly Thai To St., Hoan Kiem District, Hanoi* ☎ *024/6682–1555* ⊕ *www.sapaexpress.com.* **Vietbus** ⊠ *My Dinh Bus Station, Tu Liem, Hanoi* ☎ *024/3768–5549* ⊕ *www. vietbusexpress.vn.*

TOURS

TOURS
Fodor's Choice
★

Sapa O'Chau. Operated on a basis of social enterprise, this acclaimed tour company was started by Shu Tan, a young single mother from the Black Hmong tribe. Working with Australian volunteers she funded the first Hmong-owned homestay in Sapa and established a socially conscious trekking service. The company can organize a range of trekking itineraries, including a two-day, one-night ascent of Fansipan. Proceeds are ploughed back into the community through projects such as improvements to village schools in the area and English classes for Sapa's young tour guides and street vendors. ⊠ *8 Thac Bac Rd.* ☎ *0214/377–1166* ⊕ *www.sapaochau.org* 🗐 *Day treks from 534,000d per person per day; Fansipan treks from 1,280,000d per person.*

Fodor's Choice
★

Sapa Sisters. Entirely owned and run by women, this Hmong-operated trekking group can arrange a number of programs and activities. These include everything from multiple-day treks to market tours and homestays with families in the valley. Eschewing set itineraries, the Sisters offer guests the opportunity to arrange treks tailored to their own requirements. Email them for more details or visit their office in Sapa. ⊠ *Graceful Hotel, 9 Fansipan St.* ⊕ *www.sapasisters. com* 🗐 *Day treks from 640,000d per person.*

ESSENTIALS

Visitor Information Sapa Tourist Office. The authorities of Lao Cai Province operate a main tourist office in Sapa with branch offices in Lao Cai and Bac Ha. ⊠ *2 Fansipan St.* ☎ *0214/387–1975* ⊕ *www.sapa-tourism.com.*

EXPLORING

Nui Hoang Lien Nature Reserve. Sapa is part of this mountainous 2,995-hectare (7,400-acre) landscape covered by temperate and subtemperate forests. The reserve provides a habitat for 56 species of mammals—tigers, leopards, monkeys, and bears among them—17 of which, including the Asiatic black bear, are considered endangered. An impressive 150 species of birds, including the red-vented barbet and the collared finchbill, can be found only in these mountains. Among the area's geological resources are minerals from sediments deposited in the Mesozoic and Paleozoic periods. From the Muong Hoa River to the peak of Mt.

8

Fansipan, the eastern boundary of the reserve is formed by a ridge of marble and calcium carbonate. Also found in this region is kaolinite, or China clay, used in the making of porcelain.

Guided walking tours of the nature reserve are recommended and are easily arranged through hotels, guest houses and tour agencies in town. Motorbike drivers will be happy to take you down the road from Sapa for a full day of hiking, swimming in waterfall pools, and visiting H'mong and Thai villages. Hoteliers and tour companies can also make arrangements for you. ☎ 0214/3871–433.

Sapa Market. The center of town is a street below the muddy soccer field, but here you'll find the pulse of the community. The Sapa Market convenes daily on the slippery stone stairway that crosses this narrow, bitumen-flecked street. Much of the buying and selling takes place under the roof of the drab but roomy marketplace-on-stilts. The market expands on Saturday, when tourists from Hanoi flood into Sapa; you may actually find it quieter and more pleasant on weekdays. H'mong and Red Dao women come into town with the rising sun. Most walk in from surrounding villages, while a few catch rides on the backs of motorcycles. They are often dressed in their finest traditional garb: richly embroidered vests and dresses, aqua-and-black cotton shirts, finely detailed silver necklaces and bracelets, and elaborate headdresses that tinkle with every movement. Many of these women have picked up a few French and English words or phrases. ■ TIP➡ Part of the fun is bargaining with them, but don't express too much initial interest, or you may be labeled a sucker. Hold out for as long as you can, and then ask to see the good stuff. Invariably an elderly Dao woman will understand what you're looking for, dig deep into her bamboo basket, and produce fabric of quality superior to what she'd been showing you only moments before. Near the central market, the two-story, 8,000-square-meter (86,111-square-feet) indoor Sapa Cultural Market opened in 2013. ⊠ Dong Loi St.

Sapa Museum. You can get a useful crash course in the ethnology of the area here, with a number of exhibits devoted to the patchwork of minority tribes that live in the area. Sapa's informative museum also charts the evolution of the town from French colonial times to the present day, and a stall downstairs sells traditional handicrafts. ⊠ 103 Xuan Vien St. 🖃 Free ☉ Daily 7:30–11:30, 1:30–5.

Fodor's Choice ★

Victoria Spa. There are numerous fairly basic places in town for a massage and most do a reasonable job for the money. However, for a top-class treatment to soothe tired bones and muscles after a hard day's trekking, the spa at the Victoria Hotel is the pick of Sapa's pampering options. Choose from a number of treatments and luxuriate in the resort's gorgeous massage rooms. ⊠ Xuan Vien St. ☎ 0214/387–1522 ⊕ www.victoriahotels.asia.

WHERE TO EAT

$$$
ITALIAN

✕ **Delta Italian Restaurant.** Tourists gather at this restaurant near the market for the large portions of pasta and pizzas cooked in a genuine Italian pizza oven by the amiable owner-chef, Mr. Tung, who spent six months studying in Milan before opening the restaurant. Exquisite crepes satisfy a lighter appetite, and there's also an extensive international wine list. Upstairs, there's a pool table for customers. During peak season, from around October through mid-December, it's best to make reservations for weekend dining. $ *Average main: 180000d* ⊠ *33 Cau May St.* ☎ *0214/387–1799.*

$$$
FRENCH
Fodor's Choice
★

✕ **Hill Station Deli.** While its sister restaurant, the Hill Station Signature Restaurant, deals in refined hill tribe cuisine, the Deli pays homage to another major influence in the area—the French. Gallic favorites such as cheese, charcuterie, and wine are on the menu in a cozy little venue that warms up nicely in the winter months thanks to its dome-shape fireplace. Other Western influences also get a look in. The burgers here are the best in Sapa, and authentic Italian coffee is served throughout the day. $ *Average main: 165000d* ⊠ *7 Muong Hoa St.* ☎ *0214/388–7111* ⊕ *www.thehillstation.com.*

$$$
VIETNAMESE
Fodor's Choice
★

✕ **Hill Station Signature Restaurant.** By far the most imaginative dining option in Sapa, the Hill Station Signature Restaurant combines European design sensibilities with hill-tribe (mostly H'mong) cuisine. Opened by Danish friends Soren and Tommy, the attractive venue is a cut above the rather average establishments found elsewhere. A range of set menus are available, or choose dishes such as homemade tofu, fresh river trout, and smoked buffalo from the à la carte options. The restaurant also has a good selection of wines as well as upscale versions of the local rice-based firewater. $ *Average main: 250000d* ⊠ *37 Fansipan St.* ☎ *0214/388–7111* ⊕ *www.thehillstation.com* ◷ *No lunch.*

$$$
BISTRO
Fodor's Choice
★

✕ **Le Gecko.** Like Sapa itself, Le Gecko bears noticeable French influence with a menu that features a host of bistro classics. There's nothing particularly fussy about either the restaurant or the home-style cuisine so don't expect fancy sauces of Parisian haughtiness. Dishes on the menu include a rich boeuf bourguignon as well as more casual fare such as pizza, sandwiches, and a smattering of Vietnamese items. There's a comfortable bar area that is popular in the evenings while the outside terrace is a great spot for people-watching. $ *Average main: 160000d* ⊠ *4 Ham Rong St.* ☎ *0214/387–1504* ⊕ *www.legeckosapa.com.*

$$
VIETNAMESE
Fodor's Choice
★

✕ **Sapa Essence.** Utilizing the best local produce for a menu that is as imaginative as any in Sapa, this venue is deserving of its popularity. While many of its neighboring restaurants are content to play it safe, Sapa Essence pushes the envelope with delicious Vietnamese creations such as claypot eggplant and tofu, and beef with lemongrass and chili. Extra touches such as free fresh fruit and friendly service earn it additional kudos. $ *Average main: 140000d* ⊠ *Muong Hoa St.* ☎ *097/481–2698.*

$$
VIETNAMESE

✕ **Sapa Moment.** Of the many establishments in the center of Sapa that do a pretty good job of tackling a number of cuisines, few rise to the occasion with more aplomb than Sapa Moment. Unless you have a really keen nose for a place, it can be difficult to distinguish between the run-of-the-mill eateries, with their near-identical blend of Vietnamese dishes and Western favorites—pizza, burgers, and other stolid fare. But here, in addition to staples like spring rolls and chicken with cashew nuts, dishes such as duck in honey sauce and deer with sauteed onions and mushrooms supply the X-factor. $ *Average main: 130000d* ⊠ *33 Muong Hoa St.* ☎ *090/910–7111.*

8

$$ CAFÉ 🍴 **Sapa Rooms.** Service can be slightly scatty, but this remains one of the best contemporary cafés in Sapa. The comfortable space is stylishly decorated and its giant sofas are ideal for kicking back on. Don't expect a huge variety of dishes, but great breakfasts, cakes, and Lavazza coffee make this a fine place to while away the hours when the weather is misty outside. [$] *Average main: 70000d* ✉ *Fansipan St.* ☎ *0214/650–5228.*

WHERE TO STAY

$ HOTEL 🏨 **Auberge Dang Trung Hotel.** Owner Dang Trung, a Hanoi transplant, has one of the best things going in Sapa—a lovely, popular hotel with exquisite views of the mountains. **Pros:** bathtubs are perfect for easing weary bones. **Cons:** access is up a slightly steep incline. [$] *Rooms from: 500000d* ✉ *31 Cau May St.* ☎ *0214/387–1243* 🛏 *28 rooms* 🍽 *Breakfast.*

$$ HOTEL 🏨 **Bamboo Sapa Hotel.** Like many of Sapa's best hotels, the Bamboo Sapa enjoys a stunning location with towering views of the surrounding mountains and the valley below, and to maximize this epic outlook most rooms have private balconies. **Pros:** spacious and spotlessly clean; rooms have televisions and private bathrooms. **Cons:** lack of an elevator can be an issue for the elderly or those who are less mobile; beds are reported to be a little on the hard side. [$] *Rooms from: 768960d* ✉ *18 Muong Hoa St.* 📠 *0214/387–1075* 🌐 *www.bamboosapahotel.com.vn* 🛏 *55 rooms, 1 suite* 🍽 *Breakfast.*

$$ HOTEL 🏨 **Chau Long Hotel.** The stately French villas of Sapa have nothing on this distinctive—and decidedly incongruous—crenellated mock-chateau containing one of the town's better hotels. **Pros:** deluxe rooms feel very homey; spectacular views. **Cons:** gaudy architecture is not for everyone. [$] *Rooms from: 880000d* ✉ *24 Dong Loi St.* ☎ *0214/387–1245* 🌐 *www.chaulonghotel.com* 🛏 *33 rooms, 2 suites* 🍽 *Breakfast.*

$ HOTEL Fodor's Choice ★ 🏨 **Elysian Sapa Hotel.** One of four hotels run by the Eden chain, the Elysian Sapa offers outstanding views and good value in a convenient location on the central Cau May strip, within easy striking distance of the town's best bars, restaurants, and shops. **Pros:** as the hotel is relatively new, rooms and common areas are still very spruce; service is excellent, as is the inclusive breakfast. **Cons:** some of the rooms in the middle of the hotel have windows that open up onto hallways and staircases. [$] *Rooms from: 468270d* ✉ *38 Cau May St.* ☎ *0214/387–1238* 🌐 *www.elysiansapahotel.com* 🛏 *45 rooms* 🍽 *Breakfast.*

$$$ HOTEL 🏨 **Royal View Hotel.** Perched beneath the road on the very edge of Sapa Valley, this hotel stole a chunk of the view, and borrowed a few ideas on room design, from the nearby Auberge Dang Trung Hotel. **Pros:** five-star view; rooms that stand the test of time. **Cons:** lack of heating in dining area makes it rather chilly; downstairs bar is known to be noisy on occasion. [$] *Rooms from: 1281600d* ✉ *34 Cau May St.* ☎ *0214/387–2990, 0214/387–2992* 🛏 *28 rooms* 🍽 *Breakfast.*

$$$$ RESORT Fodor's Choice ★ 🏨 **Topas Eco-Lodge.** If Sapa town is too busy for your liking, this resort within Hoang Lien National Park has lodgings arranged around the summit of a small hill, guaranteeing absolute seclusion and some fabulous panoramic views. **Pros:** stunning views; peaceful location. **Cons:** interiors are somewhat spartan; an hour's drive from town.

$ *Rooms from: 2100000d* ⊠ *Off QL32* ☎ *0214/387–1331* ⊕ *www.topasecolodge.com* ⇆ *25 lodges* ⦿ *Breakfast.*

$$$$ 🖼 **Victoria Sapa Hotel.** The premier hotel in Sapa, the luxurious, French-
HOTEL designed Victoria sits on a hilltop overlooking the town and caters to
Fodor's Choice the fancy of its guests with heaps of amenities. **Pros:** height of luxury
★ in the mountains; private train is a classy and unusual touch. **Cons:**
in some bathrooms showers are over the bath; steps out of the bathrooms are on the high side, so care is needed. $ *Rooms from: 3417600d*
⊠ *Xuan Vien St.* ☎ *0214/871–522* ⊕ *www.victoriahotels.asia* ⇆ *76
rooms, 1 suite* ⦿ *Breakfast.*

NIGHTLIFE

Color Bar. This atmospheric spot is a little out of the way, but is worth the
journey for its friendly, bohemian vibe. Owned by an artist from Hanoi,
the venue has a mellow feel with occasional live music, a soundtrack of
laid-back tunes, and limitless ice-cold beer. ⊠ *56 Fansipan St.*

Fodor's Choice **H'mong Sisters.** Raucous and rowdy, this is by far the liveliest night spot
★ in Sapa. Busy every night of the week, the bar attracts an eclectic crowd
that spans backpackers, locals, trekkers, and members of Sapa's small
expatriate community. A pool table, a great selection of music, and gen-
erously strong drinks keep the party going until late. ⊠ *31 Muong Hoa
St.* ☎ *0214/387–3370* ⊕ *www.hmongsistersbar.jimdo.com* ⊙ *4 pm–late.*

SPORTS AND THE OUTDOORS
HIKING

A 30-minute hike from the center of town to the radio tower above
Sapa gives you a spectacular panoramic view. Climb the stone steps
from the main road. The steps lead up past well-manicured gardens and
through rocky fields. A path breaks off to the right and winds around
boulders to the tower. The town of Sapa is laid out below, and across
the valley is Mount Fansipan. Opportunities for trekking in the town's
hinterland are limitless, either independently or in the company of a
guide from one of the local hill tribes. One of the easiest (it is more of
a stroll than a hike) is the downhill walk from Sapa to Cat Cat Village.
The route is simple, but tour agencies in Sapa will be happy to supply a
map. Local guides can be hired for around 400,000d per day and their
comprehensive knowledge of the villages in the area and the narrow
paths that link them is invaluable.

Hiking Mount Fansipan, 3,143 meters (10,372 feet), requires little tech-
nical expertise, but it does take two to three days because you must
depart from Sapa and hike down into the valley, then back up the other
side. The summit of Fansipan is 19 km (12 miles) from Sapa and can
be reached only on foot. It is recommended that you bring an experienced guide to suggest the best route, help you navigate the wet, chilly
mountainside, and find places to camp. If you are serious about hiking
Fansipan, contact one of the many reputable travel operators in Sapa or
in Hanoi, which can all organize treks to the peak. Recommended companies include Sapa O Chau, Handspan, Exo Travel, and Sapa Sisters
(*see Tours*). It is up to you to choose the itinerary, the tour companies
will be happy to customize it for you. Or ask for more details at your
hotel in Sapa. The price for the most popular two-day, one-night ascent

8

THE SI LA PEOPLE OF NORTHWEST VIETNAM

Though there are roughly only 800 Si La people living in Lai Chau Province in northwest Vietnam, there are another 1,800 or so in Laos. The Si La people hunt, forage, and cultivate cereal. Tooth painting is common with elders; men paint their teeth red and women paint theirs black, but this has not continued with the younger generations. Si La women dress in indigo-dyed dresses, with embroidered collars and sleeves. The upper part of the dress is covered in metal coinlike disks. In Vietnam, the Si La speak the Tibeto-Burmese language Sila as well as standard Vietnamese.

of Fansipan varies on the size of your group. For example, prices start at around 1,300,300d per person based on a group of 15 tourists. If the group is smaller, prices will increase. It can get very cold in Sapa and even colder on the mountain, so you need to dress accordingly.

SHOPPING

The ethnic-minority communities that surround Sapa, particularly the women, have developed sophisticated trading networks, not just among themselves but for tourists as well. And what's trading hands is positively beautiful: richly dyed textiles; hand-loomed silk scarves, headdresses, and broadcloth; brocaded vests and dresses; woven bamboo baskets of all shapes and sizes; and traditional silver jewelry. Many of these wares are on display at Sapa's main market and also at weekly markets in the area such as Can Cau and Coc Ly. In Sapa, a smattering of boutiques is taking a more contemporary approach to marketing traditional craftsmanship. The hard sell tactics of the Dao and H'mong women on the streets of Sapa can be a little grating. Nevertheless, if you have the stomach for incessant pestering and the ability to bargain, some rewarding purchases can be made.

Fodor's Choice
★ **Indigo Cat.** Run by a H'mong lady and her husband, this is by far the most stylish of Sapa's small boutiques. The craftsmanship of the H'mong minority is legendary and this skill shines through in the shop's well-chosen selection of bags, clothing, pillows, and belts. ⊠ *46 Fansipan St.* ☎ *098/240–3647.*

BAC HA

100 km (62 miles) northeast of Sapa, 350 km (217 miles) northwest of Hanoi.

The main reason for venturing to Bac Ha, a small town built on a desolate highland plain northeast of Lao Cai, is the century-old Sunday morning market, one of the largest in the Northwest. Ethnic-minority villagers such as the Dao and the Flower H'mong (related to the H'mong but wearing brighter and more elaborate clothing) come from miles around to buy, sell, and trade everything from horses and dogs to medicinal herbs and beautiful handmade tapestries. The market has become a firmly established part of the tourist trail in the north and the influx of day-trippers from Sapa has certainly changed the character

Ethnic Minorities in the North

In the remote mountains and valleys of the North, ethnic-minority populations continue to live as they have for centuries, although modern society is always threatening to encroach. The history of these unique ethnic minorities is still the subject of some dispute, but many anthropologists now believe the largest of the groups, the Muong, as well as smaller groups like the Kho-mu, the Khang, the Mang, and the La Ha, have been living in the Hoang Lien Mountains and the northern foothills for thousands of years, preceding even the arrival of the Kinh—the ethnic Vietnamese who now make up 87% of the country's population.

LATE MIGRATION

Most other groups migrated from Thailand, China, or Laos—some as late as the 19th century—as a result of war, lack of land, or a simple disregard for national borders. Living in the highest elevations, near the climatic limits of hill rice cultivation, are the H'mong and Dao (pronounced zow). The clothing and jewelry of these two groups, particularly the women, are among the most colorful and elaborate in the North. The Muong and Thai (with distinct Black Thai and White Thai subgroups) are two of the larger minorities, each numbering about a million. They practice wetlands cultivation on the middle and lower slopes and generally live in airy, comfortable stilt houses in village clusters ranging from a handful of houses to several dozen.

Slash-and-burn agriculture, the traditional mainstay of ethnic-minority economies, was for centuries an ideal form of natural resource management. In the 21st century, however, as the land available for such cultivation shrinks, this method has begun to generate heated controversy in Vietnam. Indeed, northern Vietnam is one of the most deforested regions of Indochina. A migration of Kinh Vietnamese from the Red River delta farther inland and into the distant valleys is also displacing many nomadic farmers as land privatization plans take hold.

DISPLACEMENT CONTROVERSIES

Vietnam's growing energy needs are also wreaking havoc on minority life. The Hoa Binh Dam, Vietnam's first hydroelectric power project, 70 km (43 miles) southwest of Hanoi, displaced 60,000 people from the Da River valley. Most were ethnic minorities who were pushed into higher elevations, for which they had little farming experience or expertise. This form of displacement has been repeated on a larger scale at other energy initiatives, especially during the construction of the Son La Dam, currently the largest hydroelectric power station in Southeast Asia. The project required displacement of more than 91,000 ethnic minority people, the largest resettlement in Vietnam's history.

Despite odds that continue to be stacked against them, including inhospitable land, unofficial but very real bias toward the Kinh majority, and the threat of displacement, Vietnam's ethnic minorities continue to work their ancestral lands. Their distinctive traditions, such as weaving, embroidery, and other crafts, are still passed from generation to generation, ensuring that hill-tribe culture continues to exert a colorful influence high in the mountains.

8

of the market. Nevertheless, despite there being an increasing range of handicrafts for sale, it retains much of its authenticity. A highlight of the market is the lovely, high-pitched songs performed by Flower H'mong singers. If the market manager hasn't been able to arrange singers for that day, he plays a cassette of their songs over the public address system. The market gets going at about 9 am, but early birds can be seen setting up their stands and sipping *pho* (noodle soup) for breakfast as the sun comes up. A 3- to 6-km (2- to 4-mile) walk up the road past the Sao Mai Hotel (turn left at the fork) brings you to some ethnic-minority villages where residents will be more than happy to see you.

GETTING HERE AND AROUND

Many travel agencies in Sapa arrange day trips to Bac Ha, which leave at about 6 am. The going rate is around 200,000d per person in a minibus. The price includes tour guide, transportation, and lunch. The trip takes 2½ hours each way. You could opt to spend Saturday night in Bac Ha, where there are several acceptable hotels, and get an early start on Sunday morning, giving you a head start on the hundreds of day-trippers from Sapa. If you're heading back to Hanoi, you may want to travel to Bac Ha on a Sunday morning and then get dropped off in Sapa for the 2 pm bus to Lao Cai in the afternoon so that you can take the train or bus back to the capital that evening.

TOURS

Hoang Vu Tours. This Bac Ha–based operator is a one-stop shop for a range of experiences in the area including market tours, trekking expeditions, and cultural explorations. They can also help arrange transport between Bac Ha and Sapa as well as other points in the vicinity. ✉ *124 Ngoc Uyen* ☎ *0214/378–0661* ⊕ *www.bachhatourist.com* ✉ *Treks start at 534,000d per person per day; market tours start at 320,000d.*

Sapa Tours. Although it specializes in Sapa tours, this outfit is adept in familiarizing guests with the wonders of Bac Ha, its market, and the surrounding scenic splendor. Trekking is available, but the main focus is on Bac Ha market and other nearby minority bazaars. ✉ *28 Vu Pham Ham, Cau Giay, Hanoi* ☎ *024/3248–4656* ⊕ *www.sapa-tour.net* ✉ *From: 320,000d.*

ESSENTIALS

Visitor Information Bac Ha Tourist Office ✉ *Hoang A Tuong's Palace, TL 153* ☎ *0214/378–0662* ⊕ *www.sapa-tourism.com.*

EXPLORING

Fodor'sChoice ★ **Bac Ha Market.** Without a doubt Bac Ha's biggest draw, the Sunday market here retains its authenticity despite a growing influx of tourists. Market day sees local hill-tribe people (most noticeably the colorfully dressed Flower H'mong) flock from the surrounding mountains to trade their wares. Handicrafts are available for tourists, but this remains a mostly local affair with goods ranging from livestock to herbs.

Can Cau Market. Taking place every Saturday, this market is a worthy precursor to the extravaganza that is Bac Ha's Sunday trading jamboree. Indeed, Can Cau possibly feels more authentic due to its remoteness—it is 20 km (12 miles) north of Bac Ha—and the relative lack of tourist numbers. Like Bac Ha Market, it is a magnet for the local tribespeople.

The colorful Flower H'mong are a noticeable presence, as are the Blue H'mong, distinguished by their striking zigzag pattern costume. All manner of items are traded here, including livestock and traditional medicine. ✉ *Can Cau.*

Thai Giang Pho Waterfall. If you are staying in Bac Ha during the summer months, this attractive waterfall is an inviting place to cool off. Around 12 km (7 miles) east of Bac Ha, it has a large pool that is deep enough for swimming.

Vua Meo. A palace in humble Bac Ha? This unexpected and somewhat outlandish structure was built by the French to keep the fractious Flower H'mong chief Hoang A Tuong happy. The result is one of the more striking architectural sights in this part of Vietnam, resembling a fusion of a French chateau and a church. ✉ *TL 153* 🎫 *Free* 🕒 *Daily 7:30–11:30, 1:30–5.*

WHERE TO EAT AND STAY

$$ VIETNAMESE 🍴 **Cong Fu Restaurant.** Off the main road, about 200 yards from entrance to market, this restaurant, attached to a hotel of the same name, does a brisk business with lunching tourists. It serves very basic, but extremely tasty Vietnamese fare, such as pho, and a variety of noodle, meat, and chicken dishes. Service can be a little erratic, and simple orders like a cold beer sometimes take more than five minutes to arrive. [$] *Average main: 60000d* ✉ *152 Ngoc Uyen St.* ☎ *0214/388–0254* 💳 *No credit cards.*

$$ VIETNAMESE 🍴 **Hoang Yen Restaurant.** True, there's not much in the way of competition, but this is the best dining venue in Bac Ha. The menu will be familiar to students of the region's culinary landscape, with a solid selection of Vietnamese staple noodle and rice dishes along with lots of grilled, fried, and boiled meat. [$] *Average main: 120000d* ✉ *Tran Bac St.* ☎ *091/200–5952* 💳 *No credit cards.*

$ HOTEL 🏨 **Ngan Nga Bac Ha Hotel.** Opened in 2012, this is the most modern hotel in Bac Ha and makes a comfortable base in the center of town. **Pros:** service from the English-speaking staff is excellent; hotel is relatively new so rooms are up to a high standard of cleanliness. **Cons:** restaurant can be noisy; Wi-Fi is occasionally intermittent. [$] *Rooms from: 574695d* ✉ *115–117 Ngoc Uyen St.* ☎ *0214/388–0286* 🌐 *www.ngannngabachahotel.com* 🛏 *16 rooms* 🍽 *Breakfast.*

$$ HOTEL 🏨 **Sao Mai Hotel.** This is arguably the grandest place to stay in Bac Ha, renovated over the past five years, and with rooms that are more than adequate, clean, and pleasant. **Pros:** new wooden houses offer an elevated standard of comfort. **Cons:** showers take a long time to heat up. [$] *Rooms from: 704880d* ✉ *Thanh Nien St.* ☎ *0214/388–0288* 🛏 *30 rooms* 🍽 *Breakfast.*

DIEN BIEN PHU AND NEARBY

Although often overshadowed by the spectacular regions in the northeast, the scenery of broad valleys and forested peaks in Dien Bien Phu and nearby Son La and Hoa Binh provinces is equally enticing. Dien Bien Phu is most famous for its storied military history, and those with an interest in the great conflicts of the 20th century will find plenty to stimulate them. Farther southeast, Son La also offers colorful minority culture. In Hoa Binh Province, the star attraction is Mai Chau, where White Thai villages nestle in a peaceful valley.

DIEN BIEN PHU

284 km (176 miles) south of Sapa, 470 km (291 miles) west of Hanoi.

Hard by the Laos border in one of the most remote regions in Vietnam, it is easy to imagine that Dien Bien Phu might have remained in obscurity was it not for the seismic role it played in modern Vietnamese history. It was here, in 1954, that the Vietminh defeated the French colonial forces in a decisive battle. The loss effectively meant the end of French colonial power in Indochina and was another milestone in the long and bloody route toward Vietnamese independence. Even as a household name, it was not until the latter part of the 20th century that Dien Bien Phu grew into a town of any significance. It was only given town status in 1992 and was elevated to provincial capital in 2004. Nowadays, with its expansive boulevards and civic buildings, as well as its airport and proximity to Laos, the city has a slightly more bustling feel to it. The main reason to visit is to brush up on the area's evocative war history, but the surrounding Muong Thanh Valley, with its thick forests and steep terrain, is also worthy of investigation.

GETTING HERE AND AROUND

The easiest way to get to Dien Bien Phu from Hanoi is by air. Vietnam Airlines has two daily flights that start at 1,000,000d for a one-way ticket. There is no direct public bus to Dien Bien Phu, but buses to Muong Lay leave Hanoi in the morning and from Muong Lay it is possible to connect to Dien Bien Phu. Private buses run between Sapa and Dien Bien Phu and cost around 330,000d. As the buses are cramped and uncomfortable, having your own transportation—car and driver or motorbike—is infinitely preferable.

Bus Contacts Hai Van Express ⊠ *My Dinh Bus Station, Hanoi* ☎ *024/3768–5549.* **Hung Thanh Company** ⊠ *My Dinh Bus Station, Hanoi* ☎ *024/3768–5549* ⊕ *www.hungthanhtravel.vn.*

EXPLORING

Command Bunker of Colonel de Castries. Within walking distance of the Dien Bien Phu Museum, the command bunker has been remade with makeshift sandbags filled with concrete. Overhead is a reproduction of the corrugated roof from which a lone Viet Minh soldier waved a victory flag—the image, re-created several hours after the fact for a documentary film, became Vietnam's enduring symbol of victory over colonial oppression. 🕮 *5,000d* ⊙ *Daily 7–11, 1:30–5.*

Dien Bien Phu Museum. This museum has been built on the site of the battle with the French, and although there is a section dedicated to the region's ethnic-minority communities, French ignominy and Vietnamese glory are the principal topics here. The main hall recounts the events of the siege and the battle itself, with blinking maps and legends synchronized with a recorded loop outlining the battle's chronology. Outside is a collection of weapons used in and around the garrison: the Vietnamese tanks and guns look as if they were polished yesterday afternoon, the rusting French jeeps are riddled with bullet holes, and the remains of a French plane lie in a twisted heap. ✉ *7 May St.* ☎ *0215/382–4971* 🎫 *5,000d* ⏰ *Daily 7–11, 1:30–5.*

French War Memorial. French veterans organized the construction of the small, rather forlorn-looking French War Memorial, which stands across the road from the command bunker. It commemorates the 3,000 French troops buried under the rice paddies. 🎫 *Free.*

Hill A1: Eliane. Some of the battle's most intense combat took place at Hill A1, a position labeled Eliane by the French. Once considered impregnable by the French, it was the last key position to fall to the Vietminh. A decrepit French tank and a monument to Vietminh troops now stand here. 🎫 *5,000d* ⏰ *Daily 8–11:30, 1:30–5.*

Memorial Cemetery. Across the street from the Dien Bien Phu Museum, this cemetery is the final resting place for many unknown Vietminh soldiers. Here in bas-reliefs are scenes of the battle depicted in larger-than-life-size socialist realism. One of the most emotional aspects of Dien Bien Phu is here: the names of all the Vietminh casualties from the historic battle at Dien Bien Phu are carved on the back of the front wall of the cemetery. ✉ *Vo Nguyen Giap* 🎫 *Free* ⏰ *Daily 7–11, 1:30–5.*

WHERE TO EAT AND STAY

$$ INTERNATIONAL

🍴 **Lien Tuoi Restaurant.** Catering mostly to foreign tourists, this large restaurant, a short walk from Hill A1–Eliane, serves a wide selection of Chinese, Vietnamese, and Western dishes. The most popular item is chicken stewed with mushrooms. Menus are available in English and French, and be prepared to sit on plastic stools. [$] *Average main: 60000d* ✉ *Hoang Van Thai St.* ☎ *0215/382–4919* 💳 *No credit cards.*

$$ VEGETARIAN Fodor's Choice ★

🍴 **Yen Ninh Restaurant.** With meat as the staple fare of the northwest, it comes as some surprise to find that Dien Bien Phu's top restaurant is a wholly vegetarian affair—and very good it is, too. The owner is an English teacher, which ensures that service is much less spotty than it tends to be elsewhere in the more remote regions of Vietnam. Despite Dien Bien's Phu's mythical status in the country's history, there's nothing revolutionary about the food here, but the simple tofu, vegetable, and rice-based creations are fresh and tasty and the atmosphere is convivial. [$] *Average main: 80000d* ✉ *7–5 Rd.* ☎ *098/988–7513* 💳 *No credit cards.*

$ HOTEL

🏨 **Muong Thanh Hotel.** This snazzy hotel complex has cornered the (admittedly limited) business market in Dien Bien Phu due to its clean rooms and immaculate service. **Pros:** the large swimming pool is a rarity in northern Vietnam. **Cons:** ugly building; restaurant does not get good reviews. [$] *Rooms from: 420000d* ✉ *25 Phuong Him Lam St.* ☎ *0215/381–0038* 🛏 *50 rooms* 🍽 *Breakfast.*

$ HOTEL Fodor's Choice ★

🏨 **Ruby Hotel.** While some of the lodging options in Dien Bien Phu have seen better days, this hotel debuted in 2014, meaning that everything is spotless and new. **Pros:** superlative service from owner and his team. **Cons:** lack of an on-site restaurant is a drawback. [$] *Rooms*

The Battle of Dien Bien Phu

The dream of reestablishing colonial rule throughout Indochina turned into a nightmare for the French at Dien Bien Phu. History has documented General Vo Nguyen Giap's stunning victory over Colonel Christian de Castries and his 13,000 French and Vietnamese troops as one of the greatest military achievements of the modern era. The Vietminh army had been on the offensive for much of 1953, and General Henri Navarre, commander of French forces in Indochina, was intent on regaining the initiative throughout the region by building up a series of bases from which his troops could mount offensive action. One such base was at Dien Bien Phu.

Such a remote garrison would make it unlikely, thought the French, that General Giap would infiltrate the valley with ground troops. The French clearly controlled the skies and used two landing strips in the valley to shuttle in supplies, reinforcements, and batteries of howitzers and other field guns. But by late 1953 Giap had encircled the French garrison with 50,000 men and had managed, somehow, to drag into offensive position dozens of 105-millimeter artillery cannon and anti-aircraft guns up steep and densely forested slopes, all under the nose of French surveillance planes and scout missions.

The surprise assault began on March 13. Two weeks later the airstrips were within Vietminh artillery range, cutting off the base from vital troop reinforcements and forcing the French to turn to parachute drops for resupplying the base. While the French were waiting, the Vietminh were digging. An elaborate tunnel system crisscrossed the valley and gave Giap's soldiers the necessary element of surprise over the French. The French solicited assistance from their longtime allies the Americans and the British, but to no avail. Morale collapsed, and on May 7, after a series of attacks by the Vietminh, the white flag was raised over the command bunker.

Coincidentally, the next day an international conference—whose initial purpose one month earlier was the completion of a peace treaty for the Korean conflict—opened in Geneva. The result was a declaration temporarily partitioning Vietnam along the 17th parallel until national elections could be held to determine a single government (they were never held). Tellingly, the agreement was never signed, partly because of the refusal by the United States to actively participate due to the presence of the Communist Chinese at the convention.

from: 350000d ✉ 43 Muong Thanh Ward ☎ 0215/383–5568 ⊕ www. rubyhoteldienbien.com ⬎ 31 rooms ⦿ Breakfast.

SON LA

150 km (93 miles) southeast of Dien Bien Phu, 160 km (99 miles) northwest of Mai Chau, 320 km (198 miles) west of Hanoi.

Son La is a convenient overnight stop on the journey to Mai Chau or Hanoi. Even if you're not overnighting in Son La, take some time to

THE LU PEOPLE

Most of the 6,000 Lu in Vietnam live in northwestern province Lai Chau, which shares a border with China (where the Lu people also live but are counted as the Dai ethnic group). You'll also find Lu in large numbers in Thailand, Laos, and Myanmar. The Lu cultivate rice and grow corn, potatoes, and cassava (the root from which tapioca is extracted). They also weave and dye fabric. The Lu wear hand-woven, hand-dyed cotton blouses, skirts, turbans, and, on holidays, dresses. The pieces are embroidered with intricate patterns and topped off with heavy silver jewelry. In the last few years, several Lu villages have seen an influx of tourists, with visitors snapping up the Lu's beautifully embroidered dresses and headscarves. While eschewed by the younger generation, tooth-dyeing—coloring the teeth entirely black—is popular with the over-30 Lus. In Vietnam, the group speaks Tai Lu and standard Vietnamese.

explore the immediate environs. Many hill tribes reside in the area, which until 1980 was considered part of the Tay Bac Autonomous Region.

GETTING HERE AND AROUND

Several buses depart from Hanoi's My Dinh bus station to Son La. The journey takes around five hours and a one-way ticket costs between 160,000d and 250,000d. In Son La, buses stop at the town's main bus station, which is around 2 km (1 mile) south of town. Frequent buses to Son La leave from Dien Bien Phu, starting at 4:30 am, and the journey takes around four hours.

EXPLORING

Hot Springs. If you feel like soaking your tired bones for a while, have your driver or a motorbike taxi take you to the hot springs in beautiful Suoi Nuoc Nong village, a few miles south of the main road. ⚠ **Be warned, the rather murky communal pool is far from idyllic.** ⊠ *Suoi Nuoc Nong* 🖾 *5,000d* ☾ *Daily 7–6.*

Lookout Tower (Cot V3). For a commanding view of the town and the surrounding area, climb the stone steps behind the Trade Union Hotel to the lookout tower known as Cot V3. ⊠ *26–8 St.*

Old French Prison & Museum. Destroyed by American bombers, but partially rebuilt, this former French penal colony, with its tiny underground cells and dank corridors, leave a strong impression of life in captivity. The ticket includes entry to the Son La Museum, housed in a moldy colonial mansion overlooking the prison. Downstairs, the museum displays pictures of life in Son La, past and present, and upstairs is a model of a Thai village and an exhibition of ethnic minority clothing. The prison and museum are on the hill in the center of town, next to the People's Committee building. ⊠ *QL6* 🖾 *10,000d* ☾ *Daily 7:30–11, 1:30–5.*

8

WHERE TO EAT AND STAY

$$ VIETNAMESE 🍴 **Hai Phi Restaurant.** Goat meat (*thit de*) is the local delicacy here, so why not try some goat kebabs or, if you're really an adventurous eater, *tiet canh* (goat's-blood curd soup)? Goat-free dishes, such as pork and beef, are also available. The flock of goats tethered in the courtyard makes this place easy to spot. [$] *Average main: 70000d* ✉ *Hwy. 6.*

$$ VIETNAMESE 🍴 **Long Phuong Restaurant.** The countryside around Son La is rich in hill-tribe culture and this busy restaurant is a good place to try some local specialties. Goat is definitely the preferred meat in the area and it is served in several ways here. There's also a wide range of vegetarian options, for anyone who doesn't eat meat. [$] *Average main: 60000d* ✉ *Thinh Doi* ☎ *0212/385–2339* 💳 *No credit cards.*

$ HOTEL 🏨 **Hanoi Hotel.** With its modern design and clean rooms, the Hanoi Hotel is one of the better lodging options in Son La, and most of the rooms have balconies that offer decent views over the small town and out toward the surrounding rice fields and mountains. **Pros:** balconies are a nice extra. **Cons:** the massage area is a bit dank. [$] *Rooms from: 300000d* ✉ *228B Truong Chinh St.* ☎ *0212/375–3200* 🛏 *50 rooms* 💳 *No credit cards* 🍽 *Breakfast.*

$ HOTEL 🏨 **Trade Union Hotel.** The rooms at this state-owned hotel may be basic and on the dated side, but the location is central, the staff speaks reasonable English, and the experience of staying in a Communist relic is worth it for the quirk factor alone. **Pros:** fans of Communist chic will love the trimmings. **Cons:** solid mattresses and decrepit fittings won't have you rushing back. [$] *Rooms from: 491280d* ✉ *4 Xuan Thuy St.* ☎ *0212/385–5313* 🌐 *www.sonlatradeunionhotel.com* 🛏 *100 rooms* 🍽 *Breakfast.*

MAI CHAU

170 km (105 miles) southwest of Hanoi.

The Brigadoon of Vietnam, Mai Chau nestles in a serene valley of Hoa Binh Province that has been called one of the most beautiful spots in the country. Like the fictitious town that rises every 100 years, Mai Chau appears out of the mist as if in a dream. The town itself is inhabited mainly by the majority Kinh Vietnamese, but White Thai villages dot the paddy-rich valley, and this is where you're likely to spend most of your time.

The White (and later the Black) Thai migrated to Vietnam from what is now Thailand about 2,000 years ago, and they incorporate elements of both cultures. The Mai Chau Valley has a number of Thai and Muong villages where hospitality is genuine and memorable, and visiting them, either as part of a trek or independently, is easy. The valley is flat and several guesthouses, homestays, and hotels have bicycles for rent, so take off on two wheels and explore. A warm welcome and waved greeting from the children of each village is virtually guaranteed.

The homestay scene has become a burgeoning industry in recent times, and many of the tours from Hanoi include an overnight stay in a White Thai house. In fact, many of the village dwellings are closer to guesthouses than what you might associate with a homestay. Many have

Western toilets and sometimes even satellite television in the common rooms. If you overnight in a stilt house, expect a comfortable roll up mattress and a mosquito net. Authentic extras include unlimited use of a tobacco bong (thuoc lao) and giant vats of rice wine.

The Mai Chau market teems with villagers selling everything from hand-carved opium pipes to flayed pigs. Except for some women, most villagers have given up wearing traditional garb. Although many villagers still farm, tourism and panning for gold have become the most lucrative industries.

GETTING HERE AND AROUND

Buses from Hanoi to Mai Chau leave from Hanoi's My Dinh bus station. There are three buses a day, run by different companies. They leave at 7:50 am, 2 pm, and 3:15 pm. The journey takes around three hours and the fare is 80,000d. The best way to get around Mai Chau is undoubtedly by bike. All of the hotels can supply decent bikes and the pedaling along the valley floor is very easy. If, for some reason, you need to head into Mai Chau town itself then your hotel will be able to arrange a motorbike taxi.

EXPLORING

A tourist alley of sorts has sprung up in Ban Lac village, accessible from the dirt road just beyond the Mai Chau Guest House. Baskets, old crossbows, and lovely weavings are laid out on tables in front of the stilt houses. Many other silk scarves and textiles hang from the windows. And they're all for sale.

Buy some bottled water in town before heading out on a long hike through the green (or golden, depending on when you go) rice fields and into the nearby hills. Countless footpaths head off into the mountains from the main valley routes and are used by minority communities (usually women) who gather wood for cooking fires or for construction. Their baskets are usually extremely heavy, and it takes great skill to balance more than 90 kg (200 pounds) using only shoulder straps or a head brace.

The mountainsides have been largely denuded of their primary forest cover, forcing the villagers to hike more than a day to reach the larger trees needed for building stilt houses. The White Thai villagers here are very friendly and will often invite you into their homes to watch television together or to share some homemade rice wine or even lunch. Local children will often call out to passing hikers in Thai, "Pai la la?" (Hello, where are you going?) Your response: "Pa in!" (Just walking through!).

WHERE TO STAY

Many people enjoy staying in one of the White Thai villages behind the Mai Chau Lodge, where any of more than 60 households will put you up. Immaculately clean and surprisingly airy and comfortable, the traditional Thai longhouse sits on stilts about 2 meters (7 feet) up, with barely a nail used in the construction. The split-bamboo floor is soft, smooth, and springy underfoot. The going rate is 80,000d per person per night. Your hosts would accept less, but a hefty portion of the money goes to district coffers.

$$$$ HOTEL Fodor's Choice ★ 🏨 **Mai Chau Ecolodge.** Opened in 2014, this is arguably the most relaxing retreat in the valley—surrounded by green hills and rice paddies, the property is both luxurious and sympathetic to its environment. **Pros:** thoughtfully equipped accommodations; beautiful environment. **Cons:** outdoor showers are a little exposed to passing pedestrian traffic. [$] *Rooms from: 1966500d* ✉ *Na Thia Village, Na Phon Commune* ☎ *0218/381–9888* 🌐 *www.maichau.ecolodge.asia* 🛏 *43 rooms* 🍴 *Breakfast.*

$$$$ RESORT 🏨 **Mai Chau Lodge.** On the main road leading through the valley, this is the most luxurious lodging option in Mai Chau, with the best restaurant in the area, which specializes in Vietnamese cuisine and has a pleasant, shady dining area. **Pros:** great restaurant is a real plus. **Cons:** price is rather high for what you get. [$] *Rooms from: 2580000d* ☎ *0218/386–8953* 🌐 *www.maichaulodge.com* 🛏 *16 rooms* 🍴 *Breakfast.*

$$$ HOTEL 🏨 **Mai Chau Valley View.** If you are looking for something smart and comfortable in Mai Chau but don't want to splurge, then this cozy boutique option is ideal. **Pros:** Duong's inside knowledge is great for getting to know the area. **Cons:** small number of rooms means limited availability during busy periods. [$] *Rooms from: 950000d* ☎ *097/205–8696* 🌐 *www.maichauvalleyview.com* 🛏 *8 rooms* 🍴 *Breakfast.*

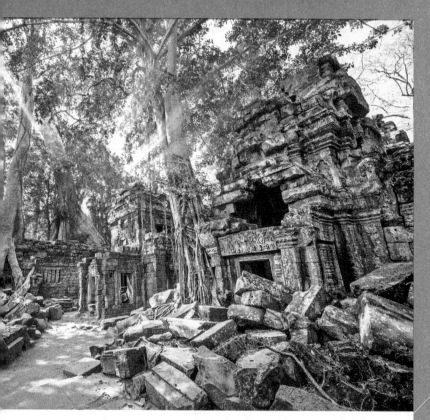

SIDE TRIP TO
ANGKOR WAT

Updated by
Adrian Vrettos

Cambodia's temples of Angkor, hailed as "the eighth wonder of the world" by some, constitute one of the world's great ancient sites and Southeast Asia's most impressive archaeological treasure. The massive structures, surrounded by tropical forest, are comparable to Central America's Mayan ruins—and far exceed them in size. Angkor Wat is the world's largest religious structure—so large that it's hard to describe its breadth to someone who hasn't seen it. And that's just one temple in a complex of hundreds.

An easy hop from Vietnam, the city of Siem Reap is the base for visiting Angkor Wat. Siem Reap, which means "Siam defeated," based on a 15th-century battle with Cambodia's neighbors to the west, has emerged as a modern, friendly and elegantly low-key city with highly sophisticated shopping, dining, and nightlife options. Many of the colonial buildings in the area were destroyed during the Khmer Rouge years, but many others have been restored and turned into world-class resorts and restaurants. After a long day at the temples you'll be happy to spend your evening strolling along the Siem Reap River, and dining at an outdoor table on a back alley in the hip old French quarter, or Alley West off the more boisterous Pub Street, which is closed to traffic in the evening. There's plenty to keep visitors occupied for two or three days, or even a week or more.

ORIENTATION AND PLANNING

GETTING ORIENTED

Cambodia is one of Southeast Asia's smallest countries—about the size of the state of Washington. The country is bordered by Thailand to the west and northwest, Laos to the northeast, and Vietnam to the east and southeast. Siem Reap is in the northeast of the country, a short flight from either Hanoi or Ho Chi Minh City.

PLANNING

WHEN TO GO

Cambodia has two seasons, both affected by the monsoon winds. The northeastern monsoon blowing toward the coast ushers in the cool, dry season in November, which lasts through February, with temperatures between 65°F (18°C) and 80°F (27°C). December and January are the coolest months. It heats up to around 95°F (35°C) and higher in March and April, when the southwestern monsoon blows inland from the Gulf of Thailand, bringing downpours that last an hour or more

most days. This rainy, humid season runs through October, with temperatures ranging from 80°F (27°C) to 95°F (35°C). Thanks to climate change, Cambodia now experiences rainstorms in the dry season, cool temperatures in the hot season, and a lot of unpredictability.

It's important to book in advance if you plan on visiting during mid-April's New Year celebrations.

GETTING HERE AND AROUND
AIR TRAVEL

Recently opened direct routes to Siem Reap from both Hanoi and Ho Chi Minh City make a side trip to Angkor Wat an easy proposition for visitors to Vietnam. From Ho Chi Minh City, there are four daily flights. The flight takes about an hour and costs from $150 one-way. There are five daily flights from Hanoi to Siem Reap, these take 1 hour 40 minutes and fares start at $150 one-way. Siem Reap International Airport is 6 km (4 miles) northwest of town. The taxi fare to any hotel in Siem Reap is $5.

Contacts Air Cambodia Angkor Air ✉ *17D Omkhun St., Siem Reap* ☎ *063/969-2681, 063/636-3666* ⊕ *www.cambodiaangkorair.com.* **Vietnam Airlines** ✉ *No. 342, Rd. 6, Svay Dang Kum, Siem Reap* ☎ *063/964488, 063/965148 reservations and ticketing* ⊕ *www.vietnamairlines.com.*

MOTO AND TUK-TUK TRAVEL

Tuk-tuk and moto (motorbike taxi) drivers have kept apace with the growing number of tourists visiting Siem Reap: they'll find you—you won't need to find them. They charge about $1 to $3 for a trip within town, but be sure to settle on the fare before setting off. There are no cruising taxis, but hotels can order one.

HEALTH AND SAFETY

Cambodia is far safer than many people realize, but you still need to exercise common sense. Keep most of your cash, valuables, and your passport in a hotel safe, and avoid walking on side streets after dark—and it's best to avoid abrupt or confrontational behavior overall. Siem Reap has less crime than the capital, Phnom Penh, but that's starting to change. ⚠ **Avoid motos late at night.**

Land mines laid during the civil war have been removed from most major tourist destinations. Cambodia has one of Asia's most atrocious road records. Accidents are common in the chaotic traffic of Phnom Penh and on the highways, where people drive like maniacs, and will not hesitate to make speedy U-turns on a busy two-way street. The better the road, the scarier the driving. Unfortunately, chauffeurs are some of the worst offenders. Wear a seat belt if they're available, and if you rent a moto, wear a helmet. If you are in a tuk-tuk, just hold on tight.

MONEY MATTERS

The Cambodian currency is the riel, but the U.S. dollar is accepted everywhere, with many high-end businesses actually requiring payment in dollars. Don't be surprised to get change in riel when you pay in dollars. *All prices are given in dollars in this chapter.* The official exchange rate is approximately 4,000 riel to one U.S. dollar or 20,000 Vietnamese Dong. It's possible to change dollars to riel just about anywhere. Banks and businesses usually charge 2% to cash travelers' checks.

ATMs are available in Siem Reap, mostly at ANZ and Canadia banks, although there are numerous other banks starting to install them. Using an ATM will cost you $5 per withdrawal. Credit cards are accepted at major hotels, restaurants, and at some boutiques. Cambodian banking hours are shorter than in many Western countries, generally from 8 am until 3 or 4 pm. ATMs are available 24 hours.

WHAT IT COSTS IN U.S. DOLLARS				
	$	**$$**	**$$$**	**$$$$**
RESTAURANTS	Under $8	$8–$12	$13–$16	over $16
HOTELS	Under $50	$50–$100	$101–$150	over $150

Restaurant prices in the reviews are the average cost of a main course at dinner or, if dinner isn't served, at lunch. Hotel prices in the reviews are the lowest cost of a standard double room in high season.

KHMER: A FEW KEY PHRASES

A knowledge of French may get you somewhere in francophone Cambodia, but these days it's far easier to find English speakers. The Cambodian language, Khmer, belongs to the Mon-Khmer family of languages, enriched by Indian Pali and Sanskrit vocabulary. It has many similarities to Thai and Lao, a reminder of their years as vassal lands in the Khmer Empire.

The following are some useful words and phrases:

Hello: joom reap soo-uh

Thank you: aw-koun

Yes: bah (male speaker), jah (female speaker)

No: aw-te

Excuse me: som-toh

Where?: ai nah?

How much?: t'lay pohn mahn?

Never mind: mun ay dtay

Zero: sohn

One: muay

Two: bpee

Three: bay

Four: buon

Five: bpram

Six: bpram muay

Seven: bpram pull

Eight: bpram bay

Nine: bpram buon

Ten: dop

Eleven: dop muay

Hundred: muay roi

Thousand: muay poan

Food: m'hohp

Water: dteuk

Expensive: t'lay nah

Morning: bprek

Night: youp

Today: tngay nee

Tomorrow: tngay sa-ik

Yesterday: mus'el mun

Bus: laan ch'nual

Ferry: salang

Village: pum

Island: koh

River: tonle

Doctor: bpet

Hospital: moonty bpet

Bank: tia-nia-kia

Post Office: praisinee

Toilet: baan tawp tdeuk

9

PASSPORTS AND VISAS

One-month single entry tourist visas, which cost $30, are available at the airports. You may need a passport photo—if you don't have one with you, it's an added $5 to have it made there. There's no added wait, and sometimes you might not even be asked for a photo.

TOURS

FAMILY

Fodor's Choice

★

Beyond Unique Escapes. Expert and ethical, this tour operater for the Siem Reap area offers the usual Angkor Temple tours, but also some more unusual temple adventures, where you can experience sunrise or sunset at a remote ruin far from the crowds. Other highly rated options include trips to villages to participate in village activities, which vary depending on the season. ⊠ *Sivatha Blvd. and Pub St. (St. 8), Old Market, Siem Reap* 🕾 *077/562565, 063/969269* ⊕ *www.beyonduniqueescapes.com* 🖾 *From: $20.*

Hanuman Travel. A longtime operator in Southeast Asia, Hanuman create tailor-made trips with an emphasis on responsible travel. ⊠ *5 Krom 2, Phuom Traeng, Siem Reap* 🕾 *023/218356, 012/807657* ✍ *marketing@ hanumantourism.com* ⊕ *www.hanuman.travel.*

IndochinEx. Bespoke eco-tourism options are offered throughout Cambodia by this company whose partners are conservationists and expert explorers. Many of the employees here previously worked for oSmoSe and other conservation groups and this has become the preferred tour operator for all the established high-end hotels. A tour with IndochinEx will be a highlight of your trip to Siem Reap. 🕾 *092/650096* ⊕ *www. indochineex.com* 🖾 *From: $65.*

Fodor's Choice ★ **oSmoSe Conservation Ecotourism Education.** An agent of positive change in the Siem Reap area, oSmoSe, a nonprofit organization, has been fighting to conserve the unique biosphere of Tonle Sap and Prek Toal by reeducating local villagers from poachers to protectors of the environment that sustains them. They also lobby against big commercial interests that have been involved in short-term exploitation of the ecosystem, and have successfully helped to reharmonize many aspects of human co-existence with nature. On their exceptional tours you get to visit a bird sanctuary with an expert guide and also experience floating villages in a fascinating and respectful way. ⊠ *St. 27, Wat Bo, Siem Reap* 🕾 *012/832812, 063/765506* ⊕ *www.osmosetonlesap.net* 🖾 *From: $105.*

VISITOR INFORMATION

Once you arrive, pick up a visitor's guide for Siem Reap, as well as any of the various pocket guides, the best of these being Cambodia Pocket Guide (*www.cambodiapocketguide.com*), widely available free at airports, hotels, and restaurants.

Web Resources Andy Brouwer (⊕ *www.andybrouwer.blogspot.com* or *www. andybrouwer.co.uk*), a longtime traveler to Cambodia, has dedicated a good part of his life to informing people about the country where he lives. **Tales of Asia** (⊕ *www.talesofasia.com*) is an excellent source of information, with travelers' stories, road reports, and up-to-date travel information. The **Ministry of Tourism** (⊕ *www.tourismcambodia.org*) has some information on its website. **Tourism Cambodia** (⊕ *www.tourismcambodia.com*) has more detailed descriptions of top attractions.

EXPLORING

Siem Reap is the base for exploring the temples at Angkor, but it has more to offer than that. There is something seductive about this city that makes visitors want to linger. You can wander around the contemporary Angkor National Museum, take a cooking class, visit a rural village, explore myriad art galleries, try a gourmet restaurant or take a stroll

Tonle Sap

Covering 2,600 square km (1,000 square miles) in the dry season, Cambodia's vast Tonle Sap, 6 miles south of Siem Reap, is the biggest freshwater lake in Southeast Asia. Its unique annual cycle of flood expansion and retreat dictates Cambodia's rice production and supplies of fish. During the rainy season the Mekong River backs into the Tonle Sap River, pushing waters into the lake, which quadruples in size. In the dry season, as the Mekong lowers the Tonle Sap River reverses its direction, draining the lake. Two-hour tours of the lake, costing $15 to $20, can be booked through reputable tour operators in Siem Reap. **oSmoSe Conservation Ecotourism Education** can also arrange trips to the **Prek Toal Biosphere Reserve**, mainland Southeast Asia's most important waterbird nesting site. It's a spectacular scene if you visit at the start of the dry season (November and December), when water remains high and thousands of rare birds begin to nest.

down the central Pub Street. You could spend an entire afternoon in the Old Market area, wandering from shop to shop, café to café, gallery to gallery. It changes every month, with ever more delights in store. Long gone are the days when high-end souvenirs (the legal kind) came from Thailand. Today numerous shops offer high-quality Cambodian silks, Kampot pepper and other Cambodian spices, and herbal soaps and toiletries made from natural Cambodian products.

SIEM REAP

Fodor'sChoice
★

Angkor National Museum. This modern, interactive museum, which opened in 2008, gracefully guides you through the rise and fall of the Angkorian Empires, covering the religions, kings, and geopolitics that drove the Khmer to create the monumental cities whose ruins are highly visible in modern day Cambodia. With more than 1,300 artifacts on glossy display, complemented by multimedia installations, this museum experience helps demystify much of the material culture that visitors encounter at the archaeological parks and sites. The atmosphere is set in the impressive gallery of a thousand Buddhas, which plunges you into the serene spirituality that still dominates the region. Seven consequent galleries, set up chronologically, highlight the Funan and Chenia pre-Angkorian epochs, followed by the golden age of the Angkorian period lead by the likes of King Soryavarman II, who built Angkor Wat. The final two galleries showcase stone inscriptions documenting some of the workings of the empires and statues of Apsara, shedding light on the cult and fashions of these celestial dancers. ■ TIP→ **The audio tour is excellent and well worth the extra $3.** ⊠ *968, Vithei Charles de Gaulle, Khrum 6, Phoum Salakanseng, Khom Svaydangum* ☎ *063/966601* ⊕ *www.angkornationalmuseum.com* ⊠ *$12* ⊙ *Daily 8:30–6 (to 6:30 Oct.–Mar.).*

Cambodia Land Mine Museum. Be sure to visit this museum, established by Akira, a former child soldier who fought for the Khmer Rouge, the

Vietnamese, and the Cambodian Army. Now he dedicates his life to removing the land mines he and thousands of others laid across Cambodia. His museum is a must-see, a socio-political eye-opener that portrays a different picture of Cambodia from the glorious temples and five-star hotels. Any tuk-tuk or taxi driver can find the museum. When in the Old Market area, visit the Akira Mine Action Gallery for more information on land mines and ways to help land-mine victims go to college.

■ TIP→ **As it is a decent distance from Siem Reap, it's best to combine this with a visit to the Banteay Srey Temple complex, only 7 km (5 miles) away.**

✉ *Siem Reap* ⊕ *Off road to Angkor, 6 km (4 miles) south of Banteay Srey Temple, 25 km (15 miles) from Siem Reap* ☎ *015/674163* ⊕ *www. cambodialandminemuseum.org* ✉ *$5* ⊗ *Daily 7:30–5:30.*

ANGKOR TEMPLE COMPLEX

6 km (4 miles) north of Siem Reap.

Fodor's Choice ★ **Angkor Temple Complex.** The Khmer Empire reached the zenith of its power, influence, and creativity from the 9th to the 13th centuries, when Angkor, the seat of the Khmer kings, was one of the largest capitals in Southeast Asia. Starting in the 15th century, the temples of Angkor's heyday were abandoned until their "discovery" in the early 1860s by French naturalist Henri Mouhot (the Cambodians living there sure knew about them). In all, there are some 300 monuments reflecting Hindu and Buddhist influence scattered throughout the jungle, but only the largest have been excavated and only a few of those reconstructed. Most of these lie within a few miles of each other and can be seen in one day, though two or three days will allow you to better appreciate them.

Although the centuries have taken their toll on the temples—some of which still hide their beauty beneath a tangle of undergrowth—they miraculously survived the ravages of the Khmer Rouge years. Many of the monks living in the temples at this time were massacred, however. The Khmer Rouge mined the area, but the mines have been removed, and the temples are now perfectly safe to visit.

Most people visit the temples of Bayon and Baphuon, which face east, in the morning—the earlier you arrive, the better the light and the smaller the crowd—and west-facing Angkor Wat in the late afternoon, though this most famous of the temples can also be a stunning sight at sunrise. The woodland-surrounded Ta Prohm can be visited any time, though it is best photographed when cloudy, whereas the distant Banteay Srei is prettiest in the late-afternoon light.

Phnom Bakheng

One of the oldest Angkor structures, dating to the 9th century, the hilltop Bakheng temple was built in the center of the first royal city site, dedicated to the Hindu god Shiva. The temple, which resembles a five-tiered pyramid, was constructed from rock hewn from the hill and faced with sandstone. Phnom Bakheng is perhaps the most popular sunset destination for Angkor visitors, as the view from the top affords a fine look at Angkor Wat and the surrounding area. Climb the stairs or take an elephant ride up.

CLOSE UP

Uncovering Angkor

The story of the "rediscovery" of Angkor is a misnomer; the temples were never lost. They have always been known and used by Cambodians. Nonetheless, the tale is like something from the pages of H. Rider Haggard, the 19th-century English author of *King Solomon's Mines* and other adventure stories.

Haggard's stories may have been set in Africa, but they evocatively parallel what was happening in Asia at the time he was writing. French colonists and missionaries in Cambodia in the early and mid-19th century heard stories from locals of a lost city deep in the jungle. Most shrugged off the stories as myth, but some adventurers, fired by romantic visions of treasure, hacked their way through the jungle and indeed found ruins, although they could make nothing of these strange piles of stone. It was left to a French botanist, Henri Mouhot, to begin serious investigation of the ruins. Mouhot traveled to Bangkok in 1858 with support from the British Royal Geographic Society. His original intention was to collect samples of the region's unique flora and insects. He ended up going much farther afield than Bangkok—supposedly, a French missionary he met in Battambang told him of the lost city, and he was

guided to the site via Tonle Sap in 1861. Mouhot filled many journals with impressions and sketches of the ruins and his notes were published in 1863, bringing the city back onto the world's radar.

Mouhot could only wonder at what type of race created such massive structures—he didn't seem to think that present-day Cambodians could have done it—but subsequent intensive international research soon revealed that Angkor had been the capital of the mighty Khmer Empire for more than three centuries, from its founding around AD 880 to the early 13th century, when it fell into decline in the shadow of a growing neighboring power, Siam.

Research also revealed that Angkor was the scene of one of the world's greatest feats of irrigation technology: thousands of experts, workers, and slaves constructed a system of reservoirs and canals to serve a city larger than medieval London or Paris. They built two huge storage basins, the Eastern and Western Barays, each covering about 17 square km (6½ square miles). Today only the Western Baray contains water, but both give an indelible impression of the sheer size of the original enterprise.

9

Angkor Thom

This was a city in its own right—the last Angkorean capital, built by King Jayavarman VII in the late 12th century. At the height of Angkor Thom's prosperity in the 12th and 13th centuries, more than 1 million people lived within its walls, and it was the richest city in Southeast Asia. The Siamese destroyed the city in the 15th century, and it became an insignificant ghost town. The south gate, towering 65 feet and crowned by four characteristic Bodhisattva faces, is so monumental it appears to dominate the entire area.

A defensive wall and moat, 3 km long by 3 km wide (2 miles by 2 miles), surrounded the city, which was entered via bridges lined with

Hiring an Angkor Guide

A guide can greatly enrich your appreciation of Angkor's temples, which are full of details you might miss on your own. English-speaking guides can be hired through the tourism office on Pokambor Avenue, across from the Raffles Grand Hotel d'Angkor. But the best way to find a guide is through your hotel or guesthouse. Ask around. Most guides who work for tour companies (and the tourism office) are freelancers, and often when you book through a tour company, you'll pay a higher price. Find a young staffer at your hotel or guesthouse and tell him or her what you want—the type of tour, what you hope to learn from your guide, your particular interests in the temples.

Prices usually run around $45 a day, not including transportation, for a well-informed, English-speaking guide.

Hanuman Travel. If you feel more comfortable booking through a travel company, Hanuman Travel is an excellent choice. The expert company, which works throughout Cambodia and surrounding countries, has established a foundation to help eradicate poverty in Cambodia's hinterlands. Your tourist dollars will go toward wells, water filters, mosquito nets, and other amenities that can greatly improve a rural family's life. ✉ 5 Krom 2, Phuom Traeng, Siem Reap, ☎ 023/218396, 023/218398 ⊕ www.hanuman.travel.

Sreang Teng. A knowledgeable, English-speaking local guide for the temple complex and other sights, Sreang Teng leads tours that seem to avoid the crowds. ✉ Siem Reap ☎ 012/426764 ⊕ www.angkorsiemreaptourguide.com.

massive stone guardians holding a mystical serpent. At its geographic center stands the 12th-century Bayon, a large, ornate Buddhist structure that rises into 54 small towers, most of which are topped with huge, strangely smiling faces. On the outer walls of the central sanctuary, and on some of the inner walls, are 1½ km (1 mile) of marvelous bas-relief murals depicting historic sea battles, scenes from daily life, and gods and mythical creatures performing legendary deeds.

Just to the north of the Bayon is the slightly older Baphuon, built in the mid-11th century by King Udayadityavarman II (a small settlement was here before King Jayavarman VII built up the area in the late 12th century). A fine example of poor planning, the temple was erected on a hill without proper supports, so that when the earth shifted in the 16th century it collapsed. Originally the temple was a Shiva sanctuary crowned with a copper-covered cupola. A magnificent reclining Buddha was added to the three-tiered temple pyramid in the 16th century. ■TIP→ **The temple is undergoing reconstruction, and is not open to the public; however, the exterior gate and elevated walkway are open.**

Elephant Terrace and the Terrace of the Leper King

Built at the end of the 12th century by King Jayavarman VII, the ornamental Elephant Terrace once formed the foundation of the royal audience hall. The gilded wooden palace that once stood here has long since disappeared. Stone-carved elephants and *garuda*, or giant eagle-people,

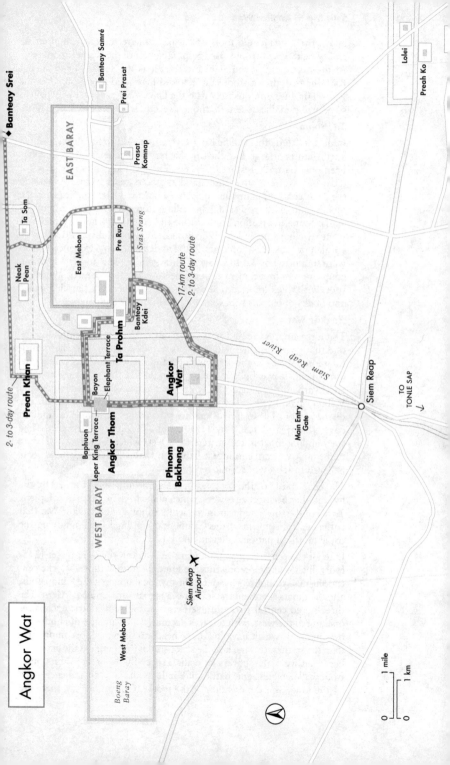

adorn the 2-meter (6½-foot) -tall wall of the terrace, which abuts an empty field where troops used to parade before the Khmer monarchs. At the north end of the Elephant Terrace is the Terrace of the Leper King, named after a stone statue found here (and now housed in the National Museum). Precisely who the Leper King was and why he was so named remains uncertain, though several legends offer speculation.

Ta Prohm

Built in 1186 by the prolific King Jayavarman VII to honor his mother, Ta Prohm is a large Buddhist monastery of five enclosures that has been only partially restored. The eerie temple looks more or less as it did when Western adventurers and explorers rediscovered Angkor in the 19th century; many buildings have been reduced to piles of stone blocks, and giant tropical fig and silk-cotton trees grow on top of the walls. Stone inscriptions reveal that the complex originally had 566 stone dwellings, including 39 major sanctuaries, and was attended by 13 high priests, 2,740 officials, 2,202 assistants, and 615 dancers, who were supported by 3,140 villages. Today you're likely to share it with a couple of hundred camera-toting tourists. Still, it's a gorgeous, magical spot, with thick knotted tree roots sprawled over half-tumbled walls, and flocks of parrots squawking in the branches high above.

Angkor Wat

The most impressive and best preserved of the Khmer temples is the one that gave the whole complex its name: Angkor Wat, the beautiful apotheosis of Khmer architecture, and the world's largest religious monument. It was built at the beginning of the 12th century by King Suryavarman II (reigned 1112–52), who dedicated it to the Hindu god Vishnu, making sure that its dimensions were suitably grand for the divine patron. Those dimensions are staggering: the temple compound covers an area of 1,500 by 1,300 meters (4,920 by 4,265 feet). The surrounding moat is 180 meters (590 feet) wide. A causeway leading to the huge western entrance is flanked by balustrades of giant serpents believed to represent cosmic fertility.

The centerpiece of the complex is the giant lotus bud formed by the five familiar beehivelike towers, which alone took 30 years to complete. Three of the towers appear in the white silhouette of Angkor Wat that is the central emblem of the Cambodian national flag, signifying the triple motto of nation, religion, and king.

Like all the other major monuments at Angkor, the 65.5-meter (215-foot) -high complex represents the Hindu/Buddhist universe. The central shrines symbolize Mt. Meru, the mythical home of the Hindu gods, and the moats represent the seven oceans that surround Mt. Meru. The three-tiered central pyramid itself rises in four concentric enclosures opening to the west, with terraces decorated with images of Hindu deities, many of which have lost their heads to looters. More impressive than the statues, towers, and the sheer size of the temple is the extensive bas-relief work that covers its walls, especially the scenes on its outer front wall depicting epic battles of Hindu mythology, an audience given by the king, and the creation of the world. On top of that, there are nearly 2,000 apsara—celestial female dancers—scattered throughout the temple complex. Two libraries flank the ancient Hindu temple.

Preah Khan

This former royal retreat was built in 1191 by King Jayavarman VII for his father, but it later became a Buddhist institution with more than 1,000 monks. The moated temple, near the north gate of Angkor Thom, is similar to Ta Prohm, but has only four enclosures. The temple houses a hall decorated with a bas-relief of heavenly apsara dancers, a two-story columnar building to keep the "sacred sword" (an important part of the royal regalia) of the kingdom, and a large lingam, or phallic symbol, representing Shiva. In the eastern part of the complex is a *baray,* one of the five huge reservoirs built to supply the growing Angkor Thom and irrigate its fields and plantations. The water was channeled from the Tonle Sap lake in an amazing feat of engineering.

Neak Pean

Sitting on an island in the middle of one of Angkor's barays, or water reservoirs, the temple of Neak Pean ("entwined serpent") is one of King Jayavarman VII's most unusual creations. He intended to create his own version of the sacred lake Anavatapta in the Himalayas, venerated for its healing powers. From a large square reservoir, gargoyles channel water into four smaller square basin sanctuaries. The temple's central tower is dedicated to the Bodhisattva Avalokitesvara, depicted riding the fabulous horse Balaha along with people escaping a disastrous pestilence and seeking the healing waters of Anavatapta.

East Mebon

The temple of East Mebon was built on a baray island by King Rajendravarman in the 10th century and now sits high and dry in the empty reservoir known as the Eastern Baray. The pyramid-shape temple, dedicated to Shiva, has all the characteristics of the temple mount construction so favored by the Khmer kings: in brick and laterite, with a 10-foot-high platform carrying five imposing towers arranged in a quincunx (one at each corner and one in the center of the ensemble). The sandstone lintels have been superbly carved and preserved, and monolithic elephants stand at the four corners of each enclosure.

Pre Rup

This grander version of the East Mebon temple is thought to have once been the center of the royal city of King Rajendravarman, who ordered its construction in 961. The five upper brick towers are adorned with fine stucco moldings. From the top of the highest platform there are sweeping views of the palm-studded countryside. If you want to avoid the crowds that gather at Angkor Wat and Phnom Bakheng at sunset but you still want a good view, this is the place to come.

Banteay Srei

If you have the time, extend your tour of Angkor to include the Banteay Srei (Citadel of Women), 38 km (24 miles) northeast of Siem Reap. The temple resembles a small fortress and it's dedicated to the Hindu goddess Sri (the Khmer version of this name was Srei, meaning "women"). This small but magnificent 10th-century temple contains fine sculptures of pink sandstone illustrating scenes from the Indian Reamker legend and gods and goddesses of the Hindu pantheon; they're surprisingly well preserved, having survived the war years. The temple achieved fame when the former French government minister and noted author and philosopher Andre Malraux was accused of plundering it during reconstruction work in the 1930s. ■TIP➡ **Admission is included in the Angkor ticket, but a tuk-tuk driver may charge an extra $20 to get here. The temple closes at 5 pm.**

Roluos Temples

About 12 km (7½ miles) east of Siem Reap on Highway 6 is a group of three temples—Preah Ko, Bakong, and Lolei—all built in the 9th century, the formative period of the Khmer Empire. The capital at that time was called Hariharalaya, when the two gods Shiva and Vishnu were both venerated; the temples were erected in their honor. A large water reservoir was fed from the Tonle Sap lake, via the Roluos River, and Lolei was then on an island. Admission to the site is included in the Angkor ticket.

There are stories of visitors who arrive in Siem Reap with the intention of seeing Angkor Wat, only to leave soon after in dismay after discovering that the wat is just one of many temples in an area covering several square miles.

Forget any idea of strolling casually from temple to temple—even a bicycle tour of the vast site is exhausting. There are two recommended circuits to gain an overview of the temples, the shortest 17 km (11 miles) and the longest 26 km (16 miles). If you have just one day, stick to the short circuit, which takes in Phnom Bakheng, the south gate of Angkor Thom, Bayon, Baphuon, the Elephant Terrace and the Terrace of the Leper King, and Ta Prohm, and ends with a visit to Angkor Wat itself to catch the sunset. If you have two days, take the longer route—do the shorter circuit on the first day, then tackle Preah Khan, Neak Pean, East Mebon, and Pre Rup (at sunset) on Day 2.

Bring a passport photo—you'll need one for your entrance ticket. Transportation within the vast complex is a necessity, and most independent travelers hire a car and driver ($20–$25 per day) or tuk-tuk ($8–$12 per day). Bicycles ($3–$4 per day) are an option for those who can stand the heat and the effort, and electric bicycles and motorbikes ($7–$10) are available for those who can't. (The latter have caused a bit of a ruckus among tuk-tuk drivers of late: so many tourists are opting for electric bikes that it's taking business away from the local drivers.) ■TIP➡ **Consider hiring a guide to interpret the site and greatly enhance your visit; the tourism office on Pokambor Avenue (across from the Raffles Grand Hotel d'Angkor) has a list of English-speaking guides.** ⊠ *5.5 km (3½ miles) north of Siem Reap* ⊕ *www.autoriteapsara.org* ✉ *$20 for 1 day, $40 for 3 days, $60 for 1 wk* ☉ *Daily 5 am–6 pm* ☞ *Skimpy clothing, such as short shorts and backless tops, violate the dress code of the complex. Shield yourself from the sun with light fabrics and bring a wide-brimmed hat or an umbrella for shade.*

WHERE TO EAT

$$$$ INTERNATIONAL

🍴 **Abacus.** Ideal for a romantic garden dinner or a fun, elegant night out with friends, Abacus offers an eclectic choice of French-international fusion cuisine. Through a weekly changing menu presented on a giant blackboard, chefs and co-owners Renaud and Pascal combine their creative talents and refined expertise to provide a high-quality, welcome change from traditional restaurants or bland hotel fare. Regulars swear by the juicy Abacus burger, but there are always plenty of options to suit any taste or disposition. The restaurant also has a bar that welcomes guests for an aperitif or an after dinner digestif. [$] *Average main: $17* ✉ *Off Rd. 6* ✥ *Take Rd. 6 toward airport, pass Angkor Hotel, and turn right at ACLEDA Bank. After 100 meters turn left* ☎ *063/763660, 012/644286* 🌐 *cafeabacus.com* ✍ *Reservations essential* 🕒 *Closed June and 1 wk in mid-Apr.* ✥ *A1*

$$$$ BISTRO

🍴 **Armand.** This is a chic little French bistro/bar that harks back to 1930s Paris, and it's set to become a hot spot in Siem Reap. It follows on from the success of the original Armand, a mainstay of Phnom Penh's dining scene, but here there are unique influences from all three partners. The manager is also a designer, and created a space inspired by Balthazars in New York and the sharp staff uniforms; another partner has a vineyard in France's Dordogne region, so the wine selection is excellent and they have the best house wine around. The stamp of Armand himself ensures that the place oozes charm and character. Come here for fine French cuisine and classic cocktails. [$] *Average main: $18* ✉ *586 Tep Vong St.* ☎ *095/684130* 🕒 *No lunch* ✥ *B2.*

$$$$ ECLECTIC
Fodor's Choice ★

🍴 **Cuisine Wat Damnak.** One of the most unique restaurants in Siem Reap, Cuisine Wat Damnak offers a real journey for the tastebuds with its five- or six-course set menus (the only options available). Beyond the apparent ambition for trendy sophistication in the indoor sala and romantic garden, the concept here is Cambodian food remodeled into creative modern dishes by French chef Joannes Riviere. Exclusively local, fresh, and seasonal ingredients are a top priority for Riviere, whose knowledge of the area allows him to source ingredients that are otherwise not easy to come by, such as shellfish unique to the Mekong and Tonle Sap lake, fresh lotus seeds, wild lily stems, and edible flowers. **TIP→ If you're interested in learning more about Riviere's culinary philosophy and techniques, you can buy a copy of his cookbook here.** [$] *Average main: $24* ✉ *Chocolate Rd., between Psa Dey Hoy market and Angkor High School, Sala Kamreuk Commune* ☎ *077/347762* 🌐 *www.cuisinewatdamnak.com* ✍ *Reservations essential* 🕒 *Closed Sun., Mon., and Apr. No lunch* ✥ *C3.*

$$ ITALIAN

🍴 **Il Forno.** Considered the best Italian restaurant in Siem Reap, Il Forno offers an enjoyable change from the Southeast Asian delights on offer at every turn. Just off Pub Street and near the Old Market, this "little corner of Italy" uses its Neopolitan woodfire oven to make delicious pizza and calzone specialties. An authentic variety of pasta dishes, platters for one or for sharing, and *primi piatti* are also on offer, all made using quality imported ingredients, and accompanied by good regional wines. For desert try the devilishly good dragonfruit and passionfruit panacotta. The brick walls and aged-effect saffron walls

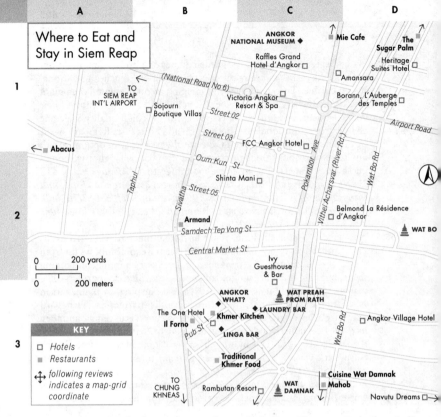

are indeed reminiscent of a rustic Italian village, as is the hospitality that creates a warmly familial setting. $ *Average main: $10* ☒ *Pari's Alley, 16 The-Lane, Old Market* ☎ *078/208174, 063/763380* ⊕ *www.ilfornorestaurantsiemreap.com* ⊕ *B3.*

$
CAMBODIAN

✕ **Khmer Kitchen.** An established staple of Siem Reap dining, the expanded and very central Khmer Kitchen is basic—in cuisine and interior design—yet pleasantly authentic, serving tasty local dishes. Fresh spring rolls, Lo Lak beef curry, or baked pumpkin are recommended among a colorful variety of options. Cooking classes are available, if you'd like to take home the skills necessary to re-create some of the traditional dishes on offer. $ *Average main: $5* ☒ *Mondul I, St. 9, Old Market* ☎ *063/964154, 012/763468* ⊕ *www.khmerkitchens.com* ▭ *No credit cards* ⊕ *B3.*

$$
CAMBODIAN
FAMILY
Fodor'sChoice
★

✕ **Mahob.** The name translates as "food," and if it's *mahob* you're after this is an excellent choice. Sothea, the owner, is a young, dynamic and creative chef who cut his teeth and honed his talents working in Siem Reap's finest establishments and farther afield internationally. Here, he has created a Cambodian menu that appeals to the Western palate but is not without an adventurous element. Try deep-fried frogs' legs coated with crispy rice flakes, or wok-fried local beef with tree red ants served with rice. If that's too much of a challenge, there's the duo *amok* soufflé of lemongrass and coconut paste with chicken and river fish, or the fun option of cooking fish or meat exactly to your liking on hot stones. For dessert the homemade ice creams are a great choice, with flavors ranging from rice milk to white Kampot pepper and lime. Set in an old Cambodian house, the restaurant also serves diners in the lovely front garden. [$] *Average main: $8* ✉ *137 Traing Village, off Charles de Gaulle Ave., Group 3* ☎ *063/966986, 017/550206* 🌐 *www.mahobkhmer.com* ✣ *C3.*

GOOD DEEDS

Angkor Hospital for Children. Not far from the Old Market on Achamen Street sits the Angkor Hospital for Children, founded in 1999 by Japanese photographer Kenro Izu. It provides pediatric care to more than 100,000 children each year. Give blood, save a life. ✉ *Tep Vong (Achamean) Rd. and Oum Chhay St., Sangkat Svay Dangkum* ☎ *063/963409* 🌐 *angkorhospital.org.*

$ ASIAN Fodor's Choice ★ 🍴 **Mie Cafe.** This top-notch restaurant reflects the upbeat, forward-thinking new generation of postdisaster Cambodia, represented here by the determined and visionary young owner, Siv Pola. Although some ingredients are imported, Pola makes fresh, local, seasonal ingredients a priority. Try the popular spicy tuna tartare with mango or the wonderfully inventive Tonle Sap Fish, a carpaccio of snake head fish fillet, marinated in fresh picked herbs, with a tempura poached egg. For dessert the hot, creamy chocolate cake is a winner. Everything is prepared with sensitivity, creativity, and great skill, right down to the home-mixed herbal teas. The somewhat out of the way location makes the open-air garden restaurant a sweet respite from noisier parts of the city, and the proudly low-budget Asian-chic style is a pleasing marriage of traditional and contemporary elements. [$] *Average main: $7* ✉ *0085 Phum Treng, Khum Slorgram* ☎ *012/791371, 069/999096* 🌐 *miecafe-siemreap.com* ⏲ *Closed Tues. and Oct.* ✣ *C1*

$ CAMBODIAN 🍴 **The Sugar Palm.** One of the best, no-frills restaurants in Siem Reap, the Sugar Palm is infused with the owner's colorful enthusiasm for traditional Khmer cuisine learned from her mother and grandmother. After years in exile in New Zealand during the Khmer Rouge regime, Kethana returned to her homeland determined to create a familial place where diners could enjoy her favorite dishes, such as her uniquely soufflélike fish *amok*, which is made to order. As you wait, sample a flavorful variety of starters such as crispy shrimp cakes with black pepper sauce or banana blossom salad with chicken. The restaurant is on the second floor of a traditional-style timber house, and its food as well as its airy, modern-traditional atmosphere has drawn all manner of diners, including superstar chef Gordon Ramsay, who filmed a cooking show here. [$] *Average main: $7* ✉ *Taphul Rd.* ☎ *063/636–2060, 063/964838* 🌐 *www.thesugarpalm.com* ⏲ *Closed Sun.* ✣ *D1*

$ CAMBODIAN 🍴 **Traditional Khmer Food.** The name says it all—this Khmer-owned and -operated restaurant gives you a hearty introduction to real Khmer cooking. The bright little spot (painted in orange and purple) is along one of the back alleys near Pub Street. It serves a wide selection of Khmer soups, curries, and meat and vegetable dishes. [$] *Average main: $5* ✉ *Mondul 1, off Pub St., Sangkat Svay Dangkum* ☎ *019/999905* 💳 *No credit cards* ✣ *B3.*

CAMBODIAN CUISINE

Cambodian cuisine is distinct from that of neighbors Thailand, Laos, and Vietnam, although some dishes are common throughout the region. Fish and rice are the mainstays, and some of the world's tastiest fish dishes are to be had in Cambodia. The country has the benefit of a complex river system that feeds Southeast Asia's largest freshwater lake, plus a coastline famous for its shrimp and crab. Beyond all that, Cambodia's rice paddies grow some of the most succulent fish around. (Besides fish, Cambodians also eat a lot of pork, more so than beef, which tends to be tough.)

Be sure to try *prahok*, the Cambodian lifeblood—a stinky cheeselike fermented fish paste that nourishes the nation. *Amok*, too, is a sure delight. Done the old-fashioned way, it takes two days to make this fish-and-coconut concoction, which is steamed in a banana leaf.

Down south, Kampot Province grows world-renowned aromatic pepper. If you're coming from a northern climate, try a seafood dish with whole green peppercorns on the stalk. You won't find it (not fresh, anyway) in your home country.

Generally, the food in Cambodia is far tamer and less flavorsome that of Thailand or Laos, but seasoned heavily with fresh herbs. Curried dishes, known as *kari*, show the ties between Indian and Cambodian cuisine. As in Thailand, it is usual in Cambodian food to use fish sauce in soups, stir-fry, and as a dipping sauce. There are many variations of rice noodles, which give the cuisine a Chinese flavor. Beef noodle soup, known simply as *kuyteav*, is a popular dish brought to Cambodia by Chinese settlers. Also, *banh chiao*, a crepelike pancake stuffed with pork, shrimp, and bean sprouts and then fried, is the Khmer version of the Vietnamese *bánh xèo*. Cambodian cuisine uses many vegetables. Mushrooms, cabbage, baby corn, bamboo shoots, fresh ginger, Chinese broccoli, snow peas, and bok choy are all found in Cambodian dishes from stir-fry to soup.

Usually, meals in Cambodia consist of three or four different dishes, reflecting the tastes of sweet, sour, salty, and bitter. The dishes are set out and you take from which dish you want and mix with your rice. Eating is usually a communal experience, and it is appropriate to share your food with others.

WHERE TO STAY

$$$$ RESORT Fodor's Choice ★ 🏨 **Amansara.** The jewel in the crown of Siem Reap hotels, Amansara offers exceptional service, atmosphere, and accommodations in an ambience of understated luxury. **Pros:** some suites have private plunge pool; rooftop open-air movies; impressive attention to detail by friendly management and staff; 10 minutes from Angkor. **Cons:** pricey; no in-room TV. [$] *Rooms from: $1770* ✉ *Road to Angkor, behind Tourism Dept.* ☎ *063/760333* 🌐 *www.amanresorts.com* 🛏 *24 suites* 🍴 *No meals* ✥ *C1.*

$$$ HOTEL 🏨 **Angkor Village Hotel.** This oasis of Khmer-style wooden buildings, lush gardens, and pools filled with lotus blossoms lies along a stone path a

couple of blocks from the river in a green neighborhood. **Pros:** central location and easy access to tuk-tuks; spa with traditional therapies; the hotel organizes activities and trips. **Cons:** road can get congested during the rainy season; some rooms are looking a little worn. $ *Rooms from: $150 ⊠ Wat Bo Rd. ☎ 063/963361 ⊕ www.angkorvillage.com ↘ 38 rooms ⋈ Breakfast ✛ D3.*

$$$$
RESORT
FAMILY

▦ **Belmond La Résidence d'Angkor.** Swathed in ancient Angkor style, this luxurious retreat, now part of the Belmond group, is within a walled compound with lovely gardens beside the river. **Pros:** attractive riverside location; family-friendly services; excellent restaurant; attentive service. **Cons:** some rooms have less than spectacular views; River Road rooms can get traffic noise. $ *Rooms from: $400 ⊠ River Rd., Wat Bo ☎ 063/963390, 800/237–1236 reservations ⊕ www.residencedangkor. com ↘ 54 rooms, 8 suites ⋈ Breakfast ✛ C2.*

$$
HOTEL

▦ **Borann, l'Auberge des Temples.** The accommodations are attractive and the rates reliable at this tranquil, small hotel, a couple of blocks east of the river behind La Noria. **Pros:** large rooms; traditional style; terrace for every room. **Cons:** small pool; patchy Wi-Fi. $ *Rooms from: $65 ⊠ Wat Bo St., north of N6, Wat Bo ☎ 063/964242 ⊕ www.borann.com ↘ 20 rooms ⋈ Breakfast ✛ D1.*

$$$
HOTEL

▦ **FCC Angkor Hotel.** Next to the Royal Residence, the former French consulate has been turned into an inviting retreat along the river, removed from the noise of the city center. **Pros:** sleek contemporary design; riverside location; on-site spa. **Cons:** could do with a sprucing up; poor lighting in some rooms. $ *Rooms from: $125 ⊠ Pokambor Ave. ☎ 063/760280, 023/992284 ⊕ www.fcccambodia.com ↘ 29 rooms, 2 Suites ⋈ Breakfast ✛ C1.*

$$$
HOTEL
Fodor's Choice
★

▦ **Heritage Suites Hotel.** In a quiet neighborhood but still close to the town center, this wonderful little boutique hotel charms with its understated luxury and discrete attention to detail. **Pros:** warm, attentive staff; quiet laid-back atmosphere; restaurant and bar are top drawer. **Cons:** hidden in Siem Reap's backstreets. $ *Rooms from: $185 ⊠ Wat Polanka Rd. ☎ 063/969100 ⊕ www.heritagesuiteshotel.com ↘ 6 rooms, 20 suites ⋈ Breakfast ✛ D1.*

$
B&B/INN

▦ **Ivy Guesthouse & Bar.** As one of the best backpacker's options, the Ivy offers cheap accommodations a short walking distance to most central spots. **Pros:** central location; low prices; near all local nightlife; free Wi-Fi. **Cons:** rooms somewhat in need of an upgrade; breakfast not included; very basic. $ *Rooms from: $8 ⊠ Central Market St. and Shinta Mani St., Old Market ☎ 012/800860 ⊕ ivy-guesthouse.com ↘ 20 rooms ⊟ No credit cards ⋈ No meals ✛ C3.*

$$$
RESORT

▦ **Navutu Dreams.** A slightly different Siem Reap experience is offered at this countryside bungalow resort, where the concept of well being is promoted via resident yoga instructors, holistic practitioners, and healthy eating options. **Pros:** free yoga classes; free airport pickup and tuk-tuk shuttles to temples and town. **Cons:** about 5 to 10 minutes out of town. $ *Rooms from: $155 ⊠ Navutu Rd. ☎ 063/964864, 092/141694 ⊕ navutudreams.com ↘ 26 rooms, 4 suites ⊘ Closed Sept. ⋈ Breakfast ✛ D3.*

9

$$$ HOTEL **The One Hotel.** There's only one suite here, but it's on the one street in town where you'd want to be and you'll have the undivided attention of the staff, including your own personal chef. **Pros:** prime location; unique experience. **Cons:** must be reserved months in advance (but last-minute deals sometimes available). [$] *Rooms from: $195* ✉ *The Passage, Old Market* ☎ *012/755311* 🌐 *www.theonehotelangkor.com* 🛏 *1 suite* 🍴 *Breakfast* ⊕ *B3.*

> **NIGHT FLIGHTS**
>
> Around sunset, the sky fills with thousands of large bats, which make their homes in the trees behind the Preah Ang Chek Preah Ang Chorm Shrine, near the gardens in front of the Raffles hotel.

$$$$ HOTEL **Raffles Grand Hotel d'Angkor.** Built in 1932 and still featuring the cage elevator from that year in the lobby, this grande dame was restored and reopened after near-destruction by occupying Khmer Rouge guerrillas. **Pros:** picturesque gardens; excellent restaurant; nicely designed and decorated. **Cons:** somewhat dependant on their name and former glory; more impersonal than smaller hotels; outside the center of Siem Reap. [$] *Rooms from: $300* ✉ *1 Vithei Charles de Gaulle, Khom Svaydangum* ☎ *063/963888* 🌐 *www.raffles.com/siem-reap* 🛏 *99 rooms, 18 suites, 2 villas* 🍴 *Breakfast* ⊕ *C1.*

$$ B&B/INN **Rambutan Resort.** This gem of a getaway is one of the better boutique accommodations around, with rooms grouped around a stone-and-palm-enclosed pool. **Pros:** good prices; friendly staff; good value. **Cons:** tricky access; small swimming pool. [$] *Rooms from: $113* ✉ *Krom 10, Rambutan La., Wat Damnak* ☎ *012/654638* 🌐 *rambutanhotelsr.com* 🛏 *43 rooms* 🍴 *Breakfast* ⊕ *C3.*

$$$ HOTEL Fodor's Choice ★ **Shinta Mani.** Not only will you sleep and eat in luxurious style, your money will also help support projects bringing clean water, transportation, and jobs to underprivileged communities, via the Shinta Mani Foundation. **Pros:** Shinta Mani is a beacon in Siem Reap for the nonstop work it does to help and promote charitable causes; good location; great facilities. **Cons:** no elevator, which limits some accessibility. [$] *Rooms from: $200* ✉ *Oun Khum and 14th Sts., Old French Quarter* ☎ *063/761998* 🌐 *www.shintamani.com* 🛏 *61 rooms 1 suite* 🍴 *Breakfast* ⊕ *C2.*

$$$ RESORT Fodor's Choice ★ **Sojourn Boutique Villas.** The layout of these villas, each with a pool or garden view, offers privacy and relaxation in lovingly maintained verdant grounds, and your stay will help the owners' ongoing support for underprivileged locals. **Pros:** poolside restaurant serves succulent Khmer specialties; extremely knowledgeable management; quality spa. **Cons:** a 10-minute tuk-tuk ride from town center; you either love or hate the 1980s-style swim-up pool bar. [$] *Rooms from: $200* ✉ *Treak Village Rd., Treak Village* ☎ *012/923437* 🌐 *www.sojournsiemreap.com* 🛏 *11 rooms* 🍴 *Breakfast* ⊕ *B1.*

$$$$ RESORT **Victoria Angkor Resort & Spa.** Just west of the Royal gardens stands this sophisticated resort modeled on a strong colonial aesthetic. **Pros:** attentive service; friendly staff; top-quality breakfast buffet. **Cons:**

a bit of a commercial feel; spa leaves much to be desired. $ *Rooms from: $200* ✉ *National Hwy. 6 and Sivatha Rd., Khom Svaydangum* ☎ *063/760428* ⊕ *www.victoriahotels-asia.com* ⬏ *120 rooms, 9 suites* ⏐◎⏐ *Breakfast* ✛ *C1.*

NIGHTLIFE AND PERFORMING ARTS

NIGHTLIFE

Most of Siem Reap's nightlife is concentrated around the Old Market, particularly on vibrant Pub Street, where some of the most popular spots are to be found. Just get a little lost, and you're sure to find a hangout that fits your style.

Angkor What?. Graffiti-splattered Angkor What? was one of the first pumping dance clubs on Pub Street, in the old quarter, and it still lures in the cool young crowd nightly. Techno, trance, dance, and ambient sounds hypnotize the revelers and keep them going until the early hours, when there is the occasional fun dance off with the bar opposite. You can also graffiti your personal philosophy on the walls. ✉ *Pub St.* ☎ *012/490755.*

Asana. A grown-up playground strewn with hammocks, wooden bar stools, and tree trunk tables, Asana is uniquely located in the one of the few remaining old traditional Khmer houses in Siem Reap. The bar attracts a fun, artsy crowd and hosts live piano performances and other artistic events. Among a list of regular snacks and drinks, try the signature cocktail—tamarind sauce, made with rum, tamarind juice, kaffir leaf, and lemony rice-paddy herbs. If you can't get enough of the drinks, they offer a cocktail class in the afternoon ($15). ✉ *St. 7 and The Lane, Old French Quarter* ☎ *092/987801.*

Bar 543. Formerly known as "Under Construction," this bar is now well and truly constructed. True to the owners' aesthetic, it's a funky, airy, minimalist space where the action takes center stage. Playing a bouncing mix of house, garage, and other uplifting beats, when it gets busy you'll find it hard not to move to the grooves. It also serves some of the tastiest bar bites in town. ✉ *Wat Bo Rd., Wat Bo.*

Charlie's. Word out on the street is "Finally! Charlie has opened his own bar." A big personality on Siem Reap's nightlife scene for many a year, Charlie has gone it alone, and his new bar, which opened in 2014,

---

THE BEST OF THE BEST

Reliable international chains have begun to open along the road to Angkor, and both the dusty airport road and the town's noisy thoroughfares are clogged with upper-end accommodations. However, why settle for a lousy location? Siem Reap offers several superb options in the quaint and quiet river area, where lush gardens are the norm and birds and butterflies thrive. Booking a room in a high-price hotel in this quarter means that your view of the hotel pool won't include the neighbors' laundry line, and will delight you with natural splendor instead of traffic jams.

9

reflects his warm and quirky character—you'll feel right at home in this retro, American-style biker bar. ⊠ *Hospital St.* ☎ *012/181–4001* ⊕ *charliessiemreap.com.*

Laundry Bar. A favorite among visitors and expats yearning for a place to chill out, this bar is a little away from the madding crowds of Pub Street and features local and touring bands. When no live bands are playing, it's also popular for its creative cocktails and funky music playlists. ⊠ *St. 9 and Psah Chas Alley 1, Old Market* ☎ *016/962026.*

Linga Bar. Known for its inventive cocktails, gay-friendly Linga Bar is named after the archaic phallus that was broadly worshipped in Angkorian times. The bar, under the same ownership as The One Hotel (⇨ *see Where to Stay*), welcomes a mixed crowd of all ages and hosts regular drag shows and live DJ sets. It celebrated its 10-year anniversary in 2014, and also moving to new premises. ⊠ *The Passage, Old Market* ☎ *012/246912, 012/540548* ⊕ *lingabar.com.*

Fodor's Choice
★

Miss Wong. A favorite haunt of creative types, eclectic expats, and guests from exclusive resorts, this bar stands out with its sexy 1920s Shanghai kitsch aesthetic—red walls, gold lanterns, and low lighting. Immersed in an era of glamorous decadence, guests are easily seduced into tasting cocktails made using local herbs, such as the apricot liqueur and kaffir lime-infused gin martini. Dim Sum and Asian fusion finger food are also on the menu. ⊠ *The-Lane* ☎ *092/428332* ⊕ *www.misswong.net.*

Nest Angkor. For a change of scene head to this restaurant-bar located in a landscaped garden, where guests are invited to sip their designer cocktails lying on canopied loungers. ⊠ *Sivatha Blvd.* ☎ *063/966381* ⊕ *nestangkor.com.*

Picasso Tapas Bar. A real hub for foreign residents, the barrel-shape Picasso is a fun option for those who crave a few tasty Spanish tapas dishes with their drinks to keep them going late into the night. ⊠ *The Alley West, Old Market.*

Fodor's Choice
★

The Yellow Submarine. This off-the-wall, four-story gastropub is the owners' gushing tribute to the Beatles, whose memorabilia—and even personal objects such as toys, paintings, and family photos—decks practically every surface. Wacky cocktails such as the bubblegum martini are complemented by snacks like crunchy popcorn-crusted prawns. It's a real hit amongst the expat crowd. ■ TIP➜ Take in the sunset over Siem Reap from the lovely fourth-floor terrace. ⊠ *9A The Lane, Old Market* ☎ *088/665–5335* ⊕ *www.theyellow-sub.com.*

PERFORMING ARTS

The 1961. Get inspired! A really interesting initiative, The 1961 is a gallery/art/events/co-work space. People gather for the quality exhibitions, to enjoy cool drinks in the outdoor pavilion, or just to find a quiet little spot to catch up on some work and have a coffee. 1961 has created quite a buzz in Siem Reap and the management is at the forefront of most major events in town. The regular exhibitions feature local and international artists and aims to bring them closer to their audiences, showcasing classic to avant garde, and visual to musical forms of art.

■ TIP→ There are spaces to rent in the ever-evolving space as well as meeting rooms, offices, and art spaces. ✉ *211 Osaphear St., Upper West River Side* ☎ *015/378088* ⊕ *the1961.com.*

FAMILY
Fodor's Choice
★

Phare. Cambodia's answer to the Cirque du Soleil is a must-see show. Previously only a traveling show, it has now found a permanent home in Siem Reap, in a cool pink high top tent behind Angkor National Museum, although one of its troupes continues to take the show on the road internationally. The high-energy performances combine Cambodian storytelling traditions with circus arts, dance, acrobatics, and acting to captivate audiences every night. The Phare School is a charitable organization that has a positive impact on poor communities. ■ TIP→ Most seating is first come first served, so try and get there early. ✉ *Comaille Rd., off Charles de Gaulle Ave.* ☎ *015/499480, 092/225320* ⊕ *www.pharecambodiancircus.org* 🍽 *$35.*

SHOPPING

ARTS AND HOMEWARES

Artisans Angkor. With 38 workshops in Siem Reap, and more than 800 craftspeople employed around the country, Artisans Angkor offers a dazzling selection of Cambodian fine arts and crafts, accessories, and silverware from all over the country, and you can see skills such as woodworking, silk painting, and lacquering. It is refreshing that the movement toward the renewal and modernization of arts, crafts and design is gathering momentum, with many of the high grade products available in Siem Reap now manufactured locally. ✉ *Stung Thmey St.* ☎ *063/963330* ⊕ *www.artisansdangkor.com.*

Fodor's Choice
★

Kandal Village. This exclusive area near the center of town is a great place to find a range of upscale shops and cafés offering tasty bites to maintain your energy levels. Get eccentric artworks from the cool Trunkh or elegant luxury gifts from talented designer Louise Loubatieres. Clothing designer Sirivan Chak Dumas presents her collections at Sirivan, and you can pick up some exquisite handmade silks from the Takeo Province at Neary Khmer. If all this shopping makes you weary, treat yourself to a relaxing treatment at Frangipani Spa. ✉ *Hap Guan St.*

Mekong Quilts. Offering employment opportunities to disadvantaged women, Mekong Quilts sells beautiful handmade, durable quilts of all designs, colors, styles, and sizes. ✉ *5 Sivatha Blvd., Old Market* ☎ *063/964498* ⊕ *www.mekong-quilts.org.*

Theam's House. This place specializes in unique lacquerware designs such as polychrome paintings and trademark colored elephants, as well as elegant traditional wood-carved Buddha statues and home style items. ✉ *25 Phum Veal, Kokchak Commune* ⊕ *www.theamshouse.com.*

9

CLOTHING

Eric Raisina. Madagascar-born, French-raised fashion designer Eric Raisina has a couple of outlets in Siem Reap where he presents his impeccably stylish couture designs. The world-acclaimed designer uses stunning Khmer silks to create clothing and accessories that clearly stand a head above the rest. You'll find this outlet net to the Shinta Mani Hotel. ■TIP→ **You can also visit his Atelier, at 75–81, Charles de Gaulle Avenue, by appointment only.** ✉ *Cassia Gallery, Oum Khun St., Sangkat Svay Dangkum* ☏ *063/963207 atelier, for appointments, 063/963210 Cassia Gallery* ⊕ *www.ericraisina.com* ⊙ *Daily 10–8.*

COSMETICS AND FOOD

Senteurs d'Angkor. This store transforms spices and herbs used traditionally in Cambodia into delightful cosmetic or deli food products. Here you can find Kampot pepper, Rattanakiri coffee, soaps made with lemongrass, turmeric, jasmine, or mango, and lots more. All the products make excellent gifts—especially for yourself. ✉ *Alley West, Old Market* ☏ *012/954815, 063/964801* ⊕ *www.senteursdangkor.com.*

MARKETS

Angkor Night Market. Expanded to be more like multiple markets now, the original is still a fun, lively flea market where you can practice your bargaining skills and get lost in a maze that includes a food hall, massage stands, bars, and an enormous variety of clothes, accessories, souvenirs, food and cosmetic products, jewelry, and more. ✉ *Sivatha Blvd., Old Market* ⊕ *www.angkornightmarket.com.*

Psar Chaa Old Market. Perfect for last-minute shopping, you'll find just about everything here, from clothing to traditional woodcrafts, fabrics, and ceramic home-style items, kitschy souvenirs, attractive silverware, and all varieties of freshly cooked or packaged foods. ✉ *Market St. and Pokombor Ave.*

UNDERSTANDING VIETNAM

Books and Movies

Vietnamese Vocabulary

BOOKS AND MOVIES

One of the best ways to get into the travel spirit for any country is to read a book or watch a film set there. Here are some recommendations to familiarize yourself with Vietnam's culture, history, and geography.

Recommended Reading

Books on Vietnam abound, written by some of the 20th-century's most renowned and emotionally articulate writers, journalists, and historians.

Historical texts on Vietnam War

Some of the most comprehensive histories of the Vietnam War are David Halberstam's *The Best and the Brightest,* Stanley Karnow's *Vietnam: A History,* Neil Sheehan's *A Bright Shining Lie,* and George C. Herring's *America's Longest War: The United States and Vietnam, 1950–1975.*

Frances FitzGerald's *Fire in the Lake* provides histories of the war from both the American and Vietnamese perspectives. Other insightful accounts of the war include Michael Herr's *Dispatches and* Nayan Chanda's *Brother Enemy: The War After the War,* which looks at the close of the Vietnam War and Vietnam's emerging conflicts with both Cambodia and China throughout the 1980s.

Novels and short fiction on Vietnam War

Several moving personal narratives (some fictionalized) have been written about the war, including *A Rumor of War* by Philip Caputo, *In Pharaoh's Army* by Tobias Wolff, *Fields of Fire* by James Webb, *Chickenhawk* by Robert Mason, and *The Things They Carried* by Tim O'Brien. A more recent account of the war is Karl Marlantes epic novel *Matterhorn,* which took the Oregon writer almost 35 years to write. For an altogether lighter read Ed Gaydos, who recounts his tour of duty in Vietnam in his memoirs *Seven in a Jeep* injecting a good dose of humor and intelligence into otherwise intolerable conditions.

Tom Mangold's *The Tunnels of Cu Chi* describes the Vietcong movement based in the tunnels around Cu Chi. Michael Lanning's *Inside the VC and the NVA* examines the workings of the North Vietnamese army and the Vietcong. *When Heaven and Earth Changed Places* is Le Ly Hayslip's story of her life before, during, and after the Vietnam War.

Texts on French Colonialism

For a history of the French role in Vietnam, read Bernard Fall's *Street Without Joy* and Jules Roy's *The Battle of Dienbienphu.* Graham Greene's literary classic *The Quiet American* is a prophetic tale of America's involvement in Vietnam. *The Lover,* by Marguerite Duras, is a fictionalized autobiographical tale of a French girl coming of age in 1930s Indochina.

Among the Tribes of Southeast Vietnam and Laos is an English translation of French explorer Captain P. Cupet's encounters with Vietnamese hill tribes at the end of the 19th century.

Texts on present-day Vietnam

To learn more about contemporary Vietnam read Henry Kamm's *Dragon Ascending: Vietnam and the Vietnamese* and Justin Wintle's fascinating experiences as one of the first writers to travel the country north to south after Vietnam first opened its doors to tourism in *Romancing Vietnam.* Look for an account of traveling through Vietnam by train in Paul Theroux's *The Great Railway Bazaar.* For a sense of Vietnam before you go, Walter Mason's *Destination Saigon* is a sometimes-funny tale of his travel experiences and people he met along the way. If you're looking for a good insight into the street food culture of Vietnam, Tracey Lister and Andreas Pohl's *Vietnamese Street Food* takes readers on a colorful journey (with recipes) across a country obsessed by the next meal, Included are a few helpful pointers on where you'll get the best pho.

For an intimate, visual rendering of the people and places of this beautiful and historical country, look to *Vietnam: Portraits and Landscapes,* featuring the stunning photography of Peter Steinhauer or

Passage to Vietnam: Through the Eyes of Seventy Photographers. For images of the war, look for *Requiem*, a moving collection of war pictures by photographers who died at work in Indochina between 1954 and 1989.

Films

Without a doubt, Vietnam has been the setting of some of film's most iconic renderings of warfare. Outside of Hollywood's offerings, Vietnamese film in the last few decades has given rise to acclaimed directors and filmmakers, including Tran Anh Hung.

Films set in Vietnam

The Lover (1991), a Jean-Jacques Annaud film based on the Marguerite Duras novel, is the tale of a young French woman coming of age in colonial Vietnam and her relationship with her Chinese lover. Régis Wargnier's *Indochine* (1992), starring Catherine Deneuve, is another film set in Vietnam during the French colonial era; it showcases the beautiful scenery of North Vietnam and is credited for putting Halong Bay on the map. Graham Greene's 1955 anti-war novel *The Quiet American* yielded two movie adaptations of the same name. The 1958 film eschews Greene's antiwar message, while the 2002 remake by Philip Noyce is more faithful to its source material. *Apocalypse Now* (1979) is Francis Ford Coppola's powerful look at the Vietnam War based on Joseph Conrad's *Heart of Darkness*; it stars Martin Sheen, Marlon Brando, and Dennis Hopper. Oliver Stone's *Platoon* (1986), with Tom Berenger, Willem Dafoe, and Charlie Sheen, is a harrowing, first-person tale of a young soldier's experience in the war. *The Deer Hunter* (1978) is a Michael Cimino film about three steelworkers from Pennsylvania who go off to fight in Vietnam; it stars Robert De Niro, John Savage, Meryl Streep, and Christopher Walken. Stanley Kubrick's *Full Metal Jacket* (1987) takes an unblinking look at the realities of the Vietnam War from the perspective of a U.S. army journalist. In Randall Wallace's *We Were Soldiers* (2002), Mel Gibson plays a colonel leading his soldiers in the first major, and bloody, battle of the Vietnam War.

Documentaries

For an inside look at the making of *Apocalypse Now*, see the documentary *Hearts of Darkness: A Filmmaker's Apocalypse* (1991). Bill Couturié, in his documentary about the Vietnam War, *Dear America: Letters Home from Vietnam* (1987), uses newsreels, amateur footage, and letters read by Robert De Niro, Sean Penn, and others to portray soldiers' experiences.

Foreign films

Nhat Minh Dang's *When the Tenth Month Comes* (1984) documents the struggle of ordinary Vietnamese villagers in the years after the war. It focuses on a young mother's grief and guilt after her husband was killed during the fighting, and the difficulties of coping with loss. Hans Petter Moland's *The Beautiful Country* (2004) tells the story of Binh, the abandoned child of a Vietnamese woman and her G.I. lover. Binh leaves the safety of his countryside home in search of his father, culminating in his journey to Texas as an illegal immigrant. Following the story of Vietnam's boat people, Ham Tran's *Journey From The Fall* (2009) is an inspirational true story of one Vietnamese family's successful resettlement in the United States. Contemporary French-Vietnamese filmmaker Tran Anh Hung's cinematographically beautiful *The Scent of Green Papaya* (1993) follows the life of a young female servant in Saigon. Tran Anh Hung's *Cyclo* (1995) portrays the rough and violent life of a bicycle-taxi driver who is inducted into the mafia-world of postwar Saigon.

VIETNAM VOCABULARY

In the mid-17th century, the Vietnamese language, which had been based on Chinese characters, was Romanized by the French Jesuit, Alexandre de Rhodes. This change made the tonal language easier for Westerners to read, but not much easier to pronounce. Vietnamese has six tones, which can significantly change the meaning of a word spelled the same way. Within a certain context, however, Vietnamese people will understand what you are trying to say even if you get the tones wrong. A bit of body language also helps get your point across.

Keep in mind that vocabulary and pronunciation vary from region to region. The soft "d" and soft "gi" are pronouced like a "z" in the north but change to "y" in the south.

	ENGLISH	VIETNAMESE	PRONUNCIATION
NUMBERS			
	one	môt	moat
	two	hai	hi
	three	ba	bah
	four	bốń	bown
	five	năm	num
	six	sáu	sow (like cow)
	seven	bay	by
	eight	tám	tom
	nine	chín	chin
	ten	mười	moy
	eleven	mười môt	moy moat
	twelve	mười hai	moy hi
	thirteen	mười ba	moy bah
	fourteen	mười bôn	moy bown
	fifteen	mười năm	moy num
	sixteen	mười sáu	moy sow
	seventeen	mười bay	muoi by
	eighteen	mười tám	moy tom
	nineteen	mười chín	moy chin
	twenty	hai mười	hi moy
	twenty-one	hai môt	hi moat

ENGLISH	VIETNAMESE	PRONUNCIATION
thirty	ba muòi	bah moy
forty	bôn muòi	bown moy
fifty	năm muòi	num moy
sixty	sáu muòi	sow moy
seventy	bay muòi	by moy
eighty	tám muòi	tom moy
ninety	chín muòi	chin moy
one hundred	môt trăm	moat chum
one thousand	môt nghìn (n)	moat nyin
one million	môt triêu	moat chew

COLORS

black	den	den
blue	xanh	sine
brown	nâu	no
green	xanh lá cây	sine la kay
orange	cam	cahm
pink	hông	hawm
purple	tím	teem
red	do	daw
white	trăng	chaang
yellow	vàng	vang

DAYS OF THE WEEK

Sunday	chu nhât	chu nyat
Monday	thú' hai	two hi
Tuesday	thú' ba	two ba
Wednesday	thú' tu'	two tu
Thursday	thú' năm	two num
Friday	thú' sáu	two sow
Saturday	thú' bay	two by

ENGLISH	VIETNAMESE	PRONUNCIATION

MONTHS

January	tháng môt	tang moat
February	tháng hai	tang hi
March	tháng ba	tang ba
April	tháng tu'	tang tu
May	tháng năm	tang num
June	tháng sáu	tang sow
July	tháng bay	tang by
August	tháng tám	tang tom
September	tháng chín	tang chin
October	tháng muòi	tang moy
November	tháng muòi môt	tang moy moat
December	tháng muòi hai	tang moy hi

USEFUL PHRASES

Do you speak English?	(Ông) có nói tiế´ng Anh không?	(ông) caw noy ting ine kawm?
I don't speak Vietnamese	Tôi không biế´t nói tiế´ng Viêt	doy kawm byet noy teng Viet
I don't understand	Tôi không hiêu	doy kawm hue
I understand	Tôi hiêu	doy hue
I don't know	Tôi không biế´t	doy kawm byet
I'm American/British	Tôi là nguòi Mỳ/Anh	doy la noy mee/ine
What's your name?	Tên (ông) là gì	ten (ong) la zee
My name is	Tôi tên là	doy ten la
How old are you?	(Ông) bao nhiêu tuôi?	bow nyoo toy
What time is it?	Mâ´y giò rôi?	may zuh zoy (n)
How?	Băng cách nào?	bong cack now?
When?	Bao giò'?	bow zuh? (n)

ENGLISH	VIETNAMESE	PRONUNCIATION
Yesterday	Hôm qua	home kwa
Today	Hôm nay	home ny (like hi)
Tomorrow	Ngày mai	ny my
This morning	Sáng nay	sang nye
Afternoon	tru'a nay	chewa nye
Tonight	lêm nay/tôi nay	dem nye/doy nye
Why?	Tai sao?	tie sow (like cow)
Who?	Ai?	eye
Where?	O' dâu	uh doe
Where is	o' dâu?	uh doe
Train station	Ga tàu	gah tow (n)
Bus station	Bê´n xe	ben say
Bus stop	Tram xe buy´t	chum say boot
Airport	Sân bay	sun bye
Post office	Bu'u diên	boo dien
Bank	Ngân hàng	nun hang
Hotel	Khách san	kack san
Temple	Chùa	chew-a
Restaurant	Nhà hàng	nya hang
Store	Cu'a hàng	kua hang
Market	Chò	Chuh
Museum	Bao tàng	bow taang
Art museum	Bao tàng mỳthuât	bow taang me twut
Gallery	Phòng tranh	fowm chine
Theater	Nhà hát	nya hat
Movie theater	Rap cine	zap see-nay
Beach	Bãi biên	bye be-in
Lake	Hô	hoe

ENGLISH	VIETNAMESE	PRONUNCIATION
Park	Công viên	cowm vee-in
Street	Phô (n)/luòng (s)	foe/dooahng
Hospital	Bênh viên	ben vee-in
Telephone	liê n thoai	dee-in twai
Restroom	Nhà vê sinh/toilette	nya vay sing
Here/there	o' dây/dăng kia	uh day/dang kee-uh
Left/right	trái/phai	chy/fye (as in 'bye')
Is it far?	Có xa không	caw sah kowm
Go	li	dee
Stop	Dú'ng lai	zoong lie
Slow	Châ m châ m	chum chum
Straight ahead	Thăng	tang
I'd like	Tôi muôn	doy mun
a room	môt phòng	moat fong
the key	chìa khóa	cheah kwa
a newspaper	tò' báo	tuh bow
magazine	ta.p chí	tup chee
a stamp	con tem	cawn tem
I'd like to buy	Tôi muôn mua	doy mun moo-a
dictionary	tu'diên	tuh dien
soap	xà phòng/xà bông (s)	sa fong/sa bowm
city map	ban dô thành phô	ban doe tine foe
postcard	bu'u thiêp	boo tip
How much is it?	Bao nhiêu?	bow nyew
Expensive/cheap	lăt/re	dut/zay /ray (s)
A little/lot	ít/nhiêu	eat/nyew
More/less	Nhiêu ho'n/ít ho'n	nyew huhn/eat huhn
Too much/enough	Nhiêu quá/du rôi	nyew kwa/ doo zoy doo roy (s)

ENGLISH	VIETNAMESE	PRONUNCIATION
Too expensive	lăt quá	dut kwa
Change money	lôi tiên	doy tee-in
I am ill	Tôi biôm	doy be awm
Call a doctor	Goi bác sy˜	goy back see
Help!	Cú'u tôi!	ku doy
Stop!	Dù'ng lai!	zoong lie
Fire!	Cháy nhà!	chay nyah
Caution!/look out!	Coi chù'ng!	coy chung
I	Tôi	doy
We	Chúng tôi	choong doy
Yes/No	Có/Không	caw/kawm
Please	Làm o'n	lamb un
Thank you	Cám o'n	cam un
That's all right	Không có chi	kawm caw chee
Excuse me, sorry	Xin lô˜ i	seen loy
Hello	Xin chào	seen chow
Goodbye	Tam biêt	tom be-it
Mr(older man)	Ông	awm
Mrs(older woman)	Bà	bah
Miss (younger woman)	co (like co-op)	Cô
Mr(young man)	Anh	ine / un(s)
Young person	Em	em
Pleased to meet you	Hân hanh du'o'c	haan hine dook gặp
How are you?	(Ông) có khoe kawm?	(ông) caw Kway không?
Very well, thanks	Khoe , cám o'n	kway, cam un
And you?	Còn (ông)?	cawn (ông)?

TRAVEL SMART
VIETNAM

GETTING HERE AND AROUND

With nearly 3,200 km (2,000 miles) of coastline, Vietnam is a narrow S-shape country stretching more than 1,600 km (1,000 miles) from north to south. Most visitors fly into Hanoi or Ho Chi Minh City, which are separated by a 2-hour flight or a 30-hour train ride. For some shorter trips out of major cities or towns, the best option is to take a train, but buses are ideal for other trips. Developing a good, countrywide transportation infrastructure has been hampered by much of the country's hilly and mountainous terrain.

Traveling during the Tet holiday means paying premium prices and should be booked as far in advance as possible. Public transportation like buses and trains are best avoided at this time as prices double and overcrowding is a problem; it's not unusual for a bus driver to pick up extra passengers and luggage along the way and delays are frequent.

TRAVEL TIMES FROM HANOI	BY AIR	BY TRAIN
Ho Chi Minh City	2 hours	34 hours
Dong Hoi	1½ hours	9–10 hours
Hue	1 hour	12 hours
Danang	1½ hours	14 hours
Nha Trang	1¾ hours	23 hours
Siem Reap Cambodia	1¾ hours	N/A

▌ AIR TRAVEL

International flights into Vietnam typically connect through hubs such as Bangkok, Singapore, Jakarta, Hong Kong, Kuala Lumpur, Phnom Penh, Siem Reap, Beijing, Seoul, Osaka, Tokyo, Dubai, Melbourne, Sydney, and Taipei and fly into Ho Chi Minh City and Hanoi. It's also possible to fly into the international airport in Danang, in central Vietnam, via Kuala Lumpur, Tokyo, Hong Kong, and Seoul. There are no direct flights between Vietnam and North America. Hanoi and Ho Chi Minh City are the main hubs for direct flights to Vietnam from the United Kingdom.

Be aware that two airlines may jointly operate a connecting flight from an Asian hub, so ask if your airline operates every segment of your flight—you may find that your preferred carrier flies only part of the way. For instance, if you purchased a ticket through an international carrier such as Air France, Cathay Pacific, Delta, Japan Airlines, or Thai International Airways but are not flying directly to Hanoi or Ho Chi Minh City, it is possible that your connecting flight into Vietnam will be on Vietnam Airlines.

Some layovers require an overnight stay in a connecting city. Before buying your ticket, check to see who covers the cost of the hotel—you or the airline—if you have to stay overnight.

AIRPORTS

The major gateways to Vietnam are Hanoi's Noi Bai Airport (HAN), 44 km (28 miles) north of the city, Ho Chi Minh City's Tan Son Nhat Airport (SGN), 7 km (4 miles) from the center, and to a lesser extent Danang International Airport (DAD), 5 km (3 miles) from the center. As the main gateways for thousands of international visitors, Ho Chi Minh City and Hanoi airports have procedures that can involve more in-depth immigration checks and baggage searches, should customs officials have any cause for suspicion. If you have arranged for a visa on arrival (VOA) waiting times can be long, so allow for at least an hour prior to check-in if you have a connecting flight, and make sure all the required paperwork, photographs and visa fee are easily accessible to avoid delays. If you have obtained your Vietnam visa in advance, you are more than likely to get through immigration, pick up your waiting bags, and breeze through customs quite quickly. All the international airports have free Wi-Fi and snack bars.

Airport Information Cam Ranh International Airport (Nha Trang Airport). ⊠ Nguyen Tat Thanh, Nha Trang ⊕ www.nhatrangairport. com. **Cat Bi Airport** (Haiphong Airport). ⊠ Le Hong Phong, Haiphong ☎ 0225/397–6408, 0225/397–6216. **Con Dao Airport** (Co Ong Airport, Sang Bay Co Ong). ⊠ Co Ong, Con Son, Con Dao ☎ 0254/383–1973 ⊕ en. vietnamairport.vn/page/107/airports/con-dao-airport. **Danang Airport** ⊠ Duy Tan, Danang ✈ 3 km (2 miles) southwest of Danang ☎ 0236/382–3391 ⊕ www. danangairportonline.com. **Dong Hoi Airport** ⊠ AH14, Loc Ninh, Quang Binh Province ☎ 0232/381–0878 ⊕ www.vietnamairport. vn. **Duong Dong Airport** (Phu Quoc Airport). ⊠ Off TL 46, Phu Quoc ⊕ www. phuquocinternationalairport.com. **Lien Khuong Airport** (Dalat Airport). ⊠ 20 Lam Dong, Dalat. **Noi Bai International Airport** ⊠ Vo Van Kiet, off QL 18, Soc Son ☎ 024/3886–5047. **Phu Bai Airport** (Hue Airport). ⊠ Huong Thuy, Phu Bai, Hue ☎ 0234/386–1131. **Tan Son Nhat Airport** ⊠ Hoang Van Thu Blvd., Phong 2, Tan Binh District, Ho Chi Minh City ☎ 028/3848–5383 ⊕ www.hochiminhcityairport.com.

INTERNATIONAL FLIGHTS

For most international visitors, flying to Vietnam usually entails a nondirect flight, with popular layovers for U.S. travelers flying Delta, American Airlines, Cathay Pacific, Emirates, or Air Canada being either Bangkok, Tokyo, or Hong Kong. From the United Kingdom, Vietnam Airlines is the only carrier offering direct flights into the country. Nondirect flights with major carriers Emirates, Air France, and Malaysia Airlines are often serviced by two different airlines; flights connect from Paris, Doha, Bangkok, or Kuala Lumpur, before flying into Vietnam's Ho Chi Minh City, Hanoi or, to a lesser extent Danang. Silk Air and Vietnam Airlines offer daily services from Danang, Ho Chi

Minh City and Hanoi to several cities in Cambodia.

AIR TRAVEL WITHIN VIETNAM

The main operator for domestic routes in Vietnam is Vietnam Airlines, which offers the most reliable service. Its smaller competitors, Jet Star Pacific (owned jointly by Vietnam Airlines and Quantas) and the privately owned VietJet Air, service fewer aircraft and despite being slightly cheaper, tend to suffer the most delays and cancellations. Flights are short and very reasonably priced; when booked in advance the two-hour trip between Hanoi and Ho Chi Minh City can cost as little as $25 (a third of the price of the 34-hour train journey). For information about domestic airports, ⊕ www.vietnamairport.vn is a good resource.

AIRLINE CONTACTS

To and from the United States American Airlines ☎ 800/433–7300 ⊕ www.aa.com. **Cathay Pacific** ☎ 020/8834–8888 ⊕ www. cathaypacific.com. **Delta** ☎ 800/221–1212 ⊕ www.delta.com **Thai Airways** ☎ 020/7491–7953 ⊕ www.thaiairways.com **United Airlines** ☎ 800/864–8331 ⊕ www.united. com **USAirways** ☎ 800/428–4322, 800/622–1015 ⊕ www.usairways.com.

To and from Australia Emirates ☎ 800/777–3999 ⊕ www.emirates.com.

Within Vietnam and Cambodia Cambodia Angkor Air ☎ 023/666–6786/8/9, 023/212564 ⊕ www.cambodiaangkorair.com. **Jetstar Pacific** ☎ 028/3547–3550 ⊕ www. jetstar.com **Silk Air** ☎ 0236/382–3391 ⊕ www. silkair.com **VietJet Air** ⊠ Hanoi ☎ 01/900–1886, 028/3551–6220 ⊕ www.vietjetair.com. **Vietnam Airlines** ☎ 024/832–0320 Northern Vietnam, 028/832–0320 Southern Vietnam, 866/677–8909 in U.S. ⊕ www.vietnamairlines. com ⊕ www.vietnamairlines.com.

FLYING TIMES

There are no direct flights to Vietnam from the United States. Flying time to the Southeast Asian hub of Bangkok is approximately 18 hours from Los Angeles, 20 hours from Chicago, and 22 hours from New York; the onward flight to Ho Chi Minh City takes an hour. Flying direct to Ho Chi Minh City from London takes 12 hours and from Sydney it's about nine hours.

▮ BOAT TRAVEL

Traveling by boat in Vietnam is generally reserved for those who want to explore the Mekong Delta, Halong Bay, or the Perfume River. The slow pace, limited routes, and high costs make it an inconvenient way to get from point A to B. For many riverside or seaside towns in Vietnam, boat rides are a natural attraction, and a great way to get a view of life on, in, or near the water. In northern Vietnam and in the Mekong Delta, ferries are often the only way to get to destinations where bridges have not yet been built or have been destroyed, or to get to islands such as Cat Ba. Bicycles and motor vehicles can usually be brought on board for a fee.

Speed boats that make sea crossings to the islands are notoriously unsafe. Designed for use on rivers, they are often not seaworthy when the water gets choppy, and the companies that run them tend to take too many passengers. Do some research and make sure you book with a reputable company, or opt for a slower trip on a large dive boat or local supply boat. Life jackets are a legal requirement on all boats; if you are told you can take it off once the boat has passed the checkpoint, you have chosen the wrong company. Ignore them, and keep the jacket on throughout the crossing.

For travel between Cambodia and Vietnam, there's a speedboat service to Phnom Penh from Chau Doc (a 3–4 hour bus journey from Ho Chi Minh City). Although very few companies service this 5–6 hour transfer, one reputable company that does, is Blue Cruiser. Tickets can be arranged at any of the tour offices in the main backpacker district (Pham Ngu Lao) in Ho Chi Minh City and include bus transportation to the Pier Café boat

dock in Chau Doc for approximately $35. Boats depart daily at 7 am and include a stop off at the Vinh Xuong border to arrange visas, before continuing onward to Phnom Penh International Port, which is near the city center.

Boat Information Blue Cruiser ⊠ *59/3B Pham Viet Chanh* ☎ *028/3926–0253* ⊕ *www.bluecruiser.com.*

▮ BORDER CROSSINGS

Air travel is the recommended way to go between Vietnam and other points in Asia. You must obtain a visa to visit most countries near Vietnam—Laos, Cambodia, and China—which can be difficult; it's best to make visa arrangements before you go to Vietnam. Cambodia and Laos currently provide visas on arrival at international airports (with a photo), but this is subject to change; inquire at these countries' embassies for the most up-to-date policies. In general, Thailand automatically grants short-term-stay visas to most Western visitors. Note also that tourist visas can be arranged quickly for most Asian countries from their respective embassies in Bangkok.

Visa Offices Chinese Embassy ⊠ *46 Hoang Dieu, Hanoi* ☎ *024/3845–3736* ⊕ *www.vn.china-embassy.org.* **Royal Embassy of Cambodia** ⊠ *4500 16th St. NW, Washington, D.C.* ☎ *202/726–7742* ⊕ *www.embassyofcambodia.org* ⊠ *71A Tran Hung Dao St., Hoan Kiem District, Hanoi* ☎ *024/942–4789* ⊕ *www.embassyofcambodia.org.*

▮ BUS TRAVEL

Public uses are often cramped, unbearably hot, packed with chain-smokers, and notoriously loud. Air-conditioned open tour buses are a better alternative; Catering to travelers, the "Open Tour" option has comfortable buses that run between Hanoi and Ho Chi Minh City, with stops in most cities along the way. Services are also available to bordering countries Laos and Cambodia. Ticket prices are based on the route and are only slightly more expensive than regular buses; $60 will buy you an open ticket from Hanoi to Ho Chi Minh City with four stops at destinations in between, and is almost half the price of a train ticket. About a dozen tour operators offer bus service, but the most reputable are Mai Linh, Phuong Trang, Hanh Cafe, and Sinh Cafe who all offer air-conditioned sleeper buses with fixed reclined seating, blankets, and onboard toilets (although these are not often operational) for longer distances. Onward journeys are best booked at least a day in advance (earlier if it happens to be a national holiday) and can easily be arranged by phone or email with the option of a cheap hotel pickup; a good option if you have a lot of luggage.

Tour companies that run bus services accept both dollars and dong. Public buses require dong.

Bus Information Mai Linh Express ⊠ *Ho Chi Minh City* ☎ *028/3939–3939* ⊕ *www. mailinhexpress.vn.* **Phuong Trang** ⊠ *Ho Chi Minh City* ☎ *028/386–0838* ⊕ *www. futabuslines.com.vn.* **Sinh Cafe** ⊠ *66 Hang Than St., Ba Dinh District, Hanoi* ☎ *024/3836– 4212* ⊕ *www.sinhcafe.com.*

▮ CAR TRAVEL

Despite changes in Vietnam's traffic laws and a new law that recognizes international drivers' licenses, it is not yet clear what specific limitations may apply to foreign drivers. This, coupled with the hazard of locals driving dangerously, means that it is not advisable to drive a car in Vietnam, although many foreigners do drive motorbikes.

CAR RENTAL

Before 2015, tourists were not permitted to drive in Vietnam at all. Now, although the laws are set to change and international drivers' permits will be accepted, there is still some uncertainty about restrictions that may be imposed, particularly on driving a car, so it's very important to check the situation before deciding

to rent. Keep an eye on embassy websites for any changes.

It is still a better option to rent a car with a driver, who will, hopefully, speak some English. Cars and minivans with drivers are readily available from private and state-run travel agencies, tourist offices, and through most hotels in bigger cities. You are charged by the kilometer, by the day, or both. A daily rate runs from $70 to $100 per day, depending on a number of criteria: the city in which you rent the vehicle; whether it has air-conditioning; the make of the car; and your bargaining skills. The agreed price should include gas and tolls, but clarify all this before you set off. Travel agencies can also arrange for English-speaking guides to accompany you and the driver. For overnight trips you're generally responsible for the driver's lodging costs as well, which may or may not be included in the quoted price; make sure to clarify this up front.

Note that most rental cars lack seat belts and the provision of child seats is unusual. You should negotiate a price in advance and check out the vehicle before you rent it. Note that the name "Land Cruiser" is overused in Vietnam, especially in Hanoi. Too many people consider a Land Cruiser—made only by Toyota—to be any four-wheel-drive vehicle that's not a Russian jeep.

EMERGENCY SERVICES

If you have hired a car and driver and the car breaks down, you should not be held responsible for the cost of repairs. Make sure everyone is clear about this before you embark on a long journey. Mechanical and engine problems with Japanese-made cars and SUVs are rare, but expect breakdowns if the vehicle was made in Russia. Most mechanical problems can be fixed, and there are mechanics on virtually every block in the cities.

In case of a traffic accident, remember that the foreigner is always at fault. So, in minor accidents, even if you've done nothing wrong it's a good idea to stay in the car and let your driver do the talking or to try to get out of the situation as quickly as possible without involving the police. Even if the case seems crystal clear, you'll likely be fighting a losing battle and will probably be asked to pay damages immediately even if you are not to blame. Many of Vietnam's civil laws provide for the underprivileged, and as a foreigner you are automatically considered privileged.

GASOLINE

Unleaded gasoline is sold by the liter in Vietnam. (There are about 4 liters to the gallon, which will usually fill a motorbike tank.) Gas stations sell at a government-regulated price of 25,000d per liter and payment must be made in Vietnamese dong. Minsks and some other makes of motorcycle take a 2%–4% oil-gas mixture; oil is added after you purchase your gasoline. Always check that the attendant has reset the meter to zero before he starts to fill your tank and check your change, especially if you are paying with a large bill. Gas sold by vendors on the street is a good option when stations are closed. The prices are slightly higher, however, and it's not unheard of for watered-down gas of the lowest octane to be sold on the street, just buy enough to get you to the next gas station and fill up there.

PARKING

Any traveling by car you do will be with a hired driver, so he (drivers are rarely women) will be the one responsible for finding adequate parking. In most small towns and at the entrance to beaches, private home owners and parking attendants will offer to look after bicycles and motorbikes for no more than 5,000d. These are the safest places to park bicycles and motorbikes and will prevent your bike or helmet from being stolen, or being removed by the police for parking illegally. At night always check what time the attendant's shift ends—if your bike is still there, he will most likely take it home for safe keeping overnight. If this happens you'll need to make other arrangements to get back to your hotel and return in the morning to be reunited with the bike.

ROAD CONDITIONS

Highways are the main transportation route for cars, public buses, trucks, tractors, motorbikes, bicycles, pedestrians, oxcarts, and a host of farm animals. Highway 1 is the primary north–south commercial route and is the backbone of Vietnam's road system. It has been upgraded along its entire length, which extends from near the Chinese border, north of Hanoi, through Ho Chi Minh City and to the heart of the Mekong Delta in the south. Other major roadways include Highway 5 from Hanoi to Haiphong; Highway 6 from Hoa Binh to Dien Bien Phu; Route 70, which bisects the northwest; Highway 7, the Nghe An Province route into Laos; Route 14 through the central highlands; Route 22, west out of Ho Chi Minh City toward Tay Ninh and the Cambodian capital of Phnom Penh; and Route 80, through the upper Mekong Delta. A second north–south route, the Truong Son Highway, is currently under construction. An ambitious project, it will follow a similar route to the famed wartime supply route known as the Ho Chi Minh Trail. Once completed, it will cut through Vietnam's western mountains and extend from the northern province of Ha Tay to Ho Chi Minh City.

Vietnam's major roads are for the most part paved, and the entire country's road network is continually being upgraded with extensive soft loans from the World Bank and the Asian Development Bank. Road conditions in the north are far worse than in the south, where the U.S. war effort built or paved many of the roads. Thoroughfares labeled national roads cover only 15,3600 km (9,544 miles) of Vietnam's transportation system; only 84% of these roads are paved. The lowest category of roads, called provincial or district roads, account for 83,000 km (51,574 miles) of the system. Only 58% of these are paved. Most dirt roads turn to mud during the rainy season and become impassable. Despite some stretches of highways having speed limits up to 100 kph (60 mph), road transportation is very slow in Vietnam. When working out approximate journey times by bus or car a more realistic average speed to work from is approximately 30 kph (20 mph).

When driving (or, more likely, being driven) around the country, try to travel during the day and be extra vigilant during rush hour—around 8 am and from 4 pm—when traffic is at its heaviest. Driving at night can be hazardous because many vehicles either don't have lights or drive with their high beams on at all times, and it is difficult to see bad spots in the road.

Driving in Ho Chi Minh and Hanoi should be left to the experts.

▌ MOTORBIKE TRAVEL

It is now legal to rent a motorbike in Vietnam if you have an International Drivers' License. It's not a good idea to do so, however, unless you have ridden one before. City traffic is chaotic, country roads may have human-size potholes, and local drivers are unlikely to stick to the rules of the road. If you are involved in an accident you, as the foreigner, will be blamed (whether it was actually your fault or not) and be liable for all costs, including hospital bills for any injured parties.

Previously, though technically illegal, the practice was widespread and so there is a good network of rental sources throughout the country, and most hotels will organize a rental for you. For a day rental, check what time you need to get back. You can rent motorbikes and scooters in major cities *(see individual city planners)* at most tourist cafés and some hotels and guesthouses for about 80,000d to 120,000d a day. A deposit is usually required, along with a passport or a photocopy of one (it's best to leave a copy). It is a legal requirement to wear a helmet, all agencies provide them at no extra cost, but a

better quality helmet (look for the safety mark and hologram sticker on the back, showing that it's passed the minimum legal safety standards) can be picked up for around 215,000d—a wise investment.

Many rental bikes are not in good condition, so always check brakes, tires, and lights before agreeing to the rental; also check the gas tank, which may have been siphoned, and ask for the location of the nearest gas station.

▌ TAXI TRAVEL

Metered taxis are common in Hanoi and Ho Chi Minh City and are becoming more common in Vietnam's smaller cities. Simply wave down a cab on the street, or ask the hotel or restaurant staff to call you a cab. In Hanoi and Ho Chi Minh City, the moment you step into a cab the meter reads between 7,500d and 14,000d; after that the rate runs about 14,000d per kilometer. Fares are always quoted in dong, and many drivers will complain if you try to pay with $1 bills. Although tipping is not required, some cabbies have developed a habit of "not having change" in the hope you'll tell them to keep it.

Although many cabbies act like reckless kings of the road, taxis are the safest way to get around Vietnam's cities.

To find addresses in Vietnam it helps to know a few local practices. You may see addresses with numbers separated by a slash, such as "361/8 Nguyen Dinh Chieu St." This means you should head for No. 361 on Nguyen Dinh Chieu Street and then look for an alley next to the building; you want No. 8 in this alley. When you see addresses with a number followed by a letter, such as "97A," this means there is more than one No. 97 on the street and you need to find the one numbered specifically with an "A." If you see "54bis," look for a building adjacent to No. 54; this is a leftover from the French that means 54½. The English word *street* (abbreviated St.) is used throughout the book rather than the Vietnamese words *pho* and *duong*. This was done to make sure street names are clear; in Vietnamese, the words pho and duong come before the names of the streets, which can prove very confusing when trying to find your way around. In addition, many Vietnamese refer to streets only by name (without adding pho or duong), so you may only see these words on street signs and maps.

Taxi Companies **Mai Linh Taxi** ✉ *Ho Chi Minh City* ☎ *028/3829–8888* ⊕ *www. mailinh.vn.* **Vinasun Taxi** ✉ *Ho Chi Minh City* ☎ *028/3827–7178* ⊕ *www.vinasuntaxi.com.*

MOTORBIKE TAXIS

Faster than regular taxis, but a less safe option, is the motorbike taxi (xe om). Xe oms are available everywhere. Most hang out on the streets with the most foot traffic, outside bus stations, and in busy tourist destinations. They will drive next to you as you walk down the street, offering their services. For a short distance it can be fun. Always wear a helmet, agree to a price before you get on, and make sure the driver knows where you want to go (your best bet is to have the address written down). Never take a xe om late at night, especially if you are on your own or have had one too many to drink. Quite often, a taxi will cost around the same. Expect to pay no more than 10,000d per kilometer.

▌ TRAIN TRAVEL

The 2,600-km (1,612-mile) rail system, built by the French, runs north–south, servicing coastal towns between Hanoi and Ho Chi Minh City. The main drawback of rail travel is that it's slow. The quickest train from Ho Chi Minh City to Hanoi, the Reunification Express, takes about 34–41 hours, depending on how many stops it makes. Trains are better for the shorter hops between Hanoi and Hue; Hanoi and Lao Cai, which gets you to Sapa; or Ho Chi Minh City and Nha Trang.

Train travel through Vietnam can be an enjoyable experience, not to mention a time saver if you take overnight trips, provided you can get a soft sleeper or at least a soft chair. Designed just for tourists, the more luxurious Livitrans that run between Hanoi and Danang, the Golden trains that connect Ho Chi Minh and Nha Trang and the privately run tourist sleeping car services between Hanoi and Sapa make for a far more comfortable experience than the Reunification Express, where regardless of what class ticket you hold, the bathrooms are often dirty and noise is often a problem; day and night, when the train stops, vendors may pop into your compartment to try to sell you soda, beer, and cigarettes. Smoking is permitted in some compartments.

Security is another concern. At all times keep the metal grille over the window shut. If you are concerned about eating food from the local vendors who board the train at every station, selling everything from rice crackers to soup, you should bring food and water with you, especially if you have cumbersome luggage that makes trips to the dining carriage impossible.

FARES AND SCHEDULES

As everywhere, fares vary based on the length of trip and the class of travel. You can purchase tickets at train stations and travel agencies can also help you make reservations.

Train service runs daily between Hanoi and Ho Chi Minh City (34–41 hours, $99 for soft sleeper with air-conditioning), daily between Hanoi and Hue (12–14 hours, $59 for a soft sleeper), daily between Hanoi and Lao Cai (9–11 hours, $43 for soft sleeper), and daily between Ho Chi Minh City and Nha Trang (15–22 hours, $43). It's also possible to take a train from Hanoi to Nanning in China (twice weekly on Tuesday and Friday, 11 hours, $22–$38), from where you can continue to Beijing. The northeastern border crossing is at Dong Dang, just north of Lang Son. Visas for China need to be arranged before you leave home—at the time of writing, the Chinese Embassy in Hanoi was not issuing visas to foreigners.

The Victoria Sapa Resort and Spa's deluxe train carriages leave Hanoi on Monday, Wednesday, and Friday evenings. They depart from Lao Cai on Tuesday and Thursday mornings and on Sunday evenings. Acquiring a berth requires that you stay at the hotel for at least one night. On Monday, Wednesday, and Thursday a four-berth compartment costs $50 and a two-berth compartment costs $80; on weekends, the price is $70 and $120, respectively.

Train Information **Danang Train Station** ⊠ *202 Hai Phong, Danang* ☎ *0236/382–3810* ⊕ *www.vietnamtrain.com.* **Dong Hoi Train Station** ⊠ *Thuan Ly, Dong Hoi* ⊕ *www.vietnamtrain.com.* **Hanoi Train Station** (*Ga Hanoi*). ⊠ *Le Duan St. at Tran Hung Dao St., Hoan Kiem District, Hanoi* ☎ *024/3942–3949 information, 090/4619–926 ticketing.* **Hue Train Station** ⊠ *2 Bui Thi Xuan, Hue* ☎ *0234/822–175* ⊕ *www.vietnamtrain.com.* **Saigon Railway Station** (*Ga Sai Gon*). ⊠ *1 Nguyen Thong St., District 3, Ho Chi Minh City* ☎ *028/3931–8952* ⊕ *www.gasaigon. com.vn.* **Victoria Sapa Resort & Spa** ⊠ *Sapa* ☎ *0214/387–1522* ⊕ *www.victoriahotels.asia.*

RESERVATIONS

It's a good idea to book ahead, especially for overnight travel, although for some trips you can only reserve a few days in advance. Tickets can either be booked at the train station, through a local tour company, or with an online booking resource such as Vietnam Impressive, Vietnam Train, or Vietnam Railways. Train tickets must be paid for in dong, unless you book through a tour company. Foreigners are charged higher fares than Vietnamese nationals. Once you disembark you may need to show your ticket again, so don't throw away your ticket stub or you may face major hassle when trying to leave the station, and may even be forced to pay again.

ESSENTIALS

■ ACCOMMODATIONS

The Vietnam National Administration of Tourism has instituted its own rating system, which vaguely conforms to international standards of quality. Yet hotels billed as five-star in Vietnam are often more like three- or four-star hotels in the United States.

Although hotel staffers are generally enthusiastic and some have received training abroad, really good service is still a rarity. A few hotels, however, are as luxurious and have as high standard of service as any international establishment in the world. Beach and mountain resorts are rapidly being developed.

In major cities and tourist destinations, the hotel industry continues to grow, with more and more international and smaller-size hotels opening. Many of the larger international hotels often aren't fully booked but it is rare that staff will have the authority to offer discounted rates, most will point you in the direction of the online booking agents that have the best deals. Smaller hotels and guesthouses may give you a better room rate than what's listed when calling to make reservations. Vietnam has a selection of other mid-size, mid-level hotels and guest houses, which go by the term "homestays." These privately owned, often family-run operations range from utilitarian to plush; they usually provide friendly service, spotless if basic rooms, and a homey environment. Although such amenities as swimming pools and exercise equipment are rare, and their restaurants are often bland and lifeless, guest rooms generally have air-conditioning and usually include satellite TV, Wi-Fi, IDD telephones, refrigerators, and showers. They may also include lots of street noise.

In smaller towns or rural areas expect much more basic accommodations. Reservations are recommended during Christmas and New Year and during Tet, the lunar new year (January or February); prices often fluctuate at that time.

APARTMENT AND HOUSE RENTALS

Airbnb, Flipkey, and to a lesser extent, home-exchange directories, list rentals as well as exchanges.

Upscale beach villas and family rentals are a relatively new thing in Vietnam, but the quality of accommodations is high; some easily compete on a design scale with the private villas at four- or five-star resorts in the region, but come at less than half the price. The highest concentration are found in the popular coastal town of Hoi An. Hanoi and Ho Chi Minh City have a number of international-standard serviced apartments. Most of these are underused, and agents are only too happy to cut deals with short-term occupants.

Contacts **Airbnb** ⊕ *www.airbnb.com.* **Flipkey** ⊕ *www.flipkey.com.* **Ocean Villas Resort** ✉ *Truong Sa, Danang* ☎ *0234/396–7094* ⊕ *www.oceanvillas.com.vn.*

■ COMMUNICATIONS

INTERNET

Free Wi-Fi is provided at most hotels throughout Vietnam and they usually also have business centers; newer boutique hotels in popular tourist destinations now offer laptops for in-room use. Internet cafés in remote areas like Sapa are rare, but there are plenty of Wi-Fi hotspots throughout the country, and most restaurants, cafés, and pho shops will lure customers by advertising an available Wi-Fi connection. However, there are government restrictions on social networking sites, so don't be surprised if you can't log on to Facebook outside of your hotel room.

LOCAL DO'S AND TABOOS

Vietnamese people rarely say "no," often simply to avoid confrontation. Anger is generally viewed as a sign of weakness, and to display it in public is considered ill mannered, so if you have a disagreement, remain calm and good-natured. Pointing at people or beckoning with your palm up is also considered extremely rude, so attract attention with your palm down. Crossing your fingers doesn't signify good luck here, and patting children on the head is viewed as a bad omen. Public displays of affection, other than putting an arm around someone of the same sex, are frowned upon. Respect for elders is a key value in Vietnam; invite older people to sit down before you do so. When visiting hill-tribe and ethnic-minority homes and villages, only enter a home if invited and ask before you photograph someone.

GREETINGS

Showing deference with a smile and a nod is typical when meeting people on the street. Handshakes are acceptable, but should be delivered with two hands. When handing an item to a person, such as money or a business card, it is customary to hold it with both hands.

SIGHTSEEING

Always dress respectfully and cover shoulders and knees when visiting a place of worship. When entering temples and pagodas, remove your footwear. On the beach, bikinis and swimwear are perfectly acceptable but, for women, going topless is illegal. When traveling to and from the beach, always cover up. Begging is rare in Vietnam, though it's not unusual to be approached by children selling trinkets, and it's best not to encourage them by buying anything. The money will not go toward their education—the more money they make, the less time they'll spend in school.

OUT ON THE TOWN

Dressing up for meals is reserved for key events and upscale restaurants. A simple "excuse me" should grab a waiter's attention in tourist restaurants, although in local haunts "em oi" will bring more success. Learning a few basic phrases in Vietnamese will help endear you in every situation, especially if an English menu or speaker is not available. Explain with good humor "*toi khong noi tieng Viet*" (I don't speak Vietnamese), then look at what other people are eating and point at something you think you'd like. Food orders come in no particular order and are served as they are cooked. To ask for the check say "*tinh tien*" or use the internationally recognized hand signal. In rural areas drunken behavior and to some extent smoking by women is frowned upon.

If you are invited to dine at someone's house, a small gift is always highly appreciated, even though the recipient may simply acknowledge the gift and carry on as before; this is not a sign of disrespect. To find something appropriate, ask staff at your hotel—it's surprisingly easy to make a mistake, particularly with flowers, as different blooms have different meanings.

PHONES

Due to cheap mobile networks and excellent countrywide coverage, cell phones have taken Vietnam by storm, so phone booths are rare, mostly found in post offices and rural village Internet cafés. Landline phones hardly exist outside of hotels and businesses. Generally, if you need to make a call within the country, all you need to do is ask and a cell phone will be thrust upon you with no expectation of payment. You cannot place collect calls from Vietnam.

AREA AND COUNTRY CODES

The country code for Vietnam is 84. When dialing a Vietnamese number from abroad, drop the initial "0" from the local area code. Some city codes follow:

Dalat, 0263; Danang, 0236; Haiphong, 0225; Halong Bay, 0203; Hanoi, 024; Ho Chi Minh City, 028; Hoi An, 0235; Hue, 0234; Nha Trang, 0258; Phan Thiet, 0252; Phong Nha, 0232; Vung Tau, 0254.

INTERNATIONAL CALLS

To call overseas from Vietnam, dial 00 + the country code (1 for the United States and Canada, 61 for Australia, 64 for New Zealand, and 44 for the United Kingdom) + the area code + the number. Remember when calling that Vietnam is 7 hours ahead of Greenwich Mean Time, 12 hours ahead of Eastern Standard Time, and 15 hours ahead of Pacific Standard Time.

Most hotels have international direct-dial (IDD), which they advertise as a selling point and which you need in order to call overseas The connection can be surprisingly clear, but calls cost a small fortune; it's better to take advantage of the free Wi-Fi and use services such as Skype, Face Time, or Viber. International calls made using a local mobile network are also cheap.

CALLING WITHIN VIETNAM

Vietnam has an incredibly efficient operator service. Call 102 for local and international directory assistance. Calling 1080 will put you in touch with an information service staffed partly by English speakers who can tell you everything from the current time to what percentage of Vietnam's population is under the age of 20. If they don't know the answer offhand, they will take your number and call you back.

Most public phones, which accept only phone cards and no coins, are found in post offices. Look for a blue sign that reads "Dien Thoai Cong Cong." Local calls cost 5–10 cents and international calls start from as little as 10 cents a minute. You can make local calls for free from most hotels. Even if your hotel room doesn't have a phone, you can usually make calls from the reception desk. Once in a while you will be charged around 25–50 cents to make a call. When making a local call, the area code is not necessary.

LONG-DISTANCE CALLS

To make an intercity or interregional telephone call, dial 0, then the city's area code + the number. For instance, to call Danang from Hanoi, dial 0236 + the number.

CELL PHONES

Cell phones in Vietnam operate on the GSM900 system. Cell phones from Europe, Australia, and Asia can receive and place roaming calls in Vietnam, but this can make local calls expensive—charges are made for duration of call, exchange rate variation, and roaming charges at both ends. It's far cheaper to buy a local prepaid SIM card to fit your cell phone, and these can be purchased at phone stores and shops displaying Vietel Telecom signs. A SIM card, local phone number and $4.70 of credit costs less than $10 and in the unlikely event that it does not fit your phone, a basic Samsung or Nokia handset will cost no more than $15. Top-up cards come in various denominations from $7 to $23.50 and can be purchased from any street vendor. The standard rate for an international call is approximately 20 cents per minute, for in-country calls and texts the price is negligible, and dependent on speed; unlimited 3G can be added for between $3.30 and $5.65 per month.

Cell-Phone Rental and Services **Vietel Telecom** ⊕ www.vieteltelecom.vn.

■ CUSTOMS AND DUTIES

When shopping abroad, keep receipts for all purchases. Upon reentering the country, be ready to show customs officials what you've bought. If you feel a duty is incorrect, appeal the assessment. If you object to the way your clearance was handled, note the inspector's badge number. In either case, first ask to see a supervisor. If the problem isn't resolved, write to the appropriate authorities, beginning with the port director at your point of entry.

Keep in mind that it is illegal to export antiques unless you get special permission to do so. If you purchase an item that looks like an antique, be sure to get a note from the owner of the store stating that it is not.

Information **U.S. Customs and Border Protection** ☎ 202/325–8000 from outside U.S., 877/227–5511 within U.S. ⊕ www.cbp.gov.

Do not attempt to bring anything that could be considered subversive (such as political or religious materials) into Vietnam, as you may receive a hefty fine, be detained, or, in extreme cases, jailed. It is a requirement to declare foreign currency over $5,000 or Vietnamese currency in excess of 15,000,000d. Contact the Embassy of Vietnam for more information on customs requirements.

Information **Embassy of Vietnam** ✉ 1233 20th St. NW, Suite 400, Washington, D.C. ☎ 202/861–0737 ⊕ www.vietnamembassy-usa.org.

■ EATING OUT

Vietnam has a variety of eateries, from street peddlers selling food and drinks from handcarts or shoulder poles to elegant international restaurants. In between are small, basic Western-style restaurants serving Vietnamese food; stalls or stands on the street, surrounded by small plastic stools, serving very cheap and often quite good rice and noodle dishes; hip venues (including hotel restaurants) serving Vietnamese, Chinese, Japanese, French, American, Italian, or other international cuisines; and tourist cafés, which cater primarily to budget travelers and serve mediocre Western and Vietnamese dishes.

Keep in mind that Vietnam's best eating isn't found only in elegant restaurants or hotel dining rooms, but also at stalls on every street corner and in every marketplace. To taste Vietnamese favorites, you need only step out of your hotel and onto the streets. These soup, rice, noodle, and seafood kitchens are usually run by several generations of a single family, and sitting down on the low plastic chairs at one of these self-contained sidewalk operations for a bowl of *bun cha* (chopped grilled meat over vermicelli-style rice noodles) feels like joining in a family gathering.

If you stick to local restaurants, food will constitute a minor part of your travel costs. Smaller restaurants—even those serving international cuisines—are surprisingly cheap. Expect to pay international prices at hotel restaurants.

Upscale international restaurants to suit nearly every palate can be found in all major tourist destinations throughout the country.

Good, strong coffee and Vietnamese tea are served with breakfast, after dinner, and any time of day at local cafés.

PRECAUTIONS

It's important to be careful of what you eat and drink in Vietnam. Fresh, leafy vegetables are known to carry parasites, so avoid those of dubious origin or those likely to have been washed in tap water. That said, dining at street-side food stands can be as safe as or safer than eating in restaurants, especially in cities. Ho Chi Minh City in particular has a celebrated street-food scene. The stands often serve fresher food than many restaurants because they have a faster turnover; they also prepare the food in front of you. Be more cautious with food stands once you are out of urban areas. It is imperative that you avoid drinking tap water, ice is always made from pure, filtered water in large factories and then delivered to households, street food stands and restaurants, ask if you are unsure. Most decent restaurants either make their own ice using filtered water or buy ice in bulk from the freezer warehouses. Your best bet is to drink bottled water, particularly La Vie and Aquafina brands; be sure to check the spelling on the container as there are many knockoffs, some quite amusing, and check the seal on the cap to make sure the bottle hasn't been refilled.

Keep in mind that monosodium glutamate (MSG) is used in many dishes in Vietnam, particularly in the ubiquitous pho. If you don't want MSG in your food, ask—the cooks may not have already added it to the dish. Many people are unfamiliar with the term MSG, so try referring to it by a popular brand name, Ajinomoto, or in Vietnamese, *mi chinh*.

MEALS AND MEALTIMES

Despite their slim build, the Vietnamese graze throughout the day and unless you are in a very small village after 8 pm you only need stand outside your hotel for two minutes before a mobile food vendor crosses your path. Breakfast vendors usually set up at first light, serving noodle soup, pho or bun bo, rice congee, chao or baguettes, banh mi, most usually sell out by 9 am. Small local restaurants offering a similar menu open at around 7 am. Tourist restaurants generally open around 8 am and hit the floor running with their full menu, including a few Western breakfast options like bacon and eggs and fresh fruit. Practically every hotel will include a breakfast buffet of Vietnamese and Western staples in their rates, although standards vary. Lunch is typically served between 11:30 and 2 and dinner is available anytime after 2:30, and usually before 8. Restaurants are generally open daily (except major holidays), and although the Vietnamese eat dinner

fairly early, most city restaurants remain open well into the night, even after they are supposed to close.

Unless otherwise noted, the restaurants listed in this guide are open daily for lunch and dinner. As a rule the only restaurants that accept credit cards are the more upscale places. However, if you do pay with plastic, these places normally add a 5% service charge to your bill.

WINE, BEER, AND SPIRITS

You'll find Heineken, Carlsberg, Tiger, and San Miguel, along with local beers such as Saigon Beer, Tiger, Ba Ba Ba (333), La Rue, Huda, and Halida. *Bia tuoi* (also known as *bia hoi* in Hanoi and Hoi An), a watery draft beer, is available on many city street corners; look for low plastic stools occupied by jovial, red-faced men. The popular rice wine (*ruou* or *deo*), which is similar to sake, is highly inebriating. You may want to skip the snake rice wine (with a cobra in the bottle) made "especially for men." Imported French, Italian, Australian, Spanish, Californian, and even Chilean wines are available in all main tourist destinations. Brave souls may want to pop open a bottle of the locally produced wine, Vang Da Lat, which bears the label "Product of the Thanh Ha Fertilizer Company."

▌ ELECTRICITY

To use electric-powered equipment purchased in the United States or Canada, bring a converter and adapter. The electrical current in Vietnam is 220 volts, 50 cycles alternating current (AC); in Cambodia it's 230 volts, 50 cycles. In the north and other parts of the country, wall outlets take the Continental-type plugs, with two round prongs; they use both the two round prong and flat-pin plugs in much of the south. Many of the international hotels can provide you with converters and adapters.

If your appliances are dual-voltage, you'll need only an adapter. Don't use 110-volt outlets marked "For Shavers Only" for high-wattage appliances such as blow dryers. Most laptops operate equally well on 110 and 220 volts and so require only an adapter and a surge protector.

Blackouts sometimes occur, especially in summer, when everyone uses fans and air-conditioners. Hotels usually have generators, but you may want to keep a flashlight handy if you're staying in a minihotel.

▌ EMERGENCIES

If something has been stolen from you, contact your hotel and ask them to help report the theft to the police or phone your embassy, especially regarding more costly items such as expensive jewelry or laptop computers. Also contact your embassy if your passport has been stolen or lost.

Pharmacies are found in every town and village and open daily from 7 to 11:30 and 2 to 8, most stock a limited range of prescription and nonprescription drugs (including antibiotics), which are available over the counter; always check the expiration date on drugs. Outside of these hours and for medical emergencies, seek assistance from local hospitals or clinics or from your hotel.

Contacts **Ambalance** ☎ *Area code plus/115.* **Fire** ☎ *Area code plus/114.* **Police** ☎ *Area code plus/113.*

Foreign Embassies **Consulate General of the United States** ✉ *4 Le Duan Blvd., District 1, Ho Chi Minh City* ☎ *028/3520–4200 24-hr emergency hotline.* **Embassy of the United States** ✉ *Lang Ha, Thanh Cong, Ba Dinh District, Hanoi* ☎ *024/3850–5000 24-hr emergency hotline* ⊕ *vietnam.usembassy.gov.*

Hospitals and Clinics **Family Medical Practice Ho Chi Minh City** ✉ *34 Le Duan, Ho Chi Minh City* ☎ *028/3822–7848* ⊕ *www.vietnammedicalpractice.com.* **Hanoi Family Medical Practice** ✉ *Van Phuc Diplomatic Compound, 298I Kim Ma, Hanoi* ☎ *024/3843–0748, 090/3401–919.* **Hoan My Danang Hospital** ✉ *161 Nguyen Van Linh, Danang*

☎ *0234/365–0676* ⊕ *www.hoanmy.com.* **Hue Central Hospital** ✉ *16 Le Loi, Hue* ☎ *0122/836–1270* ⊕ *www.bvtwhue.com.vn.*

Pharmacies **Pharmacies are open during regular shopping hours. For urgent requirements outside these hours, you should go to the nearest hospital.**

▌ HEALTH

Temperatures in Vietnam can get extremely high; drink plenty of bottled water and use common sense to avoid dehydration, heatstroke, and sunstroke. Dengue fever and malaria are risks isolated to areas in the Central Highlands—if you're not taking a prophylaxis, make sure to use mosquito repellent. Most of Vietnam is quite humid; keep a close eye on small cuts and scrapes as they can easily get infected.

Using sunscreen is recommended, especially in the south or on the coast. Sunscreen is sold in more upscale pharmacies and in stores featuring imported products. Pharmacies are plentiful and well stocked.

FOOD & DRINK

Street food is one of the more authentic ways to enjoy the Vietnam experience and is usually clean and tasty. If you do decide to indulge in frequent street dining, keep in mind the risk of parasitic infection from eating improperly handled meat. The major health risk in Vietnam is traveler's diarrhea, caused by eating contaminated fruit or vegetables or drinking contaminated water. Drink only bottled water, or water that has been boiled for several minutes, even when brushing your teeth. It's recommended you avoid eating unpeeled fruit and uncooked vegetables or those you suspect have been washed in unboiled water. Mild cases may respond to Imodium (known generically as loperamide) or Pepto-Bismol, both of which can be purchased over the counter. Drink plenty of purified water or tea—ginger (*gung*) is a good folk remedy. In severe cases, rehydrate yourself with a salt-sugar solution (½ teaspoon salt [*muoi*] and 4 tablespoons sugar [*duong*] per quart of water); if symptoms persist or worsen, seek medical assistance.

MEDICAL CARE

International clinics and hospitals in major cities offer the highest quality care but also cost more. Local hospitals are not up to the standards of Thailand, Hong Kong, or Singapore, but they are decent and occasionally employ doctors who have been trained overseas. The language barrier is an issue in local hospitals, although some doctors can speak English and French.

Hospitals and pharmacies are often undersupplied and out-of-date. Only a handful of Vietnamese doctors have top-quality Western training. Foreign insurance is not accepted in local hospitals, so you should expect to pay immediately in cash on completion of treatment. The larger hospitals in Hanoi and Ho Chi Minh City, Hue and Danang have experience treating foreigners (mainly due to motorcycle accidents, the biggest cause of injury or death of Westerners in Vietnam). Blood supply is a serious problem in Vietnam: the nation's blood banks are small and, say Western doctors, insufficiently screened.

Foreign-run medical clinics provide basic treatment, 24-hour on-call services and can arrange for emergency medical evacuation to better hospitals in other countries in the region—Medevac planes dedicated to Vietnam are on standby in Singapore. Embassies have duty officers on call to assist with logistics. If you get sick outside Hanoi or Ho Chi Minh City, get yourself to those cities as soon as possible.

Local hospitals can perform some serious emergency operations, but these hospitals are understaffed and aftercare is poor or nonexistent. If possible, it's best to avoid these hospitals altogether, but if you do end up in one, contact your embassy immediately and they will assist if you need to be evacuated to another hospital.

SHOTS AND MEDICATIONS

Tetanus-diphtheria and polio vaccinations should be up-to-date—if you haven't been immunized since childhood, consider bolstering your tetanus and polio vaccinations. If you have never contracted measles, mumps, or rubella, you should also be immunized against them. Also note: immunizations for hepatitis A and typhoid fever are advised. According to the Centers for Disease Control and Prevention (CDC), there is a risk of contracting malaria only in rural areas of Vietnam, except in the Red River delta and the coastal plain north of Nha Trang, which are safe. The CDC recommends taking mefloquine (brand name Larium) for malaria. Dengue fever occurs in Vietnam, but the risk is small except during periods of epidemic-size transmission; there is no vaccine to prevent it. Therefore, you should take precautions against mosquito bites. Malaria- and dengue-bearing mosquitoes bite at dusk and at night. No matter where you go, it's a good idea to protect yourself from mosquito-borne illnesses with a good insect repellent containing DEET, and if you're in susceptible regions, use aerosol insecticides indoors, wear clothing that covers the body, and bring mosquito nets.

If you're staying for a month or more and are traveling to rural areas, you should be vaccinated against Japanese encephalitis; for six months or more, against hepatitis B as well. Some of these vaccinations require staggered treatments, so plan ahead.

Bringing a first-aid kit with antacids, antidiarrheal, cold medicine, Band-Aids, antiseptics, aspirin, and other items you may need is a good idea. Also, know your blood type and bring enough medication to last the entire trip; you may be able to get common prescription drugs in Vietnam, but don't count on their availability or their quality. Just in case, however, have your doctor write you a prescription using the drug's generic name, because brand names vary from country to country.

Health Information **National Centers for Disease Control & Prevention** (*CDC*). ☎ *877/394–8747 international travelers' health line* ⊕ *www.cdc.gov/travel*. **World Health Organization** (*WHO*). ⊕ *www.who.int*.

OVER-THE-COUNTER REMEDIES

Pharmacies are almost as common as tea stalls in Vietnam, and many pharmacists in major cities speak English. Look for a shop with a green sign that reads *Nha Thuoc*. These usually stock painkillers (such as Panadol); eye-, nose-, and ear-drops (such as Polydexa); cold remedies (such as Tiffy); and various antibiotics— for which no prescription is needed in Vietnam. Remember to check the expiration date when buying any sort of medication.

▮ HOURS OF OPERATION

Vietnam has a tradition of afternoon siestas (especially in the countryside), which means that all activities except eating tend to stop during lunch, between 11:30 and 2. Urban life is changing rapidly in Vietnam, however, and more and more businesses are staying open during lunchtime to accommodate the increasing number of tourists and office-bound Vietnamese who use their midday break as a time to catch up on shopping or doing chores.

Cafés and restaurants are open all day, almost every day. Most sidewalk stalls serving breakfast and lunch finish by 2 and reopen for dinner about half an hour later. By 10 pm in Hanoi and 11 pm in Ho Chi Minh City, activity starts slowing down; smaller cities die down even earlier. In bigger cities more popular venues stay open much later. You can always find late-night noodle stands. Bars and nightclubs usually close at about 1 am or whenever the last customer leaves.

BANKS AND OFFICES

Vietnam for the most part has a five-day workweek. Some offices are open on Saturday morning, but many are not. Most government agencies and foreign-invested companies take the weekend off.

Banks are open on weekdays and on Saturday morning in some larger towns and cities, from 8 am to noon and then from 1:30 to 5 pm. Post offices are open seven days a week.

MUSEUMS AND SIGHTS

Most museums in Vietnam are closed on Sunday and Monday. Some are also closed on Saturday or are only open Saturday morning. It's also not uncommon to find some museums and galleries closed for a few hours at lunchtime. Pagodas are generally open from dawn to dusk, later if it's the 1st or 15th day of the lunar month.

SHOPS

Small family-run shops seem to stay open indefinitely, primarily because living and working quarters are often one and the same. Larger stores, such as supermarket chains and department stores, can stay open as late as 10 pm in major cities.

HOLIDAYS

The traditional lunar new year, known as Tet in Vietnam and celebrated throughout much of Southeast Asia, falls in January or February, depending on the lunar calendar. Note that accommodations are scarce and museums, offices, and some shops tend to shut down for days at a time during Tet. Other national holidays only tend to effect banks and government offices, these include New Year's Day, the anniversary of the founding of the Vietnamese Communist Party (February 3); Liberation Day (April 30), commemorating the day the North Vietnamese army took Saigon; International Workers Day, or May Day (May 1, the day after Liberation Day, which means a two-day holiday); Ho Chi Minh's birthday (May 19); National Day (September 2); and Christmas Day (December 25).

▮ MAIL

Main post offices (called buu dien in Vietnamese) are open daily 6:30 am to 8:30 pm; smaller and rural offices open from 7 to 5, and tend to close between 11:30 and 1:30. Mail boxes outside the post offices, but it's best to hand your mail over the counter. Sending a postcard or letter abroad should cost less than 50 cents. The local postal service is generally reliable, but for packages going abroad it's safer to use an international courier service. When mailing packages into and out of Vietnam, be aware that you usually need to show your passport and your parcels will probably be scrutinized at the post office. Note that videotapes, books, DVDs, and compact discs are especially sensitive items to ship or mail to and from Vietnam. It should take about two weeks, sometimes longer, for mail to arrive in the West from Vietnam.

Note that Vietnam does not use postal codes.

OVERNIGHT SERVICES

The U.S. Postal Service, DHL, FedEx, and UPS all have express mail services to Vietnam. Unfortunately, the service isn't always that fast: it can take from four to seven days, depending on how long the package sits in customs. DHL, FedEx, and UPS can also ship from Vietnam. Because packages sent via regular mail can take up to three months to reach North America, courier services are a far better option.

Courier Services DHL ⊠ *17 Pham Hung, Tu Liem, Hanoi* ☎ *024/3775–3999* ⊕ *www.dhl. com.vn* ⊠ *6 Thang Long St., Tan Binh District, Ho Chi Minh City* ☎ *028/3844–6203* ⊕ *www. dhl.com.vn.* **FedEx** ⊠ *14 Dang Tien Dong St., Dong Da District, Hanoi* ☎ *024/824–9054* ⊕ *www.fedex.com* ⊠ *146 Pasteur, District 1, Ho Chi Minh City* ☎ *028/119–055* ⊕ *www. fedex.com.* **FedEx** ⊠ *32 Ba Trieu, Hue* ☎ *0234/388–3738* ⊕ *www.fedex.com*

FedEx ⊠ *245 Nguyen Van Linh, Danang* ☎ *0236/365–3655* ⊕ *www.fedex.com.*

UPS ⊠ *26 Pham Van Dong, Tu Liem, Hanoi* ☎ *024/514–2888* ⊠ *18A Cong Hoa, Tan Binh District, Ho Chi Minh City* ☎ *028/811–2888* ⊕ *www.ups.com.*

POSTAL RATES

Postage is based on weight. On average, a postcard or letter to the United States or Europe costs about $1. Stamps are sold at post office (*buu dien*) branches, which are generally open daily 8–4:30, and at many hotels and shops. Usually the postal clerk will cancel the stamps on your letter and give it back to you to put into the mail slot. This policy exists in part to eliminate any possibility of stamps being peeled off your letter for resale and your letter being thrown away.

▮ MONEY

U.S. dollars are the preferred currency of exchange, but other major currencies and travelers' checks are easy to exchange at banks, exchange counters, and hotels.

Small businesses in more rural places often can't change 500,000d bills. This can be problematic because many ATMs only give out bills in this denomination. Make sure you have plenty of small change on hand to avoid potentially awkward situations.

ATMS AND BANKS

Banks and ATMs are easily found in all major cities and towns throughout Vietnam, although they have yet to catch on in rural areas like Phong Nha town, where currently there is only one ATM and it frequently runs out of cash. If you are planning on visiting smaller towns take enough Vietnamese currency to cover your expenses. Despite the easy accessibility of ATMs, the withdrawal limit is low, with most offering a maximum of 2,000,000d per transaction. For limits of 5,000,000d look for ATMs of the major banks, like Donga and HSBC. Transaction charges are set between 20,000d and 55,000d and it's possible to make multiple transactions at a time, although most Western card companies frown upon this behavior and it's not unusual for the ATM to retain your card after the third attempt. All ATMs have an English-language option and accept Visa, MasterCard, Cirrus,

Maestro, Plus, and JCB Network cards. For larger sums you'll need to go to the counter and show your passport and card. Withdrawals are charged at 2% of the total amount, Western Union has offices throughout the cities if you need to make a withdrawal outside of banking hours.

AVERAGE COSTS

Be aware that Vietnam has an official dual-pricing system, so foreigners often are expected to pay more than double what locals do for trains, buses, flights, and other goods and services. In 1999 an official decree banned dual pricing at temples and tourist sites, but despite this rule, higher entrance fees for foreigners remain the norm.

It's standard practice throughout Vietnam for tourist businesses to pay commission to guides, hotel staff, drivers, and anyone who introduces you to their business. In most circumstances the business takes the rap for the fee, but may provide an inferior tour or service because of their outlay in commissions. The worst offenders are in the busiest tourist destinations; the Mekong Delta, Nha Trang, Hoi An, Hue, and Halong Bay. Before committing, always do your research and take advice from people who have used the company. Similarly, drivers of private cars and tour buses, will park at restaurants or at shops where he has previously arranged commissions, meaning you will pay over the odds. If it's a tour bus, you are unlikely to have a choice, but with a private car you can ask to be taken elsewhere if you're unhappy with his choice.

CREDIT CARDS

Credit cards have yet to catch on as a form of payment in Vietnam, but Visa and MasterCard are accepted at most large international hotels, upscale restaurants, better shops, large tour operators, and airline agencies. Few establishments accept American Express or Diners International cards so it's best to check beforehand. For all credit card purchases you will be charged a 2%–3% transaction fee, although some restaurants, hotels, and shops sometimes insist on a service charge of up to 5%. Note that travelers' checks are accepted in Vietnam by very few places and especially not in rural areas and small towns.

CURRENCY AND EXCHANGE

The official currency is the dong. The largest denomination is 500,000 (approximately $23.50), followed by 200,000, 100,000, 50,000, 20,000 and 10,000, which all come as plastic coated bills. Smaller (paper) bills come in 5,000, 2,000, 1,000, and to a lesser extent 500 denominations. Although bank notes come in various colors and sizes, some are difficult to differentiate. Two good examples of this are the blue 500,000d bill, which looks remarkably similar to the 20,000d, and the red 200,000d, which is easily confused with the 10,000d. Keep these larger bills separate to avoid expensive mistakes. The bank exchange rate remains stable and the dong trades at approximately 21,000d to the U.S. dollar, and although some markets, local shops, hotels, and restaurants accept U.S. dollars, merchants set their own rate, which is usually lower than the bank. Sacom, Donga, or Vietcom Bank, have numerous branches all over the country and give the official government rate. International banks like HSBC have a presence in Vietnam and provide extensive banking services, including currency exchange, cash transfers, and cash advances on credit cards. At currency exchange booths you can exchange money quickly without showing your passport, but rates for smaller bills are not competitive and they will not accept torn or marked notes.

In smaller towns where banks or exchange booths are not an option, you can exchange U.S. dollars to dong in gold shops. However, this practice is technically illegal, exchange rates are usually poor, and it's not unusual to be short changed, so this should only be considered as a last resort. If there's no alternative, be sure to agree on an acceptable rate and check the currency for torn bills when it is handed over. It's also illegal for many smaller establishments to accept payments in anything but dong, but such rules are widely ignored. U.S. dollars are accepted at almost every private business, but many state enterprises—including trains—only accept dong. It's recommended that you carry both dollars and dong with you at all times.

Google does currency conversion. Just type in the amount you want to convert and an explanation of how you want it converted (e.g., "14 Swiss francs in dollars"), and then voilà. Oanda.com also allows you to print out a handy table with the current day's conversion rates. XE.com is another good currency conversion website.

▌ PACKING

For warm weather, bring cotton, linen, and any other natural-fiber clothing that allows your skin to breathe and is easy to wash. You can get your laundry done very inexpensively (a dollar a kilo) at shops and stands outside most hotels, although you may not want to give them your delicate items. Pack a light raincoat or umbrella during the rainy season and warmer clothing in winter and early spring, if you are traveling the length of Vietnam check the climate for each region as temperatures vary hugely. Dress in Vietnam is generally informal, except during meetings. Shorts are acceptable for both men and women, although women may feel more comfortable in longer shorts or skirts.

Sandals, nylon or canvas sneakers, and walking shoes are fine for the cities and more developed parts of the country. Hiking boots are recommended if you're going to head into the hills or onto trails or if you are traveling during the rainy season. Keep in mind that you must remove your shoes when entering most temples, so you may want to bring ones that are hassle-free. A hat and sunblock are always good ideas.

In your carry-on luggage, pack an extra pair of eyeglasses or contact lenses and enough of any medication you take to last a few days longer than the entire trip. You may also ask your doctor to write a spare prescription using the drug's generic name, because brand names may vary from country to country. In luggage to be checked, never pack prescription drugs or valuables. To avoid customs and security delays, carry medications in their original packaging.

Pack mosquito repellent and a first-aid kit (with, perhaps, antacids, antidiarrheal, cold medicine, Band-Aids, and antiseptics). Other items to consider are a Swiss-army knife, prophylactics, feminine hygiene products, packs of tissues (toilet paper is not always supplied in public places), moist towelettes or liquid hand sanitizer. Diapers and baby formula are available in Vietnam, but you may not be familiar with the brand and they are surprisingly expensive; unless space is tight, it's preferable to bring your own.

▌ PASSPORTS AND VISAS

Many reputable travel agencies offer pre-arranged visas, which are available to citizens of most countries, including the United States, but only to those landing in Hanoi, Ho Chi Minh City, or Danang. This makes for a convenient option for those who don't live near a Vietnamese consulate, but note that in high season, you may be stuck waiting in line for some time. You'll need to pay your visa fee in cash; as of this writing, the cost for American citizens is $45 for a one- or three-month single entry visa, $65 for a 30-day multiple-entry visa, and $95 for a longer multiple-entry visa.

Make two photocopies of the data and visa page of your passport (one for someone at home and another for you, carried separately from your passport). If you lose your passport, promptly call the nearest embassy or consulate and the local police.

U.S. passport applications for children under age 14 require consent from both parents, or legal guardians, and both must appear together to sign the application. If only one parent appears, he or she must submit a written statement from the other parent authorizing passport issuance for the child. A parent with sole authority must present evidence of it when applying; acceptable documentation includes the child's certified birth certificate listing only the applying parent, a court order specifically permitting this parent's travel with the child, or a death certificate for the nonapplying parent. Application forms and instructions are available on the website of the U.S. State Department's Bureau of Consular Affairs (⊕ *www.travel.state.gov*).

Visas for Cambodia are available online at ⊕ www.evisa.gov.kh. The fee is $30, plus a $7 processing fee, payable online. Allow at least three days for processing, after which your visa will be emailed to you. Print it out and bring it with you.

Information Embassy of Vietnam ✉ *1233 20th St. NW, Suite 400, Washington, D.C.* ☎ *202/861–0737* 🖷 *202/861–0917* ⊕ *www. vietnamembassy-usa.org.*

▋ RESTROOMS

Hotels, guesthouses, and restaurants that cater to tourists usually have Western-style toilets, at least in bigger towns. Plumbing can be an issue, so if there is a garbage can in the cubicle use it for toilet paper and save your host from dealing with any blockages. In bus and train stations, on trains themselves, and in restaurants in the countryside, you will occasionally find that squat toilets are your only option. Most of these do not flush; use the plastic ladle to splash water around and keep a stash of toilet paper handy. Many public toilets charge a 2,000d entry fee, which entitles you to a scrap of toilet paper, usually kept in a

basket near the front door. Unless you are really desperate, avoid the public toilets in parks and on street corners. In remote areas the "bathroom" may actually be a small room with a sloped cement floor or a rickety platform perched over a pond.

▋ SAFETY

Although it is widely accepted that Vietnam is safe for tourists, pickpocketing and bag snatching are becoming serious problems in Ho Chi Minh City, Nha Trang, and Hanoi; even Hoi An is beginning to see more petty crime. You may want to remove any jewelry that stands out. The rest of Vietnam's cities are safer—the biggest hassles are being stared at and being overcharged for purchases. You should take standard precautions, however.

In the big cities do not walk with your bag or purse on your street-side shoulder or leave it at your feet in a cyclo or in the basket of a bicycle, as the snatch-and-ride stealing method (on a motorbike or bicycle) is common. Put your wallet in your front pocket or in a zipped-up bag or purse, and be extra alert when you enter busy markets or crowds. Also, watch out for children or elderly people who may be acting as decoys or pickpocketing you themselves. When sitting in a street café or in a cyclo, make sure you either hold your bag in your lap with your hands through the straps or put the straps around your neck; if you do put it at your feet, wrap its handles around your ankles so no one can grab it. If someone does steal your bag, don't pursue the thief—assailants often carry knives. As for cyclos, motorbike taxis, and Easy Riders, be sure to negotiate a price before you get on, don't go with a driver you don't feel comfortable with, and don't travel by cyclo or motorbike taxi after dark, especially in cities. You should also avoid parks at night in large cities. Don't wear a money belt or a waist pack, both of which peg you as a tourist. If you carry a purse, choose one with a zipper and a thick strap that you can drape across your body; adjust the length so that the purse sits in front of you at or above hip level. Store only enough money in the purse to cover casual spending. Distribute the rest of your cash and any valuables between a deep front pocket, an inside jacket or vest pocket, and a hidden money pouch. Do not reach for the money pouch in public.

You should avoid leaving passports, cameras, laptop computers, and other valuables in your hotel room, unless the room has a safe. If it doesn't, consider leaving your valuables in the hotel's safe or with the front desk. It is advised that you leave your passport in your hotel safe and carry only a photocopy with you while out exploring. In cheaper accommodations, it's normal for the reception desk to hold your passport for the duration of your stay. If they do, demand that it is kept in the hotel safe and not, as is common, kept in an unlocked drawer with all the other guests' passports. Always check that the correct passport is returned to you when you check out.

Vietnam is a relatively safe place for women travelers. Female travelers seem to encounter more hassles—such as grabbing and heckling—in the less visited, rural areas. Walking alone or taking a solo cyclo or motorbike taxi ride at night is best avoided; if you're taking a taxi alone at night, sit in the back seat. Finally, don't venture too far down deserted beaches alone. As anywhere, use your common sense.

Dozens of Vietnamese are killed every year by unexploded war ordnances, but it is very unlikely you will visit any danger areas. If you are unsure, be sure to travel with an experienced guide.

Though both Vietnam and Cambodia are generally peaceful countries, it's important to check the Department of State website for guidance or travel alerts before making plans to travel.

Advisories U.S. Department of State
⊕ *travel.state.gov.*

▌ TAXES

VALUE-ADDED TAX

Vietnam's VAT tax is 10% on luxury items such as alcohol and cigarettes; 10% for hotels, bars, and nightclubs; and 5% for most other goods and services. Larger hotels, especially state-owned and joint-venture operations, often add another 5% service tax. Ask about added taxes before checking in or ordering.

A new VAT refund program for tourists allows travelers flying out of Hanoi, Danang or Ho Chi Minh City to be refunded for the VAT value incurred on invoiced purchases of 2,000,000d (about $100) or more made within the previous 30 days. A service charge of less than 15% of the VAT refund is charged, and certain goods—especially those whose export is prohibited—are ineligible for the refund. Refund counters in the departure area provide travelers who have cleared immigration their refunds in dollars or other currencies.

▌ TIME

Vietnam is 7 hours ahead of Greenwich Mean Time, 15 hours ahead of Los Angeles, 12 hours ahead of New York, 7 hours ahead of London, and 3 hours behind Sydney. Daylight saving time is not observed.

▌ TIPPING

Tipping is a fairly new concept in Vietnam and is appreciated but not typically expected. Many higher-end restaurants and hotels in Vietnam include 5% service fees in the bill, but if you feel you've received good service, a tip is always welcome. Although it's not necessarily expected, tour guides are more than happy to receive a tip if you enjoyed their services. When tipping service staff, do so in dong.

TIPPING GUIDELINES FOR VIETNAM

Bartender	Not expected, but if service is good leave 10% of your final bill
Bellhop	20,000d to 40,000d, depending on the level of the hotel
Hotel Concierge	20,000d or more, if he or she performs a service for you
Hotel Doorman	20,000d to 40,000d if he helps you get a cab
Hotel Maid	20,000d to 40,000d a day (either daily or at the end of your stay, in cash)
Hotel Room-Service Waiter	20,000d to 40,000d per delivery, even if a service charge has been added
Porter at Airport or Train Station	10,000d per bag
Xe Om (motorbike) Driver	20,000d to 40,000d depending on distance traveled
Taxi Driver	10%, but round up the fare to the next dollar amount
Tour Guide	10% of the cost of the tour
Cyclo driver	20,000d for shorter journeys or 10% of the cost of a tour
Waiter	10% is the norm at high-end restaurants; nothing additional if a service charge is added to the bill
Restroom attendants	Attendants in public facilities expect some small change or 5,000d

▌TOURS

TOURS AND PACKAGES

GROUP TOURS

Among companies that sell tours to Vietnam, the following are nationally known, have a proven reputation, and offer plenty of options.

Abercrombie & Kent ☎ 800/554–7016 ⊕ www.abercrombiekent.com. **Orient Flexi-Pax Tours** ☎ 800/545–5540 ⊕ www.orientflexipaxtours.com. **Pacific Bestour** ☎ 973/726–8887 in U.S. ⊕ www.bestour.

com. **Pacific Delight Tours** ☎ 800/221–7179 ⊕ www.pacificdelighttours.com. **Travcoa** ☎ 888/979–4467 ⊕ www.travcoa.com.

LOCAL OPERATORS

Most state- and privately run travel agencies in Vietnam organize tours of the whole country, both from overseas or once you arrive. Privately run companies are like Handspan, Exo, and Rose Travel Service are more likely to be able to customize trips, have better English-speaking guides, and offer you a wider range of restaurant and hotel choices. The state-run operators are generally much less flexible and provide fewer options. The main drawback to organizing your trip through tour operators in Vietnam is that you generally don't have the same recourse to consumer protection as you do with many larger, American-based companies.

Contacts Exo Travel ⊠ 66A Tran Hung Dao, 3rd fl., Hoan Kiem District, Hanoi ☎ 024/3828–2150 ⊕ www.exotravel.com. **Handspan** ⊠ 78 Ma May, Hoan Kiem District, Hanoi ☎ 024/3926–2828 ⊕ www.handspan.com. **Rose Travel Service** ⊠ 37–39 Ly Thai To, Hoi An ☎ 098/5700–700 ⊕ www.rosetravelservice.com. **Vietnam Stay** ☎ 024/3747–3482 ⊕ www.vietnamstay.com.

SPECIAL-INTEREST TOURS

Organized tours, for groups or individuals, cover a wide range of special interests, from discovering Ho Chi Minh City's street food to bird watching, to trekking through the mountains to learn about the culture of the ethnic minorities who inhabit the northeast.

Contacts Backroads ☎ 800/462–2848 ⊕ www.backroads.com. **Backyard Travel** ☎ 800/2225–9273 ⊕ www.backyardtravel.com. **Earthwatch** ⊕ www.earthwatch.org. **Hanuman** ⊠ 80 Ma May St., Hanoi ☎ 024/3926–2828 ⊕ www.hanuman.travel. **Myths and Mountains** ☎ 800/670–6984 ⊕ mythsandmountains.com. **Smithsonian Study Tours and Seminars** ☎ 202/633–3030 ⊕ www.smithsonianassociates.org. **Trufflepig** ⊠ 58 Stewart St., Suite 401, Toronto, Ontario, Canada ☎ 416/628–1272 ⊕ www.trufflepig.com. **Vietnam Veterans of America**

Foundation ✉ *8605 Cameron St., Suite 100, Silver Spring, MD* ☎ *301/585-4000* ⊕ *www. vva.org.*

DAY TOURS AND GUIDES

By law all tour guides must hold a state license, and although this law is rarely upheld in practice, in certain locations, especially those of historical importance a licensed guide will offer a better overall experience. Licensed, English-speaking guides can be arranged through travel agencies and hotels or at the ticket offices of major tourist attractions. When hiring a car and driver for excursions, you'll usually be offered the services of a tour guide as extra, as drivers are not expected to speak much English. In popular destinations like Hue, Hoi An and the big cities it's not uncommon to be approached by language students or cyclo and xe om drivers (motorbike taxis) who want to make about $10 for half a day's work guiding you around city attractions. Although this is just as viable an option as any, make sure you understand their English before you agree on an amount. When hiring an Easy Rider or motorbike tour guide off the street, wherever possible go with a recommendation from someone who has experienced the tour. Always interview your guide, take a map and mark each destination agreed in the price and take it with you on your tour. Check what's included in the final price, especially if you are taking a multiday tour, and ask about the accommodations options. In Ho Chi Minh City, Hoi An, Danang, Hue, and Hanoi, tourism students have formed free tour companies for students to practice their trade. Although not all tours on offer are free, they make for a good introduction.

Contacts Ha Noi Free Tour Guides ✉ *Hoan Kiem District, Hanoi* ☎ *097/4596-895* ⊕ *www. hanoifreetourguides.com.* **Hoi An Express** ✉ *32 Tien Giang St., Ho Chi Minh City* ☎ *028/3547-0785, 090/8039-699* ⊕ *www. hoianexpress.com.vn.* **Hoi An Free Tours** ✉ *591 Hai Ba Trung, Hoi An* ☎ *0126/363-6234*

⊕ *www.hoianfreetour.com.* **Hue Free Tours** ✉ *Hue* ⊕ *www.hue-enter.com.*

▌ VISITOR INFORMATION

Free maps and tourist publications featuring up-to-date information on towns, cities, and events are available free from most major airports and popular destinations throughout the country. The local Vietnamese papers provide slanted news coverage with little emphasis on the arts or leisure. In Vietnam, private and state-run travel agencies, tourist cafés, and hotels are your best sources of information.

ONLINE RESOURCES

The Vietnam National Administration of Tourism operates two helpful websites: ⊕ *www.vietnamtourism.com* and ⊕ *www. vietnamtourism.gov.vn.*

VIETNAM VETERANS

The office of the Vietnam Veterans of America Foundation (VVAF) in Vietnam is involved in building long-lasting ties and increasing understanding between Vietnamese and Americans. VVAF organizes cultural exchange programs and a prosthetics clinic. Veterans returning to Vietnam are encouraged to contact VVAF, either in Hanoi or at its Maryland office. At least once a year VVAF organizes tours to Vietnam; contact the Maryland office for information.

Veterans' Resource Vietnam Veterans of America Foundation ✉ *8605 Cameron St., Suite 100, Silver Spring, MD* ☎ *301/585-4000* 🖷 *301/585-0519* ⊕ *www.vva.org* ✉ *Viet Hong Bldg., 58 Tran Nhan Tong, 4th fl., Hai Ba Trung District, Hanoi* ☎ *024/733-9444* ⊕ *www. ic-vvaf.org.*

INDEX

A

Accommodations, *432*
Air Travel, *16, 424–426*
Angkor Wat, 391
Central Coast, 199
Halong Bay and North-Central
  Vietnam, 269, 279, 287–288
Hanoi, 305, 308
Ho Chi Minh City, 40–41
Mekong Delta, 111–112
Northwest, 366
South-Central Coast, 150
Alma Courtyard 🗝️ , *216*
Amansara 🗝️ , *406–407*
Ambassador's Pagoda, *317*
Amiana Resort 🗝️ , *169*
An Bang (beach), *20, 211–212*
An Bien Park, *281*
An Hai Beach, *103*
An Hoi Night Lantern Market,
  205, 208
Ana Mandara Hue Beach
  Resort 🗝️ , *254*
Ana Mandara Villas Dalat
  Resort & Spa 🗝️ , *181*
Ancient Faifo ✕ , *212*
Ang Pagoda, *140*
Angkor Hospital for Children,
  405
Angkor National Museum, *395*
Angkor Temple Complex,
  396–398, 400–402
Angkor Thom, *397–398, 400*
Angkor Wat, *14, 389–412*
children, activities for, 404–405,
  407, 411
dining, 403–406
health and safety, 392
language, 393
lodging, 406–409
money matters, 392
nightlife and the arts, 409–411
passports and visas, 393
shopping, 411–412
tours, 393–394
transportation, 391–392
visitor information, 394
when to visit, 390–391
Antiques markets, *81, 87*
Ao Ba Om, *140*
Ao Dai Museum, *54*
Apartment and house rentals,
  432
Art shops
Angkor Wat, 411
Central Coast, 257
Hanoi, 349, 351, 352
Ho Chi Minh City, 82, 86, 87
South-Central Coast, 171–172
Art Trendy Hotel 🗝️ , *338*
AssemblyHalls, *208*
ATMs, *440–441*

AVANI Haiphong Harbour View
  Hotel 🗝️ , *284*
Avani Quy Nhon Resort & Spa
  🗝️ , *192*

B

Ba Dinh Square, *321–322*
Ba Ho Waterfall, *164–165*
Ba Na Hills, *229*
Ba Vi National Park, *359–360*
Bac Ha, *378, 380–382*
Bac Ha Market, *380*
Bac Lieu Bird Sanctuary, *145*
Bai Dai Beach, *165–166*
Bai Tu Long Bay, *297, 299–300*
Banh Cuon Gia Truyen ✕ , *327*
Banh Cuon Hai Nam ✕ , *64–65*
Banh Mi Phuong ✕ , *213*
Banjiro ✕ , *232*
Banks, *440–441*
Banteay Srei, *401–402*
Banyan Tree 🗝️ , *240*
Bao Dai's Summer Palace, *175*
Bar Betta, *344*
Bar200 ✕ , *103*
Bassac Cruises, *114*
Bat Trang Ceramic Village, *353*
Bats, *408*
Battle of Dien Bien Phu, *384*
Bay Canh Island, *102*
Beaches, *20*
Central Coast, 211–212, 231–
  232, 236–237, 239–240, 248
Halong Bay and North-Central
  Vietnam, 294
Ho Chi Minh City, 96, 99, 103
Mekong Delta, 124, 128,
  131–132
South-Central Coast, 155,
  165–166, 191, 193
Ben Thanh Market, *52*
Ben Tre, *116*
Beyond Unique Escapes (tours),
  393–394
Bho Hoong Village, *245*
Bia Hoi Corner, *312*
Bicycling
Central Coast, 220, 263
Halong Bay and North-Central
  Vietnam, 297
Hanoi, 308, 348
Ho Chi Minh City, 41
Mekong Delta, 118–119
Northwest, 366–367
tours, 47, 114–115, 263
Binh An Village 🗝️ , *97*
Binh Minh's Jazz Club, *343*
Binh Tay Market, *57*
Binh Thuy Ancient House,
  135
Bird-watching
Halong Bay and North-Central
  Vietnam, 277, 292

Ho Chi Minh City, 91, 94
Mekong Delta, 115, 122, 145
Bitexco Financial Tower, *49*
Bluebird ✕ , *335–336*
Boat and ferry travel, *426*
Halong Bay and North-Central
  Vietnam, 288, 292–293
Ho Chi Minh City, 41, 95
Mekong Delta, 112
Boating and sailing
Central Coast, 220–221
Halong Bay and North-Central
  Vietnam, 297
Hanoi, 348
South-Central Coast, 170–171
Books and movies, *414–415*
Bookworm (shop), *353*
Border crossings, *426*
Botanical Gardens (Hanoi), *322*
Bowling, *79, 348*
Brilliant Hotel 🗝️ , *235*
Buddhas, *154–155*
Bun Bo Nam Bo ✕ , *327*
Buon Ma Thuot, *185–187*
Bus Travel, *16, 426–427*
Central Coast, 199–200
Halong Bay and North-Central
  Vietnam, 269, 273, 287, 288
Hanoi, 308–309
Ho Chi Minh City, 42, 92,
  94–95, 99
Mekong Delta, 112
South-Central Coast, 150, 152
Business hours, *439*

C

Ca Mau, *144–146*
Ca Mau Market, *145*
Cai Be Floating Market, *119*
Cai Rang Floating Market,
  135–136
Cam Am (beach), *20*
CAMA ATK (pub), *343*
Cambodia Land Mine Museum,
  395–396
Can Cau Market, *380–381*
Can Gio, *92–94*
Can Gio UNESCO Biosphere
  Reserve, *94*
Can Tho, *134–138*
Can Tho Museum, *136*
Cannon Fort, *293*
Cao Dai Holy See, *21, 92*
Cao Daism, *93*
Cao Temple, *229*
Car travel, *16, 427–429*
Central Coast, 200–201
Halong Bay and North-Central
  Vietnam, 269–270, 288
Hanoi, 309
Ho Chi Minh City, 42–43
Northwest, 367
South-Central Coast, 150

Caravelle Hotel ⊞ , 49
Cat Ba Island, 292–297
Cat Ba National Park, 293
Cat Tien National Park, 172–174
Caves
Central Coast, 260
Halong Bay and North-Central Vietnam, 274, 294
Mekong Delta, 124
Cell phones, 434–435
Cemeteries, 101, 383
Central Coast, 14, 195–263
beaches, 211–212, 231–232, 236–237, 239–240, 248
children, activities for, 203–204, 211–212, 213, 214, 216, 217, 218–219, 220, 221, 222, 223, 225–226, 227, 229, 231, 234, 239–240, 244, 245, 248, 250–251, 252, 254, 255, 259, 260, 262, 263
Danang, 224–240
dining, 202, 212–216, 232–234, 251–254, 260–262
history, 205, 249
Hoi An, 203–224
Hue, 241–257
lodging, 202, 216–219, 234–235, 237–238, 240, 254–256, 262
money matters, 258
nightlife and the arts, 219–220, 235, 256–257, 262–263
Phong Nha Ke Bang National Park, 257–263
shopping, 222–224, 235–236, 257
sports and the outdoors, 220–222, 238–239, 263
top reasons to go, 197
tours, 202–203, 203–204, 227, 244, 259
transportation, 199–201, 241, 258
visitor information, 204–205, 229, 244
when to visit, 198–199
Central Highlands, 172–190
Central Market, 175, 208
Central Post Office, 49
Cham artifacts, 227
Cham Islands, 208–209
Chau Doc, 120–123
Chim Sao ✕ , 333
China Bowl Pagoda, 143
Cholon Mosque, 54, 56
Christ the King Statue, 95
Chuc Thanh Pagoda, 209
Chula Fashion Showroom (shop), 353
Churches
Halong Bay and North-Central Vietnam, 276–277, 280–281
Hanoi, 315, 323, 325
Ho Chi Minh City, 51
South-Central Coast, 189

Cinematheque, 345
Cinnamon Hotel ⊞ , 73
Circus, 344–345
Citadel, The, 245–246
City Bird Park, 145
Clay Pagoda, 143
Climate, 17
Clothing shops
Angkor Wat, 412
Central Coast, 222–224, 257
Hanoi, 350, 352, 353
Ho Chi Minh City, 82, 86
Co Loa Citadel, 354–355
Co To Island, 299
Cocobox ✕ , 213
Coconut Tree Prison, 127
Coffee Tour Resort ⊞ , 187
Command Bunker of Colonel de Castries, 382
Commune ✕ , 336
Communications, 432, 433–435
Con Dao Islands, 100–106
Con Dao Museum, 101
Cosmetics, 412
Cot Co (Citadel Flag Tower), 248
Craft shops
Angkor Wat, 411
Central Coast, 222, 257
Hanoi, 350, 352, 353
Ho Chi Minh City, 82
South-Central Coast, 171–172
Credit cards, 12, 441
Crémaillère Railway, 175, 177
Crime, 31
Cruises, 114, 135, 289–290
Cu Chi, 88, 90–91
Cu Chi Wildlife Rescue Station, 91
Cu Tunnels, 90
Cua Dai Beach, 212
Cuc Phuong National Park, 277–278
Cuisine, 17, 22–23, 406
Cuisine Wat Damnak ✕ , 403
Culinary Tours, 45–46, 311
Culture, 19, 139
Currency and exchange, 441–442
Customs and duties, 435
Cyclo Resto ✕ , 65
Cyclo travel, 43, 309

D

Dac Kim Bun Cha ✕ , 330
Dai Beach, 128
Dak Lak Museum, 185
Dalat, 174–175, 177–183
Dalat Crazy House, 177
Dalat Flower Garden, 177
Daluva ✕ , 336
Dam Sen Cultural Park, 57
Dam Sen Water Park, 56
Dam Trau Beach, 103
Dambri Falls, 173
Danang, 224–240

Danang Beach, 20, 236–239
Danang Bridges, 231
Danang Museum of Cham Culture, 229–230
Dance clubs
Hanoi, 343
Ho Chi Minh City, 76, 77
Dat Doc Beach, 103
Datanla Falls, 177–178
Dau Pagoda, 358
Deck, The ✕ , 68
Dien Bien Phu, 381–384
Dien Bien Phu Museum, 382–383
Din Co Temple, 98–99
Dinh An Village (Chicken Village), 178
Dinh Tien Hoang Temple, 273
Dining, 12, 435–436
Diving
Halong Bay and North-Central Vietnam
Ho Chi Minh City, 79, 105–106
Mekong Delta, 133
South-Central Coast, 170–171
Doc Let Beach, 166
Doi Duong Beach, 155
Dong Da Market, 257
Dong Tam Snake Farm, 116
Dong Xuan Market, 312–313
Don's-A Chef's Bistro ✕ , 336–337
Dray Sap Falls, 185
Du Ca Art Gallery, 257
Du Hang Pagoda, 280
Duk Thang School, 154
Duties, 435

E

East Mebon, 401
Eat Hoi An Street-Food Tour, 203–204
Economy, 18–19
El Gaucho ✕ , 337
Electricity, 16, 436–437
Elephant Falls, 178
Elysian Sapa Hotel ⊞ , 376
Embroidery shops, 350
Emeraldo Resort ⊞ , 275
Emergencies, 16, 427–428, 437
Escape Bar, 182–183
Essence Hanoi Hotel ⊞ , 338–339
Ethnic minorities, 379
Etiquette and behavior, 433
Evason Ana Mandara ⊞ , 169
Exo Travel, 45

F

Ferry travel. ⇨ See Boat and ferry travel
Festivals and seasonal events, 17, 209, 304, 366
Film
Hanoi, 345
Ho Chi Minh City, 77, 78, 79

Fish Sauce Factories, *127*
Fishing villages, *293–294*
FITO Museum, *56*
Floating Fish Farms, *121*
Floating Markets, *119, 135–136, 141*
Food shops
Angkor Wat, 412
Central Coast, 224
Forbidden Purple City, *246*
Forts, *293, 354–355*
4P's Pizza ✕ , *68*
French War Memorial, *383*
Front Beach Park, *96*
Fusion Maia ⬚ , *238*

G

Galerie Quynh, *85*
Gallery Vivekkevin, *83*
Ganh Hao ✕ , *97*
George's Fashion Boutique (shop), *353*
Gia Long Falls, *185*
Giac Lam Pagoda, *56*
Gift and souvenir shops
Central Coast, 224, 257
Ho Chi Minh City, 82–83
Goddess Of Mercy and Linh Ung Pagoda, *230*
Go-Karting, *133*
Golden Bell Show, *345*
Golf
Central Coast, 238–239, 240
Hanoi, 348
Ho Chi Minh City, 79–80, 98, 100
Mekong Delta, 133
South-Central Coast, 161, 171, 183
Gong Shows, *184*
Gothic North Door Cathedral, *323, 325*
Government, *18*
Green Mango ✕ , *213*
Green Village Homestay ⬚ , *137*

H

Ha Chuong Hoi Quan Pagoda, *57*
Ha My Beach, *212*
Ha Tien, *123–125*
Hai Van Pass, *231*
Haiphong, *279–285*
Haiphong Cathedral, *280–281*
Haiphong Museum, *281*
Haiphong Opera House, *281*
Halia ✕ , *337*
Halong Bay and North-Central Vietnam, *14, 20, 265–300*
beaches, 294
children, activities for, 281
dining, 271, 274–275, 282–283, 290, 294–295, 299–300
Haiphong, 279–281
Halong Bay, 285–300

history, 275
lodging, 271, 275–276, 278, 284, 290–291, 295–296, 300
nightlife and the arts, 285, 291, 296–297
Ninh Binh, 271–278
safety, 289
sports and the outdoors, 291, 297
top reasons to go, 267
tours, 270–271, 273
transportation, 269–270, 273, 287–289, 292–203
visitor information, 279
when to visit, 268, 279
Han Market, *236*
Handicraft shops
Angkor Wat, 411
Central Coast, 222, 257
Hanoi, 350, 352, 353
Ho Chi Minh City, 82
South-Central Coast, 171–172
Hang Duong Cemetery, *101*
Hang Pagoda, *140*
Hang Son Doong, *260*
Hanoi, *14, 301–360*
children, activities for, 321, 341–342, 353
dining, 326–337
festivals and events. 304
French Quarter, 315–318, 332–335, 340–341
history, 324
lodging, 337–342, 357, 360
money matters, 311
nightlife and the arts, 342–347
Old Quarter, 312–315, 327, 330–332, 338–340
shopping, 314, 349–353
side trips, 354–360
sports and the outdoors, 347–349
top reasons to go, 303
tours, 310–311
transportation, 305, 308–310, 354
visitor information, 311
West Lake, 323, 325–326, 335–337, 341–342
when to visit, 304
Hanoi Bicycle Collective, *348*
Hanoi Elegance Diamond ⬚ , *339*
Hanoi Opera House, *317, 346*
Hanoi Street Food Tour, *311*
Hanoi 3B Hotel ⬚ , *339*
Hao Lo Prison, *316–317*
Hatvala ✕ , *59, 62*
Haven Beach Lounge, *98*
Health and safety, *31, 392, 437–439*
Heritage Suites Hotel ⬚ , *407*
Hidden Hanoi (tour), *311*
Highlands Eco Tours, *189*
Hiking, *106, 297, 371, 377–378*
Hill A1: Eliane (combat site), *383*

Hill Station Deli ✕ , *375*
Hill Station Signature Restaurant ✕ , *375*
History, *19, 26–29, 50, 139, 249, 324*
H'mong Sisters (bar), *377*
Ho Chi Minh, *298*
Ho Chi Minh City, *14, 37–106*
architecture, 39
beaches, 96, 99, 103
children, activities for, 52, 56, 57, 59, 65–66, 69–70, 84, 96, 97–98, 99, 105, 106
dining, 39, 58–70, 96–97, 103–104
District 3, 40, 52–53, 66–67, 73, 86–87
Dong Khoi Street, 39, 47, 49, 59, 62–64, 77–78, 81–85
history, 39, 50
lodging, 70–74, 97–98, 99, 104–105
money matters, 44
nightlife and the arts, 75–79, 98
Pham Ngu Lao, 39–40, 51–52, 64–66, 73, 77, 85–86
shopping, 81–88
side trips, 88–106
sports and the outdoors, 79–80, 98, 100, 105–106
top reasons to go, 39
tours, 44–47, 88, 90, 93–94, 106
transportation, 40–44, 88, 92, 94–95, 98, 99, 101
visitor information, 47
when to visit, 40
Ho Chi Minh City Fine Arts Museum, *52*
Ho Chi Minh City Museum, *49–51*
Ho Chi Minh Mausoleum (Hanoi), *310*
Ho Chi Minh Museum (Hanoi), *322*
Ho Chi Minh Museum (Ho Chi Minh City), *58*
Ho Chi Minh Museum (South-Central Coast), *155*
Ho Chi Minh Trail Museum, *358*
Ho Chi Minh's Residence (Hanoi), *319*
Ho Khanh's Homestay ⬚ , *262*
Ho May Eco-Tourism Park, *96*
Ho Tram, *99–100*
Ho Tram Beach Resort ⬚ , *99*
Hoa Lu, *273–274*
Hoa Tuc ✕ , *62*
Hoan Kiem Lake, *313–314*
Hoi An, *203–224*
Hoi An Arts and Crafts Manufacturing Workshop, *220*
Hoi An Lantern Festival, *209*
Holidays, *439*
Hon Ba Island, *96*
Hon Cau Island, *102*
Hon Chong Promontory, *165*

Hospital Cave, *294*
Hot springs
Northwest, 385
South-Central Coast, 165
Hotel Continental ☒ , *51, 71*
Hotel Majestic ☒ , *51, 71*
Hotel Sofitel Legend Metropole
  Hanoi ☒ , *341*
Hotels, *12.* ⇨ *See also* Lodging
  under cities
Housewares
Angkor Wat, 411
Hanoi, 350, 351, 352
Ho Chi Minh City, 83
Hue, 241–257
Hum Lounge and Restaurant
  ✕ , *62*

I

Imperial Enclosure, *246*
Imperial Museum, *246*
Indian Kitchen ✕ , *282*
Indigenous (shop), *350*
Indigo Cat (shop), *378*
Indochine Coffee ✕ , *190*
Innoviet (tours), *114*
InterContinental Danang Sun
  Peninsula Resort ☒ , *235*
Internet, *432*
Ipa-Nima (shop), *351*
I-Resort, *164*
Island of the Coconut Monk,
  116–117
Itaca Resto Lounge ✕ , *129*
Itineraries, *32–36*

J

Jade Emperor Pagoda, *52–53*
Japanese Covered Bridge, *209*
Japanese Tombs, *209–210*
Jazz, *343*
Jeep tours, *245*
Jewelry shops
Central Coast, 224, 257
Hanoi, 351
Ho Chi Minh City, 83
John McCain Memorial, *325*
Jun Village, *184*
JW Marriot Hanoi ☒ , *342*

K

Kandal Village, *411*
Kayaking, *221, 291, 297*
Khmer Museum, *143*
Kleang Pagoda, *143–144*
Kon Tum, *188–190*
Konklor Hotel ☒ . *190*
Konklor Suspension Bridge,
  189
Koto ✕ , *335*

L

La Badiane ✕ , *333*
La Maison 1888 ✕ , *233*

La Residence Hotel and Spa
  ✕ , *255*
La Veranda ☒ . *131*
La Villa ✕ , *68–69*
Lacquerware shops
Angkor Wat, 411
Ho Chi Minh City, 83
Laguna Lang Co Golf Club,
  239–240
Lak Lake, *183–185*
Lan Ha Bay, *294*
Lang Co Beach, *239–240*
Language, *16, 31, 373, 393,*
  416–421
Lanterns ✕ , *167*
Lat Village, *178*
Le Bouchon de Saigon ✕ , *63*
Le Cafe de la Poste ✕ , *180*
Le Dai Hanh Temple, *274*
Le Gecko ✕ , *375*
Les Jardins De La Carambole
  ✕ , *253*
Life's A Beach ☒ , *192*
Linh Ong Pagoda, *225*
Linh Phuoc Pagoda, *178*
Little Menu ✕ , *213–214*
Lo Voi Beach, *103*
Long Beach, *128*
Long Hai, *98–99*
Long Son Pagoda, *165*
Lookout Tower (Cot V3), *385*
Lu people, *385*
Luna Pub ✕ , *233*
L'Usine, (boutique), *82*
L'Usine ✕ , *63*

M

Mac Cuu Tombs (Linh Temple),
  124
Magonn (shop), *350*
Mahob ✕ , *404–405*
Mai Chau, *386–388*
Mai Chau Ecolodge ☒ , *388*
Mail and shipping, *439–440*
Malls and shopping centers
Central Coast, 225
Ho Chi Minh City, 83–84,
  87–88
South-Central Coast, 171
Mango Bay Resort ☒ , *132*
Marble Mountains, *21, 225–226*
Mariamman Hindu Temple, *52*
Market Restaurant and Cooking
  School, The ✕ , *214*
Markets
Angkor Wat, 412
Central Coast, 205, 208, 236,
  257
Halong Bay and North-Central
  Vietnam
Hanoi, 312–313, 351, 353
Ho Chi Minh City, 52, 53, 57,
  84, 86, 88
Mekong Delta, 117, 119,
  133–134, 135–136, 138,
  141, 145

Northwest, 374, 380–381
South-Central Coast, 171, 175
Matoc Pagoda, *144*
Meals and mealtimes, *436*
Mekong Delta, *14, 20, 107–146*
beaches, 124, 128, 131–132
children, activities for, 120
dining, 113, 117–118, 119–120,
  122, 124, 129–130, 136–137,
  141–142, 144, 146
history, 139
lodging, 113, 118, 120, 123,
  125, 130–132, 137–138, 142,
  144, 146
nightlife and the arts, 132–133
Northern Mekong Delta,
  115–125
Phu Quoc Island, 109, 125–134
shopping, 133–134, 138
South-Central Mekong Delta,
  134–146
sports and the outdoors, 133
top reasons to go, 109
tours, 114–115, 135
transportation, 111–113, 116,
  118, 121, 123–124, 125–126,
  135, 138, 143, 145
when to visit, 111
Memorial Cemetery, *383*
Memorial House, *314–315*
Mai Gallery, *349*
Mia Resort (Nha Trang) ☒ , *169*
Mia Resort Mui Ne ☒ , *160*
Mie Cafe ✕ , *405*
Miss Wong (bar), *410*
Money matters, *16, 258, 369,*
  392, 440–442. ⇨ *Also specific*
  areas
Monsoon Restaurant and Bar
  Saigon ✕ , *65–66*
Moose and Roo, The ✕ , *331*
Mosques
Halong Bay and North-Central
  Vietnam
Ho Chi Minh City, 54, 56
Mekong Delta, 121
Motorbike travel, *429*
Angkor Wat, 392
Central Coast, 201, 263
Hanoi, 309–310
Ho Chi Minh City, 43
Northwest, 368
Mubarak Moaque, *121*
Mui Ca Mau National Park,
  145–146
Mui Nai Beach, *124*
Mui Ne, *156–162*
Municipal Theater of Ho Chi
  Minh City (Saigon Opera
  House), *51, 78*
Munirangsyaram Pagoda, *136*
Murray Guest House ☒ , *123*
Museum of History (Hanoi), *317*
Museum of History and Culture,
  210
Museum of the Vietnamese
  Revolution, *317–318*

Museums and art galleries
in Angkor Wat, 411
in Buon Ma Thuot, 185
in Can Tho, 136
in Haiphong, 281
*in Hanoi, 317–318, 319, 321,
322, 349, 352, 358*
*in Ho Chi Minh City, 49–51,
52, 53, 54, 56, 58, 82, 85,
87, 101*
in Hoi An, 210
in Hue, 246, 257
in Phan Thiet, 155
in Quang Ngai, 193–194
in Sapa, 374
in Siem Reap, 395–396
in Soc Trang, 143
in Son La, 385
in Tra Vinh, 140
Music
*Halong Bay and North-Central
Vietnam, 285*
Hanoi, 346
Ho Chi Minh City, 78
My Khe Beach, *193*
My Lai Massacre, *193*
My Son Sanctuary, *230–231*
My Tho, *115–118*
My Tho Market, *117*

N

Nam Bo Boutique Hotel ☲ , *138*
Nam Cuong Hotel ☲ , *284*
Nam Hai, The ☲ , *218*
Namaste ✕ , *334*
**National Park Turtle Nesting
Tours,** *106*
Nature reserves
Ho Chi Minh City, 94
Northwest, 373–374
Navy Museum, *281*
Neak Pean, *401*
Nem Viet ✕ , *186*
Nghe Temple, *281–282*
Ngo Van So Street ✕ , *192*
Ngoc San Temple, *315*
Ngoc Vung Island, *299*
Nguyen Shack Homestay ☲ ,
138
Nha Trang Beach, *20, 166*
Niet Ban Tinh Xa Pagoda, *95*
Nine Dynastic Urns, *246*
Ninh Binh, *271–278*
Ninh Binh Legend Hotel ☲ , *276*
Noir ✕ , *66–67*
Non Nuoc Beach, *231–232*
North Beach, *166*
Northwest, The, *14, 361–388*
Dien Bien Phu, *382–388*
*dining, 368–369, 374–376, 381,
383, 386*
festivals, 366
*lodging, 369, 376–377, 381,
383–384, 386, 387–388*
money matters, 368
nightlife and the arts, 377
people, 378, 379, 385

Sapa, 371–382
shopping, 378
*sports and the outdoors, 371,
377–378*
top reasons to go, 363
tours, 368, 370–371, 373, 380
*transportation, 366–369,
372–373, 380, 382*
visitor information, 373, 380
when to visit, 364, 366
Notre Dame Cathedral, *51*
Novotel Halong Bay ☲ , *291*
**Nui Hoang Lein Nature
Reserve,** *373–374*
Nuong Da Thang ✕ , *234*

O

Ô collective, *223*
Old French Governor's House,
102
Old French Prison & Museum,
385
Old House of Tan Ky, *210*
100 Egg Mud Bath, *164*
One-Pillar Pagoda, *322–323*
Ong Bon Pagoda, *58*
Ong Lang Beach, *128*
Ong Met Pagoda, *140*
Ong Pagoda, *136, 140–141*
Opera
Haiphong, 281
Hanoi, 316, 345–346
Oriental Central Hotel ☲ , *340*
**oSmoSe Conservation Ecotour-
ism Education** (tours), *394*
Outdoor activities and sports,
20

P

Packing, *442*
Pagodas, *21*
*Central Coast, 209, 225, 226,
230, 247, 251*
*Halong Bay and North-Central
Vietnam, 280*
*Hanoi, 317, 322–323, 325,
355–356, 358, 359*
*Ho Chi Minh City, 52–53, 56,
57, 58, 95, 102*
*Mekong Delta, 117, 119, 124,
127, 136, 140, 143, 143–144*
*South-Central Coast, 165,
178–179*
**Palace of Supreme Harmony,
Thai Hoa,** *246–247*
Palaces
Central Coast, 246–247
Hanoi, 323
Ho Chi Minh City, 49, 95–96
Northwest, 381
Paradise Cave, *260*
Park Hyatt Saigon ☲ , *72*
Parks and gardens
Central Coast, 257–263
*Halong Bay and North-Central
Vietnam, 277–278, 281, 293*

Hanoi, 322, 359–360
*Ho Chi Minh City, 52, 56,
57, 96*
Mekong Delta, 127, 145–146
*South-Central Coast, 172–174,
177*
Passports and visas, *393,
442–443*
Pearls, shopping for, *134*
People, *24–25*
Pepper House ☲ , *262*
Perfume Pagoda, *21, 359*
Phan Dinh Phung Street, *323,
325*
Phan Thiet, *154–156*
Phare (circus), *411*
Phat Diem, *276–277*
Phat Diem Cathedral, *276–277*
Phnom Bakheng, *396*
Pho Gia Ttuyen (Pho Bat Dan)
✕ , *331*
Pho Na Khe Be National Park,
20
Pho Xua ✕ , *146*
Phoenix Island, *116–117*
Phong Dien Floating Market,
136
**Phong Nha Ke Bang National
Park,** *257–263*
Phonh Nha Cave, *260*
Phono Box ✕ , *282*
Phu Hai Prison, *101*
Phu Quoc Island, *109,
125–134*
Phu Quoc National Park, *127*
Phuoc Lam Pagoda, *209*
Pilgrimage Village ✕ , *255*
Pleiku, *187–188*
Po Nagar Cham Towers, *164*
Posha Inu Towers, *155*
Pre Rup, *401*
Preah Khan, *401*
Presidential Palace, *323*
Price categories, *7*
*dining, 59, 113, 153, 202, 271,
327, 370, 392*
*lodging, 71, 113, 153, 202, 271,
338, 370, 392*
Prisons
Hanoi, 316–317
Ho Chi Minh City, 101, 102
Mekong Delta, 127
Northwest, 385
Propaganda ✕ , *63*
Pub With Cold Beer, The ✕ ,
261
Puppet Theater, *346–347*

Q

Q Bar, *219*
Quan Am Pagoda, *56*
Quan An Ngon ✕ , *334*
Quan Cong Temple. *211*
Quan 49 ✕ , *156*
Quan Lan Island, *299*
Quan Thanh Temple, *325–326*
Quan Ut Ut ✕ , *66*

Quang Ngai, *192–194*
Quang Thang House, *211*
Quy Hoa Leper Colony, *191*
Quy Nhon, *191–192*
Quy Nhon Beach, *191*

R

Racha Room ✕ , *63*
Red Bridge Cooking School, *210*
Red Sand Dunes, *157*
Restaurant Benkay ✕ , *334*
Restrooms, *443*
Reunification Palace, *49*
Rex Hotel 🗔 , *72*
Rider Café ✕ , *186*
Rock climbing, *80, 297*
Rock music, *285*
Roluos Temples, *402*
Rong Houses, *189*
Rory's Beach Bar, *132–133*
Ruby Hotel 🗔 , *383–384*

S

Safety concerns, *443–444*
Saigon Café, *285*
St. Joseph's Cathedral, *315*
Salon Natasha (gallery), *349*
Sam Mountain, *121–122*
Sandals ✕ , *158*
Sao Beach, *128*
Sapa, *371–382*
Sapa Essence ✕ , *375*
Sapa Market, *374*
Sapa Museum, *374*
Sapa O'Chau (tours), *373*
Sapa Sisters (tours), *373*
Scuba diving, *221–222*
Sea Lake, *188*
Shack Vietnam, The ✕ , *168*
Shinta Mani 🗔 , *408*
Shoe shops
Central Coast, 222–224, 257
Ho Chi Minh City, 84
Shopping, *21.* ⇨ *See also* under specific cities
Shrines, *21*
Si La people, *378*
Siem Reap, *395–396*
Six Senses Con Dao 🗔 , *105*
Snorkeling
Central Coast, 221–222
Halong Bay and North-Central Vietnam
Ho Chi Minh City, 79, 105–106
Mekong Delta, 133
Soc Trang, *142–144*
Soccer, *348–349*
Sofitel Plaza Hotel 🗔 , *342*
Sojourn Boutique Villas 🗔 , *408*
Son La, *384–386*
Son My Memorial and Museum, *193–194*
Song Gia Resort 🗔 , *284*
Sophie's Art Tour, *46*

Soul Kitchen ✕ , *216*
South-Central Coast and Highlands, *14, 147–194*
beaches, 155, 165–166, 191, 193
Central Highlands, 172–190
children, activities for, 159, 160, 169, 170, 174, 177, 170
dining, 153, 155–156, 157–159, 166–168, 179–181, 184, 186–187, 189–190, 191–192
history, 193
lodging, 153, 156, 159–160, 169–170, 173–174, 181–182, 184–185, 187, 188, 190, 192, 194
Nha Trang, 162–172
nightlife and the arts, 160–161, 182–183
North of Nha Trang, 190–194
shopping, 171–172
Southern Coast, 153–162
sports and the outdoors, 161–162, 170–171, 183
top reasons to go, 149
tours, 163, 170–171, 174–175, 185, 187–188, 189
transportation, 150, 152–153, 154
visitor information, 162
when to visit, 150
Spas
Central Coast, 240, 255
Ho Chi Minh City, 84, 86, 87
Northwest, 374
South-Central Coast, 181, 192
Special-interest tours, 445–446
Spice House ✕ , *130*
Sports and the outdoors. ⇨ *See under specific cities*
Su Muon Pagoda, *127*
Sun Wheel, *231*
Suoi Tranh (waterfall), *127*
Surfing, *221*
Symbols, *12*

T

Ta Prohm, *400*
Ta Lai Longhouse 🗔 , *174*
Tadioto (music club), *343–344*
Tam Coc, *274*
Tam Coc Garden Resort 🗔 , *276*
Tam Dao Hill Station, *356–357*
Tam Son Hoi Quan Pagoda, *58*
Tam Thai Tu Pagoda, *226*
Tan Dinh Market, *53*
Tan My Design (shop), *350*
Tao Dan Park, *52*
Tapas Eco-Lodge 🗔 , *376–377*
Taxes, *444*
Taxi travel, *429–430*
Halong Bay and North-Central Vietnam, 289
Hanoi, 310–311
Ho Chi Minh City, 43–44, 95
Mekong Delta, 112

Tay Ho Temple, *326*
Tay Ninh, *92*
Tay Phuong Pagoda, *355–356*
Telephones, *434–435*
Temple Club ✕ , *63–64*
Temple of Literature (Hanoi), *319, 321*
Temple of Literature (Hue), *247*
Temples
Angkor Wat, 396–402
Central Coast, 211, 229, 247
Halong Bay and North-Central Vietnam, 273, 274, 281–282
Hanoi, 315, 325–326
Ho Chi Minh City, 52, 98–99
Mekong Delta, 124
Phan Thiet, 155
Textiles, *85*
Thach Dong Cave Pagoda, *124*
Thai Giang Pho Waterfall, *381*
Thang Long Water Puppet Theater, *347*
Thanh Toan Bridge, *247*
Thao Dien Boutique Hotel 🗔 , *74*
Thap Ba Hot Spring Center, *165*
Thap Doi Cham Towers, *191*
Thay Pagoda, *355–366*
Theater
Hanoi, 345–346
Ho Chi Minh City, 78, 79
Thich Ca Phat Dai Pagoda, *95*
Thien Ha Pagoda, *57*
Thein Mu Pagoda, *247*
Thien Vuong Pagoda, *178–179*
Thom Beach, *128*
Thuan An Beach, *248*
Tiger Cages, *102*
Time, *16, 444*
Timing the visit, *17*
Tinh Tam Lake, *248*
Tipping, *444–445*
Tomb of Dong Khanh, *248, 250*
Tomb of Duc Duc, *250*
Tomb of Gia Long, *248*
Tomb of Khai Dinh, *247–248, 250*
Tomb of Minh Mang, *250*
Tomb of Tu Duc, *248, 250*
Tombs, *209–210, 247–248, 250–251*
Tonle Sap, *395*
Tours, *445–446*
Towers
Central Coast, 248
In Nha Trang, 164
in Phan Thiet, 155
South-Central Coast, 191
Tra Ban Island, *299*
Tra Su Bird Sanctuary, *122*
Tra Vinh, *138, 140–142*
Tran Family Chapel, *211*
Tran Hung Dao Street, *318*
Train travel, *16, 430–431*
Central Coast, 201
Halong Bay and North-Central Vietnam, 270, 289

Hanoi, 310
Ho Chi Minh City, 44
Northwest, 368–369
South-Central Coast, 152–153, 175, 177
Tran Quac Pagoda, 21, 325
Trang An Landscape Complex, 274
Transportation, 16, 424–431
Tre Lon Island, 102–103
Truc Lam Pagoda, 179
Trung Nguyen Coffee Village, 185–186
Tu Hieu Pagoda, 251
Turtles, 106

U

U Minh Cajeput Forest, 146

V

Valley of Love, 179
Value-added tax, 444
Van Don Island, 299
Van Long Motel ⊡, 184–185
Van Son Tu Pagoda, 102
Van Thanh Mieu Pagoda, 119
Van Thanh Park, 57
Van Thuy Tu (The Whale Temple), 155
Vancouver Hotel ⊡, 276
Vedana Lagoon and Spa ⊡, 240
Victoria Sapa Hotel ⊡, 377

Victoria Spa, 374
Victory Monument, 186
Vietnam Central Circus, 344–345
Vietnam Military History Museum, 321
Vietnam Museum of Ethnology, 321
Vietnam National History Museum, 53
Vietnam National Tuong Theatre, 346
Vietnam veterans, 446
Vietnam Women's Museum, 318
Villa Royale ✕, 70
Villa Song Saigon ✕, 74
Villa Vista Highlands Home ⊡, 182
Vinh Hung Heritage Hotel ⊡, 217
Vinh Long, 118–120
Vinpearl Land, 127, 164
Visas, 393, 442–443
Visitor information, 446
Vocabulary, 393, 414–421
Vua Meo, 381
Vung Tau, 94–98
Vung Tau Lighthouse, 96

W

Water sports
Halong Bay and North-Central Vietnam, 291, 297
South-Central Coast, 161–162

Waterfalls
Mekong Delta, 127
Northwest, 381
South-Central Coast, 164–165, 173, 177–178, 185
Water Puppetry, 346–347
Weather, 16
Websites, 16, 446
West Lake, 323, 325–326, 335–337, 341–342
When to go, 17
Whisper of Nature ⊡, 296
White Palace, 95–96
Wildlife-watching, 106
Wooden Church, 189
Work Saigon ✕, 67

X

Xu ✕, 64
Xuan Huong Lake, 177

Y

Yellow Submarine, (bar), 410
Yen Ninh Restaurant ✕, 383
Yoga, 222

PHOTO CREDITS

Fodor's VIETNAM

Publisher: Amanda D'Acierno, *Senior Vice President*

Editorial: Arabella Bowen, *Editor in Chief*; Linda Cabasin, *Editorial Director*

Design: Tina Malaney, *Associate Art Director*; Chie Ushio, *Senior Designer*

Photography: Jennifer Arnow, *Senior Photo Editor*; Mary Robnett, *Photo Researcher*

Production: Linda Schmidt, *Managing Editor*; Evangelos Vasilakis, *Associate Managing Editor*; Angela L. McLean, *Senior Production Manager*

Maps: Rebecca Baer, *Senior Map Editor*; Mark Stroud (Moon Street Cartography); *Cartographer*

Sales: Jacqueline Lebow, *Sales Director*

Marketing & Publicity: Heather Dalton, *Marketing Director*; Katherine Punia, *Publicity Director*

Business & Operations: Susan Livingston, *Vice President, Strategic Business Planning*; Sue Daulton, *Vice President, Operations*

Fodors.com: Megan Bell, *Executive Director, Revenue & Business Development*; Yasmin Marinaro, *Senior Director, Marketing & Partnerships*

Writers: Barbara Adam, Duncan Forgan, Sophie Friedman, Caroline Mills, Adrian Vrettos

Editors: Róisín Cameron (lead project editor), Penny Phenix

Production Editor: Evangelos Vasilakis

4th Edition

ISBN 978-1-101-87822-4

ISSN 1520-4979

All details in this book are based on information supplied to us at press time. Always confirm information when it matters, especially if you're making a detour to visit a specific place. Fodor's expressly disclaims any liability, loss, or risk, personal or otherwise, that is incurred as a consequence of the use of any of the contents of this book.

SPECIAL SALES

This book is available at special discounts for bulk purchases for sales promotions or premiums. For more information, e-mail specialmarkets@penguinrandomhouse.com.

PRINTED IN THE UNITED STATES OF AMERICA

10 9 8 7 6 5 4 3 2 1

ABOUT OUR WRITERS

Barbara Adam fell in love with Vietnam during a cycling trip with her father in 2007. Four months later she quit her job as a political and financial journalist in Australia and returned to Vietnam for a career break of "three months or so." Several years down the track, Barbara now runs street-food tours in Ho Chi Minh City with her Vietnamese husband, in between wrangling their two kids and writing about Vietnam and its food. For this edition, Barbara revised and updated the Ho Chi Minh City; Mekong Delta; and South Central Coast and Highlands chapters, as well as writing parts of the Experience chapter.

After arriving on something of a whim, **Duncan Forgan** has spent the past six years living and working in Southeast Asia, and now divides his time between Vietnam and Thailand. In a previous life he was a features writer for the national newspapers in his native Scotland and an editor of various travel guides in the Middle East. When he's not comparing venues for soft-shell crab, he writes and broadcasts for a variety of outlets worldwide on Asian travel, culture, and cuisine. For this edition, Duncan revised and updated the Halong Bay and North Central Vietnam; Hanoi and the Northwest chapters.

Sophie Friedman is a transplanted New Yorker living in Southeast Asia. She has previously worked at *Time Out New York* and *The Huffington Post* and is a contributor to a number of publications, including *Conde Nast Traveler*, *Forbes Travel Guide*, and *South China Morning Post*. She wrote parts of the Experience chapter.

Having flashpacked around Europe, Southeast Asia, and India, **Caroline Mills** has a well-honed bias toward climates warmer than that of her native England, and it was no surprise to anyone when in 2010 she bought a renovated pigsty in central Vietnam. Nowadays Caroline is a freelance travel and food writer, and can be found whizzing around Hoi An and beyond on an ancient Honda Cub, reviewing shabby-chic restaurants and fabulous hotels for local travel publication *Coast Vietnam*. For this edition, Caroline revised and updated the Central Coast chapter, Travel Smart, Books and Movies, and parts of the Experience chapter.

Adrian Vrettos grew up in the United Kingdom, where he studied archaeology and anthropology. After a few years of working in London the call of the road was too strong for him so he packed a bag and set off to explore the four corners of the world, becoming a travel writer for various international publications and websites. Now based in Athens, Greece, he fills his time with website production, avid travel, reflexology, and writing. He updated the Side Trip to Angkor Wat.